Analytic Philosophy

Analytic Philosophy
Beginnings to the Present

Jordan J. Lindberg
Central Michigan University

Mayfield Publishing Company
Mountain View, California
London · Toronto

To my teachers and my students—
I've learned much from each.

Library of Congress Cataloging-in-Publication Data

Lindberg, Jordan J.
     Analytic philosophy : beginnings to the present / Jordan J. Lindberg.
          p. cm.
     Includes bibliographical references.
     ISBN 0-7674-1455-1
     1. Analysis (Philosophy)—History. I. Title

B808.5 .L5 2000
146′.4—dc21

00-029225

Manufactured in the United States of America

10   9   8   7   6   5   4   3   2   1

Mayfield Publishing Company
1280 Villa Street
Mountain View, California 94041

Sponsoring editor, Kenneth King; production, Hockett Editorial Service; manuscript editor, Sheryl Rose; design manager, Violeta Diaz; text designer, Linda M. Robertson; cover designer, Lisa Buckley; illustrations, Lotus Art; print buyer, Danielle Javier. The text was set in 9.5/12 Minion by UG/GGS Information Services and printed on 50# Finch Opaque by R. R. Donnelley & Sons Company.

Contents

Preface

Many influential works of philosophy written in the last 125 years in Northern and Central Europe and in the United States are collected in this anthology. Not every writer whose work is included in this book wrote in English and many were not citizens of either Great Britain or America. Nevertheless, their work has proved durable and their contributions have largely shaped the contemporary philosophical landscape in English-speaking countries such as England, the United States, and Australia.

The collection includes substantial and very readable selections from leading American pragmatists, the early Cambridge analysts, members of the Vienna Circle, the so-called "ordinary language philosophers" such as John Austin and Ludwig Wittgenstein, along with recent analytic and postanalytic philosophers including W. V. O. Quine, Hilary Putnam, and Thomas Nagel. As with the few other anthologies of this sort currently available, selected essays principally address problems in epistemology, metaphysics, and the philosophy of language, although one will also find notable selections from the field of ethics and metaethics.

Considerations of length and manageability preclude anthologizing many pieces that are certainly worthy of inclusion. For example, although the Austrian positivists are well represented in these pages, I an unable to include anything by authors associated with other leading centers of European positivism, e.g., the Uppsala School, the Berlin Circle, or the Warsaw Circle. In a truly comprehensive anthology of this nature, one would also find a few selections from the likes of Auguste Comte, John Stuart Mill, the American New and Critical Realists, and even from a few of the leading European phenomenologists (especially Husserl) whose work has also made a lasting impact on the tone and direction of contemporary English-speaking philosophy.

Despite the fact that this collection primarily includes writings by English and American philosophers, I am largely in sympathy with Michael Dummett when he writes that "a grave historical distortion arises from a prevalent modern habit of speaking of analytical philosophy as 'Anglo-American.'" Apart from its implicit dismissal of the work of modern Scandinavian philosophers, and of the more recent interest in analytical philosophy that has arisen in a great many other European countries, including Italy, Germany, and Spain, this terminology utterly distorts the historical context in which analytical philosophy came to birth, in the light of which it would better be called "Anglo-Austrian" than "Anglo-American."[1] However, although I agree with Dummett that it is a grave historical distortion to characterize the *roots* of contemporary analytic philosophy as exclusively "Anglo-American," it would nevertheless remain a distortion to refer to the *contemporary* analytic philosophical landscape without making reference to its predominantly Anglo-American character. Furthermore, the fact that contemporary philosophers working in the tradition today often deem themselves *postanalytic* philosophers at this point makes the term "analytic" itself somewhat suspect as a general characterization of the modern scene. Any likely term I might offer to characterize the contents of this anthology would require various appropriate caveats and qualifications.

In addition to the essays themselves, I have included short biographies of the authors, very brief summaries of the readings, bibliographies of easy-to-find primary and secondary reference materials, and reading questions to facilitate understanding and class discussion. My intention in providing these short bibliographies (mostly of books) is to provide the student of philosophy with some easy-to-find starting points for further research. There is a wide variety of superb general reference texts available, as well, for the curious reader who wants to know more about a specific figure, period, or movement in contemporary philosophy. *The Cambridge Dictionary of Philosophy, The Oxford Dictionary of Philosophy, The Oxford Companion to Philosophy, A Companion to the Philosophers,* and the *Routledge Encyclopedia of Philosophy* are all excellent places to start.

I would be very interested in hearing your thoughts about this collection and about how you think that future editions could be improved. Please feel free to send me e-mail at wildtrout@yahoo.com or through regular mail, care of the Department of Philosophy and Religion, Central Michigan University, Mt. Pleasant, MI 48858.

Acknowledgments

While preparing this anthology I received many valuable suggestions from friends and colleagues in philosophy departments across the country. In particular I want to single out the following persons for this help and encouragement: Fred Adams, Catherine Z. Elgin, Gary Fuller, Ned S. Garvin, Robert N. Johnson, Hope May, Mark Risjord, Donald Sievert, and John Wright. Some of these debts go back quite a few years. The following individuals deserve thanks for their thoughtful review of

---

[1] *Origins of Analytical Philosophy* (Cambridge, MA: Harvard University Press, 1994), pp. 1–2.

the manuscript: A. C. Genova, University of Kansas; Jeffrey Jordan, University of Delaware; Deborah Hansen Soles, Wichita State University; and Brooke Noel Moore, California State University, Chico. I also want to thank my great team of student research assistants at Central Michigan University, especially Tracy Gallatin and Jason Helton. Their hard work has made this a substantially better book. As always, I owe a huge debt of gratitude to my wife, Marcy Lindberg, for her support and encouragement. Last, but certainly not least, I want to thank Ken King, Martha Granahan, and the rest of the Mayfield staff, as well as Rachel Youngman of Hockett Editorial Service, for their trust and assistance in bringing the project to completion.

PART I / American Pragmatism

Charles Sanders Peirce

How to Make Our Ideas Clear

An eminent logician, linguist, and philosopher of science, Charles Sanders Peirce (1839–1914) was the principal figure in the birth of the philosophical movement known as *pragmatism.*

Peirce was born in Cambridge, Massachusetts, the son of a renowned American mathematician and member of the faculty at Harvard University. He was educated as a scientist at Harvard (earning the first Sc.B. degree in chemistry *summa cum laude* from Harvard in 1863), and his overall philosophical outlook was shaped in large part by his understanding of the investigative methods of the sciences. He would write in a short autobiographical essay that he was "saturated, through and through, with the spirit of the physical sciences." Although he did serve for brief periods as a lecturer both at Harvard and at Johns Hopkins University (where his students included John Dewey and Josiah Royce), most of his professional life was spent as a working scientist with the United States Coast and Geodetic Survey.

In addition to authoring various strictly scientific publications for the Geodetic Survey, Peirce was a prolific publisher of work in philosophy. Many of his research papers were issued in traditional academic venues such as the *Journal of Speculative Philosophy* and *The Monist*, but he also published important papers outside the academic mainstream in places such as *Popular Science Monthly*. His highly original writings were a source of inspiration for other American philosophers, especially William James.

Peirce came to adopt a philosophical methodology he called "pragmatism" (later he would come to prefer the title "pragmaticism" to distinguish it from the pragmatic philosophies propounded by other writers). In his essays, Peirce repeatedly emphasizes the practical, public, cooperative, and experiential over the introspective, private, individual, and purely *a priori*. He also emphasizes the fallibilistic nature of the philosophic enterprise, seeing it in the same progressive light as natural science.

Peirce's personal life was often tumultuous. His first marriage ended in divorce, and his second wife suffered from extremely poor health. Peirce made little money, lived for long periods of time in relative isolation and poverty, and often relied on his friend William James for financial assistance and for help in finding occasional work as a lecturer. Much of Peirce's most interesting and important work remained either unfinished or unpublished at the time of his death (from cancer).

In the following essay written for *Popular Science Monthly* in 1878, Peirce advances what he calls the "pragmatic maxim"—a method for clarifying (and so better understanding) our ideas or concepts. He then illustrates the importance of his maxim by applying it to various central concepts of the physical sciences in order to show how our understanding of such concepts can be clarified. In the last section of his paper, he also considers the age-old philosophical issues of the nature of truth and reality in light of his pragmatic maxim.

§1. Clearness and Distinctness

Whoever has looked into a modern treatise on logic of the common sort, will doubtless remember the two distinctions between *clear* and *obscure* conceptions, and between *distinct* and *confused* conceptions. They have lain in the books now for nigh two centuries, unimproved and unmodified, and are generally reckoned by logicians as among the gems of their doctrine.

A clear idea is defined as one which is so apprehended that it will be recognized wherever it is met with, and so that no other will be mistaken for it. If it fails of this clearness, it is said to be obscure.

This is rather a neat bit of philosophical terminology; yet, since it is clearness that they were defining, I wish the logicians had made their definition a little more plain. Never to fail to recognize an idea, and under no circumstances to mistake another for it, let it come in how recondite a form it may, would indeed imply such prodigious force and clearness of intellect as is seldom met with in this world. On the other hand, merely to have such an acquaintance with the idea as to have become familiar with it, and to have lost all hesitancy in recognizing it in ordinary cases, hardly seems to deserve the name of clearness of apprehension, since after all it only amounts to a subjective feeling of mastery which may be entirely mistaken. I take it, however, that when the logicians speak of "clearness," they mean nothing more than such a familiarity with an idea, since they regard the quality as but a small merit, which needs to be supplemented by another, which they call *distinctness.*

A distinct idea is defined as one which contains nothing which is not clear. This is technical language; by the *contents* of an idea logicians understand whatever is contained in its definition. So that an idea is *dis-*

Charles Sanders Peirce, "How to Make Our Ideas Clear" reprinted by permission of the publisher from *The Collected Papers of Charles Sanders Peirce, Volume V* edited by Charles Hartshorne and Paul Weiss, Cambridge, Mass.: The Belknap Press of Harvard University Press, Copyright © 1934, 1962 by the President and Fellows of Harvard College.

tinctly apprehended, according to them, when we can give a precise definition of it, in abstract terms. Here the professional logicians leave the subject; and I would not have troubled the reader with what they have to say, if it were not such a striking example of how they have been slumbering through ages of intellectual activity, listlessly disregarding the enginery of modern thought, and never dreaming of applying its lessons to the improvement of logic. It is easy to show that the doctrine that familiar use and abstract distinctness make the perfection of apprehension has its only true place in philosophies which have long been extinct; and it is now time to formulate the method of attaining to a more perfect clearness of thought, such as we see and admire in the thinkers of our own time.

When Descartes set about the reconstruction of philosophy, his first step was to (theoretically) permit skepticism and to discard the practice of the schoolmen of looking to authority as the ultimate source of truth. That done, he sought a more natural fountain of true principles, and thought he found it in the human mind; thus passing, in the directest way, from the method of authority to that of apriority, . . . Self-consciousness was to furnish us with our fundamental truths, and to decide what was agreeable to reason. But since, evidently, not all ideas are true, he was led to note, as the first condition of infallibility, that they must be clear. The distinction between an idea *seeming* clear and really being so, never occurred to him. Trusting to introspection, as he did, even for a knowledge of external things, why should he question its testimony in respect to the contents of our own minds? But then, I suppose, seeing men, who seemed to be quite clear and positive, holding opposite opinions upon fundamental principles, he was further led to say that clearness of ideas is not sufficient, but that they need also to be distinct, i.e., to have nothing unclear about them. What he probably meant by this (for he did not explain I himself with precision) was, that they must sustain the test of dialectical examination; that they must not only seem clear at the outset, but that discussion must never be able to bring to light points of obscurity connected with them.

Such was the distinction of Descartes, and one sees that it was precisely on the level of his philosophy. It was somewhat developed by Leibnitz. This great and singular genius was as remarkable for what he failed to see as for what he saw. That a piece of mechanism could not do work perpetually without being fed with power in some form, was a thing perfectly apparent to him; yet he did not understand that the machinery of the mind can only transform knowledge, but never originate it, unless it be fed with facts of observation. He thus missed the most essential point of the Cartesian philosophy, which is, that to accept propositions which seem perfectly evident to us is a thing which, whether it be logical or illogical, we cannot help doing. Instead of regarding the matter in this way, he sought to reduce the first principles of science to two classes, those which cannot be denied without self-contradiction, and those which result from the principle of sufficient reason ... and was apparently unaware of the great difference between his position and that of Descartes. So he reverted to the old trivialities of logic; and, above all, abstract definitions played a great part in his philosophy. It was quite natural, therefore, that on observing that the method of Descartes labored under the difficulty that we may seem to ourselves to have clear apprehensions of ideas which in truth are very hazy, no better remedy occurred to him than to require an abstract definition of every important term. Accordingly, in adopting the distinction of *clear* and *distinct* notions, he described the latter quality as the clear apprehension of everything contained in the definition; and the books have ever since copied his words. There is no danger that his chimerical scheme will ever again be over-valued. Nothing new can ever be learned by analyzing definitions. Nevertheless, our existing beliefs can be set in order by this process, and order is an essential element of intellectual economy, as of every other. It may be acknowledged, therefore, that the books are right in making familiarity with a notion the first step toward clearness of apprehension, and the defining of it the second. But in omitting all mention of any higher perspicuity of thought, they simply mirror a philosophy which was exploded a hundred years ago. That much-admired "ornament of logic"—the doctrine of clearness and distinctness—may be pretty enough, but it is high time to relegate to our cabinet of curiosities the antique *bijou*, and to wear about us something better adapted to modern uses.

The very first lesson that we have a right to demand that logic shall teach us is, how to make our ideas clear; and a most important one it is, depreciated only by minds who stand in need of it. To know what we think, to be masters of our own meaning, will make a solid foundation for great and weighty thought. It is most easily learned by those whose ideas are meager and restricted; and far happier they than such as wallow helplessly in a rich mud of conceptions. A nation, it is true, may, in the course of generations, overcome the disadvantage of an excessive wealth of language and its natural concomitant, a vast, unfathomable deep of ideas. We may see it in history, slowly perfecting its literary forms, sloughing at length its metaphysics, and, by virtue of the untirable patience which is often a compensation, attaining great excellence in every branch of mental acquirement. The page of history is not yet unrolled that is to tell us whether such a people will or will not in the long run prevail over one whose ideas (like the words of their language) are few, but which possesses a wonderful mastery over those which it has. For an individual, however, there can be no question that a few clear ideas are worth more than many confused ones. A young man would hardly be persuaded to sacrifice the greater part of his thoughts to save the rest; and the muddled head is the least apt to see the necessity of such a sacrifice. Him we can usually only commiserate, as a person with a congenital defect. Time will help him, but intellectual maturity with regard to clearness is apt to come rather late. This seems an unfortunate arrangement of Nature, inasmuch as clearness is of less use to a man settled in life, whose errors have in great measure had their effect, than it would be to one whose path lay before him. It is terrible to see how a single unclear idea, a single formula without meaning, lurking in a young man's head, will sometimes act like an obstruction of inert matter in an artery, hindering the nutrition of the brain, and condemning its victim to pine away in the fullness of his intellectual vigor and in the midst of intellectual plenty. Many a man has cherished for years as his hobby some vague shadow of an idea, too meaningless to be positively false; he has, nevertheless, passionately loved it, has made it his companion by day and by night, and has given to it his strength and his life, leaving all other occupations for its sake, and in short has lived with it and for it, until it has become, as it were, flesh of his flesh and bone of his bone; and then he has waked up some bright morning to find it gone, clean vanished away like the beautiful Melusina of the fable, and the essence of his life gone with it. I have myself known such a man; and who can tell how many histories of circle-squarers, metaphysicians, astrologers, and what not, may not be told in the old German [French!] story?

§2. The Pragmatic Maxim

The principles set forth in the first part of this essay[1] lead, at once, to a method of reaching a clearness of thought of higher grade than the "distinctness" of the logicians. It was there noticed that the action of thought is excited by the irritation of doubt, and ceases when belief is attained; so that the production of belief is the sole function of thought. All these words, however, are too strong for my purpose. It is as if I had described the phenomena as they appear under a mental microscope. Doubt and Belief, as the words are commonly employed, relate to religious or other grave discussions. But here I use them to designate the starting of any question, no matter how small or how great, and the resolution of it. If, for instance, in a horse-car, I pull out my purse and find a five-cent nickel and five coppers, I decide, while my hand is going to the purse, in which way I will pay my fare. To call such a question Doubt, and my decision Belief, is certainly to use words very disproportionate to the occasion. To speak of such a doubt as causing an irritation which needs to be appeased, suggests a temper which is uncomfortable to the verge of insanity. Yet, looking at the matter minutely, it must be admitted that, if there is the least hesitation as to whether I shall pay the five coppers or the nickel (as there will be sure to be, unless I act from some previously contracted habit in the matter), though irritation is too strong a word, yet I am excited to such small mental activity as may be necessary to deciding how I shall act. Most frequently doubts arise from some indecision, however momentary, in our action. Sometimes it is not so. I have, for example, to wait in a railway-station, and to pass the time I read the advertisements on the walls. I compare the advantages of different trains and different routes which I never expect to take, merely fancying myself to be in a state of

hesitancy, because I am bored with having nothing to trouble me. Feigned hesitancy, whether feigned for mere amusement or with a lofty purpose, plays a great part in the production of scientific inquiry. However the doubt may originate, it stimulates the mind to an activity which may be slight or energetic, calm or turbulent. Images pass rapidly through consciousness, one incessantly melting into another, until at last, when all is over—it may be in a fraction of a second, in an hour, or after long years—we find ourselves decided as to how we should act under such circumstances as those which occasioned our hesitation. In other words, we have attained belief.

In this process we observe two sorts of elements of consciousness, the distinction between which may best be made clear by means of an illustration. In a piece of music there are the separate notes, and there is the air. A single tone may be prolonged for an hour or a day, and it exists as perfectly in each second of that time as in the whole taken together; so that, as long as it is sounding, it might be present to a sense from which everything in the past was as completely absent as the future itself. But it is different with the air, the performance of which occupies a certain time, during the portions of which only portions of it are played. It consists in an orderliness in the succession of sounds which strike the ear at different times; and to perceive it there must be some continuity of consciousness which makes the events of a lapse of time present to us. We certainly only perceive the air by hearing the separate notes; yet we cannot be said to directly hear it, for we hear only what is present at the instant, and an orderliness of succession cannot exist in an instant. These two sorts of objects, what we are *immediately* conscious of and what we are *mediately* conscious of, are found in all consciousness. Some elements (the sensations) are completely present at every instant so long as they last, while others (like thought) are actions having beginning, middle, and end, and consist in a congruence in the succession of sensations which flow through the mind. They cannot be immediately present to us, but must cover some portion of the past or future. Thought is a thread of melody running through the succession of our sensations.

We may add that just as a piece of music may be written in parts, each part having its own air, so various systems of relationship of succession subsist together between the same sensations. These different systems are distinguished by having different motives, ideas, or functions. Thought is only one such system, for its sole motive, idea, and function is to produce belief, and whatever does not concern that purpose belongs to some other system of relations. The action of thinking may incidentally have other results; it may serve to amuse us, for example, and among *dilettanti* it is not rare to find those who have so perverted thought to the purposes of pleasure that it seems to vex them to think that the questions upon which they delight to exercise it may ever get finally settled and a positive discovery which takes a favorite subject out of the arena of literary debate is met with ill-concealed dislike. This disposition is the very debauchery of thought. But the soul and meaning of thought, abstracted from the other elements which accompany it, though it may be voluntarily thwarted, can never be made to direct itself toward anything but the production of belief. Thought in action has for its only possible motive the attainment of thought at rest; and whatever does not refer to belief is no part of the thought itself.

And what, then, is belief? It is the demi-cadence which closes a musical phrase in the symphony of our intellectual life. We have seen that it has just three properties: First, it is something that we are aware of; second, it appeases the irritation of doubt; and, third, it involves the establishment in our nature of a rule of action, or, say for short, a *habit*. As it appeases the irritation of doubt, which is the motive for thinking, thought relaxes, and comes to rest for a moment when belief is reached. But, since belief is a rule for action, the application of which involves further doubt and further thought, at the same time that it is a stopping-place, it is also a new starting-place for thought. That is why I have permitted myself to call it thought at rest, although thought is essentially an action. The *final* upshot of thinking is the exercise of volition, and of this thought no longer forms a part; but belief is only a stadium of mental action, an effect upon our nature due to thought, which will influence future thinking.

The essence of belief is the establishment of a habit; and different beliefs are distinguished by the different modes of action to which they give rise. If beliefs do not differ in this respect, if they appease the same

doubt by producing the same rule of action, then no mere differences in the manner of consciousness of them can make them different beliefs, any more than playing a tune in different keys is playing different tunes. Imaginary distinctions are often drawn between beliefs which differ only in their mode of expression— the wrangling which ensues is real enough, however.

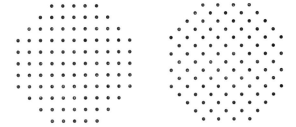

Figure 1   Figure 2

To believe that any objects are arranged among themselves as in Fig. 1, and to believe that they are arranged [as] in Fig. 2, are one and the same belief; yet it is conceivable that a man should assert one proposition and deny the other. Such false distinctions do as much harm as the confusion of beliefs really different, and are among the pitfalls of which we ought constantly to beware, especially when we are upon metaphysical ground. One singular deception of this sort, which often occurs, is to mistake the sensation produced by our own unclearness of thought for a character of the object we are thinking. Instead of perceiving that the obscurity is purely subjective, we fancy that we contemplate a quality of the object which is essentially mysterious; and if our conception be afterward presented to us in a clear form we do not recognize it as the same, owing to the absence of the feeling of unintelligibility. So long as this deception lasts, it obviously puts an impassable barrier in the way of perspicuous thinking; so that it equally interests the opponents of rational thought to perpetuate it, and its adherents to guard against it.

Another such deception is to mistake a mere difference in the grammatical construction of two words for a distinction between the ideas they express. In this pedantic age, when the general mob of writers attend so much more to words than to things, this error is common enough. When I just said that thought is an *action,* and that it consists in a *relation,* although a person performs an action but not a relation, which can only be the result of an action, yet there was no inconsistency in what I said, but only a grammatical vagueness.

From all these sophisms we shall be perfectly safe so long as we reflect that the whole function of thought is to produce habits of action; and that whatever there is connected with a thought, but irrelevant to its purpose, is an accretion to it, but no part of it. If there be a unity among our sensations which has no reference to how we shall act on a given occasion, as when we listen to a piece of music, why, we do not call that thinking. To develop its meaning, we have, therefore, simply to determine what habits it produces, for what a thing means is simply what habits it involves. Now, the identity of a habit depends on how it might lead us to act, not merely under such circumstances as are likely to arise, but under such as might possibly occur, no matter how improbable they may be. What the habit is depends on *when* and *how* it causes us to act. As for the *when,* every stimulus to action is derived from perception; as for the *how,* every purpose of action is to produce some sensible result. Thus, we come down to what is tangible and conceivably practical, as the root of every real distinction of thought, no matter how subtle it may be; and there is no distinction of meaning so fine as to consist in anything but a possible difference of practice.

To see what this principle leads to, consider in the light of it such a doctrine as that of transubstantiation. The Protestant churches generally hold that the elements of the sacrament are flesh and blood only in a tropical sense; they nourish our souls as meat and the juice of it would our bodies. But the Catholics maintain that they are literally just meat and blood; although they possess all the sensible qualities of wafer-cakes and diluted wine. But we can have no conception of wine except what may enter into a belief, either—

1. That this, that, or the other, is wine; or,

2. That wine possesses certain properties.

Such beliefs are nothing but self-notifications that we should, upon occasion, act in regard to such things as we believe to be wine according to the qualities which we believe wine to possess. The occasion of such action would be some sensible perception, the motive of it to produce some sensible result. Thus our action has exclusive reference to what affects the senses, our habit has the same bearing as our action, our belief the same as our habit, our conception the same as our belief; and we can consequently mean nothing by wine but what has certain effects, direct or indirect, upon our senses; and to talk of something as having all the sensible characters of wine, yet being in reality blood, is senseless jargon. Now, it is not my object to pursue the theological question; and having used it as a logical example I drop it, without caring to anticipate the theologian's reply. I only desire to point out how impossible it is that we should have an idea in our minds which relates to anything but conceived sensible effects of things. Our idea of anything *is* our idea of its sensible effects; and if we fancy that we have any other we deceive ourselves, and mistake a mere sensation accompanying the thought for a part of the thought itself. It is absurd to say that thought has any meaning unrelated to its only function. It is foolish for Catholics and Protestants to fancy themselves in disagreement about the elements of the sacrament, if they agree in regard to all their sensible effects, here and hereafter.

It appears, then, that the rule for attaining the third grade of clearness of apprehension is as follows: Consider what effects, that might conceivably have practical bearings, we conceive the object of our conception to have. Then, our conception of these effects is the whole of our conception of the object.

§3. Some Applications of the Pragmatic Maxim

Let us illustrate this rule by some examples; and, to begin with the simplest one possible, let us ask what we mean by calling a thing *hard.* Evidently that it will not be scratched by many other substances. The whole conception of this quality, as of every other, lies in its conceived effects. There is absolutely no difference between a hard thing and a soft thing so long as they are not brought to the test. Suppose, then, that a diamond could be crystallized in the midst of a cushion of soft cotton, and should remain there until it was finally burned up. Would it be false to say that that diamond was soft? This seems a foolish question, and would be so, in fact, except in the realm of logic. There such questions are often of the greatest utility as serving to bring logical principles into sharper relief than real discussions ever could. In studying logic we must not put them aside with hasty answers, but must consider them with attentive care, in order to make out the principles involved. We may, in the present case, modify our question, and ask what prevents us from saying that all hard bodies remain perfectly soft until they are touched, when their hardness increases with the pressure until they are scratched. Reflection will show that the reply is this: there would be no *falsity* in such modes of speech. They would involve a modification of our present usage of speech with regard to the words hard and soft, but not of their meanings. For they represent no fact to be different from what it is; only they involve arrangements of facts which would be exceedingly maladroit. This leads us to remark that the question of what would occur under circumstances which do not actually arise is not a question of fact, but only of the most perspicuous arrangement of them. For example, the question of free-will and fate in its simplest form, stripped of verbiage, is something like this: I have done something of which I am ashamed; could I, by an effort of the will, have resisted the temptation, and done otherwise? The philosophical reply is, that this is not a question of fact, but only of the arrangement of facts. Arranging them so as to exhibit what is particularly pertinent to my question—namely, that I ought to blame myself for having done wrong—it is perfectly true to say that, if I had willed to do otherwise than I did, I should have done otherwise. On the other hand, arranging the facts so as to exhibit another important consideration, it is equally true that, when a temptation has once been allowed to work, it will, if it has a certain force, produce its effect, let me struggle how I may. There is no objection to a contradiction in what would result from a false supposition. The *reductio ad absurdum* consists in showing that contradictory results would follow from a hypothesis which is consequently judged to be false. Many questions are involved in the free-will discussion, and I am far from desiring to say that both sides are equally right. On the contrary, I am of [the] opinion that one side denies important facts,

and that the other does not. But what I do say is, that the above single question was the origin of the whole doubt; that, had it not been for this question, the controversy would never have arisen; and that this question is perfectly solved in the manner which I have indicated.

Let us next seek a clear idea of Weight. This is another very easy case. To say that a body is heavy means simply that, in the absence of opposing force, it will fall. This (neglecting certain specifications of how it will fall, etc., which exist in the mind of the physicist who uses the word) is evidently the whole conception of weight. It is a fair question whether some particular facts may not *account* for gravity; but what we mean by the force itself is completely involved in its effects.

This leads us to undertake an account of the idea of Force in general. This is the great conception which, developed in the early part of the seventeenth century from the rude idea of a cause, and constantly improved upon since, has shown us how to explain all the changes of motion which bodies experience, and how to think about all physical phenomena; which has given birth to modern science, and changed the face of the globe; and which, aside from its more special uses, has played a principal part in directing the course of modern thought, and in furthering modern social development. It is, therefore, worth some pains to comprehend it. According to our rule, we must begin by asking what is the immediate use of thinking about force; and the answer is, that we thus account for changes of motion. If bodies were left to themselves, without the intervention of forces, every motion would continue unchanged both in velocity and in direction. Furthermore, change of motion never takes place abruptly; if its direction is changed, it is always through a curve without angles; if its velocity alters, it is by degrees. The gradual changes which are constantly taking place are conceived by geometers to be compounded together according to the rules of the parallelogram of forces. If the reader does not already know what this is, he will find it, I hope, to his advantage to endeavor to follow the following explanation; but if mathematics are insupportable to him, pray let him skip three paragraphs rather than that we should part company here.

A *path* is a line whose beginning and end are distinguished. Two paths are considered to be equivalent,

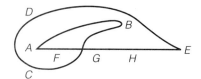

Figure 3

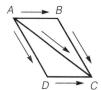

Figure 4

locities; and it becomes evident for accelerations if we consider that precisely what velocities are to positions—namely, states of change of them—that accelerations are to velocities.

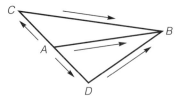

Figure 5

which, beginning at the same point, lead to the same point. Thus the two paths, *ABCDE* and *AFGHE* (Fig. 3), are equivalent. Paths which do *not* begin at the same point are considered to be equivalent, provided that, on moving either of them without turning it, but keeping it always parallel to its original position, when its beginning coincides with that of the other path, the ends also coincide. Paths are considered as geometrically added together, when one begins where the other ends; thus the path *AE* is conceived to be a sum of *AB*, *BC*, *CD*, and *DE*. In the parallelogram of Fig. 4 the diagonal *AC* is the sum of *AB* and *BC*; or, since *AD* is geometrically equivalent to *BC*, *AC* is the geometrical sum of *AB* and *AD*.

All this is purely conventional. It simply amounts to this: that we choose to call paths having the relations I have described equal or added. But, though it is a convention, it is a convention with a good reason. The rule for geometrical addition may be applied not only to paths, but to any other things which can be represented by paths. Now, as a path is determined by the varying direction and distance of the point which moves over it from the starting-point, it follows that anything which from its beginning to its end is determined by a varying direction and a varying magnitude is capable of being represented by a line. Accordingly, *velocities* may be represented by lines, for they have only directions and rates. The same thing is true of *accelerations*, or changes of velocities. This is evident enough in the case of ve-

The so-called "parallelogram of forces" is simply a rule for compounding accelerations. The rule is, to represent the accelerations by paths, and then to geometrically add the paths. The geometers, however, not only use the "parallelogram of forces" to compound different accelerations, but also to resolve one acceleration into a sum of several. Let *AB* (Fig. 5) be the path which represents a certain acceleration—say, such a change in the motion of a body that at the end of one second the body will, under the influence of that change, be in a position different from what it would have had if its motion had continued unchanged such that a path equivalent to *AB* would lead from the latter position to the former. This acceleration may be considered as the sum of the accelerations represented by *AC* and *CB*. It may also be considered as the sum of the very different accelerations represented by *AD* and *DB*, where *AD* is almost the opposite of *AC*. And it is clear that there is an immense variety of ways in which *AB* might be resolved into the sum of two accelerations.

After this tedious explanation, which I hope, in view of the extraordinary interest of the conception of force, may not have exhausted the reader's patience, we are prepared at last to state the grand fact which this conception embodies. This fact is that if the actual changes of motion which the different particles of bodies experience are each resolved in its appropriate way, each component acceleration is precisely such as is prescribed by a certain law of Nature, according to which bodies, in the relative positions which the bodies in question actually have at the moment, always receive certain accelerations, which, being compounded by geometrical addition, give the acceleration which the body actually experiences.

This is the only fact which the idea of force represents, and whoever will take the trouble clearly to apprehend what this fact is, perfectly comprehends what force is. Whether we ought to say that a force *is* an acceleration, or that it *causes* an acceleration, is a mere question of propriety of language, which has no more to do with our real meaning than the difference between the French idiom "*Il fait froid*" and its English equivalent "*It is cold.*" Yet it is surprising to see how this simple affair has muddled men's minds. In how many profound treatises is not force spoken of as a "mysterious entity," which seems to be only a way of confessing that the author despairs of ever getting a clear notion of what the word means! In a recent admired work on *Analytic Mechanics* it is stated that we understand precisely the effect of force, but what force itself is we do not understand! This is simply a self-contradiction. The idea which the word force excites in our minds has no other function than to affect our actions, and these actions can have no reference to force otherwise than through its effects. Consequently, if we know what the effects of force are, we are acquainted with every fact which is implied in saying that a force exists, and there is nothing more to know. The truth is, there is some vague notion afloat that a question may mean something which the mind cannot conceive; and when some hair-splitting philosophers have been confronted with the absurdity of such a view, they have invented an empty distinction between positive and negative conceptions, in the attempt to give their non-idea a form not obviously nonsensical. The nullity of it is sufficiently plain from the considerations given a few pages back; and, apart from those considerations, the quibbling character of the distinction must have struck every mind accustomed to real thinking.

§4. Reality

Let us now approach the subject of logic, and consider a conception which particularly concerns it, that of *reality*. Taking clearness in the sense of familiarity, no idea could be clearer than this. Every child uses it with perfect confidence, never dreaming that he does not understand it. As for clearness in its second grade, however, it would probably puzzle most men, even among those of a reflective turn of mind, to give an abstract definition of the real. Yet such a definition may perhaps be reached by considering the points of difference between reality and its opposite, fiction. A figment is a product of somebody's imagination; it has such characters as his thought impresses upon it. That those characters are independent of how you or I think is an external reality. There are, however, phenomena within our own minds, dependent upon our thought, which are at the same time real in the sense that we really think them. But though their characters depend on how we think, they do not depend on what we think those characters to be. Thus, a dream has a real existence as a mental phenomenon, if somebody has really dreamt it; that he dreamt so and so, does not depend on what anybody thinks was dreamt, but is completely independent of all opinion on the subject. On the other hand, considering, not the fact of dreaming, but the thing dreamt, it retains its peculiarities by virtue of no other fact than that it was dreamt to possess them. Thus we may define the real as that whose characters are independent of what anybody may think them to be.

But, however satisfactory such a definition may be found, it would be a great mistake to suppose that it makes the idea of reality perfectly clear. Here, then, let us apply our rules. According to them, reality, like every other quality, consists in the peculiar sensible effects which things partaking of it produce. The only effect which real things have is to cause belief, for all the sensations which they excite emerge into consciousness in the form of beliefs. The question therefore is, how is true belief (or belief in the real) distinguished from false belief (or belief in fiction). Now, . . . the ideas of truth and falsehood, in their full development, appertain exclusively to the experiential method of settling opinion. A person who arbitrarily chooses the propositions which he will adopt can use the word truth only to emphasize the expression of his determination to hold on to his choice. Of course, the method of tenacity never prevailed exclusively; reason is too natural to men for that. But in the literature of the Dark Ages we find some fine examples of it. When Scotus Erigena is commenting upon a poetical passage in which helle-bore is spoken of as having caused the death of Socrates, he does not hesitate to inform the inquiring reader that Helleborus and Socrates were two eminent Greek philosophers, and that the latter, having been overcome in argument by the former, took the matter to heart and died of it! What sort of an idea of truth could a man have who could adopt and teach, without the qualification of a perhaps, an opinion taken so entirely at random? The real spirit of Socrates, who I hope would have been delighted to have been "overcome in argument," because he would have learned something by it, is in curious contrast with the naïve idea of the glossist, for whom (as for "the born missionary" of today) discussion would seem to have been simply a struggle. When philosophy began to awake from its long slumber, and before theology completely dominated it, the practice seems to have been for each professor to seize upon any philosophical position he found unoccupied and which seemed a strong one, to entrench himself in it, and to sally forth from time to time to give battle to the others. Thus, even the scanty records we possess of those disputes enable us to make out a dozen or more opinions held by different teachers at one time concerning the question of nominalism and realism. Read the opening part of the *Historia Calamitatum* of Abelard, who was certainly as philosophical as any of his contemporaries, and see the spirit of combat which it breathes. For him, the truth is simply his particular stronghold. When the method of authority prevailed, the truth meant little more than the Catholic faith. All the efforts of the scholastic doctors are directed toward harmonizing their faith in Aristotle and their faith in the Church, and one may search their ponderous folios through without finding an argument which goes any further. It is noticeable that where different faiths flourish side by side, renegades are looked upon with contempt even by the party whose belief they adopt; so completely has the idea of loyalty replaced that of truth-seeking. Since the time of Descartes, the defect in the conception of truth has been less apparent. Still, it will sometimes strike a scientific man that the philosophers have been less intent on finding out what the facts are, than on inquiring what belief is most in harmony with their system. It is

hard to convince a follower of the *a priori* method by adducing facts; but show him that an opinion he is defending is inconsistent with what he has laid down elsewhere, and he will be very apt to retract it. These minds do not seem to believe that disputation is ever to cease; they seem to think that the opinion which is natural for one man is not so for another, and that belief will, consequently, never be settled. In contenting themselves with fixing their own opinions by a method which would lead another man to a different result, they betray their feeble hold of the conception of what truth is.

On the other hand, all the followers of science are animated by a cheerful hope that the processes of investigation, if only pushed far enough, will give one certain solution to each question to which they apply it. One man may investigate the velocity of light by studying the transits of Venus and the aberration of the stars; another by the oppositions of Mars and the eclipses of Jupiter's satellites; a third by the method of Fizeau; a fourth by that of Foucault; a fifth by the motions of the curves of Lissajoux; a sixth, a seventh, an eighth, and a ninth, may follow the different methods of comparing the measures of statical and dynamical electricity. They may at first obtain different results, but, as each perfects his method and his processes, the results are found to move steadily together toward a destined center. So with all scientific research. Different minds may set out with the most antagonistic views, but the progress of investigation carries them by a force outside of themselves to one and the same conclusion. This activity of thought by which we are carried, not where we wish, but to a foreordained goal, is like the operation of destiny. No modification of the point of view taken, no selection of other facts for study, no natural bent of mind even, can enable a man to escape the predestinate opinion. This great hope is embodied in the conception of truth and reality. The opinion which is fated[2] to be ultimately agreed to by all who investigate, is what we mean by the truth, and the object represented in this opinion is the real. That is the way I would explain reality.

But it may be said that this view is directly opposed to the abstract definition which we have given of reality, inasmuch as it makes the characters of the real depend on what is ultimately thought about them. But the answer to this is that, on the one hand, reality is independent, not necessarily of thought in general, but only of what you or I or any finite number of men may think about it; and that, on the other hand, though the object of the final opinion depends on what that opinion is, yet what that opinion is does not depend on what you or I or any man thinks. Our perversity and that of others may indefinitely postpone the settlement of opinion; it might even conceivably cause an arbitrary proposition to be universally accepted as long as the human race should last. Yet even that would not change the nature of the belief, which alone could be the result of investigation carried sufficiently far; and if, after the extinction of our race, another should arise with faculties and disposition for investigation, that true opinion must be the one which they would ultimately come to. "Truth crushed to earth shall rise again," and the opinion which would finally result from investigation does not depend on how anybody may actually think. But the reality of that which is real does depend on the real fact that investigation is destined to lead, at last, if continued long enough, to a belief in it.

But I may be asked what I have to say to all the minute facts of history, forgotten never to be recovered, to the lost books of the ancients, to the buried secrets.

"Full many a gem of purest ray serene
  The dark, unfathomed caves of ocean bear;
Full many a flower is born to blush unseen,
  And waste its sweetness on the desert air."

Do these things not really exist because they are hopelessly beyond the reach of our knowledge? And then, after the universe is dead (according to the prediction of some scientists), and all life has ceased forever, will not the shock of atoms continue though there will be no mind to know it? To this I reply that, though in no possible state of knowledge can any number be great enough to express the relation between the amount of what rests unknown to the amount of the known, yet it is unphilosophical to suppose that, with regard to any given question (which has any clear meaning), investigation would not bring forth a solution of it, if it were carried far enough. Who would have said, a few years ago, that we could ever know of what substances stars are made whose light may have been longer in reaching us than the human race has existed? Who can be sure of what we shall not know in a few hundred years? Who can guess what would be the result of continuing the pursuit of science for ten thousand years, with the activity of the last hundred? And if it were to go on for a million, or a billion, or any number of years you please, how is it possible to say that there is any question which might not ultimately be solved?

But it may be objected, "Why make so much of these remote considerations, especially when it is your principle that only practical distinctions have a meaning?" Well, I must confess that it makes very little difference whether we say that a stone on the bottom of the ocean, in complete darkness, is brilliant or not—that is to say, that it *probably* makes no difference, remembering always that that stone *may* be fished up tomorrow. But that there are gems at the bottom of the sea, flowers in the untraveled desert, etc., are propositions which, like that about a diamond being hard when it is not pressed, concern much more the arrangement of our language than they do the meaning of our ideas.

It seems to me, however, that we have, by the application of our rule, reached so clear an apprehension of what we mean by reality, and of the fact which the idea rests on, that we should not, perhaps, be making a pretension so presumptuous as it would be singular, if we were to offer a metaphysical theory of existence for universal acceptance among those who employ the scientific method of fixing belief. However, as metaphysics is a subject much more curious than useful, the knowledge of which, like that of a sunken reef, serves chiefly to enable us to keep clear of it, I will not trouble the reader with any more ontology at this moment. I have already been led much further into that path than I should have desired; and I have given the reader such a dose of mathematics, psychology, and all that is most abstruse, that I fear he may already have left me, and that what I am now writing is for the compositor and proofreader exclusively. I trusted to the importance of the subject. There is no royal road to logic, and really valuable ideas can only be had at the price of close attention. . . .

Notes

1. See his "The Fixation of Belief" in *Popular Science Monthly*, vol. 12 (1877).
2. Fate means merely that which is sure to come true, and can nohow be avoided. It is a superstition to suppose that a certain sort of events are ever fated, and it is another to suppose that the word fate can never be freed from its superstitious taint. We are all fated to die.

READING QUESTIONS

1. Peirce proposes that the function of thought is to produce belief and that "the essence of belief is the establishment of a habit." What specifically do these claims mean? Are they true? Why or why not?
2. In order to make our ideas clear, Peirce suggests that we should "consider what effects, that might conceivably have practical bearings, we conceive the object of our conception to have. Then, our conception of these effects is the whole of our conception of the object." This is an important version of his pragmatic maxim. Restate and clarify this maxim in your own words. What exactly does he mean?
3. How is Peirce's pragmatic maxim related to his assertion that "our idea of anything *is* our idea of its sensible effects"? Is he correct about this? Why or why not?
4. In §3, Peirce illustrates his pragmatic maxim by applying it to three important concepts of science: hardness, weight, and force. How, if at all, does applying the pragmatic maxim bring greater clarity to these concepts?
5. In §4, Peirce turns to an examination of the concepts of truth and reality. He writes that "the opinion which is fated to be ultimately agreed to by all who investigate, is what we mean by the truth, and the object represented in this opinion is the real." Does Peirce advance any argument for this conclusion? If so, what is it? If not, what argument could be advanced for it?
6. In your own words describe how Peirce conceives of the relationship between *reality*, on one hand, and *thought about reality*, on the other. How would you characterize this relationship? Why?

CHARLES SANDERS PEIRCE

Pragmaticism

In this selection, taken from his essay "What Pragmatism Is" (1903), Peirce works to distinguish his particular philosophical methodology from those of other philosophers who call themselves "pragmatists." Concerned that the term has come to be used too loosely or uncritically, he introduces a new label for his philosophy—*pragmaticism,* a word he hopes is "ugly enough to be safe from kidnappers." In the second half of the paper Peirce invents an imaginary dialogue in order to further clarify his view and to respond to various criticisms and misinterpretations which he believes are likely to be advanced.

Pragmaticism

After awaiting in vain, for a good many years, some particularly opportune conjuncture of circumstances that might serve to recommend his notions of the ethics of terminology, the writer has now, at last, dragged them in over head and shoulders, on an occasion when he has no specific proposal to offer nor any feeling but satisfaction at the course usage has run without any canons or resolutions of a congress. His word "pragmatism" has gained general recognition in a generalized sense that seems to argue power of growth and vitality. The famed psychologist, James, first took it up, seeing that his "radical empiricism" substantially answered to the writer's definition of pragmatism, albeit with a certain difference in the point of view. Next, the admirably clear and brilliant thinker, Mr. Ferdinand C. S. Schiller, casting about for a more attractive name for the "anthropomorphism" of his *Riddle of the Sphinx*, lit, in that most remarkable paper of his on *Axioms as Postulates*, upon the same designation "pragmatism," which in its original sense was in generic agreement with his own doctrine, for which he has since found the more appropriate specification "humanism," while he still retains "pragmatism" in a somewhat wider sense. So far all went happily. But at present, the word begins to be met with occasionally in the literary journals, where it gets abused in the merciless way that words have to expect when they fall into literary clutches. Sometimes the manners of the British have effloresced in scolding at the word as ill-chosen— ill-chosen, that is, to express some meaning that it was rather designed to exclude. So then, the writer, finding his bantling "pragmatism" so promoted, feels that it is time to kiss his child good-by and relinquish it to its higher destiny; while to serve the precise purpose of expressing the original definition, he begs to announce the birth of the word "pragmaticism," which is ugly enough to be safe from kidnappers. . . .

The bare definition of pragmaticism could convey no satisfactory comprehension of it to the most apprehensive of minds, but requires the commentary to be given below. Moreover, this definition takes no notice of one or two other doctrines without the previous acceptance (or virtual acceptance) of which pragmaticism itself would be a nullity. They are included as a part of the pragmatism of Schiller, but the present writer prefers not to mingle different propositions. The preliminary propositions had better be stated forthwith.

The difficulty in doing this is that no formal list of them has ever been made. They might all be included under the vague maxim, "Dismiss make-believes." Philosophers of very diverse stripes propose that phi-losophy shall take its start from one or another state of mind in which no man, least of all a beginner in philosophy, actually is. One proposes that you shall begin by doubting everything, and says that there is only one thing that you cannot doubt, as if doubting were "as easy as lying." Another proposes that we should begin by observing "the first impressions of sense," forgetting that our very percepts are the results of cognitive elaboration. But in truth, there is but one state of mind from which you can "set out," namely, the very state of mind in which you actually find yourself at the time you do "set out"—a state in which you are laden with an immense mass of cognition already formed, of which you cannot divest yourself if you would; and who knows whether, if you could, you would not have made all knowledge impossible to yourself? Do you call it *doubting* to write down on a piece of paper that you doubt? If so, doubt has nothing to do with any serious business. But do not make believe; if pedantry has not eaten all the reality out of you, recognize, as you must, that there is much that you do not doubt, in the least. Now that which you do not at all doubt, you must and do regard as infallible, absolute truth. Here breaks in Mr. Make Believe: "What! Do you mean to say that one is to believe what is not true, or that what a man does not doubt is *ipso facto* true?" No, but unless he can make a thing white and black at once, *he* has to regard what he does not doubt as absolutely true. Now you, *per hypothesiu*, are that man. "But you tell me there are scores of things I do not doubt. I really cannot persuade myself that there is not some one of them about which I am mistaken." You are adducing one of your make-believe facts, which, even if it were established, would only go to show that doubt has a *limen*, that is, is only called into being by a certain finite stimulus. You only puzzle yourself by talking of this metaphysical "truth" and metaphysical "falsity," that you know nothing about. All you have any dealings with are your doubts and beliefs, with the course of life that forces new beliefs upon you and gives you power to doubt old beliefs. If your terms "truth" and "falsity" are taken in such senses as to be definable in terms of doubt and belief and the course of experience (as for example they would be, if you were to define the "truth" as that to a belief in which belief would tend if it were to tend indefinitely toward absolute fixity), well and good: in that case, you are only talking about doubt and belief. But if by truth and falsity you mean something not definable in terms of doubt and belief in any way, then you are talking of entities of whose existence you can know nothing, and which Ockham's razor would clean shave off. Your problems would be greatly simplified, if, instead of saying that you want to know the "Truth," you were simply to say that you want to attain a state of belief unassailable by doubt.

Belief is not a momentary mode of consciousness; it is a habit of mind essentially enduring for some time, and mostly (at least) unconscious; and like other habits, it is (until it meets with some surprise that begins its dissolution) perfectly self-satisfied. Doubt is of an altogether contrary genus. It is not a habit, but the privation of a habit. Now a privation of a habit, in order to be anything at all, must be a condition of erratic activity that in some way must get superseded by a habit.

Among the things which the reader, as a rational person, does not doubt, is that he not merely has habits, but also can exert a measure of self-control over his future actions; which means, however, *not* that he can impart to them any arbitrarily assignable character, but, on the contrary, that a process of self-preparation will tend to impart to action (when the occasion for it shall arise), one fixed character, which is indicated and perhaps roughly measured by the absence (or slightness) of the feeling of self-reproach, which subsequent reflection will induce. Now, this subsequent reflection is part of the self-preparation for action on the next occasion. Consequently, there is a tendency, as action is repeated again and again, for the action to approximate indefinitely toward the perfection of that fixed character, which would be marked by entire absence of self-reproach. The more closely this is approached, the less room for self-control there will be; and where no self-control is possible there will be no self-reproach.

These phenomena seem to be the fundamental characteristics which distinguish a rational being. Blame, in every case, appears to be a modification, often accomplished by a transference, or "projection," of the primary feeling of self-reproach. Accordingly, we never blame anybody for what had been beyond his power of previous self-control. Now, thinking is a

species of conduct which is largely subject to self-control. In all their features (which there is no room to describe here), logical self-control is a perfect mirror of ethical self-control—unless it be rather a species under that genus. In accordance with this, what you cannot in the least help believing is not, justly speaking, wrong belief. In other words, for you it is the absolute truth. True, it is conceivable that what you cannot help believing today, you might find you thoroughly disbelieve tomorrow. But then there is a certain distinction between things you "cannot" do, merely in the sense that nothing stimulates you to the great effort and endeavors that would be required, and things you cannot do because in their own nature they are insusceptible of being put into practice. In every stage of your excogitations, there is something of which you can only say, "I cannot think otherwise," and your experientially based hypothesis is that the impossibility is of the second kind.

There is no reason why "thought," in what has just been said, should be taken in that narrow sense in which silence and darkness are favorable to thought. It should rather be understood as covering all rational life, so that an experiment shall be an operation of thought. Of course, that ultimate state of habit to which the action of self-control ultimately tends, where no room is left for further self-control, is, in the case of thought, the state of fixed belief, or perfect knowledge.

Two things here are all-important to assure oneself of and to remember. The first is that a person is not absolutely an individual. His thoughts are what he is "saying to himself," that is, is to that other self that is just coming into life in the flow of time. When one reasons, it is that critical self that one is trying to persuade; and all thought whatsoever is a sign, and is mostly of the nature of language. The second thing to remember is that the man's circle of society (however widely or narrowly this phrase may be understood), is a sort of loosely compacted person, in some respects of higher rank than the person of an individual organism. It is these two things alone that render it possible for you—but only in the abstract, and in a Pickwickian sense—to distinguish between absolute truth and what you do not doubt.

Let us now hasten to the exposition of pragmaticism itself. Here it will be convenient to imagine that somebody to whom the doctrine is new, but of rather preternatural perspicacity, asks questions of a pragmaticist. Everything that might give a dramatic illusion must be stripped off, so that the result will be a sort of cross between a dialogue and a catechism, but a good deal like the latter—something rather painfully reminiscent of Mangnall's *Historical Questions.*

Questioner: I am astounded at your definition of your pragmatism, because only last year I was assured by a person above all suspicion of warping the truth—himself a pragmatist—that your doctrine precisely was "that a conception is to be tested by its practical effects." You must surely, then, have entirely changed your definition very recently.

Pragmatist: If you will turn to Vols. VI and VII of the *Revue Philosophique*, or to the *Popular Science Monthly* for November 1877 and January 1878 [Papers No. IV and V], you will be able to judge for yourself whether the interpretation you mention was not then clearly excluded. The exact wording of the English enunciation (changing only the first person into the second), was: "Consider what effects that might conceivably have practical bearing you conceive the object of your conception to have. Then your conception of those effects is the WHOLE of your conception of the object."

Questioner: Well, what reason have you for asserting that this is so?

Pragmatist: That is what I specially desire to tell you. But the question had better be postponed until you clearly understand what those reasons profess to prove.

Questioner: What, then, is the *raison d'être* of the doctrine? What advantage is expected from it?

Pragmatist: It will serve to show that almost every proposition of ontological metaphysics is either meaningless gibberish—one word being defined by other words, and they by still others, without any real conception ever being reached—or else is downright absurd; so that all such rubbish being swept away, what will remain of philosophy will be a series of problems capable of investigation by the observational methods of the true sciences—the truth about which can be reached without those interminable misunderstandings and disputes which have made the highest of the positive sciences a mere amusement for idle intellects, a sort of chess—idle pleasure its purpose, and reading out of a book its method. In this regard, pragmaticism

is a species of prope-positivism. But what distinguishes it from other species is, first, its retention of a purified philosophy; secondly, its full acceptance of the main body of our instinctive beliefs; and thirdly, its strenuous insistence upon the truth of scholastic realism (or a close approximation to that, well stated by the late Dr. Francis Ellingwood Abbot in the Introduction to his *Scientific Theism*). So, instead of merely jeering at metaphysics, like other prope-positivists, whether by long drawn-out parodies or otherwise, the pragmaticist extracts from it a precious essence, which will serve to give life and light to cosmology and physics. At the same time, the moral applications of the doctrine are positive and potent; and there are many other uses of it not easily classed. On another occasion, instances may be given to show that it really has these effects.

Questioner: I hardly need to be convinced that your doctrine would wipe out metaphysics. Is it not as obvious that it must wipe out every proposition of science and everything that bears on the conduct of life? For you say that the only meaning that, for you, any assertion bears is that a certain experiment has resulted in a certain way: Nothing else but an experiment enters into the meaning. Tell me, then, how can an experiment, in itself, reveal anything more than that something once happened to an individual object and that subsequently some other individual event occurred?

Pragmatist: That question is, indeed, to the purpose—the purpose being to correct any misapprehensions of pragmaticism. You speak of an experiment in itself, emphasising "*in itself.*" You evidently think of each experiment as isolated from every other. It has not, for example, occurred to you, one might venture to surmise, that every connected series of experiments constitutes a single collective experiment. What are the essential ingredients of an experiment? First, of course, an experimenter of flesh and blood. Secondly, a verifiable hypothesis. This is a proposition relating to the universe environing the experimenter, or to some well-known part of it and affirming or denying of this only some experimental possibility or impossibility. The third indispensable ingredient is a sincere doubt in the experimenter's mind as to the truth of that hypothesis.

Passing over several ingredients on which we need not dwell, the purpose, the plan, and the resolve, we come to the act of choice by which the experimenter singles out certain identifiable objects to be operated upon. The next is the external (or quasi-external) ACT by which he modifies those objects. Next, comes the subsequent *reaction* of the world upon the experimenter in a perception; and finally, his recognition of the teaching of the experiment. While the two chief parts of the event itself are the action and the reaction, yet the unity of essence of the experiment lies in its purpose and plan, the ingredients passed over in the enumeration.

Another thing: in representing the pragmaticist as making rational meaning to consist in an experiment (which you speak of as an event in the past), you strikingly fail to catch his attitude of mind. Indeed, it is not in an experiment, but in *experimental phenomena*, that rational meaning is said to consist. When an experimentalist speaks of a *phenomena*, such as "Hall's phenomenon," "Zeemann's phenomenon" and its modification, "Michelson's phenomenon," or "the chess-board phenomenon," he does not mean any particular event that did happen to somebody in the dead past, but what *surely will* happen to everybody in the living future who shall fulfill certain conditions. The phenomenon consists in the fact that when an experimentalist shall come to *act* according to a certain scheme that he has in mind, then will something else happen, and shatter the doubts of skeptics, like the celestial fire upon the altar of Elijah.

And do not overlook the fact that the pragmaticist maxim says nothing of single experiments or of single experimental phenomena (for what is conditionally true *in futuro* can hardly be singular), but only speaks of *general kinds* of experimental phenomena. Its adherent does not shrink from speaking of general objects as real, since whatever is true represents a real. Now the laws of nature are true.

The rational meaning of every proposition lies in the future. How so? The meaning of a proposition is itself a proposition. Indeed, it is no other than the very proposition of which it is the meaning: it is a translation of it. But of the myriads of forms into which a proposition may be translated, what is that one which is to be called its very meaning? It is, according to the pragmaticist, that form in which the proposition becomes applicable to human conduct, not in these or those special circumstances, nor when one entertains this or that special design, but that form which is most directly applicable to self-control under every situation, and to every purpose. This is why he locates the meaning in future time; for future conduct is the only conduct that is subject to self-control. But in order that that form of the proposition which is to be taken as its meaning should be applicable to every situation and to every purpose upon which the proposition has any bearing, it must be simply the general description of all the experimental phenomena which the assertion of the proposition virtually predicts. For an experimental phenomenon is the fact asserted by the proposition that action of a certain description will have a certain kind of experimental result; and experimental results are the only results that can affect human conduct. No doubt, some unchanging idea may come to influence a man more than it had done; but only because some experiment equivalent to an experiment has brought its truth home to him more intimately than before. Whenever a man acts purposively, he acts under a belief in some experimental phenomenon. Consequently, the sum of the experimental phenomena that a proposition implies makes up its entire bearing upon human conduct. Your question, then, of how a pragmaticist can attribute any meaning to any assertion other than that of a single occurrence is substantially answered.

Questioner: I see that pragmaticism is a thoroughgoing phenomenalism. Only why should you limit yourself to the phenomena of experimental science rather than embrace all observational science? Experiment after all, is an uncommunicative informant. It never expatiates: it only answers "yes" or "no"; or rather it usually snaps out "No!" or, at best only utters an inarticulate grunt for the negation of its "no." The typical experimentalist is not much of an observer. It is the student of natural history to whom nature opens the treasury of her confidence, while she treats the cross-examining experimentalist with the reserve he merits. Why should your phenomenalism sound the meagre jews-harp of experiment rather than the glorious organ of observation?

Pragmaticist: Because pragmaticism is not definable as "thorough-going phenomenalism," although the latter doctrine may be a kind of pragmatism. The *richness* of phenomena lies in their sensuous quality. Pragmaticism does not intend to define the phenomenal equivalents of words and general ideas, but, on the contrary, eliminates their sential element, and endeavors to define the rational purport, and this it finds in the purposive bearing of the word or proposition in question.

Questioner: Well, if you choose so to make Doing the Be-all and the End-all of human life, why do you not make meaning to consist simply in doing? Doing has to be done at a certain time upon a certain object. Individual objects and single events cover all reality, as everybody knows, and as a practicalist ought to be the first to insist. Yet, your meaning, as you have described it, is *general.* Thus, it is of the nature of a mere word and not a reality. You say yourself that your meaning of a proposition is only the same proposition in another dress. But a practical man's meaning is the very thing he means. What do you make to be the meaning of "George Washington"?

Pragmaticist: Forcibly put! A good half dozen of your points must certainly be admitted. It must be admitted, in the first place, that if pragmaticism really made Doing to be the Be-all and the End-all of life, that would be its death. For to say that we live for the mere sake of action, as action, regardless of the thought it carries out, would be to say that there is no such thing as rational purport. Secondly, it must be admitted that every proposition professes to be true of a certain real individual object, often the environing universe. Thirdly, it must be admitted that pragmaticism fails to furnish any translation or meaning of a proper name, or other designation of an individual object. Fourthly, the pragmaticistic meaning is undoubtedly general; and it is equally indisputable that the general is of the nature of a word or sign. Fifthly, it must be admitted that individuals alone exist; and sixthly, it may be admitted that the very meaning of a word or significant object ought to be the very essence of reality of what it signifies. But when those admissions have been unreservedly made, you find the pragmaticist still constrained most earnestly to deny the force of your objection, you ought to infer that there is some consideration that has escaped you. Putting the admissions together, you will perceive that the pragmaticist grants that a proper name (although it is not customary to say that it has a *meaning*), has a certain denotative function peculiar, in each case, to that name and its equivalents; and that he grants that every assertion contains such a

denotative or pointing-out function. In its peculiar individuality, the pragmaticist excludes this from the rational purport of the assertion, although *the like* of it, being common to all assertions, and so, being general and not individual, may enter into the pragmaticistic purport. Whatever exists, *ex-sists*, that is, really acts upon other existents, so obtains a self-identity, and is definitely individual. As to the general, it will be a help to thought to notice that there are two ways of being general. A statue of a soldier on some village monument, in his overcoat and with his musket, is for each of a hundred families the image of its uncle, its sacrifice to the Union. That statue, then, though it is itself single, represents any one man of whom a certain predicate may be true. It is *objectively* general. The word "soldier," whether spoken or written, is general in the same way; while the name, "George Washington," is not so. But each of these two terms remains one and the same noun, whether it be spoken or written, and whenever and wherever it be spoken or written. This noun is not an existent thing: it is a *type*, or *form*, to which objects, both those that are externally existent and those which are imagined, may *conform*, but which none of them can exactly be. This is subjective generality. The pragmaticistic purport is general in both ways.

As to reality, one finds it defined in various ways; but if that principle of terminological ethics that was proposed be accepted, the equivocal language will soon disappear. For *realis* and *realitas* are not ancient words. They were invented to be terms of philosophy in the thirteenth century, and the meaning they were intended to express is perfectly clear. That is *real* which has such and such characters, whether anybody thinks it to have those characters or not. At any rate, that is the sense in which the pragmaticist uses the word. Now, just as conduct controlled by ethical reason tends toward fixing certain habits of conduct, the nature of which (as to illustrate the meaning, peaceable habits and not quarrelsome habits) does not depend upon any accidental circumstances, and *in that sense* may be said to be *destined*; so, thought, controlled by a rational experimental logic, tends to the fixation of certain opinions, equally destined, the nature of which will be the same in the end, however the perversity of thought of whole generations may cause the postponement of the ultimate fixation. If this be so, as every man of us virtually assumes that it is, in regard to each matter the truth of which he seriously discusses, then, according to the adopted definition of "real," the state of things which will be believed in that ultimate opinion is real. But, for the most part, such opinions will be general. Consequently, *some* general objects are real. (Of course, nobody ever thought that *all* generals were real; but the scholastics used to assume that generals were real when they had hardly any, or quite no, experiential evidence to support their assumption; and their fault lay just there, and not in holding that generals could be real.) One is struck with the inexactitude of thought even of analysts of power, when they touch upon modes of being. One will meet, for example, the virtual assumption that what is relative to thought cannot be real. But why not, exactly? *Red* is relative to sight, but the fact that this or that is in that relation to vision that we call being red is not *itself* relative to sight; it is a real fact.

Not only may generals be real, but they may also be *physically efficient*, not in every metaphysical sense, but in the common-sense acception in which human purposes are physically efficient. Aside from metaphysical nonsense, no sane man doubts that if I feel the air in my study to be stuffy, that thought may cause the window to be opened. My thought, be it granted, was an individual event. But what determined it to take the particular determination it did, was in part the general fact that stuffy air is unwholesome, and in part other *Forms*, concerning which Dr. Carus has caused so many men to reflect to advantage—or rather, *by* which, and the general truth concerning which Dr. Carus's mind was determined to the forcible enunciation of so much truth. For truths, on the average, have a greater tendency to get believed than falsities have. Were it otherwise, considering that there are myriads of false hypotheses to account for any given phenomenon, against one sole true one (or if you will have it so, against every true one), the first step toward genuine knowledge must have been next door to a miracle. So, then, when my window was opened, because of the truth that stuffy air is malsain, a physical effort was brought into existence by the efficiency of a general and non-existent truth. This has a droll sound because it is unfamiliar; but exact analysis is with it and not against it; and it has besides, the immense advantage of

not blinding us to great facts—such as that the ideas "justice" and "truth" are, notwithstanding the iniquity of the world, the mightiest of the forces that move it. Generality is, indeed, an indispensable ingredient of reality; for mere individual existence or actuality without any regularity whatever is a nullity. Chaos is pure nothing.

That which any true proposition asserts is *real*, in the sense of being as it is regardless of what you or I may think about it. Let this proposition be a general conditional proposition as to the future, and it is a real general such as is calculated really to influence human conduct; and such the pragmaticist holds to be the rational purport of every concept.

Accordingly, the pragmaticist does not make the *summum bonum* to consist in action, but makes it to consist in that process of evolution whereby the existent comes more and more to embody those generals which were just now said to be *destined*, which is what we strive to express in calling them *reasonable*. In its higher stages, evolution takes place more and more largely through self-control, and this gives the pragmaticist a sort of justification for making the rational purport to be general.

There is much more in elucidation of pragmaticism that might be said to advantage, were it not for the dread of fatiguing the reader. It might, for example, have been well to show clearly that the pragmaticist does not attribute any different essential mode of being to an event in the future from that which he would attribute to a similar event in the past, but only that the practical attitude of the thinker toward the two is different. It would also have been well to show that the pragmaticist does not make Forms to be the *only* realities in the world, any more than he makes the reasonable purport of a word to be the only kind of meaning there is. These things are, however, implicitly involved in what has been said.

READING QUESTIONS

1. Peirce writes that "your problems would be greatly simplified, if, instead of saying that you want to know the 'Truth,' you were simply to say that you

want to attain a state of belief unassailable by doubt." First, according to Peirce, what do the terms *belief* and *doubt* mean? Second, is Peirce correct about this?

2. Express Peirce's pragmaticism in one or two sentences. How, if at all, does his account or understanding of *pragmaticism* differ from his account or understanding of *pragmatism* as expressed in "How to Make Our Ideas Clear"?

3. Explain why Peirce considers "almost every proposition of ontological metaphysics . . . either meaningless gibberish . . . or else . . . downright absurd."

4. Why does Pierce say that the "rational meaning of every proposition lies in the future"?

5. Collect Peirce's various remarks about *what is real*. How does his understanding of *what is real* relate to his understanding of *what is believed to be real*? Also, if possible, relate his understanding of *what is real* to his remark that "every connected series of experiments constitutes a single collective experiment."

SUGGESTIONS FOR FURTHER READING (CHARLES SANDERS PEIRCE)

Primary Sources and Collected Writings

(1931–58) *Collected Papers of Charles Sanders Peirce*, edited by C. Hartshorne and P. Weiss (vols. 1–6) and by A. W Burks (vols. 7–8). Cambridge, MA: Harvard University Press.

(1940) *The Philosophy of Peirce: Selected Writings*, edited by J. Buchler. New York: Harcourt, Brace.

(1956) *Chance, Love and Logic: Philosophical Essays by C. S. Peirce, the Founder of Pragmatism*, edited by M. R. Cohen. New York: Harcourt, Brace.

(1957) *Essays in the Philosophy of Science.* New York: Liberal Arts Press.

(1966) *Charles S. Peirce: Selected Writings*, edited by P. Wiener. New York: Dover Publications.

(1977) *Semantics and Significance: The Correspondence Between Charles S. Peirce and Victoria Lady Welby*, edited by C. Hardwick. Bloomington, IN: Indiana University Press.

(1982–) *The Writings of Charles S. Peirce: A Chronological Edition*, edited by M. Fisch, C. Kloesel, E. Moore, N. Houser, et al. Bloomington, IN: Indiana University Press.

(1992) *Reasoning and the Logic of Things: The Cambridge Conferences, Lectures of 1889*, edited by Kenneth L. Ketner with an introduction by K. L. Ketner and H. Putnam. Cambridge, MA: Harvard University Press.

(1992–4) *The Essential Peirce: Selected Philosophical Writings (1867–1913)*, edited by N. Houser and C. Kloesel. Bloomington, IN: Indiana University Press.

(1998) *Charles S. Peirce: The Essential Writings*, edited by E. C. Moore, et al. Buffalo, NY: Prometheus Books.

(1998) *His Glassy Essence: An Autobiography of Charles Sanders Peirce.* Nashville: Vanderbilt University Press.

Secondary Sources

Almeder, R. (1980) *The Philosophy of Charles S. Peirce.* Totowa, NJ: Rowman and Littlefield.

Ayer, A. J. (1968) *Origins of Pragmatism: Studies in the Philosophy of Charles Sanders Peirce and William James.* New York: Macmillan.

Brent, J. (1998) *Charles Sanders Peirce: A Life.* Bloomington, IN: Indiana University Press.

Colapietro, V. (1989) *Peirce's Approach to the Self.* Buffalo, NY: University of New York Press.

Fisch, M. (1986) *Peirce, Semiotic and Pragmatism.* Bloomington, IN: Indiana State University Press.

Goudge, T. (1950) *The Thought of C. S. Peirce.* Toronto: University of Toronto Press.

Hausman, C. (1993) *Charles S. Peirce's Evolutionary Philosophy.* Cambridge: Cambridge University Press.

Hookway, C. (1985) *Peirce.* London: Routledge & Kegan Paul.

Ketner, K. L. (1995) *Peirce and Contemporary Thought: Philosophical Inquiries.* New York: Fordham University Press.

Kuklick, Bruce (1977) *The Rise of American Philosophy.* New Haven, CT: Yale University Press.

Misak, C. (1991) *The Truth and the End of Inquiry.* Oxford: Oxford University Press.

Moore, E. C. (1961) *American Pragmatism: Peirce, James, and Dewey.* New York: Columbia University Press.

Mounce, H. (1997) *The Two Pragmatisms: From Peirce to Rorty.* London: Routledge.

Murphey, M. (1961) *The Development of Peirce's Philosophy.* Cambridge, MA: Harvard University Press.

Parker, K. (1998) *The Continuity of Peirce's Thought.* Nashville. TN: Vanderbilt University Press.

Rescher, N. (1978) *Peirce's Philosophy of Science.* Notre Dame, IN: University of Notre Dame Press.

Scheffler, I. (1974) *Four Pragmatists: A Critical Introduction to Peirce, James, Mead, and Dewey*, edited by. T. Honderich. New York: Humanities Press.

Skagestad, P. (1981) *The Road of Inquiry: Charles Peirce's Pragmatic Realism.* New York: Columbia University Press.

Thompson, M. (1953) *The Pragmatic Philosophy of C. S. Peirce.* Chicago: University of Chicago Press.

WILLIAM JAMES

What Pragmatism Means

It is rare to find a professional philosopher who also enjoys a certain degree of celebrity. But for much of his life William James (1842–1910) was a prolific philosopher, America's leading psychologist, a Harvard University professor, and a public figure known throughout the world. His writings were equally influential both inside and outside the purely academic sphere.

James's father, Henry James, Sr., was a transcendentalist, a writer, and a public lecturer, and one of his four siblings, Henry James, Jr., would eventually become the famous American novelist and literary critic. The family enjoyed the benefits of wealth, and James was raised in an atmosphere of abundance and luxury. James traveled extensively, enjoyed hobnobbing with the upper class, and was able to dabble in his many interests without fear of financial ruin.

It should come as no surprise, then, that James had an eclectic education. After a period in Europe during which he studied the art of painting, he entered Harvard University and became a student of science, specifically chemistry and anatomy. In 1863 he moved on to the study of medicine. Although the bulk of his medical education was at Harvard, part of his training was obtained in Europe (where he made an effort to become acquainted with the latest developments in experimental psychology). James eventually earned his medical degree from Harvard in 1869.

Despite his high intelligence, academic accomplishments did not come easily. Throughout much of his life James suffered from various debilitating afflictions, including listlessness, loneliness, extreme bouts of depression, and chronic physical pain. Whether these symptoms were genuine or largely psychosomatic is a subject of some speculation.

His career as a philosopher was spent at Harvard (1873–1907), where he eventually rose to the rank of professor of psychology and philosophy. As an writer and university professor, James was something of a Renaissance figure in the American intellectual milieu. Throughout his life he strove to weave together his various interests in psychology, physiology, philosophy, religion, and art. In particular, his pioneering efforts in establishing psychology as a science made a lasting impact on the tone and direction of his philosophical work.

James's fame and influence as a writer and lecturer is largely responsible for the popularization of pragmatism throughout the world. Although he was quick to credit his friend Charles Sanders Peirce for the development of pragmatism as a methodological device for addressing the problems of philosophy, it was James's own commitment to a version of pragmatism that brought the movement international recognition.

In the following essay, "What Pragmatism Means," James clarifies and defends his understanding of pragmatism both as a philosophical methodology and as a theory of truth. The essay has become a staple of the literature of pragmatism—almost a manifesto for the movement. As will become evident, this is in part due to the fact that James was a great philosophical stylist as well as a serious thinker.

Some years ago, being with a camping party in the mountains, I returned from a solitary ramble to find everyone engaged in a ferocious metaphysical dispute. The *corpus* of the dispute was a squirrel—a live squirrel supposed to be clinging to one side of a tree trunk; while over against the tree's opposite side a human being was imagined to stand. This human witness tries to get sight of the squirrel by moving rapidly round the tree, but no matter how fast he goes, the squirrel moves as fast in the opposite direction, and always keeps the tree between himself and the man, so that never a glimpse of him is caught. The resultant metaphysical problem now is this: *Does the man go round the squirrel or not?* He goes round the tree, sure enough, and the squirrel is on the tree; but does he go round the squirrel? In the unlimited leisure of the wilderness, discussion had been worn threadbare. Everyone had taken sides, and was obstinate; and the numbers on both sides were even. Each side, when I appeared, therefore appealed to me to make it a majority. Mindful of the scholastic adage that whenever you meet a contradiction you must make a distinction, I immediately sought and found one, as follows: "Which party is right," I said, "depends on what you *practically mean* by 'going round' the squirrel. If you mean passing from the north of him to the east, then to the south, then to the west, and then to the north of him again, obviously the man does go round him, for he occupies these successive positions. But if on the contrary you mean being first in front of him, then on the right of him, then behind him, then on his left, and finally in front again, it is quite as obvious that the man fails to go round him, for by the compensating movements the squirrel makes, he keeps his belly turned towards the man all the time, and his back turned away. Make the distinction, and there is no occasion for any farther dispute. You are both right and both wrong according

as you conceive the verb 'to go round' in one practical fashion or the other."

Although one or two of the hotter disputants called my speech a shuffling evasion, saying they wanted no quibbling or scholastic hair-splitting, but meant just plain honest English 'round,' the majority seemed to think that the distinction had assuaged the dispute.

I tell this trivial anecdote because it is a peculiarly simple example of what I wish now to speak of as *the pragmatic method.* The pragmatic method is primarily a method of settling metaphysical disputes that otherwise might be interminable. Is the world one or many?—fated or free?—material or spiritual?—here are notions either of which may or may not hold good of the world; and disputes over such notions are unending. The pragmatic method in such cases is to try to interpret each notion by tracing its respective practical consequences. What difference would it practically make to anyone if this notion rather than that notion were true? If no practical difference whatever can be traced, then the alternatives mean practically the same thing, and all dispute is idle. Whenever a dispute is serious, we ought to be able to show some practical difference that must follow from one side or the other's being right.

A glance at the history of the idea will show you still better what pragmatism means. The term is derived from the same Greek word πράγμα, meaning action, from which our words 'practice' and 'practical' come. It was first introduced into philosophy by Mr. Charles Peirce in 1878. In an article entitled "How to Make Our Ideas Clear," in the *Popular Science Monthly* for January of that year Mr. Peirce, after pointing out that our beliefs are really rules for action, said that, to develop a thought's meaning, we need only determine what conduct it is fitted to produce: that conduct is for us its sole significance. And the tangible fact at the root of all our thought-distinctions, however subtle, is that there is no one of them so fine as to consist in anything but a possible difference of practice. To attain perfect clearness in our thoughts of an object, then, we need only consider what conceivable effects of a practical kind the object may involve—what sensations we are to expect from it, and what reactions we must prepare. Our conception of these effects, whether immediate or remote, is then for us the whole of our conception of the object, so far as that conception has positive significance at all.

This is the principle of Peirce, the principle of pragmatism. It lay entirely unnoticed by anyone for twenty years, until I, in an address before Professor Howison's philosophical union at the University of California, brought it forward again and made a special application of it to religion. By that date (1898) the times seemed ripe for its reception. The word 'pragmatism' spread, and at present it fairly spots the pages of the philosophic journals. On all hands we find the 'pragmatic movement' spoken of, sometimes with respect, sometimes with contumely, seldom with clear understanding. It is evident that the term applies itself conveniently to a number of tendencies that hitherto have lacked a collective name, and that it has 'come to stay.'

To take in the importance of Peirce's principle, one must get accustomed to applying it to concrete cases. I found a few years ago that Ostwald, the illustrious Leipzig chemist, had been making perfectly distinct use of the principle of pragmatism in his lectures on the philosophy of science, though he had not called it by that name.

"All realities influence our practice," he wrote me, "and that influence is their meaning for us. I am accustomed to put questions to my classes in this way: In what respects would the world be different if this alternative or that were true? If I can find nothing that would become different, then the alternative has no sense."

That is, the rival views mean practically the same thing, and meaning, other than practical, there is for us none. Ostwald in a published lecture gives this example of what he means. Chemists have long wrangled over the inner constitution of certain bodies called 'tautomerous.' Their properties seemed equally consistent with the notion that an instable hydrogen atom oscillates inside of them, or that they are instable mixtures of two bodies. Controversy raged; but never was decided. "It would never have begun," says Ostwald, "if the combatants had asked themselves what particular experimental fact could have been made different by one or the other view being correct. For it would then have appeared that no difference of fact could possibly ensue; and the quarrel was as unreal as if, theorizing in primitive times about the raising of dough by yeast,

one party should have invoked a 'brownie,' while another insisted on an 'elf' as the true cause of the phenomenon."

It is astonishing to see how many philosophical disputes collapse into insignificance the moment you subject them to this simple test of tracing a concrete consequence. There can be no difference anywhere that doesn't *make* a difference elsewhere—no difference in abstract truth that doesn't express itself in a difference in concrete fact and in conduct consequent upon that fact, imposed on somebody, somehow, somewhere and somewhen. The whole function of philosophy ought to be to find out what definite difference it will make to you and me, at definite instants of our life, if this world-formula or that world-formula be the true one.

There is absolutely nothing new in the pragmatic method. Socrates was an adept at it. Aristotle used it methodically. Locke, Berkeley and Hume made momentous contributions to truth by its means. Shadworth Hodgson keeps insisting that realities are only what they are 'known-as.' But these forerunners of pragmatism used it in fragments: they were preluders only. Not until in our time has it generalized itself, become conscious of a universal mission, pretended to a conquering destiny. I believe in that destiny, and I hope I may end by inspiring you with my belief.

Pragmatism represents a perfectly familiar attitude in philosophy, the empiricist attitude, but it represents it, as it seems to me, both in a more radical and in a less objectionable form than it has ever yet assumed. A pragmatist turns his back resolutely and once for all upon a lot of inveterate habits dear to professional philosophers. He turns away from abstraction and insufficiency, from verbal solutions, from bad *a priori* reasons, from fixed principles, closed systems, and pretended absolutes and origins. He turns towards concreteness and adequacy, towards facts, towards action, and towards power. That means the empiricist temper regnant, and the rationalist temper sincerely given up. It means the open air and possibilities of nature, as against dogma, artificiality and the pretense of finality in truth.

At the same time it does not stand for any special results. It is a method only. But the general triumph of that method would mean an enormous change in what

I called in my last lecture the 'temperament' of philosophy. Teachers of the ultra-rationalistic type would be frozen out, much as the courtier type is frozen out in republics, as the ultramontane type of priest is frozen out in Protestant lands. Science and metaphysics would come much nearer together, would in fact work absolutely hand in hand.

Metaphysics has usually followed a very primitive kind of quest. You know how men have always hankered after unlawful magic, and you know what a great part, in magic, *words* have always played. If you have his name, or the formula of incantation that binds him, you can control the spirit, genie, afrite, or whatever the power may be. Solomon knew the names of all the spirits, and having their names, he held them subject to his will. So the universe has always appeared to the natural mind as a kind of enigma, of which the key must be sought in the shape of some illuminating or power-bringing word or name. That word names the universe's *principle*, and to possess it is, after a fashion, to possess the universe itself. 'God,' 'Matter,' 'Reason,' 'the Absolute,' 'Energy,' are so many solving names. You can rest when you have them. You are at the end of your metaphysical quest.

But if you follow the pragmatic method, you cannot look on any such word as closing your quest. You must bring out of each word its practical cash-value, set it at work within the stream of your experience. It appears less as a solution, then, than as a program for more work, and more particularly as an indication of the ways in which existing realities may be *changed*.

Theories thus become instruments, not answers to enigmas, in which we can rest. We don't lie back upon them, we move forward, and, on occasion, make nature over again by their aid. Pragmatism unstiffens all our theories, limbers them up and sets each one at work. Being nothing essentially new, it harmonizes with many ancient philosophic tendencies. It agrees with nominalism for instance, in always appealing to particulars; with utilitarianism in emphasizing practical aspects; with positivism in its disdain for verbal solutions, useless questions, and metaphysical abstractions.

All these, you see, are *anti-intellectualist* tendencies. Against rationalism as a pretension and a method, pragmatism is fully armed and militant. But, at the outset, at least, it stands for no particular results. It has no dogmas, and no doctrines save its method. As the young Italian pragmatist Papini has well said, it lies in the midst of our theories, like a corridor in a hotel. Innumerable chambers open out of it. In one you may find a man writing an atheistic volume; in the next someone on his knees praying for faith and strength; in a third a chemist investigating a body's properties. In a fourth a system of idealistic metaphysics is being excogitated; in a fifth the impossibility of metaphysics is being shown. But they all own the corridor, and all must pass through it if they want a practicable way of getting into or out of their respective rooms.

No particular results then, so far, but only an attitude of orientation, is what the pragmatic method means. *The attitude of looking away from first things, principles, 'categories,' supposed necessities; and of looking towards last things, fruits, consequences, facts.*

So much for the pragmatic method! You may say that I have been praising it rather than explaining it to you, but I shall presently explain it abundantly enough by showing how it works on some familiar problems. Meanwhile the word pragmatism has come to be used in a still wider sense, as meaning also a certain *theory of truth.* I mean to give a whole lecture to the statement of that theory, after first paving the way, so I can be very brief now. But brevity is hard to follow, so I ask for your redoubled attention for a quarter of an hour. If much remains obscure, I hope to make it clearer in the later lectures.

One of the most successfully cultivated branches of philosophy in our time is what is called inductive logic, the study of the conditions under which our sciences have evolved. Writers on this subject have begun to show a singular unanimity as to what the laws of nature and elements of fact mean, when formulated by mathematicians, physicists and chemists. When the first mathematical, logical and natural uniformities, the first *laws*, were discovered, men were so carried away by the clearness, beauty and simplification that resulted, that they believed themselves to have deciphered authentically the eternal thoughts of the Almighty. His mind also thundered and reverberated in syllogisms. He also thought in conic sections, squares and roots and ratios, and geometrized like Euclid. He made Kepler's laws for the planets to follow; he made velocity increase proportionally to the time in falling bodies; he made the law of the sines for light to obey when refracted; he established the classes, orders, families and genera of plants and animals, and fixed the distances between them. He thought the archetypes of all things, and devised their variations; and when we rediscover any one of these his wondrous institutions, we seize his mind in its very literal intention.

But as the sciences have developed farther, the notion has gained ground that most, perhaps all, of our laws are only approximations. The laws themselves, moreover, have grown so numerous that there is no counting them; and so many rival formulations are proposed in all the branches of science that investigators have become accustomed to the notion that no theory is absolutely a transcript of reality, but that any one of them may from some point of view be useful. Their great use is to summarize old facts and to lead to new ones. They are only a man-made language, a conceptual shorthand, as someone calls them, in which we write our reports of nature; and languages, as is well known, tolerate much choice of expression and many dialects.

Thus human arbitrariness has driven divine necessity from scientific logic. If I mention the names of Sigwart, Mach, Ostwald, Pearson, Milhaud, Poincaré, Duhem, Ruyssen, those of you who are students will easily identify the tendency I speak of, and will think of additional names.

Riding now on the front of this wave of scientific logic Messrs. Schiller and Dewey appear with their pragmatistic account of what truth everywhere signifies. Everywhere, these teachers say, 'truth' in our ideas and beliefs means the same thing that it means in science. It means, they say, nothing but this, *that ideas (which themselves are but parts of our experience) become true just in so far as they help us to get into satisfactory relation with other parts of our experience,* to summarize them and get about among them by conceptual shortcuts instead of following the interminable succession of particular phenomena. Any idea upon which we can ride, so to speak; any idea that will carry us prosperously from any one part of our experience to any other part, linking things satisfactorily, working securely, simplifying, saving labor, is true for just so much, true in so far forth, true *instrumentally*. This is the 'instrumental' view of truth taught so successfully at Chicago, the view that truth in our ideas means their power to 'work,' promulgated so brilliantly at Oxford.

Messrs. Dewey, Schiller and their allies, in reaching this general conception of all truth, have only followed the example of geologists, biologists and philologists. In the establishment of these other sciences, the successful stroke was always to take some simple process actually observable in operation—as denudation by weather, say, or variation from parental type, or change of dialect by incorporation of new words and pronunciations—and then to generalize it, making it apply to all times, and produce great results by summating its effects through the ages.

The observable process which Schiller and Dewey particularly singled out for generalization is the familiar one by which any individual settles into *new opinions*. The process here is always the same. The individual has a stock of old opinions already, but he meets a new experience that puts them to a strain. Somebody contradicts them; or in a reflective moment he discovers that they contradict each other; or he hears of facts with which they are incompatible; or desires arise in him which they cease to satisfy. The result is an inward trouble to which his mind till then had been a stranger, and from which he seeks to escape by modifying his previous mass of opinions. He saves as much of it as he can, for in this matter of belief we are all extreme conservatives. So he tries to change first this opinion, and then that (for they resist change very variously), until at last some new idea comes up which he can graft upon the ancient stock with a minimum of disturbance of the latter, some idea that mediates between the stock and the new experience and runs them into one another most felicitously and expediently.

This new idea is then adopted as the true one. It preserves the older stock of truths with a minimum of modification, stretching them just enough to make them admit the novelty, but conceiving that in ways as familiar as the case leaves possible. An *outrée* explanation, violating all our preconceptions, would never pass for a true account of a novelty. We should scratch round industriously till we found something less excentric. The most violent revolutions in an individual's beliefs leave most of his old order standing. Time and space, cause and effect, nature and history, and one's own biography remain untouched. New truth is always a go-between, a smoother-over of transitions. It marries old opinion to new fact so as ever to show a minimum of jolt, a maximum of continuity. We hold a theory true just in proportion to its success in solving this 'problem of maxima and minima.' But success in solving this problem is eminently a matter of approximation. We say this theory solves it on the whole more satisfactorily than that theory; but that means more satisfactorily to ourselves, and individuals will emphasize their points of satisfaction differently. To a certain degree, therefore, everything here is plastic.

The point I now urge you to observe particularly is the part played by the older truths. Failure to take account of it is the source of much of the unjust criticism leveled against pragmatism. Their influence is absolutely controlling. Loyalty to them is the first principle—in most cases it is the only principle; for by far the most usual way of handling phenomena so novel that they would make for a serious rearrangement of our preconceptions is to ignore them altogether, or to abuse those who bear witness for them.

You doubtless wish examples of this process of truth's growth, and the only trouble is their superabundance. The simplest case of new truth is of course the mere numerical addition of new kinds of facts, or of new single facts of old kinds, to our experience—an addition that involves no alteration in the old beliefs. Day follows day, and its contents are simply added. The new contents themselves are not true, they simply *come* and *are*. Truth is *what we say about* them, and when we say that they have come, truth is satisfied by the plain additive formula.

But often the day's contents oblige a rearrangement. If I should now utter piercing shrieks and act like a maniac on this platform, it would make many of you revise your ideas as to the probable worth of my philosophy. 'Radium' came the other day as part of the day's content, and seemed for a moment to contradict our ideas of the whole order of nature, that order having come to be identified with what is called the conservation of energy. The mere sight of radium paying heat away indefinitely out of its own pocket seemed to violate that conservation. What to think? If the radiations from it were nothing but an escape of unsuspected 'potential' energy, pre-existent inside of the atoms, the principle of conservation would be saved.

The discovery of 'helium' as the radiation's outcome opened a way to this belief. So Ramsay's view is generally held to be true, because, although it extends our old ideas of energy, it causes a minimum of alteration in their nature.

I need not multiply instances. A new opinion counts as 'true' just in proportion as it gratifies the individual's desire to assimilate the novel in his experience to his beliefs in stock. It must both lean on old truth and grasp new fact; and its success (as I said a moment ago) in doing this, is a matter for the individual's appreciation. When old truth grows, then, by new truth's addition, it is for subjective reasons. We are in the process and obey the reasons. That new idea is truest which performs most felicitously its function of satisfying our double urgency. It makes itself true, gets itself classed as true, by the way it works; grafting itself then upon the ancient body of truth, which thus grows much as a tree grows by the activity of a new layer of cambium.

Now Dewey and Schiller proceed to generalize this observation and to apply it to the most ancient parts of truth. They also once were plastic. They also were called true for human reasons. They also mediated between still earlier truths and what in those days were novel observations. Purely objective truth, truth in whose establishment the function of giving human satisfaction in marrying previous parts of experience with newer parts played no role whatever, is nowhere to be found. The reasons why we call things true is the reason why they *are* true, for 'to be true' *means* only to perform this marriage-function.

The trail of the human serpent is thus over everything. Truth independent; truth that we *find* merely; truth no longer malleable to human need; truth incorrigible, in a word; such truth exists indeed superabundantly—or is supposed to exist by rationalistically minded thinkers; but then it means only the dead heart of the living tree, and its being there means only that truth also has its paleontology and its 'prescription,' and may grow stiff with years of veteran service and petrified in men's regard by sheer antiquity. But how plastic even the oldest truths nevertheless really are has been vividly shown in our day by the transformation of logical and mathematical ideas, a transformation which seems even to be invading physics. The ancient formulas are reinterpreted as special expressions of much wider principles, principles that our ancestors never got a glimpse of in their present shape and formulation.

Mr. Schiller still gives to all this view of truth the name of 'Humanism,' but, for this doctrine too, the name of pragmatism seems fairly to be in the ascendant, so I will treat it under the name of pragmatism in these lectures.

Such then would be the scope of pragmatism—first, a method; and second, a genetic theory of what is meant by truth. And these two things must be our future topics.

· · ·

You will probably be surprised to learn, then, that Messrs. Schiller's and Dewey's theories have suffered a hailstorm of contempt and ridicule. All rationalism has risen against them. In influential quarters Mr. Schiller, in particular, has been treated like an impudent schoolboy who deserves a spanking. I should not mention this, but for the fact that it throws so much sidelight upon that rationalistic temper to which I have opposed the temper of pragmatism. Pragmatism is uncomfortable away from facts. Rationalism is comfortable only in the presence of abstractions. This pragmatist talk about truths in the plural, about their utility and satisfactoriness, about the success with which they 'work,' etc., suggests to the typical intellectualist mind a sort of coarse lame second-rate makeshift article of truth. Such truths are not real truth. Such tests are merely subjective. As against this, objective truth must be something non-utilitarian, haughty, refined, remote, august, exalted. It must be an absolute correspondence of our thoughts with an equally absolute reality. It must be what we *ought* to think, unconditionally. The conditioned ways in which we *do* think are so much irrelevance and matter for psychology. Down with psychology, up with logic, in all this question!

See the exquisite contrast of the types of mind! The pragmatist clings to facts and concreteness, observes truth at its work in particular cases, and generalizes. Truth, for him, becomes a class-name for all sorts of definite working-values in experience. For the rationalist it remains a pure abstraction, to the bare name of

which we must defer. When the pragmatist undertakes to show in detail just *why* we must defer, the rationalist is unable to recognize the concretes from which his own abstraction is taken. He accuses us of denying truth; whereas we have only sought to trace exactly why people follow it and always ought to follow it. Your typical ultra-abstractionist fairly shudders at concreteness: Other things equal, he positively prefers the pale and spectral. If the two universes were offered, he would always choose the skinny outline rather than the rich thicket of reality. It is so much purer, clearer, nobler.

I hope that as these lectures go on, the concreteness and closeness to facts of the pragmatism which they advocate may be what approves itself to you as its most satisfactory peculiarity. It only follows here the example of the sister-sciences, interpreting the unobserved by the observed. It brings old and new harmoniously together. It converts the absolutely empty notion of a static relation of 'correspondence' (what that may mean we must ask later) between our minds and reality, into that of a rich and active commerce (that anyone may follow in detail and understand) between particular thoughts of ours, and the great universe of other experiences in which they play their parts and have their uses.

But enough of this at present? The justification of what I say must be postponed. I wish now to add a word in further explanation of the claim I made at our last meeting, that pragmatism may be a happy harmonizer of empiricist ways of thinking, with the more religious demands of human beings.

Men who are strongly of the fact-loving temperament, you may remember me to have said, are liable to be kept at a distance by the small sympathy with facts which that philosophy from the present-day fashion of idealism offers them. It is far too intellectualistic. Old-fashioned theism was bad enough, with its notion of God as an exalted monarch, made up of a lot of unintelligible or preposterous 'attributes'; but, so long as it held strongly by the argument from design, it kept some touch with concrete realities. Since, however, Darwinism has once for all displaced design from the minds of the 'scientific,' theism has lost that foothold; and some kind of an immanent or pantheistic deity working *in* things rather than above them is, if any, the kind recommended to our contemporary imagination. Aspirants to a philosophic religion turn, as a rule, more hopefully nowadays towards idealistic pantheism than towards the older dualistic theism, in spite of the fact that the latter still counts able defenders.

But, . . . , the brand of pantheism offered is hard for them to assimilate if they are lovers of facts, or empirically minded. It is the absolutistic brand, spurning the dust and reared upon pure logic. It keeps no connexion whatever with concreteness. Affirming the Absolute Mind, which is its substitute for God, to be the rational presupposition of all particulars of fact, whatever they may be, it remains supremely indifferent to what the particular facts in our world actually are. Be they what they may, the Absolute will father them. Like the sick lion in Aesop's fable, all footprints lead into his den, but *nulla vestigia retrorsum*. You cannot redescend into the world of particulars by the Absolute's aid, or deduce any necessary consequences of detail important for your life from your idea of his nature. He gives you indeed the assurance that all is well with *Him*, and for his eternal way of thinking; but thereupon he leaves you to be finitely saved by your own temporal devices.

Far be it from me to deny the majesty of this conception, or its capacity to yield religious comfort to a most respectable class of minds. But from the human point of view, no one can pretend that it doesn't suffer from the faults of remoteness and abstractness. It is eminently a product of what I have ventured to call the rationalistic temper. It disdains empiricism's needs. It substitutes a pallid outline for the real world's richness. It is dapper; it is noble in the bad sense, in the sense in which to be noble is to be inapt for humble service. In this real world of sweat and dirt, it seems to me that when a view of things is 'noble,' that ought to count as a presumption against its truth, and as a philosophic disqualification. The prince of darkness may be a gentleman, as we are told he is, but whatever the God of earth and heaven is, he can surely be no gentleman. His menial services are needed in the dust of our human trials, even more than his dignity is needed in the empyrean.

Now pragmatism, devoted though she be to facts, has no such materialistic bias as ordinary empiricism labors under. Moreover, she has no objection whatever to the realizing of abstractions, so long as you get about among particulars with their aid and they actually carry you somewhere. Interested in no conclusions but those which our minds and our experiences work out together, she has no *a priori* prejudices against theology. *If theological ideas prove to have a value for concrete life, they will be true, for pragmatism, in the sense of being good for so much. For how much more they are true will depend entirely on their relations to the other truths that also have to be acknowledged.*

What I said just now about the Absolute of transcendental idealism is a case in point. First, I called it majestic and said it yielded religious comfort to a class of minds, and then I accused it of remoteness and sterility. But so far as it affords such comfort, it surely is not sterile; it has that amount of value; it performs a concrete function. As a good pragmatist, I myself ought to call the Absolute true 'in so far forth,' then; and I unhesitatingly now do so.

But what does *true in so far forth* mean in this case? To answer, we need only apply the pragmatic method. What do believers in the Absolute mean by saying that their belief affords them comfort? They mean that since in the Absolute finite evil is 'overruled' already, we may, therefore, whenever we wish, treat the temporal as if it were potentially the eternal, be sure that we can trust its outcome, and, without sin, dismiss our fear and drop the worry of our finite responsibility. In short, they mean that we have a right ever and anon to take a moral holiday, to let the world wag in its own way, feeling that its issues are in better hands than ours and are none of our business.

The universe is a system of which the individual members may relax their anxieties occasionally, in which the don't-care mood is also right for men, and moral holidays in order—that, if I mistake not, is part, at least, of what the Absolute is 'known-as,' that is the great difference in our particular experiences which his being true makes for us, that is part of his cash-value when he is pragmatically interpreted. Farther than that the ordinary lay-reader in philosophy who thinks favorably of absolute idealism does not venture to sharpen his conceptions. He can use the Absolute for so much, and so much is very precious. He is pained at hearing you speak incredulously of the

Absolute, therefore, and disregards your criticisms because they deal with aspects of the conception that he fails to follow.

If the Absolute means this, and means no more than this, who can possibly deny the truth of it? To deny it would be to insist that men should never relax, and that holidays are never in order.

I am well aware how odd it must seem to some of you to hear me say that an idea is 'true' so long as to believe it is profitable to our lives. That it is good, for as much as it profits, you will gladly admit. If what we do by its aid is good, you will allow the idea itself to be good in so far forth, for we are the better for possessing it. But is it not a strange misuse of the word 'truth,' you will say, to call ideas also 'true' for this reason?

To answer this difficulty fully is impossible at this stage of my account. You touch here upon the very central point of Messrs. Schiller's, Dewey's and my own doctrine of truth, which I cannot discuss with detail until my sixth lecture. Let me now say only this, that truth is *one species of good*, and not, as is usually supposed, a category distinct from good, and coordinate with it. *The true is the name of whatever proves itself to be good in the way of belief, and good, too, for definite, assignable reasons.* Surely you must admit this, that if there were *no* good for life in true ideas, or if the knowledge of them were positively disadvantageous and false ideas the only useful ones, then the current notion that truth is divine and precious, and its pursuit a duty, could never have grown up or become a dogma. In a world like that, our duty would be to *shun* truth, rather. But in this world, just as certain foods are not only agreeable to our taste, but good for our teeth, our stomach and our tissues; so certain ideas are not only agreeable to think about, or agreeable as supporting other ideas that we are fond of, but they are also helpful in life's practical struggles. If there be any life that it is really better we should lead, and if there be any idea which, if believed in, would help us to lead that life, then it would be really *better for us* to believe in that idea, *unless, indeed, belief in it incidentally clashed with other greater vital benefits.*

'What would be better for us to believe'! This sounds very like a definition of truth. It comes very near to saying 'what we *ought* to believe': and in *that* definition none of you would find any oddity. Ought we ever not to believe what it is *better for us* to believe? And can we then keep the notion of what is better for us, and what is true for us, permanently apart?

Pragmatism says no, and I fully agree with her. Probably you also agree, so far as the abstract statement goes, but with a suspicion that if we practically did believe everything that made for good in our own personal lives, we should be found indulging all kinds of fancies about this world's affairs, and all kinds of sentimental superstitions about a world hereafter. Your suspicion here is undoubtedly well founded, and it is evident that something happens when you pass from the abstract to the concrete, that complicates the situation.

I said just now that what is better for us to believe is true *unless the belief incidentally clashes with some other vital benefit.* Now in real life what vital benefits is any particular belief of ours most liable to clash with? What indeed except the vital benefits yielded by *other beliefs* when these prove incompatible with the first ones? In other words, the greatest enemy of any one of our truths may be the rest of our truths. Truths have once for all this desperate instinct of self-preservation and of desire to extinguish whatever contradicts them. My belief in the Absolute, based on the good it does me, must run the gauntlet of all my other beliefs. Grant that it may be true in giving me a moral holiday. Nevertheless, as I conceive it—and let me speak now confidentially, as it were, and merely in my own private person—it clashes with other truths of mine whose benefits I hate to give up on its account. It happens to be associated with a kind of logic of which I am the enemy, I find that it entangles me in metaphysical paradoxes that are inacceptable, etc., etc. But as I have enough trouble in life already without adding the trouble of carrying these intellectual inconsistencies, I personally just give up the Absolute. I just *take* my moral holidays; or else as a professional philosopher, I try to justify them by some other principle.

If I could restrict my notion of the Absolute to its bare holiday-giving value, it wouldn't clash with my other truths. But we cannot easily thus restrict our hypotheses. They carry supernumerary features, and these it is that clash so. My disbelief in the Absolute means then disbelief in those other supernumerary features, for I fully believe in the legitimacy of taking moral holidays.

You see by this what I meant when I called pragmatism a mediator and reconciler and said, borrowing the word from Papini, that she 'unstiffens' our theories. She has in fact no prejudices whatever, no obstructive dogmas, no rigid canons of what shall count as proof. She is completely genial. She will entertain any hypothesis, she will consider any evidence. It follows that in the religious field she is at a great advantage both over positivistic empiricism, with its anti-theological bias, and over religious rationalism, with its exclusive interest in the remote, the noble, the simple, and the abstract in the way of conception.

In short, she widens the field of search for God. Rationalism sticks to logic and the empyrean. Empiricism sticks to the external senses. Pragmatism is willing to take anything, to follow either logic or the senses, and to count the humblest and most personal experiences. She will count mystical experiences if they have practical consequences. She will take a God who lives in the very dirt of private fact—if that should seem a likely place to find him.

Her only test of probable truth is what works best in the way of leading us, what fits every part of life best and combines with the collectivity of experience's demands, nothing being omitted. If theological ideas should do this, if the notion of God, in particular, should prove to do it, how could pragmatism possibly deny God's existence? She could see no meaning in treating as 'not true' a notion that was pragmatically so successful. What other kind of truth could there be, for her, than all this agreement with concrete reality? . . .

READING QUESTIONS

1. What does James mean by "practical" and by "experience"?
2. James asserts that "the whole function of philosophy ought to be to find out what definite difference it will make to you and me, at definite instances of our life, if this world-formula or that world-formula be the true one." Is this an adequate conception of philosophy? Why or why not?
3. James discusses pragmatism both as a philosophical method and as a theory of truth. What are the important differences here? Could one consistently defend pragmatism in one sense without necessarily defending it in the other? Why or why not?
4. In speaking of truth, James claims that "the trail of the human serpent is thus over everything." What does he mean by this? Is it true?
5. In what ways does James contrast pragmatism with rationalism? Is his characterization of rationalism fair and accurate? Why or why not? Do you consider yourself more of a pragmatist, a rationalist, or neither?
6. James claims that "*if theological ideas prove to have a value for concrete life, they will be true, for pragmatism, in the sense of being good for so much. For how much more they are true, will depend entirely on their relations to the other truths that also have to be acknowledged.*" What does James mean? Do you agree with him? Why or why not?
7. James asserts that truth is a kind of good or value. What does he mean by this? Do you share this conception of truth as a kind of good or value? Why or why not?

WILLIAM JAMES

The Moral Philosopher and the Moral Life

In the following essay, James turns to an examination of ethics. He advocates an experimental approach to moral philosophy, likening it to science, and he argues that "there is no such thing possible as an ethical philosophy dogmatically made up in advance." The process of formulating an adequate moral philosophy depends on our reflecting critically on our experiences over the course of our "moral life." The connections to his overall pragmatic approach to the problems of ethics are too obvious to miss.

The main purpose of this paper is to show that there is no such thing possible as an ethical philosophy dogmatically made up in advance. We all help to determine the content of ethical philosophy so far as we contribute to the race's moral life. In other words, there can be no final truth in ethics any more than in physics, until the last man has had his experience and said his say. In the one case as in the other, however, the hypotheses which we now make while waiting, and the acts to which they prompt us, are among the indispensable conditions which determine what that 'say' shall be.

First of all, what is the position of him who seeks an ethical philosophy? To begin with, he must be distinguished from all those who are satisfied to be ethical skeptics. He *will* not be a skeptic; therefore so far from ethical skepticism being one possible fruit of ethical philosophizing, it can only be regarded as that residual alternative to all philosophy which from the outset menaces every would-be philosopher who may give up the quest discouraged, and renounce his original aim. That aim is to find an account of the moral relations that obtain among things, which will weave them into the unity of a stable system, and make of the world what one may call a genuine universe from the ethical point of view. So far as the world resists reduction to the form of unity, so far as ethical propositions seem unstable, so far does the philosopher fail of his ideal. The subject matter of his study is the ideals he finds existing in the world; the purpose which guides him is this ideal of his own, of getting them into a certain form. This ideal is thus a factor in ethical philosophy whose legitimate presence must never be overlooked; it is a positive contribution which the philosopher himself necessarily makes to the problem. But it is his only positive contribution. At the outset of his inquiry he

William James, "The Moral Philosopher and the Moral Life" reprinted by permission of the publisher from *The Will to Believe and Other Essays* by William James, Cambridge, Mass.: Harvard University Press, Copyright © 1978 by the President and Fellows of Harvard College.

ought to have no other ideals. Were he interested peculiarly in the triumph of any one kind of good, he would *pro tanto* cease to be a judicial investigator, and become an advocate for some limited element of the case.

There are three questions in ethics which must be kept apart. Let them be called respectively the *psychological* question, the *metaphysical* question, and the *casuistic* question. The psychological question asks after the historical *origin* of our moral ideas and judgments; the metaphysical question asks what the very *meaning* of the words 'good,' 'ill,' and 'obligation' are; the casuistic question asks what is the *measure* of the various goods and ills which men recognize, so that the philosopher may settle the true order of human obligations.

I

The psychological question is for most disputants the only question. When your ordinary doctor of divinity has proved to his own satisfaction that an altogether unique faculty called 'conscience' must be postulated to tell us what is right and what is wrong, or when your popular-science enthusiast has proclaimed that 'apriorism' is an exploded superstition, and that our moral judgments have gradually resulted from the teaching of the environment, each of these persons thinks that ethics is settled and nothing more is to be said. The familiar pair of names, Intuitionist and Evolutionist, so commonly used now to connote all possible differences in ethical opinion, really refer to the psychological question alone. The discussion of this question hinges so much upon particular details that it is impossible to enter upon it at all within the limits of this paper. I will therefore only express dogmatically my own belief, which is this—that the Benthams, the Mills, and the Bains have done a lasting service in taking so many of our human ideals and showing how they must have arisen from the association with acts of simple bodily pleasures and reliefs from pain. Association with many remote pleasures will unquestionably make a thing significant of goodness in our minds; and the more vaguely the goodness is conceived of, the more mysterious will its source appear to be. But it is surely impossible to explain all our sentiments and preferences in this simple way. The more minutely psychology studies human nature, the more clearly it finds there traces of secondary affections, relating the impressions of the environment with one another and with our impulses in quite different ways from those mere associations of coexistence and succession which are practically all that pure empiricism can admit. Take the love of drunkenness; take bashfulness, the terror of high places, the tendency to sea-sickness, to faint at the sight of blood, the susceptibility to musical sounds; take the emotion of the comical, the passion for poetry, for mathematics, or for metaphysics—no one of these things can be wholly explained by either association or utility. They *go with* other things that can be so explained, no doubt; and some of them are prophetic of future utilities, since there is nothing in us for which some use may not be found. But their origin is in incidental complications to our cerebral structure, a structure whose original features arose with no reference to the perception of such discords and harmonies as these.

Well, a vast number of our moral perceptions also are certainly of this secondary and brain-born kind. They deal with directly felt fitnesses between things, and often fly in the teeth of all the prepossessions of habit and presumptions of utility. The moment you get beyond the coarser and more commonplace moral maxims, the Decalogues and Poor Richard's Almanacs, you fall into schemes and positions which to the eye of common sense are fantastic and over-strained. The sense for abstract justice which some persons have is as eccentric a variation, from the natural history point of view, as is the passion for music or for the higher philosophical consistencies which consumes the soul of others. The feeling of the inward dignity of certain spiritual attitudes, as peace, serenity, simplicity, veracity; and of the essential vulgarity of others, as querulousness, anxiety, egoistic fussiness, etc.—are quite inexplicable except by an innate preference of the more ideal attitude for its own pure sake. The nobler thing *tastes* better, and that is all that we can say. 'Experience' of consequences may truly teach us what things are *wicked*, but what have consequences to do with what is *mean* and *vulgar*? If a man has shot his wife's paramour, by reason of what subtle repugnancy in things is it that we are so disgusted when we hear that the wife and the husband have made it up and are living comfortably together again? Or if

the hypothesis were offered us of a world in which Messrs. Fourier's and Bellamy's and Morris's utopias should all be outdone, and millions kept permanently happy on the one simple condition that a certain lost should on the far-off edge of things should lead a life of lonely torture, what except a specifical and independent sort of emotion can it be which would make us immediately feel, even though an impulse arose within us to clutch at the happiness so offered, how hideous a thing would be its enjoyment when deliberately accepted as the fruit of such a bargain? To what, once more, but subtle brain-born feelings of discord can be due all these recent protests against the entire race-tradition of retributive justices?—I refer to Tolstoy with his ideas of non-resistance, to Mr. Bellamy with his substitution of oblivion for repentance (in his novel of Dr. Heidenhain's Process), to M. Guyau with his radical condemnation of the punitive ideal. All these subtleties of the moral sensibility go as much beyond what can be ciphered out from the 'laws of association' as the delicacies of sentiment possible between a pair of young lovers go beyond such precepts of the 'etiquette to be observed during engagement' as are printed in manuals of social form.

No! Purely inward forces are certainly at work here. All the higher, more penetrating ideals are revolutionary. They present themselves far less in the guise of effects of past experience than in that of probable causes of future experience, factors to which the environment and the lessons it has so far taught us must learn to bend.

This is all I can say of the psychological question now. In the last chapter of a recent work I have sought to prove in a general way the existence, in our thought, of relations which do not merely repeat the couplings of experience. Our ideals have certainly many sources. They are not all explicable as signifying corporeal pleasures to be gained, and pains to be escaped. And for having so constantly perceived this psychological fact, we must applaud the intuitionist school. Whether or not such applause must be extended to that school's other characteristics will appear as we take up the following questions.

The next one in order is the metaphysical question, of what we mean by the words 'obligation,' 'good,' and 'ill.'

II

First of all, it appears that such words can have no application or relevancy in a world in which no sentient life exists. Imagine an absolutely material world, containing only physical and chemical facts, and existing from eternity without a God, without even an interested spectator: Would there be any sense in saying of that world that one of its states is better than another? Or if there were two such worlds possible, would there be any rhyme or reason in calling one good and the other bad—good or bad positively, I mean, and apart from the fact that one might relate itself better than the other to the philosopher's private interests? But we must leave these private interests out of the account, for the philosopher is a mental fact, and we are asking whether goods and evils and obligations exist in physical facts *per se*. Surely there is no *status* for good and evil to exist in, in a purely insentient world. How can one physical fact, considered simply as a physical fact, be 'better' than another? Betterness is not a physical relation. In its mere material capacity, a thing can no more be good or bad than it can be pleasant or painful. Good for what? Good for the production of another physical fact, do you say? But what in a purely physical universe demands the production of that other fact? Physical facts simply *are* or are *not*; and neither when present or absent, can they be supposed to make demands. If they do, they can only do so by having desires; and then they have ceased to be purely physical facts, and have become facts of conscious sensibility. Goodness, badness, and obligation must be *realized* somewhere in order really to exist; and the first step in ethical philosophy is to see that no merely inorganic 'nature of things' can realize them. Neither moral relations nor the moral law can swing *in vacuo*. Their only habitat can be a mind which feels them; and no world composed of merely physical facts can possibly be a world to which ethical propositions apply.

The moment one sentient being, however, is made a part of the universe, there is a chance for goods and evils really to exist. Moral relations now have their *status*, in that being's consciousness. So far as he feels anything to be good, he *makes* it good. It *is* good, for him;

and being good for him, is absolutely good, for he is the sole creator of values in that universe, and outside of his opinion things have no moral character at all.

In such a universe as that it would of course be absurd to raise the question of whether the solitary thinker's judgments of good and ill are true or not. Truth supposes a standard outside of the thinker to which he must conform; but here the thinker is a sort of divinity, subject to no higher judge. Let us call the supposed universe which he inhabits a *moral solitude.* In such a moral solitude it is clear that there can be no outward obligation, and that the only trouble the godlike thinker is liable to have will be over the consistency of his own several ideals with one another. Some of these will no doubt be more pungent and appealing than the rest; their goodness will have a profounder, more penetrating taste; they will return to haunt him with more obstinate regrets if violated. So the thinker will have to order his life with them as its chief determinants, or else remain inwardly discordant and unhappy. Into whatever equilibrium he may settle, though, and however he may straighten out his system, it will be a right system; for beyond the facts of his own subjectivity there is nothing moral in the world.

If now we introduce a second thinker with his likes and dislikes into the universe, the ethical situation becomes much more complex, and several possibilities are immediately seen to obtain.

One of these is that the thinkers may ignore each other's attitude about good and evil altogether, and each continue to indulge his own preferences, indifferent to what the other may feel or do. In such a case we have a world with twice as much of the ethical quality in it as our moral solitude, only it is without ethical unity. The same object is good or bad there, according as you measure it by the view which this one or that one of the thinkers takes. Nor can you find any possible ground in such a world for saying that one thinker's opinion is more correct than the other's, or that either has the truer moral sense. Such a world, in short, is not a moral universe but a moral dualism. Not only is there no single point of view within it from which the values of things can be unequivocally judged, but there is not even a demand for such a point of view, since the two thinkers are supposed to be indifferent to each other's thoughts and acts. Multiply the thinkers into a pluralism, and we find realized for us in the ethical sphere something like that world which the antique skeptics conceived of—in which individual minds are the measures of all things, and in which no one 'objective' truth, but only a multitude of 'subjective' opinions, can be found.

But this is the kind of world with which the philosopher, so long as he holds to the hope of a philosophy, will not put up. Among the various ideals represented, there must be, he thinks, some which have the more truth or authority; and to these the others *ought* to yield, so that system and subordination may reign. Here in the word 'ought' the notion of *obligation* comes emphatically into view, and the next thing in order must be to make its meaning clear.

Since the outcome of the discussion so far has been to show us that nothing can be good or right except so far as some consciousness feels it to be good or thinks it to be right, we perceive on the very threshold that the real superiority and authority which are postulated by the philosopher to reside in some of the opinions, and the really inferior character which he supposes must belong to others, cannot be explained by any abstract moral 'nature of things' existing antecedently to the concrete thinkers themselves with their ideals. Like the positive attributes good and bad, the comparative ones better and worse must be *realized* in order to be real. If one ideal judgment be objectively better than another, that betterness must be made flesh by being lodged concretely in someone's actual perception. It cannot float in the atmosphere, for it is not a sort of meteorological phenomenon, like the aurora borealis or the zodiacal light. Its *esse* is *percipi*, like the *esse* of the ideals themselves between which it obtains. The philosopher, therefore, who seeks to know which ideal ought to have supreme weight and which one ought to be subordinated, must trace the *ought* itself to the *de facto* constitution of some existing consciousness, behind which, as one of the data of the universe, he as a purely ethical philosopher is unable to go. This consciousness must make the one ideal right by feeling it to be right, the other wrong by feeling it to be wrong. But now what particular consciousness in the universe *can* enjoy this

prerogative of obliging others to conform to a rule which it lays down?

If one of the thinkers were obviously divine, while all the rest were human, there would probably be no practical dispute about the matter. The divine thought would be the model to which the others should conform. But still the theoretic question would remain, What is the ground of the obligation, even here?

In our first essays at answering this question, there is an inevitable tendency to slip into an assumption which ordinary men follow when they are disputing with one another about questions of good and bad. They imagine an abstract moral order in which the objective truth resides; and each tries to prove that this pre-existing order is more accurately reflected in his own ideas than in those of his adversary. It is because one disputant is backed by this overarching abstract order that we think the other should submit. Even so, when it is a question no longer of two finite thinkers, but of God and ourselves—we follow our usual habit, and imagine a sort of *de jure* relation, which antedates and overarches the mere facts, and would make it right that we should conform our thoughts to God's thoughts, even though he made no claim to that effect, and though we preferred *de facto* to go on thinking for ourselves.

But the moment we take a steady look at the question, *we see not only that without a claim actually made by some concrete person there can be no obligation, but that there is some obligation wherever there is a claim.* Claim and obligation are, in fact, coextensive terms; they cover each other exactly. Our ordinary attitude of regarding ourselves as subject to an overarching system of moral relations, true 'in themselves,' is therefore either an out-and-out superstition, or else it must be treated as a merely provisional abstraction from that real Thinker in whose actual demand upon us to think as he does our obligation must be ultimately based. In a theistic-ethical philosophy that thinker in question is, of course, the Deity to whom the existence of the universe is due.

I know well how hard it is for those who are accustomed to what I have called the superstitious view to realize that every *de facto* claim creates in so far forth an obligation. We inveterately think that something which we call the 'validity' of the claim is what gives to it its obligatory character, and that this validity is something outside of the claim's mere existence as a matter of fact. It rains down upon the claim, we think, from some sublime dimension of being, which the moral law inhabits, much as upon the steel of the compass needle the influence of the pole rains down from out of the starry heavens. But again, how can such an inorganic abstract character of imperativeness, additional to the imperativeness which is in the concrete claim itself, *exist?* Take any demand, however slight, which any creature, however weak, may make. Ought it not, for its own sole sake, to be satisfied? If not, prove why not. The only possible kind of proof you could adduce would be the exhibition of another creature who should make a demand that ran the other way. The only possible reason there can be why any phenomenon ought to exist is that such a phenomenon actually is desired. Any desire is imperative to the extent of its amount; it *makes* itself valid by the fact that it exists at all. Some desires, truly enough, are small desires; they are put forward by insignificant persons, and we customarily make light of the obligations which they bring. But the fact that such personal demands as these impose small obligations does not keep the largest obligations from being personal demands.

If we must talk impersonally, to be sure we can say that 'the universe' requires, exacts, or makes obligatory such or such an action, whenever it expresses itself through the desires of such or such a creature. But it is better not to talk about the universe in this personified way, unless we believe in a universal or divine consciousness which actually exists. If there be such a consciousness, then its demands carry the most of obligation simply because they are the greatest in amount. But it is even then not *abstractly* right that we should respect them. It is only *concretely* right—or right after the fact, and by virtue of the fact, that they are actually made. Suppose we do not respect them, as seems largely to be the case in this queer world. That ought not to be, we say; that is wrong. But in that way is this fact of wrongness made more acceptable or intelligible when we imagine it to consist rather in the laceration of an *a priori* ideal order than in the disappointment of a living personal God? Do we, perhaps, think that we cover God and protect him and make his impotence

over us less ultimate, when we back him up with this *a priori* blanket from which he may draw some warmth of further appeal? But the only force of appeal to *us*, which either a living God or an abstract ideal order can wield, is found in the 'everlasting ruby vaults' of our own human hearts, as they happen to beat responsive and not irresponsive to the claim. So far as they do feel it when made by a living consciousness, it is life answering to life. A claim thus livingly acknowledged is acknowledged with a solidity and fullness which no thought of an 'ideal' backing can render more complete; while if, on the other hand, the heart's response is withheld, the stubborn phenomenon is there of an impotence in the claims which the universe embodies, which no talk about an eternal nature of things can glaze over or dispel. An ineffective *a priori* order is as impotent a thing as an ineffective God; and in the eye of philosophy, it is as hard a thing to explain.

We may now consider that what we distinguished as the metaphysical question in ethical philosophy is sufficiently answered, and that we have learned what the words 'good,' 'bad,' and 'obligation' severally mean. They mean no absolute natures, independent of personal support. They are objects of feeling and desire, which have no foothold or anchorage in Being, apart from the existence of actually living minds.

Wherever such minds exist, with judgments of good and ill, and demands upon one another, there is an ethical world in its essential features. Were all other things, gods and men and starry heavens, blotted out from this universe, and were there left but one rock with two loving souls upon it, that rock would have as thoroughly moral a constitution as any possible world which the eternities and immensities could harbor. It would be a tragic constitution, because the rock's inhabitants would die. But while they lived, there would be real good things and real bad things in the universe; there would be obligations, claims, and expectations; obediences, refusals, and disappointments; compunctions and longings for harmony to come again, and inward peace of conscience when it was restored; there would, in short, be a moral life, whose active energy would have no limit but the intensity of interest in each other with which the hero and heroine might be endowed.

We, on this terrestrial globe, so far as the visible facts go, are just like the inhabitants of such a rock. Whether a God exist, or whether no God exist, in yon blue heaven above us bent, we form at any rate an ethical republic here below. And the first reflection which this leads to is that ethics have as genuine and real a foothold in a universe where the highest consciousness is human, as in a universe where there is a God as well. 'The religion of humanity' affords a basis for ethics as well as theism does. Whether the purely human system can gratify the philosopher's demand as well as the other is a different question, which we ourselves must answer ere we close.

III

The last fundamental question in ethics was, it will be remembered, the *casuistic* question. Here we are, in a world where the existence of a divine thinker has been and perhaps always will be doubted by some of the lookers-on, and where, in spite of the presence of a large number of ideals in which human beings agree, there are a mass of others about which no general consensus obtains. It is hardly necessary to present a literary picture of this, for the facts are too well known. The wars of the flesh and the spirit in each man, the concupiscences of different individuals pursuing the same unshareable material or social prizes, the ideals which contrast so according to races, circumstances, temperaments, philosophical beliefs, etc.—all form a maze of apparently inextricable confusion with no obvious Ariadne's thread to lead one out. Yet the philosopher, just because he is a philosopher, adds his own peculiar ideal to the confusion (with which if he were willing to be a skeptic he would be passably content), and insists that over all these individual opinions there is a *system of truth* which he can discover if he only takes sufficient pains.

We stand ourselves at present in the place of that philosopher, and must not fail to realize all the features that the situation comports. In the first place we will not be skeptics; we hold to it that there is a truth to be ascertained. But in the second place we have just gained the insight that that truth cannot be a self-proclaiming set of laws, or an abstract 'moral reason,' but can only

exist in act, or in the shape of an opinion held by some thinker really to be found. There is, however, no visible thinker invested with authority. Shall we then simply proclaim our own ideals as the lawgiving ones? No; for if we are true philosophers we must throw our own spontaneous ideals, even the dearest, impartially in with that total mass of ideals which are fairly to be judged. But how then can we as philosophers ever find a test; how avoid complete moral skepticism on the one hand, and on the other escape bringing a wayward personal standard of our own along with us, on which we simply pin faith?

The dilemma is a hard one, nor does it grow a bit more easy as we revolve it in our minds. The entire undertaking of the philosopher obliges him to seek an impartial test. That test, however, must be incarnated in the demand of some actually existent person; and how can he pick out the person save by an act in which his own sympathies and prepossessions are implied?

One method indeed presents itself, and has as a matter of history been taken by the more serious ethical schools. If the heap of things demanded proved on inspection less chaotic than at first they seemed, if they furnished their own relative test and measure, then the casuistic problem would be solved. If it were found that all goods *qua* goods contained a common essence, then the amount of this essence involved in any one good would show its rank in the scale of goodness, and order could be quickly made; for this essence would be *the* good upon which all thinkers were agreed, the relatively objective and universal good that the philosopher seeks. Even his own private ideals would be measured by their share of it, and find their rightful place among the rest.

Various essences of good have thus been found and proposed as bases of the ethical system. Thus, to be a mean between two extremes; to be recognized by a special intuitive faculty; to make the agent happy for the moment; to make others as well as him happy in the long run; to add to his perfection or dignity; to harm no one; to follow from reason or flow from universal law; to be in accordance with the will of God; to promote the survival of the human species on this planet—are so many tests, each of which has been maintained by somebody to constitute the essence of all good things or actions so far as they are good.

No one of the measures that have been actually proposed has, however, given general satisfaction. Some are obviously not universally present in all cases—*e.g.*, the character of harming no one, or that of following a universal law; for the best course is often cruel; and many acts are reckoned good on the sole condition that they be exceptions, and serve not as examples of a universal law. Other characters, such as following the will of God, are unascertainable and vague. Others again, like survival, are quite indeterminate in their consequences, and leave us in the lurch where we most need their help: a philosopher of the Sioux nation, for example, will be certain to use the survival criterion in a very different way from ourselves. The best, on the whole, of these marks and measures of goodness seems to be the capacity to bring happiness. But in order not to break down fatally, this test must be taken to cover innumerable acts and impulses that never *aim* at happiness; so that, after all, in seeking for a universal principle we inevitably are carried onward to the *most* universal principle—that *the essence of good is simply to satisfy demand.* The demand may be for anything under the sun. There is really no more ground for supposing that all our demands can be accounted for by one universal underlying kind of motive than there is ground for supposing that all physical phenomena are cases of a single law. The elementary forces in ethics are probably as plural as those of physics are. The various ideals have no common character apart from the fact that they are ideals. No single abstract principle can be so used as to yield to the philosopher anything like a scientifically accurate and genuinely useful casuistic scale.

A look at another peculiarity of the ethical universe, as we find it, will still further show us the philosopher's perplexities. As a purely theoretic problem, namely, the casuistic question would hardly ever come up at all. If the ethical philosopher were only asking after the best *imaginable* system of goods he would indeed have an easy task; for all demands as such are *prima facie* respectable, and the best simply imaginary world would be one in which *every* demand was gratified as soon as made. Such a world would, however, have to have a physical constitution entirely different from that of the one which we inhabit. It would need not only a space, but a time, 'of *n*-dimensions,' to include all the acts and experiences incompatible with one another here

below, which would then go on in conjunction—such as spending our money, yet growing rich; taking our holiday, yet getting ahead with our work; shooting and fishing, yet doing no hurt to the beasts; gaining no end of experience, yet keeping our youthful freshness of heart; and the like. There can be no question that such a system of things, however brought about, would be the absolutely ideal system; and that if a philosopher could create universes *a priori*, and provide all the mechanical conditions, that is the sort of universe which he should unhesitatingly create.

But this world of ours is made on an entirely different pattern, and the casuistic question here is most tragically practical. The actually possible in this world is vastly narrower than all that is demanded; and there is always a *pinch* between the ideal and the actual which can only be got through by leaving part of the ideal behind. There is hardly a good which we can imagine except as competing for the possession of the same bit of space and time with some other imagined good. Every end of desire that presents itself appears exclusive of some other end of desire. Shall a man drink and smoke, *or* keep his nerves in condition?—he cannot do both. Shall he follow his fancy for Amelia, *or* for Henrietta?—both cannot be the choice of his heart. Shall he have the dear old Republican party, *or* a spirit of unsophistication in public affairs?—he cannot have both, etc. So that the ethical philosopher's demand for the right scale of subordination in ideals is the fruit of an altogether practical need. Some part of the ideal must be butchered, and he needs to know which part. It is a tragic situation, and no mere speculative conundrum, with which he has to deal.

Now *we* are blinded to the real difficulty of the philosopher's task by the fact that we are born into a society whose ideals are largely ordered already. If we follow the ideal which is conventionally highest, the others which we butcher either die and do not return to haunt us; or if they come back and accuse us of murder, everyone applauds us for turning to them a deaf ear. In other words, our environment encourages us not to be philosophers but partisans. The philosopher, however, cannot, so long as he clings to his own ideal of objectivity, rule out any ideal from being heard. He is confident, and rightly confident, that the simple taking counsel of his own intuitive preferences would be certain to end in a mutilation of the fullness of the truth. The poet Heine is said to have written 'Bunsen' in the place of 'Gott' in his copy of that author's work entitled "God in History," so as to make it read 'Bunsen in der Geschichte.' Now, with no disrespect to the good and learned Baron, is it not safe to say that any single philosopher, however wide his sympathies, must be just such a Bunsen in der Geschichte of the moral world, so soon as he attempts to put his own ideas of order into that howling mob of desires, each struggling to get breathing room for the ideal to which it clings? The very best of men must not only be insensible, but be ludicrously and peculiarly insensible, to many goods. As a militant, fighting freehanded that the goods to which he *is* sensible may not be submerged and lost from out of life, the philosopher, like every other human being, is in a natural position. But think of Zeno and of Epicurus, think of Calvin and of Paley, think of Kant and Schopenhauer, of Herbert Spencer and John Henry Newman, no longer as one-sided champions of special ideals, but as schoolmasters deciding what all must think—and what more grotesque topic could a satirist wish for on which to exercise his pen? The fabled attempt of Mrs. Partington to arrest the rising tide of the North Atlantic with her broom was a reasonable spectacle compared with their effort to substitute the content of their clean-shaven systems for that exuberant mass of goods with which all human nature is in travail, and groaning to bring to the light of day. Think, furthermore, of such individual moralists, no longer as mere schoolmasters, but as pontiffs armed with the temporal power, and having authority in every concrete case of conflict to order which good shall be butchered and which shall be suffered to survive—and the notion really turns one pale. All one's slumbering revolutionary instincts waken at the thought of any single moralist wielding such powers of life and death. Better chaos forever than an order based on any closet-philosopher's rule, even though he were the most enlightened possible member of his tribe. No! if the philosopher is to keep his judicial position, he must never become one of the parties to the fray.

What can he do, then, it will now be asked, except to fall back on skepticism and give up the notion of being a philosopher at all?

But do we not already see a perfectly definite path of escape which is open to him just because he is a philosopher, and not the champion of one particular ideal? Since everything which is demanded is by that fact a good, must not the guiding principle for ethical philosophy (since all demands conjointly cannot be satisfied in this poor world) be simply to satisfy at all times *as many demands as we can?* That act must be the best act, accordingly, which makes for the *best whole*, in the sense of awakening the least sum of dissatisfactions. In the casuistic scale, therefore, those ideals must be written highest which *prevail at the least cost*, or by whose realization the least possible number of other ideals are destroyed. Since victory and defeat there must be, the victory to be philosophically prayed for is that of the more inclusive side—of the side which even in the hour of triumph will to some degree do justice to the ideals in which the vanquished party's interests lay. The course of history is nothing but the story of men's struggles from generation to generation to find the more and more inclusive order. *Invent some manner* of realizing your own ideals which will also satisfy the alien demands—that and that only is the path of peace! Following this path, society has shaken itself into one sort of relative equilibrium after another by a series of social discoveries quite analogous to those of science. Polyandry and polygamy and slavery, private warfare and liberty to kill, judicial torture and arbitrary royal power have slowly succumbed to actually aroused complaints; and though someone's ideals are unquestionably the worse off for each improvement, yet a vastly greater total number of them find shelter in our civilized society than in the older savage ways. So far then, and up to date, the casuistic scale is made for the philosopher already far better than he can ever make it for himself. An experiment of the most searching kind has proved that the laws and usages of land are what yield the maximum of satisfaction to the thinkers taken all together. The presumption in cases of conflict must always be in favor of the conventionally recognized good. The philosopher must be a conservative, and in the construction of his casuistic scale must put the things most in accordance with the customs of the community on top.

And yet if he be a true philosopher he must see that there is nothing final in any actually given equilibrium of human ideals, but that, as our present laws and customs have fought and conquered other past ones, so they will in their turn be overthrown by any newly discovered order which will hush up the complaints that they still give rise to, without producing others louder still. "Rules are made for man, not man for rules,"—that one sentence is enough to immortalize Green's Prolegomena to Ethics. And although a man always risks much when he breaks away from established rules and strives to realize a larger ideal whole than they permit, yet the philosopher must allow that it is at all times open to any one to make the experiment, provided he fear not to stake his life and character upon the throw. The pinch is always here. Pent in under every system of moral rules are innumerable persons whom it weighs upon, and goods which it represses; and these are always rumbling and grumbling in the background, and ready for any issue by which they may get free. See the abuses which the institution of private property covers, so that even today it is shamelessly asserted among us that one of the prime functions of the national government is to help the adroiter citizens to grow rich. See the unnamed and unnamable sorrows which the tyranny, on the whole so beneficent, of the marriage institution brings to so many, both of the married and the unwed. See the wholesale loss of opportunity under our regime of so-called equality and industrialism, with the drummer and the counter-jumper in the saddle, for so many faculties and graces which could flourish in the feudal world. See our kindliness for the humble and the outcast, how it wars with that stern weeding-out which until now has been the condition of every perfection in the breed. See everywhere the struggle and the squeeze; and everlastingly the problem how to make them less. The anarchists, nihilists, and free-lovers; the free-silverites, socialists, and single-tax men; the free-traders and civil-service reformers; the prohibitionists and anti-vivisectionists; the radical Darwinians with their idea of the suppression of the weak—these and all the conservative sentiments of society arrayed against them, are simply deciding through actual experiment by what sort of conduct the maximum amount of good can be gained and kept in this world. These experiments are to be judged, not *a priori*, but by actually finding, after the fact of their making, how much more outcry or how much appeasement comes about. What closet solutions can possibly anticipate the result of trials made on such a scale? Or what can any superficial theorist's judgment be worth, in a world where every one of hundreds of ideals has its special champion already provided in the shape of some genius expressly born to feel it, and to fight to death in its behalf? The pure philosopher can only follow the windings of the spectacle, confident that the line of least resistance will always be towards the richer and the more inclusive arrangement, and that by one tack after another some approach to the kingdom of heaven is incessantly made.

IV

All this amounts to saying that, so far as the casuistic question goes, ethical science is just like physical science, and instead of being deducible all at once from abstract principles, must simply bide its time, and be ready to revise its conclusions from day to day. The presumption, of course, in both sciences, always is that the vulgarly accepted opinions are true, and the right casuistic order that which public opinion believes in; and surely it would be folly quite as great, in most of us, to strike out independently and to aim at originality in ethics as in physics. Every now and then, however, someone is born with the right to be original, and his revolutionary thought or action may bear prosperous fruit. He may replace old 'laws of nature' by better ones; he may, by breaking old moral rules in a certain place, bring in a total condition of things more ideal than would have followed had the rules been kept.

On the whole, then, we must conclude that no philosophy of ethics is possible in the old-fashioned absolute sense of the term. Everywhere the ethical philosopher must wait on facts. The thinkers who create the ideals come he knows not whence, their sensibilities are evolved he knows not how; and the question as to which of two conflicting ideals will give the best universe then and there, can be answered by him only through the aid of the experience of other men. I said some time ago, in treating of the 'first' question, that the intuitional moralists deserve credit for keeping most clearly to the psychological facts. They do much to spoil this merit on the whole, however, by mixing with it that dogmatic temper which, by absolute distinctions and unconditional 'thou shalt nots,' changes a growing, elastic, and continuous life into a superstitious system of relics and dead bones. In point of fact, there are no absolute evils, and there are no non-moral goods; and the *highest* ethical life—however few may be called to bear its burdens—consists at all times in the breaking of rules which have grown too narrow for the actual case. There is but one unconditional commandment, which is that we should seek incessantly, with fear and trembling, so to vote and to act as to bring about the very largest total universe of good which we can see. Abstract rules indeed can help; but they help the less in proportion as our intuitions are more piercing, and our vocation is the stronger for the moral life. For every real dilemma is in literal strictness a unique situation; and the exact combination of ideals realized and ideals disappointed which each decision creates is always a universe without a precedent, and for which no adequate previous rule exists. The philosopher, then, *qua* philosopher, is no better able to determine the best universe in the concrete emergency than other men. He sees, indeed, somewhat better than most men what the question always is—not a question of this good or that good simply taken, but of the two total universes with which these goods respectively belong. He knows that he must vote always for the richer universe, for the good which seems most organizable, most fit to enter into complex combinations, most apt to be a member of a more inclusive whole. But which particular universe this is he cannot know for certain in advance; he only knows that if he makes a bad mistake the cries of the wounded will soon inform him of the fact. In all this the philosopher is just like the rest of us non-philosophers, so far as we are just and sympathetic instinctively, and so far as we are open to the voice of complaint. His function is in fact indistinguishable from that of the best kind of statesman at the present day. His books upon ethics, therefore, so far as they truly touch the moral life, must more and more ally themselves with a literature which is confessedly tentative and suggestive rather than dogmatic—I mean with novels and dramas of the deeper sort, with sermons, with books on statecraft and philanthropy and social and economical reform. Treated in this way ethical treatises may be voluminous and luminous as well; but they never can be *final*, except in their abstractest and vaguest features; and they must more and more abandon the old-fashioned, clear-cut, and would-be 'scientific' form.

V

The chief of all the reasons why concrete ethics cannot be final is that they have to wait on metaphysical and theological beliefs. I said some time back that real ethical relations existed in a purely human world. They would exist even in what we called a moral solitude if the thinker had various ideals which took hold of him in turn. His self of one day would make demands on his self of another; and some of the demands might be urgent and tyrannical, while others were gentle and easily put aside. We call the tyrannical demands *imperatives*. If we ignore these we do not hear the last of it. The good which we have wounded returns to plague us with interminable crops of consequential damages, compunctions, and regrets. Obligation can thus exist inside a single thinker's consciousness; and perfect peace can abide with him only so far as he lives according to some sort of a casuistic scale which keeps his more imperative goods on top. It is the nature of these goods to be cruel to their rivals. Nothing shall avail when weighed in the balance against them. They call out all the mercilessness in our disposition, and do not easily forgive us if we are so softhearted as to shrink from sacrifice in their behalf.

The deepest difference, practically, in the moral life of man is the difference between the easy-going and the strenuous mood. When in the easy-going mood the shrinking from present ill is our ruling consideration. The strenuous mood, on the contrary, makes us quite indifferent to present ill, if only the greater ideal be attained. The capacity for the strenuous mood probably lies slumbering in every man, but it has more difficulty in some than in others in waking up. It needs the wilder passions to arouse it, the big fears, loves, and indignations; or else the deeply penetrating appeal of some one of the higher fidelities, like justice, truth, or freedom. Strong relief is a necessity of its vision; and a world where all the mountains are brought down and all the valleys are exalted is no congenial place for its habitation. This is why in a solitary thinker this mood might slumber on forever without waking. His various ideals, known to him to be mere preferences of his own, are too nearly of the same denominational value: he can play fast or loose with them at will. This too is why, in a merely human world without a God, the appeal to our moral energy falls short of its maximal stimulating power. Life, to be sure, is even in such a world a genuinely ethical symphony; but it is played in the compass of a couple of poor octaves, and the infinite scale of values fails to open up. Many of us, indeed—like Sir James Stephen in those eloquent "Essays by a Barriste"—would openly laugh at the very idea of the strenuous mood being awakened in us by those claims of remote posterity which constitute the last appeal of the religion of humanity. We do not love these men of the future keenly enough; and we love them perhaps the less the more we hear of their evolutionized perfection, their high average longevity and education, their freedom from war and crime, their relative immunity from pain and zymotic disease, and all their other negative superiorities. This is all too finite, we say; we see too well the vacuum beyond. It lacks the note of infinitude and mystery, and may all be dealt with in the don't-care mood. No need of agonizing ourselves or making others agonize for these good creatures just at present.

When, however, we believe that a God is there, and that he is one of the claimants, the infinite perspective opens out. The scale of the symphony is incalculably prolonged. The more imperative ideals now begin to speak with an altogether new objectivity and significance, and to utter the penetrating, shattering, tragically challenging note of appeal. They ring out like the call of Victor Hugo's alpine eagle, "qui parle au précipice et que le gouffre entend," and the strenuous mood awakens at the sound. It saith among the trumpets, ha, ha! it smelleth the battle afar off, the thunder of the captains and the shouting. Its blood is up; and cruelty to the lesser claims, so far from being a deterrent element, does but add to the stern joy with which it leaps to answer to the greater. All through history, in the periodical conflicts of puritanism with the don't-care temper, we see the antagonism of the strenuous and genial moods, and the contrast between the ethics of infinite and mysterious obligation from on high, and those of prudence and the satisfaction of merely finite need.

The capacity of the strenuous mood lies so deep down among our natural human possibilities that even if there were no metaphysical or traditional grounds for believing in a God, men would postulate one simply as a pretext for living hard, and getting out of the game

of existence its keenest possibilities of zest. Our attitude towards concrete evils is entirely different in a world where we believe there are none but finite demanders, from what it is in one where we joyously face tragedy for an infinite demander's sake. Every sort of energy and endurance, of courage and capacity for handling life's evils, is set free in those who have religious faith. For this reason the strenuous type of character will on the battlefield of human history always outwear the easy-going type, and religion will drive irreligion to the wall.

It would seem, too—and this is my final conclusion—that the stable and systematic moral universe for which the ethical philosopher asks is fully possible only in a world where there is a divine thinker with all-enveloping demands. If such a thinker existed, his way of subordinating the demands to one another would be the finally valid casuistic scale; his claims would be the most appealing; his ideal universe would be the most inclusive realizable whole. If he now exist, then actualized in his thought already must be that ethical philosophy which we seek as the pattern which our own must evermore approach. In the interests of our own ideal of systematically unified moral truth, therefore, we, as would-be philosophers, must postulate a divine thinker, and pray for the victory of the religious cause. Meanwhile, exactly what the thought of the infinite thinker may be is hidden from us even were we sure of his existence; so that our postulation of him after all serves only to let loose in us the strenuous mood. But this is what it does in all men, even those who have no interest in philosophy. The ethical philosopher, therefore, whenever he ventures to say which course of action is the best, is on no essentially different level from the common man. "See, I have set before thee this day life and good, and death and evil; therefore, choose life that thou and thy seed may live,"—when this challenge comes to us, it is simply our total character and personal genius that are on trial; and if we invoke any so-called philosophy, our choice and use of that also are but revelations of our personal aptitude or incapacity for moral life. From this unsparing practical ordeal no professor's lectures and no array of books can save us. The solving word, for the learned and the unlearned man alike, lies in the last resort in the dumb willingnesses and unwillingnesses of their interior characters, and nowhere else. It is not in heaven, neither is it beyond the sea; but the word is very nigh unto thee, in thy mouth and in thy heart, that thou mayest do it.

READING QUESTIONS

1. James distinguishes three kinds of questions in ethics: psychological questions, metaphysical questions, and casuistic questions. In your own words, characterize the differences among these sorts of questions.

2. James believes that "nothing can be good or right except so far as some consciousness feels it to be good or thinks it to be right." What are his reasons for drawing this conclusion? Are these reasons adequate? Why or why not?

3. James claims that "the essence of good is simply to satisfy demand." What does this mean?

4. Why does James claim that "ethical science is like physical science"?

5. Contrast Kant's moral philosophy or Mill's moral philosophy with that of James. In doing so, consider his remark that in deciding what we should and should not do, "abstract rules indeed can help; but they help the less in proportion as our intuitions are more piercing, and our vocation is the stronger for the moral life."

6. What is James's final position with regard to whether ethics depends on religion in any way? Elaborate.

SUGGESTIONS FOR FURTHER READING (WILLIAM JAMES)

Primary Sources and Collected Writings

(1975–90) *The Works of William James*, edited by F. H. Burkhardt, et al. Cambridge, MA: Harvard University Press.

(1878) *Essays in Philosophy*. Cambridge, MA: Harvard University Press, 1978.

(1890) *Principles of Psychology*. New York: Dover Publications, 1950.

(1897) *The Will to Believe and Other Essays in Popular Philosophy*. Cambridge, MA: Harvard University Press, 1979.

(1895) *Essays in Philosophy*. Cambridge, MA: Harvard University Press, 1987.

(1903) *The Varieties of Religious Experience: A Study of Human Behavior*. Cambridge, MA: Harvard University Press, 1985.

(1907) *Pragmatism: A New Name for Some Old Ways of Thinking*. Cambridge, MA: Harvard University Press, 1975.

(1909) *The Meaning of Truth: A Sequel of "Progamitism."* Cambridge, MA: Harvard University Press, 1975.

(1912) *Essays in Radical Empiricism*. Cambridge, MA: Harvard University Press, 1976.

(1920) *The Letters of William James*. edited by H. James. Boston: The Atlantic Monthly Press.

(1977) *The Writings of William James*, edited by J. J. McDermott. Chicago: University of Chicago Press.

(1984) *William James: The Essential Writings*, edited by B. W. Wilshire. Albany, NY: State University of New York Press.

Secondary Sources

Allen, G. (1967) *William James: A Biography*, New York: The Viking Press.

Ayer, A. J. (1968) *Origins of Pragmatism: Studies in the Philosophy of Charles Sanders Peirce and William James*. New York: Macmillan.

Barzun, J. (1983) *A Stroll with William James*. New York: Harper & Row.

Bird, G. (1987) *William James*. New York: Routledge and Kegan Paul.

Kuklick, B. (1977) *The Rise of American Philosophy*. New Haven, CT: Yale University Press.

Levinson, H. (1981) *The Religious Investigations of William James*. Chapel Hill, NC: University of North Carolina Press.

Myers, G. (1987) *William James: His Life and Thought*. New Haven, CT: Yale University Press.

Olin, D. (1992) *William James: Pragmatism in Focus*. London: Routledge.

Perry, R. B. (1996) *The Thought and Character of William James*. Nashville, TN: Vanderbilt University Press.

Putnam, R. A., ed. (1997) *The Cambridge Companion to William James*, Cambridge: Cambridge University Press.

Reck, A. (1967) *Introduction to William James*. Bloomington, IN: Indiana University Press.

Scheffler, I. (1974) *Four Pragmatists: A Critical Introduction to Peirce, James, Mead, and Dewey*, edited by T. Honderich. New York: Humanities Press.

Simon, L. (1998) *Genuine Reality: A Life of William James*. New York: Harcourt Brace.

John Dewey

The Problem of Logical Subject-Matter

Born the son of a grocer in Burlington, Vermont, John Dewey (1859–1952) would eventually establish himself both as an innovator in almost every area of philosophy and as a capable defender of *instrumentalism*—his version of pragmatism. He also remains to this day the most famous American philosopher of education. In addition to pursuing various purely philosophical projects, Dewey was for much of his life an engaging and outspoken proponent for practical educational reform and an activist for freedom and justice.

Dewey attended public school in Burlington (where he received average marks) before enrolling at the University of Vermont in 1875. As an undergraduate he became interested both in philosophy and in evolutionary theory. After completing his studies at Vermont, he took positions teaching science and mathematics at high schools in Pennsylvania and later in Burlington. Upon his return to Vermont, Dewey arranged for private philosophy tutorials with his former instructor, H. A. P. Torry. Shortly thereafter, Dewey composed two short philosophical monographs and sent them to W. T. Harris, a prominent American Hegelian and then editor of the *Journal of Speculative Philosophy*. Both of his articles were accepted for publication and this literary achievement gave Dewey the reassurance he needed in order to enter the graduate

program at Johns Hopkins University in Baltimore, Maryland.

While at Johns Hopkins, Dewey had the opportunity to study under Charles Sanders Peirce, who for a short time was on the faculty teaching logic, George Morris, another prominent Hegelian philosopher; and with G. Stanley Hall, a respected researcher in experimental psychology. In 1884, after just two years, Dewey received his doctoral degree with a dissertation on Kant's psychology.

Dewey's professional employment in philosophy began at the University of Michigan (1884–1894) and continued at the University of Chicago (1894–1904) and at Columbia University (1904–1930). As the chairperson of the Department of Philosophy, Psychology, Pedagogy, and Education at Chicago, Dewey was largely responsible for chartering the University of Chicago Laboratory School for Education and for bringing together a faculty composed of many of the leading philosophers and psychologists working in the pragmatic tradition, including George Herbert Mead and James Tuffs.

In 1904, Dewey left the University of Chicago for Columbia after a disagreement with the administration over the status and future of the Laboratory School. At Columbia, he continued his research on educational theory through an affiliation with Columbia Teachers College. He also expanded and deepened his research in the traditional areas of philosophy, including epistemology, metaphysics, and the philosophy of science.

As Dewey's reputation in professional circles grew, so did his public celebrity. Never reluctant to step into the ring, Dewey regularly wrote on contemporary political and social issues in such venues as *The Nation* and *The New Republic*. Overall, Dewey's literary output was remarkable. In the course of his career, he composed and published forty books along with hundreds of articles on topics in every area of philosophy and educational psychology.

After Dewey's retirement from Columbia in 1930, he continued to write and to lecture throughout the country. He also energetically pursued his interests in activism. He participated formally in the Commission of Inquiry into the Charges Against Leon Trotsky at the Moscow Trial, and when his philosophical adversary Bertrand Russell was brought to trial in New York in 1940 on charges similar to those leveled against Socrates, Dewey vigorously aided in his defense.

In the following essay, drawn from his book *Logic: The Theory of Inquiry* (1938), Dewey discusses his view of the relationship between the subject matter and theory of logic and the "methodology of scientific and practical inquiry." His conception of the nature and subject matter of logic stands in sharp contrast to that of Frege, Russell, and the early Wittgenstein. Rejecting the view that logic is "the science of necessary laws of thought" or that logic is "concerned with the formal structure of language as a system of symbols," Dewey, on the contrary, held that "all logical forms (with their characteristic properties) arise within the operation of inquiry and are concerned with control of inquiry so that it may yield warranted assertions." This view of logic brings it much closer, as a field of study, to a kind of *decision theory* or account of how we ought generally to go about deciding what to believe and how to act.

Contemporary logical theory is marked by an apparent paradox. There is general agreement as to its proximate subject-matter. With respect to this proximate subject-matter no period shows a more confident advance. Its ultimate subject-matter, on the other hand, is involved in controversies which show little sign of abating. Proximate subject-matter is the domain of the relations of propositions to one another, such as affirmation-negation, inclusion-exclusion, particular-general, etc. No one doubts that the relations expressed by such words as *is, is not, if-then, only (none but), and, or, some-all*, belong to the subject-matter of logic in a way so distinctive as to mark off a special field.

When, however, it is asked how and why the matters designated by these terms form the subject-matter of logic, dissension takes the place of consensus. Do

they stand for pure forms, forms that have independent subsistence, or are the forms in question forms *of* subject-matter? If the latter, what is that of which they are forms, and what happens when subject-matter takes on logical form? How and why?

These are questions of what I called the ultimate subject-matter of logic; and about this subject-matter controversy is rife. Uncertainty about this question does not prevent valuable work in the field of proximate subject-matter. But the more developed this field becomes, the more pressing is the question as to what it is all about. Moreover, it is not true that there is *complete* agreement in the more limited field. On the contrary, in some important matters, there is conflict even here; and there is a possibility . . . that the uncertainty and diversity that exists in the limited field is a reflection of the unsettled state of opinion about ultimate subject-matter.

To illustrate the existing uncertainty as to ultimate subject-matter, it is only necessary to enumerate some of the diverse conceptions about the nature of logic that now stand over against one another. It is said, for example, that logic is the science of necessary laws of thought, and that it is the theory of ordered relations—relations which are wholly independent of thought. There are at least three views held as to the nature of these latter relations: They are held (1) to constitute a realm of pure possibilities as such, where *pure* means independent of actuality; (2) to be ultimate invariant relations forming the *order* of nature; and (3) to constitute the rational structure of the universe. In the latter status, while independent of human thought, they are said to embody the rational structure of the universe which is reproduced in part by human reason. There is also the view that logic is concerned with processes of inference by which knowledge, especially scientific knowledge, is attained.

Of late, another conception of its subject-matter has appeared upon the scene. Logic is said to be concerned with the formal structure of language as a system of symbols. And even here there is division. Upon one view, logic is the theory of transformation of linguistic expressions, the criterion of transformation being identity of syntactical forms. According to another view, the symbolic system, which is the subject-matter of logic, is a universal algebra of existence.

In any case, as regards *ultimate* subject-matter, logic is a branch of philosophic theory; so that different views of its subject-matter are expressions of different ultimate philosophies, while logical conclusions are used in turn to support the underlying philosophies. In view of the fact that philosophizing must satisfy logical requirements there is something in this fact that should at least provoke curiosity; conceivably it affects unfavorably the autonomy of logical theory. On the face of the matter, it does not seem fitting that logical theory should be determined by philosophical realism or idealism, rationalism or empiricism, dualism or monism, atomistic or organic metaphysics. Yet even when writers on logic do not express their philosophic prepossessions, analysis discloses a connection. In some cases conceptions borrowed from one or another philosophic system are openly laid down as *foundations* of logic and even of mathematics.

This list of diverse views given above is put down by way of illustration. It is not exhaustive, but it suffices to justify one more endeavor to deal with proximate subject-matter in terms of a theory concerning the ultimate subject-matter of logic. In the present state of affairs, it is foolish to say that logic *must* be about this or that. Such assertions are verbal realisms, assuming that a word has such magical power that it can point to and select the subject to which it is applicable. Furthermore, any statement that logic *is* so-and-so, can, in the existing state of logical theory, be offered only as a hypothesis and an indication of a position to be developed.

Whatever is offered as a hypothesis must, however, satisfy certain conditions. It must be of the nature of a *vera causa*. Being a *vera causa*, does not mean, of course, that it is a *true* hypothesis, for if it were that, it would be more than a hypothesis. It means that whatever is offered as the ground of a theory must possess the property of verifiable existence in *some* domain, no matter how hypothetical it is in reference to the field in which it is proposed to apply it. It has no standing if it is drawn from the void and proffered simply *ad hoc*. The second condition that a hypothesis about ultimate logical subject-matter must satisfy is that it be able to order and account for what has been called the proximate subject-matter. If it cannot meet the test thus imposed, no amount of theoretical plausibility is of avail.

In the third place, the hypothesis must be such as to account for the arguments that are advanced in support of other theories. This condition corresponds to the capacity of a theory in any field to explain apparent negative cases and exceptions. Unless this condition is fulfilled, conclusions reached in satisfaction of the second condition are subject to the fallacy of affirming an antecedent clause because the consequent is affirmed.

From these preliminary remarks I turn to statement of the position regarding logical subject-matter that is developed in this work. The theory, in summary form, is that all logical forms (with their characteristic properties) arise within the operation of inquiry and are concerned with control of inquiry so that it may yield warranted assertions. This conception implies much more than that logical forms are disclosed or come to light when we reflect upon processes of inquiry that are in use. Of course it means that; but it also means that the forms *originate* in operations of inquiry. To employ a convenient expression, it means that while inquiry into inquiry is the *causa cognoscendi* of logical forms, primary inquiry is itself *causa essendi* of the forms which inquiry into inquiry discloses.

It is not the task of this [essay] to try to justify this hypothesis, or to show that it satisfies the three conditions laid down. But I wish to emphasize two points preparatory to expounding the *meaning* (not the justification) of the conception, an exposition that is the main task of the present [work]. One of them is that any revulsion against the position just indicated should be tempered by appreciation of the fact that all other conceptions of logical subject-matter that are now entertained are equally hypothetical. If they do not seem to be so, it is because of their familiarity. If sheer dogmatism is to be avoided, any hypothesis, no matter how unfamiliar, should have a fair chance and be judged by its results. The other point is that inquiries, numerous in variety and comprehensive in scope, do exist and are open to public examination. Inquiry is the lifeblood of every science and is constantly engaged in every art, craft and profession. In short, the hypothesis represents a *vera causa*, no matter what doubt may attend its applicability in the field of logic.

Further elucidation of the meaning of the position taken will proceed largely in terms of objections that are most likely to arise. The most basic of these objections is that the field indicated, that of inquiries, is already pre-empted. There is, it will be said, a recognized subject which deals with it. That subject is methodology; and there is a well-recognized distinction between methodology and logic, the former being an application of the latter.

It certainly cannot be shown, short of the total development of the position taken, that this objection is not just. But it may be noted that assertion *in advance* of a fixed difference between logic and the methodology of scientific and practical inquiry begs the fundamental question at issue. The fact that most of the extant treatises upon methodology have been written upon the assumption of a fixed difference between the two does not prove that the difference exists. Moreover, the relative failure of works on logic that have identified logic and methodology (I may cite the logic of Mill as an example) does not prove that the identification is doomed to failure. For the failure *may* not be inherent. In any case, *a priori* assumption of a dualism between logic and methodology can only be prejudicial to unbiased examination both of methods of inquiry and logical subject-matter.

The plausibility of the view that sets up a dualism between logic and the methodology of inquiry, between logic and scientific method, is due to a fact that is not denied. Inquiry in order to reach valid conclusions must itself satisfy logical requirements. It is an easy inference from this fact to the idea that the logical requirements are imposed upon methods of inquiry from without. Since inquiries and methods are better and worse, logic involves a standard for criticizing and evaluating them. How, it will be asked, can inquiry which has to be evaluated by reference to a standard be itself the source of the standard? How can inquiry originate logical forms (as it has been stated that it does) and yet be subject to the requirements of these forms? The question is one that must be met. It can be adequately answered only in the course of the entire discussion that follows. But the meaning of the position taken may be clarified by indicating the direction in which the answer will be sought.

The problem reduced to its lowest terms is whether inquiry can develop in its own ongoing course the logical standards and forms to which *further* inquiry shall submit. One might reply by saying that it *can* because it

has. One might even challenge the objector to produce a single instance of improvement in scientific methods not produced in and by the self-corrective process of inquiry; a single instance that is due to application of standards *ab extra*. But such a retort needs to be justified. Some kind of inquiry began presumably as soon as man appeared on earth. Of prehistoric methods of inquiry our knowledge is vague and speculative. But we know a good deal about different methods that have been used in historic times. We know that the methods which now control science are of comparatively recent origin in both physical and mathematical science.

Moreover, different methods have been not only tried, but they have been tried out; that is, tested. The developing course of science thus presents us with an immanent criticism of methods previously tried. Earlier methods failed in some important respect. In consequence of this failure, they were modified so that more dependable results were secured. Earlier methods yielded conclusions that could not stand the strain put upon them by further investigation. It is not merely that *conclusions* were found to be inadequate or false but that they were found to be so because of methods employed. Other methods of inquiry were found to be such that persistence in them not only produced conclusions that stood the strain of further inquiry but that tended to be self-rectifying. They were methods that improved with and by use.

It may be instructive to compare the improvement of scientific methods within inquiry with the improvement that has taken place in the progress of the arts. Is there any reason to suppose that advance in the art of metallurgy has been due to application of an external standard? The "norms" used at present have developed out of the processes by which metallic ores were formerly treated. There were needs to be satisfied; consequences to be reached. As they were reached, new needs and new possibilities opened to view and old processes were re-made to satisfy them. In short, some procedures worked; some succeeded in reaching the end intended; others failed. The latter were dropped; the former were retained and extended. It is quite true that modern improvements in technologies have been determined by advances in mathematics and physical science. But these advances in scientific knowledge are not external canons to which the arts have had automatically to submit themselves. They provided new instrumentalities, but the instrumentalities were not self-applying. They were used; and it was the result of their use, their failure and success in accomplishing ends and effecting consequences, that provided the final criterion of the value of scientific principles for carrying on determinate technological operations. What is said is not intended as *proof* that the logical principles involved in scientific method have themselves arisen in the progressive course of inquiry. But it is meant to show that the hypothesis that they have so arisen has a *prima facie* claim to be entertained, final decision being reserved.

I now return to exposition of the meaning of the position taken. That inquiry is related to doubt will, I suppose, be admitted. The admission carries with it an implication regarding the end of inquiry: *end* in both senses of the word, as end-in-view and as close or termination. If inquiry begins in doubt, it terminates in the institution of conditions which remove need for doubt. The latter state of affairs may be designated by the words *belief* and *knowledge*. For reasons that I shall state later I prefer the words "warranted assertibility."

Belief may be so understood as to be a fitting designation for the outcome of inquiry. Doubt is uneasy; it is tension that finds expression and outlet in the processes of inquiry. Inquiry terminates in reaching that which is settled. This settled condition is a demarcating characteristic of genuine belief. In so far, belief is an appropriate name for the end of inquiry. But belief is a "double-barreled" word. It is used objectively to name *what* is believed. In this sense, the outcome of inquiry is a settled objective state of affairs, so settled that we are ready to act upon it, overtly or in imagination. *Belief* here names the settled condition of objective subject-matter, together with readiness to act in a given way when, if, and as, that subject-matter is present in existence. But in popular usage, *belief* also means a personal matter; something that some human being entertains or holds; a position, which under the influence of psychology, is converted into the notion that belief is merely a mental or psychical state. Associations from this signification of the word *belief* are likely to creep in when it is said that the end of inquiry is settled belief. The objective meaning of *subject-matter* as that is settled through inquiry is then dimmed or even shut out.

The ambiguity of the word thus renders its use inadvisable for the purpose in hand.

The word *knowledge* is also a suitable term to designate the objective and close of inquiry. But it, too, suffers from ambiguity. When it is said that attainment of knowledge, or truth, is the end of inquiry the statement, according to the position here taken, is a truism. That which satisfactorily terminates inquiry is, by definition, knowledge; it is knowledge because it *is* the appropriate close of inquiry. But the statement may be supposed, and has been supposed, to enunciate something significant instead of a tautology. As a truism, it defines knowledge *as* the outcome of competent and controlled inquiry. When, however, the statement is thought to enunciate something significant, the case is reversed. Knowledge is then supposed to have a meaning of its own apart from connection with and reference to inquiry. The theory of inquiry is then necessarily subordinated to this meaning as a fixed external end. The opposition between the two views is basic. The idea that any knowledge in particular can be instituted apart from its being the consummation of inquiry, and that knowledge in general can be defined apart from this connection is, moreover, one of the sources of confusion in logical theory. For the different varieties of realism, idealism and dualism have their diverse conceptions of what "knowledge" really is. In consequence, logical theory is rendered subservient to metaphysical and epistemological preconceptions, so that interpretation of logical forms varies with underlying metaphysical assumptions.

The position here taken holds that since every special case of knowledge is constituted as the outcome of some special inquiry, the conception of knowledge as such can only be a generalization of the properties discovered to belong to conclusions which are outcomes of inquiry. Knowledge, as an abstract term, is a name for the product of competent inquiries. Apart from this relation, its meaning is so empty that any content or filling may be arbitrarily poured in. The general conception of knowledge, when formulated in terms of the outcome of inquiry, has something important to say regarding the meaning of inquiry itself. For it indicates that inquiry is a *continuing* process in every field with which it is engaged. The "settlement" of a particular situation by a particular inquiry is no guarantee that

that settled conclusion will always remain settled. The attainment of settled beliefs is a progressive matter; there is no belief so settled as not to be exposed to further inquiry. It is the convergent and cumulative effect of continued inquiry that defines knowledge in its general meaning. In scientific inquiry, the criterion of what is taken to be settled, or to be knowledge, is being *so* settled that it is available as a resource in further inquiry; not being settled in such a way as not to be subject to revision in further inquiry.

What has been said helps to explain why the term "warranted assertion" is preferred to the terms *belief* and *knowledge*. It is free from the ambiguity of these latter terms, and it involves reference to inquiry as that which warrants assertion. When knowledge is taken as a general abstract term related to inquiry in the abstract, it means "warranted assertibility." The use of a term that designates a potentiality rather than an actuality involves recognition that all special conclusions of special inquiries are parts of an enterprise that is continually renewed, or is a going concern.

Up to this point, it may seem as if the criteria that emerge from the processes of continuous inquiry were only descriptive, and in that sense empirical. That they are empirical in one sense of that ambiguous word is undeniable. They have grown out of the experiences of actual inquiry. But they are not empirical in the sense in which "empirical" means devoid of rational standing. Through examination of the *relations* which exist between means (methods) employed and conclusions attained as their consequence, reasons are discovered why some methods succeed and other methods fail. It is implied in what has been said (as a corollary of the general hypothesis) that rationality is an affair of the relation of *means and consequences*, not of fixed first principles as ultimate premises or as contents of what the Neo-scholastics call *criteriology*.

Reasonableness or rationality is, according to the position here taken, as well as in its ordinary usage, an affair of the relation of means and consequences. In framing ends-in-view, it is unreasonable to set up those which have no connection with available means and without reference to the obstacles standing in the way of attaining the end. It is reasonable to search for and select the means that will, with the maximum probability, yield the consequences which are intended. It is

highly unreasonable to employ as means, materials and processes which would be found, if they were examined, to be such that they produce consequences which are different from the intended end; so different that they preclude its attainment. Rationality as an abstract conception is precisely the generalized idea of the means-consequence relation as such. Hence, from this point of view, the descriptive statement of methods that achieve progressively stable beliefs, or warranted assertibility, is also a *rational* statement in case the relation between them as means and assertibility as consequence is ascertained.

Reasonableness or rationality has, however, been hypostatized. One of the oldest and most enduring traditions in logical theory has converted rationality into a faculty which, when it is actualized in perception of first truths, was called *reason* and later, *Intellectus Purus*. The idea of *reason* as the power which intuitively apprehends *a priori* ultimate first principles persists in logical philosophy. Whether explicitly affirmed or not, it is the ground of every view which holds that scientific method is dependent upon logical forms that are logically prior and external to inquiry. The original ground for this conception of reason has now been destroyed. This ground was the necessity for postulating a faculty that had the power of direct apprehension of "truths" that were axiomatic in the sense of being self-evident, or self-verifying, and self-contained, as the necessary grounds of all demonstrative reasoning. The notion was derived from the subject-matter that had attained the highest scientific formulation at the time the classic logic was formulated; namely, *Euclidean geometry*.

This conception of the nature of axioms is no longer held in mathematics nor in the logic of mathematics. Axioms are now held to be postulates, neither true nor false in themselves, and to have their meaning determined by the consequences that follow because of their implicatory relations to one another. The greatest freedom is permitted, or rather encouraged, in laying down postulates—a freedom subject only to the condition that they be rigorously fruitful of implied consequences.

The same principle holds in physics. Mathematical formulas have now taken the place in physics once occupied by propositions about eternal essences and the fixed species defined by these essences. The formulas are deductively developed by means of rules of implication. But the value of the deduced result for physical science is not determined by the correctness of the deduction.

The deductive conclusion is used to instigate and direct operations of experimental observation. The observable consequences of these operations in their systematic correlation with one another finally determine the scientific worth of the deduced principle. The latter takes its place as a means necessary to obtain the consequence of warranted assertibility. The position here taken, the general hypothesis advanced, is a generalization of the means-consequence relation characteristic of mathematical and physical inquiry. According to it, all logical forms, such as are represented by what has been called *proximate logical* subject-matter, are instances of a relation between means and consequences in properly controlled inquiry, the word "controlled" in this statement standing for the methods of inquiry that are developed and perfected in the processes of continuous inquiry. In this continuity, the conclusions of any special inquiry are subordinate to use in substantiation and maturation of methods of further inquiry. The general character of knowledge as an abstract term is determined by the nature of the methods used, not vice versa.

The character of the generalization of the relation of "first principles" and conclusions (in mathematical and physical science) may be illustrated by the meaning of first principles in logic; such as traditionally represented by the principles, say, of identity, contradiction and excluded middle. According to one view, such principles represent ultimate invariant properties of the *objects* with which methods of inquiry are concerned, and to which inquiry must conform. According to the view here expressed, they represent conditions which have been ascertained during the conduct of continued inquiry to be involved in its own successful pursuit. The two statements may seem to *amount* to the same thing. Theoretically, there is a radical difference between them. For the second position implies, as has already been stated, that the principles are generated in the very process of control of continued inquiry, while, according to the other view, they are *a priori* principles fixed antecedently to inquiry and conditioning it *ab extra.*

Neither the existence nor the indispensability of pri-mary logical principles is, then, denied. The question concerns their origin and use. In what is said upon this matter I follow in the main the account given by Peirce of "guiding" or "leading" principles. According to this view, every inferential conclusion that is drawn involves a habit (either by way of expressing it or initiating it) in the *organic* sense of habit, since life is impossible without ways of action sufficiently general to be properly named *habits.* At the outset, the habit that operates in an inference is purely biological. It operates without our being aware of it. We are aware at most of particular acts and particular consequences. Later, we are aware not only of *what* is done from time to time but of *how* it is done. Attention to the way of doing is, moreover, indispensable to control of what is done. The craftsman, for example, learns that if he operates in a certain *way* the result will take care of itself, certain materials being given. In like fashion, we discover that if we draw our inferences in a certain way, we shall, other things being equal, get dependable conclusions. The *idea* of a method of inquiry arises as an articulate expression of the habit that is involved in a class of inferences.

Since, moreover, the habits that operate are narrower and wider in scope, the formulations of methods that result from observing them have either restricted or extensive breadth. Peirce illustrates the narrower type of habit by the following case: A person has seen a rotating disk of copper come to rest when it is placed between magnets. He infers that another piece of copper will behave similarly under like conditions. At first such inferences are made without formulation of a principle. The disposition that operates is limited in scope. It does not extend beyond pieces of copper. But when it is found that there are habits involved in *every* inference, in spite of differences of subject-matter, and when these habits are noted and formulated, then the formulations are guiding or leading principles. The principles state habits operative in every inference that tend to yield conclusions that are stable and productive in further inquiries. Being free from connection with any *particular* subject-matter, they are formal, not material, though they are forms of material that is subjected to authentic inquiry.

Validity of the principles is determined by the coherency of the consequences produced by the habits they articulate. If the habit in question is such as generally produces conclusions that are sustained and developed in further inquiry, then it is valid even if in an occasional case it yields a conclusion that turns out invalid. In such cases, the trouble lies in the material dealt with rather than with the habit and general principle. This distinction obviously corresponds to the ordinary distinction between form and matter. But it does not involve the complete separation between them that is often set up in logical theories.

Any habit is a way or manner of action, not a particular act or deed. When it is formulated it becomes, as far as it is accepted, a rule, or more generally, a principle or "law" of action. It can hardly be denied that there are habits of inference and that they may be formulated as rules or principles. If there are such habits as are necessary to conduct every successful inferential inquiry, then the formulations that express them will be logical principles of all inquiries. In this statement "successful" means operative in a manner that tends in the long run, or in continuity of inquiry, to yield results that are either confirmed in further inquiry or that are corrected by use of the same procedures. These guiding logical principles are not *premises* of inference or argument. They are conditions to be satisfied such that knowledge of them provides a principle of direction and of testing. They are formulations of ways of treating subject-matter that have been found to be so determinative of sound conclusions in the past that they are taken to regulate further inquiry until definite grounds are found for questioning them. While they are derived from examination of methods previously used in their connection with the kind of conclusion they have produced, they are *operationally a priori* with respect to further inquiry.

. . . [This] discussion, as was said at the outset, is not intended to justify my position but to clarify its general meaning. In the remaining pages . . . I shall set forth certain implications of the position for the theory of logic.

1. *Logic is a progressive discipline.* The reason for this is that logic rests upon analysis of the best methods of inquiry (being judged "best" by their results with respect to continued inquiry) that exist at a given time. As the methods of the sciences improve, corresponding changes take place in logic. An enormous change has taken place in logical theory since the classic logic formulated the methods of the science that existed in its period. It has occurred in consequence of the development of the mathematical and physical science. If, however, present theory provided a coherent formulation of existing scientific methods, freed from a doctrine of logical forms inherited from a science that is no longer held, this I treatise would have no reason for existence. When in the future methods of inquiry are further changed, logical theory will also change. There is no ground for supposing that logic has been or ever will be so perfected that, save, perhaps, for minor details, it will require no further modification. The idea that logic is capable of final formulation is an *eidolon* of the theater.

2. *The subject-matter of logic is determined operationally.* This thesis is a verbal restatement of what was earlier said. The methods of inquiry are operations performed or to be performed. Logical forms are the conditions that inquiry, *qua* inquiry, has to meet. Operations, to anticipate, fall into two general types. There are operations that are performed upon and with existential material—as in experimental observation. There are operations performed with and upon symbols. But even in the latter case, "operation" is to be taken in as literal a sense as possible. There are operations like hunting for a lost coin or measuring land, and there are operations like drawing up a balance sheet. The former is performed upon existential conditions; the latter upon symbols. But the symbols in the latter case stand for *possible* final existential conditions while the conclusion, when it is stated in symbols, is a pre-condition of further operations that deal with existences. Moreover, the operations involved in making a balance sheet for a bank or any other business involve physical activities. The so-called "mental" element in operations of both these kinds has to be defined in terms of existential conditions and consequences, not vice versa.

Operations involve both material and instrumentalities, including in the latter tools and techniques. The more material and instrumentalities are shaped in advance with a view to their operating in conjunction with each other as means to consequences, the better the operations performed are controlled. Refined steel, which is the matter of the operations by which a watch-spring is formed, is itself the product of a number of preparatory operations executed with reference to getting the material into the state that fits it to be the material of the final operation. The material is thus as instrumental, from an operational point of view, as are the tools and techniques by which it is brought into a required condition. On the other hand, old tools and techniques are modified in order that they may apply more effectively to new materials. The introduction, for example, of the lighter metals demanded different methods of treatment from those to which the heavier metals previously used were subjected. Or, stated from the other side, the development of electrolytic operations made possible the use of new materials as means to new consequences.

The illustration is drawn from the operations of industrial arts. But the principle holds of operations of inquiry. The latter also proceed by shaping on one hand subject-matter so that it lends itself to the application of conceptions as modes of operation; and, on the other hand, by development of such conceptual structures as are applicable to existential conditions. Since, as in the arts, both movements take place in strict correspondence with each other, the conceptions employed are to be understood as directly operational, while the existential material, in the degree in which the conditions of inquiry are satisfied, is determined both *by* operations and with an eye *to* operations still to be executed.

3. *Logical forms are postulational.* Inquiry in order to be inquiry in the complete sense has to satisfy certain demands that are capable of formal statement. According to the view that makes a basic difference between logic and methodology, the requirements in question subsist prior to and independent of inquiry. Upon that view, they are final in themselves, not intrinsically postulational. This conception of them is the ultimate ground of the idea that they are completely and inherently *a priori* and are disclosed to a faculty called *pure reason*. The position here taken holds that they are intrinsically postulates of and for inquiry, being formulations of conditions, discovered in the course of inquiry itself, which further inquiries must satisfy if they are to yield warranted assertibility as a consequence.

Stated in terms of the means-consequence relation, they are a generalization of the nature of the means that must be employed if assertibility is to be attained as an end. Certain demands have to be met by the operations that occur in the arts. A bridge is to be built to span a river under given conditions, so that the bridge, as the consequence of the operations, will sustain certain loads. There are local conditions set by the state of the banks, etc. But there are general conditions of distance, weights, stresses and strains, changes of temperature, etc. These are formal conditions. As such they are demands, requirements, postulates, to be fulfilled.

A postulate is also a stipulation. To engage in an inquiry is like entering into a contract. It commits the inquirer to observance of certain conditions. A stipulation is a statement of conditions that are agreed to in the conduct of some affair. The stipulations involved are at first implicit in the undertaking of inquiry. As they are formally acknowledged (formulated), they become logical forms of various degrees of generality. They make definite what is involved in a demand. Every demand is a request, but not every request is a postulate. For a postulate involves the assumption of responsibilities. The responsibilities that are assumed are stated in stipulations. They involve readiness to act in certain specified ways. On this account, postulates are not arbitrarily chosen. They present claims to be met in the sense in which a claim presents a title or has authority to receive due consideration.

In engaging in transactions, human beings are not at first aware of the responsibilities that are implicit; for laws, in the legal sense, are explicit statements of what was previously only implicit in customs: namely, formal recognition of duties and rights that were *practically* involved in acceptance of the customs. One of the highly generalized demands to be met in inquiry is the following: "If anything has a certain property, and whatever has this property has a certain other property, and then the thing in question has this certain other property." This logical "law" is a stipulation. If you are going to inquire in a way which meets the requirements of inquirer, you must proceed in a way which observes this rule, just as when you make a business contract there are certain conditions to be fulfilled.

A postulate is thus neither arbitrary nor externally *a priori*. It is not the former because it issues from the relation of means to the end to be reached. It is not the latter, because it is not imposed upon inquiry from without, but is an acknowledgement of that to which the undertaking of inquiry commits us. It is empirically and temporally *a priori* in the same sense in which the law of contracts is a rule regulating in advance the making of certain kinds of business engagements. While it is derived from what is involved in inquiries that have been successful in the past, it imposes a condition to be satisfied in future inquiries, until the results of such inquiries show reason for modifying it.

Terming logical forms postulates is, thus, on the negative side, a way of calling attention to the fact that they are not given and imposed from without. Just as the postulates of, say, geometry are not self-evident first truths that are externally imposed premises but are formulations of the conditions that have to be satisfied in procedures that deal with a certain subject-matter, so with logical forms which hold for *every* inquiry. In a contract, the agreement involved is that between the consequences of the activities of two or more parties with respect to some specified affair. In inquiry, the agreement is between the consequences of a series of inquiries. But inquiry as such is not carried on by one person rather than another. When any one person engages in it, he is committed, in as far as his inquiry is genuinely such and not an insincere bluff, to stand by the results of similar inquiries by whomever conducted. "Similar" in this phrase means inquiries that submit to the same conditions or postulates.

The postulational character of logical theory requires, accordingly, the most complete and explicit formulation that is attainable of not only the subject-matter that is taken as evidential in a given inference, but also of general conditions, stated in the rules and principles of inference and discourse. A distinction of matter and form is thus instituted. But it is one in which subject-matter and form correspond strictly to each other. Hence, once more, postulates are not arbitrary or mere linguistic conventions. They must be such as control the determination and arrangement of subject-matter with respect to achieving enduringly stable beliefs. Only after inquiry has proceeded for a considerable time and has hit upon methods that work successfully, is it possible to extract the postulates that are involved. They are not presuppositions at large. They are abstract in the sense that they are derived from analytic survey of the relations between methods as means and conclusions as consequences—a principle that exemplifies the meaning of rationality.

The postulational nature of logical theory thus agrees with what has been said about logic as progressive and operational. Postulates alter as methods of inquiry are perfected; the logical forms that express modern scientific inquiry are in many respects quite unlike those that formulated the procedures of Greek science. An experimenter in the laboratory who publishes his results states the materials used, the setup of apparatus and the procedures employed. These specifications are limited postulates, demands and stipulations, for any inquirer who wishes to test the conclusion reached. Generalize this performance for procedures of inquiry as such, that is, with respect to the form of every inquiry, and logical forms as postulates are the outcome.

4. *Logic is a naturalistic theory.* The term "naturalistic" has many meanings. As it is here employed it means, on one side, that there is no breach of continuity between operations of inquiry and biological operations and physical operations. "Continuity," on the other side, means that rational operations *grow out of* organic activities, without being identical with that from which they emerge. There is an adjustment of means to consequences in the activities of living creatures, even though not directed by deliberate purpose. Human beings in the ordinary or "natural" processes of living come to make these adjustments purposely, the purpose being limited at first to local situations as they arise. In the course of time (to repeat a principle already set forth) the intent is so generalized that inquiry is freed from limitation to special circumstances. The logic in question is also naturalistic in the sense of the observability, in the ordinary sense of the word, of activities of inquiry. Conceptions derived from a mystical faculty of *intuition* or anything that is so occult as not to be open to public inspection and verification (such as the purely psychical for example) are excluded.

5. *Logic is a social discipline.* One ambiguity attending the word "naturalistic" is that it may be understood to involve reduction of human behavior to the behavior of apes, amoebas, or electrons and protons. But man is *naturally* a being that lives in association with others in communities possessing language, and therefore enjoying a transmitted culture. Inquiry is a mode of activity that is socially conditioned and that has cultural consequences. This fact has a narrower and a wider import. Its more limited import is expressed in the connection of logic with symbols. Those who are concerned with "symbolic logic" do not always recognize the need for giving an account of the reference and function of symbols. While the relations of symbols to one another is important, symbols as such must be finally understood in terms of the function which symbolization serves. The fact that all languages (which include much more than speech) consist of symbols, does not of itself settle the nature of symbolism as that is used in inquiry. But, upon any naturalistic basis, it assuredly forms the point of departure for the logical theory of symbols. Any theory of logic has to take some stand on the question whether symbols are ready-made clothing for meanings that subsist independently, or whether they are necessary conditions for the existence of meanings—in terms often used, whether language is the dress of "thought" or is something without which "thought" cannot be.

The wider import is found in the fact that every inquiry grows out of a background of culture and takes effect in greater or less modification of the conditions out of which it arises. Merely physical contacts with physical surroundings occur. But in every interaction that involves intelligent direction, the physical environment is part of a more inclusive social or cultural environment. Just as logical texts usually remark incidentally that reflection grows out of the presence of a problem and then proceed as if this fact had no further interest for the theory of reflection, so they observe that science itself is culturally conditioned and then dismiss the fact from further consideration. This wider aspect of the matter is connected with what was termed the narrower. Language in its widest sense—that is, including all means of communication such as, for example, monuments, rituals, and formalized arts—is the medium in which culture exists and through which it is transmitted. Phenomena that are not recorded cannot be even discussed. Language is the record that perpetuates occurrences and renders them amenable to public consideration. On the other hand, ideas or meanings that exist *only* in symbols that are not communicable are fantastic beyond imagination. The naturalistic conception of logic, which underlies the position here taken, is thus *cultural naturalism.* Neither inquiry nor the most abstractly formal set of symbols can escape from the cultural matrix in which they live, move and have their being.

6. *Logic is autonomous.* The position taken implies the ultimacy of inquiry in determination of the formal conditions of inquiry. Logic as inquiry into inquiry is, if you please, a circular process; it does not depend upon anything extraneous to inquiry. The force of this proposition may perhaps be most readily understood by noting what it precludes. It precludes the determination and selection of logical first principles by an *a priori* intuitional act, even when the intuition in question is said to be that of *Intellectus Purus.* It precludes resting logic upon metaphysical and epistemological assumptions and presuppositions. The latter are to be determined, if at all, by means of what is disclosed as the outcome of inquiry; they are not to be shoved under inquiry as its "foundation." On the epistemological side, it precludes, as was noted earlier in another connection, the assumption of a prior ready-made definition of knowledge which determines the character of inquiry. Knowledge is to be defined in terms of inquiry, not vice versa, both in particular and universally.

The autonomy of logic also precludes the idea that its "foundations" are psychological. It is not necessary to reach conclusions about sensations, sense-data, ideas and thought, or mental faculties generally, as material that preconditions logic. On the contrary, just as the specific meaning of these matters is determined in specific inquiries, so generally their relation to the logic of inquiry is determined by discovering the relation that the subject-matters to which these names are given bear to the effective conduct of inquiry as such. The point may be illustrated by reference to "thought." It would have been possible in the preceding pages to use the term "reflective thought" where the word "inquiry" has been used. But if that word had been used, it is certain that some readers would have supposed that "reflective thought" designated something already sufficiently known so that "inquiry" was equated to a preexisting definition of thought. The opposite view is implied in the position taken. We do not know what meaning is to be assigned to "reflective thought" except in terms of what is discovered by inquiry into inquiry; at least we do not know what it means for the purposes of logic. Personally, I doubt whether there exists anything that may be called *thought* as a strictly psychical existence. But it is not necessary to go into that question here. For even if there be such a thing, it does not determine the meaning of "thought" for logic.

Either the word "thought" has no business at all in logic or else it is a synonym of "inquiry" and its meaning is determined by what we find out about inquiry. The latter would seem to be the reasonable alternative. These statements do not mean that a sound psychology may not be of decided advantage to logical theory. For history demonstrates that unsound psychology has done great damage. But its general relation to logic is found in the light that it, as a branch of inquiry, may throw upon what is involved in inquiry. Its *generic* relation to logic is similar to that of physics or biology. Specifically, . . . its findings stand closer to logical theory than do those of the other sciences. Occasional reference to psychological subject-matter is inevitable in any case; for, . . . some logical positions that pride themselves upon their complete indifference to psychological considerations in fact rest upon psychological notions that have become so current, so embedded in intellectual tradition, that they are accepted uncritically as if they were self-evident. . . .

READING QUESTIONS

1. According to Dewey, what is the difference between the *proximate* subject-matter of logic and the *ultimate* subject-matter of logic? Why does Dewey think there is a problem about the ultimate subject matter of logic. What does Dewey think that problem is?

2. What do you think that Dewey means by the phrase "logical form"?

3. In your own words, explain Dewey's account of the ultimate subject-matter of logic. What does he mean when he states that logical forms "*originate* in operations of inquiry"?

4. Dewey believes that it is incorrect to see the "methodology of inquiry" and logic as distinct, and to view the methodology of science simply as an application of logic. What, then, is his view of the relationship between the methodology of inquiry and logic?

5. Toward the end of the essay, Dewey offers six implications of his position. Restate and elaborate on each in your own words. Do you think that this conception of logic is adequate? Why or why not?

6. Dewey claims that on his view logic is a naturalistic theory. What do you think he means by calling his view of logic "naturalistic"? In general, what does it mean to call a theory naturalistic?

SUGGESTIONS FOR FURTHER READING (JOHN DEWEY)

Primary Sources and Collected Writings

(1960–90) *The Early Works of John Dewey, 1882–1892; The Middle Works of John Dewey, 1899–1924; The Later Works of John Dewey, 1925–1953*, edited by J. A. Boydston, Carbondale, IL: Southern Illinois Press.

(1903) *Studies in Logical Theory.* Chicago: University of Chicago Press.

(1910) *The Influence of Darwin on Philosophy and Other Essays of Contemporary Thought.* New York: Henry Holt.

(1916) *Democracy and Education: An Introduction to the Philosophy of Education.* New York: Macmillan.

(1916) *Essays in Experimental Logic.* Chicago: University of Chicago Press.

(1920) *Reconstruction in Philosophy.* New York: Henry Holt.

(1922) *Human Nature and Conduct: An Introduction to Social Psychology.* New York: Henry Holt.

(1925) *Experience and Nature.* Chicago: Open Court.

(1929) *The Quest for Certainty.* New York: Minton, Balch.

(1938) *Logic: The Theory of Inquiry*. New York: Henry Holt.

(1973) *The Philosophy of John Dewey*, edited by J. J. McDermott. New York: G. P. Putnam's Sons.

Secondary Sources

Alexander, T. (1987) *John Dewey's Theory of Art, Experience, and Nature: The Horizon of Feelings*. Albany, NY: State University of New York Press.

Boisvert, R. (1988) *Dewey's Metaphysics*. New York: Fordham University Press.

Burke, T. (1998) *Dewey's New Logic: A Reply to Russell*. Chicago: University of Chicago Press.

Campbell, J. (1995) *Understanding John Dewey*, Chicago: Open Court.

Dykhuizen, G. (1973) *The Life and Mind of John Dewey*. Carbondale, IL: Southern Illinois University Press.

Gouinlock, J. (1972) *John Dewey's Philosophy of Value*. New York: Humanities Press.

Haskins, C. and D. Seiple, eds. (1999) *Dewey Reconfigured: Essays on Deweyan Pragmatism*. Albany, NY: State University of New York Press.

Hook, S. (1995) *John Dewey: An Intellectual Portrait*. New York: Prometheus Books.

Moore, E. C. (1961) *American Pragmatism: Peirce, James, and Dewey*. New York: Columbia University Press.

Rockefeller, S. (1991) *John Dewey: Religious Faith and Democratic Humanism*. New York: Columbia University Press.

Ryan, A. (1995) *John Dewey and the High Tide of American Liberalism*. New York: W. W. Norton and Co.

Scheffler, I. (1974) *Four Pragmatists: A Critical Introduction to Peirce, James, Mead, and Dewey*, edited by T. Honderich. New York: Humanities Press.

Schilpp, P. A., ed. (1939) *The Philosophy of John Dewey*. Chicago: Open Court.

Shook, J. (2000) *Dewey's Empirical Theory of Knowledge*. Nashville, TN: Vanderbilt University Press.

Sleeper, R. (1986) *The Necessity of Pragmatism*. New Haven, CT: Yale University Press.

Thayer, H. S. (1952) *The Logic of Pragmatism: An Examination of John Dewey's Logic*. New York: Humanities Press.

White, M. (1943) *The Origin of Dewey's Instrumentalism*. New York: Columbia University Press.

CLARENCE IRVING (C. I.) LEWIS

A *Pragmatic Conception of the* a Priori

Born in Stoneham, Massachusetts, and educated at Harvard University, Clarence Irving Lewis (1883–1964) became a gifted practitioner of pragmatism and a leading contributor to American philosophy in such areas as epistemology, logic, and ethical theory. Lewis remains best known today for his vigorous attempts to effectively combine elements of pragmatism and empiricism together with a generally Kantian philosophical outlook. He is also remembered as one of the principal contemporary figures in the motivation and development of modal logic.

While attending Harvard, Lewis studied under the tutelage of Josiah Royce, William James, and Ralph Barton. He received his doctorate from Harvard in 1910 and the next year began instructing at the University of California. Lewis taught at California and at Colorado until 1920, at which time he accepted a teaching and research position at Harvard.

At Harvard he wrote a number of highly influential books and articles on various central topics in symbolic logic, knowledge, and ethical theory. His *Mind and the World-Order* (1929) and *An Analysis of Knowledge and Valuation* (1946) have become classics in the theory of knowledge and, more generally, in the literature of pragmatism. His course on Kant's *Critique of Pure Reason* was also a department favorite. In 1930 Lewis was appointed the Edgar Peirce Professor of Philosophy at Harvard University, and he continued to teach and to write at Harvard until his retirement in 1953.

In "A Pragmatic Conception of the *a Priori*" (1923), Lewis takes up the difficult problem of formulating an account of the realm of the *a priori* that is sympathetic both to pragmatism and to empiricism. His proposal is reminiscent, in some ways, of Kant; however, Lewis rejects the view that the categories of the mind or the understanding are fixed and immutable. Rather, they are flexible and responsive, and answer in large part to our various needs, interests, and desires.

The conception of the *a priori* points two problems which are perennial in philosophy; the part played in knowledge by the mind itself, and the possibility of "necessary truth" or of knowledge "independent of experience." But traditional conceptions of the *a priori* have proved untenable. That the mind approaches the flux of immediacy with some godlike foreknowledge of principles which are legislative for experience, that there is any natural light or any innate ideas, it is no longer possible to believe.

Nor shall we find the clue to the *a priori* in any compulsion of the mind to incontrovertible truth or any peculiar kind of demonstration which establishes first principles. All truth lays upon the rational mind the same compulsion to belief; as Mr. Bosanquet has pointed out, this character belongs to all propositions or judgments once their truth is established.

The difficulties of the conception are due, I believe, to two mistakes: whatever is *a priori* is necessary, but we have misconstrued the relation of necessary truth to mind. And the *a priori* is independent of experience, but in so taking it, we have misunderstood its relation to empirical fact. What is *a priori* is necessary truth not because it compels the mind's acceptance, but precisely because it does not. It is given experience, brute fact, the *a posteriori* element in knowledge which the mind must accept willy-nilly. The *a priori* represents an attitude in some sense freely taken, a stipulation of the mind itself, and a stipulation which might be made in some other way if it suited our bent or need. Such truth is necessary as opposed to contingent, not as opposed to voluntary. And the *a priori* is independent of experience not because it prescribes a form which the data of sense must fit, or anticipates some preestablished harmony of experience with the mind, but precisely because it prescribes nothing to experience. That is *a priori* which is true, *no matter what.* What it anticipates is not the given, but our attitude toward it: It concerns the uncompelled initiative of mind or, as Josiah Royce would say, our categorical ways of acting.

The traditional example of the *a priori par excellence* is the laws of logic. These cannot be derived from experience since they must first be taken for granted in order to prove them. They make explicit our general modes of classification. And they impose upon experience no real limitation. Sometimes we are asked to tremble before the specter of the "alogical," in order that we may thereafter rejoice that we are saved from this by the dependence of reality upon mind. But the "alogical" is pure bogey, a word without a meaning. What kind of experience could defy the principle that everything must either be or not be, that nothing can both be and not be, or that if *x* is *y* and *y* is *z,* then *x* is *z?* If anything imaginable or unimaginable could violate such laws, then the ever-present fact of change would do it every day. The laws of logic are purely formal; they forbid nothing but what concerns the use of terms and the corresponding modes of classification and analysis. The law of contradiction tells us that nothing can be both white and not-white, but it does not and cannot tell us whether black is not-white, or soft or square is not-white. To discover *what contradicts what* we must always consult the character of experience. Similarly the law of the excluded middle formulates our decision that whatever is not designated by a certain term shall be designated by its negative. It declares our purpose to make, for every term, a complete dichotomy of experience, instead—as we might choose—of classifying on the basis of a tripartite division into opposites (as black and white) and the middle ground between the two. Our rejection of such tripartite division represents only our penchant for simplicity.

Further laws of logic are of similar significance. They are principles of procedure, the parliamentary rules of intelligent thought and speech. Such laws are independent of experience because they impose no limitations whatever upon it. They are legislative because they are addressed to ourselves—because definition, classification, and inference represent no operations of the objective world, but only our own categorical attitudes of mind.

And further, the ultimate criteria of the laws of logic are pragmatic. Those who suppose that there is, for example, *a* logic which everyone would agree to if he

Clarence I. Lewis, "A Pragmatic Conception of the *A Priori*," *The Journal of Philosophy*, XX, 7, March 29, 1923, pp. 169–177. Reprinted with the permission of the publisher.

understood it and understood himself, are more optimistic than those versed in the history of logical discussion have a right to be. The fact is that there are several logics, markedly different, each self-consistent in its own terms and such that whoever, using it, avoids false premises, will never reach a false conclusion. Mr. Russell, for example, bases *his* logic on an implication relation such that if twenty sentences be cut from a newspaper and put in a hat, and then two of these be drawn at random, one of them will certainly imply the other, and it is an even bet that the implication will be mutual. Yet upon a foundation so remote from ordinary modes of inference the whole structure of *Principia Mathematica* is built. This logic—and there are others even more strange—is utterly consistent and the results of it entirely valid. Over and above all questions of consistency, there are issues of logic which cannot be determined—nay, cannot even be argued—except on pragmatic grounds of conformity to human bent and intellectual convenience. That we have been blind to this fact itself reflects traditional errors in the conception of the *a priori*.

We may note in passing one less important illustration of the *a priori*—the proposition "true by definition." Definitions and their immediate consequences, analytic propositions generally, are necessarily true, true under all possible circumstances. Definition is legislative because it is in some sense arbitrary. Not only is the meaning assigned to words more or less a matter of choice—that consideration is relatively trivial—but the manner in which the precise classifications which definition embodies shall be effected is something not dictated by experience. If experience were other than it is, the definition and its corresponding classification might be inconvenient, fantastic, or useless, but it could not be false. Mind makes classifications and determines meanings; in so doing it creates the *a priori* truth of analytic judgments. But that the manner of this creation responds to pragmatic considerations is so obvious that it hardly needs pointing out.

If the illustrations so far given seem trivial or verbal, that impression may be corrected by turning to the place which the *a priori* has in mathematics and in natural science. Arithmetic, for example, depends *en toto* upon the operation of counting or correlating, a procedure which can be carried out at will in any world containing identifiable things—even identifiable ideas—regardless of the further characters of experience. Mill challenged this *a priori* character of arithmetic. He asked us to suppose a demon sufficiently powerful and maleficent so that every time two things were brought together with two other things, this demon should always introduce a fifth. The implication which he supposed to follow is that under such circumstances $2 + 2 = 5$ would be a universal law of arithmetic. But Mill was quite mistaken. In such a world we should be obliged to become a little clearer than is usual about the distinction between arithmetic and physics, that is all. If two black marbles were put in the same urn with two white ones, the demon could take his choice of colors, but it would be evident that there were more black marbles or more white ones than were put in. The same would be true of all objects in any wise identifiable. We should simply find ourselves in the presence of an extraordinary physical law, which we should recognize as universal in our world, that whenever two things were brought into proximity with two others, an additional and similar thing was always created by the process. Mill's world would be physically most extraordinary. The world's work would be enormously facilitated if hats or locomotives or tons of coal could be thus multiplied by anyone possessed originally of two pairs. But the laws of mathematics would remain unaltered. It is because this is true that arithmetic is *a priori*. Its laws prevent *nothing*; they are compatible with anything which happens or could conceivably happen in nature. They would be true in any possible world. Mathematical addition is not a physical transformation. Physical changes which result in an increase or decrease of the countable things involved are matters of everyday occurrence. Such physical processes present us with phenomena in which the purely mathematical has to be separated out by abstraction. Those laws and those laws only have necessary truth which we are prepared to maintain, no matter what. It is because we shall always separate out that part of the phenomenon not in conformity with arithmetic and designate it by some other category—physical change, chemical reaction, optical illusion—that arithmetic is *a priori*.

The *a priori* element in science and in natural law is greater than might be supposed. In the first place, all science is based upon definitive concepts. The formulation of these concepts is, indeed, a matter determined by the commerce between our intellectual or our pragmatic interests and the nature of experience. Definition is classification. The scientific search is for such classification as will make it possible to correlate appearance and behavior, to discover law, to penetrate to the "essential nature" of things in order that behavior may become predictable. In other words, if definition is unsuccessful, as early scientific definitions mostly have been, it is because the classification thus set up corresponds with no natural cleavage and does not correlate with any important uniformity of behavior. A name itself must represent *some* uniformity in experience or it names nothing. What does not repeat itself or recur in intelligible fashion is not a thing. Where the definitive uniformity is a clue to other uniformities, we have successful scientific definition. Other definitions cannot be said to be false; they are merely useless. In scientific classification the search is, thus, for *things worth naming*. But the naming, classifying, defining activity is essentially prior to investigation. We cannot interrogate experience in general. Until our meaning is definite and our classification correspondingly exact, experience cannot conceivably answer our questions.

In the second place, the fundamental laws of any science—or those treated as fundamental—are *a priori* because they formulate just such definitive concepts or categorical tests by which alone investigation becomes possible. If the lightning strikes the railroad track at two places, A and B, how shall we tell whether these events are simultaneous? "We . . . require a definition of simultaneity such that this definition supplies us with the method by means of which . . . we can decide whether or not both the lightning strokes occurred simultaneously. As long as this requirement is not satisfied, I allow myself to be deceived as a physicist (and of course the same applies if I am not a physicist), when I imagine that I am able to attach a meaning to the statement of simultaneity. . . .

"After thinking the matter over for some time you then offer the following suggestion with which to test simultaneity. By measuring along the rails, the con-necting line AB should be measured up and an observer placed at the midpoint M of the distance AB. This observer should be supplied with an arrangement (e.g., two mirrors inclined at 90°) which allows him visually to observe both places A and B at the same time. If the observer perceives the two flashes at the same time, then they are simultaneous.

"I am very pleased with this suggestion, but for all that I cannot regard the matter as quite settled, because I feel constrained to raise the following objection: 'Your definition would certainly be right, if I only knew that the light by means of which the observer at M perceives the lightning flashes travels along the length A—M with the same velocity as along the length B—M. But an examination of this supposition would only be possible if we already had at our disposal the means of measuring time. It would thus appear as though we were moving here in a logical circle.'

"After further consideration you cast a somewhat disdainful glance at me—and rightly so—and you declare: 'I maintain my previous definition nevertheless, because in reality it assumes absolutely nothing about light. There is only *one* demand to be made of the definition of simultaneity, namely, that in every real case it must supply us with an empirical decision as to whether or not the conception which has to be defined is fulfilled. That light requires the same time to traverse the path A—M as for the path B—M is in reality *neither a supposition nor a hypothesis* about the physical nature of light, but a *stipulation* which I can make of my own free will in order to arrive at a definition of simultaneity.' . . . We are thus led also to a definition of 'time' in physics."

As this example from the theory of relativity well illustrates, we cannot even ask the questions which discovered law would answer until we have first by *a priori* stipulation formulated definitive criteria. Such concepts are not verbal definitions, nor classifications merely; they are themselves laws which prescribe a certain uniformity of behavior to whatever is thus named. Such definitive laws are *a priori*; only so can we enter upon the investigation by which further laws are sought. Yet it should also be pointed out that such *a priori* laws are subject to abandonment if the structure which is built upon them does not succeed in simplifying our interpretation of phenomena. If, in the illustration given, the relation "simultaneous with," as defined, should not prove transitive—if event *A* should prove simultaneous with *B*, and *B* with *C*, but not *A* with *C*—this definition would certainly be rejected.

And thirdly, there is that *a priori* element in science—as in other human affairs—which constitutes the criteria of the real as opposed to the unreal in experience. An object itself is a uniformity. Failure to behave in certain categorical ways marks it as unreal. Uniformities of the type called "natural law" are the clues to reality and unreality. A mouse which disappears where no hole is, is no real mouse; a landscape which recedes as we approach is but illusion. As the queen remarked in the episode of the wishing-carpet, "If this were real, then it would be a miracle. But miracles do not happen. Therefore I shall wake presently." That the uniformities of natural law are the only reliable criteria of the real is inescapable. But such a criterion is *ipso facto a priori*. No conceivable experience could dictate the alteration of a law so long as failure to obey that law marked the content of experience as unreal.

This is one of the puzzles of empiricism. We deal with experience: what any reality may be which underlies experience, we have to learn. What we desire to discover is natural law, the formulation of those uniformities which obtain among the real. But experience as it comes to us contains not only the real but all the content of illusion, dream, hallucination, and mistake. The *given* contains both real and unreal, confusingly intermingled. If we ask for uniformities of this unsorted experience, we shall not find them. Laws which characterize all experience, of real and unreal both, are non-existent and would in any case be worthless. What we seek are the uniformities of the *real*; but *until we have such laws, we cannot sift experience and segregate the real.*

The obvious solution is that the enrichment of experience, the separation of the real from the illusory or meaningless, and the formulation of natural law, all grow up together. If the criteria of the real are *a priori* that is not to say that no conceivable character of experience would lead to alteration of them. For example, spirits cannot be photographed. But if photographs of spiritistic phenomena, taken under properly guarded conditions, should become sufficiently frequent, this *a priori* dictum would be called in question. What we should do would be to redefine our terms. Whether "spook" was spirit or matter, whether the definition of "spirit" or of "matter" should be changed; all this would constitute one inter-related problem. We should reopen together the question of definition or classification, of criteria for this sort of real, and of natural law. And the solution of one of these would mean the solution of all. Nothing could *force* a redefinition of spirit or of matter. A sufficiently fundamental relation to human bent, to human interests, would guarantee continuance unaltered even in the face of unintelligible and baffling experiences. In such problems, the mind finds itself uncompelled save by its own purposes and needs. I *may* categorize experience as I will; but *what* categorical distinctions will best serve my interests and objectify my own intelligence? What the mixed and troubled experience shall be—that is beyond me. But what I shall do with it—that is my own question, when the character of experience is sufficiently before me. I am coerced only by my own need to understand.

It would indeed be inappropriate to characterize as *a priori* a law which we are wholly prepared to alter in the light of further experience, even though in an isolated case we should discard as illusory any experience which failed to conform. But the crux of the situation lies in this; beyond such principles as those of logic, which we seem fully prepared to maintain no matter what, there must be further and more particular criteria of the real prior to any investigation of nature whatever. We cannot even interrogate experience without a network of categories and definitive concepts. And we must further be prepared to say what experimental findings will answer what questions, and how. Without tests which represent anterior principle, there is no question which experience could answer at all. Thus the most fundamental laws in any category—or those which we regard as most fundamental—are *a priori*, even though continued failure to render experience intelligible in such terms might result eventually in the abandonment of that category altogether. Matters so comparatively small as the behavior of Mercury and of starlight passing the sun's limb may, if there be persistent failure to bring them within the field of previously accepted modes of explanation, result in the abandonment of the independent categories of space and time. But without the definitions, fundamental principles, and tests, of the type which constitute such categories, no experience whatever could prove or disprove anything. And to that mind which should find independent space and time absolutely necessary conceptions, no possible experiment could prove the principles of relativity. "There must be some error in the experimental findings, or some law not yet discovered," represents an attitude which can never be rendered impossible. And the only sense in which it could be proved unreasonable would be the pragmatic one of comparison with another method of categorical analysis which more successfully reduced all such experience to order and law.

At the bottom of all science and all knowledge are categories and definitive concepts which represent fundamental habits of thought and deep-lying attitudes which the human mind has taken in the light of its total experience. But a new and wider experience may bring about some alteration of these attitudes, even though by themselves they dictate nothing as to the content of experience, and no experience can conceivably prove them invalid.

Perhaps some will object to this conception on the ground that only such principles should be designated *a priori* as the human mind *must* maintain, no matter what; that if, for example, it is shown possible to arrive at a consistent doctrine of physics in terms of relativity, even by the most arduous reconstruction of our fundamental notions, then the present conceptions are by that fact shown not to be *a priori*. Such objection is especially likely from those who would conceive the *a priori* in terms of an absolute mind or an absolutely universal human nature. We should readily agree that a decision by popular approval or a congress of scientists or anything short of such a test as would bring to bear the full weight of human capacity and interest would be ill-considered as having to do with the *a priori*. But we wish to emphasize two facts: first, that in the field of those conceptions and principles which have altered in human history, there are those which could neither be proved nor disproved by any experience, but represent the uncompelled initiative of human thought—that without this uncompelled initiative no growth of sci-

ence, nor any science at all, would be conceivable. And second, that the difference between such conceptions as are, for example, concerned in the decision of relativity versus absolute space and time, and those more permanent attitudes such as are vested in the laws of logic, there is only a difference of degree. The dividing line between the *a priori* and the *a posteriori* is that between principles and definitive concepts which *can* be maintained in the face of all experience and those genuinely empirical generalizations which *might* be proven flatly false. The thought which both rationalism and empiricism have missed is that there are principles, representing the initiative of mind, which impose upon experience no limitations whatever, but that such conceptions are still subject to alteration on pragmatic grounds when the expanding boundaries of experience reveal their infelicity as intellectual instruments.

Neither human experience nor the human mind has a character which is universal, fixed, and absolute. "The human mind" does not exist at all save in the sense that all humans are very much alike in fundamental respects, and that the language habit and the enormously important exchange of ideas has greatly increased our likeness in those respects which are here in question. Our categories and definitions are peculiarly social products, reached in the light of experiences which have much in common, and beaten out, like other pathways, by the coincidence of human purposes and the exigencies of human cooperation. Concerning the *a priori* there need be neither universal agreement nor complete historical continuity. Conceptions, such as those of logic, which are least likely to be affected by the opening of new ranges of experience, represent the most stable of our categories; but none of them is beyond the possibility of alteration.

Mind contributes to experience the element of order, of classification, categories, and definition. Without such, experience would be unintelligible. Our knowledge of the validity of these is simply consciousness of our own fundamental ways of acting and our own intellectual intent. Without this element, knowledge is impossible, and it is here that whatever truths are necessary and independent of experience must be found. But the commerce between our categorical ways of acting, our pragmatic interests, and the particular character of experience, is closer than we have realized. No explanation of any one of these can be complete without consideration of the other two.

Pragmatism has sometimes been charged with oscillating between two contrary notions; the one, that experience is "through and through malleable to our purpose," the other, that facts are "hard" and uncreated by the mind. We here offer a mediating conception: through all our knowledge runs the element of the *a priori*, which is indeed malleable to our purpose and responsive to our need. But throughout, there is also that other element of experience which is "hard," "independent," and unalterable to our will.

READING QUESTIONS

1. Lewis remarks that "the *a priori* represents an attitude in some sense freely taken, a stipulation of the mind itself, and a stipulation which might be made in some other way if it suited our bent or need." Is he correct? Are we in a position, for example, to simply choose which system of logic we will adopt?
2. Lewis states that "arithmetic is *a priori*. Its laws prevent *nothing*; they are compatible with anything which happens or could conceivably happen in nature. They would be true in any possible world." What does it mean to say that arithmetic would be true in any possible world? In what sense, if any, is arithmetic *about* the world?
3. How does Lewis think that we come to mark the distinction between what is real and what is an illusion? Is this an adequate way to mark this distinction?
4. Lewis briefly summarizes his position when he remarks that "there are principles, representing the initiative of mind, which impose upon experience no limitations whatever, but ... such conceptions are still subject to alteration on pragmatic grounds when the expanding boundaries of experience reveal their infelicity as intellectual instruments." In no more than a paragraph, explain what Lewis means by this. Do you agree?

SUGGESTIONS FOR FURTHER READING (CLARENCE I. LEWIS)

Primary Sources and Collected Writings

(1970) *Collected Papers of Clarence Irving Lewis*, edited by J. D. Goheen and J. L. Mothershead, Jr. Stanford, CA: Stanford University Press.

(1918) *A Survey of Symbolic Logic*. Berkeley, CA: University of California Press.

(1926) *The Pragmatic Element of Knowledge*. Berkeley, CA: University of California Press.

(1929) *Mind and the World-Order: Outline of a Theory of Knowledge*. New York: Charles Scribner's Sons.

(1932) *Symbolic Logic*. New York: The Century Company.

(1946) *An Analysis of Knowledge and Valuation*. La Salle, IL: Open Court.

(1955) *The Ground and Nature of the Right*. New York: Columbia University Press.

(1957) *Our Social Inheritance*. Bloomington, IN: Indiana University Press.

(1969) *Values and Imperatives: Studies in Ethics*, edited by J. Lange. Stanford CA: Stanford University Press.

Secondary Sources

Colella, E. P. (1992) *C. I. Lewis and the Social Theory of Conceptualistic Pragmatism*. Lewiston, NY: E. Mellen Press.

Knott, G. T. (1976) *Skepticism, Justification, and the Argument for Certainty: An Examination of C. I. Lewis' Foundationalism*. Athens, OH: University of Ohio Press.

Rosenthal, S. B. (1976) *The Pragmatic A Priori: A Study in the Epistemology of C. I. Lewis*. St. Louis, MO: Warren H. Green.

Saydah, J. R. (1969) *The Ethical Theory of Clarence Irving Lewis*. Athens, OH: Ohio University Press.

Schilpp, P. A., ed. (1968) *The Philosophy of C. I. Lewis*. La Salle, IL: Open Court.

PART II / Early Analytic Philosophy

GOTTLOB FREGE

GOTTLOB FREGE

On Sense and Meaning

Gottlob Frege (1848–1925) remains one of the most strikingly original and innovative logicians since Aristotle. A mathematician by vocation, Frege was born in the heart of central Europe, in the German town of Wismar. He attended the University of Jena and later obtained his doctorate in mathematics at Göttingen. After completing his formal education, Frege returned to the University of Jena where he took a teaching position in the mathematics department. Frege spent almost his entire professional life at Jena working on various problems in the nature of mathematics, along with related problems in logic, meaning, and truth.

Frege was concerned about the metaphysical and epistemological foundations of mathematics. His work centered around attempts to formulate adequate accounts of the *nature* of mathematics and of our *knowledge* of mathematics. In the process, Frege came to reject *psychologism*—the thesis that mathematics (or the meaning of mathematical propositions) is grounded simply in descriptive truths about human psychology or the so-called "laws of thought." He also rejected the idea that mathematics was some sort of empirical science. Rather, his strategy was to defend *logicism*—the thesis that the truths of mathematics are really logical truths. Frege's goal, accordingly, was to demonstrate that all the axioms and theorems of mathematics are derivable from the axioms and theorems of pure logic.

Frege's first major work in logical theory was *Begriffsschrift* ("Conceptual Notation"), which was published in 1879. In it, he brilliantly devises a formal system for representing and testing proofs. In many respects, the formal system of the *Begriffsschrift* serves as the basis of modern symbolic logic, inasmuch as it details Frege's discovery (or invention) of a conceptual vocabulary and methodology for symbolizing or representing sentences involving complex relations and quantification. With the system of the *Begriffsschrift* at hand, Frege was able to rigorously, explicitly, and precisely formulate his new logic. He was also able to express for the first time all the logically important features of any proposition requiring a symbolic formulation.

After the publication of *Begriffsschrift*, Frege went on to publish other works in logic and the philosophy of mathematics, including *Grundlagen der Arithmetik* (1884, translated as *The Foundations of Arithmetic*, 1959) and *Grundgesetze der Arithmetik* (1893, translated as *The Basic Laws of Arithmetic*, 1964). These works extended his investigations into various areas of logical theory, set theory, and the philosophy of mathematics, seeking to carry out the program in detail. *Grundlagen* goes on to lay the conceptual foundations for Frege's logicism, and *Grundgesetze* focuses in a formal way on working through the various problems of deducing the truths of mathematics from the axioms and theorems of pure logic alone.

In addition to his pioneering work in logic and the philosophy of mathematics, Frege is remembered for his significant contributions to the philosophy of language. His papers in this area are essential reading for anyone seriously interested in the problems of semantics. His many distinctions (e.g., between the sense of an expression and the referent of an expression, between a function and an object, etc.) constitute much of the contemporary vocabulary of the philosophy of language, and the significance of his work in this area is still discussed and debated to this day.

Despite Frege's importance as an original thinker, his career was quiet and uneventful. He received little public recognition or acclaim. His fame as a philosopher developed posthumously, although he was admired and respected during his lifetime by Bertrand Russell, Ludwig Wittgenstein, and Rudolf Carnap, among others.

In the following essay, "On Sense and Meaning," Frege discusses the famous distinction of the title. In the course of the paper, he works to clarify the distinction between both the sense and the meaning of a proper name and the sense and the meaning of a declarative sentence. He also considers various objections that might be raised to his view and offers his reply.

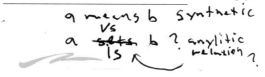

Equality* gives rise to challenging questions which are not altogether easy to answer. Is it a relation? A relation between objects, or between names or signs of objects? In my *Begriffsschrift* I assumed the latter. The reasons which seem to favor this are the following: $a = a$ and $a = b$ are obviously statements of differing cognitive values; $a = a$ holds *a priori* and, according to Kant, is to be labeled analytic, while statements of the form $a = b$ often contain very valuable extensions of our knowl-

---

Gottlob Frege, "On Sense and Meaning" translated by P. T. Geach and Max Black and reprinted with permission of the publisher from *Translations from the Philosophical Writings of Gottlob Frege*. Third Edition, Lanham, MD: Rowman and Littlefield Publishers, Inc., 1980.

*I use this word in the sense of identity and understand '$a = b$' to have the sense of 'a is the same as b' or 'a and b coincide.'

edge and cannot always be established *a priori*. The discovery that the rising sun is not new every morning, but always the same, was one of the most fertile astronomical discoveries. Even today the reidentification of a small planet or a comet is not always a matter of course. Now if we were to regard equality as a relation between that which the names 'a' and 'b' designate, it would seem that $a = b$ could not differ from $a = a$ (i.e., provided $a = b$ is true). A relation would thereby be expressed of a thing to itself, and indeed one in which each thing stands to itself but to no other thing. What we apparently want to state by $a = b$ is that the signs or names 'a' and 'b' designate the same thing, so that those signs themselves would be under discussion; a relation between them would be asserted. But this relation would hold between the names or signs only in so far as they named or designated something. It would be mediated by the connection of each of the two signs with the same designated thing. But this is arbitrary. Nobody can be forbidden to use any arbitrarily producible event or object as a sign for something. In that case the sentence $a = b$ would no longer refer to the subject matter, but only to its mode of designation; we would express no proper knowledge by its means. But in many cases this is just what we want to do. If the sign 'a' is distinguished from the sign 'b' only as an object (here, by means of its shape), not as a sign (i.e., not by the manner in which it designates something), the cognitive value of $a = a$ becomes essentially equal to that of $a = b$, provided $a = b$ is true. A difference can arise only if the difference between the signs corresponds to a difference in the mode of presentation of the thing designated. Let a, b, c be the lines connecting the vertices of a triangle with the midpoints of the opposite sides. The point of intersection of a and b is then the same as the point of intersection of b and c. So we have different designations for the same point, and these names ('point of intersection of a and b,' 'point of intersection of b and c') likewise indicate the mode of presentation; and hence the statement contains actual knowledge.

It is natural, now, to think of there being connected with a sign (name, combination of words, written mark), besides that which the sign designates, which may be called the meaning of the sign, also what I should like to call the *sense* of the sign, wherein the mode of presentation is contained. In our example, accordingly, the meaning of the expressions 'the point of intersection of *a* and *b*' and 'the point of intersection of *b* and *c*' would be the same, but not their sense. The meaning of 'evening star' would be the same as that of 'morning star,' but not the sense.

It is clear from the context that by sign and name I have here understood any designation figuring as a proper name, which thus has as its meaning a definite object (this word taken in the widest range), but not a concept or a relation, which shall be discussed further in another article. The designation of a single object can also consist of several words or other signs. For brevity, let every such designation be called a proper name.

The sense of a proper name is grasped by everybody who is sufficiently familiar with the language or totality of designations to which it belongs[1] but this serves to illuminate only a single aspect of the thing meant, supposing it to have one. Comprehensive knowledge of the thing meant would require us to be able to say immediately whether any given sense attaches to it. To such knowledge we never attain.

The regular connection between a sign, its sense, and what it means is of such a kind that to the sign there corresponds a definite sense and to that in turn a definite thing meant, while to a given thing meant (an object) there does not belong only a single sign. The same sense has different expressions in different languages or even in the same language. To be sure, exceptions to this regular behavior occur. To every expression belonging to a complete totality of signs, there should certainly correspond a definite sense; but natural languages often do not satisfy this condition, and one must be content if the same word has the same sense in the same context. It may perhaps be granted that every grammatically well-formed expression figuring as a proper name always has a sense. But this is not to say that to the sense there also corresponds a thing meant. The words 'the celestial body most distant from the Earth' have a sense, but it is very doubtful if there is also a thing they mean. The expression 'the least rapidly convergent series' has a sense but demonstrably there is nothing it means, since for every given conver-gent series, another convergent, but less rapidly convergent, series can be found. In grasping a sense, one is not certainly assured of meaning anything.

If words are used in the ordinary way, what one intends to speak of is what they mean. It can also happen, however, that one wishes to talk about the words themselves or their sense. This happens, for instance, when the words of another are quoted One's own words then first designate words of the other speaker, and only the latter have their usual meaning. We then have signs of signs. In writing, the words are in this case enclosed in quotation marks. Accordingly, a word standing between quotation marks must not be taken as having its ordinary meaning.

In order to speak of the sense of an expression 'A' one may simply use the phrase 'the sense of the expression "A."' In indirect speech one talks about the sense, e.g., of another person's remarks. It is quite clear that in this way of speaking words do not have their customary meaning but designate what is usually their sense. In order to have a short expression, we will say: In indirect speech, words are used *indirectly* or have their *indirect* meaning. We distinguish accordingly the *customary* from the *indirect* meaning of a word; and its *customary* sense from its *indirect* sense. The indirect meaning of a word is accordingly its customary sense. Such exceptions must always be borne in mind if the mode of connection between sign, sense, and meaning in particular cases is to be correctly understood.

The meaning and sense of a sign are to be distinguished from the associated idea. If what a sign means is an object perceivable by the senses, my idea of it is an internal image,[2] arising from memories of sense impressions which I have had and acts, both internal and external, which I have performed. Such an idea is often imbued with feeling; the clarity of its separate parts varies and oscillates. The same sense is not always connected, even in the same man, with the same idea. The idea is subjective: one man's idea is not that of another. There result, as a matter of course, a variety of differences in the ideas associated with the same sense. A painter, a horseman, and a zoologist will probably connect different ideas with the name 'Bucephalus.' This constitutes an essential distinction between the idea and sign's sense, which may be the common property of many people, and so is not a part or a mode of the individual mind. For one can hardly deny that mankind has a common store of thoughts which is transmitted from one generation to another.*

In the light of this, one need have no scruples in speaking simply of *the* sense, whereas in the case of an idea one must, strictly speaking, add whom it belongs to and at what time. It might perhaps be said: Just as one man connects this idea, and another that idea, with the same word, so also one man can associate this sense and another that sense. But there still remains a difference in the mode of connection. They are not prevented from grasping the same sense; but they cannot have the same idea. *Si duo idem faciunt, non est idem.* If two persons picture the same thing, each still has his own idea. It is indeed sometimes possible to establish differences in the ideas, or even in the sensations, of different men; but an exact comparison is not possible, because we cannot have both ideas together in the same consciousness.

The meaning of a proper name is the object itself which we designate by using it; the idea which we have in that case is wholly subjective; in between lies the sense, which is indeed no longer subjective like the idea, but is yet not the object itself. The following analogy will perhaps clarify these relationships. Somebody observes the Moon through a telescope. I compare the Moon itself to the meaning; it is the object of the observation, mediated by the real image projected by the object glass in the interior of the telescope, and by the retinal image of the observer. The former I compare to the sense, the latter is like the idea or experience. The optical image in the telescope is indeed one-sided and dependent upon the standpoint of observation; but it is still objective, inasmuch as it can be used by several observers. At any rate it could be arranged for several to use it simultaneously. But each one would have his own retinal image. On account of the diverse shapes of the observers' eyes, even a geometrical congruence could hardly be achieved, and an actual coincidence would be out of the question. This analogy might be developed still further, by assuming A's retinal image made visible to B; or A might also see his own retinal image in a mirror. In this way we might perhaps show how an idea

can itself be taken as an object, but as such is not for the observer what it directly is for the person having the idea. But to pursue this would take us too far afield.

We can now recognize three levels of difference between words, expressions, or whole sentences. The difference may concern at most the ideas, or the sense but not the meaning, or, finally, the meaning as well. With respect to the first level, it is to be noted that, on account of the uncertain connection of ideas with words, a difference may hold for one person, which another does not find. The difference between a translation and the original text should properly not overstep the first level. To the possible differences here belong also the coloring and shading which poetic eloquence seeks to give to the sense. Such coloring and shading are not objective, and must be evoked by each hearer or reader according to the hints of the poet or the speaker. Without some affinity in human ideas art would certainly be impossible; but it can never be exactly determined how far the intentions of the poet are realized.

In what follows there will be no further discussion of ideas and experiences; they have been mentioned here only to ensure that the idea aroused in the hearer by a word shall not be confused with its sense or its meaning.

To make short and exact expressions possible, let the following phraseology be established:

A proper name (word, sign, sign combination, expression) *expresses* its sense, *means* or *designates* its meaning. By employing a sign we express its sense and designate its meaning.

Idealists or skeptics will perhaps long since have objected: 'You talk, without further ado, of the Moon as an object; but how do you know that the name 'the Moon' has any meaning? How do you know that anything whatsoever has a meaning?' I reply that when we say 'the Moon,' we do not intend to speak of our idea of the Moon, nor are we satisfied with the sense alone, but we presuppose a meaning. To assume that in the sentence 'The Moon is smaller than the Earth' the idea of the Moon is in question, would be flatly to misunderstand the sense. If this is what the speaker wanted, he would use the phrase 'my idea of the Moon.' Now we can of course be mistaken in the presupposition, and such mistakes have indeed occurred. But the question whether the presupposition is perhaps always mistaken need not be answered here; in order to justify

---

*Hence it is inadvisable to use the word 'idea' to designate something so basically different.

mention of that which a sign means it is enough, at first, to point our intention in speaking or thinking. (We must then add the reservation: provided such a meaning exists.)

So far we have considered the sense and meaning only of such expressions, words, or signs as we have called proper names. We now inquire concerning the sense and meaning of an entire assertoric sentence. Such a sentence contains a thought.* Is this thought, now, to be regarded as its sense or its meaning? Let us assume for the time being that the sentence does mean something. If we now replace one word of the sentence by another having the same meaning, but a different sense, this can have no effect upon the meaning of the sentence. Yet we can see that in such a case the thought changes; since, e.g., the thought in the sentence 'The morning star is a body illuminated by the Sun' differs from that in the sentence 'The evening star is a body illuminated by the Sun.' Anybody who did not know that the evening star is the morning star might hold the one thought to be true, the other false. The thought, accordingly, cannot be what is meant by the sentence, but must rather be considered as its sense. What is the position now with regard to the meaning? Have we a right even to inquire about it? Is it possible that a sentence as a whole has only a sense, but no meaning? At any rate, one might expect that such sentences occur, just as there are parts of sentences having sense but no meaning. And sentences which contain proper names without meaning will be of this kind. The sentence 'Odysseus was set ashore at Ithaca while sound asleep' obviously has a sense. But since it is doubtful whether the name 'Odysseus,' occurring therein, means anything, it is also doubtful whether the whole sentence does. Yet it is certain, nevertheless, that anyone who seriously took the sentence to be true or false would ascribe to the name 'Odysseus' a meaning, not merely a sense; for it is of what the name means that the predicate is affirmed or denied. Whoever does not admit the name has meaning can neither apply nor withhold the predicate. But in that case it would be superfluous to advance to what the name means; one could be satisfied

with the sense, if one wanted to go no further than the thought. If it were a question only of the sense of the sentence, the thought, it would be needless to bother with what is meant by a part of the sentence; only the sense, not the meaning, of the part is relevant to the sense at the whole sentence. The thought remains the same whether 'Odysseus' means something or not. The fact that we concern ourselves at all about what is meant by a part of the sentence indicates that we generally recognize and expect a meaning for the sentence itself. The thought loses value for us as soon as we recognize that the meaning of one of its parts is missing. We are therefore justified in not being satisfied with the sense of a sentence, and in inquiring also as to its meaning. But now why do we want every proper name to have not only a sense, but also a meaning? Why is the thought not enough for us? Because, and to the extent that, we are concerned with its truth-value. This is not always the case. In hearing an epic poem, for instance, apart from the euphony of the language we are interested only in the sense of the sentences and the images and feelings thereby aroused. The question of truth would cause us to abandon aesthetic delight for an attitude of scientific investigation. Hence it is a matter of no concern to us whether the name 'Odysseus,' for instance, has meaning, so long as we accept the poem as a work of art.* It is the striving for truth that drives us always to advance from the sense to the thing meant.

We have seen that the meaning of a sentence may always be sought, whenever the meaning of its components is involved; and that this is the case when and only when we are inquiring after the truth-value.

We are therefore driven into accepting the *truth-value* of a sentence as constituting what it means. By the truth-value of a sentence I understand the circumstance that it is true or false. There are no further truth-values. For brevity I call the one the True, the other the False. Every assertoric sentence concerned with what its words mean is therefore to be regarded as a proper name, and its meaning, if it has one, is either the True or the False. These two objects are recognized, if only

---

*By a thought I understand not the subjective performance of thinking but its objective content, which is capable of being the common property of several thinkers.

---

*It would be desirable to have a special term for signs having only sense. If we name them, say, representations, the words of the actors on the stage would be representations; indeed the actor himself would be a representation.

implicitly, by everybody who judges something to be true—and so even by a skeptic. The designation of the truth values as objects may appear to be an arbitrary fancy or perhaps a mere play upon words, from which no profound consequences could be drawn. What I am calling an object can be more exactly discussed only in connection with concept and relation. I will reserve this for another article. But so much should already be clear, that in every judgment,* no matter how trivial, the step from the level of thoughts to the level of meaning (the objective) has already been taken.

One might be tempted to regard the relation of the thought to the True not as that of sense to meaning, but rather as that of subject to predicate. One can, indeed, say: 'The thought that 5 is a prime number is true.' But closer examination shows that nothing more has been said than in the simple sentence '5 is a prime number.' The truth claim arises in each case from the form of the assertoric sentence, and when the latter lacks its usual force, e.g., in the mouth of an actor upon the stage, even the sentence 'The thought that 5 is a prime number is true' contains only a thought, and indeed the same thought as the simple '5 is a prime number.' It follows that the relation of the thought to the True may not be compared with that of subject to predicate.

Subject and predicate (understood in the logical sense) are just elements of thought; they stand on the same level for knowledge. By combining subject and predicate, one reaches only a thought, never passes from sense to meaning, never from a thought to its truth-value. One moves at the same level but never advances from one level to the next. A truth-value cannot be a part of a thought, any more than, say, the Sun can, for it is not a sense but an object.

If our supposition that the meaning of a sentence is its truth-value is correct, the latter must remain unchanged when a part of the sentence is replaced by an expression with the same meaning. And this is in fact the case. Leibniz gives the definition: '*Eadem sunt, quae sibi mutuo substitui possunt, salva veritate.*' If we are dealing with sentences for which the meaning of their component parts is at all relevant, then what feature except the truth-value can be found that belongs to

such sentences quite generally and remains unchanged by substitutions of the kind just mentioned?

If now the truth-value of a sentence is its meaning, then on the one hand all true sentences have the same meaning and so, on the other hand, do all false sentences. From this we see that in the meaning of the sentence all that is specific is obliterated. We can never be concerned only with the meaning of a sentence; but again the mere thought alone yields no knowledge, but only the thought together with its meaning, i.e., its truth-value. Judgments can be regarded as advances from a thought to a truth-value. Naturally this cannot be a definition. Judgment is something quite peculiar and incomparable. One might also say that judgments are distinctions of parts within truth-values. Such distinction occurs by a return to the thought. To every sense attaching to a truth-value would correspond its own manner of analysis. However, I have here used the word 'part' in a special sense. I have in fact transferred the relation between the parts and the whole of the sentence to its meaning, by calling the meaning of a word part of the meaning of the sentence, if the word itself is a part of the sentence. This way of speaking can certainly be attacked, because the total meaning and one part of it do not suffice to determine the remainder, and because the word 'part' is already used of bodies in another sense. A special term would need to be invented.

The supposition that the truth-value of a sentence is what it means shall now be put to further test. We have found that the truth-value of a sentence remains unchanged when an expression is replaced by another with the same meaning: but we have not yet considered the case in which the expression to be replaced is itself a sentence. Now if our view is correct, the truth-value of a sentence containing another as part must remain unchanged when the part is replaced by another sentence having the same truth-value. Exceptions are to be expected when the whole sentence or its part is direct or indirect quotation; for in such cases as we have seen, the words do not have their customary meaning. In direct quotation, a sentence designates another sentence, and in indirect speech a thought.

We are thus led to consider subordinate sentences or clauses. These occur as parts of a sentence complex, which is, from the logical standpoint, likewise a sentence—a main sentence. But here we meet the question

---

*A judgment, for me, is not the mere grasping of a thought, but the admission of its truth.

whether it is also true of the subordinate sentence that its meaning is a truth-value. Of indirect speech we already know the opposite. Grammarians view subordinate clauses as representatives of parts of sentences and divide them accordingly into noun clauses, adjective clauses, adverbial clauses. This might generate the supposition that the meaning of a subordinate clause was not a truth-value but rather of the same kind as the meaning of a noun or adjective or adverb—in short, of a part of a sentence, whose sense was not a thought but only a part of a thought. Only a more thorough investigation can clarify the issue. In so doing, we shall not follow the grammatical categories strictly, but rather group together what is logically of the same kind. Let us first search for cases in which the sense of the subordinate clause, as we have just supposed, is not an independent thought.

The case of an abstract noun clause, introduced by 'that,' includes the case of indirect quotation, in which we have seen the words to have their indirect meaning, coincident with what is customarily their sense. In this case, then, the subordinate clause has for its meaning a thought, not a truth-value; as sense not a thought, but the sense of the words 'the thought that (etc.),' which is only a part of the thought in the entire complex sentence. This happens after 'say,' 'hear,' 'be of the opinion,' 'be convinced,' 'conclude,' and similar words.* There is a different, and indeed somewhat complicated, situation after words like 'perceive,' 'know,' 'fancy,' which are to be considered later.

That in the cases of the first kind the meaning of the subordinate clause is in fact the thought can also be recognized by seeing that it is indifferent to the truth of the whole whether the subordinate clause is true or false. Let us compare, for instance, the two sentences 'Copernicus believed that the planetary orbits are circles' and 'Copernicus believed that the apparent motion of the sun is produced by the real motion of the Earth.' One subordinate clause can be substituted for the other without harm to the truth. The main clause and the subordinate clause together have as their sense only a single thought, and the truth of the whole in-

cludes neither the truth nor the untruth of the subordinate clause. In such cases it is not permissible to replace one expression in the subordinate clause by another having the same customary meaning, but only by one having the same indirect meaning, i.e., the same customary sense. Somebody might conclude: The meaning of a sentence is not its truth-value, for in that case it could always be replaced by another sentence of the same truth-value. But this proves too much; one might just as well claim that the meaning of 'morning star' is not Venus, since one may not always say 'Venus' in place of 'morning star.' One has the right to conclude only that the meaning of a sentence is not *always* its truth value, and that 'morning star' does not always mean the planet Venus, viz., when the word has its indirect meaning. An exception of such a kind occurs in the subordinate clause just considered which has a thought as its meaning.

If one says 'It seems that . . . ' one means 'It seems to me that . . . ' or 'I think that . . . ' We therefore have the same case again. The situation is similar in the case of expressions such as 'to be pleased,' 'to regret,' 'to approve,' 'to blame,' 'to hope,' 'to fear.' If, toward the end of the battle of Waterloo, Wellington was glad that the Prussians were coming, the basis for his joy was a conviction. Had he been deceived, he would have been no less pleased so long as his illusion lasted; and before he became so convinced he could not have been pleased that the Prussians were coming—even though in fact they might have been already approaching.

Just as a conviction or a belief is the ground of a feeling, it can, as in inference, also be the ground of a conviction. In the sentence: 'Columbus inferred from the roundness of the Earth that he could reach India by traveling toward the west,' we have as the meanings of the parts two thoughts, that the Earth is round, and that Columbus by traveling to the west could reach India. All that is relevant here is that Columbus was convinced of both, and that the one conviction was a ground for the other. Whether the Earth is really round and Columbus could really reach India by traveling west, as he thought, is immaterial to the truth of our sentence; but it is not immaterial whether we replace 'the Earth' by 'the planet which is accompanied by a moon whose diameter is greater than the fourth part of its own.' Here also we have the indirect meaning of the words.

*In 'A lied in saying he had seen B,' the subordinate clause designates a thought which is said (1) to have been asserted by A (2) while A was convinced of its falsity.

Adverbial final clauses beginning 'in order that' also belong here; for obviously the purpose is a thought; therefore: indirect meaning for the words, subjunctive mood.

A subordinate clause with 'that' after 'command,' 'ask,' 'forbid,' would appear in direct speech as an imperative. Such a sentence has no meaning but only a sense. A command, a request, are indeed not thoughts, but they stand on the same level as thoughts. Hence in subordinate clauses depending upon 'command,' 'ask,' etc., words have their indirect meaning. The meaning of such a clause is therefore not a truth-value but a command, a request, and so forth.

The case is similar for the dependent question in phrases such as 'doubt whether,' 'not to know what.' It is easy to see that here also the words are to be taken to have their indirect meaning. Dependent clauses express questions and, beginning with 'who,' 'what,' 'where,' 'when,' 'how,' 'by what means,' etc., seem at times to approximate very closely to adverbial clauses in which words have their customary meanings. These cases are distinguished linguistically [in German] by the mood of the verb. With the subjunctive, we have a dependent question and indirect meanings of the words, so that a proper name cannot in general be replaced by another name of the same object.

In the cases so far considered the words of the subordinate clauses had their indirect meaning, and this made it clear that the meaning of the subordinate clause itself was indirect, i.e., not a truth-value but a thought, a command, a request, a question. The subordinate clause could be regarded as a noun, indeed one could say: as a proper name of that thought, that command, etc., which it represented in the context of the sentence structure.

We now come to other subordinate clauses, in which the words do have their customary meaning without, however, a thought occurring as sense and a truth-value as meaning. How this is possible is best made clear by examples.

Whoever discovered the elliptic form of the planetary orbits died in misery.

If the sense of the subordinate clause were here a thought, it would have to be possible to express it also in a separate sentence. But it does not work, because the grammatical subject 'whoever' has no independent sense and only mediates the relation with the consequent clause 'died in misery.' For this reason the sense of the subordinate clause is not a complete thought, and what it means is Kepler, not a truth value. One might object that the sense of the whole does contain a thought as part, viz., that there was somebody who first discovered the elliptic form of the planetary orbits; for whoever takes the whole to be true cannot deny this part. This is undoubtedly so; but only because otherwise the dependent clause 'whoever discovered the elliptic form of the planetary orbits' would have nothing to mean. If anything is asserted there is always an obvious presupposition that the simple or compound proper names used have meaning. If therefore one asserts 'Kepler died in misery,' there is a presupposition that the name 'Kepler' designates something; but it does not follow that the sense of the sentence 'Kepler died in misery' contains the thought that the name 'Kepler' designates something. If this were the case the negation would have to run not

Kepler did not die in misery

but

Kepler did not die in misery, or the name 'Kepler' has no reference.

That the name 'Kepler' designates something is just as much a presupposition for the assertion

Kepler died in misery

as for the contrary assertion. Now languages have the fault of containing expressions which fail to designate an object (although their grammatical form seems to qualify them for that purpose) because the truth of some sentence is a prerequisite. Thus it depends on the truth of the sentence:

There was someone who discovered the elliptic form of the planetary orbits

whether the subordinate clause

Whoever discovered the elliptic form of the planetary orbits

really designates an object, or only seems to do so while in fact there is nothing for it to mean. And thus it may appear as if our subordinate clause contained as a part of its sense the thought that there was somebody who discovered the elliptic form of the planetary orbits. If this were right the negation would run:

> Either whoever discovered the elliptic form of the planetary orbits did not die in misery or there was nobody who discovered the elliptic form of the planetary orbits.

This arises from an imperfection of language, from which even the symbolic language of mathematical analysis is not altogether free; even there combinations of symbols can occur that seem to mean something but (at least so far) do not mean anything, e.g., divergent infinite series. This can be avoided, e.g., by means of the special stipulation that divergent infinite series shall mean the number zero. A logically perfect language (*Begriffsschrift*) should satisfy the conditions, that every expression grammatically well constructed as a proper name out of signs already introduced shall in fact designate an object, and that no new sign shall be introduced as a proper name without being secured a meaning. The logic books contain warnings against logical mistakes arising from the ambiguity of expressions. I regard as no less pertinent a warning against apparent proper names without any meaning. The history of mathematics supplies errors which have arisen in this way. This lends itself to demagogic abuse as easily as ambiguity—perhaps more easily. 'The will of the people' can serve as an example; for it is easy to establish that there is at any rate no generally accepted meaning for this expression. It is therefore by no means unimportant to eliminate the source of these mistakes, at least in science, once and for all. Then such objections as the one discussed above would become impossible, because it could never depend upon the truth of a thought whether a proper name had meaning.

With the consideration of these noun clauses may be coupled that of types of adjective and adverbial clauses which are logically in close relation to them.

Adjective clauses also serve to construct compound proper names, though, unlike noun clauses, they are not sufficient by themselves for this purpose. These adjective clauses are to be regarded as equivalent to adjectives. Instead of 'the square root of 4 which is smaller than 0,' one can also say 'the negative square root of 4.'

We have here the case of a compound proper name constructed from the expression for a concept with the help of the singular definite article. This is at any rate permissible if the concept applies to one and only one single object.*

Expressions for concepts can be so constructed that marks of a concept are given by adjective clauses as, in our example, by the clause 'which is smaller than 0.' It is evident that such an adjective clause cannot have a thought as sense or a truth-value as meaning, any more than the noun clause could. Its sense, which can also in many cases be expressed by a single adjective, is only a part of a thought. Here, as in the case of the noun clause, there is no independent subject and therefore no possibility of reproducing the sense of the subordinate clause in an independent sentence.

Places, instants, stretches of time, logically considered, are objects; hence the linguistic designation of a definite place, a definite instant, or a stretch of time is to be regarded as a proper name. Now adverbial clauses of place and time can be used to construct such a proper name in much the same way as we have seen noun and adjective clauses can. In the same way, expressions for concepts that apply to places, etc., can be constructed. It is to be noted here also that the sense of these subordinate clauses cannot be reproduced in an independent sentence, since an essential component, viz., the determination of place or time, is missing and is just indicated by a relative pronoun or a conjunction.[3]

In conditional clauses, also, there most often recognizably occurs an indefinite indicator, with a correlative indicator in the dependent clause. (We have already seen this occur in noun, adjective, and adverbial clauses.) In so far as each indicator relates to the other, both clauses together form a connected whole, which as a rule expresses only a single thought. In the sentence

> If a number is less than 1 and greater than 0, its square is less than 1 and greater than 0

---

*In accordance with what was said above, an expression of the kind in question must actually always be assured of meaning, by means of a special stipulation, e.g., by the convention that it shall count as meaning 0 when the concept applies to no object or to more than one.

the component in question is 'a number' in the antecedent clause and 'its' in the consequent clause. It is by means of this very indefiniteness that the sense acquires the generality expected of a law. It is this which is responsible for the fact that the antecedent clause alone has no complete thought as its sense and in combination with the consequent clause expresses one and only one thought, whose parts are no longer thoughts. It is, in general, incorrect to say that in the hypothetical judgment two judgments are put in reciprocal relationship. If this or something similar is said, the word 'judgment' is used in the same sense as I have connected with the word 'thought,' so that I would use the formulation: 'A hypothetical thought establishes a reciprocal relationship between two thoughts.' This could be true only if an indefinite indicator is absent;* but in such a case there would also be no generality.

If an instant of time is to be indefinitely indicated in both the antecedent and the consequent clause, this is often achieved merely by using the present tense of the verb, which in such a case, however, does not indicate the temporal present. This grammatical form is then the indefinite indicator in the main and subordinate clauses. An example of this is: 'When the Sun is in the tropic of Cancer, the longest day in the northern hemisphere occurs. Here, also, it is impossible to express the sense of the subordinate clause in a full sentence, because this sense is not a complete thought. If we say: 'The Sun is in the tropic of Cancer,' this would refer to our present time and thereby change the sense. Neither is the sense of the main clause a thought; only the whole, composed of main and subordinate clauses, has such a sense. It may be added that several common components may be indefinitely indicated in the antecedent and consequent clauses.

It is clear that noun clauses with 'who' or 'what' and adverbial clauses with 'where,' 'when,' 'wherever,' 'whenever' are often to be interpreted as having the sense of antecedent clauses, e.g., 'who touches pitch, defiles himself.'

Adjective clauses can also take the place of conditional clauses. Thus the sense of the sentence previously used can be given in the form 'The square of a number which is less than 1 and greater than 0 is less than 1 and greater than 0.'

The situation is quite different if the common component of the two clauses is designated by a proper name. In the sentence:

Napoleon, who recognized the danger to his right flank, himself led his guards against the enemy position

two thoughts are expressed:

1. Napoleon recognized the danger to his right flank
2. Napoleon himself led his guards against the enemy position.

When and where this happened is to be fixed only by the context, but is nevertheless to be taken as definitely determined thereby. If the entire sentence is uttered as an assertion, we thereby simultaneously assert both component sentences. If one of the parts is false, the whole is false. Here we have the case that the subordinate clause by itself has a complete thought as sense (if we complete it by indication of place and time). The meaning of the subordinate clause is accordingly a truth-value. We can therefore expect that it may be replaced, without harm to the truth-value of the whole, by a sentence having the same truth-value. This is indeed the case; but it is to be noticed that for purely grammatical reasons, its subject must be 'Napoleon,' for only then can it be brought into the form of an adjective clause attaching to 'Napoleon.' But if the demand that it be expressed in this form is waived, and the connection shown by 'and,' this restriction disappears.

Subsidiary clauses beginning with 'although' also express complete thoughts. This conjunction actually has no sense and does not change the sense of the clause but only illuminates it in a peculiar fashion.* We could indeed replace the concessive clause without harm to the truth of the whole by another of the same

---

*At times there is no linguistically explicit indicator and one must be read off from the entire context.

---

*Similarly in the case of 'but,' 'yet.'

truth-value; but the light in which the clause is placed by the conjunction might then easily appear unsuitable, as if a song with a sad subject were to be sung in a lively fashion.

In the last cases the truth of the whole included the truth of the component clauses. The case is different if an antecedent clause expresses a complete thought by containing, in place of an indefinite indicator, a proper name or something which is to be regarded as equivalent. In the sentence

> If the Sun has already risen, the sky is very
> cloudy

the time is the present, that is to say, definite. And the place is also to be thought of as definite. Here it can be said that a relation between the truth-values of antecedent and consequent clauses has been asserted, viz., that the case does not occur in which the antecedent means the True and the consequent the False. Accordingly, our sentence is true if the Sun has not yet risen, whether the sky is very cloudy or not, and also if the Sun has risen and the sky is very cloudy. Since only truth-values are here in question, each component clause can be replaced by another of the same truth-value without changing the truth-value of the whole. To be sure, the light in which the subject then appears would usually be unsuitable; the thought might easily seem distorted; but this has nothing to do with its truth-value. One must always observe that there are overtones of subsidiary thoughts, which are, however, not explicitly expressed and therefore should not be reckoned in the sense. Hence, also, no account need be taken of their truth-values.*

The simple cases have now been discussed. Let us review what we have learned.

The subordinate clause usually has for its sense not a thought, but only a part of one, and consequently no truth-value is being meant. The reason for this is either that the words in the subordinate clause have indirect

meaning, so that the meaning, not the sense, of the subordinate clause is a thought; or else that, on account of the presence of an indefinite indicator, the subordinate clause is incomplete and expresses a thought only when combined with the main clause. It may happen, however, that the sense of the subsidiary clause is a complete thought, in which case it can be replaced by another of the same truth-value without harm to the truth of the whole—provided there are no grammatical obstacles.

An examination of all the subordinate clauses which one may encounter will soon provide some which do not fit well into these categories. The reason, so far as I can see, is that these subordinate clauses have no such simple sense. Almost always, it seems, we connect with the main thoughts expressed by us subsidiary thoughts which, although not expressed, are associated with our words, in accordance with psychological laws, by the hearer. And since the subsidiary thought appears to be connected with our words on its own account, almost like the main thought itself, we want it also to be expressed. The sense of the sentence is thereby enriched, and it may well happen that we have more simple thoughts than clauses. In many cases the sentence must be understood in this way, in others it may be doubtful whether the subsidiary thought belongs to the sense of the sentence or only accompanies it.* One might perhaps find that the sentence

> Napoleon, who recognized the danger to his right
> flank, himself led his guards against the enemy
> position

expresses not only the two thoughts shown above, but also the thought that the knowledge of the danger was the reason why he led the guards against the enemy position. One may in fact doubt whether this thought is just slightly suggested or really expressed. Let the question be considered whether our sentence is false if Napoleon's decision had already been made before he recognized the danger. If our sentence could be true in spite of this, the subsidiary thought should not be un-

---

*The thought of our sentence might also be expressed thus: 'Either the Sun has not risen yet or the sky is very cloudy'— which shows how this kind of sentence connection is to be understood.

*This may be important for the question whether an assertion is a lie, or an oath a perjury.

derstood as part of the sense. One would probably decide in favor of this. The alternative would make for a quite complicated situation: We would have more simple thoughts than clauses. If the sentence

Napoleon recognized the danger to his right
flank

were now to be replaced by another having the same truth value, e.g.,

Napoleon was already more than 45 years old

not only would our first thought be changed, but also our third one. Hence the truth-value of the latter might change—viz., if his age was not the reason for the decision to lead the guards against the enemy. This shows why clauses of equal truth-value cannot always be substituted for one another in such cases. The clause expresses more through its connection with another than it does in isolation.

Let us now consider cases where this regularly happens. In the sentence:

Bebel fancies that the return of Alsace-Lorraine
would appease France's desire for revenge

two thoughts are expressed, which are not, however, shown by means of antecedent and consequent clauses, viz.:

1. Bebel believes that the return of Alsace-Lorraine would appease France's desire for revenge
2. The return of Alsace-Lorraine would not appease France's desire for revenge.

In the expression of the first thought, the words of the subordinate clause have their indirect meaning, while the same words have their customary meaning in the expression of the second thought. This shows that the subordinate clause in our original complex sentence is to be taken twice over, with different meanings: once for a thought, once for a truth value. Since the truth-value is not the total meaning of the subordinate clause, we cannot simply replace the latter by another of equal truth-value. Similar considerations apply to expressions such as 'know,' 'discover,' 'it is known that.'

By means of a subordinate causal clause and the associated main clause we express several thoughts, which, however, do not correspond separately to the original clauses. In the sentence: 'Because ice is less dense than water, it floats on water' we have

1. Ice is less dense than water;
2. If anything is less dense than water, it floats on water;
3. Ice floats on water.

The third thought, however, need not be explicitly introduced, since it is contained in the remaining two. On the other hand, neither the first and third nor the second and third combined would furnish the sense of our sentence. It can now be seen that our subordinate clause

because ice is less dense than water

expresses our first thought, as well as a part of our second. This is how it comes to pass that our subsidiary clause cannot be simply replaced by another of equal truth-value; for this would alter our second thought and thereby might well alter its truth-value.

The situation is similar in the sentence

If iron were less dense than water, it would
float on water.

Here we have the two thoughts that iron is not less dense than water, and that something floats on water if it is less dense than water. The subsidiary clause again expresses one thought and a part of the other.

If we interpret the sentence already considered

After Schleswig-Holstein was separated from Denmark, Prussia and Austria quarrelled

in such a way that it expresses the thought that Schleswig-Holstein was once separated from Denmark, we have first this thought, and secondly the thought that, at a time more closely determined by the subordinate clause, Prussia and Austria quarrelled. Here also the subordinate clause expresses not only one thought but also a part of another. Therefore it may not in general be replaced by another of the same truth-value.

It is hard to exhaust all the possibilities given by language; but I hope to have brought to light at least the essential reasons why a subordinate clause may not always be replaced by another of equal truth-value without harm to the truth of the whole sentence structure. These reasons arise:

1. when the subordinate clause does not have a truth-value as its meaning, inasmuch as it expresses only a part of a thought;

2. when the subordinate clause does have a truth-value as its meaning but is not restricted to so doing, inasmuch as its sense includes one thought and part of another.

The first case arises:

a. for words having indirect meaning

b. if a part of the sentence is only an indefinite indicator instead of a proper name.

In the second case, the subsidiary clause may have to be taken twice over, viz., once in its customary meaning, and the other time in indirect meaning; or the sense of a part of the subordinate clause may likewise be a component of another thought, which, taken together with the thought directly expressed by the subordinate clause, makes up the sense of the whole sentence.

It follows with sufficient probability from the foregoing that the cases where a subordinate clause is not replaceable by another of the same value cannot be brought in disproof of our view that a truth-value is the meaning of a sentence that has a thought as its sense.

Let us return to our starting point.

When we found '$a = a$' and '$a = b$' to have different cognitive values, the explanation is that for the purpose of knowledge, the sense of the sentence, viz., the thought expressed by it, is no less relevant than its meaning, i.e., its truth-value. If now $a = b$, then indeed what is meant by 'b' is the same as what is meant by 'a,' and hence the truth-value of '$a = b$' is the same as that of '$a = a$.' In spite of this, the sense of 'b' may differ from that of 'a,' and thereby the thought expressed in '$a = b$' differs from that of '$a = a$.' In that case the two sentences do not have the same cognitive value. If we understand by 'judgment' the advance from the

thought to its truth-value, as in the present paper, we can also say that the judgments are different.

Notes

1. In the case of an actual proper name such as 'Aristotle' opinions as to the sense may differ. It might, for instance, be taken to be the following: the pupil of Plato and teacher of Alexander the Great. Anybody who does this will attach another sense to the sentence 'Aristotle was born in Stagira' than will a man who takes as the sense of the name: the teacher of Alexander the Great who was born in Stagira. So long as the thing meant remains the same, such variations of sense may be tolerated, although they are to be avoided in the theoretical structure of a demonstrative science and ought not to occur in a perfect language.

2. We may include with ideas direct experiences: here, sense-impressions and acts themselves take the place of the traces which they have left in the mind. The distinction is unimportant for our purpose, especially since memories of sense-impressions and acts always go along with such impressions and acts themselves to complete the perpetual image. One may on the other hand understand direct experience as including any object in so far as it is sensibly perceptible or spatial.

3. In the case of these sentences, various interpretations are easily possible. The sense of the sentence, 'After Schleswig-Holstein was separated from Denmark, Prussia and Austria quarrelled.' In this version, it is surely sufficiently clear that the sense is not to be taken as having as a part the thought that Schleswig-Holstein was once separated from Denmark, but that this is the necessary presupposition in order for the expression 'after the separation of Schleswig-Holstein from Denmark' to have any meaning at all. To be sure, our sentence can also be interpreted as saying that Schleswig-Holstein was once separated from Denmark. We then have a case which is to be considered later. In order to understand the difference more clearly, let us project ourselves into the mind of a Chinese who, having little knowledge of European history, believes it to be false that Schleswig-Holstein was ever separated from Denmark. He will

take our sentence, in the first version, to be neither true nor false but will deny it to have any meaning, on the ground that its subordinate clause lacks a meaning. This clause would only apparently determine a time. If he interpreted our sentence in the second way, however, he would find a thought expressed in it which he would take to be false, beside a part which would be without meaning for him.

READING QUESTIONS

1. Frege uses a number of technical terms in his paper, the most important of which are "sign," "sense," "meaning," "idea," and "object." Define these terms and discuss how they are related.
2. Frege claims that the sense of a sign contains its "mode of presentation." What does he mean by that?
3. Frege offers an account of the sense and meaning of proper names, on one hand, and of sentences, on the other. How are these accounts similar, and how are they different?
4. In speaking of the meaning of sentences, Frege writes, "we are therefore driven into accepting the *truth-value* of a sentence as constituting what it means. By the truth-value of a sentence I understand the circumstances that it is true or false. There are no further truth-values. For brevity I call the one the True, the other the False." According to Frege, why are we driven into accepting this? After reviewing his various remarks about truth-values, explain what Frege thinks a truth-value is.
5. In general, why does Frege think that there is a problem about "subordinate clauses"? What threat does it pose to his theory? What is his solution?

SUGGESTIONS FOR FURTHER READING (GOTTLOB FREGE)

Primary Sources and Collected Writings

(1879) "Begriffsschrift." In *From Frege to Gödel: A Source Book in Mathematical Logic, 1879–1931*, edited by J. van Heijenoort, 1–82. Cambridge, MA: Harvard University Press, 1967.

(1884) *The Foundations of Arithmetic: A Logico-Mathematical Enquiry into the Concept of Number*, translated by J. L. Austin. Oxford: Blackwell, 1980.

(1892–5) "Comments on Sense and Meaning." In *Posthumous Writings*, translated by P. Long and R. White, edited by H. Hermes, F. Kambartel, and F. Kaulbach, 118–25. Oxford: Blackwell, 1979.

(1964) *The Basic Laws of Arithmetic: Exposition of the System*, translated and edited by M. Furth. Berkeley, CA: University of California Press.

(1971) *On the Foundation of Geometry and Formal Theories of Arithmetic*, translated by Eike-Henner W. Kluge. New Haven, CT: Yale University Press.

(1972) *Conceptual Notation and Related Articles*, translated and edited by T. W. Bynum. Oxford: Clarendon Press.

(1979) *Posthumous Writings*, edited by H. Hermes, F. Kambartel, and F. Kaulbach, translated by P. Long and R. White. Oxford: Blackwell.

(1980) *Philosophical and Mathematical Correspondence*, translated by H. Kaal, edited by B. McGuiness. Oxford: Oxford University Press.

(1984) *Collected Papers on Mathematics, Logic and Philosophy*, edited by B. McGuiness. Oxford: Blackwell.

(1986) *Translations from the Philosophical Writings of Gottlob Frege*, edited by P. Geach and M. Black. Totowa, NJ: Rowman & Littlefield.

(1997) *The Frege Reader*, edited by M. Beaney. Oxford: Blackwell.

Secondary Sources

Beaney, M. (1996) *Frege: Making Sense*. London: Duckworth.

Bell, D. (1979) *Frege's Theory of Judgment*. Oxford: Clarendon Press.

Carl, W. (1994) *Frege's Theory of Sense and Reference*. Cambridge: Cambridge University Press.

Currie, G. (1982) *Frege: An Introduction to His Philosophy*. Totowa, NY: Barnes and Noble.

Demopoulous, W., ed. (1995) *Frege's Philosophy of Mathematics*. Cambridge, MA: Harvard University Press.

Dummett, M. (1978) *Truth and Other Enigmas*. Cambridge, MA: Harvard University Press.

————. (1981) *The Interpretation of Frege's Philosophy.* Cambridge, MA: Harvard University Press.

————. (1991) *Frege: Philosophy of Mathematics.* Cambridge, MA: Harvard University Press.

————. (1992) *Frege: Philosophy of Language*, 2nd ed. Cambridge, MA: Harvard University Press.

————. (1993) *The Sea of Language.* Oxford: Clarendon Press.

————. (1994) *Origins of Analytical Philosophy.* Cambridge, MA: Harvard University Press.

Kenney, A. (1995) *Frege.* New York: Penguin Books.

Klemke, E., ed. (1968) *Essays on Frege.* Urbana, IL: University of Illinois Press.

Resnik, M. (1980) *Frege and the Philosophy of Mathematics.* Ithaca, NY: Cornell University Press.

Salmon, N. (1986) *Frege's Puzzle.* Cambridge, MA: MIT Press.

Sluga, H. (1980) *Gottlob Frege.* London: Routledge and Kegan Paul.

————. (1993) *The Philosophy of Frege.* New York: Garland Publishing Company.

Tait, W. and L. Linsky, eds. (1997) *Early Analytic Philosophy: Frege, Russell, Wittgenstein.* La Salle, IL: Open Court Publishing Company.

Weiner, J. (1999) *Frege.* Oxford: Oxford University Press.

————. (1990) *Frege in Perspective.* Ithaca, NY: Cornell University Press.

Wright, C. (1983) *Frege's Conception of Numbers as Objects.* Aberdeen: Aberdeen University Press.

Bertrand Russell

Descriptions

Bertrand Arthur William Russell (1872–1970) was born to an aristocratic family in Wales and raised by his conservative and deeply religious grandmother from the age of four, after the unfortunate death of his parents. As a young man, Russell developed an interest both in mathematics and in questions of religion. He became a student of mathematics at Trinity College, Cambridge, in 1890. By 1893, however, his interest in mathematics had largely shifted to the philosophical foundations of mathematics (and to academic philosophy more generally). In the end, his career was spent as an advocate and practitioner of analytic philosophy, rather than as a mathematician.

As a philosopher, Russell mainly focused on pursuing topics in the philosophy of mathematics, epistemology, the philosophy of language, the philosophy of science, applied ethics, and political philosophy. His philosophical development went through many distinct phases, including an early interest in neo-Hegelian idealism, followed by periods in which he professed an extreme realism, a philosophy of logical atomism, neutral monism, and later a form of neonaturalism. Russell was in many respects his own worst critic, and he developed a reputation for reinventing himself intellectually every few years.

In addition to his academic pursuits, Russell was an active social commentator and outspoken proponent of liberalism, freethinking, and liberal ideals. He was vocal in his opposition to England's involvement in the First World War and to America's involvement in the Vietnam War, but was a proponent for the West's involvement in the Second World War. At one point he campaigned as a suffragist for Parliament. He spent his later years working actively for nuclear disarmament and for the cause of world peace.

He began his philosophical career in 1895 as a Fellow of Trinity College and went on to occupy various positions at Cambridge, the University of Chicago, the University of California at Los Angeles, and at other major research universities in places such as Great Britain, China, and the United States. Among his many students, none is more famous than Ludwig Wittgenstein, who studied the philosophy of mathematics with him at Cambridge beginning in 1911. In addition to his teaching and public lecturing, Russell was a productive writer, publishing dozens of books and literally hundreds of articles on everything that interested him.

His philosophy and his politics repeatedly put him at odds with authority. He was jailed on more than one occasion, dismissed from his teaching position at Cambridge in 1916 for political reasons, repeatedly had his life threatened, and was barred from teaching at the

City University of New York because the American courts deemed his work "lecherous, libidinous, lustful, venerous, erotomaniac, aphrodisiac, irreverent, narrow-minded, untruthful, and bereft of moral fiber." Nevertheless he was also awarded the Nobel Prize for Literature in 1950.

His personal life was tumultuous. Russell was married four times, had numerous affairs, and had difficulty maintaining close personal friendships. As a friend and spouse, he could be selfish and treacherous, but he also could be deeply concerned for the welfare of others. He loved children, but was somewhat distant from his own. He also dealt with periods of depression, insecurity, anxiety, and was at times haunted by an unshakable fear of failure. His troubled and complex relationship with Wittgenstein (who was in many ways just as tormented personally) is a subject of particular interest to intellectual historians.

In the following selection from his book *Introduction to Mathematical Philosophy* (composed while Russell was imprisoned for his antiwar activities), Russell discusses his famous theory of descriptions. The theory was first presented in 1905 in an article entitled "On Denoting," published in the journal *Mind*. In this selection, Russell succinctly recapitulates his account of the difference between indefinite and definite descriptions, their relationship to names, and of the importance of his theory in avoiding what he calls "the error of admitting unrealities."

We dealt in the preceding chapter with the words *all* and *some;* in this chapter we shall consider the word *the* in the singular, and in the next chapter we shall consider the word *the* in the plural. It may be thought excessive to devote two chapters to one word, but to the philosophical mathematician it is a word of very great

Bertrand Russell, "Descriptions" from his *Introduction to Mathematical Philosophy,* London and New York: Routledge, 1953. Reprinted with the kind permission of the publisher and The Bertrand Russell Peace Foundation.

importance: like Browning's Grammarian with the enclitic δε, I would give the doctrine of this word if I were "dead from the waist down" and not merely in a prison.

We have already had occasion to mention "descriptive functions," i.e., such expressions as "the father of *x*" or "the sine of *x*." These are to be defined by first defining "descriptions."

A "description" may be of two sorts, definite and indefinite (or ambiguous). An indefinite description is a phrase of the form "a so-and-so," and a definite description is a phrase of the form "the so-and-so" (in the singular). Let us begin with the former.

"Who did you meet?" "I met a man." "That is a very indefinite description." We are therefore not departing from usage in our terminology. Our question is: What do I really assert when I assert "I met a man"? Let us assume, for the moment, that my assertion is true, and that in fact I met Jones. It is clear that what I assert is *not* "I met Jones." I may say "I met a man, but it was not Jones"; in that case, though I lie, I do not contradict myself, as I should do if when I say I met a man I really mean that I met Jones. It is clear also that the person to whom I am speaking can understand what I say, even if he is a foreigner and has never heard of Jones.

But we may go further: not only Jones, but no actual man, enters into my statement. This becomes obvious when the statement is false, since then there is no more reason why Jones should be supposed to enter into the proposition than why anyone else should. Indeed the statement would remain significant, though it could not possibly be true, even if there were no man at all. "I met a unicorn" or "I met a sea serpent" is a perfectly significant assertion, if we know what it would be to be a unicorn or a sea serpent, i.e., what is the definition of these fabulous monsters. Thus it is only what we may call the *concept* that enters into the proposition. In the case of "unicorn," for example, there is only the concept: there is not also, some where among the shades, something unreal which may be called "a unicorn." Therefore, since it is significant (though false) to say "I met a unicorn," it is clear that this proposition, rightly analyzed, does not contain a constituent "a unicorn," though it does contain the concept "unicorn."

The question of "unreality," which confronts us at this point, is a very important one. Misled by grammar, the great majority of those logicians who have dealt with this question have dealt with it on mistaken lines. They have regarded grammatical form as a surer guide in analysis than, in fact, it is. And they have not known what differences in grammatical form are important. "I met Jones" and "I met a man" would count traditionally as propositions of the same form, but in actual fact they are of quite different forms: the first names an actual person, Jones; while the second involves a propositional function, and becomes, when made explicit: "The function 'I met x and x is human' is sometimes true." (It will be remembered that we adopted the convention of using "sometimes" as not implying more than once.) This proposition is obviously not of the form "I met x," which accounts for the existence of the proposition "I met a unicorn" in spite of the fact that there is no such thing as "a unicorn."

For want of the apparatus of propositional functions, many logicians have been driven to the conclusion that there are unreal objects. It is argued, e.g., by Meinong, that we can speak about "the golden mountain," "the round square," and so on; we can make true propositions of which these are the subjects; hence they must have some kind of logical being, since otherwise the propositions in which they occur would be meaningless. In such theories, it seems to me, there is a failure of that feeling for reality which ought to be preserved even in the most abstract studies. Logic, I should maintain, must no more admit a unicorn than zoology can; for logic is concerned with the real world just as truly as zoology, though with its more abstract and general features. To say that unicorns have an existence in heraldry, or in literature, or in imagination, is a most pitiful and paltry evasion. What exists in heraldry is not an animal, made of flesh and blood, moving and breathing of its own initiative. What exists is a picture, or a description in words. Similarly, to maintain that Hamlet, for example, exists in his own world, namely, in the world of Shakespeare's imagination, just as truly as (say) Napoleon existed in the ordinary world, is to say something deliberately confusing, or else confused to a degree which is scarcely credible. There is only one world, the "real" world: Shakespeare's imagination is part of it, and the thoughts that he had in writing Hamlet are real. So are the thoughts that we have in reading the play. But it is of the very

essence of fiction that only the thoughts, feelings, etc., in Shakespeare and his readers are real, and that there is not, in addition to them, an objective Hamlet. When you have taken account of all the feelings roused by Napoleon in writers and readers of history, you have not touched the actual man; but in the case of Hamlet you have come to the end of him. If no one thought about Hamlet, there would be nothing left of him; if no one had thought about Napoleon, he would have soon seen to it that someone did. The sense of reality is vital in logic, and whoever juggles with it by pretending that Hamlet has another kind of reality is doing a disservice to thought. A robust sense of reality is very necessary in framing a correct analysis of propositions about unicorns, golden mountains, round squares, and other such pseudo-objects.

In obedience to the feeling of reality, we shall insist that, in the analysis of propositions, nothing "unreal" is to be admitted. But, after all, if there *is* nothing unreal, how, it may be asked, *could* we admit anything unreal? The reply is that, in dealing with propositions, we are dealing in the first instance with symbols, and if we attribute significance to groups of symbols which have no significance, we shall fall into the error of admitting unrealities, in the only sense in which this is possible, namely, as objects described. In the proposition "I met a unicorn," the whole four words together make a significant proposition, and the word "unicorn" by itself is significant, in just the same sense as the word "man." But the *two* words "a unicorn" do not form a subordinate group having a meaning of its own. Thus if we falsely attribute meaning to these two words, we find ourselves saddled with "a unicorn," and with the problem how there can be such a thing in a world where there are no unicorns. "A unicorn" is an indefinite description which describes nothing. It is not an indefinite description which describes something unreal. Such a proposition as "*x* is unreal" only has meaning when "*x*" is a description, definite or indefinite; in that case the proposition will be true if "*x*" is a description which describes nothing. But whether the description "*x*" describes something or describes nothing, it is in any case not a constituent of the proposition in which it occurs; like "a unicorn" just now, it is not a subordinate group having a meaning of its own. All this results from the fact that, when "*x*" is a description, "*x* is unreal" or "*x* does not exist" is not nonsense, but is always significant and sometimes true.

We may now proceed to define generally the meaning of propositions which contain ambiguous descriptions. Suppose we wish to make some statement about "a so-and-so," where "so-and-so's" are those objects that have a certain property ϕ, i.e., those objects *x* for which the propositional function ϕ*x* is true. (E.g., if we take "a man" as our instance of "a so-and-so," ϕ*x* will be "*x* is human.") Let us now wish to assert the property ψ of "a so-and-so," i.e., we wish to assert that "a so-and-so" has that property which *x* has when ψ*x* is true. (E.g., in the case of "I met a man," ψ*x* will be "I met *x*.") Now the proposition that "a so-and-so" has the property ψ is *not* a proposition of the form "ψ*x*." If it were, "a so-and-so" would have to be identical with *x* for a suitable *x*; and although (in a sense) this may be true in some cases, it is certainly not true in such a case as "a unicorn." It is just this fact, that the statement that a so-and-so has the property ψ is not of the form ψ*x*, which makes it possible for "a so-and-so" to be, in a certain clearly definable sense, "unreal." The definition is as follows:

> The statement that "an object having the property;
> gf has the property ψ"

means:

> "The joint assertion of; gf*x* and ψ*x* is not always false."

So far as logic goes, this is the same proposition as might be expressed by "some ϕ's are ψ's"; but rhetorically there is a difference, because in the one case there is a suggestion of singularity, and in the other case of plurality. This, however, is not the important point. The important point is that, when rightly analyzed, propositions verbally about "a so-and-so" are found to contain no constituent represented by this phrase. And that is why such propositions can be significant even when there is no such thing as a so-and-so.

The definition of *existence,* as applied to ambiguous descriptions, results from what was said at the end of the preceding chapter. We say that "men exist" or "a man exists" if the propositional function "*x* is human" is sometimes true; and generally "a so-and-so" exists if "*x* is so-and-so" is sometimes true. We may put this in

other language. The proposition "Socrates is a man" is no doubt *equivalent* to "Socrates is human," but it is not the very same proposition. The *is* of "Socrates is human" expresses the relation of subject and predicate; the *is* of "Socrates is a man" expresses identity. It is a disgrace to the human race that it has chosen to employ the same word "is" for these two entirely different ideas—a disgrace which a symbolic logical language of course remedies. The identity in "Socrates is a man" is identity between an object named (accepting "Socrates" as a name, subject to qualifications explained later) and an object ambiguously described. An object ambiguously described will "exist" when at least one such proposition is true, *i.e.,* when there is at least one true proposition of the form "*x* is a so-and-so," where "*x*" is a name. It is characteristic of ambiguous (as opposed to definite) descriptions that there may be any number of true propositions of the above form— Socrates is a man, Plato is a man, etc. Thus "a man exists" follows from Socrates, or Plato, or anyone else. With definite descriptions, on the other hand, the corresponding form of proposition, namely, "*x* is the so-and-so" (where "*x*" is a name), can only be true for one value of *x* at most. This brings us to the subject of definite descriptions, which are to be defined in a way analogous to that employed for ambiguous descriptions, but rather more complicated.

We come now to the main subject of the present chapter, namely, the definition of the word *the* (in the singular). One very important point about the definition of "a so-and-so" applies equally to "the so-and-so"; the definition to be sought is a definition of propositions in which this phrase occurs, not a definition of the phrase itself in isolation. In the case of "a so-and-so," this is fairly obvious: no one could suppose that "a man" was a definite object, which could be defined by itself. Socrates is a man, Plato is a man, Aristotle is a man, but we cannot infer that "a man" means the same as "Socrates" means and also the same as "Plato" means and also the same as "Aristotle" means, since these three names have different meanings. Nevertheless, when we have enumerated all the men in the world, there is nothing left of which we can say, "This is a man, and not only so, but it is *the* 'a man,' the quintessential entity that is just an indefinite man without being anybody in particular." It is of course quite clear that whatever there is in the world is definite: if it is a man it is one definite man and not any other. Thus there cannot be such an entity as "a man" to be found in the world, as opposed to specific men. And accordingly it is natural that we do not define "a man" itself, but only the propositions in which it occurs.

In the case of "the so-and-so" this is equally true, though at first sight less obvious. We may demonstrate that this must be the case, by a consideration of the difference between a *name* and a *definite description*. Take the proposition, "Scott is the author of *Waverley*." We have here a name, "Scott," and a description, "the author of *Waverley*," which are asserted to apply to the same person. The distinction between a name and all other symbols may be explained as follows:

A name is a simple symbol whose meaning is something that can only occur as subject, *i.e.*, something of the kind that, earlier, we defined as an "individual" or a "particular." And a "simple" symbol is one which has no parts that are symbols. Thus "Scott" is a simple symbol, because, though it has parts (namely, separate letters), these parts are not symbols. On the other hand, "the author of *Waverley*" is not a simple symbol, because the separate words that compose the phrase are parts which are symbols. If, as may be the case, whatever *seems* to be an "individual" is really capable of further analysis, we shall have to content ourselves with what may be called "relative individuals," which will be terms that, throughout the context in question, are never analyzed and never occur otherwise than as subjects. And in that case we shall have correspondingly to content ourselves with "relative names." From the standpoint of our present problem, namely, the definition of descriptions, this problem, whether these are absolute names or only relative names, may be ignored, since it concerns different stages in the hierarchy of "types," whereas we have to compare such couples as "Scott" and "the author of *Waverley*," which both apply to the same object, and do not raise the problem of types. We may, therefore, for the moment, treat names as capable of being absolute; nothing that we shall have to say will depend upon this assumption, but the wording may be a little shortened by it.

We have, then, two things to compare: (1) a *name*, which is a simple symbol, directly designating an individual which is its meaning, and having this meaning in its own right, independently of the meanings of all other words; (2) a *description*, which consists of several words, whose meanings are already fixed, and from which results whatever is to be taken as the "meaning" of the description.

A proposition containing a description is not identical with what that proposition becomes when a name is substituted, even if the name names the same object as the description describes. "Scott is the author of *Waverley*" is obviously a different proposition from "Scott is Scott": the first is a fact in literary history, the second a trivial truism. And if we put anyone other than Scott in place of "the author of *Waverley*," our proposition would become false, and would therefore certainly no longer be the same proposition. But, it may be said, our proposition is essentially of the same form as (say) "Scott is Sir Walter," in which two names are said to apply to the same person. The reply is that, if "Scott is Sir Walter" really means "the person named 'Scott' is the person named 'Sir Walter,'" then the names are being used as descriptions: *i.e.*, the individual, instead of being named, is being described as the person having that name. This is a way in which names are frequently used in practice, and there will, as a rule, be nothing in the phraseology to show whether they are being used in this way or *as* names. When a name is used directly, merely to indicate what we are speaking about, it is no part of the *fact* asserted, or of the falsehood if our assertion happens to be false: it is merely part of the symbolism by which we express our thought. What we want to express is something which might (for example) be translated into a foreign language; it is something for which the actual words are a vehicle, but of which they are no part. On the other hand, when we make a proposition about "the person called 'Scott,'" "the actual name 'Scott'" enters into what we are asserting, and not merely into the language used in making the assertion. Our proposition will now be a different one if we substitute "the person called 'Sir Walter.'" But so long as we are using names *as* names, whether we say "Scott" or whether we say "Sir Walter" is as irrelevant to what we are asserting as whether we speak English or French. Thus so long as names are used *as* names, "Scott is Sir Walter" is the same trivial proposition as "Scott is Scott." This completes the proof that "Scott is the author of *Waverley*" is not the same proposition as results from substituting a name for "the author of *Waverley*," no matter what name may be substituted.

When we use a variable, and speak of a propositional function, ϕx say, the process of applying general statements about x to particular cases will consist in substituting a name for the letter "x," assuming that ϕ is a function which has individuals for its arguments. Suppose, for example, that $\phi\ x$ is "always true"; let it be, say, the "law of identity," $x = x$. Then we may substitute for "x" any name we choose, and we shall obtain a true proposition. Assuming for the moment that "Socrates," "Plato," and "Aristotle" are names (a very rash assumption), we can infer from the law of identity that Socrates is Socrates, Plato is Plato, and Aristotle is Aristotle. But we shall commit a fallacy if we attempt to infer, without further premises, that the author of *Waverley* is the author of *Waverley*. This results from what we have just proved, that, if we substitute a name for "the author of *Waverley*" in a proposition, the proposition we obtain is a different one. That is to say, applying the result to our present case: If "x" is a name, "$x = x$" is not the same proposition as "the author of *Waverley* is the author of *Waverley*," no matter what name "x" may be. Thus from the fact that all propositions of the form "$x = x$" are true we cannot infer, without more ado, that the author of *Waverley* is the author of *Waverley*. In fact, propositions of the form "the so-and-so is the so-and-so" are not always true: it is necessary that the so-and-so should *exist* (a term which will be explained shortly). It is false that the present king of France is the present king of France, or that the round square is the round square. When we substitute a description for a name, propositional functions which are "always true" may become false, if the description describes nothing. There is no mystery in this as soon as we realize (what was proved in the preceding paragraph) that when we substitute a description the result is not a value of the propositional function in question.

We are now in a position to define propositions in which a definite description occurs. The only thing that distinguishes "the so-and-so" from "a so-and-so" is the implication of uniqueness. We cannot speak of "*the* inhabitant of London," because inhabiting London is an attribute which is not unique. We cannot speak about

"the present king of France," because there is none; but we can speak about "the present king of England." Thus propositions about " the so-and-so" always imply the corresponding propositions about "a so-and-so," with the addendum that there is not more than one so-and-so. Such a proposition as "Scott is the author of Waverley" could not be true if *Waverley* had never been written, or if several people had written it; and no more could any other proposition resulting from a propositional function x by the substitution of "the author of *Waverley*" for "x." We may say that "the author of *Waverley*" means "the value of x for which 'x wrote *Waverley*' is true." Thus the proposition "the author of *Waverley* was Scotch," for example, involves:

1. x wrote "*Waverley*" is not always false;
2. "if x and y wrote *Waverley*, x and y are identical" is always true;
3. "if x wrote *Waverley*, x was Scotch" is always true.

These three propositions, translated into ordinary language, state:

1. at least one person wrote *Waverley*;
2. at most one person wrote *Waverley*;
3. whoever wrote *Waverley* was Scotch.

All these three are implied by "the author of *Waverley* was Scotch." Conversely, the three together (but no two of them) imply that the author of *Waverley* was Scotch. Hence the three together may be taken as defining what is meant by the proposition "the author of *Waverley* was Scotch."

We may somewhat simplify these three propositions. The first and second together are equivalent to: "There is a term c such that 'x wrote *Waverley*' is true when x is c and is false when x is not c." In other words, "There is a term c such that 'x wrote *Waverley*' is always equivalent to 'x is c.'" (Two propositions are "equivalent" when both are true or both are false.) We have here, to begin with, two functions of x, "x wrote *Waverley*" and "x is c," and we form a function of c by considering the equivalence of these two functions of x for all values of x; we then proceed to assert that the resulting function of c is "sometimes true," *i.e.*, that it is true for at least one value of c. (It obviously cannot be true for more than one value of c.) These two conditions together are defined as giving the meaning of "the author of *Waverley* exists."

We may now define "the term satisfying the function ϕx exists." This is the general form of which the above is a particular case. "The author of *Waverley*" is "the term satisfying the function 'x wrote *Waverley*'" And "the so-and-so" will always involve reference to some propositional function, namely, that which defines the property that makes a thing a so-and-so. Our definition is as follows:

"The term satisfying the function ϕx exists" means:

"There is a term c such that ϕx is always equivalent to 'x is c.'"

In order to define "the author of *Waverley* was Scotch," we have still to take account of the third of our three propositions, namely, "Whoever wrote *Waverley* was Scotch." This will be satisfied by merely adding that the c in question is to be Scotch. Thus "the author of *Waverley* was Scotch" is:

"There is a term c such that (1) 'x wrote *Waverley*' is always equivalent to 'x is c,' (2) c is Scotch."

And generally: "the term satisfying ϕx satisfies ψx" is defined as meaning:

"There is a term c such that (1) ϕx is always equivalent to 'x is c,' (2) ψc is true."

This is the definition of propositions in which descriptions occur.

It is possible to have much knowledge concerning a term described, *i.e.*, to know many propositions concerning "the so-and-so," without actually knowing what the so-and-so is, *i.e.*, without knowing any propositions of the form "x is the so-and-so," where "x" is a name. In a detective story propositions about "the man who did the deed" are accumulated, in the hope that ultimately they will suffice to demonstrate that it was A who did the deed. We may even go so far as to say that, in all such knowledge as can be expressed in words— with the exception of "this" and "that" and a few other words of which the meaning varies on different occa-

sions—no names, in the strict sense, occur, but what seem like names are really descriptions. We may inquire significantly whether Homer existed, which we could not do if "Homer" were a name. The proposition "the so-and-so exists" is significant, whether true or false; but if a is the so-and-so (where "a" is a name), the words "a exists" are meaningless. It is only of descriptions—definite or indefinite—that existence can be significantly asserted; for, if "a" is a name, it *must* name something: what does not name anything is not a name, and therefore, if intended to be a name, is a symbol devoid of meaning, whereas a description, like "the present king of France," does not become incapable of occurring significantly merely on the ground that it describes nothing, the reason being that it is a *complex* symbol, of which the meaning is derived from that of its constituent symbols. And so, when we ask whether Homer existed, we are using the word "Homer" as an abbreviated description: we may replace it by (say) "the author of the *Iliad* and the *Odyssey*." The same considerations apply to almost all uses of what look like proper names.

When descriptions occur in propositions, it is necessary to distinguish what may be called "primary" and "secondary" occurrences. The abstract distinction is as follows. A description has a "primary" occurrence when the proposition in which it occurs results from substituting the description for "x" in some propositional function ϕx; a description has a "secondary" occurrence when the result of substituting the description for x in ϕx gives only *part* of the proposition concerned. An instance will make this clearer. Consider "the present king of France is bald." Here "the present king of France" has a primary occurrence, and the proposition is false. Every proposition in which a description which describes nothing has a primary occurrence is false. But now consider "the present king of France is not bald." This is ambiguous. If we are first to take "x is bald," then substitute "the present king of France" for "x," and then deny the result, the occurrence of "the present king of France" is secondary and our proposition is true; but if we are to take "x is not bald" and substitute "the present king of France" for "x," then "the present king of France" has a primary occurrence and the proposition is false. Confusion of primary and secondary occurrences is a ready source of fallacies where descriptions are concerned.

Descriptions occur in mathematics chiefly in the form of *descriptive functions*, *i.e.*, "the term having the relation R to *y*," or "the R of *y*" as we may say, on the analogy of "the father of *y*" and similar phrases. To say "the father of *y* is rich," for example, is to say that the following propositional function of *c*: "*c* is rich, and '*x* begat *y*' is always equivalent to '*x* is *c*,'" is "sometimes true," *i.e.*, is true for at least one value of *c*. It obviously cannot be true for more than one value.

The theory of descriptions, briefly outlined in the present chapter, is of the utmost importance both in logic and in theory of knowledge. But for purposes of mathematics, the more philosophical parts of the theory are not essential, and have therefore been omitted in the above account, which has confined itself to the barest mathematical requisites.

READING QUESTIONS

1. What is the difference between an indefinite and a definite description?
2. Russell writes that "logic, . . . must no more admit a unicorn than zoology can; for logic is concerned with the real world just as truly as zoology, though with its more abstract and general features . . . A robust sense of reality is very necessary in framing a correct analysis of propositions about unicorns, golden mountains, round squares, and other such pseudo-objects." When Russell writes these remarks, what is his worry? In this vein, what is "the error of admitting unrealities"?
3. How does Russell analyze or understand indefinite descriptions?
4. What is the difference between a name and a description?
5. According to Russell, how can a proposition apparently be "about" something that does not exist and yet still be significant? How does his general strategy of analysis help him here? Does his strategy help him to avoid the error of admitting unrealities?
6. Discuss Russell's analysis of the proposition "The author of *Waverley* was Scottish." Is this the correct analysis?

BERTRAND RUSSELL

Logic as the Essence of Philosophy

The following selection is taken from Russell's book *Our Knowledge of the External World as a Field for Scientific Method in Philosophy* (1914). Russell argues in this essay that all of the genuine problems of philosophy are really problems of logic. In the course of this he works to clarify his understanding of the nature of logic and of the importance of recent developments in mathematical logic. He also provisionally applies his theory of logic to our knowledge of the external world.

Russell's enthusiasm for what he calls the "new logic" is obvious and even somewhat infectious. He concludes his essay by writing that it has "introduced the same kind of advance into philosophy as Galileo introduced into physics, making it possible at last to see what kinds of problems may be capable of solution, and what kinds must be abandoned as beyond human powers. And where a solution appears possible, the new logic provides a method which enables us to obtain results that do not merely embody personal idiosyncrasies, but must command the assent of all who are competent to form an opinion."

The topics we discussed in our first lecture, and the topics we shall discuss later, all reduce themselves, in so far as they are genuinely philosophical, to problems of logic. This is not due to any accident, but to the fact that every philosophical problem, when it is subjected to the necessary analysis and purification, is found ei-

---

Bertrand Russell, "Logic as the Essence of Philosophy" from his *Our Knowledge of the External World as a Field for Scientific Method in Philosophy*, London and New York: Routledge, 1993. Reprinted with the kind permission of the publisher and The Bertrand Russell Peace Foundation.

ther to be not really philosophical at all, or else to be, in the sense in which we are using the word, logical. But as the word "logic" is never used in the same sense by two different philosophers, some explanation of what I mean by the word is indispensable at the outset.

Logic, in the Middle Ages, and down to the present day in teaching, meant no more than a scholastic collection of technical terms and rules of syllogistic inference. Aristotle had spoken, and it was the part of humbler men merely to repeat the lesson after him. The trivial nonsense embodied in this tradition is still set in examinations, and defended by eminent authorities as an excellent "propaedeutic," i.e., a training in those habits of solemn humbug which are so great a help in later life. But it is not this that I mean to praise in saying that all philosophy is logic. Ever since the beginning of the seventeenth century, all vigorous minds that have concerned themselves with inference have abandoned the medieval tradition, and in one way or other have widened the scope of logic.

The first extension was the introduction of the inductive method by Bacon and Galileo—by the former in a theoretical and largely mistaken form, by the latter in actual use in establishing the foundations of modern physics and astronomy. This is probably the only extension of the old logic which has become familiar to the general educated public. But induction, important as it is when regarded as a method of investigation, does not seem to remain when its work is done: in the final form of a perfected science, it would seem that everything ought to be deductive. If induction remains at all, which is a difficult question, it will remain merely as one of the principles according to which deductions are effected. Thus the ultimate result of the introduction of the inductive method seems not the creation of a new kind of non-deductive reasoning, but rather the widening of the scope of deduction by pointing out a way of deducing which is certainly not syllogistic, and does not fit into the medieval scheme.

The question of the scope and validity of induction is of great difficulty, and of great importance to our knowledge. Take such a question as, "Will the sun rise tomorrow?" Our first instinctive feeling is that we have abundant reason for saying that it will, because it has risen on so many previous mornings. Now, I do not myself know whether this does afford a ground or not,

but I am willing to suppose that it does. The question which then arises is: "What is the principle of inference by which we pass from past sunrises to future ones? The answer given by Mill is that the inference depends upon the law of causation. Let us suppose this to be true; then what is the reason for believing in the law of causation? There are broadly three possible answers: (1) that it is itself known *a priori*; (2) that it is a postulate; (3) that it is an empirical generalization from past instances in which it has been found to hold. The theory that causation is known *a priori* cannot be definitely refuted, but it can be rendered very unplausible by the mere process of formulating the law exactly, and thereby showing that it is immensely more complicated and less obvious than is generally supposed. The theory that causation is a postulate, i.e., that it is something which we choose to assert although we know that it is very likely false, is also incapable of refutation; but it is plainly also incapable of justifying any use of the law in inference. We are thus brought to the theory that the law is an empirical generalization, which is the view held by Mill.

But if so, how are empirical generalizations to be justified? The evidence in their favor cannot be empirical, since we wish to argue from what has been observed to what has not been observed, which can only be done by means of some known relation of the observed and the unobserved; but the unobserved, by definition, is not known empirically, and therefore its relation to the observed, if known at all, must be known independently of empirical evidence. Let us see what Mill says on this subject.

According to Mill, the law of causation is proved by an admittedly fallible process called "induction by simple enumeration." This process, he says, "consists in ascribing the nature of general truths to all propositions which are true in every instance that we happen to know of." As regards its fallibility, he asserts that "the precariousness of the method of simple enumeration is in an inverse ratio to the largeness of the generalization. The process is delusive and insufficient, exactly in proportion as the subject-matter of the observation is special and limited in extent. As the sphere widens, this unscientific method becomes less and less liable to mislead; and the most universal class of truths, the law of causation for instance, and the principles of number and of geometry, are duly and satisfactorily proved by that method alone, nor are they susceptible of any other proof."

In the above statement, there are two obvious lacunae: (1) How is the method of simple enumeration itself justified? (2) What logical principle, if any, covers the same ground as this method, without being liable to its failures? Let us take the second question first.

A method of proof which, when used as directed, gives sometimes truth and sometimes falsehood—as the method of simple enumeration does—is obviously not a valid method, for validity demands invariable truth. Thus, if simple enumeration is to be rendered valid, it must not be stated as Mill states it. We shall have to say, at most, that the data render the result *probable*. Causation holds, we shall say, in every instance we have been able to test; therefore it *probable* holds in untested instances. There are terrible difficulties in the notion of probability, but we may ignore them at present. We thus have what at least *may* be a logical principle, since it is without exception. If a proposition is true in every instance that we happen to know of, and if the instances are very numerous, then, we shall say, it becomes very probable, on the data, that it will be true in any further instance. This is not refuted by the fact that what we declare to be probable does not always happen, for an event may be probable on the data and yet not occur. It is, however, obviously capable of further analysis, and of more exact statement. We shall have to say something like this: that every instance of a proposition* being true increases the probability of its being true in a fresh instance, and that a sufficient number of favorable instances will, in the absence of instances to the contrary, make the probability of the truth of a fresh instance approach indefinitely near to certainty. Some such principle as this is required if the method of simple enumeration is to be valid.

But this brings us to our other question, namely, how is our principle known to be true? Obviously, since it is required to justify induction, it cannot be proved by induction; since it goes beyond the empirical data, it cannot be proved by them alone; since it is required to justify all inferences from empirical data to what goes beyond them, it cannot itself be even ren-

dered in any degree probable by such data. Hence, *if* it is known, it is not known by experience, but independently of experience. I do not say that any such principle is known: I only say that it is required to justify the inferences from experience which empiricists allow, and that it cannot itself be justified empirically.

A similar conclusion can be proved by similar arguments concerning any other logical principle. Thus logical knowledge is not derivable from experience alone, and the empiricist's philosophy can therefore not be accepted in its entirety, in spite of its excellence in many matters which lie outside logic.

Hegel and his followers widened the scope of logic in quite a different way—a way which I believe to be fallacious, but which requires discussion if only to show how their conception of logic differs from the conception which I wish to advocate. In their writings, logic is practically identical with metaphysics. In broad outline, the way this came about is as follows. Hegel believed that, by means of *a priori* reasoning, it could be shown that the world *must* have various important and interesting characteristics, since any world without these characteristics would be impossible and self-contradictory. Thus what he calls "logic" is an investigation of the nature of the universe, in so far as this can be inferred merely from the principle that the universe must be logically self-consistent. I do not myself believe that from this principle alone anything of importance can be inferred as regards the existing universe. But, however that may be, I should not regard Hegel's reasoning, even if it were valid, as properly belonging to logic: it would rather be an application of logic to the actual world. Logic itself would be concerned rather with such questions as what self-consistency is, which Hegel, so far as I know, does not discuss. And though he criticizes the traditional logic, and professes to replace it by an improved logic of his own, there is some sense in which the traditional logic, with all its faults, is uncritically and unconsciously assumed throughout his reasoning. It is not in the direction advocated by him, it seems to me, that the reform of logic is to be sought, but by a more fundamental, more patient, and less ambitious investigation into the presuppositions which his system shares with those of most other philosophers.

The way in which, as it seems to me, Hegel's system assumes the ordinary logic which it subsequently criti-

---

*Or rather a propositional function.

cizes, is exemplified by the general conception of "categories" with which he operates throughout. This conception is, I think, essentially a product of logical confusion, but it seems in some way to stand for the conception of "qualities of Reality as a whole." Mr. Bradley has worked out a theory according to which, in all judgment, we are ascribing a predicate to Reality as a whole; and this theory is derived from Hegel. Now the traditional logic holds that every proposition ascribes a predicate to a subject, and from this it easily follows that there can be only one subject, the Absolute, for if there were two, the proposition that there were two would not ascribe a predicate to either. Thus Hegel's doctrine, that philosophical propositions must be of the form, "the Absolute is such-and-such," depends upon the traditional belief in the universality of the subject-predicate form. This belief, being traditional, scarcely self-conscious, and not supposed to be important, operates underground, and is assumed in arguments which, like the refutation of relations, appear at first sight such as to establish its truth. This is the most important respect in which Hegel uncritically assumes the traditional logic. Other less important respects—though important enough to be the source of such essentially Hegelian conceptions as the "concrete universal" and the "union of identity in difference"—will be found where he explicitly deals with formal logic.

There is quite another direction in which a large technical development of logic has taken place: I mean the direction of what is called logistic or mathematical logic. This kind of logic is mathematical in two different senses: it is itself a branch of mathematics, and it is the logic which is specially applicable to other more traditional branches of mathematics. Historically, it began as *merely* a branch of mathematics: its special applicability to other branches is a more recent development. In both respects, it is the fulfilment of a hope which Leibniz cherished throughout his life, and pursued with all the ardor of his amazing intellectual energy. Much of his work on this subject has been published recently, since his discoveries have been remade by others; but none was published by him, because his results persisted in contradicting certain points in the traditional doctrine of the syllogism. We now know that on these points the traditional doctrine is wrong, but respect for Aristotle prevented Leibniz from realizing that this was possible.

The modern development of mathematical logic dates from Boole's *Laws of Thought* (1854). But in him and his successors, before Peano and Frege, the only thing really achieved, apart from certain details, was the invention of a mathematical symbolism for deducing consequences from the premises which the newer methods shared with those of Aristotle. This subject has considerable interest as an independent branch of mathematics, but it has very little to do with real logic. The first serious advance in real logic since the time of the Greeks was made independently by Peano and Frege—both mathematicians. They both arrived at their logical results by an analysis of mathematics. Traditional logic regarded the two propositions, "Socrates is mortal" and "All men are mortal," as being of the same form;* Peano and Frege showed that they are utterly different in form. The philosophical importance of logic may be illustrated by the fact that this confusion—which is still committed by most writers—obscured not only the whole study of the forms of judgment and inference, but also the relations of things to their qualities, of concrete existence to abstract concepts, and of the world of sense to the world of Platonic ideas. Peano and Frege, who pointed out the error, did so for technical reasons, and applied their logic mainly to technical developments; but the philosophical importance of the advance which they made is impossible to exaggerate.

Mathematical logic, even in its most modern form, is not *directly* of philosophical importance except in its beginnings. After the beginnings, it belongs rather to mathematics than to philosophy. Of its beginnings, which are the only part of it that can properly be called *philosophical* logic, I shall speak shortly. But even the later developments, though not directly philosophical, will be found of great indirect use in philosophizing. They enable us to deal easily with more abstract conceptions than merely verbal reasoning can enumerate; they suggest fruitful hypotheses which otherwise could hardly be thought of; and they enable us to see quickly

---

*It was often recognized that there was *some* difference between them, but it was not recognized that the difference is fundamental, and of very great importance.

what is the smallest store of materials with which a given logical or scientific edifice can be constructed. Not only Frege's theory of number, . . . but the whole theory of physical concepts . . . is inspired by mathematical logic, and could never have been imagined without it.

In both these cases, and in many others, we shall appeal to a certain principle called "the principle of abstraction." This principle, which might equally well be called "the principle which dispenses with abstraction," and is one which clears away incredible accumulations of metaphysical lumber, was directly suggested by mathematical logic, and could hardly have been proved or practically used without its help. The principle will be explained elsewhere, but its use may be briefly indicated in advance. When a group of objects have that kind of similarity which we are inclined to attribute to possession of a common quality, the principle in question shows that membership of the group will serve all the purposes of the supposed common quality, and that therefore, unless some common quality is actually known, the group or class of similar objects may be used to replace the common quality, which need not be assumed to exist. In this and other ways, the indirect uses of even the later parts of mathematical logic are very great; but it is now time to turn our attention to its philosophical foundations.

In every proposition and in every inference there is, besides the particular subject-matter concerned, a certain *form*, a way in which the constituents of the proposition or inference are put together. If I say, "Socrates is mortal," "Jones is angry," "The sun is hot," there is something in common in these three cases, something indicated by the word "is." What is in common is the *form* of the proposition, not an actual constituent. If I say a number of things about Socrates—that he was an Athenian, that he married Xantippe, that he drank the hemlock—there is a common constituent, namely Socrates, in all the propositions I enunciate, but they have diverse forms. If, on the other hand, I take any one of these propositions and replace its constituents, one at a time, by other constituents, the form remains constant, but no constituent remains. Take (say) the series of propositions, "Socrates drank the hemlock," "Coleridge drank the hemlock," "Coleridge drank opium," "Coleridge ate

opium." The form remains unchanged throughout this series, but all the constituents are altered. Thus form is not another constituent, but is the way the constituents are put together. It is forms, in this sense, that are the proper object of philosophical logic.

It is obvious that the knowledge of logical forms is something quite different from knowledge of existing things. The form of "Socrates drank the hemlock" is not an existing thing like Socrates or the hemlock, nor does it even have that close relation to existing things that drinking has. It is something altogether more abstract and remote. We might understand all the separate words of a sentence without understanding the sentence: if a sentence is long and complicated, this is apt to happen. In such a case we have knowledge of the constituents, but not of the form. We may also have knowledge of the form without having knowledge of the constituents. If I say, "Rorarius drank the hemlock," those among you who have never heard of Rorarius (supposing there are any) will understand the form, without having knowledge of all the constituents. In order to understand a sentence, it is necessary to have knowledge both of the constituents and of the particular instance of the form. It is in this way that a sentence conveys information, since it tells us that certain known objects are related according to a certain known form. Thus some kind of knowledge of logical forms, though with most people it is not explicit, is involved in all understanding of discourse. It is the business of philosophical logic to extract this knowledge from its concrete integuments, and to render it explicit and pure.

In all inference, form alone is essential: the particular subject-matter is irrelevant except as securing the truth of the premises. This is one reason for the great importance of logical form. When I say, "Socrates was a man, all men are mortal, therefore Socrates was mortal," the connection of premises and conclusion does not in any way depend upon its being Socrates and man and mortality that I am mentioning. The general form of the inference may be expressed in some such words as: "If a thing has a certain property, and whatever has this property has a certain other property, then the thing in question also has that other property." Here no particular things or properties are mentioned: the proposition is absolutely general. All inferences, when stated fully, are instances of propositions having this kind of generality. If they seem to depend upon the subject-matter otherwise than as regards the truth of the premises, that is because the premises have not been all explicitly stated. In logic, it is a waste of time to deal with inferences concerning particular cases: we deal throughout with completely general and purely formal implications, leaving it to other sciences to discover when the hypotheses are verified and when they are not.

But the forms of propositions giving rise to inferences are not the simplest forms; they are always hypothetical, stating that if one proposition is true, then so is another. Before considering inference, therefore, logic must consider those simpler forms which inference presupposes. Here the traditional logic failed completely: it believed that there was only one form of simple proposition (i.e., of proposition not stating a relation between two or more other propositions), namely, the form which ascribes a predicate to a subject. This is the appropriate form in assigning the qualities of a given thing—we may say "this thing is round, and red, and so on." Grammar favors this form, but philosophically it is so far from universal that it is not even very common. If we say "this thing is bigger than that," we are not assigning a mere quality of "this," but a relation of "this" and "that." We might express the same fact by saying "that thing is smaller than this," where grammatically the subject is changed. Thus propositions stating that two things have a certain relation have a different form from subject-predicate propositions, and the failure to perceive this difference or to allow for it has been the source of many errors in traditional metaphysics.

The belief or unconscious conviction that all propositions are of the subject-predicate form—in other words: that every fact consists in some thing having some quality—has rendered most philosophers incapable of giving any account of the world of science and daily life. If they had been honestly anxious to give such an account, they would probably have discovered their error very quickly; but most of them were less anxious to understand the world of science and daily life, than to convict it of unreality in the interests of a super-sensible "real" world. Belief in the unreality of the world of sense arises with irresistible force in certain moods—moods which, I imagine, have some simple physiological basis, but are none the less powerfully persuasive.

The conviction born of these moods is the source of most mysticism and of most metaphysics. When the emotional intensity of such a mood subsides, a man who is in the habit of reasoning will search for logical reasons in favor of the belief which he finds in himself. But since the belief already exists, he will be very hospitable to any reason that suggests itself. The paradoxes apparently proved by his logic are really the paradoxes of mysticism, and are the goal which he feels his logic must reach if it is to be in accordance with insight. It is in this way that logic has been pursued by those of the great philosophers who were mystics—notably Plato, Spinoza, and Hegel. But since they usually took for granted the supposed insight of the mystic emotion, their logical doctrines were presented with a certain dryness, and were believed by their disciples to be quite independent of the sudden illumination from which they sprang. Nevertheless their origin clung to them, and they remained—to borrow a useful word from Mr. Santayana—"malicious" in regard to the world of science and common sense. It is only so that we can account for the complacency with which philosophers have accepted the inconsistence of their doctrines with all the common and scientific facts which seem best established and most worthy of belief.

The logic of mysticism shows, as is natural, the defects which are inherent in anything malicious. While the mystic mood is dominant, the need of logic is not felt; as the mood fades, the impulse to logic reasserts itself, but with a desire to retain the vanishing insight, or at least to prove that it *was* insight, and that what seems to contradict it is illusion. The logic which thus arises is not quite disinterested or candid, and is inspired by a certain hatred of the daily world to which it is to be applied. Such an attitude naturally does not tend to the best results. Everyone knows that to read an author simply in order to refute him is not the way to understand him; and to read the book of Nature with a conviction that it is all illusion is just as unlikely to lead to understanding. If our logic is to find the common world intelligible, it must not be hostile, but must be inspired by a genuine acceptance such as is not usually to be found among metaphysicians.

Traditional logic, since it holds that all propositions have the subject-predicate form, is unable to admit the reality of relations: all relations, it maintains, must be reduced to properties of the apparently related terms. There are many ways of refuting this opinion; one of the easiest is derived from the consideration of what are called "asymmetrical" relations. In order to explain this, I will first explain two independent ways of classifying relations.

Some relations, when they hold between A and B, also hold between B and A. Such, for example, is the relation "brother or sister." If A is a brother or sister of B then B is a brother or sister of A. Such again is any kind of similarity, say similarity of color. Any kind of dissimilarity is also of this kind: if the color of A is unlike the color of B, then the color of B is unlike the color of A. Relations of this sort are called *symmetrical*. Thus a relation is symmetrical if, whenever it holds between A and B, it also holds between B and A.

All relations that are not symmetrical are called *non-symmetrical*. Thus "brother" is non-symmetrical, because, if A is a brother of B, it may happen that B is a *sister* of A.

A relation is called *asymmetrical* when, if it holds between A and B, it *never* holds between B and A. Thus husband, father, grandfather, etc., are asymmetrical relations. So are *before, after, greater, above, to the right of,* etc. All the relations that give rise to series are of this kind.

Classification into symmetrical, asymmetrical and merely non-symmetrical relations is the first of the two classifications we had to consider. The second is into transitive, intransitive, and merely non-transitive relations, which are defined as follows.

A relation is said to be *transitive*, if, whenever it holds between A and B and also between B and C, it holds between A and C. Thus *before, after, greater, above* are transitive. All relations giving rise to series are transitive, but so are many others. The transitive relations just mentioned were asymmetrical, but many transitive relations are symmetrical—for instance, equality in any respect, exact identity of color, being equally numerous (as applied to collections), and so on.

A relation is said to be *non-transitive* whenever it is not transitive. Thus "brother" is non-transitive, because a brother of one's brother may be oneself. All kinds of dissimilarity are non-transitive.

A relation is said to be *intransitive* when, if A has the relation to B, and B to C, A never has it to C. Thus "fa-

ther" is intransitive. So is such a relation as "one inch taller" or "one year later."

Let us now, in the light of this classification, return to the question whether all relations can be reduced to predications.

In the case of symmetrical relations—i.e., relations which, if they hold between A and B, also hold between B and A—some kind of plausibility can be given to this doctrine. A symmetrical relation which is transitive, such as equality, can be regarded as expressing possession of some common property, while one which is not transitive, such as inequality, can be regarded as expressing possession of different properties. But when we come to asymmetrical relations, such as before and after, greater and less, etc., the attempt to reduce them to properties becomes obviously impossible. When, for example, two things are merely known to be unequal, without our knowing which is greater, we may say that the inequality results from their having different magnitudes, because inequality is a symmetrical relation; but to say that when one thing is *greater* than another, and not merely unequal to it, that means that they have different magnitudes, is formally incapable of explaining the facts. For if the other thing had been greater than the one, the magnitudes would also have been different, though the fact to be explained would not have been the same. Thus mere *difference* of magnitude is not *all* that is involved, since, if it were, there would be no difference between one thing being greater than another, and the other being greater than the one. We shall have to say that the one magnitude is *greater* than the *other,* and thus we shall have failed to get rid of the relation "greater." In short, both possession of the same property and possession of different properties are *symmetrical* relations, and therefore cannot account for the existence of *asymmetrical* relations.

Asymmetrical relations are involved in all series—in space and time, greater and less, whole and part, and many others of the most important characteristics of the actual world. All these aspects, therefore, the logic which reduces everything to subjects and predicates is compelled to condemn as error and mere appearance. To those whose logic is not malicious, such a wholesale condemnation appears impossible. And in fact there is no reason except prejudice, so far as I can discover, for denying the reality of relations. When once their reality is admitted, all *logical* grounds for supposing the world of sense to be illusory disappear. If this is to be supposed, it must be frankly and simply on the ground of mystic insight unsupported by argument. It is impossible to argue against what professes to be insight, so long as it does not argue in its own favor. As logicians, therefore, we may admit the possibility of the mystic's world, while yet, so long as we do not have his insight, we must continue to study the everyday world with which we are familiar. But when he contends that our world is impossible, then our logic is ready to repel his attack. And the first step in creating the logic which is to perform this service is the recognition of the reality of relations.

Relations which have two terms are only one kind of relations. A relation may have three terms, or four, or any number. Relations of two terms, being the simplest, have received more attention than the others, and have generally been alone considered by philosophers, both those who accepted and those who denied the reality of relations. But other relations have their importance, and are indispensable in the solution of certain problems. Jealousy, for example, is a relation between three people. Professor Royce mentions the relation "giving": when A gives B to C, that is a relation of three terms. When a man says to his wife: "My dear, I wish you could induce Angelina to accept Edwin," his wish constitutes a relation between four people, himself, his wife, Angelina, and Edwin. Thus such relations are by no means recondite or rare. But in order to explain exactly how they differ from relations of two terms, we must embark upon a classification of the logical forms of facts, which is the first business of logic, and the business in which the traditional logic has been most deficient.

The existing world consists of many things with many qualities and relations. A complete description of the existing world would require not only a catalogue of the things, but also a mention of all their qualities and relations. We should have to know not only this that, and the other thing, but also which was red, which yellow, which was earlier than which, which was which between two others, and so on. When I speak of a "fact," I do not mean one of the simple things in the world; I mean that a certain thing has a certain quality, or that certain things have a certain relation. Thus, for example, I should not call Napoleon a fact, but I should call it a fact that he was ambitious, or that he married Josephine. Now a fact, in this sense, is never simple, but always has two or more constituents. When it simply assigns a quality to a thing, it has only two constituents, the thing and the quality. When it consists of a relation between two things, it has three constituents, the things and the relation. When it consists of a relation between three things, it has four constituents, and so on. The constituents of facts, in the sense in which we are using the word "fact," are not other facts, but are things and qualities or relations. When we say that there are relations of more than two terms, we mean that there are single facts consisting of a single relation and more than two things. I do not mean that one relation of two terms may hold between A and B, and also between A and C, as, for example, a man is the son of his father and also the son of his mother. This constitutes two distinct facts: if we choose to treat it as one fact, it is a fact which has facts for its constituents. But the facts I am speaking of have no facts among their constituents, but only things and relations. For example, when A is jealous of B on account of C, there is only one fact, involving three people; there are not two instances of jealousy, but only one. It is in such cases that I speak of a relation of three terms, where the simplest possible fact in which the relation occurs is one involving three things in addition to the relation. And the same applies to relations of four terms or five or any other number. All such relations must be admitted in our inventory of the logical forms of facts: two facts involving the same number of things have the same form, and two which involve different numbers of things have different forms.

Given any fact, there is an assertion which expresses the fact. The fact itself is objective, and independent of our thought or opinion about it; but the assertion is something which involves thought, and may be either true or false. An assertion may be positive or negative: we may assert that Charles I was executed, or that he did *not* die in his bed. A negative assertion may be said to be a *denial*. Given a form of words which must be either true or false, such as "Charles I died in his bed," we may either assert or deny this form of words: in the one case we have a positive assertion, in the other a negative one. A form of words which must be either true or false I shall call a *proposition*. Thus a proposition is the same as what may be significantly asserted or denied. A proposition which expresses what we have called a fact, i.e., which, when asserted, asserts that a certain thing has a certain quality, or that certain things have a certain relation, will be called an atomic proposition, because, as we shall see immediately, there are other propositions into which atomic propositions enter in a way analogous to that in which atoms enter into molecules. Atomic propositions, although, like facts, they may have any one of an infinite number of forms, are only one kind of propositions. All other kinds are more complicated. In order to preserve the parallelism in language as regards facts and propositions, we shall give the name "atomic facts" to the facts we have hitherto been considering. Thus atomic facts are what determine whether atomic propositions are to be asserted or denied.

Whether an atomic proposition, such as "this is red," or "this is before that," is to be asserted or denied can only be known empirically. Perhaps one atomic fact may sometimes be capable of being inferred from another, though this seems very doubtful; but in any case it cannot be inferred from premises no one of which is an atomic fact. It follows that, if atomic facts are to be known at all, some at least must be known without inference. The atomic facts which we come to know in this way are the facts of sense-perception; at any rate, the facts of sense-perception are those which we most obviously and certainly come to know in this way. If we knew all atomic facts, and also knew that there were none except those we knew, we should, theoretically, be able to infer all truths of whatever form.* Thus logic would then supply us with the whole of the apparatus required. But in the first acquisition of knowledge concerning atomic facts, logic is useless. In pure logic, no atomic fact is ever mentioned: we confine ourselves wholly to forms, without asking ourselves what objects can fill the forms. Thus pure logic is independent of atomic facts; but conversely, they are, in a sense, independent of logic. Pure logic and atomic facts are the two poles, the wholly *a priori* and the wholly empirical. But between the two lies a vast intermediate region, which we must now briefly explore.

---

* This perhaps requires modification in order to include such facts as beliefs and wishes, since such facts apparently contain propositions as components. Such facts, though not strictly atomic, must be supposed included if the statement in the text is to be true.

"Molecular" propositions are such as contain conjunctions—*if, or, and, unless,* etc.—and such words are the marks of a molecular proposition. Consider such an assertion as, "If it rains, I shall bring my umbrella." This assertion is just as capable of truth or falsehood as the assertion of an atomic proposition, but it is obvious that either the corresponding fact, or the nature of the correspondence with fact, must be quite different from what it is in the case of an atomic proposition. Whether it rains, and whether I bring my umbrella, are each severally matters of atomic fact, ascertainable by observation. But the connection of the two involved in saying that *if* the one happens, *then* the other will happen, is something radically different from either of the two separately. It does not require for its truth that it should actually rain, or that I should actually bring my umbrella; even if the weather is cloudless, it may still be true that I should have brought my umbrella if the weather had been different. Thus we have here a connection of two propositions, which does not depend upon whether they are to be asserted or denied, but only upon the second being inferable from the first. Such propositions, therefore, have a form which is different from that of any atomic proposition.

Such propositions are important to logic, because all inference depends upon them. If I have told you that if it rains I shall bring my umbrella, and if you see that there is a steady downpour, you can infer that I shall bring my umbrella. There can be no inference except where propositions are connected in some such way, so that from the truth or falsehood of the one something follows as to the truth or falsehood of the other. It seems to be the case that we can sometimes know molecular propositions, as in the above instance of the umbrella, when we do not know whether the component atomic propositions are true or false. The *practical* utility of inference rests upon this fact.

The next kind of propositions we have to consider are *general* propositions, such as "all men are mortal," "all equilateral triangles are equiangular." And with these belong propositions in which the word "some" occurs, such as "some men are philosophers" or "some philosophers are not wise." These are the denials of general propositions, namely (in the above instances), of "all men are non-philosophers" and "all philosophers are wise." We will call propositions containing the word "some" *negative* general propositions, and those containing the word "all" *positive* general propositions. These propositions, it will be seen, begin to have the appearance of the propositions in logical textbooks. But their peculiarity and complexity are not known to the textbooks, and the problems which they raise are only discussed in the most superficial manner.

When we were discussing atomic facts, we saw that we should be able, theoretically, to infer all other truths by logic if we knew all atomic facts and also knew that there were no other atomic facts besides those we knew. The knowledge that there are no other atomic facts is positive general knowledge; it is the knowledge that "all atomic facts are in this collection"—however the collection may be given. It is easy to see that general propositions, such as "all men are mortal," cannot be known by inference from atomic facts alone. If we could know each individual man, and know that he was mortal, that would not enable us to know that all men are mortal, unless we *knew* that those were all the men there are, which is a general proposition. If we knew every other existing thing throughout the universe, and knew that each separate thing was not an immortal man, that would not give us our result unless we *knew* that we had explored the whole universe, i.e., unless we knew "all things belong to this collection of things I have examined." Thus general truths cannot be inferred from particular truths alone, but must, if they are to be known, be either self-evident or inferred from premises of which at least one is a general truth. But all *empirical* evidence is of *particular* truths. Hence, if there is any knowledge of general truths at all, there must be *some* knowledge of general truths which is independent of empirical evidence, i.e., does not depend upon the data of sense.

The above conclusion, of which we had an instance in the case of the inductive principle, is important, since it affords a refutation of the older empiricists. They believed that all our knowledge is derived from the senses and dependent upon them. We see that, if this view is to be maintained, we must refuse to admit that we know any general propositions. It is perfectly possible logically that this should be the case, but it does not appear to be so in fact, and indeed no one would dream of maintaining such a view except a theorist at the last extremity. We must therefore admit that there is general knowledge not derived from sense, and that some of this knowledge is not obtained by inference but is primitive.

Such general knowledge is to be found in logic. Whether there is any such knowledge not derived from logic, I do not know; but in logic, at any rate, we have such knowledge. It will be remembered that we excluded from pure logic such propositions as, "Socrates is a man, all men are mortal, therefore Socrates is mortal," because Socrates and *man* and *mortal* are empirical terms, only to be understood through particular experience. The corresponding proposition in pure logic is: "If anything has a certain property, and whatever has this property has a certain other property, then the thing in question has the other property." This proposition is absolutely general: it applies to all things and all properties. And it is quite self-evident. Thus in such propositions of pure logic we have the self-evident general propositions of which we were in search.

A proposition such as "If Socrates is a man, and all men are mortal, then Socrates is mortal," is true in virtue of its *form* alone. Its truth, in this hypothetical form, does not depend upon whether Socrates actually is a man, nor upon whether in fact all men are mortal; thus it is equally true when we substitute other terms for Socrates and *man* and *mortal*. The general truth of which it is an instance is purely formal, and belongs to logic. Since this general truth does not mention any particular thing, or even any particular quality or relation, it is wholly independent of the accidental facts of the existent world, and can be known, theoretically, without any experience of particular things or their qualities and relations.

Logic, we may say, consists of two parts. The first part investigates what propositions are and what forms they may have; this part enumerates the different kinds of atomic propositions, of molecular propositions, of general propositions, and so on. The second part consists of certain supremely general propositions, which assert the truth of all propositions of certain forms. This second part merges into pure mathematics, whose propositions all turn out, on analysis, to be such general formal truths. The first part, which merely enumerates forms, is the more difficult, and philosophically the more important; and it is the recent progress in this first part, more than anything else, that has rendered a truly scientific discussion of many philosophical problems possible.

The problem of the nature of judgment or belief may be taken as an example of a problem whose solution depends upon an adequate inventory of logical forms. We have already seen how the supposed universality of the subject-predicate form made it impossible to give a right analysis of serial order, and therefore made space and time unintelligible. But in this case it was only necessary to admit relations of two terms. The case of judgment demands the administration of more complicated forms. If all judgments were true, we might suppose that a judgment consisted in apprehension of a *fact*, and that the apprehension was a relation of a mind to the fact. From poverty in the logical inventory, this view has often been held. But it leads to absolutely insoluble difficulties in the case of error. Suppose I believe that Charles I died in his bed. There is no objective fact "Charles I's death in his bed" to which I can have a relation of apprehension. Charles I and death and his bed are objective, but they are not, except in my thought, put together as my false belief supposes. It is therefore necessary, in analyzing a belief, to look for some other logical form than a two-term relation. Failure to realize this necessity has, in my opinion, vitiated almost everything that has hitherto been written on the theory of knowledge, making the problem of error insoluble and the difference between belief and perception inexplicable.

Modern logic, as I hope is now evident, has the effect of enlarging our abstract imagination, and providing an infinite number of possible hypotheses to be applied in the analysis of any complex fact. In this respect it is the exact opposite of the logic practiced by the classical tradition. In that logic, hypotheses which seem *prima facie* possible are professedly proved impossible, and it is decreed in advance that reality must have a certain special character. In modern logic, on the contrary, while the *prima facie* hypotheses as a rule remain admissible, others, which only logic would have suggested, are added to our stock, and are very often found to be indispensable if a right analysis of the facts is to be obtained. The old logic put thought in fetters, while the new logic gives it wings. It has, in my opinion, introduced the same kind of advance into philosophy as Galileo introduced into physics, making it possible at last to see what kinds of problems may be capable of solution, and what kinds must be abandoned as beyond human powers. And where a solution appears possible, the new logic provides a method which enables us to obtain results that do not merely embody personal idiosyncrasies, but must command the assent of all who are competent to form an opinion.

READING QUESTIONS

1. Russell argues that "logical knowledge is not derivable from experience alone, and the empiricist's philosophy can therefore not be accepted in its entirety, in spite of its excellence in many matters outside logic." In advancing his argument, he examines Mill's proposal that our belief in the law of causation is justified on the basis of an empirical generalization. What exactly is Russell's objection to this proposal?

2. What does Russell mean when he speaks of "logical forms"?

3. Russell claims that one important limitation of "traditional logic" is its inability to admit the reality of relations. What is the importance of this, if any?

4. What is a fact? An atomic fact? A proposition? An atomic proposition? A molecular proposition? A general proposition? How are these categories related?

5. Russell writes that "if we knew all atomic facts, and also knew that there were none except those we knew, we should, theoretically, be able to infer all truths of whatever form." Why? Is this correct?

6. Russell concludes that "we must therefore admit that there is general knowledge not derived from sense, and that some of this knowledge is not obtained by inference but is primitive." What is Russell's argument for this conclusion? Is it sound?

BERTRAND RUSSELL

The Relation of Sense-Data to Physics

The following essay is a relatively clear and brief early statement of Russell's epistemology and metaphysics. Russell offers his account of the metaphysical structure of the world and of our knowledge of the world as a solution to a problem in the philosophy of science; namely, the problem of demonstrating how the science of physics and its various unobservable postulates are related to (or verified by) "observation and experiment." The overall position that Russell seeks to defend is that what we call physical objects are essentially certain series of sets of sense-data. He occasionally states his commitment to this view by saying that a physical object is a kind of logical construction out of certain series of sets of sense-data.

Russell's commitment to this metaphysical thesis primarily grew out of his work in the philosophy of mathematics. In that arena, Russell defended *logicism*—a form of reductionism that holds that the truths of mathematics can all be deduced without remainder from those of logic (plus, perhaps, those of set theory). His general approach is simply to extend this philosophical methodology to the domain of physics, arguing that "if the class of appearances will fulfill the purposes for the sake of which the thing was invented by the prehistoric metaphysicians to whom common sense is due, economy demands that we should identify the thing with the class of its appearances. . . . Our procedure here is precisely analogous to that which has swept away from the philosophy of mathematics the useless menagerie of metaphysical monsters with which it used to be infested."

I. The Problem Stated

Physics is said to be an empirical science, based upon observation and experiment.

It is supposed to be verifiable, i.e., capable of calculating beforehand results subsequently confirmed by observation and experiment.

What can we learn by observation and experiment?

Bertrand Russell, "The Relation of Sense-Data to Physics" from his *Mysticism and Logic and Other Essays,* London: Allen & Unwin, 1919. Reprinted with the kind permission of the publisher and The Bertrand Russell Peace Foundation.

Nothing, so far as physics is concerned, except immediate data of sense: certain patches of color, sounds, tastes, smells, etc., with certain spatio-temporal relations.

The supposed contents of the physical world are *prima facie* very different from these: molecules have no color, atoms make no noise, electrons have no taste, and corpuscles do not even smell.

If such objects are to be verified, it must be solely through their relation to sense-data: they must have some kind of correlation with sense-data, and must be verifiable through their correlation *alone.*

But how is the correlation itself ascertained? A correlation can only be ascertained empirically by the correlated objects being constantly *found* together. But in our case, only one term of the correlation, namely, the sensible term, is ever *found:* the other term seems essentially incapable of being found. Therefore, it would seem, the correlation with objects of sense, by which physics was to be verified, is itself utterly and for ever unverifiable.

There are two ways of avoiding this result.

1. We may say that we know some principle *a priori*, without the need of empirical verification, e.g., that our sense-data have *causes* other than themselves, and that something can be known about these causes by inference from their effects. This way has been often adopted by philosophers. It may be necessary to adopt this way to some extent, but in so far as it is adopted physics ceases to be empirical or based upon experiment and observation alone. Therefore this way is to be avoided as much as possible.

2. We may succeed in actually defining the objects of physics as functions of sense-data. Just in so far as physics leads to expectations, this *must* be possible, since we can only *expect* what can be experienced. And in so far as the physical state of affairs is inferred from sense-data, it must be capable of expression as a function of sense-data. The problem of accomplishing this expression leads to much interesting logico-mathematical work.

In physics as commonly set forth, sense-data appear as functions of physical objects: when such-and-such waves impinge upon the eye, we see such-and-such colors, and so on. But the waves are in fact inferred from the colors, not vice versa. Physics cannot be regarded as validly based upon empirical data until the waves have been expressed as functions of the colors and other sense-data.

Thus if physics is to be verifiable we are faced with the following problem: Physics exhibits sense-data as functions of physical objects, but verification is only possible if physical objects can be exhibited as functions of sense-data. We have therefore to solve the equations giving sense-data in terms of physical objects, so as to make them instead give physical objects in terms of sense-data.

II. Characteristics of Sense-Data

When I speak of a 'sense-datum', I do not mean the whole of what is given in sense at one time. I mean rather such a part of the whole as might be singled out by attention: particular patches of color, particular noises, and so on. There is some difficulty in deciding what is to be considered *one* sense-datum: often attention causes divisions to appear where, so far as can be discovered, there were no divisions before. An observed complex fact, such as that this patch of red is to the left of that patch of blue, is also to be regarded as a datum from our present point of view: epistemologically, it does not differ greatly from a simple sense-datum as regards its function in giving knowledge. Its *logical* structure is very different, however, from that of sense: *sense* gives acquaintance with particulars, and is thus a two-term relation in which the object can be *named* but not *asserted*, and is inherently incapable of truth or falsehood, whereas the observation of a complex fact, which may be suitably called perception, is not a two-term relation, but involves the propositional form on the object-side, and gives knowledge of a truth, not mere acquaintance with a particular. This logical difference, important as it is, is not very relevant to our present problem; and it will be convenient to regard data of perception as included among sense-data for the purposes of this paper. It is to be observed that the particulars which are constituents of a datum of perception are always sense-data in the strict sense.

Concerning sense-data, we know that they are there while they are data, and this is the epistemological basis of all our knowledge of external particulars. (The meaning of the word 'external' of course raises problems which will concern us later.) We do not know, except by means of more or less precarious inferences, whether the objects which are at one time sense-data continue to exist at times when they are not data. Sense-data at the times when they are data are all that we directly and primitively know of the external world; hence in epistemology the fact that they are *data* is all-important. But the fact that they are all we directly know gives, of course, no presumption that they are all that there is. If we could construct an impersonal metaphysic, independent of the accidents of our knowledge and ignorance, the privileged position of the actual data would probably disappear, and they would probably appear as a rather haphazard selection from a mass of objects more or less like them. In saying this, I assume only that it is probable that there are particulars with which we are not acquainted. Thus the special importance of sense-data is in relation to epistemology, not to metaphysics. In this respect, physics is to be reckoned as metaphysics: it is impersonal, and nominally pays no special attention to sense-data. It is only when we ask how physics can be *known* that the importance of sense-data re-emerges.

III. Sensibilia

I shall give the name *sensibilia* to those objects which have the same metaphysical and physical status as sense-data without necessarily being data to any mind. Thus the relation of a *sensibile* to a sense-datum is like that of a man to a husband: a man becomes a husband by entering into the relation of marriage, and similarly a *sensibile* becomes a sense-datum by entering into the relation of acquaintance. It is important to have both terms; for we wish to discuss whether an object which is at one time a sense-datum can still exist at a time when it is not a sense-datum. We cannot ask, 'Can sense-data exist without being given?' for that is like asking, 'Can husbands exist without being married?' We must ask, 'Can *sensibilia* exist without being given?' and also 'Can a particular *sensibile* be at one time a sense-datum, and at another not?' Unless we have the word *sensibile* as well as the word 'sense-datum', such questions are apt to entangle us in trivial logical puzzles.

It will be seen that all sense-data are *sensibilia*. It is a metaphysical question whether all *sensibilia* are sense-data, and an epistemological question whether there exist means of inferring *sensibilia* which are not data from those that are.

A few preliminary remarks, to be amplified as we proceed, will serve to elucidate the use which I propose to make of *sensibilia*.

I regard sense-data as not mental, and as being, in fact, part of the actual subject-matter of physics. There are arguments, shortly to be examined, for their subjectivity, but these arguments seem to me only to prove *physiological* subjectivity, i.e., casual dependence on the sense-organs, nerves, and brain. The appearance which a thing presents to us is casually dependent upon these, in exactly the same way as it is dependent upon intervening fog or smoke or colored glass. Both dependencies are contained in the statement that the appearance which a piece of matter presents when viewed from a given place is a function not only of the piece of matter, but also of the intervening medium. (The terms used in this statement—'matter', 'view from a given place', 'appearance', 'intervening medium'—will all be defined in the course of the present paper.) We have not the means of ascertaining how things appear from places not surrounded by brain and nerves and sense-organs, because we cannot leave the body; but continuity makes it not unreasonable to suppose that they present *some* appearance at such places. Any such appearance would be included among *sensibilia*. If—*per impossible*—there were a complete human body with no mind inside it, all those *sensibilia* would exist, in relation to that body, which would be sense-data if there were a mind in the body. What the mind adds to *sensibilia*, in fact, is *merely* awareness: everything else is physical or physiological.

IV. Sense-Data Are Physical

Before discussing this question it will be well to define the sense in which the terms 'mental' and 'physical' are to be used. The word 'physical', in all preliminary discussions, is to be understood as meaning 'what is dealt with by physics'. Physics, it is plain, tells us something about some of the constituents of the actual world; what these constituents are may be doubtful, but it is they that are to be called physical, whatever their nature may prove to be.

The definition of the term 'mental' is more difficult, and can only be satisfactorily given after many difficult controversies have been discussed and decided. For present purposes therefore I must content myself with assuming a dogmatic answer to these controversies. I shall call a particular 'mental' when it is aware of something, and I shall call a fact 'mental' when it contains a mental particular as a constituent.

It will be seen that the mental and the physical are not necessarily mutually exclusive, although I know of no reason to suppose that they overlap.

The doubt as to the correctness of our definition of the 'mental' is of little importance in our present discussion. For what I am concerned to maintain is that sense-data are physical, and this being granted it is a matter of indifference in our present inquiry whether or not they are also mental. Although I do not hold, with Mach and James and the 'new realists', that the difference between the mental and the physical is *merely* one of arrangement, yet what I have to say in the present paper is compatible with their doctrine and might have been reached from their standpoint.

In discussions on sense-data, two questions are commonly confused, namely:

(1) Do sensible objects persist when we are not sensible of them? in other words, do *sensibilia* which are data at a certain time sometimes continue to exist at times when they are not data? And (2) are sense-data mental or physical?

I propose to assert that sense-data are physical, while yet maintaining that they probably never persist unchanged after ceasing to be data. The view that they do not persist is often thought, quite erroneously in my opinion, to imply that they are mental; and this has, I believe, been a potent source of confusion in regard to our present problem. If there were, as some have held, a *logical impossibility* in sense-data persisting after ceasing to be data, that certainly would tend to show that they were mental; but if, as I contend, their non-persistence is merely a probable inference from empirically ascertained causal laws, then it carries no such implication with it, and we are quite free to treat them as part of the subject-matter of physics.

Logically a sense-datum is an object, a particular of which the subject is aware. It does not contain the subject as a part, as for example beliefs and volitions do. The existence of the sense-datum is therefore not logically dependent upon that of the subject; for the only way, so far as I know, in which the existence of *A* can be *logically* dependent upon the existence of *B* is when *B* is part of *A*. There is therefore no *a priori* reason why a particular which is a sense-datum should not persist after it has ceased to be a datum, nor why other similar particulars should not exist without ever being data. The view that sense-data are mental is derived, no doubt, in part from their physiological subjectivity, but in part also from a failure to distinguish between sense-data and 'sensations'. By a sensation I mean the fact consisting in the subject's awareness of the sense-datum. Thus a sensation is a complex of which the subject is a constituent and which therefore is mental. The sense-datum, on the other hand, stands over against the subject as that external object of which is sensation the subject is aware. It is true that the sense-datum is in many cases in the subject's body, but the subject's body is as distinct from the subject as tables and chairs are, and is in fact merely a part of the material world. So soon, therefore, as sense-data are clearly distinguished from sensations, and as their subjectivity is recognized to be physiological not physical, the chief obstacles in the way of regarding them as physical are removed.

V. 'Sensibilia' and 'Things'

But if 'sensibilia' are to be recognized as the ultimate constituents of the physical world, a long and difficult journey is to be performed before we can arrive either at the 'thing' of common sense or at the 'matter' of physics. The supposed impossibility of combining the different sense-data which are regarded as appearances of the same 'thing' to different people has made it seem as though these 'sensibilia' must be regarded as mere subjective phantasms. A given table will present to one man a rectangular appearance, while to another it appears to have two acute angles and two obtuse angles; to

one man it appears brown, while to another, towards whom it reflects the light, it appears white and shiny. It is said, not wholly without plausibility, that these different shapes and different colors cannot coexist simultaneously in the same place, and cannot therefore both be constituents of the physical world. This argument I must confess appeared to me until recently to be irrefutable. The contrary opinion has, however, been ably maintained by Dr. T. P. Nunn in an article entitled: "Are Secondary Qualities Independent of Perception?" The supposed impossibility derives its apparent force from the phrase: '*in the same place*', and it is precisely in this phrase that its weakness lies. The conception of space is too often treated in philosophy—even by those who on reflection would not defend such treatment—as though it were as given, simple, and unambiguous as Kant, in his psychological innocence, supposed. It is the unperceived ambiguity of the word 'place' which, as we shall shortly see, has caused the difficulties to realists and given an undeserved advantage to their opponents. Two 'places' of different kinds are involved in every sense-datum, namely the place *at* which it appears and the place *from* which it appears. These belong to different spaces, although, as we shall see, it is possible, with certain limitations, to establish a correlation between them. What we call the different appearances of the same thing to different observers are each in a space private to the observer concerned. No place in the private world of one observer is identical with a place in the private world of another observer. There is therefore no question of combining the different appearances in the one place; and the fact that they cannot all exist in one place affords accordingly no ground whatever for questioning their physical reality. The 'thing' of common sense may in fact be identified with the whole class of its appearances—where, however, we must include among appearances not only those which are actual sense-data, but also those 'sensibilia', if any, which on grounds of continuity and resemblance, are to be regarded as belonging to the same system of appearances, although there happen to be no observers to whom they are data.

An example may make this clearer. Suppose there are a number of people in a room, all seeing, as they say, the same tables and chairs, walls and pictures. No two of these people have exactly the same sense-data, yet there is sufficient similarity among their data to enable them to group together certain of these data as appearances of one 'thing' to the several spectators, and others as appearances of another 'thing'. Besides the appearances which a given thing in the room presents to the actual spectators, there are, we may suppose, other appearances which it would present to other possible spectators. If a man were to sit down between two others, the appearance which the room would present to him would be intermediate between the appearances which it presents to the two others: and although this appearance would not exist as it is without the sense organs, nerves and brain, of the newly arrived spectator, still it is not unnatural to suppose that, from the position which he now occupies, *some* appearance of the room existed before his arrival. This supposition, however, need merely be noticed and not insisted upon.

Since the 'thing' cannot, without indefensible partiality, be identified with any single one of its appearances, it came to be thought of as something distinct from all of them and underlying them. But by the principle of Occam's razor, if the class of appearances will fulfill the purposes for the sake of which the thing was invented by the prehistoric metaphysicians to whom common sense is due, economy demands that we should identify the thing with the class of its appearances. It is not necessary to *deny* a substance or substratum underlying these appearances; it is merely expedient to abstain from asserting this unnecessary entity. Our procedure here is precisely analogous to that which has swept away from the philosophy of mathematics the useless menagerie of metaphysical monsters with which it used to be infested.

VI. Constructions versus Inferences

Before proceeding to analyze and explain the ambiguities of the word 'place', a few general remarks on method are desirable. The supreme maxim in scientific philosophizing is this:

> *Wherever possible, logical constructions are to be substituted for inferred entities.*

Some examples of the substitution of construction for inference in the realm of mathematical philosophy may serve to elucidate the uses of this maxim. Take first the case of irrationals. In old days, irrationals were inferred as the supposed limits of series of rationals which had no rational limit; but the objection to this procedure was that it left the existence of irrationals merely optative, and for this reason the stricter methods of the present day no longer tolerate such a definition. We now define an irrational number as a certain class of ratios, thus constructing it logically by means of ratios, instead of arriving at it by a doubtful inference from them. Take again the case of cardinal numbers. Two equally numerous collections appear to have something in common: this something is supposed to be their cardinal number. But so long as the cardinal number is inferred from the collections, not constructed in terms of them, its existence must remain in doubt, unless in virtue of a metaphysical postulate *ad hoc*. By defining the cardinal number of a given collection as the class of all equally numerous collections, we avoid the necessity of this metaphysical postulate, and thereby remove a needless element of doubt from the philosophy of arithmetic. A similar method, as I have shown elsewhere, can be applied to classes themselves, which need not be supposed to have any metaphysical reality, but can be regarded as symbolically constructed fictions.

The method by which the construction proceeds is closely analogous in these and all similar cases. Given a set of propositions nominally dealing with the supposed inferred entities, we observe the properties which are required of the supposed entities in order to make these propositions true. By dint of a little logical ingenuity, we then construct some logical function of less hypothetical entities which has the requisite properties. This constructed function we substitute for the supposed inferred entities, and thereby obtain a new and less doubtful interpretation of the body of propositions in question. This method, so fruitful in the philosophy of mathematics, will be found equally applicable in the philosophy of physics, where, I do not doubt, it would have been applied long ago but for the fact that all who have studied this subject hitherto have been completely ignorant of mathematical logic. I myself cannot claim originality in the application of this method to physics, since I owe the suggestion and the stimulus for its application entirely to my friend and collaborator Dr. Whitehead, who is engaged in applying it to the more mathematical portions of the region intermediate between sense-data and the points, instants and particles of physics.

A complete application of the method which substitutes constructions for inferences would exhibit matter wholly in terms of sense-data, and even, we may add, of the sense-data of a single person, since the sense-data of others cannot be known without some element of inference. This, however, must remain for the present an ideal, to be approached as nearly as possible, but to be reached, if at all, only after a long preliminary labor of which as yet we can only see the very beginning. The inferences which are unavoidable can, however, be subjected to certain guiding principles. In the first place, they should always be made perfectly explicit, and should be formulated in the most general manner possible. In the second place, the inferred entities should, whenever this can be done, be similar to those whose existence is given, rather than, like the Kantian *Ding an sich*, something wholly remote from the data which nominally support the inference. The inferred entities which I shall allow myself are of two kinds: (*a*) the sense-data of other people, in favor of which there is the evidence of testimony, resting ultimately upon the analogical argument in favor of minds other than my own; (*b*) the 'sensibilia' which would appear from places where there happen to be no minds, and which I suppose to be real although they are no one's data. Of these two classes of inferred entities, the first will probably be allowed to pass unchallenged. It would give me the greatest satisfaction to be able to dispense with it, and thus establish physics upon a solipsistic basis; but those—and I fear they are the majority—in whom the human affections are stronger than the desire for logical economy, will, no doubt, not share my desire to render solipsism scientifically satisfactory. The second class of inferred entities raises much more serious questions. It may be thought monstrous to maintain that a thing can present any appearance at all in a place where no sense organs and nervous structure exist through which it could appear. I do not myself feel the monstrosity; nevertheless I should regard these supposed appearances only in the light of a hypothetical scaffolding, to be used while the edifice of physics is being raised, though possibly capable of being removed as soon as the edifice is completed. These 'sensibilia' which are not data to anyone are therefore to be taken rather as an illustrative hypothesis and as an aid in preliminary statement than as a dogmatic part of the philosophy of physics in its final form.

VII. Private Space and the Space of Perspectives

We have now to explain the ambiguity in the word 'place', and how it comes that two places of different sorts are associated with every sense-datum, namely the place *at* which it is and the place *from* which it is perceived. The theory to be advocated is closely analogous to Leibniz's monadology, from which it differs chiefly in being less smooth and tidy.

The first fact to notice is that, so far as can be discovered, no sensible is ever a datum to two people at once. The things seen by two different people are often closely similar, so similar that the same *words* can be used to denote them, without which communication with others concerning sensible objects would be impossible. But, in spite of this similarity, it would seem that some difference always arises from difference in the point of view. Thus each person, so far as his sense-data are concerned, lives in a private world. This private world contains its own space, or rather spaces, for it would seem that only experience teaches us to correlate the space of sight with the space of touch and with the various other spaces of other senses. This multiplicity of private spaces, however, though interesting to the psychologist, is of no great importance in regard to our present problem, since a merely solipsistic experience enables us to correlate them into the one private space which embraces all our own sense-data. The place *at* which a sense-datum is, is a place in private space. This place therefore is different from any place in the private space of another percipient. For if we assume, as logical economy demands, that all position is relative, a place is only definable by the things in or around it, and therefore the same place cannot occur in two private worlds which have no common constituent. The question, therefore, of combining what we call different appearances of the same thing in the same place does not arise, and the fact that a given object appears to different spectators to have different shapes and colors affords no argument against the physical reality of all these shapes and colors.

In addition to the private spaces belonging to the private worlds of different percipients, there is, however, another space, in which one whole private world counts as a point, or at least as a spatial unit. This might be described as the space of points of view, since each private world may be regarded as the appearance which the universe presents from a certain point of view. I prefer, however, to speak of it as the space of *perspectives*, in order to obviate the suggestion that a private world is only real when someone views it. And for the same reason, when I wish to speak of a private world without assuming a percipient, I shall call it a 'perspective'.

We have now to explain how the different perspectives are ordered in one space. This is effected by means of the correlated 'sensibilia' which are regarded as the appearances, in different perspectives, of one and the same thing. By moving, and by testimony, we discover that two different perspectives, though they cannot both contain the same 'sensibilia', may nevertheless contain very similar ones; and the spatial order of a certain group of 'sensibilia' in a private space of one perspective is found to be identical with, or very similar to, the spatial order of the correlated 'sensibilia' in the private space of another perspective. In this way one 'sensibile' in one perspective is correlated with one 'sensibile' in another. Such correlated 'sensibilia' will be called 'appearances of one thing'. In Leibniz's monadology, since each moaned mirrored the whole universe, there was in each perspective a 'sensibile' which was an appearance of each thing. In our system of perspectives, we make no such assumption of completeness. A given thing will have appearances in some perspectives, but presumably not in certain others. The 'thing' being defined as the class of its appearances, if κ is the class of perspectives in which a certain thing θ appears, then θ is a member of the multiplicative class of κ, κ being a class of mutually exclusive classes of 'sensibilia'. And similarly a perspective is a member of the multiplicative class of the things which appear in it.

The arrangement of perspectives in a space is effected by means of the differences between the appearances of a given thing in the various perspectives. Suppose, say, that a certain penny appears in a number of different perspectives; in some it looks larger and in some smaller, in some it looks circular, in others it presents the appearance of an ellipse of varying eccentric-

ity. We may collect together all those perspectives in which the appearance of the penny is circular. These we will place on one straight line, ordering them in a series by the variations in the apparent size of the penny. Those perspectives in which the penny appears as a straight line of a certain thickness will similarly be placed upon a plane (though in this case there will be many different perspectives in which the penny is of the same size; when one arrangement is completed these will form a circle concentric with the penny), and ordered as before by the apparent size of the penny. By such means, all those perspectives in which the penny presents a visual appearance can be arranged in a three-dimensional spatial order. Experience shows that the same spatial order of perspectives would have resulted if, instead of the penny, we had chosen any other thing which appeared in all the perspectives in question, or any other method of utilizing the differences between the appearances of the same things in different perspectives. It is this empirical fact which has made it possible to construct the one all-embracing space of physics.

The space whose construction has just been explained, and whose elements are whole perspectives, will be called 'perspective space'.

VIII. The Placing of 'Things' and 'Sensibilia' in Perspective Space

The world which we have so far constructed is a world of six dimensions, since it is a three-dimensional series of perspectives, each of which is itself three-dimensional. We have now to explain the correlation between the perspective space and the various private spaces contained within the various perspectives severally. It is by means of this correlation that the one three-dimensional space of physics is constructed; and it is because of the unconscious performance of this correlation that the distinction between perspective space and the percipient's private space has been blurred, with disastrous results for the philosophy of physics. Let us revert to our penny: the perspectives in which the penny appears larger are regarded as being nearer to the penny than those in which it appears smaller, but as far as experience goes the apparent size of the penny will not grow beyond a certain limit, namely, that where (as we say) the penny is so near the eye that if it were any nearer it could not be seen. By touch we may prolong the series until the penny touches the eye, but no further. If we have been traveling along a line of perspectives in the previously defined sense, we may, however, by imagining the penny removed, prolong the line of perspectives by means, say, of another penny; and the same may be done with any other line of perspectives defined by means of the penny. All these lines meet in a certain place, that is, in a certain perspective. This perspective will be defined as 'the place where the penny is'.

It is now evident in what sense two places in constructed physical space are associated with a given 'sensibile'. There is first the place which is the perspective of which the 'sensibile' is a member. This is the place *from* which the 'sensibile' appears. Secondly there is the place where the other thing is of which the 'sensibile' is a member, in other words an appearance; this is the place *at* which the 'sensibile' appears. The 'sensibile' which is a member of one perspective is correlated with another perspective, namely, that which is the place where the thing is of which the 'sensibile' is an appearance. To the psychologist the 'place from which' is the more interesting, and the 'sensibile' accordingly appears to him subjective and where the percipient is. To the physicist the 'place at which' is the more interesting, and the 'sensibile' accordingly appears to him physical and external. The causes, limits and partial justification of each of these two apparently incompatible views are evident from the above duplicity of places associated with a given 'sensibile'.

We have seen that we can assign to a physical thing a place in the perspective space. In this way different parts of our body acquire positions in perspective space, and therefore there is a meaning (whether true or false need not much concern us) in saying that the perspective to which our sense-data belong is inside our head. Since our mind is correlated with the perspective to which our sense-data belong, we may regard this perspective as being the position of our mind in perspective space. If, therefore, this perspective is, in the above defined sense, inside our head, there is a good meaning for the statement that the mind is in the head. We can now say of the various appearances of a given thing that some of them are nearer to the thing than others; those are nearer which belong to perspectives that are nearer to 'the place where the thing is'. We can thus find a meaning, true or false, for the statement that more is to be learned about a thing by examining it close to than by viewing it from a distance. We can also find a meaning for the phrase, 'the things which intervene between the subject and a thing of which an appearance is a datum to him'. One reason often alleged for the subjectivity of sense-data is that the appearance of a thing may change when we find it hard to suppose that the thing itself has changed—for example, when the change is due to our shutting our eyes, or to our screwing them up so as to make the thing look double. If the thing is defined as the class of its appearances (which is the definition adopted above), there is of course necessarily *some* change in the thing whenever any one of its appearances changes. Nevertheless there is a very important distinction between two different ways in which the appearances may change. If after looking at a thing I shut my eyes, the appearance of my eyes changes in every perspective in which there is such an appearance, whereas most of the appearances of the thing will remain unchanged. We may say, as a matter of definition, that a thing changes when, however near to the thing an appearance of it may be, there are changes in appearances as near as, or still nearer to, the thing. On the other hand we shall say that the change is in some other thing if all appearances of the thing which are at not more than a certain distance from the thing remain unchanged, while only comparatively distant appearances of the thing are altered. From this consideration we are naturally led to the consideration of *matter*, which must be our next topic.

IX. The Definition of Matter

We defined the 'physical thing' as the class of its appearances, but this can hardly be taken as a definition of matter. We want to be able to express the fact that the appearance of a thing in a given perspective is causally affected by the matter between the thing and the perspective. We have found a meaning for 'between a thing and a perspective'. But we want matter to be something other than the whole class of appearances of a thing, in order to state the influence of matter on appearances.

We commonly assume that the information we get about a thing is more accurate when the thing is nearer. Far off, we see it is a man; then we see it is Jones; then we see he is smiling. Complete accuracy would only be attainable as a limit: if the appearances of Jones as we approach him tend towards a limit, that limit may be taken to be what Jones really is. It is obvious that from the point of view of physics the appearances of a thing close to 'count' more than the appearances far off. We may therefore set up the following tentative definition:

The *matter* of a given thing is the limit of its appearances as their distance from the thing diminishes.

It seems probable that there is something in this definition, but it is not quite satisfactory, because empirically there is no such limit to be obtained from sense-data. The definition will have to be eked out by constructions and definitions. But probably it suggests the right direction in which to look.

We are now in a position to understand in outline the reverse journey from matter to sense-data which is performed by physics. The appearance of a thing in a given perspective is a function of the matter composing the thing and of the intervening matter. The appearance of a thing is altered by intervening smoke or mist, by blue spectacles or by alterations in the sense-organs or nerves of the percipient (which also must be reckoned as part of the intervening medium). The nearer we approach to the thing, the less its appearance is affected by the intervening matter. As we travel further and further from the thing, its appearances diverge more and more from their initial character; and the causal laws of their divergence are to be stated in terms of the matter which lies between them and the thing. Since the appearances at very small distances are less affected by causes other than the thing itself, we come to think that the limit towards which these appearances tend as the distance diminishes is what the thing 'really is', as opposed to what it merely seems to be. This, together with its necessity for the statement of causal laws, seems to be the source of the entirely erroneous feeling that matter is more 'real' than sense-data.

Consider for example the infinite divisibility of matter. In looking at a given thing and approaching it, one sense-datum will become several, and each of these will again divide. Thus *one* appearance may represent *many*

things, and to this process there seems no end. Hence in the limit, when we approach indefinitely near to the thing, there will be an indefinite number of units of matter corresponding to what, at a finite distance, is only one appearance. This is how infinite divisibility arises.

The whole causal efficacy of a thing resides in its matter. This is in some sense an empirical fact, but it would be hard to state it precisely, because 'causal efficacy' is difficult to define.

What can be known empirically about the matter of a thing is only approximate, because we cannot get to know the appearances of the thing from very small distances, and cannot accurately infer the limit of these appearances. But it *is* inferred *approximately* by means of the appearances we can observe. It then turns out that these appearances can be exhibited by physics as a function of the matter in our immediate neighborhood; e.g., the visual appearance of a distant object is a function of the light-waves that reach the eyes. This leads to confusions of thought, but offers no real difficulty.

One appearance, of a visible object for example, is not sufficient to determine its other simultaneous appearances, although it goes a certain distance towards determining them. The determination of the hidden structure of a thing, so far as it is possible at all, can only be effected by means of elaborate dynamical inferences.

X. Time

It seems that the one all-embracing time is a construction, like the one all-embracing space. Physics itself has become conscious of this fact through the discussions connected with relativity.

Between two perspectives which both belong to one person's experience, there will be a direct time-relation of before and after. This suggests a way of dividing history in the same sort of way as it is divided by different experiences, but without introducing experience or anything mental: we may define a 'biography' as everything that is (directly) earlier or later than, or simultaneous with, a given 'sensibile'. This will give a series of perspectives, which *might* all form parts of one person's experience, though it is not necessary that all or any of them should actually do so. By this means, the history of the world is divided into a number of mutually exclusive biographies.

We have now to correlate the times in the different biographies. The natural thing would be to say that the appearances of a given (momentary) thing in two different perspectives belonging to different biographies are to be taken as simultaneous; but this is not convenient. Suppose A shouts to B, and B replies as soon as he hears A's shout. Then between A's hearing of his own shout and his hearing of B's there is an interval; thus if we made A's and B's hearing of the same shout exactly simultaneous with each other, we should have events exactly simultaneous with a given event but not with each other. To obviate this, we assume a 'velocity of sound'. That is, we assume that the time when B hears A's shout is half-way between the time when A hears his own shout and the time when he hears B's. In this way the correlation is effected.

What has been said about sound applies of course equally to light. The general principle is that the appearances, in different perspectives, which are to be grouped together as constituting what a certain thing is at a certain moment, are not to be all regarded as being at that moment. On the contrary they spread outward from the thing with various velocities according to the nature of the appearances. Since no *direct* means exist of correlating the time in one biography with the time in another, this temporal grouping of the appearances belonging to a given thing at a given moment is in part conventional. Its motive is partly to secure the verification of such maxims as that events which are exactly simultaneous with the same event are exactly simultaneous with one another, partly to secure convenience in the formulation of causal laws.

XI. The Persistence of Things and Matter

Apart from any of the fluctuating hypotheses of physics, three main problems arise in connecting the world of physics with the world of sense, namely:

1. the construction of a single space;
2. the construction of a single time;
3. the construction of permanent things or matter.

We have already considered the first and second of these problems; it remains to consider the third.

We have seen how correlated appearances in different perspectives are combined to form one 'thing' at one moment in the all-embracing time of physics. We have now to consider how appearances at different times are combined as belonging to one 'thing', and how we arrive at the persistent 'matter' of physics. The assumption of permanent substance, which technically underlies the procedure of physics, cannot of course be regarded as metaphysically legitimate: just as the one thing simultaneously seen by many people is a construction, so the one thing seen at different times by the same or different people must be a construction, being in fact nothing but a certain grouping of certain 'sensibilia'.

We have seen that the momentary state of a 'thing' is an assemblage of 'sensibilia', in different perspectives, not all simultaneous in the one constructed time, but spreading out from 'the place where the thing is' with velocities depending upon the nature of the 'sensibilia'. The time *at* which the 'thing' is in this state is the lower limit of the times at which these appearances occur. We have now to consider what leads us to speak of another set of appearances as belonging to the same 'thing' at a different time.

For this purpose, we may, at least to begin with, confine ourselves within a single biography. If we can always say when two 'sensibilia' in a given biography are appearances of one thing, then, since we have seen how to connect 'sensibilia' in different biographies as appearances of the same momentary state of a thing, we shall have all that is necessary for the complete construction of the history of a thing.

It is to be observed, to begin with, that the identity of a thing for common sense is not always correlated with the identity of matter for physics. A human body is one persisting thing for common sense, but for physics its matter is constantly changing. We may say, broadly, that the common-sense conception is based upon continuity in appearances at the ordinary distances of sense-data, while the physical conception is based upon the continuity of appearances at very small distances from the thing. It is probable that the common-sense conception is not capable of complete precision. Let us therefore concentrate our attention upon the conception of the persistence of matter in physics.

The first characteristic of two appearances of the same piece of matter at different times is *continuity*. The two appearances must be connected by a series of intermediaries, which, if time and space form compact series, must themselves form a compact series. The color of the leaves is different in autumn from what it is in summer; but we believe that the change occurs gradually, and that, if the colors are different at two given times, there are intermediate times at which the colors are intermediate between those at the given times.

But there are two considerations that are important as regards continuity.

First, it is largely hypothetical. We do not observe any one thing continuously, and it is merely a hypothesis to assume that, while we are not observing it, it passes through conditions intermediate between those in which it is perceived. During uninterrupted observation, it is true, continuity is nearly verified; but even here, when motions are very rapid, as in the case of explosions, the continuity is not actually capable of direct verification. Thus we can only say that the sense-data are found to *permit* a hypothetical complement of 'sensibilia' such as will preserve continuity, and that therefore there *may* be such a complement. Since, however, we have already made such use of hypothetical 'sensibilia', we will let this point pass, and admit such 'sensibilia', as are required to preserve continuity.

Secondly, continuity is not a sufficient criterion of material identity. It is true that in many cases, such as rocks, mountains, tables, chairs, etc., where the appearances change slowly, continuity is sufficient, but in other cases, such as the parts of an approximately homogeneous fluid, it fails us utterly. We can travel by sensibly continuous gradations from any one drop of the sea at any one time to any other drop at any other time. We infer the motions of sea water from the effects of the current, but they cannot be inferred from direct sensible observation together with the assumption of continuity.

The characteristic required in addition to continuity is conformity with the laws of dynamics. Starting from what common sense regards as persistent things, and making only such modifications as from time to time seem reasonable, we arrive at assemblages of 'sensibilia' which are found to obey certain simple laws, namely those of dynamics. By regarding 'sensibilia' at different times as belonging to the same piece of matter, we are able to define *motion*, which presupposes the assumption or construction of something persisting throughout the time of motion. The motions which are regarded as occurring, during a period in which all the 'sensibilia' and the times of their appearance are given, will be different according to the manner in which we combine 'sensibilia' at different times as belonging to the same piece of matter. Thus even when the whole history of the world is given in every particular, the question what motions take place is still to a certain extent arbitrary even after the assumption of continuity. Experience shows that it is possible to determine motions in such a way as to satisfy the laws of dynamics, and that this determination, roughly and on the whole, is fairly in agreement with the common-sense opinions about persistent things. This determination, therefore, is adopted, and leads to a criterion by which we can determine, sometimes practically, sometimes only theoretically, whether two appearances at different times are to be regarded as belonging to the same piece of matter. The persistence of all matter throughout all time can, I imagine, be secured by definition.

To recommend this conclusion, we must consider what it is that is proved by the empirical success of physics. What is proved is that its hypotheses, though unverifiable where they go beyond sense-data, are at no point in contradiction with sense-data, but, on the contrary, are ideally such as to render all sense-data calculable when a sufficient collection of 'sensibilia' is given. Now physics has found it empirically possible to collect sense-data into series, each series being regarded as belonging to one 'thing', and behaving, with regard to the laws of physics, in a way in which series not belonging to one thing would in general not behave. If it is to be unambiguous whether two appearances belong to the same thing or not, there must be only one way of grouping appearances so that the resulting things obey the laws of physics. It would be very difficult to prove that this is the case, but for our present purposes we may let this point pass, and assume that there is only one way. Thus we may lay down the following definition: *physical things are those series of appearances whose matter obeys the laws of physics.* That such series exist is an empirical fact, which constitutes the verifiability of physics.

XII. Illusions, Hallucinations, and Dreams

It remains to ask how, in our system, we are to find a place for sense-data which apparently fail to have the usual connection with the world of physics. Such sense-data are of various kinds, requiring somewhat different treatment. But all are of the sort that would be called 'unreal', and therefore, before embarking upon the discussion, certain logical remarks must be made upon the conceptions of reality and unreality.

Mr. A. Wolf says:

'The conception of mind as a system of transparent activities is, I think, also untenable because of its failure to account for the very possibility of dreams and hallucinations. It seems impossible to realize how a bare, transparent activity can be directed to what is not there, to apprehend what is not given.'

This statement is one which, probably, most people would endorse. But it is open to two objections. First it is difficult to see how an activity, however un-'transparent', can be directed towards a nothing: a term of a relation cannot be a mere nonentity. Secondly, no reason is given, and I am convinced that none can be given, for the assertion that dream-objects are not 'there' and not 'given'. Let us take the second point first.

1. The belief that dream-objects are not given comes, I think, from failure to distinguish, as regards waking life, between the sense-datum and the corresponding 'thing'. In dreams, there is no such corresponding 'thing' as the dreamer supposes; if, therefore, the 'thing' were given in waking life, as, e.g., Meinong maintains, then there would be a difference in respect of givenness between dreams and waking life. But if, as we have maintained, what is given is never the thing, but merely one of the 'sensibilia' which compose the thing, then what we apprehend in a dream is just as much given as what we apprehend in waking life.

Exactly the same argument applies as to the dream-objects being 'there'. They have their position in the private space of the perspective of the dreamer; where they fail is in their correlation with other private spaces and therefore with perspective space. But in the only sense in which 'there' can be a datum, they are 'there' just as truly as any of the sense-data of waking life.

2. The conception of 'illusion' or 'unreality', and the correlative conception of 'reality', are generally used in a way which embodies profound logical confusions. Words that go in pairs, such as 'real' and 'unreal', 'existent' and 'non-existent', 'valid' and 'invalid', etc., are all derived from the one fundamental pair, 'true' and 'false'. Now 'true' and 'false' are applicable only—except in derivative significations—to *propositions*. Thus wherever the above pairs can be significantly applied, we must be dealing either with propositions or with such incomplete phrases as only acquire meaning when put into a context which, with them, forms a proposition. Thus such pairs of words can be applied to *descriptions*, but not to proper names: in other words, they have no application whatever to data, but only to entities or non-entities described in terms of data.

Let us illustrate by the terms 'existence' and 'non-existence'. Given any datum x, it is meaningless either to assert or to deny that x 'exists'. We might be tempted to say: 'Of course x exists, for otherwise it could not be a datum'. But such a statement is really meaningless, although it is significant and true to say, 'My present sense-datum exists', and it may also be true that 'x is my present sense-datum'. The inference from these two propositions to 'x exists' is one which seems irresistible to people unaccustomed to logic; yet the apparent proposition inferred is not merely false, but strictly meaningless. To say 'My present sense-datum exists' is to say (roughly): 'There is an object of which "my present sense-datum" is a description'. But we cannot say: 'There is an object of which "x" is a description,' because 'x' is (in the case we are supposing) a name, not a description. Dr. Whitehead and I have explained this point fully elsewhere ... with the help of symbols, without which it is hard to understand; I shall not therefore here repeat the demonstration of the above propositions, but shall proceed with their application to our present problem.

The fact that 'existence' is only applicable to descriptions is concealed by the use of what are grammatically proper names in a way which really transforms them into descriptions. It is, for example, a legitimate question whether Homer existed; but here 'Homer' means 'the author of the Homeric poems', and is a description. Similarly we may ask whether God exists; but then 'God' means 'the Supreme Being' or 'the *ens realissimum*' or whatever other description we may prefer. If 'God' were a proper name, God would have to be a datum; and then no question could arise as to His existence. The distinction between existence and other predicates, which Kant obscurely felt, is brought to light by the theory of descriptions, and is seen to remove 'existence' altogether from the fundamental notions of metaphysics.

What has been said about 'existence' applies equally to 'reality', which may, in fact, be taken as synonymous with 'existence'. Concerning the immediate objects in illusions, hallucinations, and dreams, it is meaningless to ask whether they 'exist' or are 'real'. There they are, and that ends the matter. But we may legitimately inquire as to the existence or reality of 'things' or other 'sensibilia' inferred from such objects. It is the unreality of these 'things' and other 'sensibilia', together with a failure to notice that they are not data, which has led to the view that the objects of dreams are unreal.

We may now apply these considerations in detail to the stock arguments against realism, though what is to be said will be mainly a repetition of what others have said before.

1. We have first the variety of normal appearances, supposed to be incompatible. This is the case of the different shapes and colors which a given thing presents to different spectators. Locke's water which seems both hot and cold belongs to this class of cases. Our system of different perspectives fully accounts for these cases, and shows that they afford no argument against realism.

2. We have cases where the correlation between different senses is unusual. The bent stick in water belongs here. People say it looks bent but is straight: this only means that it is straight to the touch, though bent to sight. There is no 'illusion', but only a false inference, if we think that the stick would feel bent to the touch. The stick would look just as bent in a photograph, and, as Mr. Gladstone used to say, 'the photograph cannot lie'. The case of seeing double also belongs here, though in this case the cause of the unusual correlation is physiological, and would therefore not operate in a photograph. It is a mistake to ask whether the 'thing' is duplicated when we see it double. The 'thing' is a whole system of 'sensibilia', and it is only those visual 'sensibilia' which are data to the percipient that are duplicated. The phenomenon has a purely physiological explanation; indeed, in view of our having two eyes, it is in less need of explanation than the single visual sense-datum which we normally obtain from the things on which we focus.

3. We come now to cases like dreams, which may, at the moment of dreaming, contain nothing to arouse suspicion, but are condemned on the ground of their supposed incompatibility with earlier and later data. Of course it often happens that dream-objects fail to behave in the accustomed manner: heavy objects fly, solid objects melt, babies turn into pigs or undergo even greater changes. But none of these unusual occurrences *need* happen in a dream, and it is not on account of such occurrences that dream-objects are called 'unreal'. It is their lack of continuity with the dreamer's past and future that makes him, when he wakes, condemn them; and it is their lack of correlation with other private worlds that makes others condemn them. Omitting the latter ground, our reason for condemning them is that the 'things' which we infer from them cannot be combined according to the laws of physics with the 'things' inferred from waking sense-data. This might be used to condemn the 'things' inferred from the data of dreams. Dream-data are no doubt appearances of 'things', but not of such 'things' as the dreamer supposes. I have no wish to combat psychological theories of dreams, such as those of the psychoanalysts. But there certainly are cases where (whatever psychological causes may contribute) the presence of physical causes also is very evident. For instance, a door banging may produce a dream of a naval engagement, with images of battleships and sea and smoke. The whole dream will be an appearance of the door banging, but owing to the peculiar condition of the body (especially the brain) during sleep, this appearance is not that expected to be produced by a door banging, and thus the dreamer is led to entertain false beliefs. But his sense-data are still physical, and are such as a completed physics would include and calculate.

4. The last class of illusions are those which cannot be discovered within one person's experience, except through the discovery of discrepancies with the experi-

ences of others. Dreams might conceivably belong to this class, if they were jointed sufficiently neatly into waking life; but the chief instances are recurrent sensory hallucinations of the kind that lead to insanity. What makes the patient, in such cases, become what others call insane is the fact that, within his own experience, there is nothing to show that the hallucinatory sense-data do not have the usual kind of connection with 'sensibilia' in other perspectives. Of course he may learn this through testimony, but he probably finds it simpler to suppose that the testimony is untrue and that he is being willfully deceived. There is, so far as I can see, no theoretical criterion by which the patient can decide, in such a case, between the two equally satisfactory hypotheses of his madness and of his friends' mendacity.

From the above instances it would appear that abnormal sense-data, of the kind which we regard as deceptive, have intrinsically just the same status as any others, but differ as regards their correlations or causal connections with other 'sensibilia' and with 'things'. Since the usual correlations and connections become part of our unreflective expectations, and even seem, except to the psychologist, to form part of our data, it comes to be thought, mistakenly, that in such cases the data are unreal, whereas they are merely the causes of false inferences. The fact that correlations and connections of unusual kinds occur adds to the difficulty of inferring things from sense and of expressing physics in terms of sense-data. But the unusualness would seem to be always physically or physiologically explicable, and therefore raises only a complication, not a philosophical objection.

I conclude, therefore, that no valid objection exists to the view which regards sense-data as part of the actual substance of the physical world, and that, on the other hand, this view is the only one which accounts for the empirical verifiability of physics. In the present paper, I have given only a rough preliminary sketch. In particular, the part played by *time* in the construction of the physical world is, I think, more fundamental than would appear from the above account. I should hope that, with further elaboration, the part played by unperceived 'sensibilia' could be indefinitely diminished, probably by invoking the history of a 'thing' to eke out the inferences derivable from its momentary appearance.

READING QUESTIONS

1. What does Russell mean by the terms *sense-data* and *sensibilia*? How are these categories related, and how are they different? What does Russell mean when he states that "sense-data are physical"?

2. Russell claims that the "supreme maxim in scientific philosophizing is this: Wherever possible, logical constructions are to be substituted for inferred entities." What is the difference between a logical construction and an inferred entity? What difference does it make from the standpoint of epistemology?

3. Carefully discuss Russell's penny example. How does he use this example to illustrate his conception of "perspective space"? How does he go about "assigning a physical thing a place in perspective space," such as a penny?

4. As a philosopher interested in the epistemological and metaphysical foundations of physics, Russell pays special attention to the problem of defining "matter" and to the nature of time. How does Russell conceive of these categories? How do his conceptions differ from your own?

5. Russell writes that "physical things are those series of appearances whose matter obeys the laws of physics." First, what does this mean? Second, what, then, is the metaphysical status of illusions, hallucinations, and dreams? How does an illusion of a physical object differ from an actual physical object?

SUGGESTIONS FOR FURTHER READING (BERTRAND RUSSELL)

Primary Sources and Collected Writings

(1983–) *The Collected Papers of Bertrand Russell*, various editors. A total of 30 volumes are anticipated. London: Routledge.

(1897) *An Essay on the Foundations of Geometry*. Cambridge: Cambridge University Press.

(1900) *A Critical Exposition of the Philosophy of Leibniz*. Cambridge: Cambridge University Press.

(1903) *The Principles of Mathematics*. New York: W. W. Norton, 1995.

(1910) *Philosophical Essays*. London: Longmans, Green.

(1910–13) *Principia Mathematica* (with A. N. White-head). Cambridge: Cambridge University Press, 1962.

(1912) *The Problems of Philosophy.* Oxford: Oxford University Press, 1974.

(1914) *Our Knowledge of the External World as a Field for Scientific Investigation in Philosophy.* London: Routledge, 1993.

(1918) *Mysticism and Logic and Other Essays.* London: Allen and Unwin, 1919.

(1919) *Introduction to Mathematical Philosophy.* London: Routledge, 1993.

(1921) *The Analysis of Mind.* London: Routledge, 1992.

(1927) *The Analysis of Matter.* London: Routledge, 1992.

(1927) *An Outline of Philosophy.* London: Routledge, 1996.

(1940) *An Inquiry into Meaning and Truth.* London: Routledge, 1992.

(1948) *Human Knowledge: Its Scope and Limits.* London: Routledge, 1992.

(1956) *Logic and Knowledge: Essays 1901–1950*, edited by R. C. Marsh. London: George Allen & Unwin.

(1957) *Why I Am Not a Christian and Other Essays on Religion and Related Subjects.* London: George Allen and Unwin.

(1959) *My Philosophical Development.* London: Routledge, 1993.

(1967–9) *Autobiography.* London: Allen and Unwin.

(1992) *The Selected Letters of Bertrand Russell.* London: Penguin Press.

Secondary Sources

Ayer, A. J. (1972) *Bertrand Russell.* New York: Viking Press.

Eames, E. R. (1969) *Bertrand Russell's Theory of Knowledge.* London: George Allen and Unwin.

Evans, G. (1982) *The Varieties of Reference*, edited by J. McDowell. New York: Oxford University Press.

Grayling, A. C. (1996) *Russell.* Oxford: Oxford University Press.

Griffin, N. (1991) *Russell's Idealist Apprenticeship.* Oxford: Clarendon Press.

Hylton, P. (1990) *Russell, Idealism, and the Emergence of Analytic Philosophy.* Oxford: Clarendon Press.

Irvine, A. D., ed. (1999) *Bertrand Russell: Critical Assessments.* London: Routledge.

Jager, R. (1972) *The Development of Bertrand Russell's Philosophy.* London: Allen and Unwin.

Monk, R. (1996) *Bertrand Russell: The Spirit of Solitude, 1872–1921.* New York: Free Press.

———. (1999) *Russell.* London: Routledge.

———, and A. Palmer, eds. (1996). *Bertrand Russell and the Origins of Analytic Philosophy.* Toronto: University of Toronto Press.

Pears, D. F. (1967) *Bertrand Russell and the British Tradition in Philosophy.* New York: Random House.

Sainsbury, R. M. (1979) *Russell.* London: Routledge.

Savage, C. W. and C. Anderson, eds. (1989) *Rereading Russell: Essays in Bertrand Russell's Metaphysics and Epistemology.* Minneapolis, MN: University of Minnesota Press.

Schilpp, P. A., ed. (1944) *The Philosophy of Bertrand Russell.* Evanston, IL: Northwestern University Press.

Slater, J. (1994) *Bertrand Russell.* Bristol: Thoemmes Press.

Wood, A. (1957) *Bertrand Russell: The Passionate Sceptic.* London: Allen and Unwin.

Ludwig Wittgenstein

Tractatus Logico-Philosophicus

Brooding, brilliant, and enigmatic, Ludwig Wittgenstein (1889–1951) is arguably the most influential and controversial philosopher of the contemporary period. Virtually every aspect of his work has had an enduring effect on philosophy. His writings on various topics in the philosophy of mathematics, the philosophy of mind, the philosophy of logic, the philosophy of language, metaphysics, and epistemology have been especially fruitful sources of insight, inspiration, and argument.

Wittgenstein was the youngest of a family of eight children in Vienna, Austria. His father was a wealthy and powerful industrialist, and Wittgenstein enjoyed the benefits of an excellent early education. His first serious academic pursuits were in the area of engineering, although he was acquainted with the work of various philosophers, including, especially, Arthur Schopenhauer, whose *The World as Will and Representation* made a lasting impact on Wittgenstein's life. He began his higher education at a technical university in Berlin and later transferred to the University of Manchester in England to study aeronautics.

It was in Manchester (while working on various problems relating to the design of propellers) that Wittgenstein first became interested in issues in the foundations of mathematics. Inspired by his reading of Bertrand Russell's *The Principles of Mathematics* and intrigued by Russell's obvious enthusiasm for the logical work of Gottlob Frege, Wittgenstein made a point of visiting Frege in 1911. Frege suggested to Wittgenstein that he travel to Trinity College, Cambridge, to study the philosophy of mathematics with Russell. Soon Wittgenstein had dropped his pursuit of engineering and was in Cambridge attending Russell's lectures.

Wittgenstein was a student at Cambridge from 1911 to 1913, working almost exclusively on problems in the foundations of mathematics, logical theory, and the philosophy of language. He began as Russell's student and protégé but quickly became Russell's collaborator and sharp critic. It would be fair to say that their relationship was often rocky and difficult. Wittgenstein was an emotional and erratic man, but he was also a completely original genius with an unusual gift for philosophy. Often Russell and Wittgenstein struggled simply to understand each other. In his autobiography, Russell writes that Wittgenstein "was perhaps the most perfect example I have ever known of genius as traditionally conceived, passionate, profound, intense, and dominating. He has a kind of purity which I have never known equaled except by G. E. Moore."

Wittgenstein returned to Austria in 1914 to enlist in the army at the outbreak of the First World War. He served with distinction and often on the front lines, living for periods of time under heavy fire. Toward the end of the war he was captured by the Italians and finished his military service in a prisoner-of-war camp. It was while imprisoned that he finished his early masterpiece, *Tractatus Logico-Philosophicus* (1918, first published in German in 1921, and translated into English in 1922).

The *Tractatus* represents a synthesis of elements of Russell's logical atomism, Frege's philosophy of mathematics and logic, Schopenhauer's idealism, and Wittgenstein's own unique contributions to philosophy.

After being released from prison camp at the end of the war, Wittgenstein decided not to return to Cambridge and to professional philosophy. Rather, he became an elementary school teacher in a country village in lower Austria, later served as the architect for a house built for his sister, and worked as a gardener in a monastery. At various times he considered entering the priesthood. Wittgenstein was visited by the young Cambridge philosopher, P. F. Ramsey, by members of the Vienna Circle (who found great inspiration in his *Tractatus*), and by a few others, but for the most part he lived in relative isolation until he eventually did return to Cambridge and to professional philosophy in 1929.

PREFACE

This book will perhaps be understood only by those who have themselves already thought the thoughts which are expressed in it—or similar thoughts. It is therefore not a textbook. Its purpose would be achieved if there were one person who read it with understanding and to whom it gave pleasure.

The book deals with the problems of philosophy and shows, as I believe, that the method of formulating these problems rests on a misunderstanding of the logic of our language. Its whole meaning might be summed up as follows: What can be said at all can be said clearly; and what we cannot speak thereof we must be silent.

The book will, therefore, draw a limit to thought, or rather—not to thought, but to the expression of

Ludwig Wittgenstein, *Tractatus Logico-Philosophicus,* translated by Daniel Kolak and published as *Wittgenstein's Tractatus* by Mayfield Publishing Company. Copyright © 1998 Daniel Kolak. Reprinted with the permission of the publisher.

thought; for, in order to draw a limit to thought we should have to be able to think both sides of this limit (we should therefore have to be able to think what cannot be thought).

The limit can, therefore, only be drawn in language and what lies on the other side of the limit will be simply nonsense.

How far my efforts agree with those of other philosophers I cannot judge. Indeed what I have here written makes no claim to novelty in points of detail; and therefore I give no sources, because it makes no difference to me whether what I have thought has already been thought before me by someone else.

I will only mention that to the great works of Frege and the writings of my friend Bertrand Russell I owe for much of the stimulation of my thoughts.

If this work has a value it consists in two things. First that in it thoughts are expressed, and this value will be the greater the better the thoughts are expressed—the more the nail has been hit on the head, the greater will be its value. Here I am conscious that I have fallen far short of the possible. Simply because my powers are insufficient to cope with the task. May others come and do it better.

On the other hand the *truth* of the thoughts communicated here seems to me unassailable and definitive. I therefore believe that the problems have in essentials been finally solved. And if I am not mistaken in this, then the value of this work secondly consists in the fact that it shows how little has been achieved when these problems have been solved.

---

1 The world is all that is the case.

  1.1 The world is the totality of facts, not of things.

    1.11 The world is determined by the facts, and by these being all the facts.

    1.12 For the totality of facts determines all that is the case and also all that is not the case.

    1.13 The facts in logical space are the world.

  1.2 The world can be broken down into facts.

    1.21 Each one can be the case or not be the case while all else remains the same.

2 What is the case—a fact—is the existence of elementary facts.

  2.01 An elementary fact is a combination of objects (items, things).

    2.011 It is essential that such objects can be constituents of an elementary fact.

2.012 In logic nothing is accidental: if something *can* be a constituent of an elementary fact, it must already include within itself the possibility of that elementary fact.

2.0121 It would, so to speak, appear as an accident, if it turned out that an elementary fact accommodated something that could already exist on its own.

For something to be a constituent of an elementary fact, it must already include this possibility in itself.

(Something logical cannot be merely possible. Logic deals with every possibility, and all possibilities are its facts.)

Just as we cannot think of spatial objects outside space nor temporal objects outside time, so we cannot think of *any* object outside the possibility of its combining with other things.

If I can think of an object combining with others into an elementary fact, I cannot think of it without the *possibility* of such combinations.

2.0122 This thing [the constituting object] is independent [of the elementary fact] to the extent that it can occur in all *possible* elementary facts, but this form of independence is a form of connection with elementary facts and thus ultimately a form of dependence. (Words cannot appear in two different roles: by themselves, and in sentences.)

2.0123 If I know an object, I also know all the possibilities of its occurrence in elementary facts.

(Every such possibility [what will soon be defined as *form*] must lie in the nature of the object.)

New possibilities cannot be found in the future [i.e., the form cannot be altered by new possibilities discovered in the future].

2.01231 To know an object, I need not know its external [material] qualities, but I need to know all its internal [formal] properties.

2.0124 If all objects are given, then thereby are all *possible* elementary facts also given.

2.013 Everything exists, as it were, in a space of possible elementary facts. I can imagine this space empty, but nothing without this space.

2.0131 A spatial object must be surrounded by an infinite space. (A point in space is a place for an argument.)

A spot in the visual field need not be red but it must have some color: it is surrounded by color-space. Notes must have some pitch, tactile objects some degree of hardness, and so on.

2.014 Objects contain the possibility of all elementary facts.

2.0141 The possibility of an object being part of an elementary fact is its form.

2.02 Objects are simple.

2.0201 Every complex assertion [involving compounds of objects] can be broken down into an assertion about simple constituents using sentences that describe the complex completely.

2.021 Objects form the substance of the world. That is why they cannot be compound.

2.0211 Were the world without substance, whether one sentence made sense would depend on whether another sentence was true.

2.0212 It would then be impossible to form a picture of the world (true or false).

2.022 Obviously, a world that exists only in thought, however different from the real world, must have something—a form—in common with it.

2.023 This fixed form consists of objects.

2.0231 The substance of the world *can* only determine such a form and not the material properties. Material properties can only be presented by means of sentences—they can only be constituted by the configuration of objects.

2.0232 Roughly speaking, objects are colorless.

2.0233 Two objects of the same logical form—apart from their external properties—are only distinct from one another in that they are different.

2.02331 Either a thing has unique properties, and then we can immediately distinguish it from others using a description as well as refer to it; or, on the other hand, there are several things that have a common set of all their properties, in which case it is impossible to distinguish them.

For if something is distinguished by nothing, I cannot distinguish it—otherwise it would be distinguished.

2.024 Substance is that which exists independently of what is the case.

2.025 It is form and content.

2.0251 Space, time, and color (the state of being colored) are forms of objects.

2.026 Only if objects exist can the world have a fixed form.

2.027 The fixed, the existent, and the object are one.

2.0271 The object is the fixed, the existent; the configuration of objects is the changing, the variable.

2.0272 The configuration of objects forms the elementary fact.

In an elementary fact the objects hang in one another like the links of a chain.

2.03 In an elementary fact the objects hang in one another like the links of a chain.

2.031 In an elementary fact the objects combine with one another in a definite way.

2.032 The definite way in which objects are connected in an elementary fact is the structure of the elementary fact.

2.033 Form is the possibility of structure.

2.034 The structure of a fact consists of the structures of its elementary facts.

2.04 The world is a totality of all existing elementary facts.

2.05 The totality of all existing elementary facts determines which elementary facts do not exist.

2.06 The existence and nonexistence of elementary facts is reality.

(We also call the existence of elementary facts a positive fact, and their nonexistence a negative fact.)

2.061 Elementary facts exist independently of one another.

2.062 From the existence or nonexistence of one elementary fact we cannot infer the existence or nonexistence of any other elementary fact.

2.063 The sum total of reality is the world.

2.1 We make pictures of facts to ourselves.

2.11 Such a picture represents an elementary fact in logical space, the existence and nonexistence of elementary facts.

2.12 Such a picture is a model of reality.

2.13 To the objects correspond, in such a picture, the elements of the picture.

2.131 The picture's elements stand, in the picture, for the objects.

2.14 The picture consists in its elements being combined in a definite way.

2.141 The picture is a fact.

2.15 The definite way in which the picture elements combine represents how things are related.

Let us call this combination of elements the *structure* of the picture, and let us call the possibility of this structure the *form of representation* of the picture.

2.151 The form of representation is the possibility that things combine in the same way as do the pictorial elements.

2.1511 In this way the picture makes contact with, or reaches up to, reality.

2.1512 It lies against reality like a ruler.

2.15121 Only the end points of the marks on the ruler touch the object being measured.

2.1513 A picture conceived in this way includes the representing relation, which makes the picture a picture.

2.1514 The representing relation consists of the correlations of picture elements with things.

2.1515 These correlations are the antennae of the picture's elements, which put the picture in touch with reality.

2.16 To be a picture, a fact must have something in common with what it depicts.

2.161 A picture cannot depict anything unless the picture and the depicted have something identical in common.

2.17 What a picture must have in common with reality to be capable of depicting it the way it does—rightly or wrongly—is its form of representation.

2.171 A picture can represent any reality whose form it has.

A spatial picture, anything spatial; a colored picture, anything colored; etc.

2.172 A picture cannot, however, depict its form of representation; it can only show it.

2.173 A picture represents its subject from the outside (its point of view is its form of representation), and that is how it represents its subject rightly or wrongly.

2.174 A picture cannot place itself outside its form of representation.

2.18 What any such picture, of any form, must have in common with reality to be capable of representing it the way it does—rightly or wrongly—is logical form, that is, the form of reality.

2.181 A picture whose form of representation is logical is a logical picture.

2.182 Every such picture is *also* a logical picture. (Whereas, for example, every picture is not a spatial picture.)

2.19 Logical pictures are depictions of the world.

2.2 A picture must have the logical form of representation in common with what it depicts.

2.201 A picture depicts reality by representing the possible existence and nonexistence of elementary facts.

2.202 Such a picture represents a possible elementary fact in logical space.

2.203 Such a picture contains the possibility of the elementary fact that it represents.

2.21 Such a picture agrees with reality or not; it is right or wrong, true or false.

2.22 Such a picture represents what it represents independently of its truth or falsity, via its representational form.

2.221 What this picture represents is its sense.

2.222 Its truth or falsity consists in the agreement or disagreement of its sense with reality.

2.223 To see whether the picture is true or false we must compare it with reality.

2.224 We cannot see whether the picture is true or false merely by looking at it.

2.225 There is no such picture that is true a priori.

3 A thought is a logical picture of a fact.

3.001 "An elementary fact is thinkable" means: we can form a mental picture of it.

3.01 The totality of all true thoughts is a picture of the world.

3.02 A thought contains the possibility of the facts that it thinks. What is thinkable is also possible.

3.03 Thought cannot be of anything illogical, else we would have to think illogically.

3.031 As the old saying goes: God can create anything so long as it does not contradict the laws of logic. The truth is that we could not even *say* what an illogical world might look like.

3.032 It is as impossible to say something that contradicts logic as it is to draw a figure that contradicts the laws of space or to specify the coordinates of a nonexistent point.

3.0321 An elementary fact contradicting the laws of physics can be represented spatially, but not one that contradicts the laws of geometry.

3.04 A thought that was correct a priori would ensure its truth in virtue of its possibility.

3.05 To know that a thought is true a priori you would have to recognize its truth from the thought itself (without any corresponding fact).

3.1 In a sentence the thought expresses itself perceptibly.

3.11 We use a sentence (spoken or written, etc.) as a projection of a possible fact.

The method of projection is our thinking the sense of the sentence.

3.12 The sign with which a thought expresses itself, I will call a sentential sign. And a sentence is a sentential sign conceived in its projective relation to the world.

3.13 The sentence has everything that the projection has, except what is projected.

Therefore, the possibility of what is projected is in the sentence, but not the projection itself.

And so the sentence does not yet contain its sense; what it does contain is the possibility of expressing that sense.

("The content of the sentence" means the content of a sentence that makes sense.)

The sentence contains the [empty, logical] form of its sense, without any content.

3.14 What constitutes a sentence is that its elements, the words, stand in a determinate relation to one another.

A sentential sign is a fact.

3.141 A sentence is not merely a mixture of words. (Just as a musical theme is not merely a mixture of notes.)

A sentence is articulate.

3.142 Only facts can express a sense; a class of names cannot.

3.143 That a sentential sign is a fact is concealed in its usual form of expression, whether written or printed.

For example, in a printed sentence there is no essential difference between the sentence and the word.

(Thus it was possible for Frege to call the sentence a compound name.)

3.1431 The essential nature of the sentential sign can be seen very clearly once we think of it as composed not of written signs but of spatial objects (such as tables, chairs, and books).

Then the mutual spatial layout of these objects expresses the sense of the sentence.

3.1432 We must not say, "The complex sign 'aRb' says that *a* stands to *b* in relation R," but, rather, "*That* '*a*' stands to '*b*' in a certain relation says *that aRb*."

3.144 Facts can be described but not named. (Names are like points, sentences like arrows—they designate.)

3.2 In sentences, thoughts can be expressed such that the objects of the thoughts correspond to the elements of the sentential signs.

3.201 I call these elements "simple signs," and such a sentence "completely analyzed."

3.202 A simple sign used in a sentence I will call a *name.*

3.203 A name signifies an object. The designated object is what the name means. ("*A*" is the same sign as "*A*".)

3.21 The configuration of simple signs in the sentential sign corresponds to the configuration of objects in the fact.

3.22 In a sentence a name signifies an object.

3.221 Objects can only be *named.* Signs represent them. I can only speak *about* objects: I *cannot put them into words.* A sentence can only say *how* a thing is, not *what* it is.

3.23 The demand for the possibility of simple signs is the demand that sense be determinate.

3.24 A sentence about a complex stands in an internal relation to a sentence about its constituent part.

A complex can be given only by its description, which either will fit or not fit. A sentence that mentions a complex that does not exist is not meaningless, merely false.

When a sentence element designates a complex, this shows up in the indeterminateness of the sentences in which it occurs.

We then *know* that everything is not yet determined by this sentence. (The notation for generality *contains* a prototype.)

The contraction of the symbol of a complex into a simple symbol can be expressed by means of a definition.

3.25 There is one and only one complete analysis of a sentence.

3.251 A sentence expresses itself clearly and distinctly: a sentence is articulate.

3.26 A name cannot be further analyzed using definitions. It is a primitive sign.

3.261 Every defined sign signifies *via* the signs by which it is defined; the definitions show the way.

Two signs, one primitive and one defined in terms of primitive signs, cannot signify the same way. Names *cannot* be further broken down into pieces by means of definitions. (This cannot be done to any sign that signifies independently and on its own.)

3.262 What a sign fails to express gets shown by its application. What a sign conceals, its application declares.

3.263 The meanings of primitive signs can be explained through clarifications. Clarifications are sentences containing the primitive signs. Therefore, they can only be understood when the meanings of these signs is already known.

3.3 Only sentences make sense; only in the context of a sentence does a name signify anything.

3.31 Any part of a sentence that characterizes the sense of the sentence I call an *expression* (a symbol).

(A sentence is itself an expression.)

Expressions are everything essential for the sense of the sentence that sentences can have in common with each other.

An expression characterizes the form and content.

3.311 An expression presupposes the forms of all the sentences in which it can occur. It is the common characteristic mark of a class of sentences.

3.312 It therefore presents itself in the general form of the sentences that it characterizes.

And in this form the expression will be *constant* and all else *variable.*

3.313 The expression is thus presented by a variable whose values are the sentences containing the expressions.

(In the limiting case the variable becomes constant and the expression becomes a sentence.)

Such a variable I call a *sentence variable.*

3.314 An expression means something only in the context of a sentence. All variables can be understood as sentence variables.

(Including variable names.)

3.315 If we turn an expression into a variable, the resulting variable sentence will have a class of sentences as its values. This class in general still depends upon what we, by arbitrary convention, mean by parts of that original sentence. But if we change all the signs whose designations have been arbitrarily turned into variables, there still always exists this type of class. This, however, is now no longer a matter of convention but depends solely on the nature of the sentence. It corresponds to a logical form—a logical prototype.

3.316 The values of sentence variables are set by stipulation.

The stipulation of values *is* the variable.

3.317 Values for a sentence variable are stipulated by indicating which sentences have that variable as a common mark.

The description of those sentences is the stipulation.

The stipulation thus concerns only the symbols, not their meaning.

And all that is essential to the stipulation is *that it merely describes the symbols without stating anything about what they designate.*

The way in which we describe the sentences doesn't matter.

3.318 I conceive a sentence—like Frege and Russell—as a function of the expressions it contains.

3.32 A sign is the perceptible aspect of a symbol.

3.321 Two different symbols can therefore have one and the same sign (written or spoken, etc.) in common—in which case each will signify in a different way.

3.322 Using the same sign to signify two different objects can never show a common characteristic. For the sign is of course arbitrary. So we could instead choose two different signs, and then where would there be what was common in the symbolization?

3.323 In ordinary language it often happens that the same word signifies in two different ways—and therefore belongs to two different symbols—or that two words, which signify in different ways, are apparently applied in the same way in the sentence.

Thus the word "is" appears as a copula, as a sign for identity, and as an expression for existence; "exist" appears as an intransitive verb, like "go"; and "identical" appears as an adjective; we speak of *something*, and also of *something* happening.

(In the sentence, "Green is green"—where the first word is a proper name and the last an adjective—not only do these words have different meanings, they are *different symbols.*)

3.324 This is how the most fundamental confusions can easily arise (philosophy is full of them).

3.325 To avoid such errors we must employ a symbolic language that excludes them, by never applying the same sign in different symbols and by not applying signs in the same way that signify in different ways: a symbolic language, that is to say, that obeys the rules of *logical* grammar—of logical syntax.

(The logical symbolism of Frege and Russell is such a language that, however, still does not exclude all errors.)

3.326   To recognize a symbol by its sign we must observe the sense in which it is used.

3.327   The sign determines a logical form only together with its use according to logical syntax.

3.328   An unused sign is meaningless. That is the point of Occam's razor. (When everything behaves as if a sign has meaning, that sign does have a meaning.)

3.33   The meaning of a sign should never play a role in logical syntax. It must be possible to formulate logical syntax without mentioning the *meaning* of a sign; it ought *only* to presuppose the description of the expressions.

3.331   From this observation we get a comprehensive view of Russell's "theory of types" and can see Russell's mistake: in drawing up his symbolic rules, he had to speak about the things his signs mean.

3.332   No sentence can assert anything about itself, because a sentence cannot be contained in itself (that is the essence of the "theory of types").

3.333   A function cannot be its own argument because the sign for a function already contains the prototype of its argument, and so cannot contain itself.

   If, for example, we suppose that the function $F(fx)$ could be its own argument, there would then be a sentence "$F(F(fx))$" in which case the outer function F and inner function F must have different meanings; for the inner has the form $\phi(fx)$ and the outer one has the form $\psi(\phi(fx))$. The two functions have only the letter "F" in common, which by itself signifies nothing.

   This is immediately clear if instead of "$F(F(fu))$" we write "$(\exists\phi):F(\phi u).\phi u = Fu$".
   Hereby Russell's paradox vanishes.

3.334   All the rules of logical syntax become self-evident once we know how every single sign signifies.

3.34   A sentence has essential and accidental features.

The accidental features arise in the way the sentence is produced, the essential features are the ones without which the sense of the sentence would be lost.

3.341   What is essential about a sentence is what all sentences that can express the same sense have in common.

   Likewise, generally, what is essential about a symbol is what all symbols capable of fulfilling the same function have in common.

3.3411   So one could therefore say that the real name is that which all symbols that signify an object have in common. It would then follow, step by step, that no sort of composition at all would turn out to be essential to the name.

3.342   In our notations there is indeed something arbitrary, but *this* is not arbitrary; namely, that *if* we have determined anything arbitrarily, then something else *must* necessarily be the case. (This results from the *essence* of the notation.)

3.3421   A particular method of symbolizing may be unimportant, but that it is a *possible* way of symbolizing is always important. And that's the way it often goes in philosophy: again and again the particular detail turns out to be unimportant, whereas the possibility of each detail discloses something essential about the world.

3.343   Definitions are rules for the translation of one language into another. Every correct symbolism must be translatable into every other according to such rules. *This* is what they all have in common.

3.344   A symbol signifies in virtue of what is common to all those symbols by which it can be replaced according to the rules of logical syntax.

3.3441   Here is how we can express what is common to all notations for truth-functions: for instance, it is common to them that they all *can be replaced* by the notations of "~p" ("not p") and "p v q" ("p or q").

(This indicates the way in which a special possible notation can supply us with general information.)

3.3442 The sign of a complex cannot be arbitrarily resolved in the analysis in such a way that its resolution would be different in every sentential structure.

3.4 A sentence determines a place in logical space. The existence of this logical place is guaranteed by the existence of the expressions of which the sentence is composed—by the existence of the meaningful sentence.

3.41 The sentential sign with logical coordinates: that is the logical place.

3.411 Both in geometry and in logic, a place is a possibility: something can exist in it.

3.42 Although a sentence may determine only one place in logical space, the whole logical space must already be given by it.

(Otherwise negation, logical sum, logical product, etc., would always introduce new elements—in coordination.)

(The logical scaffolding around the picture determines the whole logical space. The sentence reaches through the whole logical space.)

3.5 A sentential sign, applied and thought, is a thought.

4 A sentence that makes sense is a thought.

4.001 The totality of sentences is the language.

4.002 Human beings possess the capacity of constructing languages in which every sense can be expressed without our having any idea how and what each word means, just as we speak without knowing how the individual sounds are produced.

Ordinary language is a part of the human organism and no less complicated than it.

It is humanly impossible to gather from it the logic of language.

Language disguises thought, so that from the external form of the clothes one cannot infer the form of the thought beneath, because the external form of the clothes is designed not to reveal the form of the body but for different purposes.

The silent adjustments to understand ordinary language are extremely complicated.

4.003 Most of the statements and questions found in philosophy are not false but nonsensical. We cannot, therefore, answer such questions at all but only show them to be nonsensical. Most questions and statements of the philosophers result from our inability to understand the logic of our language.

(They are of the same variety as the question, "Is the Good more or less identical than the Beautiful?")

No wonder that the deepest problems are actually *not* problems.

4.0031 All philosophy is a "critique of language." (But not at all in Mauthner's sense.) Russell's merit is to have shown that the apparent logical form of a sentence need not be its real form.

4.01 A sentence is a picture of reality.

A sentence is a model of reality as we think it is.

4.011 At first glance a sentence—say as it is laid out on the printed page—does not seem to be a picture of the reality that it is about. But neither does the musical score appear at first glance to be a picture of a musical piece; nor does our phonetic spelling (the letters of the alphabet) seem to be a picture of our spoken language. And yet these symbolisms turn out to be pictures—even in the ordinary sense of the word—of what they represent.

4.012 Obviously, a sentence of the form "aR b" looks like a picture. Here the sign is obviously a likeness of what is signified.

4.013 And if we penetrate into the essence of this visualization, we see that it is not hindered by *apparent irregularities* (such as the use of ♯'s and ♭'s in musical notation).

For even these irregularities depict what they are to express, only in a different way.

4.014 The gramophone record, the musical thought, the score, the sound waves, all stand to one another in that internal relation of depicting that holds between language and the world.

They all have the logical structure in common.

(Like the two youths, their two horses, and their lilies in the fairy tale. In a certain sense they are all one.)

4.0141 In the fact that there is a general rule by which the musician is able to read the symphony from the score, and that there is a rule by which one can reconstruct the symphony from the grooves in the gramophone record and from this again—by means of the first rule—construct the score, herein lies the internal similarity between these things that at first glance seem so completely different. And the rule is the law of projection that projects the symphony into the language of the musical score. It is the rule of translation of this language into the language of the gramophone record.

4.015 The possibility of all similes, of all the imagery of our language, rests on the logic of representation.

4.016 To understand the essential nature of a sentence, consider hieroglyphic writing, which pictures the facts it describes.

And from it came the alphabet without the essence of the representation being lost.

4.02 This we see from the fact that we understand the sense of a sentence without having had it explained to us.

4.021 A sentence is a picture of reality, for if I understand the sentence, I know the fact represented by it. And I understand the sentence without its sense having been explained to me.

4.022 A sentence *shows* its sense.

A sentence *shows* how things are *if* it is true. And it *says* that that is how they are.

4.023 A sentence determines reality to the degree that one only needs to say "yes" or "no" to it, and nothing more, to make it agree with reality.

Reality must therefore be completely described by the sentence.

A sentence is the description of a fact.

Just as a description describes an object by its external properties, so a sentence describes reality by its internal properties.

A sentence constructs a world with the help of a logical scaffolding, so that one can actually see in the sentence all the logical features of reality *if* it is true. One can *draw conclusions* from a false sentence.

4.024 To understand a sentence means to know what is the case if it is true.

(One therefore understands it independently of knowing whether it is true.)

One understands the sentence if one understands its expressions.

4.025 The translation of one language into another is not a process of translating each sentence of one language into a sentence of the other language but only the constituent parts.

(And the dictionary translates not only substantives but also adverbs and conjunctions, etc., and it treats them all alike.)

4.026 The meanings of simple signs (the words) must be explained to us before we can understand them.

By means of sentences we explain ourselves.

4.027 It is essential to sentences that they can communicate a new sense to us.

4.03 A sentence must communicate a new sense with old words.

A sentence communicates a fact to us, therefore it must be *essentially* concerned with the fact.

And the connection is that it is its logical picture.

A sentence asserts something only insofar as it is a picture.

4.031 In a sentence the fact is, as it were, put together as an experiment.

Instead of saying "The sense of this sentence is such and such," we can say, "This sentence represents such and such a fact."

4.0311 One name stands for one thing, and another for another, and they are connected together. And so the whole—like a *tableau vivant* [living picture]—presents an elementary fact.

4.0312 The possibility of sentences is based upon the principle that things are represented by their signs.

My fundamental thought is that the "logical constants" do not represent anything, that the *logic* of the facts cannot be represented.

4.032 A sentence is a picture of its fact only insofar as it is logically articulated.

(Even the sentence "ambulo" is composite, for with a different ending its stem yields a different sense, as does its ending with a different stem.)

4.04 In a sentence there must be exactly as many things distinguishable as there are in the fact that it represents.

They must both possess the same logical (mathematical) multiplicity. (Compare Hertz's *Mechanics* on dynamic models.)

4.041 Naturally, this mathematical multiplicity cannot itself be represented. Yet one cannot miss it in the representation.

4.0411 Say we wanted to express what is expressed by "$(x).f(x)$" by putting an index in front of "fx", like: "Gen.fx", it simply would not do, for we would not know what was generalized. If we tried to show by an index "$_g$", like:

"$f(x_g)$", it still would not do, for we would not know the scope of the generalization.

Suppose we tried to do it by introducing a mark into the argument places, like

"$(G,G).F(G,G)$",

it would not do: we could not determine the identity of the variables, etc.

All these ways of symbolizing are inadequate because they do not have the requisite mathematical multiplicity.

4.0412 Likewise, the idealist explanation of the seeing of spatial relations through "spatial glasses" does not work, because it cannot explain the multiplicity of these relations.

4.05 The reality is compared with the sentence.

4.06 Sentences can be true or false only by being pictures of the reality.

4.061 If one does not notice that sentences make sense independently of the facts, one can easily believe that true and false are relations of equal value between signs and what the signs represent.

One could then say, for instance, that "p" truly signifies what "$\sim p$" falsely signifies, etc.

4.062 Can we not make ourselves understood by means of false sentences just as we have done up to now with true ones, so long as we know that they are meant to be false? No! For a sentence is true when what it asserts is the case; and if by "p" we mean "$\sim p$" and that's what is the case, then "p" in the new conception is true and not false.

4.0621 But it is important that the signs "p" and "$\sim p$" *can* say the same thing. For it shows that the sign "$\sim$" corresponds to nothing in reality.

That negation occurs in a sentence is not enough to characterize its sense ($\sim\sim p = p$).

The sentences "p" and "$\sim p$" have opposite senses, but one and the same reality corresponds to them.

4.063 Here is an analogy to illustrate the concept of truth. A black spot on white paper; the form of the spot can be described by saying for each point on the sheet whether it is black or white. To the fact that some point is black corresponds a positive fact, and to the fact that some point is white (not black) corresponds a negative fact. If I indicate a point on the sheet (a Fregean truth-value) this corresponds to the supposition presented for judgment, etc., etc.

However, to be able to say whether a point is black or white, I must first know under what conditions a point is called white or black; I cannot say "p" is true (or false), unless I know in advance the circumstances in which "p" is called true, and in so doing I determine the sense of the sentence.

The point at which this simile breaks down is this: we can still pick a point on the paper even if we don't know what black and white are; but to a sentence that does not make sense, there corresponds nothing at all, for it signifies nothing (a truth-value) whose properties are called "false" or "true"; the verb of the sentence is not "is true" or "is false", as Frege thought, but that which "is true" must already contain the verb.

4.064 Every sentence must *already* have a sense; assertion cannot give it a sense, for what it asserts is the sense itself. The same goes for negation, etc.

4.0641 One can say: the negation must already be related to the logical place determined by the negated sentence.

The negating sentence determines a *different* logical place from the negated sentence.

The negating sentence determines a logical place using the logical place of the negated sentence by describing it as lying outside its logical place.

That the negated sentence can again be negated shows that what is negated is already a sentence and not just something assumed in advance of the sentence.

4.1 A sentence presents the existence and nonexistence of elementary facts.

4.11 The totality of true sentences is the whole of natural science (or the totality of the natural sciences).

4.111 Philosophy is not one of the natural sciences.

(The word "philosophy" must mean something that stands above and below the natural sciences, not alongside them.)

4.112 The goal of philosophy is the logical clarification of thought. Philosophy is not a theory but an activity. A philosophical work consists essentially of clarifications.

The end result of philosophy is not a number of "philosophical sentences" but to make sentences clear.

Philosophy should make clear and sharpen the contrast of thoughts that are otherwise opaque and blurred.

4.1121 Psychology is no more related to philosophy than is any other natural science.

The theory of knowledge is the philosophy of psychology.

Does not my study of symbolism correspond to the study of thought processes that philosophers have held to be so essential to the philosophy of logic? Only they got involved for the most part in inessential psychological investigations, and there is an analogous danger with my method.

4.1122 The Darwinian theory has nothing to do with philosophy, any more than does any hypothesis in the natural sciences.

4.113 Philosophy limits the domain of natural science.

4.114 It must limit the thinkable and thereby the unthinkable.

It must limit the unthinkable from within through the thinkable.

4.115 It will show what cannot be said by clearly presenting all that can be said.

4.116 Everything that can be thought at all can be thought clearly. Everything that can be said can be said clearly.

4.12 Sentences can represent the whole reality, but they cannot represent what they must have in common with reality to be able to represent it—the logical form.

To be able to represent logical form, we would have to be able to place ourselves with sentences outside logic, that is, outside the world.

4.121 Sentences cannot represent the logical form; the logical form mirrors itself in the sentences.

Language reflects what it cannot represent.

That which expresses *itself* in language, *we* cannot express by means of language.

Sentences *show* the logical form of reality.

They exhibit it.

4.1211 Thus a sentence "*fa*" shows it is about *a,* two sentences "*fa*" and "*ga*" show they are about the same object.

If two sentences contradict each other, their structure shows it; likewise, if one of them implies the other. And so on.

4.1212 What *can* be shown *cannot* be said.

4.1213 Now we understand our feeling that we possess the right logical conception, if only all is right in our symbolism.

4.122 In some sense we can talk about formal properties of objects and elementary facts, or about the structural properties of facts and about relations of form and restructure.

(Instead of "structural property" I can just as well say "internal property"; instead of "structural relation," "internal relation." I introduce these expressions to show the reason for the confusion between internal relations and proper (external) relations, so common among philosophers.)

However, one cannot use sentences to assert such internal properties and relations; rather, this shows itself in the sentences that present the relevant facts and objects in question.

4.1221 An internal property of a fact can be called a feature of that fact (in the sense that we speak of facial features).

4.123 A property is internal if it is logically impossible for its object to not possess it.

(One shade of blue and another stand, *eo ipso*, in the internal relation of lighter to darker. It is logically inconceivable that those two objects could not be related in this fashion.)

(Here to the shifting use of the words "property" and "relation" there corresponds the shifting use of the word "object.")

4.124 The internal property of a possible fact cannot be expressed using sentences; rather, it shows *itself* in the sentence that presents the statement, by means of an internal property of that sentence.

It would be as nonsensical to ascribe a formal property to a sentence as to deny it the formal property.

4.1241 Forms cannot be distinguished from one another by saying that one has this or that property and the other does not, for this presupposes that either property can be ascribed to either form.

4.125 That an internal relation holds between possible facts expresses itself in language by means of the internal relation that holds between the sentences that present them.

4.1251 Now this settles the disputed question, "Are all relations internal or external?"

4.1252 A series ordered by an *internal* relation I call a formal series.

The number series is governed not by an external relation but by an internal one.

The same holds of the series of sentences

$$\text{``}aRb\text{''}$$
$$\text{``}(\exists x){:}aRx.xRb\text{''}$$
$$\text{``}(\exists x,y){:}aRx.xRy.yRb\text{''},$$
and so on.

(If *b* is related to *a* in one of these ways, I call *b* a successor of *a*.)

4.126 In the same sense that we can speak of formal properties, we can now speak of formal concepts.

(I introduce this expression to show the source of confusion between formal concepts and proper concepts, which infects all of traditional logic.)

Something's being an instance of a formal concept cannot be expressed by a sentence but is shown in the sign for that object. (The name shows that it designates an object, the numeral that it designates a number, etc.)

Unlike actual concepts, formal concepts cannot be presented by a function.

This is because their marks—formal properties—cannot be expressed using functions.

The expression of a formal property is an internal property of certain symbols.

A mark of a formal concept is symbolized by a distinctive internal property of all sentences that include instances of the concept.

The expression of a formal concept is a sentential variable in which this distinctive internal property alone is constant.

4.127 The sentential variable signifies the formal concept and its values signify the objects that are its instances.

4.1271 Each variable is a sign for a formal concept.

Each variable represents the constant form of its values, which can be viewed as the formal properties of the values.

4.1272 The variable name "*x*" is thus the actual sign for the pseudoconcept, *object*.

Whenever the word "object" ("thing," etc.) is used correctly, it is expressed by a variable name in conceptual notation.

For instance, in the sentence "There exist 2 objects that . . . ," it is expressed by "$(\exists x,y) \ldots$"

Used as an actual concept-word, it creates nonsensical pseudosentences.

Thus for instance we cannot say "There are objects," in the way we say "There are books." And it is equally impossible to say "There are 100 objects" or "There are χ objects."

And it makes no sense to speak of the *total number of objects*.

This also applies to words like "complex," "fact," "function," "number," etc.

These all refer to formal concepts and are represented in conceptual notation not by functions or classes (as Frege and Russell believed) but by variables.

"1 is a number," "There is only one zero," and all similar expressions are nonsense.

(To say "There is only one 1," "2 + 2 at 3 o'clock equals 4," would be equally nonsense.)

4.12721 The formal concept is already given by an object that is an instance of the formal concept.

Therefore it is impossible to introduce as primitive ideas both the formal concept and the objects that are instances of it. For example, one cannot introduce as primitive ideas both the concept of a function and specific functions, as Russell does, or the concept of a number along with particular numbers.

4.1273 To express the general sentence "b is a successor of a" in logical notation, we need an expression for the general term of the formal series

$$\text{``}aRb\text{''}$$
$$\text{``}(\exists x){:}aRx.xRb\text{''}$$
$$\text{``}(\exists x,y){:}aRx.xRy.yRb\text{''},$$
$$\cdots$$

To express a general term of a formal series, we must use a variable because the concept "term of the formal series" is itself a *formal* concept. (This is what Frege and Russell overlooked; their way of expressing such general sentences is wrong; it contains a vicious circle.)

We can determine the general term of a formal series by stating its first term along with the general form of the operation by which the next term can be produced out of the preceding sentence.

4.1274 It makes no sense to ask whether a formal concept exists. For there is no sentence that could possibly answer this question.

(For example, one cannot ask, "Are there unanalyzable subject-predicate sentences?")

4.128 Logical forms are uncountable.

Therefore, in logic there are no pre-eminent numbers, and therefore there is no philosophical monism or dualism, etc.

4.2 The sense of a sentence is in its agreement and disagreement with the possibilities of the existence and nonexistence of elementary facts.

4.21 The simplest sentence, the elementary sentence, asserts the existence of an elementary fact.

4.211 It is a characteristic of an elementary sentence that no elementary sentence can contradict it.

4.22 An elementary sentence consists of names. It is a connection, a linkage of names.

4.221 Obviously, in analyzing sentences, we must arrive at elementary sentences consisting of names in immediate connection.

This raises the question of how such sentential connections arise.

4.2211 Even if the world is infinitely complex, so that every fact consists of infinitely many elementary facts and every elementary fact consists of infinitely many objects, even so there must be objects and elementary facts.

4.23 A name occurs in a sentence only in the context of an elementary sentence.

4.24 Names are the simplest symbols, and so I indicate them by single letters ("x", "y", "z").

An elementary sentence I write as a function of names in the form "f(x)", "ϕ(x,y)", etc.

Or I indicate it by the letters "p", "q", "r".

4.241 When I use two different signs to signify one and the same object, I indicate this by placing the sign "$=$" between them.

Thus, "$a = b$" means that the sign "b" can be substituted for the sign "a".

(If I use an equation to introduce a new sign "b", saying that this will be a substitute for some already known sign "a", then (like Russell) I write the definition of the equation in the form "$a = b$ Def". A definition is a rule about signs.)

4.242 Expressions having the form "$a = b$" are merely expedient aids in presentation;

they assert nothing about the significations of the signs "*a*" and "*b*".

4.243 Can we understand two names unless we know whether they signify the same object or two different objects? Can we understand a sentence containing two names without knowing whether they signify the same thing or not?

If I know that an English word and a German word signify the same thing, then it is impossible for me not to know that they are synonymous, it is impossible for me not to be able to translate them into one another.

Expressions like "*a* = *a*", and others derived from them, are not elementary sentences, nor is there any other way in which they could make sense. (This will be shown later.)

4.25 If the elementary sentence is true, the elementary fact exists; if the elementary sentence is false, the elementary fact does not exist.

4.26 The specification of all true elementary sentences describes the world completely. The world is completely described by the specification of all elementary sentences plus the specification of which ones are true and which false.

4.27 With respect to the existence and nonexistence of *n* elementary facts, there are

$$Kn = \sum_{v=0}^{n} \binom{n}{v}$$

possibilities.

It is possible for all combinations of elementary facts to exist, and for the others not to exist.

4.28 To these combinations correspond an equal number of possibilities of truth—and falsehood—for *n* elementary sentences.

4.3 Truth—possibilities of elementary sentences signify the possibilities of the existence and nonexistence of elementary facts.

4.31 We can show truth—possibilities by the following sort of schemata ("T" means "true,"

"F" means "false"; the columns of T's and F's under the row of elementary sentences symbolize their truth—possibilities perspicuously):

p	*q*	*r*
T	T	T
F	T	T
T	F	T
T	T	F
F	F	T
F	T	F
T	F	F
F	F	F

p	*q*
T	T
F	T
T	F
F	F

p
T
F

4.4 A sentence is an expression of agreement and disagreement with the truth-possibilities of elementary sentences.

4.41 The truth-possibilities of elementary sentences are the conditions of the truth and falsehood of the sentence.

4.411 It is likely that the introduction of the elementary sentences provides the foundation for understanding all other kinds of sentences. Indeed, understanding general sentences *obviously* depends on an understanding the elementary sentences.

4.42 With respect to the agreement and disagreement of a sentence with the truth-possibilities of n elementary sentences, there are

$$\sum_{k=o}^{Kn} \left(\frac{K}{k}\right) = Ln$$

possibilities.

4.43 Agreement with truth-possibilities can be expressed by correlating the mark "T" (true) with them in the schema.

The absence of this mark means disagreement.

4.431 Formulation of the truth-possibilities of the elementary sentences expresses the truth-conditions of the sentence.

The sentence is the expression of its truth-conditions.

(Frege was therefore right to put them at the beginning, as explaining the signs of his *Begriffsschrift* [logical notation]. But Frege's explanation of the concept of truth is false: if "the true" and "the false" were real objects and the arguments in ~p, etc., then the sense of "~p" would in no way be determined by Frege's determination.)

4.44 The sign resulting from the correlation of the mark "T" with the truth-possibilities is a sentential sign.

4.441 Clearly, a complex of the signs "F" and "T" has no corresponding object (or complex of objects), just as no objects correspond to the horizontal and vertical lines [as in 4.31] or to the brackets [as in 5.461]. There are no "logical objects."

Naturally, the same applies to all signs expressing what is expressed by the schemata of T's and F's.

4.442 For instance, the following is a sentential sign:

" p	q	
T	T	T
F	T	T
T	F	
F	F	T "

(Frege's assertion sign "|-" is logically altogether meaningless: in Frege (and in Russell) it only shows that these authors hold as true the sentences marked in this way. "|-" belongs as little to the sentences as their number. A sentence cannot possibly assert of itself that it is true.)

If the sequence of the truth-possibilities in the schema is fixed by a rule of combination, then the last column is by itself an expression of the truth-conditions. Writing this column as a row, the sentence becomes:

"(TT-T)(p, q)" or, more clearly "(TTFT)(p,q)".

(The number of terms in the right-hand pair determines the number of places in the left-hand pair.)

4.45 For n elementary sentences, there are L_n possible groups of truth-conditions.

The groups of truth-conditions that belong to the truth-possibilities of a given number of elementary sentences can be ordered into a series.

4.46 Among the possible groups of truth-conditions are two limiting cases.

In one case the sentence is true for all the truth-possibilities of the elementary sentences: the truth-conditions are *tautological*.

In the second case the sentence is false for all truth-possibilities: the truth-conditions are *self-contradictory*.

In the first case we call the sentence a tautology; in the second case we call it a contradiction.

4.461 A sentence shows what it says; a tautology and a contradiction show that they say nothing.

Because a tautology is true unconditionally, it has no truth-conditions; likewise, on no condition is a contradiction true.

Tautologies and contradictions do not make any sense.

(Like a point with two arrows emerging in opposite directions.)

(For example, in knowing that it is either raining or not raining, I know nothing about the weather.)

4.4611 However, neither are tautologies nor contradictions nonsensical. They belong to the symbolism, just as "O" belongs to the symbolism of arithmetic.

4.462 Tautologies and contradictions are not pictures of the reality. They present no possible facts. For tautologies admit *all* possible facts, and contradictions admit *none.*

In the tautology the conditions of agreement with the world—the presenting relations—cancel each other out, so that in the tautology no aspect of reality can present itself.

4.463 The truth-conditions of a sentence determine the play left to the facts.

(The sentence, the picture, the model are in a negative sense like a solid body, which restricts the free movement of another; in a positive sense, they are like a bound space into which a body may be placed.)

A tautology leaves the whole infinite logical space open to reality; a contradiction fills in the whole logical space, leaving no point to reality. Thus neither of them can determine reality in any way.

4.464 The truth of tautology is certain, that of sentences possible, and that of contradiction impossible.

(Certain, possible, impossible: here we have a hint of the gradation needed in probability theory.)

4.465 The logical product of a tautology and a sentence says the same thing as the sentence. This logical product is therefore identical with the sentence. For the essence of a symbol cannot be altered without altering its sense.

4.466 A definite logical combination of signs corresponds to a definite logical combination of the objects signified by the signs (their semantic content).

That is, sentences that are true for every fact [i.e., tautologies] cannot be combinations of signs at all, for otherwise only particular combinations of objects would correspond to them.

(And there isn't any logical combination to which there corresponds *no* combination of the designated objects.)

Tautology and contradiction are the limiting cases of the combinations of signs, their point of disintegration.

4.4661 Of course the signs are still combined even in tautologies—that is, they stand in certain relations to one another, but these relations are meaningless, in no way are they essential to the symbol.

4.5 We are in a position now to state the most general form of a sentence—that is, to describe the sentence of any symbolic language whatsoever such that every sense can be expressed by a symbol satisfying the description and every symbol satisfying the description can express a sense, provided that the signification of each name is well chosen.

Clearly, only what is essential to the most general form of a sentence may be included in its description—otherwise, it would not be the most general form.

The existence of a general form of a sentence is proved in that no sentence can be given whose form could not have been foreseen (i.e., constructed). The general form of a sentence is soandso is the case.

4.51 Suppose *all* elementary sentences were given me: then we can simply ask what sentences I can build out of them. And these are *all* the sentences and *that* is how they are bound.

4.52 Sentences are all that follows from the totality of elementary sentences (and of course from its being the *totality of then all*). (Thus we might say that in a certain sense *all* sentences are generalizations of elementary sentences.)

4.53 The general form of a sentence is a variable.

5 A sentence is a truth-function of elementary sentences.

(An elementary sentence is a truth-function of itself.)

5.01 Elementary sentences are the truth-arguments of sentences.

5.02 It is quite natural to confuse the arguments of functions with the indices of names. For I recognize equally well from the argument and from the index what is meant by the signs containing them.

In Russell's "$+_c$", for instance, "c" is an index indicating that the whole sign is the addition sign for cardinal numbers. But this way of symbolizing is an arbitrary convention, and we could have chosen a simple sign instead of "$+_c$". In "$\sim p$", on the other hand, "p" is not an index but an argument: the sense of "$\sim p$" *cannot* be understood unless one already understands the sense of "p". (In the name Julius Caesar, "Julius" is an index. The index is always part of the description of the designated object to whose name we attach it, for example, *the* Caesar of the Julius gens.)

The confusion of argument and index stems, unless I am mistaken, from Frege's theory about the meaning of sentences and functions. For Frege, the sentences of logic are names and their arguments are the indices of these names.

5.1 The truth-functions can be ordered in a series.

This is the foundation for the theory of probability.

5.101 The truth-functions of every number of elementary sentences can be arranged in the following sort of schema:

(TTTT) (p,q) Tautology (if p then p, and if q then q)
[$p \supset p.q \supset q$]
(FTTT)(p,q) in words: Not both p and q.   [$\sim(p.q)$]
(TFTT) (p,q) ″   ″ If q then p. [$q \supset p$]
(TTFT) (p,q) ″   ″ If p then q. [$p \supset q$]
(TTTF) (p,q) ″   ″ p or q. [$p \lor q$]
(FFTT) (p,q) ″   ″ Not q. [$\sim q$]
(FTFT) (p,q) ″   ″ Not p. [$\sim p$]

(FTTF) (p,q) in words: p or q, but not both.
[$p. \sim q\text{: v: } q. \sim p$]
(TFFT) (p,q) ″   ″ If p, then q; and if q, then p.
[$p \equiv q$]
(TFTF) (p,q) ″   ″ p
(TTFF) (p,q) ″   ″ q
(FFFT) (p,q) ″   ″ Neither p nor q.
[$\sim p. \sim q$ or $p|q$]
(FFTF) (p,q) ″   ″ p and not q.   [$p. \sim q$]
(FTFF) (p,q) ″   ″ q and not p.   [$q. \sim p$]
(TFFF) (p,q) ″   ″ p and q. [$p.q$]
(FFFF) (p,q) Contradiction (p and not p; and q and not q.)   [$p. \sim p.q. \sim q$]

The truth-possibilities of a sentence's truth-arguments that make the sentence true I shall call its *truth-grounds*.

5.11 If the truth-grounds common to several sentences are also the truth-grounds of some one sentence, then we say that the truth of that sentence follows from the truth-grounds of the others.

5.12 In particular, the truth of a sentence "p" follows from the truth of a sentence "q" if all the truth-grounds of "q" are the truth-grounds "p".

5.121 The truth-grounds of q are extracted from the truth-grounds of p: p follows from q.

5.122 If p follows from q, the sense of "p" is extracted from the sense of "q".

5.123 If God creates a world in which certain sentences are true, then God thereby creates a world in which all the sentences that follow from them are true. Similarly, God could not create a world in which sentence "p" were true without creating all the objects designated by it.

5.124 A sentence affirms every sentence that follows from it.

5.1241 "$p.q$" is one of the sentences that affirms "p" while also affirming one of the sentences that affirms "q".

Two sentences oppose each other when no meaningful sentence affirms them both.

5.13 Whether the truth of one sentence follows from the truth of other sentences can be seen in the structure of the sentences.

5.131 That the truth of one sentence follows from the truth of others is expressed by relations in which the forms of those sentences stand to one another: nor need we set up these relations between them by combining them with one another into a single sentence. These relations are internal and exist simultaneously with, and through, the existence of the sentences.

5.1311 When from p v q and $\sim p$ we infer q, the relation between the forms of the sentences "p v q" and "$\sim p$" is concealed by our method of symbolizing. But if instead of "p v q" we write "$p|q.|.p|q$" and instead of "$\sim$p" we write "$p|p$" (where "$p|q$ = neither p nor q, then the inner connection [the inference from $(p|q.|.p|q)$ and $(p|p)$ to $(q|.q|q)$] becomes apparent.

(The possibility of inference from $(x).fx$ to fa to fa shows us that the symbol $(x).fx$ has itself generality already in it.)

5.132 If p follows from q, I can make an inference from q to p, deduce p from q.

The manner of inference can only be drawn from the two sentences.

Only they alone can offer any possible justification for the inference.

"Laws of inference," which—as in Frege and Russell—supposedly justify inferences, are senseless and completely superfluous.

5.133 All inference takes place a priori.

5.134 From an elementary sentence no other can be inferred.

5.135 There is no possible way to make an inference from the existence of one fact to the existence of another, entirely different, fact.

5.136 There is no causal linkage to justify any such inference.

5.1361 The future *cannot* be inferred from the present.

Superstition is the belief in causal "linkage."

5.1362 Free will consists in the impossibility of our knowing future actions now. Future actions could only be known if causality were a form of logical inference and had some such *inner* necessity. The connection between knowledge and the known is that of logical necessity.

("A knows that p is the case" makes no sense if p is a tautology.)

5.1363 If the truth of a sentence does not *follow* from the fact of its seeming obvious to us, then obviousness in no way justifies our belief in its truth.

5.14 If a sentence follows from another, then the latter says more than the former and the former says less than the latter.

5.141 If p follows from q and q follows from p, then they are one and the same sentence.

5.142 A tautology follows from all propositions: it says nothing.

5.143 A contradiction is that which is common to sentences that *no* sentence has in common with any other. A tautology is that which is common to all sentences that have nothing in common with each other.

Contradiction vanishes, so to speak, outside, and tautology inside, all sentences.

Contradiction is the outer boundary of sentences; tautology is the insubstantial point at their center.

5.15 If Tr is the number of truth-grounds of sentence "r", Trs the number of truth-grounds of sentence "s" that are at the same time truth-grounds of "r", then let us call the ratio $Trs: Tr$ the measure of the *probability* given by sentence "r" to sentence "s".

5.151 In a schema like the one in 5.101, let Tr be the number of "T's" in sentence s that stand in those columns where sentence r

has "T's". Then sentence *r* gives to sentence *s* the probability *Trs: Tr*.

5.1511 There is no separate object unique to probability sentences.

5.152 Sentences that have no truth-arguments in common with each other we call independent.

Two elementary sentences give each other the probability ½.

If p follows from q, then sentence "*q*" gives sentence "*p*" the probability 1. The certainty of the logical conclusion is a limiting case of probability.

(Application to tautology and contradiction.)

5.153 A sentence is in itself neither probable nor improbable. An event occurs or does not occur, there is no middle course.

5.154 An urn contains an equal number of black balls and white balls. I draw one ball after another and put them back in the urn. Then I can determine by the experiment that the number of black balls drawn and the number of white balls drawn approximate each other as the drawing continues.

So *this* is not a mathematical truth.

If then I say, "It's equally probable that I will draw a white and a black ball," this means, "all the circumstances known to me (including the laws of nature that I assume by hypothesis to be true) give to the occurrence of the one event no *more* probability than to the occurrence of the other. That is, they give—as can easily be seen from the above explanations—to each event the probability ½.

What I can verify by the experiment is that the occurrence of the two events is independent of the circumstances about which I have only schematic knowledge.

5.155 The unit for a probability statement is: the circumstances—which I only know in part—give a certain degree of probability to the occurrence of a particular event.

5.156 Thus probability is a generalization.

It involves a general description of the form of a sentence.

We use probability in place of certainty—our knowledge of a fact may be incomplete, but at least we know *something* about its form.

(A sentence may be an incomplete picture of a certain fact, but it is always *a* complete picture.)

A probability sentence is, as it were, an extract from other sentences.

5.2 The structures of sentences stand to one another in internal relations.

5.21 We can emphasize these internal relations in our form of expression, by representing one sentence as the result of an operation that produces it out of other sentences (the bases of the operation).

5.22 The operation is the expression of a relation between the structures of its result and of its bases.

5.23 The operation is what has to happen to a sentence to turn it into another one.

5.231 Naturally, that will depend on their formal properties, the internal similarity of their forms.

5.232 A series is ordered by an internal relation equivalent to that of generating one term from another.

5.233 There can be no other than truth-functional operations.

5.234 The truth-functions of the elementary sentences are the results of operations with the elementary sentences as bases. (These operations I call truth-operations).

5.2341 The sense of a truth-function of p is a function of the sense of p.

Negation, logical addition, logical multiplication, etc., etc., are operations.

(Negation reverses the sense of sentences.)

5.24 An operation shows itself in a variable; it shows how we can get from one sentence form to another.

It expresses the difference between the forms.

(And the bases themselves are what the bases of an operation and the result have in common.)

5.241 An operation does not characterize a form but only the difference between forms.

5.242 The same operation that produces "q" from "p" produces "r" from "q", and so on. There is but one way of expressing this: "p", "q", "r", etc., are variables that give general expression to certain formal relations.

5.25 The occurrence of an operation does not characterize the sense of a sentence.

For the operation does not assert anything, only its result does, and this depends on the bases of the operation.

(Operation and function must not be confused with one another.)

5.251 A function cannot be its own argument, but the result of an operation can be the base of that very operation.

5.252 This is the only possible way of stepping from one term of a formal series to a term in another formal series (from type to type in the hierarchies of Russell and Whitehead). (Russell and Whitehead did not allow such steps but took them repeatedly themselves.)

5.2521 When an operation is repeatedly applied to its own results, I call it a *successive application*. (Thus, "$0'0'0'a$" is the end result of three successive applications of the operation "$0'\xi$" to "a".)

Similarly, I speak of the successive application of *multiple* operations to a number of sentences.

5.2522 For the general term of the formal series a, $0'a$, $0'0'a$, ... I use the sign "$[a, x, 0'x]$". The bracketed expression is a variable. The first term marks the beginning of the formal series, the second is the form of a term x selected arbitrarily from the formal series, and the third is the formal term immediately following x in the series.

5.2523 The concept of the successive application of an operation is equivalent to the concept "and so on."

5.253 One operation can reverse the effect of another. Operations can cancel each other out.

5.254 Operations can vanish (e.g., negation in "$\sim\sim p$".$\sim\sim p = p$).

5.3 All sentences are the result of truth-operations on the elementary sentences.

The truth-operation is the way in which a truth-function arises from elementary sentences.

According to the nature of truth-operations, truth-functions generate further truth-functions in the same way that elementary sentences generate their own truth-functions. Every truth-operation creates from truth functions of elementary sentences another truth-functions of elementary sentences, that is, another sentence. The result of every truth-operation on the results of truth-operations on elementary sentences is also the result of one truth-operation on elementary sentences.

Every sentence is the result of truth-operations on elementary sentences.

5.31 The schemata in 4.31 are also meaningful even when "p", "q", "r", etc., are not elementary sentences.

And one can easily see that the sentence in 4.442 expresses a single truth-function of elementary sentences even when "p" and "q" are truth-functions of elementary sentences.

5.32 All truth-functions are results of successive applications of a finite number of truth-operations to elementary sentences.

5.4 It is here that the nonexistence of "logical objects" or "logical constants" (in the sense of Frege and Russell) shows itself.

5.41 For: all results of truth-operations on truth-functions are always identical whenever they are one and the same truth function of elementary sentences.

5.42 That v, ⊃, etc., are not relations in the sense of right and left, etc., is obvious.

The possibility of defining crosswise the primitive signs of Frege and Russell shows by itself that they are not primitive nor do they signify any relations.

And it is obvious that the "⊃" that we define by means of "~" and "v" is identical with that by which we define "V" with the help of "; ~", and that this second "v" is identical with the first, and so on.

5.43 That from a fact *p* infinitely many *others* should follow, namely, ~~*p*, ~~~~*p*, etc., seems impossible. And it seems even stranger that the infinite number of sentences of logic (mathematics) follow from half a dozen "primitive sentences."

Actually, all the sentences of logic say the same thing. Namely, nothing.

5.44 Truth-functions are not material functions.

If, for an example, a double negation is an affirmation, is the negation—in any sense—contained in the affirmation? Does "~~*p*" negate ~*p*, or does it affirm *p*, or both?

In no sense is the sentence "~~*p*" about negation, for negation is not an object; on the other hand, the possibility of negation is already presupposed in affirmation.

And if there were an object called "~", then "~~p" would have to say something different from what "*p*" says, since in that case the one sentence would be about ~ and the other would not.

5.441 The disappearance of apparent logical constants happens also in "~($\exists x$).~*fx*", which is equivalent to "(*x*).*fx*", and in "($\exists x$).*fx.x*; = *a*", which is equivalent to "*fa*".

5.442 When a sentence is given us, so is given *with* it the results of all truth-operations that have it as their basis.

5.45 If logical primitive signs, then any correct logic must clearly show their relative status and justify their presence [*Dasein*]. The construction of logic *out of* its primitive signs must be clearly shown.

5.451 If logic has primitive ideas, these must be independent of one another. If a primitive idea is introduced, it must be introduced for all the contexts in which it occurs at all. One cannot therefore introduce it first for *one* context and then again for another.

For instance, once negation is introduced it must be clearly understandable both in sentences of the form "~*p*" and in sentences like "~*p* v *q*)", "($\exists x$).~*fx*", etc. We cannot introduce it first for one class of cases and then all over again for the other, for then it would be very doubtful whether the term meant the same in both cases, and there would be no ground for using the same kind of connective in both cases.

(In short, what Frege said [in *The Fundamental Laws of Arithmetic*] about the introduction of signs by means of definitions holds, *mutatis mutandis*, for the introduction of primitive signs.)

5.452 The introduction of any new device into the symbolism must always be a momentous event. No new symbol may be "innocently" introduced in logic using brackets or in a footnote with a perfectly innocent face.

(Thus in *Principia Mathematica* Russell and Whitehead suddenly present a definition and a fundamental law in words. Why the sudden appearance of words? It requires justification but of course they don't give any because they can't, the whole procedure is forbidden.)

But if at some point there is a need for a new symbol, we must first ask: when will the use of this device now become unavoidable? Its proper place in logic must be clearly shown.

5.453 All use of numbers in logic requires justification.

Or, on the contrary: it must be cleared up that there are no numbers in logic.

There are no privileged numbers.

5.454 In logic there is no side-by-side and no classification can be given.

In logic no distinction can be made between the general and the specific.

5.4541 The solutions to logical problems should be simple, since they set the standard of simplicity.

People have always quietly accepted the idea that there must be a realm in which answers to all questions fit perfectly together—a priori—into a closed, regular structure.

A domain ruled by one law: "Simplicity is the hallmark of truth."

5.46 When we have properly introduced the logical signs, we have introduced the sense of all their combinations at the same time; that is, not only "pvq" but "~(pv~q)" as well, etc., etc. We should then already have introduced the effect of all possible combinations of brackets; and we would thereby have made clear that the proper general primitive signs of logic are not "pvq", "(∃(x).fx", etc., but rather the most general form of their combinations.

5.461 The apparently unimportant fact that logical pseudorelations like v and ⊃—unlike real relations—need brackets is significant.

The use of brackets with these apparently indefinable signs indicates that they are not the real indefinable signs of logic. And surely no one could believe that brackets have an independent meaning.

5.4611 The logical operation signs are punctuation marks.

5.47 Clearly, whatever can be said *from the very* beginning about the form of all sentences, must be sayable *all at once.*

All logical operations can be expressed in terms of the elementary sentences themselves. For "*fa*" says the same thing as

$$\text{"}(\exists x).fx.x = a\text{".}$$

Where there is complexity, there is argument and function, and where these are present, there are already all the logical constants.

One could say: the sole logical constant is what *all* sentences, by their nature, have in common.

This however is the general form of a sentence.

5.471 The general form of a sentence is the essence of a sentence.

5.4711 The essence of a sentence gives the essence of all description and therefore reveals the essence of the world.

5.472 The description of the most general form of a sentence is itself the description of the one and only general primitive sign in logic.

5.473 Logic must take care of itself.

If a sign is *possible*, it is capable of signifying something. Everything that is possible in logic is also permitted. ("Socrates is identical" does not mean anything because there is no such quality as "identical". The sentence is nonsensical because we have not made some arbitrary determination but not because of the symbol being impermissible in itself.)

That is the sense in which we cannot make mistakes in logic.

5.4731 The self-evidence that Russell talked so much about can be completely dispensed with in logic because language itself absolutely forbids all logical mistakes. What makes logic a priori is the impossibility of thinking illogically.

5.4732 We cannot give the wrong sense to a sign.

5.47321 Naturally, Occam's razor is no arbitrary rule, nor one that is merely justified by successful application: its message is that *unnecessary* signs in a symbolic language are meaningless, they refer to nothing.

5.4733 Frege says: any well-formed sentence must have a sense; and I say: every possible sentence is well-formed, and if it doesn't make sense, that can only be because we have failed to give any reference for some of its constituents.

(Even if we think we have.)

Thus, "Socrates is identical" says nothing, because we have given *no adjectival* meaning to the word "identical." For when it appears as a sign for identity, it symbolizes in an entirely different way—the signifying relation is different—therefore the symbol is in the two cases entirely different; the two symbols have the sign in common with one another only by accident.

5.474 The number of fundamental operations we need depends *solely* on our notation.

5.475 We need only construct a system of signs with the right number of dimensions—with a fitting mathematical variety.

5.476 Clearly, then, the question is not how many fundamental ideas have to be given expression, but rather how to express a rule.

5.5 Each truth-function is a result of successive applications of the operation

$$\text{``}(\text{-----}\mathrm{T})(\xi,\dots)\text{''}.$$

This operation negates all the sentences in the right-hand brackets and so I call it the negation of those sentences.

5.501 When the terms of a bracketed expression are sentences—and their order inside the brackets is irrelevant—I indicate this by a sign of the form "$(\bar{\xi})$". "ξ" is a variable whose values are terms of the bracketed expression and the bar over it signifies that it is the representative of all the values inside the brackets.

(E.g., if ξ has three values, P, Q, and R, then

$$(\bar{\xi}) = (\mathrm{P,Q,R}).)$$

The values of the variable are prescribed.

The prescription is a description of the sentences having the variable as their representative.

We can distinguish three types of description: 1. Direct enumeration. In this case we substitute for the variable the constants that are its values. 2. Giving a function fx whose values for all values of x are the sentences that are to be described. 3. Giving a formal law, according to which those sentences are constructed, in which case the bracketed expression has as its members all the terms of a formal series.

5.502 Instead of "$(\text{-----}\mathrm{T})(\xi,\dots)$", I can thus write "$\mathrm{N}(\bar{\xi})$".

"$\mathrm{N}(\bar{\xi})$" is the negation of all the values of the sentence variable ξ.

5.503 It is obviously easy to express using this operation how sentences may and may not be constructed. So it must be possible to express this exactly.

5.51 If ξ has but one value, then $\mathrm{N}(\bar{\xi}) = \sim p$ (not p); if it has two values, then $\mathrm{N}(\bar{\xi}) = \sim p . \sim q$ (neither p nor q).

5.511 How can the all-embracing logic that mirrors the world rely on so many special hooks and manipulations? Only because all these devices are all connected into an infinitely fine network, the great mirror.

5.512 "$\sim p$" is true when "p" is false. Therefore, in the sentence "$\sim p$", when true, "p" is false. How then can the stroke "$\sim$" make it agree with reality?

Here's how: in "$\sim p$" it is not the "$\sim$" that negates but, rather, the negating is done by what all the signs of this notation have in common.

That is, the common rule governing the construction of "$\sim p$", "$\sim\sim\sim p$", "$\sim pv \sim p$", "$\sim p . \sim p$", etc., ad infinitum, is the common factor that mirrors the negation.

5.513 It could be said that what is common to all symbols that assert p as well as q, is the sentence "$p.q$", and that what is common to all symbols that affirm either p or q is the proposition "$p \vee q$".

And in this way we can say: two sentences are opposed to one another, if they have nothing in common and: every sentence has only one negative, because there is only one sentence that lies entirely outside it.

In Russell's notation, too, it appears evident that "$q.p \vee \sim p$" is equivalent to "q", that "$pv \sim p$" says nothing.

5.514 If a notation is established, there is in it a rule that governs how all the sentences that negate p are constructed, a rule that governs the construction of all sentences that affirm p, a rule that governs the construction of all sentences that affirm p or q, and so on. These rules are equivalent to the symbols and in them their sense is mirrored.

5.515 It must be shown in our symbols that only sentences can be combined with each other by "v", "." [and], etc.

And this is indeed so, for the symbol *p* in *p* v *q* itself presupposes "v", "~", etc. If the sign "*p*" in "*p* v *q*" does not stand for a complex sign, then by itself it cannot make sense. But then the signs "*p* v *p*", "*p.p*", etc., whose sense must be the same as *p*'s, must also not make sense. But if "*p* v *p*" does not make sense, then "*p* v *q*" cannot make sense either.

5.5151 Does the sign of a negative sentence have to be constructed by means of the sign of the positive? Couldn't we use a negative fact to express a negative sentence? (Like: if "*a*" does not stand in a certain relation to "*b*", then we could rely on this Act to express that *aRb* is not the case.)

Yet even in such a case the negative sentence is constructed by our relying indirectly on the positive.

The positive *sentence* necessarily presupposes the existence of the negative *sentence* and *vice versa*.

5.52 Suppose the value of ξ are all the values of a given function *fx* for all values of x, then $N(\bar{\xi}) = \sim (\exists x). fx$.

5.521 I separate the concept *all* from the truth-function.

Frege and Russell introduced generality together with logical product or logical sum. This made the sentences "$(\exists x).fx$" and "$(x).fx$", which involve both concepts, difficult to understand.

5.522 What is most peculiar about the generality sign is that it indicates a logical archetype and, second, that it draws attention to constants.

5.523 The sign for generality appears as an argument.

5.524 Once objects are given, that itself gives us *all* objects.

Once elementary sentences are given, that in itself is enough for *all* elementary sentences to be given.

5.525 It is wrong to render the sentence "$(\exists x).fx$" in the words, "*fx* is *possible*," as Russell does.

Certainty, possibility or impossibility of a fact are expressed, not by a sentence, but by an expression's being a tautology, a meaningful sentence, or a contradiction.

The precedent to which one would always like to appeal must reside in the symbol itself.

5.526 The world can be completely described using fully generalized sentences, that is, without first correlating any name with a particular object.

Then, to arrive at the ordinary mode of expression, we simply need to add, after sentences like "There is an *x* and there are not an *x* and a *y*, such that . . . ," the words "and this *x* is *a*."

5.5261 A fully generalized sentence is composite just as every other sentence is. (This shows itself in that "$(\exists x,\phi).(\phi x)$" mentions "$\phi$" and "*x*" separately. Both signs independently stand in a signifying relation to the world, as in ungeneralized sentences.)

A characteristic of a composite symbol: it has something in common with *other* symbols.

5.5262 The truth or falsehood of *every* sentence alters something about the general structure of the world. And the play that is allowed to its structure by the totality of elementary sentences is just that which is limited by the completely general statements.

(If an elementary sentence is true, then, at any rate, there is *one more* elementary sentence that is true.)

5.53 Identity of the object I express by identity of the sign and not by means of a sign of identity. Difference of the objects I express by difference of the signs.

5.5301 That identity is not a relation between objects is obvious. This becomes very clear if, for example, one considers the sentence" $(x):fx.\supset.x = a$". This sentences says simply that *only a* satisfies function *f*, not that only objects having a certain relation to *a* satisfy function *f*.

One might then say that *only a* has this relation to *a*, but this would have to be expressed using the identity sign.

5.5302 Russell's definition of "=" is unsatisfactory, because according to it we cannot assert of two objects that all their properties are in common. (Even if this sentence is never right, it still makes sense.)

5.5303 Roughly put: to assert that *two* objects are identical is nonsense, whereas to assert that *one* thing is identical with itself says nothing.

5.531 I also don't write "$f(a,b).a = b$" but "$f(a,a)$" (or, "$f(b,b)$"). And it's not "$f(a,b).\sim a = b$", but "$f(a,b)$". Likewise, I do not write "$(\exists x,y). f(x,y).x = y$", but, rather, "$(\exists x).f(x,x)$"; and it's not "$(\exists x,y).f(x,y). \sim x$, eq y" but "$(\exists x.y).f(x,x)$"; and it's not "$(;fxx,y).f(x,y). \sim x = y$", but "$(\exists x.y).f(x,y)$".

5.532 And analogously: not "$(\exists x,y).f(x,y).x = y$" but "$(\exists x).f(x,x)$"; and not "$(\exists x,y).f(x,y).\sim x = y$" but "$(\exists x,y).f(x,y).$"

(Thus Russell's "$(\exists x,y).fxyxy$" becomes "$(\exists x,y).f(x,y).v.(\exists x).f(x,x)$".)

5.5321 Thus "$(x):f(x)\supset x = a$" can be written, for instance, "$(\exists x).f(x).\supset.fa:\sim(\exists x,y).fx.fy$".

And the sentence "*Only one x* satisfies *f( )*" will be: "$(\exists x).fx:\sim(\exists x,y).fx.fy$".

5.533 Therefore, the identity sign is not an essential part of logical notation.

5.534 And now we see that pseudosentences such as "$a = a$", "$a = b. b = c.\supset a = c$", "$(x).x = x$", " $(\exists x).x = a$", etc., cannot even be written down using correct conceptual notation.

5.535 This clears up all the problems having to do with such pseudo-sentences.

The resolution of all problems having to do with Russell's "axiom of infinity" can now be given.

What the Axiom of Infinity is supposed to show would be expressed in language by there being infinitely many names with different meanings.

5.5351 In some cases it may be tempting to use expressions of the form "$a = a$" or "$p\supset p$" and other such expressions. This is exactly what happens when one wants to say something about the archetype Sentence, Thing, etc. So Russell in his *Principles of Mathematics* renders nonsense such as "*p* is a sentence" symbolically as "$p\supset p$", and then places it in front of sentences as an antecedent hypothesis so as to show that their places for arguments can only be occupied by sentences.

(It is meaningless to use "$p\supset p$" as an antecedent to ensure that the arguments of the consequent will have the right form. First, with a non-sentence as argument, the antecedent becomes not merely false but meaningless; second, using the wrong sort of arguments makes the sentence itself meaningless. So in this way it saves itself from the wrong arguments just as well, or as badly, as the meaningless antecedent that was supposed to have done this in the first place.)

5.5352 Similarly, some have tried to express the thought "There are no things" by writing "$\sim(\exists x).x = x$". If this were actually a sentence, wouldn't the sentence be just as true if "there *were* things" but such that no thing was identical with itself?

5.54 In their general form, sentences occur in other sentences only as bases of truth-operations.

5.541 At first glance, it appears as if there were another way in which one sentence could occur in another.

Especially in certain forms of sentences in psychology, such as "A believes that p is the case" or "A thinks p," etc.

Here it appears superficially as if the sentence p stood in some sort of relation to an object A.

(And these sentences have actually been so taken in modern theory of knowledge [Russell, Moore, etc.].)

5.542 Clearly, however, "A believes that p," "A thinks p," "A says p," are of the form "p says p," and this in no way involves a correlation of fact to object, but rather the correlation of facts by means of the correlation of their objects.

5.5421 This also shows that the soul—the subject, etc.—as conceived in contemporary superficial psychology, does not exist.

For a composite soul would no longer be a soul.

5.5422 The correct explanation of the form of the sentence "A judges that p" must show the impossibility of a judgment being a piece of nonsense. (Russell's theory does not satisfy this condition.)

5.5423 Perceiving a complex means perceiving the way its components are related.

This also explains the sort of phenomena illustrated by the following figure, which can be seen as a cube in two different ways:

For we really see two different facts.

(If I look first at the corners marked *a* and only glance at the *b's*, the *a's* appear in front and vice versa.)

5.55 The question about all the possible forms of elementary sentences must now be answered a priori.

Elementary sentences consist of names. However, since we cannot specify the number of names having different meanings, we cannot give the composition of elementary sentences.

5.551 One fundamental principle is this: whenever we can answer a question using logic we must be able to answer it without a lot of fuss.

(And if we ever have to look at the world for the answer to such a question, this shows us that we have gone off on a completely wrong track.)

5.552 The "experience" we need to understand logic is not that soandso is the case, but simply that it *is:* that, however, is not an experience.

Logic precedes every experience— that something is soandso.

It is before the How, not before the What.

5.5521 If this were not the case, how could we apply logic? Let me put it this way: since even if there were no world there would still be logic, how could it possibly be the case that there be logic given that there is a world?

5.553 Russell said that there were simple relations between different numbers of things (individuals). But between what numbers? And how is this to be decided? By experience? (There is no privileged number.)

5.554 To enumerate any specific forms would be entirely arbitrary.

5.5541 Russell supposes it is possible to answer a priori the question whether I can get into a situation in which I need the sign for a relation having 27 terms to signify something.

5.5542 But can it even be legitimate to ask such a question? How can we set up a form of a sign unless we first know that it is possible that something corresponds to it?

Does it make any sense to ask what must there *be* such that something can be the case?

5.555 It is clear that we have a concept of elementary sentences independently of their particular logical forms.

But when we have a system for creating symbols, what is most important for logic is the system itself, not the individual symbols it produces.

And in any case, how could logic demand that I must deal with forms that I can invent? Logic demands that I must deal with that which makes it possible for me to invent forms.

5.556 There can be no hierarchy of forms of elementary sentences. We can only foresee what we ourselves can construct.

5.5561 Empirical reality is bounded by the totality of objects. This boundary reveals itself throughout the totality of elementary sentences.

The hierarchies are and must be independent of reality.

5.5562 If we know on purely logical grounds that there must be elementary sentences, this must be known by anyone who understands sentences in their unanalyzed form.

5.5563 All the sentences of ordinary language are actually, just as they are, logically and completely in order. The completely simple thing that we must here formulate is not a mere likeness of the truth but the truth in its totality.

(Our problems are not abstract but, on the contrary, about as concrete as you can get.)

5.557 The *application* of logic is what decides what elementary sentences there are.

Logic cannot foresee in advance what belongs to its application.

Clearly, logic must never collide with its application.

But logic must always remain in touch with its application.

Therefore, logic and its application must not overlap each other.

5.5571 Since I cannot make a list of elementary sentences a priori, any attempt to make such a list must lead to nonsense.

5.6 *The boundary of my language* is the boundary of my world.

5.61 Logic fills the world: the boundary of logic is also the boundary of the world.

So in logic we cannot say "The world has this in it and this, but not that."

For that would apparently presuppose that some possibilities were thereby being excluded, which cannot possibly be the case, since this would require that logic should extend beyond the boundary of the world; for only then could it have a view from the other side of the boundary.

What we cannot think, that we cannot think: we cannot therefore *say* what we cannot think.

5.62 This thought itself shows how much truth there is in solipsism.

What the solipsist intends to say is absolutely correct. The problem is that the truth cannot speak but only shows itself.

That the world is my world reveals itself in the fact that the boundary of language (the language that I alone understand) is the boundary of my world.

5.621 The world and life are one.

5.63 I am my world. (The microcosm.)

5.631 The thinking, perceiving subject does not exist.

If I were to write a book, *The World as I Found It*, I would also have to include an account of my body in it, and report which parts are subject to my will and which are not, etc. This then would be a method of isolating the subject, or rather of showing that in an important sense there is no subject; that is to say, of it alone in this book mention could *not* be made.

5.632 The subject does not belong to the world but is the boundary of the world.

5.633 Where *in* the world could a metaphysical subject be?

You say this is just like the case with the eye and the visual field. But you do *not* really see the eye.

And there is nothing *in the visual field* to let you infer that it is being seen through an eye.

5.6331 For the form of the visual is clearly not like this:

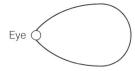

Eye

5.634 This is connected with the fact that no aspect of our experience is a priori.

Everything we see could be other than it is.

Everything we describe could be other than it is.

There is no arrangement of things a priori.

5.64 Here we can see that solipsism thoroughly thought out coincides with pure realism. The *I* in solipsism shrinks to an extensionless point and there remains the reality coordinated with it.

5.641 Thus there really is a sense in which philosophy can speak about the self in a nonpsychological way.

The *I* occurs in philosophy through the fact that the "world is my world."

The philosophical *I* is not the human being, not the human body, nor the human soul with which psychology deals. The philosophical self is the metaphysical subject, the boundary—nowhere in the world.

6 The general form of a truth-function is $[\bar{p},\bar{\xi},N(\bar{\xi})]$.
This is the general form of a sentence.

6.001 This says only that every sentence is the result of successive applications of the operation $N'\bar{\xi}$ to the elementary sentences.

6.002 If we are given the general form of the way in which a sentence is constructed, then we are thereby also given the general form of the way in which by an operation out of one sentence we can create another.

6.01 The general form of the operation Ω' (*mmmm*) is therefore:

$$[\bar{\xi},N],\bar{\xi}'\,(n)\,(=[n,\bar{\xi}\,N\,(\bar{\xi})]).$$

This is the most general form of transition from one sentence to another.

6.02 And thus we come to numbers: I define

$$x = \Omega^0,\, x \,\text{Def. and}$$
$$\Omega'\Omega^y,\, x = \Omega^{y+1},\, x\,\text{Def.}$$

According, then, to these symbolic rules write the series $x,\, \Omega'x,\, \Omega'\Omega'x,\, \Omega'\Omega'\Omega'x \ldots .$
as: $\Omega^0,\, x,\, \Omega^{0+1},\, x,\, \Omega^{0+1+1},\, x,\, \Omega^{0+1+1+1},\, x \ldots .$
Therefore I write in place of "$[x, \xi, \Omega'\,\xi]$",
"$[\Omega^0, x, \Omega^y, x, \Omega^{y}+1, x]$".
And I define:
$$0 + 1 = 1\,\text{Def.}$$
$$0 + 1 + 1 = 2\,\text{Def.}$$
$$0 + 1 + 1 + 1 = 3\,\text{Def.}$$
and so on.

6.021 A number is the exponent of an operation.

6.022 The concept "number" is simply what is common to all numbers, the general form of a number.

The concept "number" is the variable number.

And the concept of numerical equality is the general form of all particular cases of numerical equality.

6.03 The general form for integers is $[0,\xi,\xi + 1]$.

6.031 The theory of classes is altogether superfluous in mathematics.

This is connected with the fact that the generality that we need in mathematics is not an *accidental* one.

6.1 The sentences of logic are tautologies.

6.11 The sentences of logic therefore say nothing. (They are analytic sentences.)

6.111 Theories that make a sentence of logic appear to have real content are always false. It might be thought, for example, that the words "true" and "false" denote two properties among other properties, and then it would look like a remarkable fact that every sentence possesses one of these properties. This now seems no more obvious than the sentence "All roses are either red or yellow" would seem, even if it were true. Indeed, the logical sentence acquires all the characteristics of a sentence of natural science, and this is a sure sign that it has been wrongly construed.

6.112 The correct explanation of logical sentences must give them a peculiar position among all sentences.

6.113 It is the characteristic mark of logical sentences that one can perceive in the symbol alone that they are true; and this fact contains in itself the whole philosophy of logic. And so also it is one of the most important facts that the truth or falsehood of nonlogical sentences can *not* be recognized from the sentences alone.

6.12 The fact that the sentences of logic are tautologies shows the formal—logical—properties of language, of the world.

That its constituent parts connected together *in this way* form a tautology is a characteristic of its constituent parts.

To be able to form a tautology, sentences connected together in a definite way must have definite properties of structure. That they form a tautology when *so* connected shows therefore that they possess these properties of structure.

6.1201 That for example the sentences "*p*" and "~*p*" in the conjunction "~(*p*.~*p*)" from a tautology shows that they contradict each other. That the sentences "*p*⊃*q*" "*p*", and "*q*" conjoined into "(*p*⊃*q*) . (*p*):u2):*q*)" form a tautology shows that *q* follows from *p* and *p*⊃*q*. That "(*x*),*fx*: ⊃: *fa*" forms a tautology shows that *fa* follows from (*x*). *fx*. etc., etc.

6.1202 Clearly, we could have used for this purpose contradictions instead of tautologies.

6.1203 To recognize a tautology as such, we can, in cases in which no sign of generality occurs in the tautology, make use of the following intuitive method: I write instead of "*p*", "*q*", "*r*", etc., " *TpF*", "*TqF*", "*TrF*", etc. The truth-combinations I express by brackets, for example:

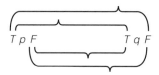

and the coordination of the truth or falsity of the whole sentence with the truth-combinations of the truth-arguments by lines in the following way:

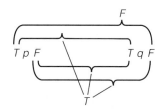

This sign, for example, would therefore present the sentence *p*⊃*q*. Now I will proceed to inquire whether a sentence such as ~(*p*. ~*p*) (The Law of Contradiction) is a tautology. The form "~ξ" is written in our notation

the form "ξ. *n*" thus:

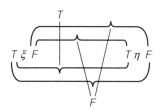

Hence the sentence~$(p. \sim q)$ runs thus:

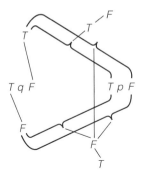

If here we put "p" instead of "q" and examine the combination of the outermost T and F with the innermost, it is seen that the truth of the whole sentence is coordinated with *all* the truth-combinations of its argument, its falsity with none of the truth-combinations.

6.121 The sentences of logic demonstrate the logical properties of sentences, by combining them into sentences that say nothing.

This could be called a zero-method. Sentences are brought into equilibrium in a logical sentence, and then this state of equilibrium shows how these sentences must be logically constructed.

6.122 This shows that we can carry on without logical sentences, since in proper notation we can recognize the formal properties of the sentences merely by inspecting them.

6.1221 If, for example, two sentences "p" and "q" form a tautology, then clearly q follows from p.

For instance, that "q" follows from "$p\sim.q.p$" can be seen from these two sentences themselves, but we can also show it by combining them into "$p\sim q.p:\sim:q$" and then showing that this is a tautology.

6.1222 This throws light on the question of why logical sentences can no more be confirmed empirically than they can be refuted empirically. Not only must a sentence of logic be incapable of being contradicted by any possible experience, it must likewise be incapable of being confirmed by experience.

6.1223 It becomes clear now why we often feel as though "logical truths" must be "*postulated*" by us. Actually, we can postulate them insofar as we can postulate a proper notation.

6.1224 It now also becomes clear why logic was thought of as the theory of forms and of inference.

6.123 Clearly, the laws of logic cannot themselves obey further logical laws.

(Russell was wrong in supposing that there is a special law of contradiction for every "type"; one law is sufficient, since it is not applied to itself.)

6.1231 General validity is *not* the mark of logical sentences.

For to be general only means to be accidentally valid for all objects. An ungeneralized sentence can be a tautology just as well as a generalized one.

6.1232 General logical validity could be called essential rather than the accidental general validity of sentences like "All people are mortal." Sentences like Russell's "axiom of reducibility" are not logical sentences, which explains our feeling that, if true, they can only be true by lucky coincidence.

6.1233 We can conceive a world in which the axiom of reducibility is invalid. But clearly, logic has nothing to do with the question of whether our world is really like that or not.

6.124 The sentences of logic describe the scaffolding of the world, or rather, they present it. They are not *about* anything. They presuppose that names mean something, that elementary sentences make sense [express thoughts]: and that is their connection to the world. Clearly, that some combinations of essentially determinate symbols are tautologies says something about the world. That's the decisive point. We said that in the symbols that we use, there is something arbitrary, something not. In logic only the latter expresses; but this means that in logic it is not *we* who express, by means of signs, what we want; in logic the nature of inevitably necessary signs *speaks for itself.* Thus in learning the logical syntax of any symbolic language we are *given* all the sentences of logic.

6.125 It is possible, even with the old conception of logic, to give from the start a description of all "true" logical sentences.

6.1251 Hence there can *never* be surprises in logic.

6.126 By calculating the logical properties of the *symbol,* we can calculate whether a sentence belongs to logic.

And that's what we do when we "prove" a sentence in logic. For without bother about sense and meaning, we form the logical sentences out of others by mere *symbolic rules.*

Here is how we prove a sentence in logic: we create it out of other sentences by successively applying certain operations that again generate tautologies out of the first. (Only a tautology can *follow* from a tautology.)

6.1261 In logic, process and result are equivalent. (Hence, no surprises.)

6.1262 Proof in logic is nothing but a mechanical procedure for facilitating the recognition of it as a tautology.

6.1263 Indeed, it would be an incredible coincidence if a meaningful sentence could be proved *logically* from others, just as a sentence in logic can. Clearly, proving logically that some meaningful sentence is true is completely different from a proof in logic.

6.1264 The meaningful sentence asserts something, and its proof shows that it is so; in logic every sentence is the form of a proof.

Every sentence in logic is a symbolic presentation of a *modus ponens.* (And the *modus ponens* cannot be expressed by a sentence.)

6.1265 Logic can always be conceived in such a way that every sentence is its own proof.

6.127 All sentences in logic are of equal rank, rather than some being essentially primitive from which the others are derived.

Every tautology shows itself that it is a tautology.

6.1271 Clearly, the number of "primitive sentences of logic" is arbitrary, since we could deduce logic from one primitive sentence simply by forming, for example, the logical product of Frege's primitive sentences. (Frege might say that this would no longer be immediately self-evident. But what is amazing is that a thinker as precise as Frege nevertheless appealed to the degree of selfevidence as his criterion of what a logical sentence is.)

6.13 Logic is not a theory about the world but a reflection of it, its mirror image.

Logic is transcendent.

6.2 Mathematics is a logical method.

Mathematical sentences are equations and, therefore, pseudo-statements.

6.21 Mathematical sentences express no thoughts.

6.211 In our daily lives we never need mathematical sentences, we use them only to infer from sentences that are not a part of mathematics to other sentences that also are not mathematical.

(In philosophy the question "Why do we really use that word, that sentence?" always leads to valuable insights.)

6.22 The logic of the world that the sentences of logic show to be tautologies, mathematics shows to be equations.

6.23 If two expressions are connected by the sign of equality, this means that they can be substituted for one another. But whether this is the case must be visible in the two expressions themselves.

That two expressions can be substituted for one another characterizes their logical form.

6.231 A property of affirmation is that it can be conceived as double denial.

A property of "$1 + 1 + 1 + 1$" is that it can be conceived as "$(1 + 1) + (1 + 1)$."

6.232 According to Frege, all these expressions have the same meaning but different senses.

But what is essential about an equation is that it is not necessary to show that both expressions, which are connected by the sign of equality, have the same meaning: this can be seen from the two expressions themselves.

6.2321 And that the sentences of mathematics can be proved means nothing more than this: their correctness can be seen without our having to compare the sentences, what they express, with the facts, in terms of correctness.

6.2322 The identity of the meaning of two expressions cannot be *asserted*. To be able to assert anything about their meaning, I must first know their meaning, and if I already know their meaning, I then know whether they mean the same or something else.

6.2323 The equation merely characterizes the point of view from which I consider the two expressions, that is, from the point of view of their equality of meaning.

6.233 The question of whether we need intuition for the solution of mathematical problems must be answered in this way: here language itself is the necessary intuition.

6.2331 The process of calculation brings about just this intuition.

Calculation is not an experiment.

6.234 Mathematics is a method of logic.

6.2341 The essence of the mathematical method is working with equations. As a consequence of this method, every sentence in mathematics must be self-evident.

6.24 The way mathematics arrives at its equations is by the method of substitution.

For equations express the substitutability of two expressions, and we proceed from a number of equations to new ones, replacing expressions by others in accordance with the equations.

6.241 Thus the proof of the proposition $2 \times 2 = 4$ runs:

$$(\Omega^\nu)^{\mu'} x = \Omega^{\nu \cdot \iota x\, \mu'} x \, \text{Def.}$$
$$\Omega^{2 \times 2'} x = (\Omega^2)^{2'} x = (\Omega^2)^{1 + 1'} x = \Omega^{2'}\Omega^{2'} x =$$
$$\Omega^{1 + 1'} x$$
$$= (\Omega'\Omega)' (\Omega'\Omega)' x = \Omega'\Omega'\Omega'\Omega' x =$$
$$\Omega^{1 + 1 + 1 + 1'} x = \Omega^{4'} x.$$

6.3 The investigation of logic means the investigation of *all* conformity to *laws*. And outside logic, all is accident.

6.31 The so-called law of induction cannot in any way be a logical law, for obviously it is a meaningful sentence. And therefore it cannot be an a priori law either.

6.32 The law of causality is not a law but the form of a law.

6.321 "Law of causality" is a general name. And just as in mechanics there are, for instance, minimum-laws, such as that of least action, so in physics there are causal laws, laws of the form of causality.

6.3211 People thought that there must be *a* "law of least action" even before they knew exactly what it was. (Here, as always, a priori certainty turns out to be something purely logical.)

6.33 We do not *believe* a priori in a law of conservation; rather, we *know* a priori the possibility of a logical form.

6.34 All sentences, such as the law of causation, the law of continuity in nature, the law of least expenditure in nature, etc., etc., all these are a priori intuitions of possible forms of sentences in science.

6.341 Newtonian mechanics, for instance, brings the description of the universe into a unified form. Imagine a white surface with irregular black spots. We then say: Whatever kind of picture these make I can always get as near as I like to its description, provided I cover the surface with some sufficiently fine square network and then say of each square that it is either white or black. In this way I bring the description of the surface into a unified form. The form itself is arbitrary because I could have applied with equal success a net with, say, a triangular or hexagonal mesh. It might be that the description would then have been simpler, that is, we might well have described the surface more accurately with a triangular and coarser, rather than with the finer, square mesh, or vice versa, and so on. To such different networks correspond different systems of describing the world. Mechanics determine a form of description by saying that all sentences in the description of the world must be obtained in a given way from a certain number of already given sentences, the mechanical axioms. It thus provides the bricks for building the edifice of science and says: Whatever building you would erect, you must construct it in some manner with these, and only these, bricks.

(Just as within the system of numbers we must be able to write down any arbitrary number, so within the system of mechanics we must be able to write down any arbitrary physical sentence.)

6.342 And now we can see the position of logic in relation to mechanics. (We construct the network out of indifferent kinds of figures, such as triangles and hexagons together.) That such a picture can be described by a network of a given form asserts *nothing* about the picture. (For this

holds of every picture of this kind.) But *this* does characterize the picture in that it can be described *completely* by a particular net with a *particular* size mesh.

Likewise, that the world can be described by Newtonian mechanics says nothing about the world, but it does say something, namely, that the world can be described in that particular way. The fact, too, that the world can be described more simply by one system of mechanics rather than by some other says something about the world.

6.343 Mechanics can be seen as an attempt to construct according to a single plan all *true* sentences that we need for the description of the world.

6.3432 Let us not forget that the mechanical description of the world must always be general. There is, for instance, never any mention of *particular* material points in it, but always only of *some points or other*.

6.35 Although the spots in our picture are geometrical figures, geometry can obviously say nothing about their actual form and position. But the network is *purely* geometrical, and all its properties can be given a priori.

Laws, like the law of causation, etc., are of the network and not of what the network describes.

6.36 If there were a law of causality, it might go like this: "There are natural laws."

But clearly, no one can say this: it shows itself.

6.361 In Hertz's terminology we might say: Only *uniform* connections are *thinkable*.

6.3611 We cannot compare any process with the "passage of time"—there is no such thing—but only with another process (say, with the movement of the chronometer).

The description of the temporal sequence of events is thus only possible if we support ourselves on another process.

The same is true of space. When, for instance, we say that neither of two (mutually exclusive) events can occur, because there is *no cause* why one rather than nother should occur, it is clearly a matter of our being unable to describe *one* of the two events unless there is some sort of asymmetry. And if there *is* such an asymmetry, we can regard this as the cause of the occurrence of the one and of the nonoccurrence of the other.

6.63111 The Kantian problem of the right and left hands that cannot cover each other already exists in the plane, and already there even in one-dimensional space where two congruent figures, *a* and *b*, cannot be made to cover each other without moving them out

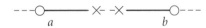

of this space. The right and left hands are in fact completely congruent. And the fact that they cannot be made to cover each other has nothing to do with it.

A right-hand glove could be put on a left hand if it could be turned around in four-dimensional space.

6.362 What can be described can also happen, and what is excluded by the law of causality cannot be described.

6.363 The process of induction is the process of assuming the *simplest* law that can be reconciled with our experience.

6.3631 However, this process has no logical foundation, only a psychological one.

Clearly, there are no reasons for believing that the simplest course of events will really happen.

6.36311 That the sun will rise tomorrow is a hypothesis, which means that we do not *know* whether the sun will rise.

6.37 Nothing forces one thing to happen because something else has happened. The only kind of necessity is *logical* necessity.

6.371 The entire modern worldview is based on the illusion that the so-called laws of nature can explain natural phenomena.

6.372 People thus treat the laws of nature as if they were unassailable, which is how the ancients treated God and Fate.

And they are right but also wrong, except the ancients were far clearer, in that they recognized a clear endpoint—whereas the moderns make it seem as if *everything* is explained.

6.373 The world exists independently of my will.

6.374 Even if everything we wished for would happen, this would only have been granted, so to say, by fate, for there is no *logical* connection between the will and the world that could guarantee such a thing; and the assumed physical connection itself is not something we can will.

6.375 Just as there is only *logical* necessity, so there is only *logical* impossibility.

6.3751 For instance, that two colors could be at one place in the visual field at the same time is logically impossible, since it is excluded by the logical structure of color.

Let us look at how this contradiction presents itself in physics. It goes something like this: That a particle cannot have two different velocities at the same time, i.e., that it cannot be at two different places at the same time, i.e., that particles at different places at the same time cannot be identical.

(Clearly, the logical product of two elementary sentences can be neither a tautology nor a contradiction. The assertion that a point in the visual field is two different colors at the same time is a contradiction.)

6.4 All sentences are of equal value.

6.41 The meaning of the world must lie outside the world. In the world everything is as it is, everything happens as it does happen; there is no value *in* it—if there were any, the value would be worthless.

For a value to be worth something, it must lie outside all happening and outside being this way or that. For all happening and being this way or that is accidental.

The nonaccidental cannot be found in the world, for otherwise this too would then be accidental.

The value of the world lies outside it.

6.42 Likewise, there can be no sentences in ethics. Sentences cannot express anything higher.

6.421 Clearly, ethics cannot be put into words.

Ethics is transcendent.

(Ethics and esthetics are one.)

6.422 As soon as we set up an ethical law having the form "thou shalt . . . ," our first thought is: So then what if I don't do it? But clearly ethics has nothing to do with punishment and reward in the ordinary sense. The question about the consequences of my action must therefore be irrelevant. At least these consequences will not be events. For there must be something right in that formulation of the question. There must be some sort of ethical reward and ethical punishment, but this must lie in the action itself.

6.423 We cannot speak of the will as if it were the ethical subject. And the will as a phenomenon is only of interest to psychology.

6.43 If good or bad willing changes the world, it only changes the boundaries of the world, not the facts, not the things that can be expressed in language.

6.431 In death, too, the world does not change but only ceases.

6.4311 Death is not an event in life. Death is not lived through.

If by *eternity* we mean not endless temporal duration but timelessness, then to live eternally is to live in the present.

In the same way as our visual field is without boundary, our life is endless.

6.4312 The temporal immortality of the human soul—its eternal survival after death—is not only without guarantee, this assumption could never have the desired effect. Is a riddle solved by the fact that I survive forever? Is eternal life not as enigmatic as our present one? The solution of the riddle of life in space and time lies *outside* of space and time.

(Certainly it does not involve solutions to any of the problems of natural science.)

6.432 *How* the world is is completely indifferent to what is higher. God does not reveal himself *in* the world.

6.4321 The facts all belong to the setting up of the problem, not to its solution.

6.44 It's not *how* the world is that is mystical, but *that* it is.

6.45 To view the world *sub specie aeterni* is the view of it as a—bounded—whole.

The feeling of the world as a bounded whole is the mystical feeling.

6.5 If the answer cannot be put into words, the question, too, cannot be put into words.

The *riddle* does not exist.

If a question can be put at all, then it *can* also be answered.

6.51 Skepticism is *not* irrefutable, only nonsensical, insofar as it tries to raise doubts about what cannot be asked.

For doubt can only exist provided there is a question; a question can exist only provided there is an answer, and this can only be the case provided something *can* be *said*.

6.52 We feel that even if *all possible* scientific questions were answered, the problems of life would still not have been touched at all.

To be sure, there would then be no question left, and just this is the answer.

6.521 The vanishing of this problem is the solution to the problem of life.

(Is this not the very reason why people to whom, after long bouts of doubt, the meaning of life became clear, could not then say what this meaning is?)

6.522 The inexpressible indeed exists. This *shows* itself. It is the mystical.

6.53 The right method in philosophy would be to say nothing except what can be said using sentences such as those of natural science—which of course has nothing to do with philosophy—and then, to show those wishing to say something metaphysical that they failed to give any meaning to certain signs in their sentences. Although they would not be satisfied—they would feel you weren't teaching them any philosophy—*this* would be the only right method.

6.54 My sentences are illuminating in the following way: to understand me you must recognize my sentences—once you have climbed out through them, on them, over them—as senseless. (You must, so to speak, throw away the ladder after you have climbed up on it.)

You must climb out through my sentences; then you will see the world correctly.

7 Of what we cannot speak we must be silent.

READING QUESTIONS

1. Wittgenstein writes that "the world is the totality of facts, not of things" (1.1). Why does he say this? Is it true?

2. How do the following metaphysical categories relate to each other: world, fact, elementary fact, object? How are we to understand his remark that "everything exists . . . in a space of possible elementary facts" (2.013)?

3. According to Wittgenstein, what is a picture? What is the difference between the *structure* of a picture and the *form of representation* of a picture?

4. Wittgenstein writes that "a thought is a logical picture of a fact" (3). What does the word "logical" add to this proposition?

5. Wittgenstein uses the term *name* in a very precise way. What does he mean by calling a "simple sign" a name? How are names related to propositions, according to Wittgenstein? What accounts for the significance of a name?

6. "A sentence determines a place in logical space" (3.4). What does this mean and how is it related to his other remarks about the nature or reality of logical space? Is "logical space" a metaphor?

7. At 4.01, Wittgenstein remarks that "a sentence is a picture of reality." How does this remark connect to his earlier discussions of the metaphysical structure of the world, the nature of a picture, and his account of a thought?

8. Review Wittgenstein's remarks about the nature of philosophy from 4.1 to 4.1213. How, if at all, does his conception of philosophy fit his theory of language and his account of the metaphysical structure of the world? Do you agree or disagree with this conception of philosophy? Why?

9. At 4.2, Wittgenstein remarks that "the sense of a sentence is in its agreement and disagreement with the possibilities of the existence and nonexistence of elementary facts." What does he mean by this? Later he remarks that "a sentence is a truth-function of elementary sentences" (5). How, if at all, are these remarks related? In answering these questions, consider the diagram at 5.101 and his remark at 5.32.

10. What argument can be advanced for Wittgenstein's claim at 5.4711 that "the essence of a sentence gives the essence of all description and therefore reveals the essence of the world"?

11. Review 5.6 to 5.641. According to Wittgenstein, *where* and *what* am I? Is the correct answer "*nowhere* and *nothing*"? Carefully justify your interpretation of these difficult passages.

12. Wittgenstein regularly comments on the nature and status of logic throughout the *Tractatus*. He claims that "the sentences of logic are tautologies" and "therefore say nothing" (6.1, 6.11). But he also claims that "logic is not a theory about the world but a reflection of it, its mirror image. Logic is transcendent" (6.13). What does he mean? What

ultimately *is* the status of logic, according to Wittgenstein?

13. Review 6.4 to 6.45. According to Wittgenstein, in what ways are ethics and logic on a similar footing? How do you interpret his remark that "the value of the world lies outside it" (6.41)? Is it true?

14. Carefully read 6.53 to 7, then consider the *Tractatus* as a whole. Are we supposed to conclude that his entire work, as a work of philosophy, is really senseless? If so, how could his sentences be "illuminating" at all?

15. Return to Wittgenstein's "Preface." He writes in the end that "the *truth* of the thoughts communicated here seems to me unassailable and definitive. I therefore believe that the problems have in essentials been finally solved. And if I am not mistaken in this, then the value of this work secondly consists in the fact that it shows how little has been achieved when these problems have been solved." To what problems is he referring? In light of your reading as a whole, in what sense, if any, could the thoughts communicated in the *Tractatus* be true thoughts? Why does Wittgenstein believe that little has been achieved when these problems (whatever they are) have been solved?

SUGGESTIONS FOR FURTHER READING (THE EARLY WITTGENSTEIN)

Primary Sources and Collected Writings

(1912–1951) *Philosophical Occasions*, edited by J. C. Klagge and A. Nordmann. Indianapolis, IN: Hackett, 1993.

(1914–1916) *Notebooks 1914–16*, edited by G. H. von Wright and G. E. M. Anscombe, translated by G. E. M. Anscombe. Oxford: Blackwell, 1961.

(1918) *Tractatus Logico-Philosophicus*, translated by C. K. Ogden and F. P. Ramsey. London: Routledge, 1922. Translated by D. F. Pears and B. F. McGuiness. London: Routledge, 1961.

Secondary Sources

Anscombe, G. E. M. (1959) *An Introduction to Wittgenstein's Tractatus.* London: Hutchinson University Library.

Arrington, R. L., and H. Glock, eds.(1996) *Wittgenstein and Quine.* New York: Routledge.

Black, M. (1964) *A Companion to Wittgenstein's Tractatus.* Cambridge: Cambridge University Press.

Bradley, R. (1995) *The Nature of All Being: A Study of Wittgenstein's Modal Atomism.* Oxford: Oxford University Press.

Fogelin, R. J. (1987) *Wittgenstein*, 2nd ed. London: Routledge.

Glock, H. (1996) *A Wittgenstein Dictionary.* London: Blackwell.

Grayling, A. C. (1988) *Wittgenstein.* Oxford: Oxford University Press.

———(1986) *Insight and Illusion.* Oxford: Oxford University Press.

Hacker, P. M. S. (1999) *Wittgenstein.* London: Routledge.

———. (1996) *Wittgenstein's Place in Twentieth-Century Analytic Philosophy.* Oxford: Blackwell.

Janik, A. (1973) *Wittgenstein's Vienna.* New York: Simon and Schuster.

Kenny, A. (1974) *Wittgenstein.* Cambridge, MA: Harvard University Press.

Monk, R. (1990) *Ludwig Wittgenstein: The Duty of Genius.* New York: Free Press.

Mounce, H. O. (1990) *Wittgenstein's Tractatus: An Introduction.* Chicago: University of Chicago Press.

Pears, D. (1987) *The False Prison.* Oxford: Oxford University Press.

Sluga, H., and D. Stern, eds. (1996) *The Cambridge Companion to Wittgenstein.* Cambridge: Cambridge University Press.

PART III / Positivistic Philosophy

HANS HAHN, RUDOLF CARNAP,
AND OTTO NEURATH

The Scientific Conception of the World: The Vienna Circle

In 1929, Moritz Schlick received an offer of employment from the University of Bonn. Although tempted by the offer, Schlick ultimately chose to decline it and to remain in Vienna so that he could continue his research in philosophy in close consultation with the other members of the Vienna Circle. The offer from Bonn coincided with his trip abroad to Stanford University to spend a year as a visiting professor in the Department of Philosophy. The other leading members of the Vienna Circle (especially Hans Hahn, Rudolf Carnap, and Otto Neurath) were aware that Schlick was seriously considering a move to Bonn and were very pleased to hear that he intended to return from Stanford and to stay in Vienna.

Written primarily by Otto Neurath, *Wissenschaftliche Weltauffassung: Der Wiener Kreis* [The Scientific Conception of the World: The Vienna Circle] was intended both as a statement of philosophic principles and as a gift to Schlick to be given to him upon his return from California in honor of his decision to stay in Vienna. The document has come to have a wider and more lasting historical significance, though, because it constitutes a manifesto, of sorts, of the Viennese positivist movement written by its leading practitioners and advocates.

To the historian of philosophy, the document is valuable for a number of specific reasons: It records, in an easily readable fashion, the positivists' conception of the problems of philosophy, its proper method, and its main lines of inquiry. It also chronicles their conception of the history of philosophy leading up to the formation of the Vienna Circle and names those whom they believe to be sympathetic to their overall philosophical outlook. Equally crucial, it also clearly and concisely explains their position on the unity and importance of the sciences, on the elimination of metaphysics as a field of critical inquiry, and on the collaborative nature of the philosophic enterprise.

PREFACE

At the beginning of 1929 Moritz Schlick received a very tempting call to Bonn. After some vacillation he decided to remain in Vienna. On this occasion, for the first time it became clear to him and us that there is such a thing as the 'Vienna Circle' of the scientific con-

Hans Hahn, Rudolf Carnap, and Otto Neurath, "The Scientific Conception of the World: The Vienna Circle" reprinted from Otto Neurath, *Empiricism and Sociology*, Dordrecht: Kluwer Academic Publishers, 1973, pp. 299–318. Reprinted with kind permission of Kluwer Academic Publishers.

ception of the world, which goes on developing this mode of thought in a collaborative effort. This circle has no rigid organization; it consists of people of an equal and basic scientific attitude; each individual endeavors to fit in, each puts common ties in the foreground, none wishes to disturb the links through idiosyncrasies. In many cases one can deputize for another, the work of one can be carried on by another.

The Vienna Circle aims at making contact with those similarly oriented and at influencing those who stand further off. Collaboration in the Ernst Mach Society is the expression of this endeavor; Schlick is the chairman of this society and several members of Schlick's circle belong to the committee.

On 15–16 September 1929, the Ernst Mach Society, with the Society for Empirical Philosophy (Berlin), will hold a conference in Prague, on the epistemology of the exact sciences, in conjunction with the conference of the German Physical Society and the German Association of Mathematicians which will take place there at the same time. Besides technical questions, questions of principle are to be discussed. It was decided that on the occasion of this conference the present pamphlet on the Vienna Circle of the scientific conception of the world was to be published. It is to be handed to Schlick in October 1929 when he returns from his visiting professorship at Stanford University, California, as token of gratitude and joy at his remaining in Vienna. The second part of the pamphlet contains a bibliography compiled in collaboration with those concerned. It is to give a survey of the area of problems in which those who belong to, or are near to, the Vienna Circle are working.

Vienna, August 1929
For the Ernst Mach Society
Hans Hahn
Otto Neurath   Rudolf Carnap

1. The Vienna Circle of the Scientific Conception of the World

1.1 Historical Background

Many assert that metaphysical and theologizing thought is again on the increase today, not only in life but also in science. Is this a general phenomenon or merely a change restricted to certain circles? The assertion itself is easily confirmed if one looks at the topics of university courses and at the titles of philosophic publications. But likewise the opposite spirit of enlightenment and *anti-metaphysical factual research* is growing stronger today, in that it is becoming conscious of its existence and task. In some circles the mode of thought grounded in experience and averse to speculation is stronger than ever, being strengthened precisely by the new opposition that has arisen.

In the research work of all branches of empirical science this *spirit of a scientific conception of the world* is alive. However only a very few leading thinkers give it systematic thought or advocate its principles, and but rarely are they in a position to assemble a circle of like-minded colleagues around them. We find anti-metaphysical endeavors especially in England, where the tradition of the great empiricists is still alive; the investigations of Russell and Whitehead on logic and the analysis of reality have won international significance. In the U.S.A. these endeavors take on the most varied forms; in a certain sense James belongs to this group too. The new Russia definitely is seeking for a scientific world conception, even if partly leaning on older materialistic currents. On the continent of Europe, a concentration of productive work in the direction of a scientific world conception is to be found especially in Berlin (Reichenbach, Petzoldt, Grelling, Dubislav and others) and in Vienna.

That Vienna was specially suitable ground for this development is historically understandable. In the second half of the nineteenth century, liberalism was long the dominant political current. Its world of ideas stems from the enlightenment, from empiricism, utilitarianism and the free trade movement of England. In Vienna's liberal movement, scholars of world renown occupied leading positions. Here an anti-metaphysical spirit was cultivated, for instance, by men like Theodor Gomperz who translated the works of J. S. Mill, Suess, Jodl and others.

Thanks to this spirit of enlightenment, Vienna has been leading in a scientifically oriented people's education. With the collaboration of Victor Adler and Friedrich Jodl, the society for popular education was founded and carried forth; 'popular university courses' and the 'people's college' were set up by the well-known historian Ludo Hartmann whose anti-metaphysical attitude and materialist conception of history expressed itself in all his actions. The same spirit also inspired the movement of the 'Free School' which was the forerunner of today's school reform.

In this liberal atmosphere lived Ernst Mach (born 1838) who was in Vienna as student and as *privatdozent* (1861–64). He returned to Vienna only at an advanced age when a special chair of the philosophy of the inductive sciences was created for him (1895). He was especially intent on cleansing empirical science, and in the first place, physics, of metaphysical notions. We recall his critique of absolute space which made him a forerunner of Einstein, his struggle against the metaphysics of the thing-in-itself and of the concept of substance, and his investigations of the construction of scientific concepts from ultimate elements, namely sense data. In some points the development of science has not vindicated his views, for instance in his opposition to atomic theory and in his expectation that physics would be advanced through the physiology of the senses. The essential points of his conception however were of positive use in the further development of science. Mach's chair was later occupied by Ludwig Boltzmann (1902–06) who held decidedly empiricist views.

The activity of the physicists Mach and Boltzmann in a philosophical professorship makes it conceivable that there was a lively dominant interest in the epistemological and logical problems that are linked with the foundations of physics. These problems concerning foundations also led toward a renewal of logic. The path towards these objectives had also been cleared in Vienna from quite a different quarter by Franz Brentano (during 1874–80 professor of philosophy in the theological faculty, and later lecturer in the philosophical faculty). As a Catholic priest Brentano understood scholasticism; he started directly from the scholastic logic and from Leibniz's endeavors to reform logic, while leaving aside Kant and the idealist system-builders. Brentano and his students time and again showed their understanding of men like Bolzano (*Wissenschaftslehre*, 1837) and others who were working toward a rigorous new foundation of logic. In particular Alois Höfler (1853–1922) put this side of Brentano's philosophy in the foreground before a forum in which, through Mach's and Boltzmann's influence, the adherents of

the scientific world conception were strongly represented. In the Philosophical Society at the University of Vienna numerous discussions took place under Höfler's direction, concerning questions of the foundation of physics and allied epistemological and logical problems. The Philosophical Society published *Prefaces and Introductions to Classical Works on Mechanics* (1899), as well as the individual papers of Bolzano (edited by Höfler and Hahn, 1914 and 1921). In Brentano's Viennese circle there was the young Alexius von Meinong (1870–82, later professor in Graz), whose theory of objects (1907) has certainly some affinity to modern theories of concepts and whose pupil Ernst Mally (Graz) also worked in the field of logistics. The early writings of Hans Pichler (1909) also belong to these circles.

Roughly at the same time as Mach, his contemporary and friend Josef Popper-Lynkeus worked in Vienna. Beside his physical and technical achievements we mention his large-scale, if unsystematic philosophical reflections (1899) and his rational economic plan (*A General Peacetime Labour Draft*, 1878). He consciously served the spirit of enlightenment, as is also evident from his book on Voltaire. His rejection of metaphysics was shared by many other Viennese sociologists, for example Rudolf Goldscheid. It is remarkable that in the field of political economy, too, there was in Vienna a strictly scientific method, used by the marginal utility school (Carl Menger, 1871); this method took root in England, France and Scandinavia, but not in Germany. Marxist theory likewise was cultivated and extended with special emphasis in Vienna (Otto Bauer, Rudolf Hilferding, Max Adler and others).

These influences from various sides had the result, especially since 1900, that there was in Vienna a sizeable number of people who frequently and assiduously discussed more general problems in close connection with empirical sciences. Above all these were epistemological and methodological problems of physics, for instance Poincaré's conventionalism, Duhem's conception of the aim and structure of physical theories (his translator was the Viennese Friedrich Adler, a follower of Mach, at that time *privatdozent* in Zürich); also questions about the foundations of mathematics, problems of axiomatics, logistic and the like. The following were the main strands from the history of science and philosophy that came together here, marked by those of their representatives whose works were mainly read and discussed:

1. Positivism and empiricism: Hume, Enlightenment, Comte, J. S. Mill, Richard Avenarius, Mach.

2. Foundations, aims and methods of empirical science (hypotheses in physics, geometry, etc.): Helmholtz, Riemann, Mach, Poincaré, Enriques, Duhem, Boltzmann, Einstein.

3. Logistic and its application to reality: Leibniz, Peano, Frege, Schröder, Russell, Whitehead, Wittgenstein.

4. Axiomatics: Pasch, Peano, Vailati, Pieri, Hilbert.

5. Hedonism and positivist sociology: Epicurus, Hume, Bentham, J. S. Mill, Comte, Feuerbach, Marx, Spencer, Müller-Lyer, Popper-Lynkeus, Carl Menger (the elder).

1.2 The Circle Around Schlick

In 1922 Moritz Schlick was called from Kiel to Vienna. His activities fitted well into the historical development of the Viennese scientific atmosphere. Himself originally a physicist, he awakened to new life the tradition that had been started by Mach and Boltzmann and, in a certain sense, carried on by the anti-metaphysically inclined Adolf Stöhr. (In Vienna successively: Mach, Boltzmann, Stöhr, Schlick; in Prague: Mach, Einstein, Philipp Frank.)

Around Schlick, there gathered in the course of time a circle whose members united various endeavors in the direction of a scientific conception of the world. This concentration produced a fruitful mutual inspiration. Not one of the members is a so-called 'pure' philosopher; all of them have done work in a special field of science. Moreover they come from different branches of science and originally from different philosophic attitudes. But over the years a growing uniformity appeared; this too was a result of the specifically scientific attitude: "What can be said at all, can be said clearly" (Wittgenstein); if there are differences of opinion, it is in the end possible to agree, and therefore agreement is demanded. It became increasingly clearer that a position not only free from metaphysics, but opposed to metaphysics was the common goal of all.

The attitudes toward questions of life also showed a noteworthy agreement, although these questions were not in the foreground of themes discussed within the Circle. For these attitudes are more closely related to the scientific world-conception than it might at first glance appear from a purely theoretical point of view. For instance, endeavors toward a new organization of economic and social relations, toward the unification of mankind, toward a reform of school and education, all show an inner link with the scientific world-conception; it appears that these endeavors are welcomed and regarded with sympathy by the members of the Circle, some of whom indeed actively further them.

The Vienna Circle does not confine itself to collective work as a closed group. It is also trying to make contact with the living movements of the present, so far as they are well disposed toward the scientific world-conception and turn away from metaphysics and theology. The Ernst Mach Society is today the place from which the Circle speaks to a wider public. This society, as stated in its program, wishes to "further and disseminate the scientific world-conception. It will organize lectures and publications about the present position of the scientific world-conception, in order to demonstrate the significance of exact research for the social sciences and the natural sciences. In this way intellectual tools should be formed for modern empiricism, tools that are also needed in forming public and private life." By the choice of its name, the society wishes to describe its basic orientation: science free of metaphysics. This, however, does not mean that the society declares itself in programmatic agreement with the individual doctrines of Mach. The Vienna Circle believes that in collaborating with the Ernst Mach Society it fulfils a demand of the day: we have to fashion intellectual tools for everyday life, for the daily life of the scholar but also for the daily life of all those who in some way join in working at the conscious re-shaping of life. The vitality that shows itself in the efforts for a rational transformation of the social and economic order permeates the movement for a scientific world-conception too. It is typical of the present situation in Vienna that when the Ernst Mach Society was founded in November 1928, Schlick was chosen chairman; round him the common work in the field of the scientific world-conception had concentrated most strongly.

Schlick and Philipp Frank jointly edit the collection of *Monographs on the Scientific World-Conception* [*Schriften zur wissenschaftlichen Weltauffassung*] in which members of the Vienna Circle preponderate.

2. The Scientific World Conception

The scientific world conception is characterized not so much by theses of its own, but rather by its basic attitude, its points of view and direction of research. The goal ahead is *unified* science. The endeavor is to link and harmonize the achievements of individual investigators in their various fields of science. From this aim follows the emphasis on *collective efforts*, and also the emphasis on what can be grasped intersubjectively; from this springs the search for a neutral system of formulas, for a symbolism freed from the slag of historical languages; and also the search for a total system of concepts. Neatness and clarity are striven for, and dark distances and unfathomable depths rejected. In science there are no 'depths'; there is surface everywhere: all experience forms a complex network, which cannot always be surveyed and can often be grasped only in parts. Everything is accessible to man; and man is the measure of all things. Here is an affinity with the Sophists, not with the Platonists; with the Epicureans, not with the Pythagoreans; with all those who stand for earthly being and the here and now. The scientific world-conception knows *no unsolvable riddle.* Clarification of the traditional philosophical problems leads us partly to unmask them as pseudo-problems, and partly to transform them into empirical problems and thereby subject them to the judgment of experimental science. The task of philosophical work lies in this clarification of problems and assertions, not in the propounding of special 'philosophical' pronouncements. The method of this clarification is that of *logical analysis;* of it, Russell says (*Our Knowledge of the External World*, p. 4) that it "has gradually crept into philosophy through the critical scrutiny of mathematics . . . It represents, I believe, the same kind of advance as was introduced into physics by Galileo: the substitution of piecemeal, detailed and verifiable results for large untested generalities recommended only by a certain appeal to imagination."

It is *the method of logical analysis* that essentially distinguishes recent empiricism and positivism from the earlier version that was more biological-psychological in its orientation. If someone asserts "there is a God", "the primary basis of the world is the unconscious", "there is an entelechy which is the leading principle in the living organism", we do not say to him: "what you say is false"; but we ask him: "what do you mean by these statements?" Then it appears that there is a sharp boundary between two kinds of statements. To one belong statements as they are made by empirical science; their meaning can be determined by logical analysis or, more precisely, through reduction to the simplest statements about the empirically given. The other statements, to which belong those cited above, reveal themselves as empty of meaning if one takes them in the way that metaphysicians intend. One can, of course, often re-interpret them as empirical statements; but then they lose the content of feeling which is usually essential to the metaphysician. The metaphysician and the theologian believe, thereby misunderstanding themselves, that their statements say something, or that they denote a state of affairs. Analysis, however, shows that these statements say nothing but merely express a certain mood and spirit. To express such feelings for life can be a significant task. But the proper medium for doing so is art, for instance lyric poetry or music. It is dangerous to choose the linguistic garb of a theory instead: a theoretical content is simulated where none exists. If a metaphysician or theologian wants to retain the usual medium of language, then he must himself realize and bring out clearly that he is giving not description but expression, not theory or communication of knowledge, but poetry or myth. If a mystic asserts that he has experiences that lie above and beyond all concepts, one cannot deny this. But the mystic cannot talk about it, for talking implies capture by concepts and reduction to scientifically classifiable states of affairs.

The scientific world-conception rejects metaphysical philosophy. But how can we explain the wrong paths of metaphysics? This question may be posed from several points of view: psychological, sociological and logical. Research in a psychological direction is still in its early stages; the beginnings of more penetrating explanation may perhaps be seen in the investigations of Freudian psychoanalysis. The state of sociological investigation is similar; we may mention the theory of the 'ideological superstructure'; here the field remains open to worthwhile further research.

More advanced is the clarification of *the logical origins of metaphysical aberration*, especially through the works of Russell and Wittgenstein. In metaphysical theory, and even in the very form of the questions, there are two basic logical mistakes: too narrow a tie to the form of *traditional languages* and a confusion about the logical achievement of thought. Ordinary language for instance uses the same part of speech, the substantive, for things ('apple') as well as as for qualities ('hardness'), relations ('friendship'), and processes ('sleep'); therefore it misleads one into a thing-like conception of functional concepts (hypostasis, substantialization). One can quote countless similar examples of linguistic misleading that have been equally fatal to philosophers.

The second basic error of metaphysics consists in the notion that *thinking* can either lead to knowledge out of its own resources without using any empirical material, or at least arrive at new contents by an inference from given states of affair. Logical investigation, however, leads to the result that all thought and inference consists of nothing but a transition from statements to other statements that contain nothing that was not already in the former (tautological transformation). It is therefore not possible to develop a metaphysic from 'pure thought'.

In such a way logical analysis overcomes not only metaphysics in the proper, classical sense of the word, especially scholastic metaphysics and that of the systems of German idealism, but also the hidden metaphysics of Kantian and modern *apriorism*. The scientific world-conception knows no unconditionally valid knowledge derived from pure reason, no 'synthetic judgments a priori' of the kind that lie at the basis of Kantian epistemology and even more of all pre-and post-Kantian ontology and metaphysics. The judgments of arithmetic, geometry, and certain fundamental principles of physics that Kant took as examples of a priori knowledge will be discussed later. It is precisely in the rejection of the possibility of synthetic knowledge a priori that the basic thesis of modern empiricism lies. The scientific world-conception knows only empirical statements about things of all kinds, and analytic statements of logic and mathematics.

In rejecting overt metaphysics and the concealed variety of apriorism, all adherents of the scientific world-conception are at one. Beyond this, the Vienna Circle maintain the view that the statements of (critical) *realism* and *idealism* about the reality or non-reality of the external world and other minds are of a metaphysical character, because they are open to the same objections as are the statements of the old metaphysics: they are meaningless, because unverifiable and without content. For us, *something is 'real' through being incorporated into the total structure of experience.*

Intuition which is especially emphasized by metaphysicians as a source of knowledge is not rejected as such by the scientific world-conception. However, rational justification has to pursue all intuitive knowledge step by step. The seeker is allowed any method; but what has been found must stand up to testing. The view which attributes to intuition a superior and more penetrating power of knowing, capable of leading beyond the contents of sense experience and not to be confined by the shackles of conceptual thought—this view is rejected.

We have characterized the *scientific world-conception* essentially by *two features. First it is empiricist and positivist*: there is knowledge only from experience, which rests on what is immediately given. This sets the limits for the content of legitimate science. *Second*, the scientific world-conception is marked by application of a certain method, namely *logical analysis*. The aim of scientific effort is to reach the goal, unified science, by applying logical analysis to the empirical material. Since the meaning of every statement of science must be statable by reduction to a statement about the given, likewise the meaning of any concept, whatever branch of science it may belong to, must be statable by step-wise reduction to other concepts, down to the concepts of the lowest level which refer directly to the given. If such an analysis were carried through for all concepts, they would thus be ordered into a reductive system, a 'constitutive system'. Investigations towards such a constitutive system, the 'constitutive theory', thus form the framework within which logical analysis is applied by the scientific world-conception. Such investigations show very soon that traditional Aristotelian scholastic logic is quite inadequate for this purpose. Only modern symbolic logic ('logistic') succeeds in gaining the required precision of concept definitions and of statements, and in formalizing the intuitive process of inference of ordinary thought, that is to bring it into a rigorous automatically controlled form by means of a symbolic mechanism. Investigations into constitutive theory show that the lowest layers of the constitutive system contain concepts of the experience and qualities of the individual psyche; in the layer above are physical objects; from these are constituted other minds and lastly the objects of social science. The arrangement of the concepts of the various branches of science into the constitutive system can already be discerned in outline today, but much remains to be done in detail. With the proof of the possibility and the outline of the shape of the total system of concepts, the relation of all statements to the given and with it the general structure of *unified science* become recognizable too.

A scientific description can contain only the *structure* (form of order) of objects, not their 'essence'. What unites men in language are structural formulas; in them the content of the common knowledge of men presents itself. Subjectively experienced qualities—redness, pleasure—are as such only experiences, not knowledge; physical optics admits only what is in principle understandable by a blind man too.

3. Fields of Problems

3.1 Foundations of Arithmetic

In the writings and discussions of the Vienna Circle many different problems are treated, stemming from various branches of science. Attempts are made to arrange the various lines of problems systematically and thereby to clarify the situation.

The problems concerning the foundations of arithmetic have become of special historical significance for the development of the scientific world-conception because they gave impulse to the development of a new logic. After the very fruitful developments of mathematics in the 18th and 19th century during which more attention was given to the wealth of new results than to subtle examination of their conceptual foundations, this examination became unavoidable if mathematics were not to lose the traditionally celebrated certainty of

its structure. This examination became even more urgent when certain contradictions, the 'paradoxes of set theory', arose. It was soon recognized that these were not just difficulties in a special part of mathematics, but rather they were general logical contradictions, 'antinomies', which pointed to essential mistakes in the foundations of traditional logic. The task of eliminating these contradictions gave a very strong impulse to the further development of logic. Here efforts for *clarification of the concept of number* met with those for an internal *reform of logic*. Since Leibniz and Lambert, the idea had come up again and again to master reality through a greater precision of concepts and inferential processes, and to obtain this precision by means of a symbolism fashioned after mathematics. After Boole, Venn and others, especially Frege (1884), Schröder (1890) and Peano (1895) worked on this problem. On the basis of these preparatory efforts *Whitehead* and *Russell* (1910) were able to establish a coherent system of logic in symbolic form ('logistic'), not only avoiding the contradictions of traditional logic, but far exceeding that logic in intellectual wealth and practical applicability. From this logical system they derived the concepts of arithmetic and analysis, thereby giving mathematics a secure foundation in logic.

Certain difficulties however remained in this attempt at overcoming the foundation crisis of arithmetic (and set theory) and have so far not found a definitively satisfactory solution. At present three different views confront each other in this field; besides the 'logicism' of Russell and Whitehead, there is Hilbert's 'formalism' which regards arithmetic as a playing with formulas according to certain rules, and Brouwer's 'intuitionism' according to which arithmetic knowledge rests on a not further reducible intuition of duality and unity [*Zwei-einheit*]. The debates are followed with great interest in the Vienna Circle. Where the decision will lead in the end cannot yet be foreseen; in any case, it will also imply a decision about the structure of logic; hence the importance of this problem for the scientific world-conception. Some hold that the three views are not so far apart as it seems. They surmise that essential features of all three will come closer in the course of future development and probably, using the far-reaching ideas of Wittgenstein, will be united in the ultimate solution.

The conception of mathematics as tautological in character, which is based on the investigations of Russell and Wittgenstein, is also held by the Vienna Circle. It is to be noted that this conception is opposed not only to apriorism and intuitionism, but also to the older empiricism (for instance of J. S. Mill), which tried to derive mathematics and logic in an experimental-inductive manner as it were.

Connected with the problems of arithmetic and logic are the investigations into the nature of the *axiomatic method* in general (concepts of completeness, independence, monomorphism, unambiguity and so on) and on the establishment of axiom-systems for certain branches of mathematics.

3.2 Foundations of Physics

Originally the Vienna Circle's strongest interest was in the method of empirical science. Inspired by ideas of Mach, Poincaré, and Duhem, the problems of mastering reality through scientific systems, especially through *systems of hypotheses and axioms,* were discussed. A system of axioms, cut loose from all empirical application, can at first be regarded as a system of implicit definitions; that is to say, the concepts that appear in the axioms are fixed, or as it were defined, not from their content but only from their mutual relations through the axioms. Such a system of axioms attains a meaning for reality only by the addition of further definitions, namely the 'coordinating definitions', which state what objects of reality are to be regarded as members of the system of axioms. The development of empirical science, which is to represent reality by means of as uniform and simple a net of concepts and judgments as possible, can now proceed in one of two ways, as history shows. The changes imposed by new experience can be made either in the axioms or in the coordinating definitions. Here we touch the problem of conventions, particularly treated by Poincaré.

The methodological problem of the application of axiom systems to reality may in principle arise for any branch of science. That these investigations have thus far been fruitful almost solely for physics, however, can be understood from the present stage of historical development of science: in regard to precision and refinement of concepts, physics is far ahead of the other branches of science.

Epistemological analysis of the leading concepts of natural science has freed them more and more from *metaphysical admixtures* which had clung to them from ancient time. In particular, Helmholtz, Mach, Einstein, and others have cleansed the concepts of *space, time, substance, causality, and probability.* The doctrines of absolute space and time have been overcome by the theory of relativity; space and time are no longer absolute containers but only ordering manifolds for elementary processes. Material substance has been dissolved by atomic theory and field theory. Causality was divested of the anthropomorphic character of 'influence' or 'necessary connection' and reduced to a relation among conditions, a functional coordination. Further, in place of the many laws of nature which were considered to be strictly valid, statistical laws have appeared; following the quantum theory there is even doubt whether the concept of strictly causal lawfulness is applicable to phenomena in very small space-time regions. The concept of probability is reduced to the empirically graspable concept of relative frequency.

Through the application of the *axiomatic method* to these problems, the empirical components always separate from the merely conventional ones, the content of statements from definitions. No room remains for a priori synthetic judgments. That knowledge of the world is possible rests not on human reason impressing its form on the material, but on the material being ordered in a certain way. The kind and degree of this order cannot be known beforehand. The world might be ordered much more strictly than it is; but it might equally be ordered much less without jeopardizing the possibility of knowledge. Only step by step can the advancing research of empirical science teach us in what degree the world is regular. The method of induction, the inference from yesterday to tomorrow, from here to there, is of course only valid if regularity exists. But this method does not rest on some a priori presupposition of this regularity. It may be applied wherever it leads to fruitful results, whether or not it be adequately founded; it never yields certainty. However, epistemological reflection demands that an inductive inference should be given significance only insofar as it can be tested empirically. The scientific world-conception will not condemn the success of a piece of research because it has been gathered by means that are inadequate, logically unclear or empirically unfounded. But it will always strive at testing with clarified aids, and demand an indirect or direct reduction to experience.

3.3 Foundations of Geometry

Among the questions about the foundations of physics, the problem of *physical space* has received special significance in recent decades. The investigations of Gauss (1816), Bolyai (1823), Lobatchevski (1835) and others led to *non-Euclidean geometry*, to a realization that the hitherto dominant classical geometric system of Euclid was only one of an infinite set of systems, all of equal logical merit. This raised the question, which of these geometries was that of actual space. Gauss had wanted to resolve this question by measuring the angles of a large triangle. This made *physical geometry* into an empirical science, a branch of physics. The problems were further studied particularly by Riemann (1868), Helmholtz (1868) and Poincaré (1904). Poincaré especially emphasized the link of physical geometry with all other branches of physics: the question concerning the nature of actual space can be answered only in connection with a total system of physics. Einstein then found such a total system, which answered the question in favor of a certain non-Euclidean system.

Through this development, physical geometry became more and more clearly separated from pure *mathematical* geometry. The latter gradually became more and more formalized through further development of logical analysis. First it was arithmetized, that is, interpreted as the theory of a certain number system. Next it was axiomatized, that is, represented by means of a system of axioms that conceives the geometrical elements (points, etc.) as undefined objects, and fixes only their mutual relations. Finally geometry was logicized, namely represented as a theory of certain structural relations. Thus geometry became the most important field of application for the axiomatic method and for the general theory of relations. In this way, it gave the strongest impulse to the development of the two methods which in turn became so important for the development of logic itself, and thereby again for the scientific world-conception.

The relations between mathematical and physical geometry naturally led to the problem of the application of axiom systems to reality which, as mentioned, played a big role in the more general investigations about the foundations of physics.

3.4 Problems of the Foundations of Biology and Psychology

Metaphysicians have always been fond of singling out biology as a special field. This came out in the doctrine of a special life force, the theory of *vitalism*. The modern representatives of this theory endeavor to bring it from the unclear, confused form of the past into a conceptually clear formulation. In place of the life force, we have 'dominants' (Reinke, 1899) or 'entelechies' (Driesch, 1905). Since these concepts do not satisfy the requirement of reducibility to the given, the scientific world-conception rejects them as metaphysical. The same holds true of so-called 'psycho-vitalism' which puts forward an intervention of the soul, a 'role of leadership of the mental in the material'. If, however, one digs out of this metaphysical vitalism the empirically graspable kernel, there remains the thesis that the processes of organic nature proceed according to laws that cannot be reduced to physical laws. A more precise analysis shows that this thesis is equivalent to the assertion that certain fields of reality are not subject to a uniform and pervasive regularity.

It is understandable that the scientific world-conception can show more definite confirmation for its views in those fields which have already achieved conceptual precision than in others: in physics more than in psychology. The linguistic forms which we still use in psychology today have their origin in certain ancient metaphysical notions of the soul. The formation of concepts in psychology is made difficult by these defects of language: metaphysical burdens and logical incongruities. Moreover there are certain factual difficulties. The result is that hitherto most of the concepts used in psychology are inadequately defined; of some, it is not known whether they have meaning or only simulate meaning through usage. So, in this field nearly everything in the way of epistemological analysis still remains to be done; of course, analysis here is more difficult than in physics. The attempt of behaviorist psychology to grasp the psychic through the behavior of bodies, which is at a level accessible to perception, is, in its principled attitude, close to the scientific world-conception.

3.5 Foundations of the Social Sciences

As we have specially considered with respect to physics and mathematics, every branch of science is led to recognize that, sooner or later in its development, it must conduct an epistemological examination of its foundations, a logical analysis of its concepts. So too with the social sciences, and in the first place with history and economics. For about a hundred years, a process of elimination of metaphysical admixtures has been operating in these fields. Of course the purification has not yet reached the same degree as in physics; on the other hand, the task of cleansing is less urgent perhaps. For it seems that even in the heyday of metaphysics and theology, the metaphysical strain was not particularly strong here; maybe this is because the concepts in this field, such as war and peace, import and export, are closer to direct perception than concepts like atom and ether. It is not too difficult to drop concepts like 'folk spirit' and instead to choose, as our object, groups of individuals of a certain kind. Scholars from the most diverse trends, such as Quesnay, Adam Smith, Ricardo, Comte, Marx, Menger, Walras, Müller-Lyer, have worked in the sense of the empiricist, anti-metaphysical attitude. The object of history and economics are people, things and their arrangement.

4. Retrospect and Prospect

The modern scientific world-conception has developed from work on the problems just mentioned. We have seen how in physics, the endeavors to gain tangible results, at first even with inadequate or still insufficiently clarified scientific tools, found itself forced more and more into methodological investigations. Out of this developed the method of forming hypotheses and, further, the axiomatic method and logical analysis; thereby concept formation gained greater clarity and strength. The same methodological problems were met also in the development of foundations research in physical geometry, mathematical geometry and arithmetic, as we have seen. It is mainly from all these sources that the problems arise with which representatives of the scientific world-conception particularly concern themselves at present. Of course it is still clearly noticeable from

which of the various problem areas the individual members of the Vienna Circle come. This often results in differences in lines of interests and points of view, which in turn lead to differences in conception. But it is characteristic that an endeavor toward precise formulation, application of an exact logical language and symbolism, and accurate differentiation between the theoretical content of a thesis and its mere attendant notions, diminish the separation. Step by step the common fund of conceptions is increased, forming the nucleus of a scientific world-conception around which the outer layers gather with stronger subjective divergence.

Looking back we now see clearly what is the *essence of the new scientific world-conception* in contrast with traditional philosophy. No special 'philosophic assertions' are established, assertions are merely clarified; and at that assertions of empirical science, as we have seen when we discussed the various problem areas. Some representatives of the scientific world-conception no longer want to use the term 'philosophy' for their work at all, so as to emphasize the contrast with the philosophy of (metaphysical) systems even more strongly. Whichever term may be used to describe such investigations, this much is certain: *there is no such thing as philosophy as a basic or universal science alongside or above the various fields of the one empirical science*; there is no way to genuine knowledge other than the way of experience; there is no realm of ideas that stands over or beyond experience. Nevertheless the work of 'philosophic' or 'foundational' investigations remains important in accord with the scientific world-conception. For the logical clarification of scientific concepts, statements and methods liberates one from inhibiting prejudices. Logical and epistemological analysis does not wish to set barriers to scientific enquiry; on the contrary, analysis provides science with as complete a range of formal possibilities as is possible, from which to select what best fits each empirical finding (example: non-Euclidean geometries and the theory of relativity).

The representatives of the scientific world-conception resolutely stand on the ground of simple human experience. They confidently approach the task of removing the metaphysical and theological debris of millennia. Or, as some have it: returning, after a metaphysical interlude, to a unified picture of this world which had, in a sense, been at the basis of magical beliefs, free from theology, in the earliest times.

The increase of metaphysical and theologizing leanings which shows itself today in many associations and sects, in books and journals, in talks and university lectures, seems to be based on the fierce social and economic struggles of the present: one group of combatants, holding fast to traditional social forms, cultivates traditional attitudes of metaphysics and theology whose content has long since been superseded; while the other group, especially in central Europe, faces modern times, rejects these views and takes its stand on the ground of empirical science. This development is connected with that of the modern process of production, which is becoming ever more rigorously mechanized and leaves ever less room for metaphysical ideas. It is also connected with the disappointment of broad masses of people with the attitude of those who preach traditional metaphysical and theological doctrines. So it is that in many countries the masses now reject these doctrines much more consciously than ever before, and along with their socialist attitudes tend to lean towards a down-to-earth empiricist view. In previous times, *materialism* was the expression of this view; meanwhile, however, modern empiricism has shed a number of inadequacies and has taken a strong shape in the *scientific world-conception.*

Thus, the scientific world-conception is close to the life of the present. Certainly it is threatened with hard struggles and hostility. Nevertheless there are many who do not despair but, in view of the present sociological situation, look forward with hope to the course of events to come. Of course not every single adherent of the scientific world-conception will be a fighter. Some, glad of solitude, will lead a withdrawn existence on the icy slopes of logic; some may even disdain mingling with the masses and regret the 'trivialized' form that these matters inevitably take on spreading. However, their achievements too will take a place among the historic developments. We witness the spirit of the scientific world-conception penetrating in growing measure the forms of personal and public life, in education, upbringing, architecture, and the shaping of economic and social life according to rational principles. *The scientific world-conception serves life, and life receives it.*

APPENDIX

1. *Members of the Vienna Circle*
   Gustav Bergmann
   Rudolf Carnap
   Herbert Feigl
   Philipp Frank
   Kurt Gödel
   Hans Hahn
   Viktor Kraft
   Karl Menger
   Marcel Natkin
   Otto Neurath
   Olga Hahn-Neurath
   Theodor Radakovic
   Moritz Schlick
   Friedrich Waismann

2. *Those Sympathetic to the Vienna Circle*
   Walter Dubislav
   Josef Frank
   Kurt Grelling
   Hasso Härlen
   E. Kaila
   Heinrich Loewy
   F. P. Ramsey
   Hans Reichenbach
   Kurt Reidemeister
   Edgar Zilsel

3. *Leading Representatives of the Scientific World-Conception*
   Albert Einstein
   Bertrand Russell
   Ludwig Wittgenstein

READING QUESTIONS

1. In §1.1 and §1.2 the authors defend their claim that "Vienna was specially suitable ground for" the development of positivism. What specific facts do they cite in support of this claim?

2. In §2 the authors claim that "the scientific world conception is characterized not so much by theses of its own, but rather by its basic attitude, its points of view and direction of research." In a general way, outline the main features of the scientific world conception, its methodology, and its main commitments.

3. In §3, the authors outline various fields of problems that interest the logical positivists. What do these various fields have in common? Are there areas of philosophy that are *not* of interest to the positivists? Why?

4. In §4, the authors assert that "there is no such thing as philosophy as a basic or universal science alongside or above the various fields of the one empirical science." First, why do the positivists believe that there is really only one empirical science? Second, how does philosophy (as a field of inquiry) relate to science (as a field of inquiry), on this conception?

5. In a few short paragraphs, document your own conception of the nature and methods of philosophy. In what ways does your conception of philosophy differ from that of the logical positivists? In what ways is it the same?

SUGGESTIONS FOR FURTHER READING (THE VIENNA CIRCLE)

Secondary Sources and Collected Writings

Achinstein, P., and S. Barker, eds. (1969) *The Legacy of Logical Positivism.* Baltimore: Johns Hopkins University Press.

Ayer, A. J., ed. (1959) *Logical Positivism.* New York: The Free Press.

Fischer, K. R., ed. (1995) *The Golden Age of Austrian Philosophy: A Source Book.* Vienna: WUV Verlag.

Fleming, D., and B. Bailyn, eds. (1969) *The Intellectual Migration: Europe and America, 1930–1960.* Cambridge, MA: Harvard University Press.

Frank, P. (1949) *Modern Science and Its Philosophy.* Cambridge: Cambridge University Press.

Friedman, M. (1999) *Reconsidering Logical Positivism.* Cambridge: Cambridge University Press.

Giere, M. (1992) *The Vienna Circle with Self-Descriptions and Photographs.* Reinbeck bei Hamburg: Rowohlt.

Giere, R. N., and A. W. Richardson, eds. (1996) *Origins of Logical Empiricism.* Minneapolis, MN: University of Minnesota Press.

Gower, B., ed. (1987) *Logical Positivism in Perspective.* Totowa, NJ: Barnes & Noble.

Haller, R., ed. (1993) *Neo-Positivism: A Historical Introduction to the Philosophy of the Vienna Circle.* Darmstadt: Wissenschaftliche Buchgesellschaft.

Hanfling, O. (1981) *Logical Positivism.* Oxford: Blackwell.

Kraft, V. (1950) *The Vienna Circle: The Origin of Neo-Positivism: A Chapter in the History of Recent Philosophy,* translated by A. Pap. New York: Philosophical Library, 1953.

Menger, K. (1994) *Reminiscences of the Vienna Circle and the Mathematical Colloquium,* edited by L. Golland, B. McGuiness, and A. Sklar. Dordrecht: Kluwer Academic.

Ryle, G. (1956) *The Revolution in Philosophy.* New York: Macmillan.

Sarkar, S., ed. (1996) *Science and Philosophy in the Twentieth Century: Basic Works of Logical Empiricism.* New York: Garland.

Uebel, T. E., ed. (1991) *Rediscovering the Forgotten Vienna Circle.* Dordrecht: Kluwer Academic.

Sir Alfred Jules (A. J.) Ayer

The Elimination of Metaphysics

A great philosophical stylist, if not a particularly original philosopher, A. J. Ayer's monumentally significant *Language, Truth, and Logic* (1936) brought logical positivism international attention from the philosophic community and from nonphilosophers alike. Ayer was only twenty-six years old when his book was first issued, and in many respects his remaining life in philosophy was a continued pursuit and refinement of the outlook or orientation expressed in *Language, Truth, and Logic.* Ayer never deviated far from its essential tenets.

Ayer was born in 1910 in London and was educated at Eton and at Christ Church, Oxford, graduating in

1932. After graduation, Ayer spent a year in Vienna immersing himself in the philosophy of logical positivism. His academic career as a professional philosopher began with an appointment as a lecturer at Oxford in 1933, a position he held until 1940. The war interrupted his academic career, but he returned to teaching as a fellow and dean at Wadham College, Oxford, in 1945, and a year later took a position as Grote Professor of the Philosophy of Mind and Logic at the University of London. In 1959 he returned to Oxford as Wykeham Professor of Logic, a position he held until 1978. Ayer was active in liberal politics his entire life, and in 1973 he was knighted for service to his country.

Ayer's constructive philosophy closely follows the lines of Viennese positivism, the logicism of Russell, the empiricism of Hume, and the attention to language one finds in writers such as Gilbert Ryle and John L. Austin. His genius primarily lies in his ability to combine and refine philosophical outlooks and in his ability to write clear, concise, and captivating philosophical prose.

In addition to *Language, Truth, and Logic*, Ayer penned the essentially phenomenalist *Foundations of Empirical Knowledge* (1940), *Philosophical Essays* (1954), and *The Problem of Knowledge* (1956), a lucid and engaging introduction to epistemology. In his later years Ayer turned to the history of philosophy and authored books on the philosophies of Russell, Moore, Hume, and Voltaire, along with a book on pragmatism and on the history of analytic philosophy. Ayer died in 1989.

In the following chapter from *Language, Truth, and Logic*, Ayer advances a version of the positivist's *criterion of verifiability* or test of the literal significance of any given purported proposition. He then argues that if we apply this criterion to the various kinds of propositions often met with in philosophy, we will discover that all of the propositions of "transcendent metaphysics" are complete nonsense.

Ayer's criterion shares an affinity with another classic criterion of modern philosophy, that of David Hume: "If we take in our hand any volume; of divinity or school metaphysics, for instance; let us ask, Does it contain any abstract reasoning concerning quantity or number? No. Does it contain any experimental reasoning concerning matter of fact and existence? No. Com-

mit it then to the flames: For it can contain nothing but sophistry and illusion" (*An Inquiry Concerning Human Understanding*, Sec. VII).

In many respects, this chapter of Ayer's work represents an outline of the argument of his book as a whole and serves as a good introduction to the positivist's general philosophy of language.

The traditional disputes of philosophers are, for the most part, as unwarranted as they are unfruitful. The surest way to end them is to establish beyond question what should be the purpose and method of a philosophical enquiry. And this is by no means so difficult a task as the history of philosophy would lead one to suppose. For if there are any questions which science leaves it to philosophy to answer, a straightforward process of elimination must lead to their discovery.

We may begin by criticizing the metaphysical thesis that philosophy affords us knowledge of a reality transcending the world of science and common sense. Later on, when we come to define metaphysics and account for its existence, we shall find that it is possible to be a metaphysician without believing in a transcendent reality; for we shall see that many metaphysical utterances are due to the commission of logical errors, rather than to a conscious desire on the part of their authors to go beyond the limits of experience. But it is convenient for us to take the case of those who believe that it is possible to have knowledge of a transcendent reality as a starting-point for our discussion. The arguments which we use to refute them will subsequently be found to apply to the whole of metaphysics.

One way of attacking a metaphysician who claimed to have knowledge of a reality which transcended the phenomenal world would be to enquire from what premises his propositions were deduced. Must he not begin, as other men do, with the evidence of his senses?

A. J. Ayer, "The Elimination of Metaphysics" from his *Language, Truth, and Logic,* Second Edition, New York: Dover Publications, Inc., 1952. Used with the permission of the publisher.

And if so, what valid process of reasoning can possibly lead him to the conception of a transcendent reality? Surely from empirical premises nothing whatsoever concerning the properties, or even the existence, of anything super-empirical can legitimately be inferred. But this objection would be met by a denial on the part of the metaphysician that his assertions were ultimately based on the evidence of his senses. He would say that he was endowed with a faculty of intellectual intuition which enabled him to know facts that could not be known through sense-experience. And even if it could be shown that he was relying on empirical premises, and that his venture into a non-empirical world was therefore logically unjustified, it would not follow that the assertions which he made concerning this non-empirical world could not be true. For the fact that a conclusion does not follow from its putative premise is not sufficient to show that it is false. Consequently one cannot overthrow a system of transcendent metaphysics merely by criticizing the way in which it comes into being. What is required is rather a criticism of the nature of the actual statements which comprise it. And this is the line of argument which we shall, in fact, pursue. For we shall maintain that no statement which refers to a "reality" transcending the limits of all possible sense-experience can possibly have any literal significance; from which it must follow that the labors of those who have striven to describe such a reality have all been devoted to the production of nonsense.

It may be suggested that this is a proposition which has already been proved by Kant. But although Kant also condemned transcendent metaphysics, he did so on different grounds. For he said that the human understanding was so constituted that it lost itself in contradictions when it ventured out beyond the limits of possible experience and attempted to deal with things in themselves. And thus he made the impossibility of a transcendent metaphysic not, as we do, a matter of logic, but a matter of fact. He asserted, not that our minds could not conceivably have had the power of penetrating beyond the phenomenal world, but merely that they were in fact devoid of it. And this leads the critic to ask how, if it is possible to know only what lies within the bounds of sense-experience, the author can be justified in asserting that real things do exist beyond, and how he can tell what are the boundaries beyond which the human understanding may not venture, unless he succeeds in passing them himself. As Wittgenstein says, "in order to draw a limit to thinking, we should have to think both sides of this limit," a truth to which Bradley gives a special twist in maintaining that the man who is ready to prove that metaphysics is impossible is a brother metaphysician with a rival theory of his own.

Whatever force these objections may have against the Kantian doctrine, they have none whatsoever against the thesis that I am about to set forth. It cannot here be said that the author is himself overstepping the barrier he maintains to be impassable. For the fruitlessness of attempting to transcend the limits of possible sense-experience will be deduced, not from a psychological hypothesis concerning the actual constitution of the human mind, but from the rule which determines the literal significance of language. Our charge against the metaphysician is not that he attempts to employ the understanding in a field where it cannot profitably venture, but that he produces sentences which fail to conform to the conditions under which alone a sentence can be literally significant. Nor are we ourselves obliged to talk nonsense in order to show that all sentences of a certain type are necessarily devoid of literal significance. We need only formulate the criterion which enables us to test whether a sentence expresses a genuine proposition about a matter of fact, and then point out that the sentences under consideration fail to satisfy it. And this we shall now proceed to do. We shall first of all formulate the criterion in somewhat vague terms, and then give the explanations which are necessary to render it precise.

The criterion which we use to test the genuineness of apparent statements of fact is the criterion of verifiability. We say that a sentence is factually significant to any given person, if and only if, he knows how to verify the proposition which it purports to express—that is, if he knows what observations would lead him, under certain conditions, to accept the proposition as being true, or reject it as being false. If, on the other hand, the putative proposition is of such a character that the assumption of its truth, or falsehood, is consistent with any assumption whatsoever concerning the nature of his future experience, then, as far as he is concerned, it is, if not a tautology, a mere pseudo-proposition. The sentence expressing it may be emotionally significant to him; but it is not literally significant. And with regard to questions the procedure is the same. We enquire in every case what observations would lead us to answer the question, one way or the other; and, if none can be discovered, we must conclude that the sentence under consideration does not, as far as we are concerned, express a genuine question, however strongly its grammatical appearance may suggest that it does.

As the adoption of this procedure is an essential factor in the argument of this book, it needs to be examined in detail.

In the first place, it is necessary to draw a distinction between practical verifiability, and verifiability in principle. Plainly we all understand, in many cases believe, propositions which we have not in fact taken steps to verify. Many of these are propositions which we could verify if we took enough trouble. But there remain a number of significant propositions, concerning matters of fact, which we could not verify even if we chose; simply because we lack the practical means of placing ourselves in the situation where the relevant observations could be made. A simple and familiar example of such a proposition is the proposition that there are mountains on the farther side of the moon. No rocket has yet been invented which would enable me to go and look at the farther side of the moon, so I am unable to decide the matter by actual observation. But I do know what observations would decide it for me, if, as is theoretically conceivable, I were once in a position to make them. And therefore I say that the proposition is verifiable in principle, if not in practice, and is accordingly significant. On the other hand, such a metaphysical pseudo-proposition as "the Absolute enters into, but is itself incapable of, evolution and progress," is not even in principle verifiable. For one cannot conceive of an observation which would enable one to determine whether the Absolute did, or did not, enter into evolution and progress. Of course it is possible that the author of such a remark is using English words in a way in which they are not commonly used by English-speaking people, and that he does, in fact, intend to assert something which could be empirically verified. But until he makes us understand how the proposition that he wishes to express would be verified, he fails to communicate anything to us. And if he admits, as I think

the author of the remark in question would have admitted, that his words were not intended to express either a tautology or a proposition which was capable, at least in principle, of being verified, then it follows that he has made an utterance which has no literal significance even for himself.

A further distinction which we must make is the distinction between the "strong" and the "weak" sense of the term "verifiable." A proposition is said to be verifiable, in the strong sense of the term, if, and only if, its truth could be conclusively established in experience. But it is verifiable, in the weak sense, if it is possible for experience to render it probable. In which sense are we using the term when we say that a putative proposition is genuine only if it is verifiable?

It seems to me that if we adopt conclusive verifiability as our criterion of significance, as some positivists have proposed, our argument will prove too much. Consider, for example, the case of general propositions of law—such propositions, namely, as "arsenic is poisonous"; "all men are mortal"; "a body tends to expand when it is heated." It is of the very nature of these propositions that their truth cannot be established with certainty by any finite series of observations. But if it is recognized that such general propositions of law are designed to cover an infinite number of cases, then it must be admitted that they cannot, even in principle, be verified conclusively. And then, if we adopt conclusive verifiability as our criterion of significance, we are logically obliged to treat these general propositions of law in the same fashion as we treat the statements of the metaphysician.

In face of this difficulty, some positivists have adopted the heroic course of saying that these general propositions are indeed pieces of nonsense, albeit an essentially important type of nonsense. But here the introduction of the term "important" is simply an attempt to hedge. It serves only to mark the authors' recognition that their view is somewhat too paradoxical, without in any way removing the paradox. Besides, the difficulty is not confined to the case of general propositions of law, though it is there revealed most plainly. It is hardly less obvious in the case of propositions about the remote past. For it must surely be admitted that, however strong the evidence in favor of historical statements may be, their truth can never become more than highly probable. And to maintain that they also constituted an important, or unimportant, type of nonsense would be unplausible, to say the very least. Indeed, it will be our contention that no proposition, other than a tautology, can possibly be anything more than a probable hypothesis. And if this is correct, the principle that a sentence can be factually significant only if it expresses what is conclusively verifiable is self-stultifying as a criterion of significance. For it leads to the conclusion that it is impossible to make a significant statement of fact at all.

Nor can we accept the suggestion that a sentence should be allowed to be factually significant if, and only if, it expresses something which is definitely confusable by experience. Those who adopt this course assume that, although no finite series of observations is ever sufficient to establish the truth of a hypothesis beyond all possibility of doubt, there are crucial cases in which a single observations, or series of observations, can definitely confute it. But, as we shall show later on, this assumption is false. A hypothesis cannot be conclusively confuted any more than it can be conclusively verified. For when we take the occurrence of certain observations as proof that a given hypothesis is false, we presuppose the existence of certain conditions. And though, in any given case, it may be extremely improbable that this assumption is false, it is not logically impossible. We shall see that there need be no self-contradiction in holding that some of the relevant circumstances are other than we have taken them to be, and consequently that the hypothesis has not really broken down. And if it is not the case that any hypothesis can be definitely confuted, we cannot hold that the genuineness of a proposition depends on the possibility of its definite confutation.

Accordingly, we fall back on the weaker sense of verification. We say that the question that must be asked about any putative statement of fact is not, Would any observations make its truth or falsehood logically certain? but simply, Would any observations be relevant to the determination of its truth or falsehood? And it is only if a negative answer is given to this second question that we conclude that the statement under consideration is nonsensical.

To make our position clearer, we may formulate it in another way. Let us call a proposition which records an actual or possible observation an experiential proposition. Then we may say that it is the mark of a genuine factual proposition, not that it should be equivalent to an experiential proposition, or any finite number of experiential propositions, but simply that some experiential propositions can be deduced from it in conjunction with certain other premises without being deducible from those other premises alone.

This criterion seems liberal enough. In contrast to the principle of conclusive verifiability, it clearly does not deny significance to general propositions or to propositions about the past. Let us see what kinds of assertion it rules out.

A good example of the kind of utterance that is condemned by our criterion as being not even false but nonsensical would be the assertion that the world of sense-experience was altogether unreal. It must, of course, be admitted that our senses do sometimes deceive us. We may, as the result of having certain sensations, expect certain other sensations to be obtainable which are, in fact, not obtainable. But, in all such cases, it is further sense-experience that informs us of the mistakes that arise out of sense-experience. We say that the senses sometimes deceive us, just because the expectations to which our sense-experiences give rise do not always accord with what we subsequently experience. That is, we rely on our senses to substantiate or confute the judgements which are based on our sensations. And therefore the fact that our perceptual judgements are sometimes found to be erroneous has not the slightest tendency to show that the world of sense-experience is unreal. And, indeed, it is plain that no conceivable observation, or series of observations, could have any tendency to show that the world revealed to us by sense-experience was unreal. Consequently, anyone who condemns the sensible world as a world of mere appearance, as opposed to reality, is saying something which, according to our criterion of significance, is literally nonsensical.

An example of a controversy which the application of our criterion obliges us to condemn as fictitious is provided by those who dispute concerning the number of substances that there are in the world. For it is admitted both by monists, who maintain that reality is one substance, and by pluralists, who maintain that reality is many, that it is impossible to imagine any empirical situation which would be relevant to the solution of their dispute. But if we are told that no possible observation could give any probability either to the assertion that reality was one substance or to the assertion that it was many, then we must conclude that neither assertion is significant. We shall see later on that there are genuine logical and empirical questions involved in the dispute between monists and pluralists. But the metaphysical question concerning "substance" is ruled out by our criterion as spurious.

A similar treatment must be accorded to the controversy between realists and idealists, in its metaphysical aspect. A simple illustration, which I have made use of in a similar argument elsewhere, will help to demonstrate this. Let us suppose that a picture is discovered and the suggestion made that it was painted by Goya. There is a definite procedure for dealing with such a question. The experts examine the picture to see in what way it resembles the accredited works of Goya, and to see if it bears any marks which are characteristic of a forgery; they look up contemporary records for evidence of the existence of such a picture, and so on. In the end, they may still disagree, but each one knows what empirical evidence would go to confirm or discredit his opinion. Suppose, now, that these men have studied philosophy, and some of them proceed to maintain that this picture is a set of ideas in the perceiver's mind, or in God's mind, others that it is objectively real. What possible experience could any of them have which would be relevant to the solution of this dispute one way or the other? In the ordinary sense of the term "real," in which it is opposed to "illusory," the reality of the picture is not in doubt. The disputants have satisfied themselves that the picture is real, in this sense, by obtaining a correlated series of sensations of sight and sensations of touch. Is there any similar process by which they could discover whether the picture was real, in the sense in which the term "real" is opposed to "ideal"? Clearly there is none. But, if that is so, the problem is fictitious according to our criterion. This does not mean that the realist-idealist controversy may be dismissed without further ado. For it can legitimately be regarded as a dispute concerning the analysis of existential propositions, and so as involving a logical problem which can be definitively solved. What we have just shown is that the question at issue between idealists and realists becomes fictitious when, as is often the case, it is given a metaphysical interpretation.

There is no need for us to give further examples of the operation of our criterion of significance. For our object is merely to show that philosophy, as a genuine branch of knowledge, must be distinguished from metaphysics. We are not now concerned with the historical question how much of what has traditionally passed for philosophy is actually metaphysical. We shall, however, point out later on that the majority of the "great philosophers" of the past were not essentially metaphysicians, and thus reassure those who would otherwise be prevented from adopting our criterion by considerations of piety.

As to the validity of the verification principle, in the form in which we have stated it, a demonstration will be given in the course of this book. For it will be shown that all propositions which have factual content are empirical hypotheses; and that the function of an empirical hypothesis is to provide a rule for the anticipation of experience. And this means that every empirical hypothesis must be relevant to some actual, or possible, experience, so that a statement which is not relevant to any experience is not an empirical hypothesis, and accordingly has no factual content. But this is precisely what the principle of verifiability asserts.

It should be mentioned here that the fact that the utterances of the metaphysician are nonsensical does not follow simply from the fact that they are devoid of factual content. It follows from that fact, together with the fact that they are not *a priori* propositions. And in assuming that they are not *a priori* propositions, we are once again anticipating the conclusions of a later chapter in this book. For it will be shown there that *a priori* propositions, which have always been attractive to philosophers on account of their certainty, owe this certainty to the fact that they are tautologies. We may accordingly define a metaphysical sentence as a sentence which purports to express a genuine proposition, but does, in fact, express neither a tautology nor an empirical hypothesis. And as tautologies and empirical hypotheses form the entire class of significant propositions, we are justified in concluding that all metaphysical assertions are nonsensical. Our next task is to show how they come to be made.

The use of the term "substance," to which we have already referred, provides us with a good example of the way in which metaphysics mostly comes to be written. It happens to be the case that we cannot, in our language, refer to the sensible properties of a thing without introducing a word or phrase which appears to stand for the thing itself as opposed to anything which may be said about it. And, as a result of this, those who are infected by the primitive superstition that to every name a single real entity must correspond assume that it is necessary to distinguish logically between the thing itself and any, or all, of its sensible properties. And so they employ the term "substance" to refer to the thing itself. But from the fact that we happen to employ a single word to refer to a thing, and make that word the grammatical subject of the sentences in which we refer to the sensible appearances of the thing, it does not by any means follow that the thing itself is a "simple entity," or that it cannot be defined in terms of the totality of its appearances. It is true that in talking of "its" appearances we appear to distinguish the thing from the appearances, but that is simply an accident of linguistic usage. Logical analysis shows that what makes these "appearances" the "appearances of" the same thing is not their relationship to an entity other than themselves, but their relationship to one another. The metaphysician fails to see this because he is misled by a superficial grammatical feature of his language.

A simpler and clearer instance of the way in which a consideration of grammar leads to metaphysics is the case of the metaphysical concept of Being. The origin of our temptation to raise questions about Being, which no conceivable experience would enable us to answer, lies in the fact that, in our language, sentences which express existential propositions and sentences which express attributive propositions may be of the same grammatical form. For instance, the sentences "Martyrs exist" and "Martyrs suffer" both consist of a noun followed by an intransitive verb, and the fact that they have grammatically the same appearance leads one to assume that they are of the same logical type. It is seen that in the proposition "Martyrs suffer," the members of a certain species are credited with a certain attribute, and it is sometimes assumed that the same thing is true of such a proposition as "Martyrs exist." If this were actually the case, it would, indeed, be as legitimate to speculate about the Being of martyrs as it is to speculate about their suffering. But, as Kant pointed out, existence is not an attribute. For, when we ascribe an attribute to a thing, we covertly assert that it exists: so that if existence were itself an attribute, it would follow that all positive existential propositions were tau-

tologies, and all negative existential propositions self-contradictory; and this is not the case. So that those who raise questions about Being which are based on the assumption that existence is an attribute are guilty of following grammar beyond the boundaries of sense.

A similar mistake has been made in connection with such propositions as "Unicorns are fictitious." Here again the fact that there is a superficial grammatical resemblance between the English sentences "Dogs are faithful" and "Unicorns are fictitious," and between the corresponding sentences in other languages, creates the assumption that they are of the same logical type. Dogs must exist in order to have the property of being faithful, and so it is held that unless unicorns in some way existed they could not have the property of being fictitious. But, as it is plainly self-contradictory to say that fictitious objects exist, the device is adopted of saying that they are real in some non-empirical sense—that they have a mode of real being which is different from the mode of being of existent things. But since there is no way of testing whether an object is real in this sense, as there is for testing whether it is real in the ordinary sense, the assertion that fictitious objects have a special non-empirical mode of real being is devoid of all literal significance. It comes to be made as a result of the assumption that being fictitious is an attribute. And this is a fallacy of the same order as the fallacy of supposing that existence is an attribute, and it can be exposed in the same way.

In general, the postulation of real non-existent entities results from the superstition, just now referred to, that, to every word or phrase that can be the grammatical subject of a sentence, there must somewhere be a real entity corresponding. For as there is no place in the empirical world for many of these "entities," a special non-empirical world is invoked to house them. To this error must be attributed, not only the utterances of a Heidegger, who bases his metaphysics on the assumption that "Nothing" is a name which is used to denote something peculiarly mysterious, but also the prevalence of such problems as those concerning the reality of propositions and universals whose senselessness, though less obvious, is no less complete.

These few examples afford a sufficient indication of the way in which most metaphysical assertions come to be formulated. They show how easy it is to write sentences which are literally nonsensical without seeing that they are nonsensical. And thus we see that the view that a number of the traditional "problems of philosophy" are metaphysical, and consequently fictitious, does not involve any incredible assumptions about the psychology of philosophers.

Among those who recognize that if philosophy is to be accounted a genuine branch of knowledge it must be defined in such a way as to distinguish it from metaphysics, it is fashionable to speak of the metaphysician as a kind of misplaced poet. As his statements have no literal meaning, they are not subject to any criteria of truth or falsehood: but they may still serve to express, or arouse, emotion, and thus be subject to ethical or æsthetic standards. And it is suggested that they may have considerable value, as means of moral inspiration, or even as works of art. In this way, an attempt is made to compensate the metaphysician for his extrusion from philosophy.

I am afraid that this compensation is hardly in accordance with his deserts. The view that the metaphysician is to be reckoned among the poets appears to rest on the assumption that both talk nonsense. But this assumption is false. In the vast majority of cases the sentences which are produced by poets do have literal meaning. The difference between the man who uses language scientifically and the man who uses it emotively is not that the one produces sentences which are incapable of arousing emotion, and the other sentences which have no sense, but that the one is primarily concerned with the expression of true propositions, the other with the creation of a work of art. Thus, if a work of science contains true and important propositions, its value as a work of science will hardly be diminished by the fact that they are inelegantly expressed. And similarly, a work of art is not necessarily the worse for the fact that all the propositions comprising it are literally false. But to say that many literary works are largely composed of falsehoods, is not to say that they are composed of pseudo-propositions. It is, in fact, very rare for a literary artist to produce sentences which have no literal meaning. And where this does occur, the sentences are carefully chosen for their rhythm and balance. If the author writes nonsense, it is because he considers it most suitable for bringing about the effects for which his writing is designed.

The metaphysician, on the other hand, does not intend to write nonsense. He lapses into it through being deceived by grammar, or through committing errors of reasoning, such as that which leads to the view that the sensible world is unreal. But it is not the mark of a poet simply to make mistakes of this sort. There are some, indeed, who would see in the fact that the metaphysician's utterances are senseless a reason against the view that they have æsthetic value. And, without going so far as this, we may safely say that it does not constitute a reason for it.

It is true, however, that although the greater part of metaphysics is merely the embodiment of humdrum errors, there remain a number of metaphysical passages which are the work of genuine mystical feeling; and they may more plausibly be held to have moral or æsthetic value. But, as far as we are concerned, the distinction between the kind of metaphysics that is produced by a philosopher who has been duped by grammar, and the kind that is produced by a mystic who is trying to express the inexpressible, is of no great importance: what is important to us is to realise that even the utterances of the metaphysician who is attempting to expound a vision are literally senseless; so that henceforth we may pursue our philosophical researches with as little regard for them as for the more inglorious kind of metaphysics which comes from a failure to understand the workings of our language.

READING QUESTIONS

1. Ayer writes that "the fruitlessness of attempting to transcend the limits of possible sense-experience will be deduced, not from a psychological hypothesis concerning the actual constitution of the human mind, but from the rule which determines the literal significance of language." Why does Ayer believe that this will be a more successful strategy? Why does he believe that the empiricist's and the Kantian's respective replies to the metaphysician will fail to convince?

2. What is the *criterion of verifiability*? Express the criterion three different ways. How is the criterion supposed to be understood? Is it a test of meaningfulness, for example? What else could it be?

3. What is the distinction between practical verifiability and verifiability in principle? What is the distinction between strong verifiability and weak verifiability? Why are these distinctions important? What kind of verifiability does Ayer argue for? What is his argument?

4. Ayer applies the criterion of verifiability to some of the traditional disputes of philosophy (e.g., the dispute between the monist and the pluralist and the dispute between the realist and the idealist). How does he think that applying the criterion could help to resolve these disputes?

5. What is an *a priori* proposition? What does it mean to say that an *a priori* proposition expresses a tautology?

6. Briefly outline Ayer's account of how we come to make metaphysical assertions (when they are, in fact, nonsense). Why does Ayer think that it is an error to think of the "metaphysician as a kind of misplaced poet"?

SUGGESTIONS FOR FURTHER READING (A. J. AYER)

Primary Sources

(1936) *Language, Truth, and Logic.* 2nd ed., 1946. London: Victor Gollancz.

(1940) *Foundations of Empirical Knowledge.* New York: Macmillan.

(1947) *Thinking and Meaning.* London: H. K. Lewis.

(1954) *Philosophical Essays.* New York: Macmillan.

(1956) *The Problem of Knowledge.* New York: Macmillan.

(ed.) (1959) *Logical Positivism.* New York: The Free Press.

(1963) *The Concept of a Person and Other Essays.* New York: Macmillan.

(1968) *The Origins of Pragmatism.* New York: Macmillan.

(1969) *Metaphysics and Common-Sense.* New York: Macmillan.

(1971) *Russell and Moore: The Analytical Heritage.* New York: Macmillan.

(1972) *Probability and Evidence.* New York: Macmillan.

(1972) *Bertrand Russell.* New York: Viking Press.

(1973) *The Central Questions of Philosophy.* New York: Holt, Rinehart, and Winston.

(1977) *Part of My Life.* London: Harper Collins.

(1980) *Hume.* Oxford: Oxford University Press.

(1980) *Philosophy in the Twentieth Century.* London: Weidenfeld.

(1981) *Philosophy and Morality and Other Essays.* Oxford: Clarendon Press.

(1984) *More of My Life.* London: Harper Collins.

(1986) *Wittgenstein.* Chicago: University of Chicago Press.

(1988) *Bertrand Russell.* Chicago: University of Chicago Press.

Secondary Sources

Achinstein, P., and S. Barker (1969) *The Legacy of Logical Positivism.* Baltimore, MD: Johns Hopkins Press.

Foster, J. (1985) *A. J. Ayer.* London: Routledge.

Gower, B., ed. (1987) *Logical Positivism in Perspective: Essays on "Language, Truth, and Logic".* Beckenham: Croom Helm.

Griffiths, A. P. (1992) *A. J. Ayer: Memorial Essays.* Cambridge: Cambridge University Press.

Hahn, L. E., ed. (1972) *The Philosophy of A. J. Ayer.* La Salle, IL: Open Court.

Hanfling, O. (1999) *Ayer.* London: Routledge.

Honderich, T. (1981) *Essays on A. J. Ayer.* Cambridge: Cambridge University Press.

Joad, C. E. (1950) *Critique of Logical Positivism.* London: Victor Gollancz.

Macdonald, G., and C. Wright., eds. (1986) *Fact, Science, and Morality: Essays on A. J. Ayers's "Language, Truth, and Logic".* Oxford: Blackwell.

MORITZ SCHLICK

Positivism and Realism

Friedrich Albert Moritz Schlick (1882–1936) was born in Berlin. He studied at the universities in Berlin, Heidelberg, and Lausanne, eventually earning his doctorate in physics in 1904 from the University of Berlin with a dissertation on the reflection of light in a non-homogeneous medium. His studies in physics left him familiar with and appreciative of the methods and standards of scientific research. This familiarity, in time, would play a significant role in the development of his distinctive philosophical outlook.

Schlick's teaching and research career began with his appointment as an associate professor at the University of Rostock in 1911. It was at Rostock that his serious interests in the philosophy of science and in epistemology first developed. In 1921, he received a professorship at the University of Kiel, but left after only one year in order to accept the chair of *Naturphilosophie* at the University of Vienna, a chair originally created for the early Viennese positivist Ernst Mach.

In the course of the time that he spent in Vienna, Schlick's philosophical outlook underwent major development, culminating in his becoming an outspoken proponent for positivistic philosophy. Changes in his philosophical orientation were largely due to the influence of the writings of Ludwig Wittgenstein and the regular discussions he engaged in with fellow members of the Vienna Circle (perhaps especially with Rudolf Carnap). Along with many other members of the Circle, Schlick came ultimately to accept and espouse the principle doctrines of positivism, i.e., verificationism, the meaninglessness of traditional metaphysics, the conception of philosophy as pure method, and so on. His own particular interests in philosophy never strayed far from the core issues of epistemology, the philosophy of language, and the philosophy of science. Schlick remained a professor and chair at Vienna until his untimely death. He was assassinated by a deranged student while making his way to a lecture on campus.

In "Positivism and Realism" Schlick undertakes two projects: First, he clarifies and develops his version of verificationism. Second, he applies his version of verificationism to the so-called "problem of the external world." The section of his essay in which he pursues this second project is reprinted below. After examining the arguments, he concludes that "the denial of the existence of a transcendent external world [is] just as much a metaphysical proposition as its assertion."

Therefore, both theses are, in actuality, completely meaningless.

III. What Does 'Reality' Mean? What Does 'External World' Mean?

Let us ask: What meaning has it, if the 'realist' says 'there is an external world'? or even: What meaning attaches to the claim (which the realist attributes to the positivist) 'there is no external 'world'?

To answer the question, it is necessary, of course, to clarify the significance of the words 'there is' and 'external world'. Let us begin with the first. 'There is *x*' amounts to saying '*x* is real' or '*x* is actual'. So what does it mean if we attribute actuality (or reality) to an object? It is an ancient and very important insight of logic or philosophy, that the proposition '*x* is actual' is totally different in kind from a proposition that attributes any sort of *property* to *x* (such as '*x* is hard'). In other words, actuality, reality or existence is not a property. The statement 'the dollar in my pocket is round' has a totally different logical form from the statement 'the dollar in my pocket is actual'. In modern logic this distinction is expressed by an altogether different symbolism, but it had already been very sharply emphasized by Kant, who, as we know, in his critique of the so-called ontological proof of God's existence had correctly found the error of this proof in the fact that existence was treated like a property there.

In daily life we very often have to speak of actuality or existence, and for that very reason it cannot be hard to discover the meaning of this talk. In a legal battle it often has to be established whether some document really exists, or whether this has merely been falsely claimed, say, by one of the parties; nor is it wholly unimportant to me, whether the dollar in my pocket is

Moritz Schlick, selection from "Positivism and Realism" from his *Philosophical Papers,* Vol. II, Dordrecht: Kluwer Academic Publishers, 1980, pp. 259–284. Reprinted with kind permission of Kluwer Academic Publishers.

merely imaginary or actually real. Now everybody knows in what way such a reality-claim is verified, nor can there be the least doubt about it; the reality of the dollar is proved by this, and this alone, that by suitable manipulations I furnish myself certain tactual or visual sensations, on whose occurrence I am accustomed to say: this is a dollar. The same holds of the document, only there we should be content, on occasion, with certain statements by others claiming to have seen the document, that is, to have had perceptions of a quite specific kind. And the 'statements of others' again consist in certain acoustic, or—if they were written utterances—visual perceptions. There is need of no special controversy about the fact that the occurrence of certain sense-perceptions among the data *always* constitutes the sole criterion for propositions about the reality of a 'physical' object or event, in daily life no less than in the most refined assertions of science. That there are okapis in Africa can be established only by observing such animals. But it is not necessary that the object or event 'itself' should have to be perceived. We can imagine, for example, that the existence of a trans-Neptunian planet might be inferred by observation of perturbations with just as much certainty as by direct perception of a speck of light in the telescope. The reality of the atom provides another example, as does the back side of the moon.

It is of great importance to state that the occurrence of some one particular experience in verifying a reality-statement is often not recognized as such a verification, but that it is throughout a question of regularities, of law-like connections; in this way true verifications are distinguished from illusions and hallucinations. If we say of some event or object—which must be marked out by a description—that it *is real*, this means, then, that there is a quite specific connection between perceptions or other experiences, that under given circumstances certain data are presented. By this alone is it verified, and hence this is also its only stateable meaning.

This, too, was already formulated, in principle, by Kant, whom nobody will accuse of 'positivism'. Reality, for him, is a category, and if we apply it anywhere, and claim of an object that it is real, then all this asserts, in Kant's opinion, is that it belongs to a law-governed connection of perceptions.

It will be seen that for us (as for Kant; and the same must apply to any philosopher who is aware of his task)

it is merely a matter of saying what is meant when we ascribe real existence to a thing in life or in science; it is in no sense a matter of correcting the claims of ordinary life or of research. I must confess that I should charge with folly and reject *a limine* every philosophical system that involved the claim that clouds and stars, mountains and the sea, were not actually real, that the 'physical world' did not exist, and that the chair against the wall ceases to be every time I turn my back on it. Nor do I seriously impute such a claim to any thinker. It would, for example, be undoubtedly a quite mistaken account of Berkeley's philosophy if his system were to be understood in this fashion. He, too, in no way denied the reality of the physical world, but merely sought to explain what we mean when we attribute reality to it. Anyone who says here that unperceived things are ideas in the mind of God is not in fact denying their existence, but is seeking, rather, to understand it. Even John Stuart Mill was not wanting to deny the reality of physical objects, but rather to explain it, when he declared them to be 'permanent possibilities of sensation', although I do consider his mode of expression to have been very unsuitably chosen.

So if 'positivism' is understood to mean a view that denies reality to bodies, I should simply have to declare it absurd; but I do not believe that such an interpretation of positivist opinions, at least as regards their competent exponents, would be historically just. Yet, however that may be, we are concerned only with the issue itself. And on this we have established as follows: our principle, that the question about the meaning of a proposition is identical with the question about its verification, leads us to recognize that the claim that a thing is real is a statement about lawful connections of experiences; it does *not*, however, imply this claim to be false. (There is therefore no denial of reality to physical objects in favor of sensations.)

But opponents of the view presented profess themselves by no means satisfied with this assertion. So far as I can see, they would answer as follows: 'You do, indeed, acknowledge completely the reality of the physical world, but—as we see it—only in words. You simply *call* real what we should describe as mere conceptual constructions. When *we* use the word "reality", we mean by it something quite different from you. Your definition of the real reduces it to experiences; but we mean something quite independent of all experiences. We mean something that possesses the same independence that you obviously concede only to the data, in that you reduce everything else to them, as the not-further-reducible'.

Although it would be a sufficient rebuttal to request our opponents to reflect once more upon how reality-statements are verified, and how verification is connected with *meaning*, I do in fact recognize the need to take account of the psychological attitude from which this argument springs, and therefore beg attention to the following considerations, whereby a modification of this attitude may yet, perhaps, be effected.

Let us first enquire whether, on our view, a 'content of consciousness' is credited with a reality that is denied to a physical object. We ask, therefore: does the claim that a feeling or sensation is real have a meaning different from the claim that a physical object is real? For us, this can mean only: are different types of verification involved in the two cases? The answer is: no!

To clarify this, we need to enter a little into the logical form of reality-statements. The general logical recognition that an existence-statement can be made about a datum only if it is marked out by a description, but not if it is given by an immediate indication, is also valid, of course, for the 'data of consciousness'. In the language of symbolic logic, this is expressed by the fact that an existence-claim must contain an 'operator'. In Russell's notation, for example, a reality-statement has the form $(\exists x)fx$, or in words, 'there is an x that has the property f'. The form of words 'there is a', where 'a' is supposed to be the individual name of a directly indicated object, therefore means no more than 'this here'; this form of words is meaningless, and in Russell's symbolism it cannot even be written down. We have to grasp the idea that Descartes' proposition 'I am'—or, to put it better, 'contents of consciousness exist'—is absolutely meaningless; it expresses nothing, and contains no knowledge. This is due to the fact that 'contents of consciousness' occurs in this connection as a mere *name* for the given; no characteristic is asserted, whose presence could be tested. A proposition has meaning, and is verifiable, only if I can state under what circumstances it would be true, and under what circumstances it would be false. But how am I to describe the circumstances under which the proposition 'My contents of consciousness exist' would be false? Every attempt

would lead to ridiculous absurdities, to such propositions, say, as 'It is the case that nothing is the case', or the like. Hence I am self-evidently unable to describe the circumstances that make the proposition true (just try it!). Nor is there any doubt whatever that Descartes, with his proposition, had really obtained no knowledge, and was actually no wiser than before.

No, the question about the reality of an experience has meaning only where this reality can also be meaningfully *doubted*. I can ask, for example: Is it really true that I felt joy on hearing that news? This can be verified or falsified exactly as when we ask, say: Is it true that Sirius has a companion (that this companion is real)? That I felt joy on a particular occasion can be verified, for example, by examination of other people's statements about my behavior at the time, by my finding of a letter that I then wrote, or simply by the return to me of an exact memory of the emotion I experienced. Here, therefore, there is not the slightest difference of principle: to be real always means to stand in a definite connection with the given. Nor is it otherwise, say, with an experience that is present at this very moment. I can quite meaningfully ask, for example (in the course, say, of a physiological experiment): Do I now actually feel a pain or not? (Notice that 'pain', here, does not function as an individual name for a 'this here', but represents a conceptual term for a describable class of experiences.) Here, too, the question is answered by establishing that in conjunction with certain circumstances (experimental conditions, concentration of attention, etc.) an experience with certain describable properties occurs. Such describable properties would be, for example: similarity to an experience that has occurred under certain other circumstances; tendency to evoke certain reactions; and so on.

However we may twist and turn, it is impossible to interpret a reality-statement otherwise than as fitting into a perceptual context. It is absolutely the *same* kind of reality that we have to attribute to the data of consciousness and to physical events. Scarcely anything in the history of philosophy has created more confusion than the attempt to pick out one of the two as true 'being'. Wherever the term 'real' is intelligibly used, it has one and the same meaning.

Our opponent, perhaps, will still feel his position unshaken by what we have said, having the impression, rather, that the arguments here presented presuppose a starting-point at which he cannot, from the outset, station himself. He has to concede that the decision about the reality or unreality of anything in experience takes place, in every case, in the manner outlined, but he claims that in this way we only arrive at what Kant called *empirical* reality. It designates the area governed by the observations of daily life and of science, but beyond this boundary there lies something else, *transcendent* reality, which cannot be inferred by strict logic, and is thus no postulate of the understanding, though it is a postulate of sound *reason.* It is the only true *external world,* and this alone is at issue in the philosophical problem of the existence of the external world. The discussion thereupon abandons the question about the meaning of the term 'reality', and turns to that about the meaning of the term 'external world'.

The term 'external world' is obviously used in two different ways: firstly in the usage of daily life, and secondly as a technical term in philosophy.

Where it occurs in everyday life, it has, like the majority of expressions employed in practical affairs, an intelligibly stateable meaning. In contrast to the 'internal world', which covers memories, thoughts, dreams, wishes and feelings, the 'external world' means nothing else, here, but the world of mountains and trees, houses, animals and men. What it means to maintain the existence of a certain object in this world, is known to every child; and it was necessary to point out that it really means absolutely nothing *more* than what the child knows. We all know how to verify the proposition, say, that 'There is a castle in the park before the town'. We perform certain acts, and if certain exactly specifiable states-of-affairs come about, then we say: 'Yes, there really is a castle there'; otherwise we say: 'That statement was an error or a lie.' And if somebody now asks us: 'But was the castle there in the night as well, when nobody saw it?' we answer: 'Undoubtedly! for it would have been impossible to build it in the period from early this morning till now, and besides, the state of the building shows that it was not only already *in situ* yesterday, but has been there for a hundred years, and hence since before we were born'. We are thus in possession of quite specific empirical criteria for whether houses and trees were also there when we were not seeing them, and whether they already existed before our birth, and will exist after our death. That is to say, the claim that these things 'exist independently of us' has a perfectly clear, testable meaning, and is obviously to be answered in the affirmative. We are very well able to distinguish such things in a stateable way from those that only occur 'subjectively', 'in dependence upon ourselves'. If, owing to an eye-defect, I see, for example, a dark speck when I look at the wall opposite me, I say of it that it is there only when I look, whereas I say of the wall that it is also there when I am not looking. The verification of this difference is in fact very easy, and both claims assert precisely what is contained in these verifications and nothing more.

So if the term 'external world' is taken in the everyday sense, the question about its existence simply means: Are there, in addition to memories, wishes and ideas, also stars, clouds, plants and animals, and my own body? We have just affirmed once more that it would be utterly absurd to say no to this question. There are obviously houses and clouds and animals existing independently of us, and I have already said earlier that a thinker who denied the existence of the external world in this sense would have no claim to our attention. Instead of telling us what we mean when we speak of mountains and plants, he wishes to persuade us that there are no such things at all!

But now how about science? When it speaks of the external world, does it, unlike daily life, mean something other than things such as houses and trees? It seems to me that this is by no means the case. For atoms and electric fields, or whatever else the physicist may speak of, are precisely what houses and trees consist of, according to his teaching; the one must therefore be real in the same sense as the other. The objectivity of mountains and clouds is just exactly the same as that of protons and energies; the latter stand in no greater contrast to the 'subjectivity' of feelings, say, or hallucinations, than do the former. We have long since convinced ourselves, in fact, that the existence of even the most subtle of the 'invisible' things postulated by the scientist is verified, in principle, in exactly the same way as the reality of a tree or a star.

In order to settle the dispute about realism, it is of the greatest importance to alert the physicist to the fact that his external world is nothing else but the *nature* which also surrounds us in daily life, and is not the 'transcendent world' of the metaphysicians. The difference between the two is again quite particularly evident in the philosophy of Kant. Nature, and everything of which the physicist can and must speak, belongs, in Kant's view, to empirical reality, and the meaning of this (as already mentioned) is explained by him exactly as we have also had to do. Atoms, in Kant's system, have no transcendent reality—they are not 'things-in-themselves'. Thus the physicist cannot appeal to the Kantian philosophy; his arguments lead only to the empirical external world that we all acknowledge, not to a transcendent one; his electrons are not metaphysical entities.

Many scientists speak, nonetheless, of the necessity of having to postulate the existence of an external world as a *metaphysical* hypothesis. They never do this, indeed, within their own science (although all the necessary hypotheses of a science ought to occur *within* it), but only at the point where they leave this territory and begin to philosophize. The transcendent external world is actually something that is referred to exclusively in philosophy, never in a science or in daily life. It is simply a technical term, whose meaning we now have to inquire into.

How does the transcendent or metaphysical external world differ from the empirical one? In philosophical systems it is thought of as subsisting somehow behind the empirical world, where the word 'behind' is also supposed to indicate that this world is not *knowable* in the same sense as the empirical, that it lies beyond a boundary that divides the accessible from the inaccessible.

This distinction originally has its ground in the view formerly shared by the majority of philosophers, that to know an object requires that it be immediately given, directly experienced; knowledge is a kind of intuition, and is perfect only if the known is directly present to the knower, like a sensation or a feeling. So what cannot be immediately experienced or intuited remains, on this view, unknowable, ungraspable, transcendent, and belongs to the realm of things-in-themselves. Here, as I have elsewhere had to state on numerous occasions, we simply have a confusion of knowing with mere acquaintance or experiencing. But such a confusion is certainly not committed by modern scientists; I do not believe that any physicist considers knowledge of the electron to consist in its entering

bodily, by an act of intuition, into the scientist's consciousness; he will take the view, rather, that for complete knowledge the only thing needed is for the regularity of an electron's behavior to be so exhaustively stated that all formulas in which its properties occur in any way are totally confirmed by experience. In other words, the electron, and all physical realities likewise, are *not* unknowable things-in-themselves, and do not belong to a transcendent, metaphysical reality, if this is characterized by the fact that it embraces the unknowable.

Thus we again return to the conclusion that all the physicist's hypotheses can relate only to *empirical* reality, if by this we mean the knowable. It would in fact be a self-contradiction to wish to assume something unknowable as a hypothesis. For there must always be specific *reasons* for setting up a hypothesis, since it is, after all, supposed to fulfill a specific purpose. What is assumed in the hypothesis must therefore have the property of fulfilling this purpose, and of being precisely so constituted as to be justified by these reasons. But in virtue of this very fact certain statements are made of it, and these contain *knowledge* of it. And they contain, indeed, *complete* knowledge of it, since *only* that can be hypothetically assumed for which there are reasons in experience.

Or does the scientific 'realist' wish to characterize the talk of not immediately experienced objects as a metaphysical hypothesis for some reason other than the non-existent one of its unknowability? To this, perhaps, he will answer 'yes'. In fact it can be seen from numerous statements in the literature, that the physicist by no means couples his claim of a transcendent world with the claim that it is unknowable; on the contrary, he (quite rightly) takes the view that the nature of extra-mental things is reflected with perfect correctness in his equations. Hence the external world of the physical realist is not that of traditional metaphysics. He employs the technical term of the philosophers, but what he designates by means of it has seemed to us to be merely the external world of everyday life, whose existence is doubted by nobody, not even the 'positivist'.

So what is this other reason that leads the 'realist' to regard his external world as a metaphysical assumption? Why does he want to distinguish it from the empirical external world that we have described? The answer to this question leads us back again to an earlier point in our argument. For the 'realistic' physicist is perfectly content with our description of the external world, except on one point: he thinks that we have not lent it enough *reality*. It is not by its unknowability or any other feature that he takes his 'external world' to differ from the empirical one; it is simply and solely by the fact that another, higher reality attaches to it. This often finds expression even in the terminology; the word 'real' is often reserved for this external world, in contrast to the merely 'ideal', 'subjective' content of consciousness, and the mere 'logical constructions' into which 'positivism' is accused of dissolving reality.

But now even the physical realist has a dim feeling that, as we know, reality is not a 'property'; hence he cannot simply pass from our empirical external world to his transcendent one by attributing to it the feature of 'reality' over and above the features that we, too, ascribe to all physical objects; yet that is how he talks, and this illegitimate leap, whereby he leaves the realm of the meaningful, would in fact be 'metaphysical', and is also felt to be such by himself.

We now have a clear view of the situation, and can judge it on the basis of the preceding considerations.

Our principle, that the truth and falsity of all statements, including those about the reality of a physical object, can be tested only in the 'given', and that *therefore* the meaning of all statements can likewise be formulated and understood only by means of the given—this principle has been wrongly construed as if it claimed or presupposed that only the given is real. Hence the 'realist' feels compelled to contradict the principle, and to set up the counterclaim, that the meaning of a reality-statement is by no means exhausted in mere assertions of the form 'Under these particular circumstances this particular experience will occur' (where these assertions, on our view, are in any case an infinite multitude); the meaning, he says, in fact lies *beyond this* in something else, which must be referred to, say, as 'independent existence', 'transcendent being' or the like, and of which our principle provides no account.

To this we ask: Well, then, *how* does one give an account of it? What do these words 'independent existence' and 'transcendent being' means? In other words, what testable difference does it make in the world, whether an object has transcendent being or not?

Two answers are given here. The first runs: It makes a quite enormous difference. For a scientist who believes in a 'real external world' will feel and work quite differently from one who merely aims at 'describing sensations'. The former will regard the starry heaven, whose aspect recalls to him the inconceivable sublimity and size of the universe, and his own human smallness, with feelings of awe and devotion quite different from those of the latter, to whom the most distant galactic systems are but 'complexes of his own sensations'. The first will be devoted to his task with an enthusiasm, and will feel in his knowing of the objective world a satisfaction, that are denied to the second, since he takes himself to be concerned only with constructions of his own.

To this first answer we have this to say: If, in the behavior of two thinkers, there should anywhere occur a difference such as has here been described—and it would in fact involve an observable state-of-affairs—and were we to insist upon so expressing this difference as to say that the first believes in a real external world, and the other not—well, even so, the *meaning* of our assertion still consists solely in what we observe in the behavior of the two. That is to say, the words 'absolute reality', or 'transcendent being', or whatever other terms we may use for it, now *signify* absolutely nothing else but certain states of feeling which arise in the two whenever they contemplate the universe, or make reality-statements, or philosophize. The fact of the matter is, that employment of the words 'independent existence', 'transcendent reality' and so on, is simply and solely the expression of a feeling, a psychological attitude of the speaker (which may in the end, moreover, apply to all metaphysical propositions). If someone assures us that there is a real external world in the supra-empirical sense of the term, he thinks, no doubt, that he has thereby conveyed a truth about the world; but in actuality his words express a quite different state of affairs, namely the mere presence of certain feelings, which provoke him to specific reactions of a verbal or other nature.

If the self-evident still needs to be specially dwelt on, I should like to underline—but in that case with maximum emphasis, and with stress upon the *seriousness* of what I am saying—that the non-metaphysician does not differ from the metaphysician by the fact, say, that he lacks those feelings to which the other gives expression by way of the propositions of a 'realistic' philosophy, but only by the fact that he has recognized that these propositions by no means have the meaning that they seem to have, and are therefore to be avoided. He will give expression to the same feelings in a *different* way. In other words, this confrontation of the two types of thinker, set up in the 'realist's' first answer, was misleading and erroneous. If anyone is so unfortunate as not to feel the sublimity of the starry heaven, then the blame lies on something other than a logical analysis of the concepts of reality and the external world. To suppose that the opponent of metaphysics is incapable, say, of justly estimating the greatness of Copernicus, because in a certain sense the Ptolemaic view reflects the empirical situation just as well as the Copernican, seems to me no less strange than to believe that the 'positivist' cannot be a good father to his family, because according to his theory his children are merely complexes of his own sensations, and it is therefore senseless to make provision for their welfare after his death. No, the world of the non-metaphysician is the same world as that of everybody else; it lacks nothing that is needed in order to make meaningful all the statements of science and all the actions of daily life. He merely refuses to add meaningless statements to his description of the world.

We come to the *second* answer that can be given to the question about the meaning of the claim that there is a transcendent reality. It simply consists in admitting that it makes absolutely no difference for experience whether we postulate something else existing behind the empirical world or not; metaphysical realism cannot therefore be actually tested or verified. Thus it cannot be further stated what is meant by this claim; yet something *is* meant thereby, and the meaning can also be understood without verification.

This is nothing else but the view criticized in the previous section, that the meaning of a proposition has nothing to do with its verification, and it only remains for us to repeat once more our earlier general criticism, as applied to this particular case. We must reply, therefore: Well now! You are giving the name 'existence' or 'reality' here to something that is utterly inexpressible and cannot be explained or stated in any fashion. You think, nonetheless, that these words have a meaning. As to that, we shall not quarrel with you. But this much is certain: by the admission just made, this meaning cannot in any way become manifest, cannot be expressed by any oral or written communication, or by

any gesture or act. For if this were possible, a testable empirical situation would exist; there would be something *different* in the world, if the proposition 'There is a transcendent world' were true, from if it were false. This differentness would then signify the meaning of the words 'real external world', and hence it would be an empirical meaning—that is, this real external world would again be merely the empirical world which we, too, acknowledge, like everyone else. Even to speak, merely, of another world, is logically impossible. There can be no discussion about it, for a non-verifiable existence cannot enter as meaning into any possible proposition. Anyone who still believes in such a thing—or imagines he believes—can only do so in silence. There are arguments only for something that can be said.

The results of our discussion can be summarized as follows.

1. The principle, that the meaning of every proposition is exhaustively determined by its verification in the given, seems to me a legitimate, unassailable core of the 'positivist' schools of thought.

But within those schools it has seldom come clearly to light, and has often been mingled with so many untenable principles, that a logical clean-up is necessary. If we want to call the result of this clean-up 'positivism', which might well be justified on historical grounds, we should have, perhaps, to affix a differentiating adjective: the term 'logical' or 'logistic positivism' is often used; otherwise the expression 'consistent empiricism' has seemed to me appropriate.

2. This principle does not mean, nor does it follow from it, that only the given is real; such a claim would actually be meaningless.

3. Consistent empiricism, therefore, does *not* deny, either, the existence of an external world; it merely points out the empirical meaning of this existence-claim.

4. It is not an 'as if theory'. It does not say, for example, that everything behaves as if there were physical independent bodies; on the contrary, for it, too, everything is real that the non-philosophizing scientist declares to be real. The subject-matter of physics does not consist of sensations, but of laws. The formulation employed by some positivists, that bodies 'are mere com-

plexes of sensations' is therefore to be rejected. The only correct view is that propositions about bodies can be transformed into propositions of like meaning about the regularity of occurrence of sensations.

5. Logical positivism and realism are therefore not opposed; anyone who acknowledges our principle must actually be an empirical realist.

6. There is opposition only between consistent empiricism and the meta-physician, and it is directed as much against the realist as the idealist (the former is designated in our discussion as a 'realist', in quotation marks).

7. The denial of the existence of a transcendent external world would be just as much a metaphysical proposition as its assertion; the consistent empiricist does not therefore deny the transcendent, but declares both its denial and its affirmation to be equally devoid of meaning.

This last distinction is of the greatest importance. I am convinced that the main resistances to our viewpoint stem from the fact that the difference between the falsity and the meaninglessness of a proposition is not heeded. The proposition 'Talk of a metaphysical external world is meaningless' does *not* say 'There is no metaphysical external world', but something *toto coelo* different. The empiricist does not say to the metaphysician: 'Your words assert something false', but 'Your words assert nothing at all!' He does not contradict the metaphysician, but says: 'I do not understand you'.

READING QUESTIONS

1. Schlick's essay concerns the so-called "question as to the reality of the external world." He indicates that on this question "there seem to be two parties: that of 'realism', which believes in the reality of the external world, and that of 'positivism', which does not believe in this." In fact, Schlick thinks, there is no such dualism, because neither view is really intelligible—it is a "meaningless pseudo-problem." Why?

2. Why does Schlick (and others) think that there is a difference between the logical form of the statement

"the dollar in my pocket is round" and "the dollar in my pocket is actual"?

3. Schlick states that "if we say of some event or object—which must be marked out by a description—that it is *real*, this means, then, that there is a quite specific connection between perceptions or other experiences, that under given circumstances certain data are presented. By this alone it is verified, and hence this is also its only stateable meaning." Briefly outline his argument for this thesis. From his various remarks, construct his answer to the objection that, on this view, illusions and hallucinations are, therefore, going to be *real*.

4. Schlick states that "the form of words 'there is *a*', where '*a*' is supposed to be the individual name of a directly indicated object, therefore means no more than 'this here'; this form of words is meaningless, and in Russell's symbolism it cannot even be written down." This is supposed to be contrasted with the case of genuine "reality statements," which have the logical form: $(\exists x)fx$. Carefully catalogue the differences between these two logical forms. What is the significance of the fact that these logical forms are different, on Schlick's view? Are they nevertheless related in some way?

5. Schlick believes that many scientists (and nonscientists) still want to assert that there is a "transcendent or metaphysical external world" and not merely an "empirical" one. But he asks, "what testable difference does it make in the world whether an object has transcendent being or not?" What are the two answers that are offered, and what are his replies to these two answers? Are these replies adequate? Why or why not?

SUGGESTIONS FOR FURTHER READING (MORITZ SCHLICK)

Primary Sources and Collected Writings

(1979) *Philosophical Papers*, edited by B. van de Velde-Schlick and H. Mulder. Dordrecht: D. Reidel.

(1917) *Space and Time in Contemporary Physics*. Oxford: Clarendon, 1920.

(1918) *General Theory of Knowledge*, 2nd ed., 1925. New York: Springer Verlag, 1974.

(1930) *Problems of Ethics*, edited by D. Rynin. New York: Dover, 1962.

(1948) *Philosophy of Nature*, translated by A. von Zeppelin. New York: Philosophical Library, 1968.

(1986) *The Problems of Philosophy in Their Interconnection*, edited by H. Mulder et al. Dordrecht: D. Reidel, 1987.

Secondary Sources

Ayer, A. J., ed (1959) *Logical Positivism*. New York: The Free Press.

Gadol, E. T. (1982) *Rationality and Science*. Vienna: Springer Verlag.

Giere R., and A. Richardson, eds. (1996) *The Origins of Logical Empiricism*. Minneapolis, MN: University of Minnesota Press.

Haller, R., ed. (1982) *Schlick and Neurath ein Symposion*. Amsterdam: Editions Rodopi.

Johnston, W. M. (1972) *The Austrian Mind*. Berkeley, CA: University of California Press.

Kraft, V. (1950) *The Vienna Circle*, translated by A. Pap. New York: Philosophical Library, 1953.

McGuiness, B., and F. Waismann, eds. (1967) *Wittgenstein and the Vienna Circle*, translated by J. Schulte and B. McGuiness. Oxford: Blackwell (1979).

Oberdan, T. (1993). *Protocols, Truth and Convention*. Amsterdam: Editions Rodopi.

Passmore, J. A. (1957) *A Hundred Years of Philosophy*, 2nd ed. London: Duckworth, 1966.

Reichenbach, H. (1951) *The Rise of Scientific Philosophy*. Los Angeles, CA: University of California Press.

Solmon, W., and G. Wolters, eds. (1993) *Logic, Language, and the Structure of Scientific Theories*. Pittsburgh, PA: University of Pittsburgh Press.

Otto Neurath

Physicalism

Born in Austria, Otto Neurath (1882–1945) was an dynamic and outspoken member of the Vienna Circle and a political activist for socialist causes. He was educated at the University of Vienna and at Berlin, where he earned his Ph.D. in the history of economics. He was greatly influenced by the writings of Karl Marx. Neurath's first teaching position was at the Vienna Academy of Commerce as professor of political economy. He later took a teaching position at the University of Vienna. During his time in Vienna he also founded and directed the Social and Economic Museum (from 1924 to 1934).

Neurath led an overtly political life. He was employed by the Austrian planning ministry during the First World War. He also worked for the Bavarian government after the war on the project of socializing the economy. When the Communists reestablished control over Bavaria, he was arrested for treason and only narrowly escaped execution due to the intervention of Max Weber and sympathetic Austrian officials.

Neurath's early writings were mostly on topics in economics, with the exception of a series of articles on logic written with his second wife (who also happened to be Hans Hahn's sister). In addition to his many political interests, Neurath was an active participant in the Vienna Circle and in the development of positivistic philosophy. He was personally responsible for bringing together many of the members of the Vienna Circle and was closely involved in the establishment of *Erkenntnis* as the leading journal of positivism.

Neurath rejected the view, held by Schlick, that empirical knowledge had a secure foundation in direct sense experience, arguing instead for a version of holism. He also believed that it was possible to unify the physical sciences on a completely physicalistic basis. It was this belief that motivated the project of the *Encyclopedia of Unified Science*, written in collaboration with Carl Hempel and Rudolf Carnap. Neurath's commitment to physicalism can also be found in his many writings on the principle of verification and on the epistemological status of protocol statements.

Neurath was forced to leave Austria for Holland in 1934. He eventually settled in England, residing in Oxford, where he ultimately died. Neurath contributed to the development and refinement of positivism both through his many writings and through the personal influence he exerted on other positivistic writers, especially Moritz Schlick and Rudolf Carnap.

In the following essay, Neurath outlines a holistic epistemological framework for unified science. In the process, he critiques various commitments that were widely shared by leading members of the Vienna Circle on the grounds that they depend on various objectionable metaphysical assumptions.

The members of the Vienna Circle (Moritz Schlick, Rudolf Carnap, Philipp Frank, Hans Hahn, Herbert Feigl, Fritz Waismann, Kurt Gödel, Otto Neurath and others) are working out a 'Logical Empiricism'. Following Mach and Poincaré, but above all Russell and Wittgenstein, all the sciences are treated uniformly. Carnap's *Logischer Aufbau der Welt* (1928) shows in which direction future systematic work will move. Wittgenstein's *Tractatus Logico-Philosophicus* (1921) clarified, among other things, the position of logic and mathematics; besides the statements that make additions to what is meaningful, there are the 'tautologies' that show us which transformations are possible within language. By its syntax the language of science excludes anything that is meaningless from the very beginning.

At first the Vienna Circle analyzed 'physics' in the narrower sense almost exclusively; now psychology, biology, sociology are more and more drawn into the discussions. The task of this movement is unified science and nothing less. This radical standpoint, a consequence of the direction of development so far, is to be sketched in the following, for those who know the foundations of these endeavors.

All members of the Vienna Circle agree that there is no 'philosophy' with its own special statements. Some people, however, still wish to separate the discussions of the conceptual foundations of the sciences from the body of scientific work and allow this to continue as 'philosophizing'. Closer reflections show that even this

Otto Neurath, "Physicalism" in Morris Cohen, *Philosophical Papers*, Dordrecht: Kluwer Academic Publishers, 1983, pp. 52–57. Reprinted with kind permission of Kluwer Academic Publishers.

separation is not feasible, and that the definition of concepts is part and parcel of the work of unified science.

Wittgenstein and others, who admit only scientific statements as 'legitimate', nevertheless also acknowledge 'non-legitimate' formulations as preparatory 'explanations' which later should no longer be used within pure science. Within the framework of these explanations the attempt is also made to construct the scientific language with the help, so to speak, of prelinguistic means. Here we also find the attempt to confront language with reality; to use reality to verify whether the language is serviceable. Some of this can be translated into the legitimate language of science, for example, as far as reality is replaced by the totality of other statements with which a new statement is confronted: more about this later. But much of what Wittgenstein and others say about elucidations and the confrontation of language and reality cannot be maintained if unified science is built on the basis of scientific language from the beginning; scientific language itself is a physical formation whose structure, as physical arrangement (ornament), can be discussed by means of the very same language without contradictions.

Let us now attempt to carry out the Vienna Circle's demands within the sciences consistently and apply them to everything that we express by language. We start with scientific language as a physical formation.

'Making predictions' is what all of science is about. At the beginning of the process are observation statements, which, of course, contain measurements of time and space, if only in an approximate manner. There are always spatio-temporal formulations behind which we cannot reach at all without saying something meaningless. 'Saying' itself is a spatio-temporal arrangement.

With the help of observation statements we formulate laws; according to Schlick these laws are not to be seen as proper statements but as directives for finding predictions of individual courses of events; these predictions can then be tested by more observation statements.

The study of language can perfectly well be combined with the study of physical processes; for one always stays in the same field. In staying within the closed area of language one can express everything.

Thus *statements are always compared with statements*, certainly not with some 'reality', nor with 'things', as the Vienna Circle also thought up till now.

This preliminary stage had some idealistic and some realistic elements; these can be completely eliminated if the transition is made to pure unified science.

'Induction' that leads to laws is a matter of 'decision', it cannot be deduced. The attempts to give 'induction' a logical foundation are therefore bound to fail. If a statement is made, it is to be confronted with the totality of existing statements. If it agrees with them, it is joined to them; if it does not agree, it is called 'untrue' and rejected; or the existing complex of statements of science is modified so that the new statement can be incorporated; the latter decision is mostly taken with hesitation. *There can be no other concept of 'truth' for science.*

Under certain circumstances it must be possible to link the laws of all sciences with each other to make *one* definite prediction. One can only know whether a certain house will burn down if one can take into account how the building components behave, how the human groups behave who push on to fight the fire. The various scientific disciplines together make up the 'unified science'. It is the task of scientific work to create unified science with all its laws.

A prediction can be checked [controlled] by observation statements only if we indicate where and when a predicted change is to take place. It does not make any fundamental difference how this is defined in detail by statements. What matters is that all statements contain references to the spatio-temporal order, the order that we know from physics. Therefore this view is to be called 'physicalism' . . . Unified science contains only physicalist formulations. The fate of physics in the narrower sense thus becomes the fate of all the sciences, as far as statements about the smallest particles are concerned. For 'physicalism' it is essential that *one* kind of *order* is the foundation of all laws, whichever science is concerned, geology, chemistry or sociology.

The Vienna Circle is making particularly vigorous efforts to give unified science a solid framework through 'syntax', along the lines of the logicians, of Wittgenstein and others, and to eliminate everything that is 'meaningless', i.e., all metaphysics, by a proper use of language. It is a defect of language that it admits something like a 'neighbor without a neighbor', a 'command without a commander' ('categorical imperative') within its rules. The defects of syntax reveal the

standard of scientific study. An unblemished syntax is the foundation of an unblemished unified science. Language is essential for science; within language all transformations of science take place, not by confrontation of language with a 'world', a totality of 'things' whose variety language is supposed to reflect. An attempt like that would be metaphysics. *The one scientific language can speak about itself, one part of language can speak about the other*; it is impossible to turn back behind or before language.

This also corresponds perfectly to the 'behavioristic' approach of 'unified science'. Thinking in terms of language as physical process is the starting point of all science. It is quite possible to speak about the behavior of someone who does not speak; it is however, impossible to discuss some pre-linguistic circumstance with pre-linguistic means—this at once seems to us to be meaningless.

Carnap, who has so far probably advanced the work of the Vienna Circle the most towards empiricism, made an attempt to create a constitutive constructive system; in this he distinguished two languages: a 'monologizing' (phenomenalist) one and an 'intersubjective' (physicalist) one. He tries to deduce the physicalist one from the phenomenalist. However, in my opinion it can be shown that this division cannot be carried out, that on the contrary only one language comes into question from the start, and that is the language of physics. One can learn the language of physics from earliest childhood. If someone makes predictions and wants to check them himself, he must count on changes in the system of his senses, he must use clocks and rulers; in short, the man who supposedly is in isolation already makes use of the intersensual and 'intersubjective' language. The forecaster of yesterday and the controller of today are, so to speak, two persons.

The words 'blue' or 'hard' or 'shrieking' are then used in a physical sense alone. They either indicate that a man shows a certain behavior under certain conditions, that he speaks words or exhibits nervous changes ('field statements'), just as, for example, a test body in the neighborhood of a charged ball in some experiment; or they indicate that there is a certain oscillation somewhere. If someone says: "I see blue", this is coordinated as a 'statement about reality', if one accepts the statement as being about spatio-temporal changes that have taken place outside the man, or as an 'hallucinatory' statement if certain changes are assumed to be only within the human body, that is in certain areas of perception in the brain, whatever their delimitations are. Finally one can also speak of a 'lie', namely if only the speech center and word formation participate in making the statement. In all cases, however, the statements are physicalist.

The statements themselves also form part of other statements as physicalist elements. A comparison of 'statements' with other entities is meaningless, as mentioned before. If someone says, "I see blue", we base on this the construction of statements about changes in his eye nerves, in his brain, but we do the same if he says, "I feel anger". The statements about 'organ sensations', which play an important part along with statements about other behavior, are then joined to the structure of the system of physicalist statements. 'Behaviorism' in its widest sense makes use of statements about organ sensations as well as of statements about sense perceptions (in order to combine all physicalist statements about human behavior). This widens the scope of our considerations, compared, for example, with those of Carnap, who so far has made behavioristic use of 'statements about feelings (anger, etc.)' only as *statements*. The statement, 'I feel anger', is only vaguer than the statement, 'I see blue', but just as serviceable as a statement about reality.

Unified science based on physicalism recognizes only statements with spatio-temporal data. 'Equivalent statements' are constructed physicalistically; for statements are physicalist structures, written or spoken words. If, to a command, "Do this, if the table is red", the statement is added, "The table is red", something definite happens. The same happens if it were said, for example, "Mensa est rubra". The two formulations would be equivalent physicalistically. On the other hand 'tautologies' do not add anything meaningful. "Two times two equals four" is always true. The addition of this condition to a command or statement does not make any difference, it is always fulfilled.

In the framework of physicalism, 'psychology' becomes a system of behaviorism in its widest sense. Also sociology has to be formulated in physicalist language as 'social behaviorism'. We can speak of men, things and their correlations, but not of 'norms in themselves', 'values' or 'essences'. There is only one kind of

science; the separation into 'natural sciences' and 'mental (moral) sciences', which in any case plays a minor role outside Germany, is not elicited by any practical or theoretical considerations within the framework of unified science. The demand for this separation comes mostly from metaphysical groups.

Since there is no philosophy with meaningful statements, there is even less a 'philosophy of nature' or a 'philosophy of culture'; these are dichotomies that have their sources in theology and idealism. 'Physicalism' is perfectly monistic; idealistic philosophy, including phenomenology, is alien to it.

We find related endeavors in Berlin (Reichenbach, Dubislav, Grelling and others), Paris and Warsaw. In Berlin attention is given less to unified science, more to certain questions of the foundations of physics and mathematics in the narrower sense, while in Warsaw mainly logic and metalogic, as well as the foundations of mathematics, are treated. In Paris 'rationalism' is furthered in a similar sense by a circle of resolute antimetaphysicians.

The standpoint of the Vienna Circle is set forth in essays in the journal *Erkenntnis*, in the publications of the 'Verein Ernst Mach—Wien', as well as in the *Schriften zur wissenschaftlichen Weltauffassung* [Monographs on the Scientific World-Conception], edited by Schlick and Frank, with works by Waismann, Carnap, Mises, Schlick, Frank. An 'Empirical Sociology', a behavioristic sociology in the framework of physicalism, was published by the author of this article.

If one wants to speak of the further development of physicalism, it can probably be expected that the attempt that Carnap undertook in his *Logischer Aufbau der Welt* (1928) will be repeated in order to create the syntax for unified science in the sense of physicalism as represented here. The work on unified science replaces all former philosophy. At this point 'science without a world-view' confronts 'world-views' of all kinds, 'philosophies' of all kinds. Physicalism is the form work in unified science takes in our time. Whatever else is said in pronouncements is either 'meaningless' or merely a means to emotion, 'poetry'. For physicalism as it is represented here quite strictly, everything that was put forward as philosophy by scholastics, Kantians, phenomenologists, is *meaningless* except that part of their formulations that can be translated into scientific, that is physicalist, statements.

READING QUESTIONS

1. Neurath puts a great deal of emphasis on "scientific language as a physical formation." What does he mean by this, and what is its significance from the standpoint of positivism?
2. " 'Making predictions' is what science is all about." Is this true? What is science all about?
3. Neurath remarks that *"statements are always compared with statements*, certainly not with some 'reality', nor with 'things', as the Vienna Circle has thought up till now. . . . If a statement is made, it is to be confronted with the totality of existing statements. If it agrees with them, it is joined to them; if it does not agree, it is called 'untrue' and rejected; or the existing complex of statements of science is modified so that the new statement can be incorporated . . . there can be no other concept of 'truth' for science.*" Evaluate this claim. Is this a general fact about truth, compatible with any theory of truth? If not, is it a substantial theory of truth itself? Why or why not?
4. What does Neurath mean by the term *physicalism*? What does he mean by *unified science*?

OTTO NEURATH

Protocol Sentences

A protocol sentence is ostensibly a report of one's immediate sensory experiences or memories.* A protocol sentence is generally supposed to be pretheoretical, noninferential (basic), and essentially grounded in one's present private sensations. The purpose of articulating protocol sentences, it was thought, was so that they could serve as noninferentially justified premises or epistemological supports for more general claims or

---

*Throughout this article, Neurath refers to a particular essay by Rudolf Carnap entitled "Die Physikalische Sprache als Univeralsprache der Wissenschaft," *Erkenntnis* 3 (1931/1932). Translated into English by Max Black and published as *The Unity of Science,* London: Kegan Paul, 1934.

theories whose relation to facts about immediate experience is not clear. The idea of a protocol sentence survives today in many foundationalistic epistemologies, in the concept of a *basic statement* or a *noninferentially justified justifier.*

In this essay, Neurath contests the idea of a conclusively established, pure protocol statement and rejects its associated epistemology. In keeping with his physicalism, he argues instead for a more holistic epistemology in which protocol sentences do not appear as foundational, basic, or unrevisable. On the contrary, he argues that "protocol sentences are factual sentences like [any] others" and are, therefore, on the same epistemological footing as so-called 'non-protocol' sentences.

With the progress of knowledge, the number of expressions which are formulated with a high degree of precision in the language of Unified Science is continually on the increase. Even so, no such scientific term is wholly precise; for they are all based upon terms which are essential for *protocol sentences*; and it is immediately obvious to everyone that these terms must be vague.

The fiction of an ideal language constructed out of pure atomic sentences is no less metaphysical than the fiction of Laplace's demon. The language of science, with its ever increasing development of symbolic systems, cannot be regarded as an approximation to such an ideal language. The sentence "Otto is observing an angry person" is less precise than the sentence "Otto is observing a thermometer reading 24 degrees," insofar as the expression "angry person" cannot be so exactly defined as "thermometer reading 24 degrees." But "Otto" itself is in many ways a vague term. The phrase "Otto is observing" could be replaced by the phrase "The man, whose carefully taken photograph is listed no. 16 in the file, is observing": but the term "photo-

---

graph listed no. 16 in the file" still has to be replaced by a system of mathematical formulas, which is unambiguously correlated with another system of mathematical formulas, the terms of which take the place of "Otto," "angry Otto," "friendly Otto," etc.

What is originally given to us is our *ordinary natural language* with a stock of imprecise, unanalyzed terms. We start by purifying this language of metaphysical elements and so reach the *physicalistic ordinary language.* In accomplishing this we may find it very useful to draw up a list of proscribed words.

There is also the *physicalistic language of advanced science* which we can so construct that it is free from metaphysical elements from the start. We can use this language only for special sciences, indeed only for parts of them.

If one wished to express all of the unified science of our time in one language, one would have to combine terms of ordinary language with terms of the language of advanced science, since, in practice, the two overlap. There are some terms which are used only in ordinary language, others which occur only in the language of advanced science, and still others which appear in both languages. Consequently, in a scientific treatise concerned with the entire field of unified science only a "slang" comprising words of both languages will serve.

We believe that every word of the physicalistic ordinary language will prove to be replaceable by terms taken from the language of advanced science, just as one may also formulate the terms of the language of advanced science with the help of the terms of ordinary language. Only the latter is a very unfamiliar proceeding, and sometimes not easy. Einstein's theories are expressible (somehow) in the language of the Bantus—but not those of Heidegger, unless linguistic abuses to which the German language lends itself are introduced into Bantu. A physicist must, in principle, be able to satisfy the demand of the talented writer who insisted that: "One ought to be able to make the outlines of any rigorously scientific thesis comprehensible in his own terms to a hackney-coach driver."

The language of advanced science and ordinary language coincide today primarily in the domain of arithmetic. But, in the system of radical physicalism, even the expression "2 times 2 is 4," a *tautology,* is linked to protocol sentences. Tautologies are defined in terms of

sentences which state how tautologies function as codicils appended to certain commands under certain circumstances. For instance: "Otto says to Karl 'Go outside when the flag waves *and* when 2 times 2 is four.'" The addition of the tautology here does not alter the effect of the command.

Even considerations of rigorous scientific method restrict us to the use of a *"universal slang."* Since there is as yet no general agreement as to its composition, each scholar who concerns himself with these matters must utilize a universal slang to which he himself has contributed new terms.

There is no way of taking conclusively established pure protocol sentences as the starting point of the sciences. No *tabula rasa* exists. We are like sailors who must rebuild their ship on the open sea, never able to dismantle it in dry dock and to reconstruct it there out of the best materials. Only the metaphysical elements can be allowed to vanish without trace. Vague linguistic conglomerations always remain in one way or another as components of the ship. If vagueness is diminished at one point, it may well be increased at another.

We shall, from the very first, teach children the universal-slang—purged of all metaphysics—as the language of the historically transmitted unified science. Each child will be so trained that it starts with a simplified universal-slang, and advances gradually to the use of the universal-slang of adults. In this connection, it is meaningless to segregate this children's language from that of the adults. One would, in that case, have to distinguish several universal-slangs. The child does not learn a *primitive* universal-slang from which the universal-slang of the adults derives. He learns a "poorer" universal-slang, which is gradually filled in. The expression "ball of iron" is used in the language of adults as well as in that of children. In the former it is defined by a sentence in which terms such as "radius" and "π" occur, while in the children's definition words such as "nine-pins," "present from Uncle Rudi," etc. are used. But "Uncle Rudi" also crops up in the language of rigorous science, if the physical ball is defined by means of protocol sentences in which "Uncle Rudi" appears as "the observer who perceives a ball."

Carnap, on the other hand, speaks of a *primitive* protocol language. His comments on the primitive protocol language—on the protocol sentences which "require no verification"—are only marginal to his significant anti-metaphysical views, the mainspring of which is not affected by the objections here brought forward. Carnap speaks of a primary language, also referred to as an experiential or as a phenomenalistic language. He maintains that "at the present stage of inquiry, the question of the precise characterization of this language cannot be answered." These comments might induce younger men to search for a protocol language of the sort described: and this might easily lead to metaphysical deviations. Although metaphysical speculation cannot altogether be restrained by argument, it is important, as a means of keeping waverers in line, to maintain physicalism in its most radical version.

Apart from tautologies, unified science consists of factual sentences. These may be sub-divided into

a. protocol sentences
b. non-protocol sentences.

Protocol sentences are factual sentences of the same form as the others, except that, in them, a personal noun always occurs several times in a specific association with other terms. A complete protocol sentence might, for instance, read: "Otto's protocol at 3:17 o'clock: [At 3:16 o'clock Otto said to himself: (at 3:15 o'clock there was a table in the room perceived by Otto)]." This factual sentence is so constructed that, within each set of brackets, further factual sentences may be found, *viz*.: "At 3:16 o'clock Otto said to himself: (At 3:15 o'clock there was a table in the room perceived by Otto)" and "At 3:15 o'clock there was a table in the room perceived by Otto." These sentences are, however, not protocol sentences.

Each term occurring in these sentences may, to some extent, be replaced at the very outset by a group of terms of the language of advanced science. One may introduce a system of physicalistic designations in place of "Otto," and this system of designations may, in turn, further be defined by referring to the "position" of the name "Otto" in a group of signs composed of the names "Karl," "Heinrich," etc. All the words used in the expression of the above protocol sentence are either words of the universal-slang or may without difficulty be replaced at any moment by words of the universal-slang.

For a protocol sentence to be complete it is essential that the name of some person occur in it. "Now joy," or "Now red circle," or "A red die is lying on the table" are not complete protocol sentences. They are not even candidates for a position within the innermost set of brackets. For this they would, on our analysis, at least have to read "Otto now joy," or "Otto now sees a red circle," or "Otto now sees a red die lying on the table"—which would roughly correspond to the children's language. That is, in a full protocol sentence the expression within the innermost set of brackets is a sentence which again features a personal noun and a term from the domain of perception-terms. The relative extent to which terms of ordinary language and of the language of advanced science are used is of no significance, since the universal-slang may be used with considerable flexibility.

The expression "said to himself," after the first bracket, recommends itself when, as above, one wants to construct various groups of sentences, as, for instance, sentences incorporating reality-terms, or hallucination-terms, or dream-terms, and especially when one wants to identify unreality as such. For instance, one could say: "Otto actually said to himself, 'There was nothing in the room but a bird perceived by Otto' but, in order to amuse himself, he wrote, 'There was nothing in the room but a table perceived by Otto.'" This is especially pertinent to the discussion in the next section, in which we reject Carnap's thesis to the effect that protocol sentences are those "which require no verification."

The transformation of the sciences is effected by the discarding of sentences utilized in a previous historical period, and, frequently, their replacement by others. Sometimes the same form of words is retained, but their definitions are changed. *Every law and every physicalistic sentence of unified-science or of one of its subsciences is subject to such change. And the same holds for protocol sentences.*

In unified science we try to construct a non-contradictory system of protocol sentences and non-protocol sentences (including laws). When a new sentence is presented to us we compare it with the system at our disposal, and determine whether or not it conflicts with that system. If the sentence does conflict with the system, we may discard it as useless (or false), as, for instance, would be done with "In Africa lions sing only in major scales." One may, on the other hand, *accept* the sentence and so change the system that it remains consistent even after the adjunction of the new sentence. The sentence would then be called "true."

The fate of being discarded may befall even a protocol sentence. No sentence enjoys the *noli me tangere* which Carnap ordains for protocol sentences. Let us consider a particularly drastic example. We assume that we are acquainted with a scholar called "Kalon," who can write with both hands simultaneously. He writes with his left hand, "Kalon's protocol at 3:17 o'clock: [At 16 minutes 30 seconds past 3 o'clock Kalon said to himself: (There was *nothing* in the room at 3:16 o'clock except a table perceived by Kalon)]." At the same time, with his right hand, he writes, "Kalon's protocol at 3:17 o'clock: [At 16 minutes 30 seconds past 3 o'clock Kalon said to himself: (There was *nothing* in the room at 3:16 o'clock except a bird perceived by Kalon)]." What is he—and what are we—to make of the conjunction of these two sentences? We may, of course, make statements such as "Marks may be found on this sheet of paper, sometimes shaped this way and sometimes that." With respect to these marks on paper, however, Carnap's word "verification" finds no application. "Verification" can only be used with reference to sentences, that is, with reference to sequences of marks which are used in a context of a reaction-test and which may systematically be replaced by other marks. Synonymous sentences may be characterized as stimuli which under specific reaction-tests evoke the same responses. Chains of ink marks on paper and chains of air vibrations which may under specific conditions be co-ordinated with one another are called "sentences."

Two conflicting protocol sentences cannot both be used in the system of unified science. Though we may not be able to tell which of the two is to be excluded, or whether both are not to be excluded, it is clear that not both are verifiable, that is, that both do not fit into the system.

If a protocol sentence must in such cases be discarded, may not the same occasionally be called for when the contradiction between protocol sentences on the one hand and a system comprising protocol sentences and non-protocol sentences (laws, etc.) on the other is such that an extended argument is required to disclose it? On Carnap's view, one could be obliged to alter only non-protocol sentences and laws. *We also allow for the possibility of discarding protocol sentences. A defining condition of a sentence is that it be subject to verification, that is to say, that it may be discarded.*

Carnap's contention that protocol sentences do not require verification, however it may be understood, may without difficulty be related to the belief in *immediate experiences* which is current in traditional academic philosophy. According to this philosophy there are, indeed, certain *basic elements* out of which the world-picture is to be constructed. On this academic view, these *atomic experiences* are, of course, above any kind of critical scrutiny; they do not require verification.

Carnap is trying to introduce a kind of *atomic protocol*, with his demand that "a clear-cut distinction be made in scientific procedure between the adoption of a protocol and the interpretation of the protocol sentences," as a result of which "no indirectly acquired sentences would be accepted into the protocol." The above formulation of a complete protocol sentence shows that, insofar as personal nouns occur in a protocol, interpretation must *always* already have taken place. When preparing scientific protocols, it may be useful to phrase the expression within the innermost set of brackets as simply as possible, as, for instance, "At 3 o'clock Otto was seeing red," or—another protocol—"At 3 o'clock Otto was hearing C sharp," etc. But a protocol of such a sort is not primitive in Carnap's sense, since one cannot, after all, get around Otto's act of perception. There are no sentences in the universal-slang which one may characterize as "more primitive" than any others. All are of equal primitiveness. Personal nouns, words denoting perceptions, and other words of little primitiveness occur in all factual sentences, or, at least, in the hypotheses from which they derive. All of which means that *there are neither primitive protocol sentences nor sentences which are not subject to verification.*

The universal-slang, in the sense explained above, is the same for the child as for the adult. It is the same for a Robinson Crusoe as for a human society. If Crusoe wants to relate what he registered ("protokolliert") yesterday with what he registers today, that is, when he wants to have any sort of recourse to a language, he cannot but have recourse to the inter-subjective language. The Crusoe of yesterday and the Crusoe of today stand to one another in precisely the relation in which Crusoe stands to Friday. Consider a man who has both lost his memory and been blinded, who is now learning afresh to read and to write. The notes which he himself took in the past and which now, with the aid of a special apparatus, he reads again are for him as much the notes of some other man as notes actually written by someone else. And the same would still be the case after he had realized the tragic nature of his circumstances, and had pieced together the story of his life.

In other words, *every* language *as such* is intersubjective. The protocols of one moment must be subject to incorporation in the protocols of the next, just as the protocols of A must be subject to incorporation in the protocols of B. *It is therefore meaningless to talk, as Carnap does, of a private language,* or of a set of disparate protocol languages which may ultimately be drawn together. The protocol languages of the Crusoe of yesterday and of the Crusoe of today are as close and as far apart from one another as are the protocol languages of Crusoe and of Friday. If, under certain circumstances, the protocol languages of yesterday's Crusoe and of today's are called the *same* language, then one may also, under the same circumstances, call the protocol language of Crusoe and that of Friday the same language.

In Carnap's writings we also encounter an emphasis on the "I" familiar to us from idealistic philosophy. In the universal-slang it is as meaningless to talk of a *personal* protocol as to talk of a *here* or a *now*. In the physicalistic language personal nouns are simply replaced by coordinates and coefficients of physical states. One can distinguish an *Otto-protocol* from a *Karl-protocol*, but not a protocol of one's own from a protocol of others. The whole puzzle of *other minds* is thus resolved.

Methodological solipsism and *methodological positivism* do not become any the more serviceable because of the addition of the word "methodological."

For instance, had I said above, "Today, the 27th of July, I examine protocols both of my own and of others," it would have been more correct to have said "Otto Neurath's protocol at 10:00 a.m., July 27, 1932; [At 9:35 o'clock Otto Neurath said to himself: (Otto Neurath occupied himself between 9:40 and 9:57 with a protocol by Neurath and one by Kalon, to both of which the following two sentences belong: . . .)]." Even though Otto Neurath himself formulates the protocol concerning the utilization of these protocols, he does not link his own protocol with the system of unified science in any different way from that in which he links Kalon's. It may well happen that Neurath discards one of Neurath's protocols, and adopts in its stead one of Kalon's. The fact that men generally retain their own protocol sentences more obstinately than they do those of other people is a historical accident which is of no real significance for our purposes. Carnap's contention that "every individual can adopt only his own protocol as an epistemological basis" cannot be accepted, for the argument presented in its favor is *not* sound: "S_1 can, indeed, also utilize the protocol of S_2—and the incorporation of both protocol languages in physicalistic language makes this utilization particularly easy. The utilization is, however, indirect: S_1 must first state in his own protocol that he sees a piece of writing of such and such a form." *But Neurath must describe Neurath's protocol in a manner analogous to that in which he describes Kalon's!* He describes how Neurath's protocol looks to him as well as how Kalon's does.

In this way we can go on to deal with everyone's protocol sentences. Basically, it makes no difference at all whether Kalon works with Kalon's or with Neurath's protocols, or whether Neurath occupies himself with Neurath's or with Kalon's protocols. In order to make this quite clear, we could conceive of a sorting machine into which protocol sentences are thrown. The laws and other factual sentences (including protocol sentences) serving to mesh the machine's gears sort the protocol sentences which are thrown into the machine and cause a bell to ring if a contradiction ensues. At this point one must either replace the protocol sentence whose introduction into the machine has led to the contradiction by some other protocol sentence, or rebuild the entire machine. *Who* rebuilds the machine, or *whose* protocol sentences are thrown into the machine is of no consequence whatsoever. Anyone may test his own protocol sentences as well as those of others.

Summing Up

Unified science utilizes a universal-slang, in which terms of the physicalistic ordinary language necessarily also occur.

Children can be trained to use the universal-slang. Apart from it we do not employ any specially distinguishable "basic" protocol sentences, nor do different people make use of different protocol languages.

We find no use in unified science for the expressions "methodological solipsism" and "methodological positivism."

One cannot start with conclusively established, pure protocol sentences. Protocol sentences are factual sentences like the others, containing names of persons or names of groups of people linked in specific ways with other terms, which are themselves also taken from the universal-slang.

The Vienna Circle devotes itself more and more to the task of expressing unified science (which includes sociology as well as chemistry, biology as well as mechanics, psychology—more properly termed "behavioristics"—as well as optics) in a unified language, and with the displaying of the inter-connections of the various sciences which are so often neglected; so that one may without difficulty relate the terms of any science to those of any other. The word "man" which is prefixed to "makes assertions" is to be defined in just the same way as the word "man" occurring in sentences which contain the words "economic system" and "production."

The Vienna Circle has received powerful encouragement from various sources. The achievements of Mach, Poincaré, and Duhem have been turned to as good account as the contributions of Frege, Schröder, and Russell. Wittgenstein's writings have been extraordinarily stimulating, both through what has been taken from them and through what has been rejected. His original plan—to use philosophy as a ladder which it is necessary to climb in order to see things clearly—may, however, be considered to have come to grief. The main issue in this, as in all other intellectual activities, will always be to bring the sentences of unified science—both protocol sentences and non-protocol sentences—into consonance with one another. For this, a *logical syntax* of the sort toward which Carnap is working is required—Carnap's *logical reconstruction of the world* being the first step in this direction.

The discussion I have initiated here—for Carnap will certainly find much in the corrections to correct again and to develop—serves, as do so many of our other efforts, to secure ever more firmly the common, broad foundations on which all the adherents of physicalism base their studies. Discussions of peripheral issues, such as this one, are, however, going to play a continuously diminishing role. The rapid progress of the work of the Vienna Circle shows that the planned cooperative project dedicated to the construction of unified science is in constant development. The less time we find it necessary to devote to the elimination of ancient confusions and the more we can occupy ourselves with the formulation of the inter-connections of the sciences, the quicker and more successful will this construction be. To this end it is of the first importance that we learn how to use the physicalistic language, on behalf of which Carnap, in his article, entered the lists.

READING QUESTIONS

1. Neurath begins by proposing that, although it is not yet possible, the day will come in which "every word of the physicalistic ordinary language will prove to be replaceable by terms taken from the language of advanced science, just as one may also formulate the terms of the language of advanced science with the help of the terms of ordinary language." In general, how might this become possible? On what presuppositions does the success or failure of such a project depend?

2. Neurath writes that "*there is no way of taking conclusively established pure protocol sentences as the starting point of the sciences. No tabula rasa exists. We are like sailors who must rebuild their ship on the open sea, never able to dismantle it in dry dock and to reconstruct it there out of the best materials.*" What is the epistemological impact of this outlook, if Neurath is correct?

3. How specifically does Neurath characterize protocol sentences?
4. Neurath objects to Carnap's thesis that "protocol sentences are those 'which require no verification'." On his view, there are no such things—"the fate of being discarded may befall even a protocol sentence," he writes. Why? What is his argument?
5. Neurath argues that "it is . . . meaningless to talk, as Carnap does, of a private language." What is a "private language"? In arguing for his view, Neurath considers a case involving Robinson Crusoe. How, if at all, does an examination of this case support his contention that there are no private languages?

SUGGESTIONS FOR FURTHER READING (OTTO NEURATH)

Primary Sources and Collected Writings

(1921)*Anti-Spengler*. Munich: Callwey.
(1930) *Modern Man in the Making*. New York: Knopf.
(1936) *International Picture Language*. London: Kegan Paul.
(1938) (with Rudolf Carnap and C. Morris) *Foundations of the Unity of Science: Towards an International Encyclopedia of Unified Science*. Chicago, IL: University of Chicago Press.
(1973) *Empiricism and Sociology*. Dordrecht: Kluwer Academic Publishers.
(1981) *Gesammelte philosophiche und methodologische Schriften* (Collected Philosophical and Methodological Writings), edited by R. Haller and H. Rutte. Vienna: Holder-Pichler-Tempsky.
(1983) *Philosophical Papers*. Dordrecht: D. Reidel.
(1987) *Unified Science*. Dordrecht: Kluwer Academic Publishers.
(1991) *Gesammelte bildpadagagische Schriften*, edited by R. Haller and R. Kinross. Vienna: Holder-Pichler-Tempsky.

Secondary Sources

Cartwright, N., J. Cat, and T. Uebel (1995) *Philosophy Between Science and Politics*. Cambridge: Cambridge University Press.

Nemeth, E., and F. Stadler, eds. (1996) *Otto Neurath: Encyclopedia of Utopia*. Dordrecht: Kluwer Academic Publishers.
Neurath, M., and R. S. Cohen, eds. (1973) *Empiricism and Sociology*. Dordrecht: D. Reidel.
Uebel, T. E., ed. (1991) *Rediscovering the Forgotten Vienna Circle*. Dordrecht: Kluwer Academic Publishers.
———. (1992) *Overcoming Logical Positivism from Within: The Emergence of Neurath's Naturalism in the Vienna Circle's Protocol Sentence Debate*. Amsterdam: Editions Rodopoi.
Zolo, D. (1989) *Reflexive Epistemology: The Philosophical Legacy of Otto Neurath*. Dordrecht: Kluwer Academic Publishers.

RUDOLF CARNAP

On the Character of Philosophic Problems

Rudolf Carnap (1891–1970) was born in Ronsdorf, Germany. His father died when Carnap was seven, and the remaining family relocated to Barmen, where Carnap studied at the local gymnasium. From Barmen, Carnap went on to study philosophy, mathematics, and physics at the universities of Freiburg and Jena (1910–1914). While attending the University of Jena, Carnap had the opportunity to study under Gottlob Frege, completing three of his courses on topics in mathematical philosophy.

Although intrigued by the intricacies of the philosophy of mathematics, Carnap was much more interested in various problems in theoretical physics. He also became greatly influenced by his teacher, Bruno Bauch, who professed a generally Kantian philosophical outlook, and who encouraged Carnap to pursue his interests in the philosophical foundations of the sciences. Carnap began work on a dissertation on problems of experimental physics, but was forced to suspend his academic work in order to serve in the First World War. He remained a soldier until 1917, at which time he returned to his education, briefly attending the University of Berlin so that he could study the theory of relativity. Albert Einstein was a member of the faculty at Berlin during those years.

By the time that Carnap took up his dissertation again, his research interests had shifted from problems in the pure sciences to various issues on the borderline between philosophy and the sciences. He completed his dissertation and committed himself to pursuing various projects in epistemology, the philosophy of language, and the philosophy of science.

In 1923 Carnap met Moritz Schlick and two years later was invited by Schlick to Vienna to meet with him and with other members of the Vienna Circle. Within a short time (also at Schlick's invitation) he accepted a position at the University of Vienna and became an active figure himself in the work of the Vienna Circle. Carnap would go on to become one of the most important members of the Circle, and his work continues to this day to be closely associated with the best of Viennese positivism.

In 1928 he published his first major book, *Der Logische Aufbau der Welt* (translated and published as *The Logical Structure of the World* in 1967). In the *Aufbau*, Carnap embraces the program of phenomenalistic reconstructionism, motivated in large part by his appreciation of Russell's *Our Knowledge of the External World* and by the generally Humean outlook on the problems of philosophy that it professes.

In 1931, Carnap left Vienna and accepted the chair of natural philosophy at the German University in Prague. His appointment in Prague did not last long, however. Because of the rise of Nazism on the Continent, Carnap left Europe for the United States at the end of 1935. Only a few months after his arrival, he obtained a position in the philosophy department at the University of Chicago. Carnap remained in Chicago until 1952, with the exception of brief spells spent at the University of Illinois and at Harvard as a visiting professor. From 1952 to 1954 Carnap was appointed a professor at the Institute for Advanced Study at Princeton. He later left Princeton for a chair that was opened at the University of California, Los Angeles, by the death of his longtime friend and fellow positivist, Hans Reichenbach. Carnap remained at UCLA until he retired from teaching in 1961. He died in Santa Monica, California.

In the following early essay, "On the Character of Philosophic Problems," Carnap presents a general theory of philosophy in the positivistic tradition. One of his major concerns has to do with evaluating the status of 'philosophical' propositions, i.e., the nature of the propositions of philosophy themselves, in light of the overall program of positivism. Critics of positivism often point out that the *verifiability theory of meaning*, upon which the most important doctrines of positivism ultimately rest, does not clearly pass its own test for genuine significance—that is, the theory itself, when expressed as a proposition, appears to be meaningless on the grounds that it is neither an empirical thesis nor an outright tautology.

Rejecting Wittgenstein's apparent response to this conundrum (that is, that the propositions of philosophy are really meaningless nonsense), Carnap suggests that the questions of philosophy are really "questions of the syntax of the language of science which permit expression in a formal mode of speech" (i.e., they are all questions about language itself, not questions about the world) and that the propositions of philosophy are really proposals or suggestions "for the syntactical formulation of the language of science." A philosophical proposition, in other words, is a proposal or a suggestion as to how we should understand the language of science.

Philosophy Is the Logic of Science

Philosophers have ever declared that their problems lie at a different level from the problems of the empirical sciences. Perhaps one may agree with this assertion; the question is, however, where should one seek this level. The metaphysicians wish to seek their object *behind* the objects of empirical science; they wish to enquire after

Rudolf Carnap, "On the Character of Philosophic Problems" translated by W. M. Malisoff from *Philosophy of Science* 1 (1934), pp. 5–19. Reprinted with the kind permission of Lippincott-William and Wilkins.

the essence, the ultimate cause of things. But the logical analysis of the pretended propositions of metaphysics has shown that they are not propositions at all, but empty word arrays, which on account of notional and emotional connections arouse the false appearance of being propositions. This conception that the "propositions" of metaphysics, including those of ethics, have no theoretical content, is to be sure still disputed. We shall not, however, enter here on its demonstration, but, under its guidance, will limit ourselves to non-metaphysical and non-ethical (non-evaluating) philosophical problems.

In order to discover the correct standpoint of the philosopher, which differs from that of the empirical investigator, we must not penetrate *behind* the objects of empirical science into presumably some kind of transcendent level; on the contrary we must take a *step back* and *take science itself as the object. Philosophy is the theory of science* (wherein here and in the following "science" is always meant in the comprehensive sense of the collective system of the knowledge of any kind of entity; physical and psychic, natural and social entities). This must be appraised more closely. One may consider science from various viewpoints; e.g., whether one can institute a psychological investigation considering the activities of observation, deduction, formulation of theories, etc., or sociological investigations concerning the economical and cultural conditions of the pursuit of science. These provinces—although most important—are not meant here. Psychology and sociology are empirical sciences; they do not belong to philosophy even though they are often pursued by the same person, and have torn loose from philosophy as independent branches of science only in our own times. Philosophy deals with science only from the *logical* viewpoint. *Philosophy is the logic of science,* i.e., the logical analysis of the concepts, propositions, proofs, theories of science, as well as of those which we select in available science as common to the possible methods of constructing concepts, proofs, hypotheses, theories. [What one used to call epistemology or theory of knowledge is a mixture of applied logic and psychology (and at times even metaphysics); insofar as this theory is logic it is included in what we call logic of science; insofar, however, as it is psychology, it does not belong to philosophy, but to empirical science.]

The interpretation that philosophy is the logic of science is not to be justified here. It has been represented previously and is represented now by various philosophic groups, among others also by our Vienna circle. With this thesis the question as to the character of philosophic problems is not by any means already solved. Very much comes into question right at this point. We should consequently ask here: what character, what logical nature, do the questions and answers of the logic of science have? For those who are with us in the conception that philosophy is the logic of science the question of the character of philosophic problems will be answered thereby as well.

Are the Propositions of the Logic of Science Meaningless?

Our antimetaphysical position has been formulated by Hume in the classical manner:

> It seems to me, that the only objects of the abstract science or of demonstration are quantity and number, and that all attempts to extend this more perfect species of knowledge beyond these bounds are mere sophistry and illusion. As the component parts of quantity and number are entirely similar, their relations become intricate and involved; and nothing can be more curious, as well as useful, than to trace, by a variety of mediums their equality or inequality, through their different appearances. But as all other ideas are clearly distinct and different from each other, we can never advance farther, by our utmost scrutiny, than to observe this diversity, and, by an obvious reflection, pronounce one thing not to be another. Or if there be any difficulty in these decisions, it proceeds entirely from the undeterminate meaning of words, which is corrected by juster definitions.—Hume, An Enquiry Concerning Human Understanding, XII, 3.

Against this the following objection, which on first appearance seems indeed destructive, has been repeatedly raised: "If every proposition which does not belong either to mathematics or to the empirical investigation of facts, is meaningless, how does it fare then with your own propositions? You positivists and antimetaphysicians yourselves cut off the branch on which you sit." This objection indeed touches upon a decisive point. It should be of interest to every philosopher as well as metaphysician to comprehend the character of the propositions of the logic of science; but to the antimetaphysician, who identifies philosophy and the logic of science, this is the *deciding question*, upon the satisfactory answer of which the security of his standpoint depends.

Wittgenstein has represented with especial emphasis the thesis of the meaninglessness of metaphysical propositions and of the identity of philosophy and the logic of science; especially through him has the Vienna circle been developed on this point. How now does Wittgenstein dispose of the objection that his own propositions are also meaningless? He doesn't at all; he agrees with it! He is of the opinion that the non-metaphysical *philosophy* also has no propositions; it operates with words, *the meaninglessness of which in the end it itself must recognize*:

> "Philosophy is not a theory but an activity. A philosophical work consists essentially of elucidations. The result of philosophy is not a number of "philosophical propositions," but to make propositions clear."

> "My propositions are elucidatory in this way: he who understands me finally recognizes them as senseless, when he has climbed out through them, on them, over them. (He must so to speak throw away the ladder, after he has climbed up on it.) He must surmount these propositions; then he sees the world rightly. Whereof one cannot speak, thereof one must be silent." (Tractatus Logico-philosophicus)

We shall try in the following to give in place of this radically negative answer a *positive answer* to the question of the character of the propositions of the logic of science and thereby of philosophy.

Connotative and Formal Consideration

(Inhaltliche und formale Betrachtung)

To construct science means to construct a system of propositions which stand in certain fundamental coherence with one another. The logic of science is thus the logical analysis of this system, of its elements and of the methods of tying these elements. In such an analysis we can start from but two different viewpoints; we shall call them connotative (inhaltlich) and formal.

It is usual in the logic of science to put something like the following and similar questions: What is the meaning of this or that concept? In what relation does the meaning of this concept stand with respect to that? Is the meaning of this concept more fundamental than of that? What meaning (Inhalt, Gehalt) does this proposition have? (Or: What does this proposition say?) Is the meaning of this proposition contained in the meaning of that? Does this proposition say more than that? Is what this proposition asserts, necessary or contingent or impossible? Is what these two propositions say compatible?

All these questions refer to the *meaning* of concepts and propositions. We call them therefore questions of meaning or of *connotation* (inhaltliche). In contrast to this we understand by *formal* questions and propositions such as relate only to the formal structure of the propositions, i.e., to the arrangement and kind of symbols (e.g., words) out of which a proposition is constructed, *without reference to the meaning* of the symbols and propositions. Formal (in the sense here defined) are, e.g., (most of) the rules of grammar.

According to prevalent conception the connotative questions of the logic of science are much richer and fruitful than the formal; though the formal do belong to the logic of science, they are at most a small, insignificant section. But this opinion is wrong. The logic of science can progress without exception according to the formal method without thereby restricting the wealth of questioning. It is possible in case of purely formal procedure, that is from a viewpoint in which one does not reckon with the meaning, finally to arrive to the answering of all those questions which are formulated as connotative questions. This possibility is to be shown illustratively in the following. Therewith the question of the character of *philosophy as logic of science* is answered: it is *the formal structure theory of the language of science,* we shall call it: The logical syntax of the language of science.

Logical Syntax of Language

By the "logical syntax" (or also briefly "syntax") of a language we shall understand the *system* of the *formal* (i.e., not referring to meaning) *rules* of that language, as well as to the consequences of these rules. Therein we deal first with the *formative rules* (Formregeln), which decree how from the symbols (e.g., words) of the language propositions can be built up, secondly with the *transformation rules* (Unformungsregeln), which decree how from given propositions new ones can be derived. If the rules are set up strictly formally they furnish mechanical operations with the symbols of the language. The formation and transformation of propositions resembles chess: like chess figures words are here combined and manipulated according to definite rules. But thereby we do not say that language is nothing but a game of figures; it is not denied that the words and propositions have a meaning; one merely averts methodically from meaning. One may express it also thus: *language* is treated as a *calculus.*

That the formal, calculus-like representation of the formative rules is possible is evident. What linguists call rules of syntax are indeed such formal (or at least formally expressible) rules for the formation of propositions. We can see, however, clearly that the transformation rules, which one usually calls logical rules of deduction, have the same formal, that is, syntactical character. (And that is the reason why we call the combined system of rules syntax, in widening the terminology of linguists). Since Aristotle the efforts of logicians (more or less consciously) were directed toward formulating the deductive rules as formally as possible, i.e., possibly so that with their help the conclusion could be "calculated" mechanically from the premises. This was attained first in a strict manner only in modern symbolic logic; the traditional logic was too much hindered by the defect of the language of words.

For a certain part of the language of science we already know a strictly formal theory, namely *Hilbert's* mathematics. It considers the symbols and formulas of mathematics without reference to meaning, in order to investigate relations of deducibility, sufficiency, consistency, etc. This mathematics is hence (in our manner of expression) the logical syntax of mathematical language. The logical syntax of the language of science meant here is an analogous extension with reference to the language of all of science.

One of the most important concepts of logic and thereby of the logic of science is that of (logical) inference (Folgerung-entailment). Can this concept be formulated purely formally? It is often stated that the relation of entailment depends on the meaning of the propositions. In a certain sense we can agree with that; for when the meaning of two propositions is known, it is thereby determined whether one is the entailment of the other or not. The decisive point, however, is: is it also possible to formulate the concept "entailment" purely formally? If the transformation rules of language are set up purely formally, we call a proposition an inference (entailment) of other propositions if it can be constructed from those propositions by the application of the transformation rules. The question, whether a certain proposition is an inference (entailment) of certain other propositions or not, is therefore completely analogous to the question whether a certain position in chess can be played from another or not. This question is answered by chess theory, i.e., a combinatorial or mathematical investigation which is based on the chess rules; that question is thus a formal one, it is answered by a *Combinatorial Calculus or Mathematics of Language,* which rests on the transformation rules of language, that is what we have called the *syntax* of language. Briefly: "entailment" is defined as deducibility according to the transformation rules; since these rules are formal, "entailment" is also a formal, syntactical concept.

The concept "entailment" is, as *Lewis* has correctly seen, quite different from the concept of "(material) *implication.*" (Russell, *Principles of Mathematics*). Implication does not depend on the sense of the propositions, but only on their *truth-value*; but entailment on the contrary is not quite determined by the truth values. From this, however, one may not conclude that in the determination of entailment reference to the *meaning* is necessary; it suffices to refer to the formal structure of the propositions.

The Content of a Proposition

On the basis of the concept "entailment" one can define the following classification of propositions which is fundamental to the logic of science. A proposition is called *analytic* (or tautological) if it is an entailment of every proposition (more exactly: if it is deducible without premises, or is the entailment of the empty class of propositions). A proposition is called *contradictory* if any proposition at all is its entailment. A proposition is called *synthetic* if it is neither analytical nor contradictory. Example: "It is raining here" is synthetic; "It is raining or it is not raining" is analytic; "It is raining and it is not raining" is contradictory. An analytic proposition is true in every possible case and therefore does not state which case is on hand. A contradictory propostion on the contrary says too much, it is not true in any possible case. A synthetic proposition is true only in certain cases, and states therefore that one of these cases is being considered—all (true or false) statements of fact are synthetic. The concepts "analytic," "contradictory," "synthetic" can be defined in analogous manner also for classes of propositions; several propositions are said to be *incompatible* (unverträglich) with one another, if their class is contradictory.

And now we come to the principal concept of the logic of science, the concept of the (Inhalt) content of a proposition. Can this central concept of the connotative (inhaltliche) method of consideration be formulated purely formally also? We can be easily convinced that that is possible. For what, to be sure, do we want to know when we ask concerning the content or meaning of a proposition S? We wish to know what S conveys to us; what we experience through S; what we can take out of S. In other words: we ask what we can deduce from S; more accurately: what propositions are entailments of S which are not already entailments of any proposition at all, and therefore declare nothing. We define therefore: by the *content* (Gehalt) of a proposition S we understand the class of entailments from S which are not analytic. Thereby the concept "Gehalt" is connected to the syntactical concepts defined earlier; it is then also a syntactic, a purely formal concept. From this definition it is apparent that the content of an analytic proposition is empty, since no non-analytic proposition is an entailment of it. Further, that the content of S_2 is obtained from that of S_1 when and only when S_2 is an entailment of S_1; that two propositions are of equal content when and only when each is the entailment of the other. Thus the defined concept "Content" corresponds completely to what we mean when we (in a vague manner) are accustomed to speak of the "meaning" (Inhalt) of a proposition; at any rate, insofar as by "meaning" something logical is meant. Often in the investigation of the "meaning" or "sense" of a proposition one also means: What does one think of or imagine in this proposition? This, however, is a psychological question with which we have nothing to do in a logical investigation.

Connotative and Formal Modes of Expression

(Inhaltliche und formale Redeweise)

We have set out from the fact that a language can be considered in two different ways: in a connotative and in a formal manner. Now, however, we have established that with the aid of the formal method the questions of the connotative approach can also be answered finally. Fundamentally really there is no difference between the two approaches, but only a difference between two modes of expression: in the investigation of a language, its concepts and propositions and the relations between them, one can employ either the connotative or the formal mode of expression. The connotative mode of expression is more customary and obvious; but one must use it with great care, it frequently begets muddles and pseudo-problems. We shall consider several examples of propositions in connotative form and their translation into formal mode of speech; in the case of several of these examples (6a–10a) only on translation do we see that we are dealing with assertions concerning the language.

Connotative Mode of Speech:	*Formal Mode of Speech*
1a. The propositions of arithmetical language gives the properties of numbers and relations between them.	1b. The propositions of arithmetical language are constructed in such and such a manner from predicates of one or more values and number expressions as arguments.
2a. The expression '5'and '3 + 2' mean the same number.	2b. 3b. The expressions '5' and '3 + 2' are synonymous in the arithmetical language (i.e., always interchangeable with one another).
3a. '5' and '3 + 2' do not mean the same number but two equal numbers	

On the basis of the connotative formulation *1a* there arise easily a number of metaphysical pseudo-problems concerning the nature of numbers, whether the numbers are real or ideal, whether they are extra- or intramental and the like. The danger of these pseudo-problems disappears when we use the formal mode of expression, where we speak of "number expressions" instead of "numbers." Also the philosophic conflict between *2a* and *3a* disappears in the formal mode of expression: both theses have the same translation.

4a. The word "luna" of the Latin language signifies the moon.

4b. On the basis of the syntactical translation rules between the Latin and the English languages the word "moon" is coordinated with the word "luna."

5a. The concept "red" signifies an ultimate quality; the concept "man" has a more ultimate meaning than the concept "grandson."

5b. The word "red" is an undefined fundamental symbol of language; the word "man" stands on a lower level that the word "grandson" in the definition family-tree of concepts.

6a. The moon is a thing; the sum of 3 and 2 is not a thing but a number.

6b. "Moon is the designation of a thing; "3+2" is not a designation of a thing but a designation of a number.

7a. A property is not a thing.

7b. A property-word is not a thing-word.

8a. This particular (fact, event, condition) is logically necessary: ... logically impossible; ... logically possible.

8b. This proposition is analytic; ...contradictory; ... not contradictory.

9a. This particular (fact, event condition) is physically necessary; ... physically impossible; ... physically possible.

9b. This proposition is deducible from the class of physical laws; ... is incompatible with ...; ... is compatible.

10a. Reality consists of facts, not of things.

10b. Science is a system of propositions, not of names.

Philosophy Is the Syntax of the Language of Science

We had started with the presupposition: Philosophy of science is the logic of science, the logical analysis of concepts, propositions, structures of propositions of science. Since now the data of every logical analysis can be translated in the formal mode of expression, all the questions and theorems of philosophy consequently find their place in the formal structure theory of language, that is, in the realm which we have called the syntax of the language of science. Here it must, however, be noted that a philosophic theorem, formulated as a proposition of syntax, can be meant in different ways:

A. As *Assertion*; e.g.,
  1. In the language of science available today (or a part of it: of physics, biology, ...) such and such holds.
  2. In every language (or: in every language of such and such a nature) such and such holds.
  3. There is a language for which such and such holds.
B. As *Proposal*; e.g.,
  1. I propose to build up the language of science (or of mathematics, of psychology, ...) so that it acquires such and such properties.
  2. I wish (along with other things) to investigate a language which possesses such and such properties.

The common confusion in philosophic discussions, not only among metaphysicians but also in the philosophy of science, is principally called forth by lack of a clear conception that the object of discussion is the language of science; and further because one does not clearly state (and mostly does not know oneself) whether a thesis is meant as an assertion or as a proposal. Let us consider, for example, in the discussion of the logical foundations of mathematics a point of conflict between the logisticists (Frege, Russell) and the axiomatists (Peano, Hilbert); let the theses be formulated by 12a, 13a. Then we translate the theses in order to formulate them more exactly into the formal mode of expression: 12b, 13b.

12a. The *numbers* are classes of classes of things.	12b. The number-symbols are class symbols of second rank.
13a. The numbers are unique ultimate entities.	13b. The number-symbols are individual-symbols (i.e. symbols of null rank, which appear only as arguments).

If now we interpret 12b and 13b in the manner A3, the conflict disappears: one can say that a language of arithmetic is constructible which has the property 12b; but also one as well which has the property 13b. But perhaps the theses 12b, 13b are meant as proposals in the sense B_1. In that case one is not dealing with a discussion about true or false, but with a discussion as to whether this or that mode of expression is simpler or more pertinent (for certain purposes of a scientific methodical nature). In any case the discussion is oblique and fruitless as long as the discussers do not agree as to which of the interpretation A or B is meant. The situation is similar with regard to the philosophical combat concerning the theses 14a, 15a:

14a. To the ultimate given belong relations.	14b. To the undefined fundamental signs belong two- (or more-) valued predicates.
15a. Relations are never given ultimately but depend always on the nature of the members of the relation.	15b. All two- or more-valued predicates are defined on the basis of one-valued predicates.

The discussion becomes clear only when 14b and 15b are considered as proposals; the problem then consists of putting up languages of this or that form and to compare them to one another.

In the following example we deal with the conflict of two theses 16a, 17a, which correspond more or less to positivism and to realism.

16a. *A thing* is a complex of sensations.	16b. Every proposition in which a thing-name occurs, is of equal content with a class of propositions in which no thing-names but sensation-names occur.
17a. A thing is a complex of atoms.	17b. Every proposition in which a thing-name occurs is of equal content with a proposition in which no thing names but space-time coordinates and physical functions occur.

16b, 17b can be interpreted here in the sense A_1, namely as assertions concerning the syntactical structure of our language of science. In spite of that they do not contradict one another; since a proposition concerning a thing can be transformed in more than one way with equal content. We see: in using the formal mode of expression the pseudo-problem "What is a thing?" disappears, and therewith the opposition between the positivist and the realist answer disappears.

If we represent the position that all philosophical problems are questions of the syntax of the language of science, we do not mean it to be a proposal or even a prescription for limitation to a definite, seemingly very narrow field of questions. Much more is meant: as soon as one exactly formulates some question of philosophy as logic of science, one notes that it is a question of the logical analysis of the language of science; and further investigation then teaches that each such question allows itself to be formulated as a formal question, to wit a question of the syntax of the language of science. All theorems of philosophy take on an exact, discussable form only when we formulate them as assertions or proposals of the syntax of the language of science.

The Problem of the Foundations of the Sciences

In order to make clearer our position concerning the character of philosophic problems, we shall cast a brief glance on the problems which one customarily designates as the philosophic foundation problems of the individual sciences.

The philosophic *problems of the foundations of mathematics* are the questions of the syntax of mathematical language, and to be sure not as of an isolated language, but as of a part language of the language of science. This addendum is important. The logistic trend (Frege, Russell) is right in the demand that the foundation laying of mathematics must not only construct the mathematical calculus but also must make clear the meaning of mathematical concepts, since the application of mathematics to reality rests on this meaning. We restate it in formal mode of speech: mathematical concepts attain their meaning by the fact that the rules of their application in empirical science are given. If we investigate not only the syntactical rules of mathematical language merely, but also the rules which relate to the appearance of mathematical symbols in synthetic propositions, we formulate thereby the meaning of mathematical concepts (e.g., the meaning of the symbol "2" is formulated by establishing how this symbol can appear in synthetic propositions, and according to what rules such propositions can be derived from propositions without number expressions. If a rule is set up with the aid of which one can derive from the proposition "In this room there are Peter and Paul and otherwise no person" the proposition "In this room there are 2 people," the meaning of "2" is established by that rule).

The *problems of the foundations of physics* are questions of the syntax of physical language: the problem of the verification of physical laws is the question concerning the syntactic deductive coherence between the physical laws (i.e., general propositions of a certain form) and the protocol propositions (singular propositions of a certain form); the problem of induction is the question whether and which transformation rules lead from protocol propositions to laws; the problem of the finitude or infinity and other structure properties of time and space is the question concerning the syntactical transformation rules with reference to number expressions which appear in the physical propositions as time and space coordinates; the problem of causalty is the question concerning the syntactical structures of the physical laws (whether unique or probability functions) and concerning a certain property of completeness of the system of these laws (determinism-indeterminism).

The philosophical *problems of the foundation of biology* refer above all to the relation between biology and physics. Here the following two problems are to be distinguished:

1. Can the concepts of biology be defined on the basis of the concepts of physics? (If yes, the language of biology is a part language of physical language).
2. Can the laws of biology be derived from the laws of the physics of the inorganic? The second question forms the kernel of the vitalism-problem, if we purge this problem from the usual metaphysical admixtures.

Among the *problems of the foundations of psychology* there are analogously to the above-mentioned: 1. Can the concepts of psychology be defined on the basis of the concepts of physics? 2. Can the laws of psychology be derived from those of physics? The so-called psycho-physical problem is usually formulated as a problem of the relation of two object-realms: the realm of psychic events and the realm of physical events. But this formulation leads to a maze of pseudo-problems. In using the formal mode of expression it becomes clear that one is dealing only with the relation of both part-languages, that of psychology and that of physics, and to be sure more accurately with the manner of the syntactical derivation relations (translation rules) between the propositions of both these languages. With the formulation of the psycho-physical problem in the formal mode of expression the problem surely is not yet solved; it may still be quite difficult to find the solution. But at least the necessary condition is satisfied whereby a solution may be sought: the question at least is put clearly.

A point of principle must now be noted so that our position will be understood correctly. When we say that philosophical questions are questions of the syntax of the language of science which permit expression in a formal mode of speech, we do not say thereby that the answers to these questions can be found by a mere calculating about with logical formulas without recourse to experience. A proposal for the syntactical formulation of the language of science is, when seen as a principle, a proposal for a freely chosable convention; but what induces us to prefer certain forms of language to others is the recourse to the empirical material which scientific investigation furnishes. (It is, e.g., a question of convention whether one takes as the fundamental laws of physics deterministic or statistical laws; but only by attention to the empirical material, syntactically put: to the protocol propositions, can we decide with which of these two forms we can arrive at a well-correlated, relatively simple construction of a system.) From this it follows that the task of the philosophy of science can be pursued only in a close cooperation between logicians and empirical investigators.

READING QUESTIONS

1. Carnap writes that "philosophy is the theory of science" and that it investigates "the logic of science." He does not defend this claim directly, but indicates that it is a view of philosophy that is characteristic of positivism, and he hints that a justification for this claim can be found elsewhere. Consider this and other positivistic writings you have encountered. How might one justify this claim?

2. What is the difference between connotative questions and formal questions? When Carnap discusses the "logical syntax of language," what does he mean?

3. What is 'entailment'? What does the concept of 'entailment' have to do with the rules of chess?

4. How does Carnap propose that we understand the categories of 'analytic', 'contradictory', and 'synthetic,' if we restrict ourselves only to considering the formal or syntactic aspects of language? How does Carnap propose that we understand the con-

tent or meaning of a proposition utilizing only formal or syntactic considerations? Why is the concept of entailment important here?

5. Consider Carnap's various translations from the connotative mode of speech to the formal mode of speech. Do these translations in fact say the same thing? If not, why?

6. Carnap considers the possibility that philosophical propositions could be taken both as assertions and as proposals. What is the difference?

7. Carnap proposes that when two contrary philosophical positions are expressed in the formal mode, then it becomes apparent that "one is not dealing with a discussion about true or false, but with a discussion as to whether this or that mode of expression is simpler or more pertinent (for certain purposes of a scientific methodical nature)." Philosophers, therefore, are in the business of evaluating various proposed modes of expression in an effort to uncover which ones they should adopt. Does this seem correct? Is a philosophical proposition really a kind of proposal?

8. Carnap suggests that philosophical propositions are really proposals "for the syntactical formulation of the language of science" and that these, in turn, are "freely choosable" conventions, which we make on the basis of whether it gives us "recourse to the empirical material which scientific investigation furnishes." Do you agree with this, or do you believe that at least some genuine propositions of philosophy are really true or false, that is, not proposals but assertions? Why or why not?

RUDOLF CARNAP

Empiricism, Semantics, and Ontology

In this essay, originally written in 1950, Carnap addresses questions of ontology (or what exists) in the tradition of both pragmatism and empiricism. In the process, he distinguishes so-called "internal questions," or questions about what exists, raised within the context or framework of a language rich enough to permit us to talk about physical objects, from so-called "external questions," or questions about the adequacy or appropriateness of accepting an entire linguistic framework for the purposes of expression and discovery. In Carnap's view, internal questions are questions about what exists and about which propositions are true and which are false. External questions, on the other hand, are questions about the practical implications of accepting, rejecting, and utilizing various proposed linguistic frameworks.

1. The Problem of Abstract Entities

Empiricists are in general rather suspicious with respect to any kind of abstract entities like properties, classes, relations, numbers, propositions, etc. They usually feel much more in sympathy with nominalists than with realists (in the medieval sense). As far as possible they try to avoid any reference to abstract entities and to restrict themselves to what is sometimes called a nominalistic language, i.e., one not containing such references. However, within certain scientific contexts it seems hardly possible to avoid them. In the case of mathematics, some empiricists try to find a way out by treating the whole of mathematics as a mere calculus, a formal system for which no interpretation is given or can be given. Accordingly, the mathematician is said to speak not about numbers, functions, and infinite classes, but merely about meaningless symbols and formulas manipulated according to given formal rules. In physics it is more difficult to shun the suspected entities, because the language of physics serves for the communication of reports and predictions and hence cannot be taken as a mere calculus. A physicist who is suspicious of abstract entities may perhaps try to de-

Rudolf Carnap, "Empiricism, Semantics, and Ontology" from his *Meaning and Necessity*, 2nd ed. Chicago, IL: University of Chicago Press, 1958, pp. 205–221. Reprinted with the kind permission of the University of Chicago Press.

clare a certain part of the language of physics as uninterpreted and uninterpretable, that part which refers to real numbers as space-time coordinates or as values of physical magnitudes, to functions, limits, etc. More probably he will just speak about all these things like anybody else but with an uneasy conscience, like a man who in his everyday life does with qualms many things which are not in accord with the high moral principles he professes on Sundays. Recently the problem of abstract entities has arisen again in connection with semantics, the theory of meaning and truth. Some semanticists say that certain expressions designate certain entities, and among these designated entities they include not only concrete material things but also abstract entities, e.g., properties as designated by predicates and propositions as designated by sentences.[1] Others object strongly to this procedure as violating the basic principles of empiricism and leading back to a metaphysical ontology of the Platonic kind.

It is the purpose of this article to clarify this controversial issue. The nature and implications of the acceptance of a language referring to abstract entities will first be discussed in general; it will be shown that using such a language does not imply embracing a Platonic ontology but is perfectly compatible with empiricism and strictly scientific thinking. Then the special question of the role of abstract entities in semantics will be discussed. It is hoped that the clarification of the issue will be useful to those who would like to accept abstract entities in their work in mathematics, physics, semantics, or any other field; it may help them to overcome nominalistic scruples.

2. Linguistic Frameworks

Are there properties, classes, numbers, propositions? In order to understand more clearly the nature of these and related problems, it is above all necessary to recognize a fundamental distinction between two kinds of questions concerning the existence or reality of entities. If someone wishes to speak in his language about a new kind of entities, he has to introduce a system of new ways of speaking, subject to new rules; we shall call this procedure the construction of a linguistic *framework* for the new entities in question. And now we must distinguish two kinds of questions of existence: first, questions of the existence of certain entities of the new kind *within the framework*; we call them *internal questions*; and second, questions concerning the existence or reality *of the system of entities as a whole*, called *external questions*. Internal questions and possible answers to them are formulated with the help of the new forms of expressions. The answers may be found either by purely logical methods or by empirical methods, depending upon whether the framework is a logical or a factual one. An external question is of a problematic character which is in need of closer examination.

The world of things. Let us consider as an example the simplest kind of entities dealt with in the everyday language: the spatio-temporally ordered system of observable things and events. Once we have accepted the thing language with its framework for things, we can raise and answer internal questions, e.g., "Is there a white piece of paper on my desk?", "Did King Arthur actually live?", "Are unicorns and centaurs real or merely imaginary?", and the like. These questions are to be answered by empirical investigations. Results of observations are evaluated according to certain rules as confirming or disconfirming evidence for possible answers. (This evaluation is usually carried out, of course, as a matter of habit rather than a deliberate, rational procedure. But it is possible, in a rational reconstruction, to lay down explicit rules for the evaluation. This is one of the main tasks of a pure, as distinguished from a psychological, epistemology.) The concept of reality occurring in these internal questions is an empirical, scientific, non-metaphysical concept. To recognize something as a real thing or event means to succeed in incorporating it into the system of things at a particular space-time position so that it fits together with the other things recognized as real, according to the rules of the framework.

From these questions we must distinguish the external question of the reality of the thing world itself. In contrast to the former questions, this question is raised neither by the man in the street nor by scientists, but only by philosophers. Realists give an affirmative answer, subjective idealists a negative one, and the controversy goes on for centuries without ever being solved. And it cannot be solved because it is framed in

a wrong way. To be real in the scientific sense means to be an element of the system; hence this concept cannot be meaningfully applied to the system itself. Those who raise the question of the reality of the thing world itself have perhaps in mind not a theoretical question as their formulation seems to suggest, but rather a practical question, a matter of a practical decision concerning the structure of our language. We have to make the choice whether or not to accept and use the forms of expression in the framework in question.

In the case of this particular example, there is usually no deliberate choice because we all have accepted the thing language early in our lives as a matter of course. Nevertheless, we may regard it as a matter of decision in this sense: we are free to choose to continue using the thing language or not; in the latter case we could restrict ourselves to a language of sense-data and other "phenomenal" entities, or construct an alternative to the customary thing language with another structure, or, finally, we could refrain from speaking. If someone decides to accept the thing language, there is no objection against saying that he has accepted the world of things. But this must not be interpreted as if it meant his acceptance of a *belief* in the reality of the thing world; there is no such belief or assertion or assumption, because it is not a theoretical question. To accept the thing world means nothing more than to accept a certain form of language, in other words, to accept rules for forming statements and for testing, accepting, or rejecting them. The acceptance of the thing language leads, on the basis of observations made, also to the acceptance, belief, and assertion of certain statements. But the thesis of the reality of the thing world cannot be among these statements, because it cannot be formulated in the thing language or, it seems, in any other theoretical language.

The decision of accepting the thing language, although itself not of a cognitive nature, will nevertheless usually be influenced by theoretical knowledge, just like any other deliberate decision concerning the acceptance of linguistic or other rules. The purposes for which the language is intended to be used, for instance, the purpose of communicating factual knowledge, will determine which factors are relevant for the decision. The efficiency, fruitfulness, and simplicity of the use of the thing language may be among the decisive factors. And the questions concerning these qualities are indeed of a theoretical nature. But these questions cannot be identified with the question of realism. They are not yes-no questions but questions of degree. The thing language in the customary form works indeed with a high degree of efficiency for most purposes of everyday life. This is a matter of fact, based upon the content of our experiences. However, it would be wrong to describe this situation by saying: "The fact of the efficiency of the thing language is confirming evidence for the reality of the thing world"; we should rather say instead: "This fact makes it advisable to accept the thing language."

The system of numbers. As an example of a system which is of a logical rather than a factual nature let us take the system of natural numbers. The framework for this system is constructed by introducing into the language new expressions with suitable rules: (1) numerals like "five" and sentence forms like "there are five books on the table"; (2) the general term "number" for the new entities, and sentence forms like "five is a number"; (3) expressions for properties of numbers (e.g., "odd", "prime"), relations (e.g., "greater than"), and functions (e.g., "plus"), and sentence forms like "two plus three is five"; (4) numerical variables ("m", "n", etc.) and quantifiers for universal sentences ("for every n, . . .") and existential sentences ("there is an n such that . . .") with the customary deductive rules.

Here again there are internal questions, e.g., "Is there a prime number greater than a hundred?" Here, however, the answers are found, not by empirical investigation based on observations, but by logical analysis based on the rules for the new expressions. Therefore the answers are here analytic, i.e., logically true.

What is now the nature of the philosophical question concerning the existence or reality of numbers? To begin with, there is the internal question which, together with the affirmative answer, can be formulated in the new terms, say, by "There are numbers" or, more explicitly, "There is an n such that n is a number." This statement follows from the analytic statement "five is a number" and is therefore itself analytic. Moreover, it is rather trivial (in contradistinction to a statement like "There is a prime number greater than a

million," which is likewise analytic but far from trivial), because it does not say more than that the new system is not empty; but this is immediately seen from the rule which states that words like "five" are substitutable for the new variables. Therefore nobody who meant the question "Are there numbers?" in the internal sense would either assert or even seriously consider a negative answer. This makes it plausible to assume that those philosophers who treat the question of the existence of numbers as a serious philosophical problem and offer lengthy arguments on either side, do not have in mind the internal question. And, indeed, if we were to ask them: "Do you mean the question as to whether the framework of numbers, *if* we were to accept it, would be found to be empty or not?", they would probably reply: "Not at all; we mean a question *prior* to the acceptance of the new framework." They might try to explain what they mean by saying that it is a question of the ontological status of numbers; the question whether or not numbers have a certain metaphysical characteristic called reality (but a kind of ideal reality, different from the material reality of the thing world) or subsistence or status of "independent entities." Unfortunately, these philosophers have so far not given a formulation of their question in terms of the common scientific language. Therefore our judgment must be that they have not succeeded in giving to the external question and to the possible answers any cognitive content. Unless and until they supply a clear cognitive interpretation, we are justified in our suspicion that their question is a pseudo-question, that is, one disguised in the form of a theoretical question while in fact it is non-theoretical; in the present case it is the practical problem whether or not to incorporate into the language the new linguistic forms which constitute the framework of numbers.

The system of propositions. New variables, "p", "q", etc., are introduced with a rule to the effect that any (declarative) sentence may be substituted for a variable of this kind; this includes, in addition to the sentences of the original thing language, also all general sentences with variables of any kind which may have been introduced into the language. Further, the general term "proposition" is introduced. "p is a proposition" may be defined by "p or not p" (or by any other sentence form yielding only analytic sentences). Therefore, every sentence of the form ". . . is a proposition" (where any sentence may stand in the place of the dots) is analytic. This holds, for example, for the sentence:

a. "Chicago is large is a proposition."

(We disregard here the fact that the rules of English grammar require not a sentence but a that-clause as the subject of another sentence; accordingly, instead of (*a*) we should have to say "That Chicago is large is a proposition".) Predicates may be admitted whose argument expressions are sentences; these predicates may be either extensional (e.g., the customary truth-functional connectives) or not (e.g., modal predicates like "possible", "necessary", etc.). With the help of the new variables, general sentences may be formed, e.g.,

b. "For every *p*, either *p* or not-*p*."

c. "There is a *p* such that *p* is not necessary and not-*p* is not necessary."

d. "There is a *p* such that *p* is a proposition."

(*c*) and (*d*) are internal assertions of existence. The statement "There are propositions" may be meant in the sense of (*d*); in this case it is analytic (since it follows from (*a*)) and even trivial. If, however, the statement is meant in an external sense, then it is non-cognitive.

It is important to notice that the system of rules for the linguistic expressions of the propositional framework (of which only a few rules have here been briefly indicated) is sufficient for the introduction of the framework. Any further explanations as to the nature of the propositions (i.e., the elements of the system indicated, the values of the variables "*p*", "*q*", etc.) are theoretically unnecessary because, if correct, they follow from the rules. For example, are propositions mental events (as in Russell's theory)? A look at the rules shows us that they are not, because otherwise existential statements would be of the form: "If the mental state of the person in question fulfils such and such conditions, then there is a *p* such that. . . ." The fact that no references to mental conditions occur in existential statements (like (*c*), (*d*), etc.) shows that propositions are not mental entities. Further, a statement of the existence of linguistic entities (e.g., expressions, classes of expressions, etc.) must con-

tain a reference to a language. The fact that no such reference occurs in the existential statements here, shows that propositions are not linguistic entities. The fact that in these statements no reference to a subject (an observer or knower) occurs (nothing like: "There is a *p* which is necessary for Mr. *X*"), shows that the propositions (and their properties, like necessity, etc.) are not subjective. Although characterizations of these or similar kinds are, strictly speaking, unnecessary, they may nevertheless be practically useful. If they are given, they should be understood, not as ingredient parts of the system, but merely as marginal notes with the purpose of supplying to the reader helpful hints or convenient pictorial associations which may make his learning of the use of the expressions easier than the bare system of the rules would do. Such a characterization is analogous to an extra-systematic explanation which a physicist sometimes gives to the beginner. He might, for example, tell him to imagine the atoms of a gas as small balls rushing around with great speed, or the electromagnetic field and its oscillations as quasi-elastic tensions and vibrations in an ether. In fact, however, all that can accurately be said about atoms or the field is implicitly contained in the physical laws of the theories in question.[2]

The system of thing properties. The thing language contains words like "red", "hard", "stone", "house", etc., which are used for describing what things are like. Now we may introduce new variables, say "*f*", "*g*", etc., for which those words are substitutable and furthermore the general term "property". New rules are laid down which admit sentences like "Red is a property," "Red is a color," "These two pieces of paper have at least one color in common" (i.e., "There is an *f* such that *f* is a color, and . . ."). The last sentence is an internal assertion. It is of an empirical, factual nature. However, the external statement, the philosophical statement of the reality of properties—a special case of the thesis of the reality of universals—is devoid of cognitive content.

The systems of integers and rational numbers. Into a language containing the framework of natural numbers we may introduce first the (positive and negative) integers as relations among natural numbers and then the rational numbers as relations among integers. This involves introducing new types of variables, expressions substitutable for them, and the general terms "integer" and "rational number".

The system of real numbers. On the basis of the rational numbers, the real numbers may be introduced as classes of a special kind (segments) of rational numbers (according to the method developed by Dedekind and Frege). Here again a new type of variables is introduced, expressions substitutable for them (e.g., "$\sqrt{2}$"), and the general term "real number".

The spatio-temporal coordinate system for physics. The new entities are the space-time points. Each is an ordered quadruple of four real numbers, called its coordinates, consisting of three spatial and one temporal coordinates. The physical state of a spatio-temporal point or region is described either with the help of qualitative predicates (e.g., "hot") or by ascribing numbers as values of a physical magnitude (e.g., mass, temperature, and the like). The step from the system of things (which does not contain space-time points but only extended objects with spatial and temporal relations between them) to the physical coordinate system is again a matter of decision. Our choice of certain features, although itself not theoretical, is suggested by theoretical knowledge, either logical or factual. For example, the choice of real numbers rather than rational numbers or integers as coordinates is not much influenced by the facts of experience but mainly due to considerations of mathematical simplicity. The restriction to rational coordinates would not be in conflict with any experimental knowledge we have, because the result of any measurement is a rational number. However, it would prevent the use of ordinary geometry (which says, e.g., that the diagonal of a square with the side 1 has the irrational value $\sqrt{2}$) and thus lead to great complications. On the other hand, the decision to use three rather than two or four spatial coordinates is strongly suggested, but still not forced upon us, by the result of common observations. If certain events allegedly observed in spiritualistic séances, e.g., a ball moving out of a sealed box, were confirmed beyond any reasonable doubt, it might seem advisable to use four spatial coordinates. Internal questions are here, in general, empirical questions to be answered by empirical investigations. On the other hand, the external questions of the reality of physical space and physical time are pseudo-questions. A question like "Are there (really) space-time points?" is ambiguous. It may be meant as an internal question; then the affirmative answer is, of course, analytic and trivial. Or it may be meant in the external sense: "Shall we introduce such and such forms into our language?"; in this case it is not a theoretical but a practical question, a matter of decision rather than assertion, and hence the proposed formulation would be misleading. Or finally, it may be meant in the following sense: "Are our experiences such that the use of the linguistic forms in question will be expedient and fruitful?" This is a theoretical question of a factual, empirical nature. But it concerns a matter of degree; therefore a formulation in the form "real or not?" would be inadequate.

3. What Does Acceptance of a Kind of Entities Mean?

Let us now summarize the essential characteristics of situations involving the introduction of a new kind of entities, characteristics which are common to the various examples outlined above.

The acceptance of a new kind of entities is represented in the language by the introduction of a framework of new forms of expressions to be used according to a new set of rules. There may be new names for particular entities of the kind in question; but some such names may already occur in the language before the introduction of the new framework. (Thus, for example, the thing language contains certainly words of the type of "blue" and "house" before the framework of properties is introduced; and it may contain words like "ten" in sentences of the form "I have ten fingers" before the framework of numbers is introduced.) The latter fact shows that the occurrence of constants of the type in question—regarded as names of entities of the new kind after the new framework is introduced—is not a sure sign of the acceptance of the new kind of entities. Therefore the introduction of such constants is not to be regarded as an essential step in the introduction of the framework. The two essential steps are rather the following. First, the introduction of a general term, a predicate of higher level, for the new kind of entities, permitting us to say of any particular entity that it belongs to this kind (e.g., "Red is a *property*," "Five is a *number*"). Second, the introduction of variables of the new type. The new entities are values of these variables;

the constants (and the closed compound expressions, if any) are substitutable for the variables.[3] With the help of the variables, general sentences concerning the new entities can be formulated.

After the new forms are introduced into the language, it is possible to formulate with their help internal questions and possible answers to them. A question of this kind may be either empirical or logical; accordingly a true answer is either factually true or analytic.

From the internal questions we must clearly distinguish external questions, i.e., philosophical questions concerning the existence or reality of the total system of the new entities. Many philosophers regard a question of this kind as an ontological question which must be raised and answered *before* the introduction of the new language forms. The latter introduction, they believe, is legitimate only if it can be justified by an ontological insight supplying an affirmative answer to the question of reality. In contrast to this view, we take the position that the introduction of the new ways of speaking does not need any theoretical justification because it does not imply any assertion of reality. We may still speak (and have done so) of "the acceptance of the new entities" since this form of speech is customary; but one must keep in mind that this phrase does not mean for us anything more than acceptance of the new framework, i.e., of the new linguistic forms. Above all, it must not be interpreted as referring to an assumption, belief, or assertion of "the reality of the entities." There is no such assertion. An alleged statement of the reality of the system of entities is a pseudo-statement without cognitive content. To be sure, we have to face at this point an important question; but it is a practical, not a theoretical question; it is the question of whether or not to accept the new linguistic forms. The acceptance cannot be judged as being either true or false because it is not an assertion. It can only be judged as being more or less expedient, fruitful, conducive to the aim for which the language is intended. Judgments of this kind supply the motivation for the decision of accepting or rejecting the kind of entities.[4]

Thus it is clear that the acceptance of a linguistic framework must not be regarded as implying a metaphysical doctrine concerning the reality of the entities in question. It seems to me due to a neglect of this important distinction that some contemporary nominalists label the admission of variables of abstract types as "Platonism".[5] This is, to say the least, an extremely misleading terminology. It leads to the absurd consequence, that the position of everybody who accepts the language of physics with its real number variables (as a language of communication, not merely as a calculus) would be called Platonistic, even if he is a strict empiricist who rejects Platonic metaphysics.

A brief historical remark may here be inserted. The non-cognitive character of the questions which we have called here external questions was recognized and emphasized already by the Vienna Circle under the leadership of Moritz Schlick, the group from which the movement of logical empiricism originated. Influenced by ideas of Ludwig Wittgenstein, the Circle rejected both the thesis of the reality of the external world and the thesis of its irreality as pseudo-statements;[6] the same was the case for both the thesis of the reality of universals (abstract entities, in our present terminology) and the nominalistic thesis that they are not real and that their alleged names are not names of anything but merely *flatus vocis*. (It is obvious that the apparent negation of a pseudo-statement must also be a pseudo-statement.) It is therefore not correct to classify the members of the Vienna Circle as nominalists, as is sometimes done. However, if we look at the basic anti-metaphysical and pro-scientific attitude of most nominalists (and the same holds for many materialists and realists in the modern sense), disregarding their occasional pseudo-theoretical formulations, then it is, of course, true to say that the Vienna Circle was much closer to those philosophers than to their opponents.

4. Abstract Entities in Semantics

The problem of the legitimacy and the status of abstract entities has recently again led to controversial discussions in connection with semantics. In a semantical meaning analysis certain expressions in a language are often said to designate (or name or denote or signify or refer to) certain extra-linguistic entities.[7] As long as physical things or events (e.g., Chicago or Caesar's death) are taken as designata (entities designated), no serious doubts arise. But strong objections have been raised, especially by some empiricists, against abstract entities as designata, e.g., against semantical statements of the following kind:

1. "The word 'red' designates a property of things";
2. "The word 'color' designates a property of properties of things";
3. "The word 'five' designates a number";
4. "The word 'odd' designates a property of numbers";
5. "The sentence 'Chicago is large' designates a proposition."

Those who criticize these statements do not, of course, reject the use of the expressions in question, like "red" or "five"; nor would they deny that these expressions are meaningful. But to be meaningful, they would say, is not the same as having a meaning in the sense of an entity designated. They reject the belief, which they regard as implicitly presupposed by those semantical statements, that to each expression of the types in question (adjectives like "red", numerals like "five", etc.) there is a particular real entity to which the expression stands in the relation of designation. This belief is rejected as incompatible with the basic principles of empiricism or of scientific thinking. Derogatory labels like "Platonic realism", "hypostatization", or " 'Fido'-Fido principle" are attached to it. The latter is the name given by Gilbert Ryle to the criticized belief, which, in his view, arises by a naïve inference of analogy: just as there is an entity well known to me, viz., my dog Fido, which is designated by the name "Fido", thus there must be for every meaningful expression a particular entity to which it stands in the relation of designation or naming, i.e., the relation exemplified by "Fido"-Fido. The belief criticized is thus a case of hypostatization, i.e., of treating as names expressions which are not names. While "Fido" is a name, expressions like "red", "five", etc., are said not to be names, not to designate anything.

Our previous discussion concerning the acceptance of frameworks enables us now to clarify the situation with respect to abstract entities as designata. Let us take as an example the statement:

a. " 'Five' designates a number."

The formulation of this statement presupposes that our language L contains the forms of expressions which we have called the framework of numbers, in particular, numerical variables and the general term "number". If L contains these forms, the following is an analytic statement in L:

b. "Five is a number."

Further, to make the statement (a) possible, L must contain an expression like "designates" or "is a name of" for the semantical relation of designation. If suitable rules for this term are laid down, the following is likewise analytic:

c. " 'Five' designates five."

(Generally speaking, any expression of the form " '. . .' designates . . ." is an analytic statement provided the term " . . ." is a constant in an accepted framework. If the latter condition is not fulfilled, the expression is not a statement.) Since (a) follows from (c) and (b), (a) is likewise analytic.

Thus it is clear that *if* someone accepts the framework of numbers, then he must acknowledge (c) and (b) and hence (a) as true statements. Generally speaking, if someone accepts a framework for a certain kind of entities, then he is bound to admit the entities as possible designata. Thus the question of the admissibility of entities of a certain type or of abstract entities in general as designata is reduced to the question of the acceptability of the linguistic framework for those entities. Both the nominalistic critics, who refuse the status of designators or names to expressions like "red", "five", etc., because they deny the existence of abstract entities, and the skeptics, who express doubts concerning the existence and demand evidence for it, treat the question of existence as a theoretical question. They do, of course, not mean the internal question; the affirmative answer to *this* question is analytic and trivial and too obvious for doubt or denial, as we have seen. Their doubts refer rather to the system of entities itself; hence they mean the external question. They believe that only after making sure that there really is a system of entities of the kind in question are we justified in accepting the framework by incorporating the linguistic forms into our language. However, we have seen that the external question is not a theoretical question but rather the practical question whether or not to accept those linguistic forms. This acceptance is not in need of a theoretical justification (except with respect to expediency and fruitfulness), because it does not imply a belief or assertion. Ryle says that the "Fido"-Fido principle is "a grotesque theory". Grotesque or not, Ryle is wrong in calling it a theory. It is rather the practical decision to accept certain frameworks. Maybe Ryle is historically right with respect to those whom he mentions as previous representatives of the principle, viz., John Stuart Mill, Frege, and Russell. If these philosophers regarded the acceptance of a system of entities as a theory, an assertion, they were victims of the same old, metaphysical confusion. But it is certainly wrong to regard *my* semantical method as involving a belief in the reality of abstract entities, since I reject a thesis of this kind as a metaphysical pseudo-statement.

The critics of the use of abstract entities in semantics overlook the fundamental difference between the acceptance of a system of entities and an internal assertion, e.g., an assertion that there are elephants or electrons or prime numbers greater than a million. Whoever makes an internal assertion is certainly obliged to justify it by providing evidence, empirical evidence in the case of electrons, logical proof in the case of the prime numbers. The demand for a theoretical justification, correct in the case of internal assertions, is sometimes wrongly applied to the acceptance of a system of entities. Thus, for example, Ernest Nagel asks for "evidence relevant for affirming with warrant that there are such entities as infinitesimals or propositions." He characterizes the evidence required in these cases—in distinction to the empirical evidence in the case of electrons—as "in the broad sense logical and dialectical." Beyond this no hint is given as to what might be regarded as relevant evidence. Some nominalists regard the acceptance of abstract entities as a kind of superstition or myth, populating the world with fictitious or at least dubious entities, analogous to the belief in centaurs or demons. This shows again the confusion mentioned, because a superstition or myth is a false (or dubious) internal statement.

Let us take as example the natural numbers as cardinal numbers, i.e., in contexts like "Here are three books." The linguistic forms of the framework of numbers, including variables and the general term "number", are generally used in our common language of communication; and it is easy to formulate explicit rules for their use. Thus the logical characteristics of this framework are sufficiently clear (while many internal questions, i.e., arithmetical questions, are, of course, still open). In spite of this, the controversy concerning the external question of the ontological reality of the system of numbers continues. Suppose that one philosopher says: "I believe that there are numbers as real entities. This gives me the right to use the linguistic forms of the numerical framework and to make semantical statements about numbers as designata of numerals." His nominalistic opponent replies: "You are wrong; there are no numbers. The numerals may still be used as meaningful expressions. But they are not names, there are no entities designated by them. Therefore the word "number" and numerical variables must not be used (unless a way were found to introduce them as merely abbreviating devices, a way of translating them into the nominalistic thing language)." I cannot think of any possible evidence that would be regarded as relevant by both philosophers, and therefore, if actually found, would decide the controversy or at least make one of the opposite theses more probable than the other. (To construe the numbers as classes or properties of the second level, according to the Frege-Russell method, does, of course, not solve the controversy, because the first philosopher would affirm and the second deny the existence of the system of classes or properties of the second level.) Therefore I feel compelled to regard the external question as a pseudo-question, until both parties to the controversy offer a common interpretation of the question as a cognitive question; this would involve an indication of possible evidence regarded as relevant by both sides.

There is a particular kind of misinterpretation of the acceptance of abstract entities in various fields of science and in semantics, that needs to be cleared up. Certain early British empiricists (e.g., Berkeley and Hume) denied the existence of abstract entities on the ground that immediate experience presents us only with particulars, not with universals, e.g., with this red patch, but not with redness or color-in-general; with this scalene triangle, but not with scalene triangularity or triangularity-in-general. Only entities belonging to a type of which examples were to be found within immediate experience could be accepted as ultimate constituents of reality. Thus, according to this way of thinking, the existence of abstract entities could be asserted only if one could show either that some abstract entities fall within the given, or that abstract entities can be defined in terms of the types of entity which are given. Since these empiricists found no abstract entities within the realm of sense-data, they either denied their existence, or else made a futile attempt to define universals in terms of particulars. Some contemporary philosophers, especially English philosophers following Bertrand Russell, think in basically similar terms. They emphasize a distinction between the data (that which is immediately given in consciousness, e.g., sense-data, immediately past experiences, etc.) and the constructs based on the data. Existence or reality is ascribed only to the data; the constructs are not real entities; the corresponding linguistic expressions are merely ways of speech not actually designating anything (reminiscent of the nominalists' *flatus vocis*). We shall not criticize here this general conception. (As far as it is a principle of accepting certain entities and not accepting others, leaving aside any ontological, phenomenalistic and nominalistic pseudo-statements, there cannot be any theoretical objection to it.) But if this conception leads to the view that other philosophers or scientists who accept abstract entities thereby assert or imply their occurrence as immediate data, then such a view must be rejected as a misinterpretation. References to space-time points, the electromagnetic field, or electrons in physics, to real or complex numbers and their functions in mathematics, to the excitatory potential or unconscious complexes in psychology, to an inflationary trend in economics, and the like, do not imply the assertion that entities of these kinds occur as immediate data. And the same holds for references to abstract entities as designata in semantics. Some of the criticisms by English philosophers against such references give the impression that, probably due to the misinterpretation just indicated, they accuse the semanticist not so much of bad metaphysics (as some nominalists would do) but of bad psychology. The fact that they regard a semantical method involving abstract entities not merely as doubtful and perhaps wrong, but as manifestly absurd, preposterous and grotesque, and that they show a deep horror and indignation against this method, is perhaps to be explained by a misinterpretation of the kind described. In fact, of course, the se-

manticist does not in the least assert or imply that the abstract entities to which he refers can be experienced as immediately given either by sensation or by a kind of rational intuition. An assertion of this kind would indeed be very dubious psychology. The psychological question as to which kinds of entities do and which do not occur as immediate data is entirely irrelevant for semantics, just as it is for physics, mathematics, economics, etc., with respect to the examples mentioned above.[8]

5. Conclusion

For those who want to develop or use semantical methods, the decisive question is not the alleged ontological question of the existence of abstract entities but rather the question whether the use of abstract linguistic forms or, in technical terms, the use of variables beyond those for things (or phenomenal data), is expedient and fruitful for the purposes for which semantical analyses are made, viz., the analysis, interpretation, clarification, or construction of languages of communication, especially languages of science. This question is here neither decided nor even discussed. It is not a question simply of yes or no, but a matter of degree. Among those philosophers who have carried out semantical analyses and thought about suitable tools for this work, beginning with Plato and Aristotle and, in a more technical way on the basis of modern logic, with C. S. Peirce and Frege, a great majority accepted abstract entities. This does, of course, not prove the case. After all, semantics in the technical sense is still in the initial phases of its development, and we must be prepared for possible fundamental changes in methods. Let us therefore admit that the nominalistic critics may possibly be right. But if so, they will have to offer better arguments than they have so far. Appeal to ontological insight will not carry much weight. The critics will have to show that it is possible to construct a semantical method which avoids all references to abstract entities and achieves by simpler means essentially the same results as the other methods.

The acceptance or rejection of abstract linguistic forms, just as the acceptance or rejection of any other linguistic forms in any branch of science, will finally be decided by their efficiency as instruments, the ratio of the results achieved to the amount and complexity of the efforts required. To decree dogmatic prohibitions of certain linguistic forms instead of testing them by their success or failure in practical use, is worse than futile; it is positively harmful because it may obstruct scientific progress. The history of science shows examples of such prohibitions based on prejudices deriving from religious, mythological, metaphysical, or other irrational sources, which slowed up the developments for shorter or longer periods of time. Let us learn from the lessons of history. Let us grant to those who work in any special field of investigation the freedom to use any form of expression which seems useful to them; the work in the field will sooner or later lead to the elimination of those forms which have no useful function. *Let us be cautious in making assertions and critical in examining them, but tolerant in permitting linguistic forms.*

Notes

1. The terms "sentence" and "statement" are here used synonymously for declarative (indicative, propositional) sentences.

2. In my book *Meaning and Necessity* (Chicago, 1947) I have developed a semantical method which takes propositions as entities designated by sentences (more specifically, as intentions of sentences). In order to facilitate the understanding of the systematic development, I added some informal, extrasystematic explanations concerning the nature of propositions. I said that the term "proposition" "is used neither for a linguistic expression nor for a subjective, mental occurrence, but rather for something objective that may or may not be exemplified in nature. . . . We apply the term 'proposition' to any entities of a certain logical type, namely, those that may be expressed by (declarative) sentences in a language" (p. 27). After some more detailed discussions concerning the relation between propositions and facts, and the nature of false propositions, I added: "It has been the purpose of the preceding remarks to facilitate the understanding of our conception of propositions. If, however, a reader should find these explanations more puzzling than clarifying, or even unacceptable, he may disregard them"

(p. 31) (that is, disregard these extra-systematic explanations, not the whole theory of the propositions as intensions of sentences, as one reviewer understood). In spite of this warning, it seems that some of those readers who were puzzled by the explanations did not disregard them but thought that by raising objections against them they could refute the theory. This is analogous to the procedure of some laymen who by (correctly) criticizing the ether picture or other visualizations of physical theories thought they had refuted those theories. Perhaps the discussions in the present paper will help in clarifying the role of the system of linguistic rules for the introduction of a framework for entities on the one hand, and that of extrasystematic explanations concerning the nature of the entities on the other.

3. W. V. Quine was the first to recognize the importance of the introduction of variables as indicating the acceptance of entities. "The ontology to which one's use of language commits him comprises simply the objects that he treats as falling . . . within the range of values of his variables" (["Notes on Existence and Necessity," *Journal of Philosophy* 40 (1943)], p. 118; compare also his ["Designation and Existence," *Journal of Philosophy* 36 (1939), 701–709] and ["On Universals," *Journal of Symbolic Logic* 12 (1947), 74–84]).

4. For a closely related point of view on these questions see the detailed discussions in Herbert Feigl, "Existential Hypotheses," *Philosophy of Science,* 17 (1950), 35–62.

5. Paul Bernays, "Sur le platonisme dans les mathématiques" (*L'Enseignement math.*, 34 (1935), 52–69). W. V. Quine, see previous footnote and a recent paper ["On What There Is," *Review of Metaphysics* 2 (1948), 21–38]. Quine does not acknowledge the distinction which I emphasize above, because according to his general conception there are no sharp boundary lines between logical and factual truth, between questions of meaning and questions of fact, between the acceptance of a language structure and the acceptance of an assertion formulated in the language. This conception, which seems to deviate considerably from customary ways of thinking, will be explained in his article ["Semantics and Abstract Objects," *Proceedings of the Academy of Arts and Sci-*

ences 80 (1951), 90–96]. When Quine in the article ["On What There Is," *Review of Metaphysics* 2 (1948), 21–38] classifies my logistic conception of mathematics (derived from Frege and Russell) as "platonic realism" (p. 33), this is meant (according to a personal communication from him) not as ascribing to me agreement with Plato's metaphysical doctrine of universals, but merely as referring to the fact that I accept a language of mathematics containing variables of higher levels. With respect to the basic attitude to take in choosing a language form (an "ontology" in Quine's terminology, which seems to me misleading), there appears now to be agreement between us: "the obvious counsel is tolerance and an experimental spirit" (["On What There Is," *Review of Metaphysics* 2 (1948)], p. 38).

6. See Carnap, *Scheinprobleme in der Philosophie; das Fremdpsychische und der Realismusstreit*, Berlin, 1928. Moritz Schlick, *Positivismus und Realismus*, reprinted in *Gesammelte Aufsätze*, Wien, 1938.

7. See [I] *Meaning and Necessity* (Chicago, 1947). The distinction I have drawn in the latter book between the method of the name-relation and the method of intension and extension is not essential for our present discussion. The term "designation" is used in the present article in a neutral way; it may be understood as referring to the name-relation or to the intension-relation or to the extension-relation or to any similar relations used in other semantic methods.

8. Wilfrid Sellars ("Acquaintance and Description Again," in *Journal of Philos.*, 46 (1949), 496–504; see pp. 502 f.) analyzes clearly the roots of the mistake "of taking the designation relation of semantic theory to be a reconstruction of *being present to an experience*."

READING QUESTIONS

1. What is "the problem of abstract entities"? For what kind of philosopher is this a genuine problem? Why?

2. What does Carnap mean when he speaks of a 'linguistic framework'? Specifically, what are the differences between internal questions and external questions?

3. Carnap writes that "to recognize something as a real thing or event means to succeed in incorporating it into the system of things at a particular space-time position so that it fits together with the other things recognized as real, according to the rules of the framework." Do you agree that this is what it means to recognize something as a real thing or event? Why or why not?

4. Why does Carnap believe that "to accept the thing world means nothing more than to accept a certain form of language"? Why doesn't he believe that this will imply one's acceptance of "a *belief* in the reality of the thing world"? Does it follow that "an alleged statement of the reality of the system of entities is a pseudo-statement without cognitive content"? Why or why not?

5. Carnap proposes that "the acceptance of a new kind of entities is represented in the language by the introduction of new forms of expressions to be used according to a new set of rules." Briefly outline how Carnap believes that this introduction can occur.

6. After discussing how new linguistic forms can be introduced into a language, Carnap writes that, "we have to face at this point an important question; but it is a practical, not a theoretical question; it is the question of whether or not to accept the new linguistic forms. The acceptance cannot be judged as being either true or false because it is not an assertion. It can only be judged as being more or less expedient, fruitful, conducive to the aim for which the language is intended. Judgments of this kind supply the motivation for the decision of accepting or rejecting the kind of entities." If Carnap is correct, what, in general, does this say about our ontology?

7. What is Gilbert Ryle's objection to "taking abstract entities as designata"? What is Carnap's reply to Ryle's objection? Is this an adequate reply?

SUGGESTIONS FOR FURTHER READING (RUDOLF CARNAP)

Primary Sources

(1928) *The Logical Structure of the World and Pseudo-problems in Philosophy*, translated by R. George. Berkeley: University of California Press, 1969.

(1929) *Survey of Symbolic Logic*. Vienna: Springer Verlag.

(1934) *The Logical Syntax of Language*. London: Routledge & Kegan Paul, 1937.

(1935) *Philosophy and Logical Syntax*. London: Kegan Paul, Trench, Trubner.

(1939) *Foundations of Logical Mathematics*. Chicago, IL: University of Chicago Press.

(1942) *Introduction to Semantics*. Cambridge, MA: Harvard University Press.

(1943) *Formalization of Logic*. Cambridge, MA: Harvard University Press.

(1947) *Meaning and Necessity*, 2nd ed. Chicago, IL: University of Chicago Press, 1956.

(1950) *The Logical Foundations of Probability*. Chicago, IL: University of Chicago Press.

(1966) *Philosophical Foundations of Physics: An Introduction to the Philosophy of Science*, edited by M. Gardner. New York: Basic Books.

(1971, 1980) *Studies in Inductive Logic and Probability*, Vol. 1, edited by R. Carnap and R. Jeffrey; Vol. 2, edited by R. Jeffrey. Berkeley, CA: University of California Press.

(1990) (and W.v.O. Quine) *Dear Carnap, Dear Van: The Quine-Carnap Correspondence and Related Works*, edited by R. Creath. Berkeley, CA: University of California Press.

Secondary Sources

Coffa, J. A. (1991) *The Semantic Tradition from Kant to Carnap: To the Vienna Station*, edited by L. Wessels. Cambridge: Cambridge University Press.

Goldfarb, W., and T. Ricketts (1992) *Science and Subjectivity*, edited by D. Bell and W. Vossenkuhl. Berlin: Akedemie Verlag.

Goodman, N. (1951) *The Structure of Appearance*. Cambridge, MA: Harvard University Press.

Hintikka, J., ed. (1975) *Rudolf Carnap, Logical Empiricist*. Dordrecht: D. Reidel.

Oberdan, T. (1992) *Protocols, Truths, and Convention*. Amsterdam: Editions Rodopoi.

Richardson, A. (1997) *Carnap's Construction of the World: The Aufbau and the Emergence of Logical Empiricism*. Cambridge: Cambridge University Press.

Salmon, W., and G. Wolters, eds. (1994) *Logic, Language, and the Structure of Scientific Theories*. Pittsburgh, PA: University of Pittsburgh Press

Schilpp, P. A., ed. (1963) *The Philosophy of Rudolf Carnap*. La Salle, IL: Open Court.

Spohn, W., ed. (1991) *Hans Reichenbach, Rudolf Carnap: A Centenary*. Dordrecht: Kluwer Academic Publishers.

Carl G. Hempel

Problems and Changes in the Empiricist Criterion of Meaning

Carl Gustav Hempel (who was nicknamed Peter since his childhood) was born in Oranienburg, Germany, in 1905. Hempel began his studies in Berlin, but transferred to the University of Göttingen in 1923 to study mathematics with David Hilbert and Edmund Landan. While at Göttingen, he also studied symbolic logic with Heinrich Behmann before moving to the University of Heidelberg, where he pursued specialized studies in various topics in mathematics, physics, and philosophy. He next went to the University of Berlin. In Berlin, Hempel attended Hans Reichenbach's courses on mathematics, on the philosophy of space and time, and on probability. He also began his dissertation (on probability) under Reichenbach, but completed his degree with the psychologist Wolfgang Köhler after the Nazis removed Reichenbach from his professorship in 1933. Sympathetic to the major thrust of positivistic philosophy, Hempel regularly attended the gatherings of the Society for Scientific Philosophy or the "Berlin Circle."

In 1934, Hempel received his doctorate from Berlin and, fleeing the plague of Nazism sweeping Germany, moved with his wife to Brussels to do advanced research with Paul Oppenheim. In 1937, he left Brussels and came to the United States after it became clear to him that a German invasion of Brussels was imminent. The move to America was partially inspired by an invitation from the University of Chicago to become a phi-losophy research associate, a position arranged by Hempel's friend Rudolf Carnap, who was at that time on the faculty at Chicago.

In 1939, Hempel left Chicago and took a position at City College in New York for a year, then moved on to Queen's College in Flushing, New York, where he remained until 1948. He became a naturalized citizen of the United States in 1944. During the time he spent at Queen's, he published a number of pioneering and exceptionally influential articles on confirmation and on the nature of scientific explanation. After leaving Queen's, Hempel accepted a position at Yale and worked on the *International Encyclopedia of Unified Science* with Otto Neurath and Rudolf Carnap.

In 1955, Hempel left Yale for a position at Princeton as Stuart Professor of Philosophy, a chair he held until 1973. After his mandatory retirement from Princeton he continued to teach as University Professor of Philosophy at the University of Pittsburgh. Hempel eventually retired completely from college teaching in 1985, but is remembered as a gifted and inspiring educator whose strong personality and active intellect had a remarkable effect on his students. Hempel died near Princeton, New Jersey, in 1997.

In the following essay, written in 1950, Hempel reviews and critiques the history of attempts to formulate an adequate empiricist criterion of meaning. In the first half of his paper he specifically examines various direct attempts at formulating a criterion that will rule out the supposed propositions of metaphysics, while at the same time leaving intact and meaningful various propositions of the sciences, especially propositions expressing general laws. Hempel concludes that previous attempts to locate an adequate criterion have failed, either by making the criterion so restrictive that it rules out too much or so liberal that it allows too much in.

In the second half of his paper, Hempel considers Carnap's attempt to formulate "an artificial language whose vocabulary and grammar were so chosen as to preclude altogether the possibility of forming sentences of any kind which the empiricist meaning criterion is meant to rule out." Although in some ways he is more enthusiastic about the prospects of formulating an ade-quate criterion of cognitive significance along these lines, he points out a number of problems with this type of proposal, which remain unresolved. In particular, he advances concerns about adequately capturing the holistic nature of the language of the empirical sciences. He concludes his argument with some remarks about the logical status of any really adequate empiricist criterion of meaning.

1. Introduction

The fundamental tenet of modern empiricism is the view that all non-analytic knowledge is based on experience. Let us call this thesis the principle of empiricism.[1] Contemporary logical empiricism has added[2] to it the maxim that a sentence makes a cognitively meaningful assertion, and thus can be said to be either true or false, only if it is either (1) analytic or self-contradictory or (2) capable, at least in principle, of experiential test. According to this so-called *empiricist criterion of cognitive meaning, or of cognitive significance,* many of the formulations of traditional metaphysics and large parts of epistemology are devoid of cognitive significance—however rich some of them may be in non-cognitive import by virtue of their emotive appeal or the moral inspiration they offer. Similarly certain doctrines which have been, at one time or another, formulated within empirical science or its border disciplines are so contrived as to be incapable of test by any conceivable evidence; they are therefore qualified as pseudo-hypotheses, which assert nothing, and which therefore have no explanatory or predictive force whatever. This verdict applies, for example, to the neo-vitalist speculations about entelechies or vital forces, and to the "telefinalist hypothesis" propounded by Lecomte du Noüy.

Carl Hempel, "Problems and Changes in the Empiricist Criterion of Meaning", *Revue Internationale de Philosophie* 4, no. 11 (15 January 1950), pp. 41–63. Reprinted with kind permission of the editors of *Revue Internationale de Philosophie.*

The preceding formulations of the principle of empiricism and of the empiricist meaning criterion provide no more, however, than a general and rather vague characterization of a basic point of view, and they need therefore to be elucidated and amplified. And while in the earlier phases of its development, logical empiricism was to a large extent preoccupied with a critique of philosophic and scientific formulations by means of those fundamental principles, there has been in recent years an increasing concern with the positive tasks of analyzing in detail the logic and methodology of empirical science and of clarifying and restating the basic ideas of empiricism in the light of the insights thus obtained. In the present article, I propose to discuss some of the problems this search has raised and some of the results it seems to have established.

2. Changes in the Testability Criterion of Empirical Meaning

As our formulation shows, the empiricist meaning criterion lays down the requirement of experiential testability for those among the cognitively meaningful sentences which are neither analytic nor contradictory; let us call them sentences with empirical meaning, or empirical significance. The concept of testability, which is to render precise the vague notion of being based—or rather baseable—on experience, has undergone several modifications which reflect an increasingly refined analysis of the structure of empirical knowledge. In the present section, let us examine the major stages of this development.

For convenience of exposition, we first introduce three auxiliary concepts, namely those of observable characteristic, of observation predicate, and of observation sentence. A property or a relation of physical objects will be called an *observable characteristic* if, under suitable circumstances, its presence or absence in a given instance can be ascertained through direct observation. Thus, the terms "green", "soft", "liquid", "longer than", designate observable characteristics, while "bivalent", "radioactive", "better electric conductor", and "introvert" do not. Terms which designate observable characteristics will be called *observation predicates*. Finally, by an *observation sentence* we shall understand any sentence which—correctly or incorrectly—asserts of one or more specifically named objects that they have, or that they lack, some specified observable characteristic. The following sentences, for example, meet this condition: "The Eiffel Tower is taller than the buidings in its vicinity," "The pointer of this instrument does not cover the point marked '3' on the scale," and even, "The largest dinosaur on exhibit in New York's Museum of Natural History had a blue tongue"; for this last sentence assigns to a specified object a characteristic—having a blue tongue—which is of such a kind that under suitable circumstances (e.g., in the case of my Chow dog) its presence or absence can be ascertained by direct observation. Our concept of observation sentence is intended to provide a precise interpretation of the vague idea of a sentence asserting something that is "in principle" ascertainable by direct observation, even though it may happen to be actually incapable of being observed by myself, perhaps also by my contemporaries, and possibly even by any human being who ever lived or will live. Any evidence that might be adduced in the test of an empirical hypothesis may now be thought of as being expressed in observation sentences of this kind.[3]

We now turn to the changes in the conception of testability and thus of empirical meaning. In the early days of the Vienna Circle, a sentence was said to have empirical meaning if it was capable, at least in principle, of complete verification by observational evidence; i.e., if observational evidence could be described which, if actually obtained, would conclusively establish the truth of the sentence.[4] With the help of the concept of observation sentence, we can restate this requirement as follows: A sentence S has empirical meaning if and only if it is possible to indicate a finite set of observation sentences, $O_1, O_2, \ldots, O_n$, such that if these are true, then S is necessarily true, too. As stated however, this condition is satisfied also if S is an analytic sentence or if the given observation sentences are logically incompatible with each other. By the following formulation, we rule these cases out and at the same time express the intended criterion more precisely:

2.1. *Requirement of complete verifiability in principle:*

A sentence has empirical meaning if and only if it is not analytic and follows logically from some finite and logically consistent class of observation sentence.[5]

This criterion, however, has several serious defeats. The first of those here to be mentioned has been pointed out by various writers:

a. The verifiability requirement rules out all sentences of universal form and thus all statements purporting to express general laws; for these cannot be conclusively verified by any finite set of observational data. And since sentences of this type constitute an integral part of scientific theories, the verifiability requirement must be regarded as overly restrictive in this respect. Similarly, the criterion disqualifies all sentences such as "For any substance there exists some solvent," which contain both universal and existential quantifiers (i.e., occurrences of the terms "all" and "some" or their equivalents); for no sentences of this kind can be logically deduced from any finite set of observation sentences.

Two further defects of the verifiability requirement do not seem to have been widely noticed:

b. Suppose that S is a sentence which satisfies the proposed criterion, whereas N is a sentence such as "The absolute is perfect," to which the criterion attributes no empirical meaning. Then the alternation SvN (i.e., the expression obtained by connecting the two sentences by the word "or"), likewise satisfies the criterion; for if S is a consequence of some finite class of observation sentences then trivially SvN is a consequence of the same class. But clearly, the empiricist criterion of meaning is not intended to countenance sentences of this sort. In this respect, therefore, the requirement of complete verifiability is too inclusive.

c. Let "P" be an observation predicate. Then the purely existential sentence "(Ex) P(x)" ("There exists at least one thing that has the property P") is completely verifiable, for it follows from any observation sentence asserting of some particular object that it has the property P. But its denial, being equivalent to the universal sentence "(x) ∼ P(x)" ("Nothing has the property P") is clearly not completely verifiable, as follows from comment (a) above. Hence, under the criterion (2.1), the denials of certain empirically—and thus cognitively—significant sentences are empirically meaningless; and as they are neither analytic nor contradictory, they are cognitively meaningless. But however we may delimit the domain of significant discourse, we shall have to insist that if a sentence falls within that domain, then so must its denial. To put the matter more explicitly: The sentences to be qualified as cognitively meaningful are precisely those which can be significantly said to be either true or false. But then, adherence to (2.1) would engender a serious dilemma, as is shown by the consequence just mentioned: We would either have to give up the fundamental logical principle that if a sentence is true or false, then its denial is false or true, respectively (and thus cognitively significant); or else, we must deny, in a manner reminiscent of the intuitionistic conception of logic and mathematics, that "(x) ∼ P(x)" is logically equivalent to the negation of "(Ex) P (x)". Clearly, the criterion (2.1), which has disqualified itself on several other counts, does not warrant such drastic measures for its preservation; hence, it has to be abandoned.[6]

Strictly analogous considerations apply to an alternative criterion, which makes complete falsifiability in principle the defining characteristic of empirical significance. Let us formulate this criterion as follows: A sentence has empirical meaning if and only if it is capable, in principle, of complete refutation by a finite number of observational data; or, more precisely:

2.2. *Requirement of complete falsifiability in principle:*

A sentence has empirical meaning if and only if its denial is not analytic and follows logically from some finite logically consistent class of observation sentences.[7]

This criterion qualifies a sentence as empirically meaningful if its denial satisfies the requirement of complete verifiability; as is to be expected, it is therefore inadequate on similar grounds as the latter:

a. It rules out purely existential hypotheses, such is "There exists at least one unicorn," and all sentences whose formulation calls for mixed—i.e., universal and existential—quantification; for none of these can possibly be conclusively falsified by a finite number of observation sentences.

b. If a sentence S is completely falsifiable whereas N is a sentence which is not, then their conjunction, S.N (i.e., the expression obtained by connecting the two sentences by the word "and") is completely falsifiable; for if the denial of S is entailed by some class of observation sentences, then the denial of S.N is, *a fortiori*, entailed by the same class. Thus, the criterion allows empirical signifiance to many sentences which an adequate empiricist criterion should rule out, such as, says, "All swans are white and the absolute is perfect."

c. If "P" is an observation predicate, then the assertion that all things have the property P is qualified as significant, but its denial, being equivalent to a purely existential hypothesis, is disqualified (cf. (*a*)). Hence, criterion (2.2) gives rise to the same dilemma as (2.1).

In sum, then, interpretations of the testability criterion in terms of complete verifiability or of complete falsifiability are inadequate because they are overly restrictive in one direction and overly inclusive in another, and because both of them require incisive changes in the fundamental principles of logic.

Several attempts have been made to avoid these difficulties by construing the testability criterion as demanding merely a partial and possibly indirect confirmability of empirical hypotheses by observational evidence.

2.3. A formulation suggested by Ayer[8] is characteristic of these attempts to set up a clear and sufficiently comprehensive criterion of confirmability. It states, in effect, that a sentence S has empirical import if from S in conjunction with suitable subsidiary hypotheses it is possible to derive observation sentences which are not derivable from the subsidiary hypotheses alone.

This condition is suggested by a closer consideration of the logical structure of scientific testing; but it is much too liberal as it stands. Indeed, as Ayer himself has pointed out in the second edition of his book, *Language, Truth, and Logic*,[9] his criterion allows empirical import to any sentence whatever. Thus, e.g., if S is the sentence "The absolute is perfect," it suffices to choose as a subsidiary hypothesis the sentence "If the absolute is perfect then this apple is red" in order to make possible the deduction of the observation sentence "This apple is red," which clearly does not follow from the subsidiary hypothesis alone.[10]

2.4. To meet this objection, Ayer has recently proposed a modified version of his testability criterion. The modification restricts, in effect, the subsidiary hypotheses mentioned in (2. 3) to sentences which are either analytic or can independently be shown to be testable in the sense of the modified criterion.[11]

But it can readily be shown that this new criterion, like the requirement of complete falsifiablity, allows empirical significance to any conjunction S.N, where S satisfies Ayer's criterion while N is a sentence such as "The absolute is perfect," which is to be disqualified by that criterion. Indeed: whatever consequences can be deduced from S with the help of permissible subsidiary hypotheses can also be deduced from S.N by means of the same subsidiary hypotheses, and as Ayer's new criterion is formulated essentially in terms of the deducibility of a certain type of consequence from the given sentence, it countenances S.N together with S. Another difficulty has been pointed out by Professor A. Church , who has shown[12] that if there are any three observation sentences none of which alone entails any of the others, then it follows for any sentence S whatsoever that either it or its denial has empirical import according to Ayer's revised criterion.

3. Translatability into an Empiricist Language as a New Criterion of Cognitive Meaning

I think it is useless to continue the search for an adequate criterion of testability in terms of deductive relationships to observation sentences. The past development of this search—of which we have considered the major stages—seems to warrant the expectation that as long as we try to set up a criterion of testability for individual sentences in a natural language, in terms of logical relationship to observation sentences, the result will be either too restrictive or too inclusive, or both. In particular it appears likely that such criteria would allow empirical import in the manner of (2.1) (*b*) or of (2.2) (*b*), either to any alternation or to any conjunction of two sentences of which at least one is qualified as empirically meaningful; and this peculiarity has undesirable consequences because the liberal grammatical rules of English as of any other natural language countenance as sentences certain expressions ("The absolute is perfect" was our illustration) which even by the most liberal empiricist standards make no assertion whatever; and these would then have to be permitted as components of empirically significant statements.

The predicament would not arise, of course, in an artificial language whose vocabulary and grammar were so chosen as to preclude altogether the possibility of forming sentences of any kind which the empiricist meaning criterion is intended to rule out. Let us call any such language an *empiricist language*. This reflection suggests an entirely different approach to our problem: Give a general characterization of the kind of language that would qualify as empiricist, and then lay down the following:

3.1. *Translatability criterion of cognitive meaning:* A sentence has cognitive meaning if and only if it is translatable into an empiricist language.

This conception of cognitive import, while perhaps not explicitly stated, seems to underlie much of the more recent work done by empiricist writers; as far as I can see it has its origin in Carnap's essay, *Testability and Meaning* (especially part IV).

As any language so also any empiricist language can be characterized by indicating its vocabulary and the rules determining its logic; the latter include the syntactical rules according to which sentences may be formed by means of the given vocabulary. In effect, therefore, the translatability criterion proposes to characterize the cognitively meaningful sentences by the vocabulary out of which they may be constructed, and by the syntactical principles governing their construction. What sentences are singled out as cognitively significant will depend, accordingly, on the choice of the vocabulary and of the construction rules. Let us consider a specific possibility:

3.2. We might qualify a language L as empiricist if satisfies the following conditions:

a. *The vocabulary of L* contains:

1. The customary locutions of logic which are used in the formulation of sentences; including in particular the expressions "not", "and", "or", "if . . . then . . .", "all", "some", "the class of all things such that. . . .", " . . . is an element of class . . .";

2. Certain *observation predicates*. These will be said to constitute the basic empirical vocabulary of L;

3. Any expression definable by means of those referred to under (1) and (2).

b. *The rules of sentence formation for L* are those laid down in some contemporary logical system such as *Principia Mathematica.*

Since all defined terms can be eliminated in favor of primitives, these rules stipulate in effect that a language L is empiricist if all its sentences are expressible, with the help of the usual logical locutions, in terms of observable characteristics of physical objects. Let us call any language of this sort a thing-language in the narrower sense. Alternatively, the basic empirical vocabulary of an empiricist language might be construed as consisting of phenomenalistic terms, each of them referring to some aspect of the phenomena of perception or sensation. The construction of adequate phenomenalistic languages, however, presents considerable difficulties,13 and in recent empiricism, attention has been focused primarily on the potentialities of languages whose basic empirical vocabulary consists of observation predicates; for the latter lend themselves more directly to the description of that type of intersubjective evidence which is invoked in the test of scientific hypotheses.

If we construe empiricist languages in the sense of (3.2), then the translatability criterion (3.1) avoids all of the short-comings pointed out in our discussion of earlier forms of the testability criterion:

a. Our characterization of empiricist languages makes explicit provision for universal and existential quantification, i.e., for the use of the terms "all" and "some"; hence, no type of quantified statement is generally excluded from the realm of cognitively significant discourse;

b. Sentences such as "The absolute is perfect" cannot be formulated in an empiricist language (cf. (*d*) below); hence there is no danger that a conjunction or alternation containing a sentence of that kind as a component might be qualified as cognitively significant;

c. In a language L with syntactical rules conforming to *Principia Mathematica*, the denial of a sentence is always again a sentence of L. Hence, the translatability criterion does not lead to the consequence, which is entailed by both (2.1) and (2.2), that the denials of certain significant sentences are non-significant;

d. Despite its comprehensiveness, the new criterion does not attribute cognitive meaning to *all* sentences; thus, e.g., the sentences "The absolute is perfect" and "Nothingness nothings" cannot be translated into an empiricist language because their key terms are not definable by means of purely logical expressions and observation terms.

4. The Problem of Disposition Terms and of Theoretical Constructs

Yet, the new criterion is still too restrictive—as are, incidentally, also its predecessors—in an important respect which now calls for consideration. If empiricist languages are defined in accordance with (3.2), then, as was noted above, the translatability criterion (3.1) allows cognitive import to a sentence only if its constitutive empirical terms are explicitly definable by means of observation predicates. But as we shall argue presently, many terms even of the physical sciences are not so definable; hence the criterion would oblige us to reject, as devoid of cognitive import, all scientific hypotheses containing such terms—an altogether intolerable consequence.

The concept of temperature is a case in point. At first glance, it seems as though the phrase "Object x has a temperature of c degrees centigrade," or briefly "$T(x) = c$" could be defined by the following sentence, (D): $T(x) = c$ if and only if the following condition is satisfied: If a thermometer is in contact with x, then it registers c degrees on its scale.

Disregarding niceties, it may be granted that the definiens given here is formulated entirely in reference to observables. However, it has one highly questionable aspect: In *Principia Mathematica* and similar systems, the phrase "if p then q" is construed as being synonymous with "not p or q"; and under this so-called material interpretation of the conditional, a statement of the form "if p then q" is obviously true if (though not only if) the sentence standing in the place of "p" is false. If, therefore, the meaning of "if . . . then . . ." in the definiens of (D) is understood in the material sense, then that definiens is true if (though not only if) x is an object not in contact with a thermometer—no matter what numerical value we may give to c. And since the definiendum would be true under the same circumstances, the definition (D) would qualify as true the assignment of any temperature value whatsoever to any object not in contact with a thermometer! Analogous considerations apply to such terms as "electrically charged", "magnetic", "intelligent", "electric resistance", etc., in short to all disposition terms, i.e., which express the disposition of one or more objects to react in a determinate way under specified circumstances: A definition of such terms by means of observation predicates cannot be effected in the manner of (D), however natural and obvious a mode of definition this may at first seem to be.[14]

There are two main directions in which a resolution of the difficulty might be sought. On the one hand, it could be argued that the definition of disposition terms in the manner of (D) is perfectly adequate provided that the phrase "if . . . then . . ." in the definiens is construed in the sense it is obviously intended to have, namely as implying, in the case of (D), that even if x is not actually in contact with a thermometer, still if it *were* in such contact, then the thermometer *would* register c degrees. In sentences such as this, the phrase "if . . . then . . ." is said to be used counterfactually; and it is in this "strong" sense, which implies a counterfactual conditional, that the definiens of (D) would have to be construed. This suggestion would provide an answer to the problem of defining disposition terms if it were not for the fact that no entirely satisfactory account of the exact meaning of counterfactual conditionals seems to be available at present. Thus, the first way out of the difficulty has the status of a program rather than that of a solution. The lack of an adequate theory of counterfactual conditionals is all the more deplorable as such a theory is needed also for the analysis of the concept of general law in empirical science and of certain related ideas. A clarification of this cluster of problems constitutes at present one of the urgent desiderata in the logic and methodology of science.[15]

An alternative way of dealing with the definitional problems raised by disposition terms was suggested, and developed in detail, by Carnap. It consists in permitting the introduction of new terms, within an empiricist language, by means of so-called reduction sentences, which have the character of partial or conditional definitions.[16] Thus, e.g., the concept of temperature in our last illustration might be introduced by means of the following reduction sentence, (R): If a thermometer is in contact with an object x, then $T(x) = c$ if and only if the thermometer registers c degrees.

This rule, in which the conditional may be construed in the material sense, specifies the meaning of "temperature", i.e., of statements of the form "$T(x) = c$", only partially, namely in regard to those objects which are in contact with a thermometer; for all other objects, it simply leaves the meaning of "$T(x) = c$" undetermined. The specification of the meaning of "temperature" may then be gradually extended to cases not covered in (R) by laying down further reduction sentences, which reflect the measurement of temperature by devices other than thermometers.

Reduction sentences thus provide a means for the precise formulation of what is commonly referred to as operational definitions.[17] At the same time, they show that the latter are not definitions in the strict sense of the word, but rather partial specifications of meaning.

The preceding considerations suggest that in our characterization (3.2) of empiricist languages we broaden the provision a (3) by permitting in the vocabulary of L all those terms whose meaning can be specified in terms of the basic empirical vocabulary by means of definitions or reduction sentences. Languages satisfying this more inclusive criterion will be referred to as thing-languages in the wider sense.

If the concept of empiricist language is broadened in this manner, then the translatability criterion (3.1) covers—as it should—also all those statements whose constituent empirical terms include "empirical constructs", i.e., terms which do not designate observables, but which can be introduced by reduction sentences on the basis of observation predicates.

Even in this generalized version, however, our criterion of cognitive meaning may not do justice to advanced scientific theories, which are formulated in terms of "theoretical constructs", such as the terms "absolute temperature", "gravitational potential", "electric field", "ϕ function", etc. There are reasons to think that neither definitions nor reduction sentences are adequate to introduce these terms on the basis of observation predicates. Thus, e.g., if a system of reduction sentences for concept of electric field were available, then—to oversimplify the point a little—it would be possible to describe, in terms of observable characteristics, some necessary and some sufficient conditions for the presence, in a given region, of an electric field of any mathematical description, however complex. Actually, however, such criteria can at best be given only for some sufficiently simple kinds of fields.

Now theories of the advanced type here referred to may be considered as hypothetico-deductive systems in which all statements are logical consequences of a set of fundamental assumptions. Fundamental as well as derived statements in such a system are formulated either in terms of certain theoretical constructs which are not defined within the system and thus play the rôle of primitives, or in terms of expressions defined by means of the latter. Thus, in their logical structure such sys-

tems equal the axiomatized uninterpreted systems studied in mathematics and logic. They acquire applicability to empirical subject matter, and thus the status of theories of empirical science, by virtue of an empirical interpretation. The latter is effected by a translation of some of the sentences of the theory—often derived rather than fundamental ones—into an empiricist language, which may contain both observation predicates and empirical constructs. And since the sentences which are thus given empirical meaning are logical consequences of the fundamental hypotheses of the theory, that translation effects, indirectly, a partial interpretation of the latter and of the constructs in terms of which they are formulated.[18]

In order to make translatability into an empiricist language an adequate criterion of cognitive import, we broaden therefore the concept of empiricist language so as to include thing-languages in the narrower and in the wider sense as well as all interpreted theoretical systems of the kind just referred to.[19] With this understanding, (3.1) may finally serve as a general criterion of cognitive meaning.

5. On "the Meaning" of an Empirical Statement

In effect, the criterion thus arrived at qualifies a sentence as cognitively meaningful if its non-logical constituents refer, directly or in certain specified indirect ways, to observables. But it does not make any pronouncement on what "the meaning" of a cognitively significant sentence is, and in particular it neither says nor implies that that meaning can be exhaustively characterized by what the totality of possible tests would reveal in terms of observable phenomena. Indeed, *the content of a statement with empirical import cannot, in general, be exhaustively expressed by means of any class of observation sentences.*

For consider first, among the statements permitted by our criterion, any purely existential hypothesis or any statement involving mixed quantification. As was pointed out earlier, under (2.2) (*a*), statements of these kinds entail no observation sentences whatever; hence their content cannot be expressed by means of a class of observation sentences.

And secondly, even most statements of purely universal form (such as "All flamingoes are pink") entail observation sentences (such as "That thing is pink") only when combined with suitable other observation sentences (such as "That thing is a flamingo").

This last remark can be generalized: The use of empirical hypotheses for the prediction of observable phenomena requires, in practically all cases, the use of subsidiary empirical hypotheses.[20] Thus, e.g., the hypotheses that the agent of tuberculosis is rod-shaped does not by itself entail the consequence that upon looking at a tubercular sputum specimen through a microscope, rod-like shapes will be observed: a large number of subsidiary hypotheses, including the theory of the microscope, have to be used as additional premises in deducing that prediction.

Hence, what is sweepingly referred to as "the (cognitive) meaning" of a given scientific hypothesis cannot be adequately characterized in terms of potential observational evidence alone, nor can it be specified for the hypothesis taken in isolation: In order to understand "the meaning" of a hypothesis within an empiricist language, we have to know not merely what observation sentences it entails alone or in conjunction with subsidiary hypotheses, but also what other, nonobservational, empirical sentences are entailed by it, what sentences in the given language would confirm or disconfirm it, and for what other hypotheses the given one would be confirmatory or disconfirmatory. In other words, the cognitive meaning of a statement in an empiricist language is reflected in the totality of its logical relationships to all other statements in that language and not to the observation sentences alone. In this sense, the statements of empirical science have a surplus meaning over and above what can be expressed in terms of relevant observation sentences.[21]

6. The Logical Status of the Empiricist Criterion of Meaning

What kind of a sentence, it has often been asked, is the empiricist meaning criterion itself? Plainly it is not an empirical hypothesis; but it is not analytic or self-contradictory either; hence, when judged by its own standard, is it not devoid of cognitive meaning? In that case, what claim of soundness or validity could possibly be made for it?

One might think of construing the criterion as a definition which indicates what empiricists propose to understand by a cognitively significant sentence; thus understood, it would not have the character of an assertion and would be neither true nor false. But this conception would attribute to the criterion a measure of arbitrariness which cannot be reconciled with the heated controversies it has engendered and even less with the fact, repeatedly illustrated in the present article, that the changes in its specific content have always been determined by the objective of making the criterion a more adequate index of cognitive import. And this very objective illuminates the character of the empiricist criterion of meaning: It is intended to provide a clarification and *explication* of the idea of a sentence which makes an intelligible assertion.[22] This idea is admittedly vague, and it is the task of philosophic explication to replace it by a more precise concept. In view of this difference of precision we cannot demand, of course, that the "new" concept, the explicatum, be strictly synonymous with the old one, the explicandum.[23] How, then, are we to judge the adequacy of a proposed explication, as expressed in some specific criterion of cognitive meaning?

First of all, there exists a large class of sentences which are rather generally recognized as making intelligible assertions, and another large class of which this is more or less generally denied. We shall have to demand of an adequate explication that it take into account these spheres of common usage; hence an explication which, let us say, denies cognitive import to descriptions of past events or to generalizations expressed in terms of observables has to be rejected as inadequate. As we have seen, this first requirement of adequacy has played an important role in the development of the empiricist meaning criterion.

But an adequate explication of the concept of cognitively significant statement must satisfy yet another, even more important, requirement: Together with the explication of certain other concepts, such as those of confirmation and of probability, it has to provide the framework for a general theoretical account of the structure and the foundations of scientific knowledge. Explication, as here understood, is not a mere description of the accepted usages of the terms under consideration: it has to go beyond the limitations, ambiguities, and inconsistencies of common usage and has to show how we had better construe the meanings of those terms if we wish to arrive at a consistent and comprehensive theory of knowledge. This type of consideration, which has been largely influenced by a study of the structure of scientific theories, has prompted the more recent extensions of the empiricist meaning criterion. These extensions are designed to include in the realm of cognitive significance various types of sentences which might occur in advanced scientific theories, or which have to be admitted simply for the sake of systematic simplicity and uniformity[24] but on whose cognitive significance or non-significance a study of what the term "intelligible assertion" means in everyday discourse could hardly shed any light at all.

As a consequence, the empiricist criterion of meaning, like the result of any other explication, represents a linguistic proposal which itself is neither true nor false, but for which adequacy is claimed in two respects: First in the sense that the explication provides a reasonably close *analysis* of the commonly accepted meaning of the explicandum—and this claim implies an empirical assertion; and secondly in the sense that the explication achieves a "*rational reconstruction*" of the explicandum, i.e., that it provides, together perhaps with other explications, a general conceptual framework which permits a consistent and precise restatement and theoretical systematization of the contexts in which the explicandum is used—and this claim implies at least an assertion of a logical character.

Though a proposal in form, the empiricist criterion of meaning is therefore far from being an arbitrary definition; it is subject to revision if a violation of the requirements of adequacy, or even a way of satisfying those requirements more fully, should be discovered. Indeed, it is to be hoped that before long some of the open problems encountered in the analysis of cognitive significance will be clarified and that then our last version of the empiricist meaning criterion will be replaced by another, more adequate one.

Notes

1. This term is used by Benjamin (2) in an examination of the foundations of empiricism. For a recent discussion of the basic ideas of empiricism see Russell (27), Part Six.
2. In his stimulating article, "Positivism," W. T. Stace argues, in effect, that the testability criterion of meaning is not logically entailed by the principle of empiricism. (See (29), especially section 11.) This is correct: According to the latter, a sentence expresses knowledge only if it is either analytic or corroborated by empirical evidence; the former goes further and identifies the domain of cognitively significant discourse with that of potential knowledge; i.e., it grants cognitive import only to sentence for which—unless they are either analytic or contradictory—a test by empirical evidence is conceivable.
3. Observation sentences of this kind belong to what Carnap has called the thing-language (cf., e.g., (7), pp. 52–53). That they are adequate to formulate the data which serve as the basis for empirical tests is clear in particular for the intersubjective testing procedures used in science as well as in large areas of empirical inquiry on the common-sense level. In epistemological discussions, it is frequently assumed that the ultimate evidence for beliefs about empirical matters consists in perceptions and sensations whose description calls for a phenomenalistic type of language. The specific problems connected with the phenomenalistic approach cannot be discussed here; but it should be mentioned that at any rate all the critical considerations presented in this article in regard to the testability criterion are applicable, *mutalis mulandis*, to the case of a phenomenalistic basis as well.
4. Originally, the permissible evidence was meant to be restricted to what is observable by the speaker and perhaps his fellow-beings during their lifetimes. Thus construed, the criterion rules out, as cognitively meaningless, all statements about the distant future or the remote past, as has been pointed out, among others, by Ayer in (1), Chapter by Pap in (21), Chapter 13, esp. pp. 333 ff.; and by Russell in (27 pp. 445–447. This difficulty is avoided, however, if we permit the evidence to consist of any finite set of "logically possible observation data," each of them formulated in an observation sentence. Thus, e.g., the sentence S_1, "The tongue of the largest dinosaur in New York's Museum of Natural History was blue or black" is completely verifiable in our sense; for it is a logical consequence of the sentence S_2, "The tongue of the largest dinosaur in New York's Museum of Natural History was blue"; and this is an observation sentence, as has been shown above.

And if the concept of *verifiability in principle* and the more general concept of *confirmability in principle*, which will be considered later, are construed as referring to *logically possible evidence* as expressed by observation sentences, then it follows similarly that the class of statements which are verifiable, or at least confirmable, in principle includes such assertions as that the planet Neptune and the Antarctic Continent existed before they were discovered, and that atomic warfare, if not checked, may lead to the extermination of this planet. The objections which Russell (cf. (27), pp. 445 and 447) raises against the verifiability criterion by reference to those examples do not apply therefore if the criterion is understood in ther manner here suggested. Incidentally, statements of the kind mentioned by Russell, which are not actually verifiable by any human being, were explicitly recognized as cognitively significant already by Schlick (in (28), Part V), who argued that the impossibility of verifying them was "merely empirical." The characterization of verifiability with the help of the concept of observation sentence as suggested here might serve as a more explicit and rigorous statement of that conception.

5. As has frequently been emphasized in empiricist literature, the term "verifiability" is to indicate, of course, the conceivability, or better, the logical possibility of evidence of an observational kind which, if actually encountered, would constitute conclusive evidence for the given sentence; it is not intended to mean the technical possibility of performing the tests needed to obtain such evidence, and even less does it mean the possibility of actually finding directly observable phenomena which constitute conclusive evidence for that sentence—which would be tantamount to the actual existence of such evidence and would thus imply the truth of the given sentence. Analogous remarks apply to the terms "falsifiability" and "confirmability". This point has been disregarded in some recent critical discussions of the verifiability criterion. Thus, e.g., Russell (cf. (27), p. 448) construes verifiability as the actual existence of a set of conclusively verifying occurrences. This conception, which has never been advocated by any logical empiricist, must naturally turn out to be inadequate since according to it the empirical meaningfulness of a sentence could not be established without gathering empirical evidence, and moreover enough of it to permit a conclusive proof of the sentences in question! It is not surprising, therefore, that his extraordinary interpretation of verifiability leads Russell to the conclusion: "In fact, that a proposition is verifiable is itself not verifiable" (*l.c.*) Actually, under the empiricist interpretation of complete verifiability, any statement asserting the verifiability of some sentence S whose text is quoted, is either analytic or contradictory; for the decision whether there exists a class of observation sentences which entail S, i.e., whether such observation sentences can be formulated, no matter whether they are true or false—that decision is a matter of pure logic and requires no factual information whatever.

A similar misunderstanding is in evidence in the following passage in which W. H. Werkmeister claims to characterize a view held by logical positivists: "A proposition is said to be 'true' when it is 'verifiable in principle'; i.e., when we know the conditions which, when realized, will make 'verification' possible (cf. Ayer)." (cf. (31), p. 145). The quoted thesis, which, again, was never held by any logical positivist, including Ayer, is in fact logically absurd. For we can readily describe conditions which, if realized, would verify the sentence "The outside of the Chrysler Building is painted a bright yellow"; but similarly, we can describe verifying conditions for its denial; hence, according to the quoted principle, both the sentence and its denial would have to be considered true. Incidentally, the passage under discussion does not accord with Werkmeister's perfectly correct observation, *l.c.*, p. 40, that verifiability is intended to characterize the meaning of a sentence—which shows that verifiability is meant to be a criterion of cognitive significance rather than of truth.

6. The arguments here adduced against the verifiability criterion also prove the inadequacy of a view closely related to it, namely that two sentences have the same cognitive significance if any set of observation sentences which would verify one of them would also verify the other, and conversely. Thus,

e.g., under this criterion, any two general laws would have to be assigned the same cognitive significance, for no general law is verified by any set of observation sentences. The view just referred to must be clearly distinguished from a position which Russell examines in his critical discussion of the positivistic meaning criterion. It is "the theory that two propositions whose verified consequences are identical have the same significance" ((27), p. 448). This view is untenable indeed, for what consequences of a statement have actually been verified at a given time is obviously a matter of historical accident which cannot possibly serve to establish identity of cognitive significance. But I am not aware that any logical positivist ever subscribed to that "theory."

7. The idea of using theoretical falsifiability by observational evidence as the "criterion of demarcation" separating empirical science from mathematics and logic on the one hand and from metaphysics on the other is due to K. Popper (cf. (22), section 1–7 and 19–24; also sec. (23), vol. II, pp. 282–285). Whether Popper would subscribe to the proposed restatement of the falsifiability criterion, I do not know.

8. (1), Ch. I—The case against the requirements of verifiability and of falsifiability, and favor of a requirement of partial confirmability and disconfirmability is very clearly presented also by Pap in (21), Chapter 13.

9. (1), 2d ed., pp. 11–12.

10. According to Stace (cf. (29), p. 218), the criterion of partial and indirect testability, which he calls the positivist principle, presupposes (and thus logically entails) another principle, which he terms the *Principle of Observable Kinds*: "A sentence, in order to be significant, must assert or deny facts which are of a kind or class such that it is logically possible directly to observe some facts which are instances of that class or kind. And if a sentence purports to assert or deny facts which are of a class or kind such that it would be logically impossible directly to observe any instance of that class or kind, then the sentence is non-significant." I think the argument Stace offers to prove that this principle is entailed by the requirement of testability is inconclusive (mainly because of the incorrect tacit assumption

that "on the transformation view of deduction," the premises of a valid deductive argument must be necessary conditions for the conclusion (*l.c.*, p. 225)). Without pressing this point any further, I should like to add here a remark on the principle of observable kinds itself. Professor Stace does not say how we are to determine what "facts" a given sentence asserts or denies, or indeed whether it asserts or denies any "facts" at all. Hence, the exact import of the principle remains unclear. No matter, however, how one might choose the criteria for the factual reference off sentences, this much seems certain: If a sentence expresses any fact at all, say *f*, then it satisfies the requirement laid down in the first sentence of the principle; for we can always form a class containing *f* together with the fact expressed by some observation sentence of our choice, which makes *f* a member of a class of facts at least one of which is capable, in principle, of direct observation. The first part of the principle of observable kinds is therefore all-inclusive, somewhat like Ayer's original formulation of the empiricist meaning criterion.

11. This restriction is expressed in recursive form and involves no vicious circle. For the full statement of Ayer's criterion, see (1), 2d edition, p. 13.

12. Church (11).

13. Important contributions to the problem have been made by Carnap (5) and by Goodman (15).

14. This difficulty in the definition of disposition terms was first pointed out and analyzed by Carnap (in (6); see esp. section 7).

15. The concept of strict implication as introduct by C. I. Lewis would be of no avail for the interpretation of the strong "if . . . then . . ." as here understood, for it refers to a purely logical relationship of entailment, whereas the concept under consideration will, in general, represent a nomological relationship, i.e., one based on empirical laws. For recent discussions of the problems of counterfactuals and laws, see Langford (18); Lewis (20), pp. 210–230; Chisholm (10); Goodman (14); Reichenbach (26), Chapter VIII; Hempel and Oppenheim (16), Part III; Popper (24).

16. Cf. Carnap (6); a brief elementary exposition of the central idea may be found in Carnap (7), Part III.

The partial definition (R) formulated above for the expression "T(x) = c" illustrates only the simplest type of reduction sentence, the so-called bilateral reduction sentence.

17. On the concept of operational definition, which was developed by Bridgman, see, for example, Bridgman (3, 4) and Feigl (12).

18. The distinction between a formal deductive system and the empirical theory resulting from it by an interpretation has been elaborated in detail by Reichenbach in his penetrating studies of the relations between pure and physical geometry; cf., e.g., Reichenbach (25). The method by means of which a formal system is given empirical content is characterized by Reichenbach as "coordinating definition" of the primitives in the theory by means of specific empirical concepts. As is suggested by our discussion of reduction and the interpretation of theorical constructs, however, the process in question may have to be construed as a partial interpretation of the non-logical terms of the system rather than as a complete definition of the latter in terms of the concepts of a thing-language.

19. These systems have not been characterized here as fully and as precisely as would be desirable. Indeed, the exact character of the empirical interpretation of theoretical constructs and of the theories in which they function is in need of further investigation. Some problems which arise in this connection—such as whether, or in what sense, theoretical constructs may be said to denote—are obviously also of considerable epistemological interest. Some suggestions as to the interpretation of theoretical constructs may be found in Carnap (8), section 24, and in Kaplan (17); for an excellent discussion of the epistemological aspects of the problem, see Feigl (13).

20. This point is clearly taken into consideration in Ayer's criteria of cognitive significance, which were discussed in section 2.

21. For a fuller discussion of the issues here involved cf. Feigl (13) and the comments on Feigl's position which will be published together with that article.

22. In the preface to the second edition of his book, Ayer takes a very similar position: he holds that the testability criterion is a definition which, however, is not entirely arbitrary, because a sentence which did not satisfy the criterion "would not be capable of being understood in the sense in which either scientific hypotheses or commonsense statements are habitually understood" ((1), p. 16).

23. Cf. Carnap's characterization of explication in his article (9), which examines in outline the explication of the concept of probability. The Frege-Russell definition of integers as classes of equivalent classes, and the semantical definition of truth—cf. Tarski (30)—are outstanding examples of explication. For a lucid discussion of various aspects of logical analysis see Pap (21), Chapter 17.

24. Thus, e.g., our criterion qualifies as significant certain statements containing, say, thousands of existential or universal quantifiers—even though such sentences may never occur in everyday nor perhaps even in scientific discourse. For indeed, from a systematic point of view it would be arbitrary and unjustifiable to limit the class of significant statements to those containing no more than some fixed number of quantifiers. For further discussion of this point, cf. Carnap (6), sections 17, 24, 25.

References

1. Ayer, A. J., *Language, Truth and Logic*, Oxford Univ. Press, 1936; 2nd ed., Gollancz, London, 1946.

2. Benjamin, A. C., *Is empiricism self-refuting?* (*Journal of Philos.*, vol. 38, 1941).

3. Bridgman, P. W., *The Logic of Modern Physics*, The Macmillan Co., New York, 1927.

4. Bridgman, P. W., *Operational analysis* (*Philos. of Science*, vol. 5, 1938).

5. Carnap, R., *Der logische Aufbau der Welt*, Berlin, 1928.

6. Carnap, R., *Testability and meaning* (*Philos. of Science*, vol. 3, 1936, and vol. 4, 1937).

7. Carnap, R., *Logical foundations of the unity of science*, In: *Internat. Encyclopedia of Unified Science*, I, 1; Univ. of Chicago Press, 1938.

8. Carnap, R., *Foundations of logic and mathematics. Internal Encyclopedia of Unified Science*, I, 3; Univ. of Chicago Press, 1939.

9. Carnap, R., *The two concepts of probability* (*Philos. and Phenom. Research*, vol. 5, 1945).

10. Chisholm, R. M., *The contrary-to-fact conditional* (*Mind*, vol. 55, 1946).

11. Church, A., Review of (1), 2nd. ed. (*The Journal of Symb. Logic*, vol. 14, 1949, pp. 52–53).

12. Feigl, H., *Operationism and scientific method* (*Psychol. Review*, vol. 52, 1945). (Also reprinted in Feigl and Sellars, *Readings in Philosophical Analysis*, New York, 1949.)

13. Feigl, H., *Existential hypotheses; realistic vs. phenomenalistic interpretations*, (*Philos. of Science*, vol. 17, 1950).

14. Goodman, N. *The problem of counterfactual conditionals* (*Journal of Philos.*, vol. 44, 1947).

15. Goodman, N., *The Structure of Appearance*, Harvard University Press, Cambridge, Mass., 1951.

16. Hempel, C. G., and Oppeheim, P., *Studies in the logic of explanation* (*Philos. of Science*, vol. 15, 1948).

17. Kaplan, A., *Definition and specification of meaning* (*Journal of Philos.*, vol. 43, 1946).

18. Langford, C. H., Review in *The Journal of Symb. Logic*, vol. 6 (1941), pp. 67–68.

19. Lecomte du Noüy, *Human Destiny*, New York, London, Toronto, 1947.

20. Lewis, C. I., *An Analysis of Knowledge and Valuation*, Open Court Publ., La Salle, Ill., 1946.

21. Pap, A., *Elements of Analytic Philosophy*, The Macmillan Co., New York, 1949.

22. Popper, K., *Logik der Forschung*, Springer, Wien, 1935.

23. Popper, K., *The Open Society and Its Enemies*, 2 vols., Routledge, London, 1945.

24. Popper, K., *A note on natural laws and so-called "contrary-to-fact conditionals"* (*Mind*, vol. 58, 1949).

25. Reichenbach, H., *Philosophie der Raum-Zeit-Lehre*, Berlin, 1928.

26. Reichenbach, H., *Elements of Symbolic Logic*, The Macmillan Co., New York, 1947.

27. Russell, B., *Human Knowledge*, Simon and Schuster, New York, 1948.

28. Schlick, M., *Meaning and Verification* (*Philos. Review*, vol. 45, 1936). (Also reprinted in Feigl and Sellars, *Readings in Philosophical Analysis*, New York, 1949).

29. Stace, W. T., *Positivism* (*Mind*, vol. 53, 1944).

30. Tarski, A., *The semantic conception of truth and the foundations of semantics* (*Philos. and Phenom. Research*, vol. 4, 1944). (Also reprinted in Feigl and Sellars, *Readings in Philosophical Analysis*, New York, 1949.)

31. Werkmeister, W. H., *The Basis and Structure of Knowledge*, Harper, New York and London, 1948.

32. Whitehead, A. N., and Russell, B., *Principia Mathematica*, 3 vols., 2nd ed., Cambridge, 1925–1927.

READING QUESTIONS

1. What does Hempel mean by 'observable characteristic', 'observation predicate', and 'observation sentence'?

2. Examine the requirement of complete verifiability in principle. What are the three "serious defects" with this proposal that Hempel outlines? Are these, in fact, serious defects? How might a defender of the requirement respond to Hempel's objections?

3. Examine the requirement of complete falsifiability in principle. What are the three reasons that Hempel advances for thinking that this requirement is "inadequate"? Is the requirement, in fact, inadequate? How might a defender of the requirement respond to Hempel's objections?

4. According to Hempel, what is Ayer's formulation of the empiricist criterion of cognitive meaning? Why does Hempel think that it is "much too liberal as it stands"?

5. What is an 'empiricist language'? Intuitively, why would translatability into an empiricist language constitute an acceptable criterion of cognitive significance for a positivist?

6. What is the "problem of disposition terms and of theoretical constructs"? According to Hempel, what is Carnap's solution to the problem of disposition terms? Is this solution adequate?

7. Hempel claims that "the content of a statement with empirical import cannot, in general, be exhaustively expressed by means of any class of observation sentences." Rather, "the cognitive meaning of a statement in an empiricist language is reflected in the

totality of its logical relationships to all other statements in that language and not to the observation statements alone." If this is correct, what impact does it have on translatability into an empiricist language as a criterion of cognitive significance?

8. What is Hempel's position on the question of the "logical status of the empiricist criterion of meaning"?

SUGGESTIONS FOR FURTHER READING (CARL HEMPEL)

Primary Sources

(1936) (and P. Oppenheim) *Der Typusbegriff im Lichte der neuen Logik*. Leiden: A. W. Sijthoff.

(1952) "Fundamentals of Concept Formation in Empirical Science." In *International Encyclopedia of Unified Science*, Vol. II. Chicago, IL: University of Chicago Press.

(1963) (and R. G. Colodny, eds.) *Frontiers of Science and Philosophy*. Pittsburgh, PA: Pittsburgh University Press.

(1965) *Aspects of Scientific Explanation and Other Essays in the Philosophy of Science*. New York: The Free Press.

(1966) *Philosophy of Natural Science*. Englewood Cliffs, NJ: Prentice-Hall.

(1983) (with H. Putnam and W. K. Essler, eds.) *Methodology, Epistemology, and Philosophy of Science: Essays in Honour of Wolfgang Stegmuller on the Occasion of His Sixtieth Birthday*. Dordrecht: D. Reidel.

(1979) "Scientific Rationality: Analytic vs. Pragmatic Perspectives." In *Rationality Today/La rationalité aujourd'hui*, edited by T. Geraets, 46–58. Ottawa: University of Ottawa Press.

(1993) "Empiricism in the Vienna Circle and in the Berlin Society for Exact Philosophy: Recollections and Reflections." In *Scientific Philosophy: Origins and Developments*, edited by F. Stadtler. Dordrecht: Kluwer Academic Publishers.

(2000) *Selected Philosophical Essays*, edited by R. Jeffrey. Cambridge: Cambridge University Press.

Secondary Sources

Dray, W. H. (1957) *Laws and Explanation in History*. London: Oxford University Press.

Essler, W. K., H. Putnam, and W. Stegmuller, eds. (1985) *Epistemology, Methodology, and Philosophy of Science: Essays in Honor of Carl G. Hempel on the Occasion of His Eightieth Birthday*. Dordrecht: D. Reidel.

Kyburg, H. E., and E. Nagel, eds. (1963) *Induction: Some Current Issues*. Middletown, CT: Wesleyan University Press.

Mandelbaum, M. (1984) *Philosophy, History, and the Sciences*. Baltimore, MD: Johns Hopkins University Press.

Morgenbesser, B. (1960) *Philosophy of Science*. New York: World.

Rescher, N., ed. (1969) *Essays in Honour of Carl G. Hempel: A Tribute on the Occasion of His Sixty-Fifth Birthday*. Dordrecht: D. Reidel.

Scheffler, I. (1963) *The Anatomy of Inquiry*. New York: Knopf.

CHARLES L. STEVENSON

The Emotive Meaning of Ethical Terms

Charles Leslie Stevenson was born in Cincinnati, Ohio, in 1908. He attended Yale University, where he received his first bachelor's degree in 1930. After leaving Yale, he attended Cambridge University and earned a second bachelor's degree in 1933. He then returned to the United States and attended Harvard, quickly acquiring his Ph.D. by 1935. Stevenson's overall philosophical outlook was strongly influenced by his appreciation for the moral philosophies of David Hume and G. E. Moore.

Stevenson began his teaching career at Harvard, remaining there until 1939, at which time he returned to Yale as assistant professor of philosophy. In 1946 he moved to the University of Michigan in Ann Arbor, where he remained as a professor until 1977. From 1977 until his death in 1979 he was a professor at Bennington College in Vermont. Among his many academic honors, Stevenson was appointed a Guggenheim Memorial Foundation Fellow for the years 1945 and 1946. His 1944 book, *Ethics and Language,* remains one of the most important and influential texts in contemporary analytical metaethics.

In the following essay, written in 1937, Stevenson advances an emotivistic account of the language of ethics. His purpose, however, is not to show that the language of ethics lacks meaning altogether (which was the position of many of the leading logical positivists when it came to the question of how to construe the language of ethics), but rather to show that the language of ethics possesses "emotive meaning" and that the propositions of ethics are not mere descriptions of the world, but are instead used by speakers to influence, change, or intensify the attitudes of others.

I

Ethical questions first arise in the form "Is so and so good?" or "Is this alternative better than that?" These questions are difficult partly because we don't quite know what we are seeking. We are asking, "Is there a needle in that haystack?" without even knowing just what a needle is. So the first thing to do is to examine the questions themselves. We must try to make them clearer, either by defining the terms in which they are expressed, or by any other method that is available.

The present paper is concerned wholly with this preliminary step of making ethical questions clear. In order to help answer the question "Is X good?" we must *substitute* for it a question which is free from ambiguity and confusion.

Charles L. Stevenson, "The Emotive Meaning of Ethical Terms," *Mind* 46 (1937), pp. 14–31. Reprinted by permission of Oxford University Press.

It is obvious that in substituting a clearer question we must not introduce some utterly different kind of question. It won't do (to take an extreme instance of a prevalent fallacy) to substitute for "Is X good?" the question "Is X pink with yellow trimmings?" and then point out how easy the question really is. This would beg the original question, not help answer it. On the other hand, we must not expect the substituted question to be strictly "identical" with the original one. The original question may embody hypostatization, anthropomorphism, vagueness, and all the other ills to which our ordinary discourse is subject. If our substituted question is to be clearer, it must remove these ills. The questions will be identical only in the sense that a child is identical with the man he later becomes. Hence we must not demand that the substitution strike us, on immediate introspection, as making no change in meaning.

Just how, then, must the substituted question be related to the original? Let us assume (inaccurately) that it must result from replacing "good" by some set of terms which define it. The question then resolves itself to this: How must the defined meaning of "good" be related to its original meaning?

I answer that it must be *relevant.* A defined meaning will be called "relevant" to the original meaning under these circumstances: Those who have understood the definition must be able to say all that they then want to say by using the term in the defined way. They must never have occasion to use the term in the old, unclear sense. (If a person did have to go on using the word in the old sense, then to this extent his meaning would not be clarified, and the philosophical task would not be completed.) It frequently happens that a word is used so confusedly and ambiguously that we must give it *several* defined meanings, rather than one. In this case only the whole set of defined meanings will be called "relevant," and any one of them will be called "partially relevant." This is not a rigorous treatment of *relevance,* by any means; but it will serve for the present purposes.

Let us now turn to our particular task—that of giving a relevant definition of "good." Let us first examine some of the ways in which others have attempted to do this.

The word "good" has often been defined in terms of *approval,* or similar psychological attitudes. We may take as typical examples: "good" means *desired by me*

(Hobbes); and "good" means *approved by most people* (Hume, in effect). It will be convenient to refer to definitions of this sort as "interest theories," following Mr. R. B. Perry, although neither "interest" nor "theory" is used in the most usual way.

Are definitions of this sort relevant?

It is idle to deny their *partial* relevance. The most superficial inquiry will reveal that "good" is exceedingly ambiguous. To maintain that "good" is *never* used in Hobbes's sense, and never in Hume's, is only to manifest an insensitivity to the complexities of language. We must recognize, perhaps, not only these senses, but a variety of similar ones, differing both with regard to the kind of interest in question, and with regard to the people who are said to have the interest.

But this is a minor matter. The essential question is not whether interest theories are *partially* relevant, but whether they are *wholly* relevant. This is the only point for intelligent dispute. Briefly: Granted that some senses of "good" may relevantly be defined in terms of interest, is there some *other* sense which is *not* relevantly so defined? We must give this question careful attention. For it is quite possible that when philosophers (and many others) have found the question "Is X good?" so difficult, they have been grasping for this *other* sense of "good," and not any sense relevantly defined in terms of interest. If we insist on defining "good" in terms of interest, and answer the question when thus interpreted, we may be begging *their* question entirely. Of course this *other* sense of "good" may not exist, or it may be a complete confusion; but that is what we must discover.

Now many have maintained that interest theories are *far* from being completely relevant. They have argued that such theories neglect the very sense of "good" which is most vital. And certainly, their arguments are not without plausibility.

Only . . . what *is* this "vital" sense of "good"? The answers have been so vague, and so beset with difficulties, that one can scarcely determine.

There are certain requirements, however, with which this "vital" sense has been expected to comply— requirements which appeal strongly to our common sense. It will be helpful to summarize these, showing how they exclude the interest theories.

In the first place, we must be able sensibly to *disagree* about whether something is "good." This condition rules out Hobbes's definition. For consider the following argument: "This is good." "That isn't so; it's not good." As translated by Hobbes, this becomes: "I desire this." "That isn't so, for *I* don't." The speakers are not contradicting one another, and think they are, only because of an elementary confusion in the use of pronouns. The definition, "good" means *desired by my community*, is also excluded, for how could people from different communities disagree?

In the second place, "goodness" must have, so to speak, a magnetism. A person who recognizes X to be "good" must *ipso facto* acquire a stronger tendency to act in its favor than he otherwise would have had. This rules out the Humian type of definition. For according to Hume, to recognize that something is "good" is simply to recognize that the majority approve of it. Clearly, a man may see that the majority approve of X without having, himself, a stronger tendency to favor it. This requirement excludes any attempt to define "good" in terms of the interest of people *other* than the speaker.

In the third place, the "goodness" of anything must not be verifiable solely by use of the scientific method. "Ethics must not be psychology." This restriction rules out all of the traditional interest theories, without exception. It is so sweeping a restriction that we must examine its plausibility. What are the methodological implications of interest theories which are here rejected?

According to Hobbes's definition, a person can prove his ethical judgments, with finality, by showing that he is not making an introspective error about his desires. According to Hume's definition, one may prove ethical judgments (roughly speaking) by taking a vote. *This* use of the empirical method, at any rate, seems highly remote from what we usually accept as proof, and reflects on the complete relevance of the definitions which imply it.

But aren't there more complicated interest theories which are immune from such methodological implications? No, for the same factors appear; they are only put off for a while. Consider, for example, the definition: "X is good" means *most people would approve of X if they knew its nature and consequences*. How, according to this definition, could we prove that a certain X was good? We should first have to find out, empirically, just what X was like, and what its consequences would be. To this extent the empirical method, as required by the definition, seems beyond intelligent objection. But what remains? We should next have to discover whether most people would approve of the sort of thing we had discovered X to be. This couldn't be determined by popular vote—but only because it would be too difficult to explain to the voters, beforehand, what the nature and consequences of X really were. Apart from this, voting would be a pertinent method. We are again reduced to counting noses, as a *perfectly final* appeal.

Now we need not scorn voting entirely. A man who rejected interest theories as irrelevant might readily make the following statement: "If I believed that X would be approved by the majority, when they knew all about it, I should be strongly *led* to say that X was good." But he would continue: "*Need* I say that X was good, under the circumstances? Wouldn't my acceptance of the alleged 'final proof' result simply from my being democratic? What about the more aristocratic people? They would simply say that the approval of most people, even when they knew all about the object of their approval, simply had nothing to do with the goodness of anything, and they would probably add a few remarks about the low state of people's interests." It would indeed seem, from these considerations, that the definition we have been considering has presupposed democratic ideals from the start; it has dressed up democratic propaganda in the guise of a definition.

The omnipotence of the empirical method, as implied by interest theories and others, may be shown unacceptable in a somewhat different way. Mr. G. E. Moore's familiar objection about the open question is chiefly pertinent in this regard. No matter what set of scientifically knowable properties a thing may have (says Moore, in effect), you will find, on careful introspection, that it is an open question to ask whether anything having these properties is *good*. It is difficult to believe that this recurrent question is a totally confused one, or that it seems open only because of the ambiguity of "good." Rather, we must be using some sense of "good" which is not definable, relevantly, in terms of anything scientifically knowable. That is, the scientific method is not sufficient for ethics.

These, then, are the requirements with which the "vital" sense of "good" is expected to comply: (1) goodness must be a topic for intelligent disagreement; (2) it must be "magnetic"; and (3) it must not be discoverable solely through the scientific method.

II

Let us now turn to my own analysis of ethical judgments. First let me present my position dogmatically, showing to what extent I vary from tradition.

I believe that the three requirements, given above, are perfectly sensible; that there is some *one* sense of "good" which satisfies all three requirements; and that no traditional interest theory satisfies them all. But this does not imply that "good" must be explained in terms of a platonic idea, or of a categorical imperative, or of an unique, unanalyzable property. On the contrary, the three requirements can be met by a *kind* of interest theory. *But we must give up a presupposition which all the traditional interest theories have made.*

Traditional interest theories hold that ethical statements are *descriptive* of the existing state of interests—that they simply *give information* about interests. (More accurately, ethical judgments are said to describe what the state of interests is, was, or will be, or to indicate what the state of interests *would* be under specified circumstances.) It is this emphasis on description, on information, which leads to their incomplete relevance. Doubtless there is always *some* element of description in ethical judgments, but this is by no means all. Their major use is not to indicate facts, but to *create an influence*. Instead of merely describing people's interests, they *change* or *intensify* them. They *recommend* an interest in an object, rather than state that the interest already exists.

For instance: When you tell a man that he oughtn't to steal, your object isn't merely to let him know that people disapprove of stealing. You are attempting, rather, to get *him* to disapprove of it. Your ethical judgment has a quasi-imperative force which, operating through suggestion, and intensified by your tone of voice, readily permits you to begin to *influence*, to *modify*, his interests. If in the end you do not succeed in getting *him* to disapprove of stealing, you will feel that you've failed to convince him that stealing is wrong. You will continue to feel this, even though he fully acknowledges that you disapprove of it, and that almost everyone else does. When you point out to him the consequences of his actions—consequences which you suspect he already disapproves of—these *reasons* which support your ethical judgment are simply a means of facilitating your influence. If you think you can change his interests by making vivid to him how others will disapprove of him, you will do so; otherwise not. So the consideration about other people's interest is just an additional means you may employ, in order to move him, and is not a part of the ethical judgment itself. Your ethical judgment doesn't merely describe interests to him, it directs his very interests. The difference between the traditional interest theories and my view is like the difference between describing a desert and irrigating it.

Another example: A munition maker declares that war is a good thing. If he merely meant that he approved of it, he would not have to insist so strongly, nor grow so excited in his argument. People would be quite easily convinced that he approved of it. If he merely meant that most people approved of war, or that most people would approve of it if they knew the consequences, he would have to yield his point if it were proved that this wasn't so. But he wouldn't do this, nor does consistency require it. He is not *describing* the state of people's approval; he is trying to *change* it by his influence. If he found that few people approved of war, he might insist all the more strongly that it was good, for there would be more changing to be done.

This example illustrates how "good" may be used for what most of us would call bad purposes. Such cases are as pertinent as any others. I am not indicating the *good* way of using "good." I am not influencing people, but am describing the way this influence sometimes goes on. If the reader wishes to say that the munition maker's influence is bad—that is, if the reader wishes to awaken people's disapproval of the man, and to make him disapprove of his own actions—I should at another time be willing to join in this undertaking. But this is not the present concern. I am not using ethical terms, but am indicating how they *are* used. The munition maker, in his use of "good," illustrates the persuasive character of the word just as well as does the unselfish man who, eager to encourage in each of us a desire for the happiness of all, contends that the supreme good is peace.

Thus ethical terms are *instruments* used in the complicated interplay and readjustment of human interests. This can be seen plainly from more general observations. People from widely separated communities have different moral attitudes. Why? To a great extent because they have been subject to different social influences. Now clearly this influence doesn't operate through sticks and stones alone; words play a great part. People praise one another, to encourage certain inclinations, and blame one another, to discourage others. Those of forceful personalities issue commands which weaker people, for complicated instinctive reasons, find it difficult to disobey, quite apart from fears of consequences. Further influence is brought to bear by writers and orators. Thus social influence is exerted, to an enormous extent, by means that have nothing to do with physical force or material reward. The ethical terms facilitate such influence. Being suited for use in *suggestion*, they are a means by which men's attitudes may be led this way or that. The reason, then, that we find a greater similarity in the moral attitudes of one community than in those of different communities is largely this: ethical judgments propagate themselves. One man says "This is good"; this may influence the approval of another person, who then makes the same ethical judgment, which in turn influences another person, and so on. In the end, by a process of mutual influence, people take up more or less the same attitudes. Between people of widely separated communities, of course, the influence is less strong; hence different communities have different attitudes.

These remarks will serve to give a general idea of my point of view. We must now go into more detail. There are several questions which must be answered: How does an ethical sentence acquire its power of influencing people—why is it suited to suggestion? Again, what has this influence to do with the *meaning* of ethical terms? And finally, do these considerations really lead us to a sense of "good" which meets the requirements mentioned in the preceding section?

Let us deal first with the question about *meaning*. This is far from an easy question, so we must enter into a preliminary inquiry about meaning in general. Although a seeming digression, this will prove indispensable.

III

Broadly speaking, there are two different *purposes* which lead us to use language. On the one hand we use words (as in science) to record, clarify, and communicate *beliefs*. On the other hand we use words to give vent to our feelings (interjections), or to create moods (poetry), or to incite people to actions or attitudes (oratory).

The first use of words I shall call "descriptive"; the second, "dynamic." Note that the distinction depends solely upon the *purpose* of the *speaker*.

When a person says "Hydrogen is the lightest known gas," his purpose *may* be simply to lead the hearer to believe this, or to believe that the speaker believes it. In that case the words are used descriptively. When a person cuts himself and says "Damn," his purpose is not ordinarily to record, clarify, or communicate any belief. The word is used dynamically. The two ways of using words, however, are by no means mutually exclusive. This is obvious from the fact that our purposes are often complex. Thus when one says "I want you to close the door," part of his purpose, ordinarily, is to lead the hearer to believe that he has this want. To that extent the words are used descriptively. But the major part of one's purpose is to lead the hearer to *satisfy* the want. To that extent the words are used dynamically.

It very frequently happens that the same sentence may have a dynamic use on one occasion, and may not have a dynamic use on another; and that it may have different dynamic uses on different occasions. For instance: A man says to a visiting neighbor, "I am loaded down with work." His purpose may be to let the neighbor know how life is going with him. This would *not* be a dynamic use of words. He may make the remark, however, in order to drop a hint. This *would* be dynamic usage (as well as descriptive). Again, he may make the remark to arouse the neighbor's sympathy. This would be a *different* dynamic usage from that of hinting.

Or again, when we say to a man, "Of course you won't make those mistakes any more," we *may* simply be making a prediction. But we are more likely to be using "suggestion," in order to encourage him and hence *keep* him from making mistakes. The first use would be descriptive; the second, mainly dynamic.

From these examples it will be clear that we can't determine whether words are used dynamically or not, merely by reading the dictionary—even assuming that everyone is faithful to dictionary meanings. Indeed, to know whether a person is using a word dynamically, we must note his tone of voice, his gestures, the general circumstances under which he is speaking, and so on.

We must now proceed to an important question: What has the dynamic use of words to do with their *meaning*? One thing is clear—we must not define "meaning" in a way that would make meaning vary with dynamic usage. If we did, we should have no use for the term. All that we could say about such "meaning" would be that it is very complicated, and subject to constant change. So we must certainly distinguish between the dynamic use of words and their meaning.

It doesn't follow, however, that we must define "meaning" in some non-psychological fashion. We must simply restrict the psychological field. Instead of identifying meaning with *all* the psychological causes and effects that attend a word's utterance, we must identify it with those that it has a *tendency* (causal property, dispositional property) to be connected with. The tendency must be of a particular kind, moreover. It must exist for all who speak the language; it must be persistent; and must be realizable more or less independently of determinate circumstances attending the word's utterance. There will be further restrictions dealing with the interrelation of words in different contexts. Moreover, we must include, under the psychological responses which the words tend to produce, not only immediately introspectable experiences, but *dispositions* to react in a given way with appropriate stimuli. I hope to go into these matters in a subsequent paper. Suffice it now to say that I think "meaning" may be thus defined in a way to include "propositional" meaning as an important kind. Now a word may *tend* to have causal relations which in fact it sometimes doesn't; and it may sometimes have causal relations which it *doesn't tend* to have. And since the tendency of words which constitutes their meaning must be of a particular kind, and may include, as responses, dispositions to reactions, of which any of *several* immediate experiences may be a sign, then there is nothing surprising in the fact that words have a permanent meaning, in spite of the fact that the immediately introspectable experiences which attend their usage are so highly varied.

When "meaning" is defined in this way, meaning will not include dynamic use. For although words are sometimes accompanied by dynamic purposes, they do not *tend* to be accompanied by them in the way above mentioned. E.g., there is no tendency realizable independently of the determinate circumstances under which the words are uttered.

There will be a kind of meaning, however, in the sense above defined, which has an intimate relation to dynamic usage. I refer to "emotive" meaning (in a sense roughly like that employed by Ogden and Richards). The emotive meaning of a word is a tendency of a word, arising through the history of its usage, to produce (result from) *affective* responses in people. It is the immediate aura of feeling which hovers about a word. Such tendencies to produce affective responses cling to words very tenaciously. It would be difficult, for instance, to express merriment by using the interjection "alas." Because of the persistence of such affective tendencies (among other reasons) it becomes feasible to classify them as "meanings."

Just *what* is the relation between emotive meaning and the dynamic use of words? Let us take an example. Suppose that a man is talking with a group of people which includes Miss Jones, aged 59. He refers to her, without thinking, as an "old maid." Now even if his purposes are perfectly innocent—even if he is using the words purely descriptively—Miss Jones won't think so. She will think he is encouraging the others to have contempt for her, and will draw in her skirts, defensively. The man might have done better if instead of saying "old maid" he had said "elderly spinster." The latter words could have been put to the same descriptive use, and would not so readily have caused suspicions about the dynamic use.

"Old maid" and "elderly spinster" differ, to be sure, only in emotive meaning. From the example it will be clear that certain words, because of their emotive meaning, are suited to a certain kind of dynamic use—so well suited, in fact, that the hearer is likely to be misled when we use them in any other way. The more

pronounced a word's emotive meaning is, the less likely people are to use it purely descriptively. Some words are suited to encourage people, some to discourage them, some to quiet them, and so on.

Even in these cases, of course, the dynamic purposes are not to be identified with any sort of meaning; for the emotive meaning accompanies a word much more persistently than do the dynamic purposes. But there is an important contingent relation between emotive meaning and dynamic purpose: the former assists the latter. Hence if we define emotively laden terms in a way that neglects their emotive meaning, we are likely to be confusing. *We lead people to think that the terms defined are used dynamically less often than they are.*

IV

Let us now apply these remarks in defining "good." This word may be used morally or non-morally. I shall deal with the non-moral usage almost entirely, but only because it is simpler. The main points of the analysis will apply equally well to either usage.

As a preliminary definition, let us take an inaccurate approximation. It may be more misleading than helpful, but will do to begin with. Roughly, then, the sentence "X is good" means *We like X.* ("We" includes the hearer or hearers.)

At first glance this definition sounds absurd. If used, we should expect to find the following sort of conversation: A. "This is good." B. "But I *don't* like it. What led you to believe that I did?" The unnaturalness of B's reply, judged by ordinary word-usage, would seem to cast doubt on the relevance of my definition.

B's unnaturalness, however, lies simply in this: he is assuming that "We like it" (as would occur implicitly in the use of "good") is being used descriptively. This won't do. When "We like it" is to take the place of "This is good," the former sentence must be used not purely descriptively, but dynamically. More specifically, it must be used to promote a very subtle (and for the non-moral sense in question, a very easily resisted) kind of *suggestion*. To the extent that "we" refers to the hearer, it must have the dynamic use, essential to suggestion, of leading the hearer to *make* true what is said, rather than merely to believe it. And to the extent that "we" refers to the speaker, the sentence must have not only the descriptive use of indicating belief about the speaker's interest, but the quasi-interjectory, dynamic function of giving direct expression to the interest. (This immediate expression of feelings assists in the process of suggestion. It is difficult to disapprove in the face of another's enthusiasm.)

For an example of a case where "We like this" is used in the dynamic way that "This is good" is used, consider the case of a mother who says to her several children, "One thing is certain, *we all like to be neat.*" If she really believed this, she wouldn't bother to say so. But she is not using the words descriptively. She is *encouraging* the children to like neatness. By telling them that they like neatness, she will lead them to *make* her statement true, so to speak. If, instead of saying "We all like to be neat" in this way, she had said "It's a good thing to be neat," the effect would have been approximately the same.

But these remarks are still misleading. Even when "We like it" is used for suggestion, it isn't quite like "This is good." The latter is more subtle. With such a sentence as "This is a good book," for example, it would be practically impossible to use instead "We like this book." When the latter is used, it must be accompanied by so exaggerated an intonation, to prevent its becoming confused with a descriptive statement, that the force of suggestion becomes stronger, and ludicrously more overt, than when "good" is used.

The definition is inadequate, further, in that the definiens has been restricted to dynamic usage. Having said that dynamic usage was different from meaning, I should not have to mention it in giving the *meaning* of "good."

It is in connection with this last point that we must return to emotive meaning. The word "good" has a pleasing emotive meaning which fits it especially for the dynamic use of suggesting favorable interest. But the sentence "We like it" has no such emotive meaning. Hence my definition has neglected emotive meaning entirely. Now to neglect emotive meaning is likely to lead to endless confusions, as we shall presently see; so I have sought to make up for the inadequacy of the definition by letting the restriction about dynamic usage take the place of emotive meaning. What I should do, of course, is to find a definiens whose emotive meaning, like that of "good," simply does *lead* to dynamic usage.

Why didn't I do this? I answer that it isn't possible, if the definition is to afford us increased clarity. No two words, in the first place, have quite the same emotive meaning. The most we can hope for is a rough approximation. But if we seek for such an approximation for "good," we shall find nothing more than synonyms, such as "desirable" or "valuable"; and these are profitless because they do not clear up the connection between "good" and favorable interest. If we reject such synonyms, in favor of non-ethical terms, we shall be highly misleading. For instance: "This is good" has something like the meaning of "I *do* like this; do so as well." But this is certainly not accurate. For the imperative makes an appeal to the conscious efforts of the hearer. Of course he can't like something just by trying. He must be led to like it through suggestion. Hence an ethical sentence differs from an imperative in that it enables one to make changes in a much more subtle, less fully conscious way. Note that the ethical sentence centers the hearer's attention not on his interests, but on the object of interest, and thereby facilitates suggestion. Because of its subtlety, moreover, an ethical sentence readily permits counter-suggestion, and leads to the give and take situation which is so characteristic of arguments about values.

Strictly speaking, then, it is impossible to define "good" in terms of favorable interest if emotive meaning is not to be distorted. Yet it is possible to say that "This is good" is *about* the favorable interest of the speaker and the hearer or hearers, and that it has a pleasing emotive meaning which fits the words for use in suggestion. This is a rough description of meaning, not a definition. But it serves the same clarifying function that a definition ordinarily does; and that, after all, is enough.

A word must be added about the moral use of "good." This differs from the above in that it is about a different kind of interest. Instead of being about what the hearer and speaker *like*, it is about a stronger sort of approval. When a person *likes* something, he is pleased when it prospers, and disappointed when it doesn't. When a person *morally approves* of something, he experiences a rich feeling of security when it prospers, and is indignant, or "shocked" when it doesn't. These are rough and inaccurate examples of the many factors which one would have to mention in distinguishing the two kinds of interest. In the moral usage, as well as in the non-moral, "good" has an emotive meaning which adapts it to suggestion.

And now, are these considerations of any importance? Why do I stress emotive meanings in this fashion? Does the omission of them really lead people into errors? I think, indeed, that the errors resulting from such omissions are normous. In order to see this, however, we must return to the restrictions, mentioned in section I, with which the "vital" sense of "good" has been expected to comply.

V

The first restriction, it will be remembered, had to do with disagreement. Now there is clearly some sense in which people disagree on ethical points; but we must not rashly assume that all disagreement is modeled after the sort that occurs in the natural sciences. We must distinguish between "disagreement in belief" (typical of the sciences) and "disagreement in interest." Disagreement in belief occurs when A believes p and B disbelieves it. Disagreement in interest occurs when A has a favorable interest in X, when B has an unfavorable one in it, and when neither is content to let the other's interest remain unchanged.

Let me give an example of disagreement in interest. A. "Let's go to a cinema tonight." B. "I don't want to do that. Let's go to the symphony." A continues to insist on the cinema, B on the symphony. This is disagreement in a perfectly conventional sense. They can't agree on where they want to go, and each is trying to redirect the other's interest. (Note that imperatives are used in the example.)

It is disagreement in *interest* which takes places in ethics. When C says "This is good," and D says "No, it's bad," we have a case of suggestion and counter-suggestion. Each man is trying to redirect the other's interest. There obviously need be no domineering, since each may be willing to give ear to the other's influence; but each is trying to move the other nonetheless. It is in this sense that they disagree. Those who argue that certain interest theories make no provision for disagreement have been misled, I believe, simply because the traditional theories, in leaving out emotive

meaning, give the impression that ethical judgments are used descriptively only; and of course when judgments are used purely descriptively, the only disagreement that can arise is disagreement *in belief*. Such disagreement may be disagreement in belief *about* interests; but this is not the same as disagreement *in* interest. My definition doesn't provide for disagreement in belief about interests, any more than does Hobbes's; but that is no matter, for there is no reason to believe, at least on common-sense grounds, that this kind of disagreement exists. There is only disagreement *in* interest. (We shall see in a moment that disagreement in interest does not remove ethics from sober argument—that this kind of disagreement may often be resolved through empirical means.)

The second restriction, about "magnetism," or the connection between goodness and actions, requires only a word. This rules out *only* those interest theories which do *not* include the interest of the speaker, in defining "good." My account does include the speaker's interest; hence is immune.

The third restriction, about the empirical method, may be met in a way that springs naturally from the above account of disagreement. Let us put the question in this way: When two people disagree over an ethical matter, can they completely resolve the disagreement through empirical considerations, assuming that each applies the empirical method exhaustively, consistently, and without error?

I answer that sometimes they can, and sometimes they cannot; and that at any rate, even when they can, the relation between empirical knowledge and ethical judgments is quite different from the one which traditional interest theories seem to imply.

This can best be seen from an analogy. Let's return to the example where A and B couldn't agree on a cinema or a symphony. The example differed from an ethical argument in that imperatives were used, rather than ethical judgments; but was analogous to the extent that each person was endeavoring to modify the other's interest. Now how would these people argue the case, assuming that they were too intelligent just to shout at one another?

Clearly, they would give "reasons" to support their imperatives. A might say, "But you know, Garbo is at the Bijou." His hope is that B, who admires Garbo, will acquire a desire to go to the cinema when he knows what play will be there. B may counter, "But Toscanini is guest conductor tonight, in an all-Beethoven program." And so on. Each supports his imperative ("*Let's* do so and so") by reasons which may be empirically established.

To generalize from this: disagreement in interest may be rooted in disagreement in belief. That is to say, people who disagree in interest would often cease to do so if they knew the precise nature and consequences of the object of their interest. To this extent disagreement in interest may be resolved by securing agreement in belief, which in turn may be secured empirically.

This generalization holds for ethics. If A and B, instead of using imperatives, had said, respectively, "It would be *better* to go to the cinema," and "It would be better to go to the symphony," the reasons which they would advance would be roughly the same. They would each give a more thorough account of the object of interest, with the purpose of completing the redirection of interest which was begun by the suggestive force of the ethical sentence. On the whole, of course, the suggestive force of the ethical statement merely exerts enough pressure to start such trains of reasons, since the reasons are much more essential in resolving disagreement in interest than the persuasive effect of the ethical judgment itself.

Thus the empirical method is relevant to ethics simply because our knowledge of the world is a determining factor to our interests. But note that empirical facts are not inductive grounds from which the ethical judgment problematically follows. (This is what traditional interest theories imply.) If someone said "Close the door," and added the reason "We'll catch cold," the latter would scarcely be called an inductive ground of the former. Now imperatives are related to the reason which support them in the same way that ethical judgments are related to reasons.

Is the empirical method *sufficient* for attaining ethical agreement? Clearly not. For empirical knowledge resolves disagreement in interest only to the extent that such disagreement is rooted in disagreement in belief. Not all disagreement in interest is of this sort. For instance: A is of a sympathetic nature, and B isn't. They are arguing about whether a public dole would be good. Suppose that they discovered all the consequences of

the dole. Isn't it possible, even so, that A will say that it's good, and B that it's bad? The disagreement in interest may arise not from limited factual knowledge, but simply from A's sympathy and B's coldness. Or again, suppose, in the above argument, that A was poor and unemployed, and that B was rich. Here again the disagreement might not be due to different factual knowledge. It would be due to the different social positions of the men, together with their predominant self-interest.

When ethical disagreement is not rooted in disagreement in belief, is there *any* method by which it may be settled? If one means by "method" a *rational* method, then there is no method. But in any case there is a "way." Let's consider the above example, again, where disagreement was due to A's sympathy and B's coldness. Must they end by saying, "Well, it's just a matter of our having different temperaments"? Not necessarily. A, for instance, may try to *change* the temperament of his opponent. He may pour out his enthusiasms in such a moving way—present the sufferings of the poor with such appeal—that he will lead his opponent to see life through different eyes. He may build up, by the contagion of his feelings, an influence which will modify B's temperament, and create in him a sympathy for the poor which didn't previously exist. This is often the only way to obtain ethical agreement, if there is any way at all. It is persuasive, not empirical or rational; but that is no reason for neglecting it. There is no reason to scorn it, either, for it is only by such means that our personalities are able to grow, through our contact with others.

The point I wish to stress, however, is simply that the empirical method is instrumental to ethical agreement only to the extent that disagreement in interest is rooted in disagreement in belief. There is little reason to believe that all disagreement is of this sort. Hence the empirical method is not sufficient for ethics. In any case, ethics is not psychology, since psychology doesn't endeavor to *direct* our interests; it discovers facts about the ways in which interests are or can be directed, but that's quite another matter.

To summarize this section: my analysis of ethical judgments meets the three requirements for the "vital" sense of "good" that were mentioned in section I. The traditional interest theories fail to meet these requirements simply because they neglect emotive meaning.

This neglect leads them to neglect dynamic usage, and the sort of disagreement that results from such usage, together with the method of resolving the disagreement. I may add that my analysis answers Moore's objection about the open question. Whatever scientifically knowable properties a thing may have, it *is* always open to question whether a thing having these (enumerated) qualities is good. For to ask whether it is good is to ask for *influence*. And whatever I may know about an object, I can still ask, quite pertinently, to be influenced with regard to my interest in it.

VI

And now, have I really pointed out the "vital" sense of "good"?

I suppose that many will still say "No," claiming that I have simply failed to set down *enough* requirements which this sense must meet, and that my analysis, like all others given in terms of interest, is a way of begging the issue. They will say: "When we ask 'Is X good?' we don't want mere influence, mere advice. We decidedly don't want to be influenced through persuasion, nor are we fully content when the influence is supported by a wide scientific knowledge of X. The answer to our question will, of course, modify our interests. But this is only because an unique sort of *truth* will be revealed to us—a truth which must be apprehended *a priori*. We want our interests to be guided by this truth, and by nothing else. To substitute for such a truth mere emotive meaning and suggestion is to conceal from us the very object of our search."

I can only answer that I do not understand. What is this truth to be *about*? For I recollect no platonic idea, nor do I know what to *try* to recollect. I find no indefinable property, nor do I know what to look for. And the "self-evident" deliverances of reason, which so many philosophers have claimed, seem, on examination, to be deliverances of their respective reasons only (if of anyone's) and not of mine.

I strongly suspect, indeed, that any sense of "good" which is expected both to unite itself in synthetic *a priori* fashion with other concepts, and to influence interests as well, is really a great confusion. I extract from this meaning the power of influence alone, which I find

the only intelligible part. If the rest is confusion, however, then it certainly deserves more than the shrug of one's shoulders. What I should like to do is to *account* for the confusion—to examine the psychological needs which have given rise to it, and to show how these needs may be satisfied in another way. This is *the* problem, if confusion is to be stopped at its source. But it is an enormous problem, and my reflections on it, which are at present worked out only roughly, must be reserved until some later time.

I may add that if "X is good" is essentially a vehicle for suggestion, it is scarcely a statement which philosophers, any more than many other men, are called upon to make. To the extent that ethics predicates the ethical terms of anything, rather than explains their meaning, it ceases to be a reflective study. Ethical statements are social instruments. They are used in a cooperative enterprise in which we are mutually adjusting ourselves to the interests of others. Philosophers have a part in this, as do all men, but not the major part.

READING QUESTIONS

1. Stevenson argues that any relevant definition of 'good' must meet three requirements. What are these requirements? Why are these requirements important? Do you agree with Stevenson's criticism of Hobbes and with Hume?

2. Stevenson claims that the "major use" of ethical claims "is not to indicate facts, but to *create an influence*." What is the difference between indicating a fact (a *descriptive* use of language) and creating an influence (a *dynamic* use of language)?

3. What is the 'emotive meaning' of a word? As Stevenson asks, what is the relation between emotive meaning and the dynamic use of words?

4. According to Stevenson, what is the difference between the moral and the nonmoral uses of the term *good*? Is his way of drawing the distinction correct? Why or why not?

5. What is the difference between a "disagreement in belief" and a "disagreement in interest"? In arguing that "it is a disagreement in *interest* which takes place in ethics," Stevenson claims that this view sat-

isfies the three requirements for any relevant definition of 'good'. How does he think that his theory does this? Is he correct?

6. On his view, in what ways are empirical facts relevant to the resolution of ethical disagreements? In what ways are they not relevant?

SUGGESTIONS FOR FURTHER READING (CHARLES L. STEVENSON)

Primary Sources

(1944) *Ethics and Language.* New Haven, CT: Yale University Press.

(1948) "Meaning: Descriptive and Emotive." In *Philosophical Review* 57, 127–144.

(1963) *Facts and Values: Studies in Ethical Analysis.* New Haven, CT: Yale University Press.

Secondary Sources

Blackburn, S. (1984) *Spreading the Word.* Oxford: Oxford University Press.

Frankena, W. (1963) *Ethics.* Englewood Cliffs, NJ: Prentice-Hall.

Goldman, A., and J. Kim, eds. (1978) *Values and Morals: Essays in Honor of William Frankena, Charles Stevenson, and Richard Brandt.* Dordrecht: D. Reidel.

Hare, R. M. (1952) *The Language of Morals.* Oxford: Oxford University Press.

Hudson, W. D. (1983) *Modern Moral Philosophy,* 2nd ed. New York: Macmillan.

Urmson, J. O. (1968) *The Emotive Theory of Ethics.* London: Hutchinson.

Warnock, G. J. (1967) *Contemporary Moral Philosophy.* New York: Macmillan.

Warnock, M. (1960) *Ethics Since 1900.* London: Oxford University Press.

PART IV / Ordinary Language Philosophy

George Edward (G. E.) Moore

Proof of an External World

G. E. Moore (1873–1958) is remembered, along with Bertrand Russell, as a leading early defender and master practitioner of analytic philosophy. Moore was born near London, the fifth child in a family of eight. Moore's grandfather, his namesake, among other things had published several "popular" philosophy books during the course of his life.

Moore enrolled in Trinity College, Cambridge, in 1892 as a student of the classics. One of his fellow students was the young Bertrand Russell, and it was Russell who, in addition to members of the faculty, encouraged him to seriously pursue the study of philosophy. Under the influence of their teachers, both Russell and Moore quickly came to accept absolute idealism, then the dominant philosophical outlook in Cambridge. Nevertheless, they both soon broke with their teachers over this issue—Moore leading the way. Moore's paper "The Refutation of Idealism" (*Mind*, 1903) marks in print his move in metaphysics from idealism to realism.

Moore began teaching at Cambridge in 1904. In 1921, he succeeded G. F. Stout as the editor of the journal *Mind*, a position that he would hold for more than 25 years. In 1925, Moore was named Professor of Mental Philosophy and Logic at Cambridge, a chair that he held until 1939. Moore was also elected a Fellow of the British Academy in 1918 and was a recipient of the Order of Merit in 1951. He had a distinguished and productive academic career and was widely re-

garded as one of the most careful, precise, and lucid philosophers of his day. He was also known as a great teacher of philosophy.

Although Moore wrote on virtually every topic in philosophy, his most highly regarded achievement remains his celebrated work in moral philosophy, *Principia Ethica* (1903), in which he argues that right actions are those which maximize the good (consequentialism), that goodness is a simple and unanalyzable quality or property (non-naturalism), and that we can know what is good through our moral intuitions (intuitionism). *Principia Ethica* has become a classic of twentieth-century moral philosophy and is considered by many to be the starting point for any serious work in analytical metaethics.

During World War II, Moore came to America to teach at Smith College in Massachusetts. At the same time, he also lectured periodically at Princeton. Later he taught briefly at Mills College in Oakland, CA, and at the University of California in Berkeley. In 1942, he returned to the East Coast to teach at Columbia and at Swarthmore College in Pennsylvania. Moore returned to Cambridge in 1944 and spent much of the rest of his life at home because of declining health.

In the following essay from 1939, Moore addresses the problem of philosophical skepticism by offering a proof of the existence of an external world. Moore argues that any "rigorous proof" for such a claim must satisfy three conditions. First, the premises must be different from conclusion. Second, it must be the case that we know that the premises are true. And third, the conclusion must follow logically from the premises. He claims that his proof satisfies these conditions.

In the preface to the second edition of Kant's *Critique of Pure Reason* some words occur, which, in Professor Kemp Smith's translation, are rendered as follows:

> It still remains a scandal to philosophy . . . that the existence of things outside of us . . . must be accepted merely on *faith*, and that, if anyone thinks good to doubt their existence, we are unable to counter his doubts by any satisfactory proof.

It seems clear from these words that Kant thought it a matter of some importance to give a proof of "the existence of things outside of us" or perhaps rather (for it seems to me possible that the force of the German words is better rendered in this way) of "the existence of *the* things outside of us"; for had he not thought it important that a proof should be given, he would scarcely have called it a "scandal" that no proof had been given. And it seems clear also that he thought that the giving of such a proof was a task which fell properly within the province of philosophy; for, if it did not, the fact that no proof had been given could not possibly be a scandal to *philosophy*.

Now, even if Kant was mistaken in both of these two opinions, there seems to me to be no doubt whatever that it is a matter of some importance and also a matter which falls properly within the province of philosophy to discuss the question what sort of proof, if any, can be given of "the existence of things outside of us." And to discuss this question was my object when I began to write the present lecture. But I may say at once that, as you will find, I have only, at most, succeeded in saying a very small part of what ought to be said about it.

George Edward Moore, "Proof of an External World" from his *Philosophical Papers,* London, Allen & Unwin, 1959. I am indebted to Timothy Moore for his kind permission to reprint his father's article.

The words "it . . . remains a scandal to philosophy . . . that we are unable . . ." would, taken strictly, imply that, at the moment at which he wrote them, Kant himself was unable to produce a satisfactory proof of the point in question. But I think it is unquestionable that Kant himself did not think that he personally was at the time unable to produce such a proof. On the contrary, in the immediately preceding sentence, he has declared that he has, in the second edition of his *Critique,* to which he is now writing the Preface, given a "rigorous proof" of this very thing; and has added that he believes this proof of his to be "the only possible proof." It is true that in this preceding sentence he does not describe the proof which he has given as a proof of "the existence of things outside of us" or of "the existence of the things outside of us," or of "the existence of the things outside of us," but describes it instead as a proof of "the objective reality of outer intuition." But the context leaves no doubt that he is using these two phrases, "the objective reality of outer intuition" and "the existence of things (*or* 'the things') outside of us," in such a way that whatever is a proof of the first is also necessarily a proof of the second. We must, therefore, suppose that when he speaks as if *we* are unable to give a satisfactory proof, he does not mean to say that he himself, as well as others, is *at the moment* unable; but rather that, until he discovered the proof which he has given, both he himself and everybody else *were* unable. Of course, if he is right in thinking that he has given a satisfactory proof, the state of things which he describes came to an end as soon as his proof was published. As soon as that happened, anyone who read it was able to give a satisfactory proof by simply repeating that which Kant had given, and the "scandal" to philosophy had been removed once for all.

If, therefore, it were certain that the proof of the point in question given by Kant in the second edition is a satisfactory proof, it would be certain that at least one satisfactory proof can be given; and all that would remain of the question which I said I proposed to discuss would be, firstly, the question as to what *sort* of a proof this of Kant's is, and secondly the question whether (contrary to Kant's own opinion) there may not perhaps be other proofs, of the same or of a different sort, which are also satisfactory. But I think it is by no means certain that Kant's proof is satisfactory. I think it is by no means certain that he did succeed in removing once for all the state of affairs which he considered to be a scandal to philosophy. And I think, therefore, that the question whether it is possible to give *any* satisfactory proof of the point in question still deserves discussion.

But what is the point in question? I think it must be owned that the expression "things outside of us" is rather an odd expression, and an expression the meaning of which is certainly not perfectly clear. It would have sounded less odd if, instead of "things outside of us" I had said "external things," and perhaps also the meaning of this expression would have seemed to be clearer; and I think we make the meaning of "external things" clearer still if we explain that this phrase has been regularly used by philosophers as short for "things external to *our minds*." The fact is that there has been a long philosophical tradition, in accordance with which the three expressions "external things," "things external to *us*," and "things external to *our minds*" have been used as equivalent to one another, and have, each of them, been used as if they needed no explanation. The origin of this usage I do not know. It occurs already in Descartes; and since he uses the expressions as if they needed no explanation, they had presumably been used with the same meaning before. Of the three, it seems to me that the expression "external to *our minds*" is the clearest, since it at least makes clear that what is meant is not "external to *our bodies*"; whereas both the other expressions might be taken to mean this: and indeed there has been a good deal of confusion, even among philosophers, as to the relation of the two conceptions "external things" and "things external to *our bodies*." But even the expression "things external to our minds" seems to me to be far from perfectly clear; and if I am to make really clear what I mean by "proof of the existence of things outside of us," I cannot do it by merely saying that by "outside of us" I mean "external to our minds."

There is a passage in which Kant himself says that the expression "outside of us" "carries with it an unavoidable ambiguity." He says that "sometimes it means something which exists *as a thing in itself* distinct from us, and sometimes something which merely belongs to external *appearance*"; he calls things which are "outside of us" in the first of these two senses "objects which might be called external in the transcenden-

tal sense," and things which are so in the second "*empirically external* objects"; and he says finally that, in order to remove all uncertainty as to the latter conception, he will distinguish empirically external objects from objects which might be called "external" in the transcendental sense, "by calling them outright things which are *to be met with in space.*"

I think that this last phrase of Kant's, "things which are to be met with in space," does indicate fairly clearly what sort of things it is with regard to which I wish to inquire what sort of proof, if any, can be given that there are any things of that sort. My body, the bodies of other men, the bodies of animals, plants of all sorts, stones, mountains, the sun, the moon, stars, and planets, houses and other buildings, manufactured articles of all sorts—chairs, tables, pieces of paper, etc., are all of them "things which are to be met with in space." In short, all things of the sort that philosophers have been used to call "physical objects," "material things," or "bodies" obviously come under this head. But the phrase "things that are to be met with in space" can be naturally understood as applying also in cases where the names "physical object," "material thing," or "body" can hardly be applied. For instance, shadows are sometimes to be met with in space, although they could hardly be properly called "physical objects," "material things," or "bodies"; and although in one usage of the term "thing" it would not be proper to call a shadow a "thing," yet the phrase "things which are to be met with in space" can be naturally understood as synonymous with "whatever can be met with in space," and this is an expression which can quite properly be understood to include shadows. I wish the phrase "things which are to be met with in space" to be understood in this wide sense; so that if a proof can be found that there ever have been as many as two different shadows it will follow at once that there have been at least two "things which were to be met with in space," and this proof will be as good a proof of the point in question as would be a proof that there have been at least two "physical objects" of no matter what sort.

The phrase "things which are to be met with in space" can, therefore, be naturally understood as having a very wide meaning—a meaning even wider than that of "physical object" or "body," wide as is the meaning of these latter expressions. But wide as is its meaning, it is not, in one respect, so wide as that of another phrase which Kant uses as if it were equivalent to this one; and a comparison between the two will, I think, serve to make still clearer what sort of things it is with regard to which I wish to ask what proof, if any, can be given that there are such things.

The other phrase which Kant uses as if it were equivalent to "things which are to be met with in space" is used by him in the sentence immediately preceding that previously quoted in which he declares that the expression "things outside of us" "carries with it an unavoidable ambiguity." In this preceding sentence he says that an "empirical object" "is called *external*, if it is presented (*vorgestellt*) *in space*." He treats, therefore, the phrase "presented in space" as if it were equivalent to "to be met with in space." But it is easy to find examples of "things," of which it can hardly be denied that they are "presented in space," but of which it could, quite naturally, be emphatically denied that they are "to be met with in space." Consider, for instance, the following description of one set of circumstances under which what some psychologists have called a "negative after-image" and others a "negative after-sensation" can be obtained. "If, after looking steadfastly at a white patch on a black ground, the eye be turned to a white ground, a grey patch is seen for some little time." (Foster's *Text-book of Physiology*, IV, iii, 3, page 1266; quoted in Stout's *Manual of Psychology*, 3rd edition, page 280.) Upon reading these words recently, I took the trouble to cut out of a piece of white paper a four-pointed star, to place it on a black ground, to "look steadfastly" at it, and then to turn my eyes to a white sheet of paper: and I did find that I saw a grey patch for some little time—I not only saw a grey patch, but I saw it *on* the white ground, and also this grey patch was of roughly the same shape as the white four-pointed star at which I had "looked steadfastly" just before—it also was a four-pointed star. I repeated the simple experiment successfully several times. Now each of those grey four-pointed stars, one of which I saw in each experiment, was what is called an "after-image" or "after-sensation"; and can anybody deny that each of these after-images can be quite properly said to have been "presented in space"? I saw each of them on a real white background, and, if so, each of them was "presented" on a real white background. But though they

were "presented in space" everybody, I think, would feel that it was gravely misleading to say that they were "to be met with in space." The white star at which I "looked steadfastly," the black ground on which I saw it, and the white ground on which I saw the after-images, were, of course, "to be met with in space": they were, in fact, "physical objects" or surfaces of physical objects. But one important difference between them, on the one hand, and the grey after-images, on the other, can be quite naturally expressed by saying that the latter were *not* "to be met with in space." And one reason why this is so is, I think, plain. To say that so and so was at a given time "to be met with in space" naturally suggests that there are conditions such that *anyone* who fulfilled them might, conceivably, have "perceived" the "thing" in question—might have seen it, if it was a visible object, have felt it, if it was a tangible one, have heard it, if it was a sound, have smelt it, if it was a smell. When I say that the white four-pointed paper star, at which I looked steadfastly, was a "physical object" and was "to be met with in space," I am implying that *anyone*, who had been in the room at the time, and who had normal eyesight and a normal sense of touch, might have seen and felt it. But, in the case of those grey after-images which I saw, it is not conceivable that anyone besides myself should have seen any one of them. It is, of course, quite conceivable that other people, if they had been in the room with me at the time, and had carried out the same experiment which I carried out, would have seen grey after-images *very like* one of those which I saw: there is no absurdity in supposing even that they might have seen after-images *exactly* like one of those which I saw. But there is an absurdity in supposing that any one of the after-images which I saw could also have been seen by anyone else: in supposing that two different people can ever see the *very same* after-image. One reason, then, why we should say that none of those grey after-images which I saw was "to be met with in space," although each of them was certainly "presented in space" to me, is simply that none of them could conceivably have been seen by anyone else. It is natural so to understand the phrase "to be met with in space," that to say of anything which a man perceived that it was to be met with in space is to say that it might have been perceived by *others* as well as by the man in question.

Negative after-images of the kind described are, therefore, one example of "things" which, though they must be allowed to be "presented in space," are nevertheless *not* "to be met with in space," and are *not* "external to our minds" in the sense with which we shall be concerned. And two other important examples may be given.

The first is this. It is well known that people sometimes see things double, an occurrence which has also been described by psychologists by saying that they have a "double image," or two "images," of some object at which they are looking. In such cases it would certainly be quite natural to say that each of the two "images" is "presented in space": they are seen, one in one place, and the other in another, in just the same sense in which each of those grey after-images which I saw was seen at a particular place on the white background at which I was looking. But it would be utterly unnatural to say that, when I have a double image, each of the two images is "to be met with in space." On the contrary it is quite certain that *both* of them are not "to be met with in space." If both were, it would follow that somebody else might see the *very same* two images which I see; and, though there is no absurdity in supposing that another person might see a pair of images exactly similar to a pair which I see, there is an absurdity in supposing that anyone else might see the *same identical pair*. In every case, then, in which anyone sees anything double, we have an example of at least one "thing" which, though "presented in space" is certainly not "to be met with in space."

And the second important example is this. Bodily pains can, in general, be quite properly said to be "presented in space." When I have a toothache, I feel it *in* a particular region of my jaw or *in* a particular tooth; when I make a cut on my finger smart by putting iodine on it, I feel the pain *in* a particular place in my finger; and a man whose leg has been amputated may feel a pain *in* a place where his foot might have been if he had not lost it. It is certainly perfectly natural to understand the phrase "presented in space" in such a way that if, in the sense illustrated, a pain is felt *in* a particular place, that pain is "presented in space." And yet of pains it would be quite unnatural to say that they are "to be met with in space," for the same reason as in the case of after-images or double images. It is quite conceivable that another person should feel a pain exactly like one which I feel, but there is an absurdity in supposing that he could feel *numerically the same* pain which I feel. And pains are in fact a typical example of the sort of "things" of which philosophers say that they are *not* "external" to our minds, but "within" them. Of any pain which *I* feel they would say that it is necessarily *not* external to my mind but *in it*.

And finally it is, I think, worth while to mention one other class of "things," which are certainly not "external" objects and certainly not "to be met with in space," in the sense with which I am concerned, but which yet some philosophers would be inclined to say are "presented in space," though they are not "presented in space" in quite the same sense in which pains, double images, and negative after-images of the sort I described are so. If you look at an electric light and then close your eyes, it sometimes happens that you see, for some little time, against the dark background which you usually see when your eyes are shut, a bright patch similar in shape to the light at which you have just been looking. Such a bright patch, if you see one, is another example of what some psychologists have called "after-images" and others "after-sensations"; but, unlike the negative after-images of which I spoke before, it is seen when your eyes are shut. Of such an after-image, seen with closed eyes, some philosophers might be inclined to say that this image too was "presented in space," although it is certainly not "to be met with in space." They would be inclined to say that it is "presented in space," because it certainly is presented as at some little distance from the person who is seeing it: and how can a thing be presented as at some little distance from me without being "presented in space"? Yet there is an important difference between such after-images, seen with closed eyes, and after-images of the sort I previously described—a difference which might lead other philosophers to deny that these after-images, seen with closed eyes, are "presented in space" at all. It is a difference which can be expressed by saying that when your eyes are shut, you are not seeing any part of *physical* space at all—of the space which is referred to when we talk of "things which are to be met with in *space*." An after-image seen with closed eyes certainly is presented in *a* space, but it may be questioned whether it is proper to say that it is presented in *space*.

It is clear, then, I think, that by no means everything which can naturally be said to be "presented in space" can also be naturally said to be a "thing which is to be met with in space." Some of the "things," which are presented in space, are very emphatically *not* to be met with in space: or, to use another phrase, which may be used to convey the same notion, they are emphatically *not* "physical realities" at all. The conception "presented in space" is therefore, in one respect, much wider than the conception "to be met with in space": many "things" fall under the first conception which do not fall under the second—many after-images, one at least of the pair of "images" seen whenever anyone sees double, and most bodily pains, are "presented in space," though none of them are to be met with in space. From the fact that a "thing" is presented in space, it by no means follows that it is to be met with in space. But just as the first conception is, in one respect, wider than the second, so, in another, the second is wider than the first. For there are many "things" to be met with in space, of which it is not true that they are presented in space. From the fact that a "thing" is to be met with in space, it by no means follows that it is presented in space. I have taken "to be met with in space" to imply, as I think it naturally may, that a "thing" *might be* perceived; but from the fact that a thing *might be* perceived, it does not follow that it *is* perceived; and if it is not actually perceived, then it will not be presented in space. It is characteristic of the sorts of "things," including shadows, which I have described as "to be met with in space," that there is no absurdity in supposing with regard to any one of them which *is*, at a given time, perceived, both (1) that it might have existed at that very time, without being perceived; (2) that it might have existed at another time, without being perceived at that other time; and (3) that during the whole period of its existence, it need not have been perceived at any time at all. There is, therefore, no absurdity in supposing that many things, which were at one time to be met with in space, never were "presented" at any time at all, and that many things which *are* to be met with in space now, are not now "presented" and also never were and never will be. To use a Kantian phrase, the conception of "things which are to be met with in space" embraces not only objects of actual experience, but also objects of *possible*

experience; and from the fact that a thing is or was an object of *possible* experience, it by no means follows that it either was or is or will be "presented" at all.

I hope that what I have now said may have served to make clear enough what sorts of "things" I was originally referring to as "things outside us" or "things external to our minds." I said that I thought that Kant's phrase "things that are to be met with in space" indicated fairly clearly the sorts of "things" in question; and I have tried to make the range clearer still, by pointing out that this phrase only serves the purpose, if (*a*) you understand it in a sense, in which many "things," e.g., after-images, double images, bodily pains, which might be said to be "presented in space," are nevertheless *not* to be reckoned as "things that are to be met with in space," and (*b*) you realize clearly that there is no contradiction in supposing that there have been and are "to be met with in space" things which never have been, are not now, and never will be perceived, nor in supposing that among those of them which have at some time been perceived many existed at times at which they were not being perceived. I think it will now be clear to everyone that, since I do not reckon as "external things" after-images, double images, and bodily pains, I also should not reckon as "external things," any of the "images" which we often "see with the mind's eye" when we are awake, nor any of those which we see when we are asleep and dreaming; and also that I was so using the expression "external" that from the fact that a man was at a given time having a visual hallucination, it will follow that he was seeing at that time something which was *not* "external" to his mind, and from the fact that he was at a given time having an auditory hallucination, it will follow that he was at the time hearing a sound which was *not* "external" to his mind. But I certainly have not made my use of these phrases, "external to our minds" and "to be met with in space," so clear that in the case of every kind of "thing" which might be suggested, you would be able to tell at once whether I should or should not reckon it as "external to our minds" and "to be met with in space." For instance, I have said nothing which makes it quite clear whether a reflection which I see in a looking-glass is or is not to be regarded as "a thing that is to be met with in space" and "external to our minds," nor have I said anything which makes it quite clear whether the sky is or is not to be so regarded. In the case of the sky, everyone, I think, would feel that it was quite inappropriate to talk of it as "a thing that is to be met with in space"; and most people, I think, would feel a strong reluctance to affirm, without qualification, that reflections which people see in looking-glasses are "to be met with in space." And yet neither the sky nor reflections seen in mirrors are in the same position as bodily pains or after-images in the respect which I have emphasized as a reason for saying of these latter that they are *not* to be met with in space—namely, that there is an absurdity in supposing that *the very same* pain which I feel could be felt by someone else or that *the very same* after-image which I see could be seen by someone else. In the case of reflections in mirrors we should quite naturally, in certain circumstances, use language which implies that another person may see the same reflection which we see. We might quite naturally say to a friend: "Do you see that reddish reflection in the water there? I can't make out what it's a reflection of," just as we might say, pointing to a distant hillside: "Do you see that white speck on the hill over there? I can't make out what it is." And in the case of the sky, it is quite obviously *not* absurd to say that other people see it as well as I.

It must, therefore, be admitted that I have not made my use of the phrase "things to be met with in space," nor therefore that of "external to our minds," which the former was used to explain, so clear that in the case of every kind of "thing" which may be mentioned, there will be no doubt whatever as to whether things of that kind are or are not "to be met with in space" or "external to our minds." But this lack of a clear-cut definition of the expression "things that are to be met with in space," does not, so far as I can see, matter for my present purpose. For my present purpose it is, I think, sufficient if I make clear, in the case of many kinds of things, that I am so using the phrase "things that are to be met with in space," that, in the case of each of these kinds, from the proposition that there are things of that kind it *follows* that there are things to be met with in space. And I have, in fact, given a list (though by no means an exhaustive one) of kinds of things which are related to my use of the expression "things that are to be met with in space" in this way. I mentioned among others the bodies of men and of ani-

mals, plants, stars, houses, chairs, and shadows; and I want now to emphasize that I am so using "things to be met with in space" that, in the case of each of these kinds of "things," from the proposition that there are "things" of that kind it *follows* that there are things to be met with in space: e.g., from the proposition that there are plants or that plants exist it *follows* that there are things to be met with in space, from the proposition that shadows exist, it *follows* that there are things to be met with in space, and so on, in the case of all the kinds of "things" which I mentioned in my first list. That this should be clear is sufficient for my purpose, because, if it is clear, then it will also be clear that, as I implied before, if you have proved that two plants exist, or that a plant and a dog exist, or that a dog and a shadow exist, etc., etc., you will *ipso facto* have proved that there are things to be met with in space: you will not require *also* to give a separate proof that from the proposition that there are plants it *does* follow that there are things to be met with in space.

Now with regard to the expression "things that are to be met with in space" I think it will readily be believed that I may be using it in a sense such that no proof is required that from "plants exist" there follows "there are things to be met with in space"; but with regard to the phrase "things external to our minds" I think the case is different. People may be inclined to say: "I can see quite clearly that from the proposition 'At least two dogs exist at the present moment' there *follows* the proposition 'At least two things are to be met with in space at the present moment,' so that if you can prove that there are two dogs in existence at the present moment you will *ipso facto* have proved that two things at least are to be met with in space at the present moment. I can see that you do not also require a separate proof that from 'Two dogs exist' 'Two things are to be met with in space' does *follow;* it is quite obvious that there couldn't be a dog which wasn't to be met with in space. But it is not by any means so clear to me that if you can prove that there are two dogs or two shadows, you will *ipso facto* have proved that there are two things *external to our minds.* Isn't it possible that a dog, though it certainly must be 'to be met with in space,' might *not* be an external object—an object external to our minds? Isn't a separate proof required that anything that is to be met with in space must be external to our minds? Of course, if you are using 'external' as a mere synonym for 'to be met with in space,' no proof will be required that dogs are external objects: in that case, if you can prove that two dogs exist, you will *ipso facto* have proved that there are some external things. But I find it difficult to believe that you, or anybody else, do really use 'external' as a mere synonym for 'to be met with in space'; and if you don't, isn't some proof required that whatever is to be met with in space must be external to our minds?"

Now Kant, as we saw, asserts that the phrases "outside of us" or "external" are in fact used in two very different senses; and with regard to one of these two senses, that which he calls the "transcendental" sense, and which he tries to explain by saying that it is a sense in which "external" means "existing *as a thing in itself* distinct from us," it is notorious that he himself held that things which are to be met with in space are *not* "external" in that sense. There is, therefore, according to him, *a* sense of "external," a sense in which the word has been commonly used by philosophers—such that, if "eternal" be used in that sense, then from the proposition "Two dogs exist" it will *not* follow that there are some external things. What this supposed sense is I do not think that Kant himself ever succeeded in explaining clearly; nor do I know of any reason for supposing that philosophers ever have used "external" in a sense, such that in *that* sense things that are to be met with in space are *not* external. But how about the other sense, in which, according to Kant, the word "external" has been commonly used—that which he calls "empirically external"? How is this conception related to the conception "to be met with in space"? It may be noticed that, in the passages which I quoted, Kant himself does not tell us at all clearly what he takes to be the proper answer to this question. He only makes the rather odd statement that, in order to remove all uncertainty as to the conception "empirically external," he will distinguish objects to which it applies from those which might be called "external" in the transcendental sense, by "calling them outright things which are *to be met with in space*." These odd words certainly suggest, as one possible interpretation of them, that in Kant's opinion the conception "empirically external" is *identical* with the conception "to be met with in space"—that he does think that "external," when used in this second

sense, is a mere synonym for "to be met with in space." But, if this is his meaning, I do find it very difficult to believe that he is right. Have philosophers, in fact, ever used "external" as a mere synonym for "to be met with in space"? Does he himself do so?

I do not think they have, nor that he does himself; and, in order to explain how they have used it, and how the two conceptions "external to our minds" and "to be met with in space" are related to one another, I think it is important expressly to call attention to a fact which hitherto I have only referred to incidentally: namely, the fact that those who talk of certain things as "external to" our minds, do, in general, as we should naturally expect, talk of other "things," with which they wish to contrast the first, as "in" our minds. It has, of course, been often pointed out that when "in" is thus used, followed by "my mind," "your mind," "his mind," etc., "in" is being used metaphorically. And there are some metaphorical uses of "in," followed by such expressions, which occur in common speech, and which we all understand quite well. For instance, we all understand such expressions as "I had you in mind when I made that arrangement" or "I had you in mind when I said that there are some people who can't bear to touch a spider." In these cases "I was thinking of you" can be used to mean the same as "I had you in mind." But it is quite certain that this particular metaphorical use of "in" is not the one in which philosophers are using it when they contrast what is "in" my mind with what is "external" to it. On the contrary, in their use of "external," you will be external to my mind even at a moment when I have you in mind. If we want to discover what this peculiar metaphorical use of "*in* my mind" is, which is such that nothing, which is, in the sense we are now concerned with, "external" to my mind, can ever be "in" it, we need, I think, to consider instances of the sort of "things" which they would say are "in" my mind in this special sense. I have already mentioned three such instances, which are, I think, sufficient for my present purpose: any bodily pain which I feel, any after-image which I see with my eyes shut, and any image which I "see" when I am asleep and dreaming, are typical examples of the sort of "thing" of which philosophers have spoken as "*in* my mind." And there is no doubt, I think, that when they have spoken of such things as my body, a sheet of paper, a star—in short "physical objects" generally—as "external," they have meant to emphasize some important difference which they feel to exist between such things as these and such "things" as a pain, an after-image seen with closed eyes, and a dream-image. But *what* difference? What difference do they feel to exist between a bodily pain which I feel or an after-image which I see with closed eyes, on the one hand, and my body itself, on the other—what difference which leads them to say that whereas the bodily pain and the after-image are "in" my mind, my body itself is *not* "in" my mind—not even when I am feeling it and seeing it or thinking of it? I have already said that one difference which there is between the two, is that my body is to be met with in space, whereas the bodily pain and the after-image are not. But I think it would be quite wrong to say that this is *the* difference which has led philosophers to speak of the two latter as "in" my mind, and of my body as *not* "in" my mind.

The question what the difference is which has led them to speak in this way, is not, I think, at all an easy question to answer; but I am going to try to give, in brief outline, what I *think* is a right answer.

It should, I think, be noted, first of all, that the use of the word "mind," which is being adopted when it is said that any bodily pains which I feel are "in my mind," is one which is not quite in accordance with any usage common in ordinary speech, although we are very familiar with it in philosophy. Nobody, I think, would say that bodily pains which I feel are "in my mind," unless he was also prepared to say that it is *with* my mind that I feel bodily pains; and to say this latter is, I think, not quite in accordance with common non-philosophic usage. It is natural enough to say that it is with my mind that I remember, and think, and imagine, and feel *mental* pains—e.g., disappointment, but not, I think, quite so natural to say that it is with my mind that I feel *bodily* pains, e.g., a severe headache; and perhaps even less natural to say that it is with my mind that I see and hear and smell and taste. There is, however, a well-established philosophical usage according to which seeing, hearing, smelling, tasting, and having a bodily pain are just as much *mental* occurrences or processes as are remembering, or thinking, or imagining. This usage was, I think, adopted by philosophers, because they saw a real resemblance between

such statements as "I saw a cat," "I heard a clap of thunder," "I smelled a strong smell of onions," "My finger smarted horribly," on the one hand, and such statements as "I remembered having seen him," "I was thinking out a plan of action," "I pictured the scene to myself," "I felt bitterly disappointed," on the other—a resemblance which puts all these statements in one class together, as contrasted with other statements in which "I" or "my" is used, such as, e.g., "I was less than four feet high," "I was lying on my back," "My hair was very long." What is the resemblance in question? It is a resemblance which might be expressed by saying that all the first eight statements are the sort of statements which furnish data for psychology, while the three latter are not. It is also a resemblance which may be expressed, in a way now common among philosophers, by saying that in the case of all the first eight statements, if we make the statement more specific by adding a date, we get a statement such that, if it is true, then it *follows* that I was "having an experience" at the date in question, whereas this does not hold for the three last statements. For instance, if it is true that I saw a cat between 12 noon and 5 minutes past, today, it *follows* that I was "having some experience" between 12 noon and 5 minutes past, today; whereas from the proposition that I was less than four feet high in December 1877, it does not *follow* that I had any experiences in December 1877. But this philosophic use of "having an experience" is one which itself needs explanation, since it is not identical with any use of the expression that is established in common speech. An explanation, however, which is, I think, adequate for the purpose, can be given by saying that a philosopher, who was following this usage, would say that I was at a given time "having an experience" if and only if either (1) I was conscious at the time or (2) I was dreaming at the time or (3) something else was true of me at the time, which resembled what is true of me when I am conscious and when I am dreaming, in a certain very obvious respect in which what is true of me when I am dreaming resembles what is true of me when I am conscious, and in which what would be true of me, if at any time, for instance, I had a vision, would resemble both. This explanation is, of course, in some degree vague; but I think it is clear enough for our purpose. It amounts to saying that, in this philosophic usage of "having an experience," it would be said of me that I was, at a given time, having *no* experience, if I was at the time neither conscious nor dreaming nor having a vision nor *anything else of the sort*; and, of course, this is vague in so far as it has not been specified what else would be *of the sort*: this is left to be gathered from the instances given. But I think this is sufficient: often at night when I am asleep, I am neither conscious nor dreaming nor having a vision nor *anything else of the sort*—that is to say, I am having no experiences. If this explanation of this philosophic usage of "having an experience" is clear enough, then I think that what has been meant by saying that any pain which I feel or any after-image which I see with my eyes closed is "*in my mind*," can be explained by saying that what is meant is neither more nor less than that there would be a contradiction in supposing *that very same pain* or *that very same after-image* to have existed at a time at which I was having no experience; or, in other words, that from the proposition, with regard to any time, that *that* pain or *that* after-image existed at that time, it *follows* that I was having some experience at the time in question. And if so, then we can say that the felt difference between bodily pains which I feel and after-images which I see, on the one hand, and my body on the other, which has led philosophers to say that any such pain or after-image is "*in* my mind," whereas my body *never* is but is always "outside of" or "external to" my mind, is just this, that whereas there is a contradiction in supposing a pain which I feel or an after-image which I see to exist at a time when I am having no experience, there is no contradiction in supposing my body to exist at a time when I am having no experience; and we can even say, I think, that just this and nothing more is what they have meant by these puzzling and misleading phrases "in my mind" and "external to my mind."

But now, if to say of anything, e.g., my body, that it is external to *my* mind, means merely that from a proposition to the effect that it existed at a specified time, there in no case follows the further proposition that *I* was having an experience at the time in question, then to say of anything that it is external to *our* minds, will mean similarly that from a proposition to the effect that it existed at a specified time, it in no case follows that any of *us* were having experiences at the time in

question. And if by *our* minds be meant, as is, I think, usually meant, the minds of human beings living on the earth, then it will follow that any pains which animals may feel, any after-images they may see, any experiences they may have, though not external to *their* minds, yet are external to *ours*. And this at once makes plain how different is the conception "external to our minds" from the conception "to be met with in space"; for, of course, pains which animals feel or after-images which they see are no more to be met with in space than are pains which *we* feel or after-images which *we* see. From the proposition that there are external objects—objects that are not in any of *our* minds, it does *not* follow that there are things to be met with in space; and hence "external to our minds" is not a mere synonym for "to be met with in space": that is to say, "external to our minds" and "to be met with in space" are two different conceptions. And the true relation between these conceptions seems to me to be this. We have already seen that there are ever so many kinds of "things," such that, in the case of each of these kinds, from the proposition that there is at least one thing of that kind there *follows* the proposition that there is at least one thing to be met with in space: e.g., this follows from "There is at least one star," from "There is at least one human body," from "There is at least one shadow," etc. And I think we can say that of every kind of thing of which this is true, it is also true that from the proposition that there is at least one "thing" of that kind there *follows* the proposition that there is at least one thing external to our minds: e.g., from "There is at least one star" there follows not only "There is at least one thing to be met with in space" but also "There is at least one external thing," and similarly in all other cases. My reason for saying this is as follows. Consider any kind of thing, such that anything of that kind, if there is anything of it, must be "to be met with in space": e.g., consider the kind "soap bubble." If I say of anything which I am perceiving, "That is a soap bubble," I am, it seems to me, certainly implying that there would be no contradiction in asserting that it existed before I perceived it and that it will continue to exist, even if I cease to perceive it. This seems to me to be part of what is meant by saying that it is a real soap bubble, as distinguished, for instance, from a hallucination of a soap bubble. Of course, it by no means follows, that if it really is a soap bubble, it did in fact exist before I perceived it or will continue to exist after I cease to perceive it: soap bubbles are an example of a kind of "physical object" and "thing to be met with in space," in the case of which it is notorious that particular specimens of the kind often do exist only so long as they are perceived by a particular person. But a thing which I perceive would not be a soap bubble unless its existence at any given time were *logically independent* of my perception of it at that time; unless that is to say, from the proposition, with regard to a particular time, that it existed at that time, it *never* follows that I perceived it at that time. But, if it is true that it would not be a soap bubble, unless it *could* have existed at any given time without being perceived by me at that time, it is certainly also true that it would not be a soap bubble, unless it *could* have existed at any given time, without its being true that I was having any experience of any kind at the time in question: it would not be a soap bubble, unless, whatever time you take, from the proposition that it existed at that time it does *not* follow that I was having any experience at that time. That is to say, from the proposition with regard to anything which I am perceiving that it is a soap bubble, there *follows* the proposition that it is external to *my* mind. But if, when I say that anything which I perceive is a soap bubble, I am implying that it is external to *my* mind, I am, I think, certainly also implying that it is also external to all other minds: I am implying that it is not a thing of a sort such that things of that sort *can* only exist at a time when somebody is having an experience. I think, therefore, that from any proposition of the form "There's a soap bubble!" there does really *follow* the proposition "There's an external object!" "There's an object external to *all* our minds!" And, if this is true of the kind "soap bubble," it is certainly also true of any other kind (including the kind "unicorn") which is such that, if there are any things of that kind, it follows that there are *some* things to be met with in space.

I think, therefore, that in the case of all kinds of "things," which are such that if there is a pair of things, both of which are of one of these kinds, or a pair of things one of which is of one of them and one of them of another, then it will follow at once that there are some things to be met with in space, it is true also that if I can prove that there are a pair of things, one of which is of one of these kinds and another of another, or a pair both of which are of one of them, then I shall have proved *ipso facto* that there are at least two "things outside of us." That is to say, if I can prove that there exist now both a sheet of paper and a human hand, I shall have proved that there are now "things outside of us"; if I can prove that there exist now both a shoe and sock, I shall have proved that there are now "things outside of us"; etc.; and similarly I shall have proved it, if I can prove that there exist now two sheets of paper, or two human hands, or two shoes, or two socks, etc. Obviously, then, there are thousands of different things such that, if, at any time, I can prove any one of them, I shall have proved the existence of things outside of us. Cannot I prove any of these things?

It seems to me that, so far from its being true, as Kant declares to be his opinion, that there is only one possible proof of the existence of things outside of us, namely the one which he has given. I can now give a large number of different proofs, each of which is a perfectly rigorous proof; and that at many other times I have been in a position to give many others. I can prove now, for instance, that two human hands exist. How? By holding up my two hands and saying, as I make a certain gesture with the right, "Here is one hand," and adding, as I make a certain gesture with the left, "and here is another." And if, by doing this, I have proved *ipso facto* the existence of external things, you will all see that I can also do it now in numbers of other ways: there is no need to multiply examples.

But did I prove just now that two human hands were then in existence? I do want to insist that I did; that the proof which I gave was a perfectly rigorous one; and that it is perhaps impossible to give a better or more rigorous proof of anything whatever. Of course, it would not have been a proof unless three conditions were satisfied; namely, (1) unless the premise which I adduced as proof of the conclusion was different from the conclusion I adduced it to prove; (2) unless the premise which I adduced was something which I *knew* to be the case, and not merely something which I believed but which was by no means certain, or something which, though in fact true, I did not know to be so; and (3) unless the conclusion did really follow from the premise. But all these three conditions were in fact satisfied by my proof. (1) The premise which I adduced in proof was quite certainly different from the conclusion, for the conclusion was merely "Two human hands exist at this moment," but the premise was something far more specific than this—something which I expressed by showing you my hands, making certain gestures, and saying the words "Here is one hand, and here is another." It is quite obvious that the two were different, because it is quite obvious that the conclusion might have been true, even if the premise had been false. In asserting the premise I was asserting much more than I was asserting in asserting the conclusion. (2) I certainly did at the moment *know* that which I expressed by the combination of certain gestures with saying the words "There is one hand and here is another." I *knew* that there was one hand in the place indicated by combining a certain gesture with my first utterance of "here" and that there was another in the different place indicated by combining a certain gesture with my second utterance of "here." How absurd it would be to suggest that I did not know it, but only believed it, and that perhaps it was not the case! You might as well suggest that I do not know that I am now standing up and talking—that perhaps after all I'm not, and that it's not quite certain that I am! And finally (3) it is quite certain that the conclusion did follow from the premise. This is as certain as it is that if there is one hand here and another here *now*, then it follows that there are two hands in existence *now*.

My proof, then, of the existence of things outside of us did satisfy three of the conditions necessary for a rigorous proof. Are there any other conditions necessary for a rigorous proof, such that perhaps it did not satisfy one of them? Perhaps there may be; I do not know; but I do want to emphasize that, so far as I can see, we all of us do constantly take proofs of this sort as absolutely conclusive proofs of certain conclusions—as finally settling certain questions, as to which we were previously in doubt. Suppose, for instance, it were a question whether there were as many as three misprints on a certain page in a certain book. A says there are, B is inclined to doubt it. How could A prove that he is right? Surely he *could* prove it by taking the book, turning to

the page, and pointing to three separate places on it, saying "There's one misprint here, another here, and another here": surely that is a method by which it *might* be proved! Of course, A would not have proved, by doing this, that there were at least three misprints on the page in question, unless it was certain that there was a misprint in each of the places to which he pointed. But to say that he *might* prove it in this way, is to say that it *might* be certain that there was. And if such a thing as that could ever be certain, then assuredly it was certain just now that there was one hand in one of the two places I indicated and another in the other.

I did, then, just now, give a proof that there were *then* external objects; and obviously, if I did, I could *then* have given many other proofs of the same sort that there were external objects *then*, and could now give many proofs of the same sort that there are external objects *now*.

But, if what I am asked to do is to prove that external objects have existed *in the past*, then I can give many different proofs of this also, but proofs which are in important respects of a different sort from those just given. And I want to emphasize that, when Kant says it is a scandal not to be able to give a proof of the existence of external objects, a proof of their existence in the past would certainly *help* to remove the scandal of which he is speaking. He says that, if it occurs to anyone to question their existence, we ought to be able to confront him with a satisfactory proof. But by a person who questions their existence, he certainly means not merely a person who questions whether any exist at the moment of speaking, but a person who questions whether any have *ever* existed; and a proof that some have existed in the past would certainly therefore be relevant to *part* of what such a person is questioning. How then can I prove that there have been external objects in the past? Here is one proof. I can say: "I held up two hands above this desk not very long ago; therefore two hands existed not very long ago; therefore at least two external objects have existed at some time in the past, Q.E.D." This is a perfectly good proof, provided I *know* what is asserted in the premise. But I *do* know that I held up two hands above this desk not very long ago. As a matter of fact, in this case you all know it too. There's no doubt whatever that I did. Therefore I have given a perfectly conclusive proof that external objects have existed in the past; and you will all see at once that, if this is a conclusive proof, I could have given many others of the same sort, and could now give many others. But it is also quite obvious that this sort of proof differs in important respects from the sort of proof I gave just now that there were two hands existing *then*.

I have, then, given two conclusive proofs of the existence of external objects. The first was a proof that two human hands existed at the time when I gave the proof; the second was a proof that two human hands had existed at a time previous to that at which I gave the proof. These proofs were of a different sort in important respects. And I pointed out that I could have given, then, many other conclusive proofs of both sorts. It is also obvious that I could give many others of both sorts now. So that, if these are the sort of proof that is wanted, nothing is easier than to prove the existence of external objects.

But now I am perfectly well aware that, in spite of all that I have said, many philosophers will still feel that I have not given any satisfactory proof of the point in question. And I want briefly, in conclusion, to say something as to why this dissatisfaction with my proofs should be felt.

One reason why, is, I think, this. Some people understand "proof of an external world" as including a proof of things which I haven't attempted to prove and haven't proved. It is not quite easy to say *what* it is that they want proved—*what* it is that is such that unless they got a proof of it, they would not say that they had a proof of the existence of external things; but I can make an approach to explaining what they want by saying that if I had proved the propositions which I used as *premises* in my two proofs, then they would perhaps admit that I had proved the existence of external things, but, in the absence of such a proof (which, of course, I have neither given nor attempted to give), they will say that I have not given what they mean by a proof of the existence of external things. In other words, they want a proof of what I assert *now* when I hold up my hands and say "Here's one hand and here's another"; and, in the other case, they want a proof of

what I assert *now* when I say "I did hold up two hands above this desk just now." Of course, what they really want is not merely a proof of these two propositions, but something like a general statement as to how *any* propositions of this sort may be proved. This, of course, I haven't given; and I do not believe it can be given: if this is what is meant by proof of the existence of external things, I do not believe that any proof of the existence of external things is possible. Of course, in some cases what might be called a proof of propositions which seem like these can be got. If one of you suspected that one of my hands was artificial he might be said to get a proof of my proposition "Here's one hand, and here's another," by coming up and examining the suspected hand close up, perhaps touching and pressing it, and so establishing that it really was a human hand. But I do not believe that any proof is possible in nearly all cases. How am I to prove now that "Here's one hand, and here's another"? I do not believe I can do it. In order to do it, I should need to prove for one thing, as Descartes pointed out, that I am not now dreaming. But how can I prove that I am not? I have, no doubt, conclusive reasons for asserting that I am not now dreaming; I have conclusive evidence that I am awake: but that is a very different thing from being able to prove it. I could not tell you what all my evidence is; and I should require to do this at least, in order to give you a proof.

But another reason why some people would feel dissatisfied with my proofs is, I think, not merely that they want a proof of something which I haven't proved, but that they think that, if I cannot give such extra proofs, then the proofs that I have given are not conclusive proofs at all. And this, I think, is a definite mistake. They would say: "If you cannot prove your premise that here is one hand and here is another, then you do not know it. But you yourself have admitted that, if you did not know it, then your proof was not conclusive. Therefore your proof was not, as you say it was, a conclusive proof." This view that, if I cannot prove such things as these, I do not know them, is, I think, the view that Kant was expressing in the sentence which I quoted at the beginning of this lecture, when he implies that so long as we have no proof of the existence of external things, their existence must be accepted merely on *faith*. He means to say, I think, that if I cannot prove that there is a hand here, I must accept it merely as a matter of faith—I cannot know it. Such a view, though it has been very common among philosophers, can, I think, be shown to be wrong—though shown only by the use of premises which are not known to be true, unless we do know of the existence of external things. I can know things, which I cannot prove; and among things which I certainly did know, even if (as I think) I could not prove them, were the premises of my two proofs. I should say, therefore, that those, if any, who are dissatisfied with these proofs merely on the ground that I did not know their premises, have no good reason for their dissatisfaction.

READING QUESTIONS

1. Concerning the existence of "external things," Moore distinguishes between "things which are presented in space" and "things which are to be met with in space." What is the difference? Give some examples of each.

2. According to Moore, how do the two conceptions "external to our minds" and "to be met with in space" differ? In what ways are they logically related, if any?

3. How, according to Moore, does holding up my two hands constitute the basis for a proof of an external world?

4. Carefully catalogue the reasons that Moore offers for thinking that his proof satisfies the three conditions that he lays down for any rigorous proof. Do you believe that he has satisfied these conditions? Why or why not?

5. In reference to the adequacy of his proof, Moore writes that "so far as I can see, we all of us do constantly take proofs of this sort as absolutely conclusive proofs of certain conclusions—as finally settling certain questions, as to which we were previously in doubt." In what ways, if any, is this fact relevant to establishing the adequacy of his proof?

6. Moore maintains that even though the conditions for having a rigorous proof have been satisfied by his argument, there will still be persons who will ex-

press doubt concerning the legitimacy of his supposed proof. According to Moore, why will they remain skeptical? What does he believe that they want in a proof? Why does Moore believe that it will not be possible to satsfy them?

SUGGESTIONS FOR FURTHER READING (GEORGE EDWARD (G. E.) MOORE)

Primary Sources and Collected Writings

(1903) *Principia Ethica*, rev. ed., edited with an introduction by T. Baldwin. Cambridge: Cambridge University Press, 1993.

(1912) *Ethics*. Oxford: Oxford University Press.

(1922) *Philosophical Studies*. New York: Harcourt, Brace.

(1953) *Some Main Problems of Philosophy*. London: Allen and Unwin.

(1959) *Philosophical Papers*. London: Allen and Unwin.

(1962) *Commonplace Book, 1919–1935*, edited by C. Lewy. New York: Macmillan.

(1966) *Lectures on Philosophy*, edited by C. Lewy. London: Allen and Unwin.

(1986) *G. E. Moore: The Early Essays*. Philadelphia, PA: Temple University Press.

(1991) *The Elements of Ethics*, edited by T. Regan. Philadelphia, PA: Temple University Press.

(1993) *Selected Writings*, edited by T. Baldwin. New York: Routledge.

Secondary Sources

Ambrose, A., and M. Lazerowitz, eds. (1970) *G. E. Moore: Essays in Retrospect*. New York: Humanities Press.

Baldwin, T. (1990) *G. E. Moore*. New York: Routledge.

Fratantaro, S. (1998) *The Methodology of G. E. Moore*. Burlington, VT: Ashgate Publishing Company.

Klein, E. D. (1969). *Studies in the Philosophy of G. E. Moore*. Chicago, IL: Quadrangle Books.

Klemke, E. D. (1999) *A Defense of Realism: Reflections on the Metaphysics of G. E. Moore*. Amhearst, NY: Humanity Books.

Levy, P. (1979) *G. E. Moore and the Cambridge Apostles.* New York: Holt, Rinehart and Winston.

Regan, T. (1986) *Bloomsbury's Prophet.* Philadelphia, PA: Temple University Press.

Schlipp, P. A., ed. (1993) *The Philosophy of G. E. Moore,* 3d edition. La Salle, IL: Open Court.

Stroll, A. (1994) *Moore and Wittgenstein on Certainty.* Oxford: Oxford University Press.

Stroud, B. (1984) *The Significance of Philosophical Skepticism.* Oxford: Clarendon Press.

Whilte, A. (1958) *G. E. Moore: A Critical Exposition.* Oxford: Oxford University Press.

Wittgenstein, L. (1969) *On Certainty.* Oxford: Basil Blackwell.

LUDWIG WITTGENSTEIN

From *Philosophical Investigations*

In 1929 Ludwig Wittgenstein (1889–1951) returned to Cambridge and to work in academic philosophy. After submitting *Tractatus Logico-Philosophicus* as his dissertation and being examined by Bertrand Russell and G. E. Moore, he was awarded his doctoral degree. He was appointed to a fellowship by Trinity College in 1930 and later became a professor of philosophy there in 1939—the same year that he became a naturalized British citizen. He officially remained a professor at Cambridge until 1947, although during the Second World War he found work as a porter in Guy's Hospital in London and later took a job as a laboratory assistant in Newcastle.

His return to Cambridge marked the beginning of major changes in his overall philosophical outlook. Wittgenstein did not immediately repudiate the philosophical views that he had developed before and during the First World War, but he did set about modifying them in various substantial ways. As the years progressed, Wittgenstein became more and more convinced that there were fundamental problems in the *Tractatus* that could not be resolved adequately within its existing philosophical framework. By 1936,

his thinking had undergone changes substantial enough to justify characterizing it as a new outlook on the methods and problems of philosophy.

Between 1930 and 1946 Wittgenstein struggled to produce what was to become his monumental *Philosophical Investigations* (1953). Like his *Tractatus, Philosophical Investigations* is composed as a series of remarks on various central topics in philosophy (the nature of language and language-learning, rules and rule-following, understanding talk about the mental, etc.) and on the methods and aims of philosophical thinking. *Philosophical Investigations* develops a profoundly antifoundationalistic approach to its subject matter, one in which the idea that philosophy ought to offer explanations of various phenomena (or of the possibility of phenomena) is superseded by the idea that philosophy should be a purely descriptive or therapeutic enterprise.

Philosophical Investigations was published after Wittgenstein's death, along with a number of other texts or partial texts that he authored over the intervening years. In many respects Wittgenstein detested professional philosophy, the process of academic publishing, and the atmosphere of academic life. Yet many remember him fondly as a great teacher, although he regularly advised his best students to give up any idea of becoming university professors and suggested that they turn instead to some "practical" pursuit, such as medicine, engineering, or carpentry.

Wittgenstein died in Cambridge, succumbing to cancer. His final words, intriguingly, were, "Tell them I've had a wonderful life!"

1. "When they (my elders) named some object, and accordingly moved towards something, I saw this and I grasped that the thing was called

Ludwig Wittgenstein, selections from his *Philosophical Investigations*, Third Edition, translated by Elizabeth Anscombe. Copyright © 1953 Prentice-Hall, Inc. Reprinted by permission of Prentice-Hall, Inc., Upper Saddle River, NJ.

by the sound they uttered when they meant to point it out. Their intention was shown by their bodily movements, as it were the natural language of all peoples: the expression of the face, the play of the eyes, the movement of other parts of the body, and the tone of voice which expresses our state of mind in seeking, having, rejecting, or avoiding something. Thus, as I heard words repeatedly used in their proper places in various sentences, I gradually learned to understand what objects they signified; and after I had trained my mouth to form these signs, I used them to express my own desires."

(Augustine, *Confessions*, 1. 8.)

These words, it seems to me, give us a particular picture of the essence of human language. It is this: the individual words in language name objects—sentences are combinations of such names.—In this picture of language we find the roots of the following idea: Every word has a meaning. This meaning is correlated with the word. It is the object for which the word stands.

Augustine does not speak of there being any difference between kinds of word. If you describe the learning of language in this way, you are, I believe, thinking primarily of nouns like "table", "chair", "bread", and of people's names, and only secondarily of the names of certain actions and properties; and of the remaining kinds of word as something that will take care of itself.

Now think of the following use of language: I send someone shopping. I give him a slip marked "five red apples". He takes the slip to the shopkeeper, who opens the drawer marked "apples"; then he looks up the word "red" in a table and finds a color sample opposite it; then he says the series of cardinal numbers—I assume that he knows them by heart—up to the word "five" and for each number he takes an apple of the same color as the sample out of the drawer.—It is in this and similar ways that one operates with words.—"But how does he know where and how he is to look up the word 'red' and what he is to do with the word 'five'?"—Well, I assume that he *acts* as I have described. Explanations come to an end somewhere.—But what is the meaning of the word "five"?—No such thing was in question here, only how the word "five" is used.

2. That philosophical concept of meaning has its place in a primitive idea of the way language functions. But one can also say that it is the idea of a language more primitive than ours.

Let us imagine a language for which the description given by Augustine is right. The language is meant to serve for communication between a builder A and an assistant B. A is building with building stones: there are blocks, pillars, slabs and beams. B has to pass the stones, and that in the order in which A needs them. For this purpose they use a language consisting of the words "block", "pillar", "slab", "beam". A calls them out;—B brings the stone which he has learned to bring at such-and-such a call.—Conceive this as a complete primitive language.

3. Augustine, we might say, does describe a system of communication; only not everything that we call language is this system. And one has to say this in many cases where the question arises "Is this an appropriate description or not?" The answer is: "Yes, it is appropriate, but only for this narrowly circumscribed region, not for the whole of what you were claiming to describe."

It is as if someone were to say: "A game consists in moving objects about on a surface according to certain rules . . ."—and we replied: You seem to be thinking of board games, but there are others. You can make your definition correct by expressly restricting it to those games.

4. Imagine a script in which the letters were used to stand for sounds, and also as signs of emphasis and punctuation. (A script can be conceived as a language for describing sound patterns.) Now imagine someone interpreting that script as if there were simply a correspondence of letters to sounds and as if the letters had not also completely different functions. Augustine's conception of language is like such an oversimple conception of the script.

5. If we look at the example in §1, we may perhaps get an inkling how much this general notion of the meaning of a word surrounds the working of language with a haze which makes clear vision impossible. It disperses the fog to study the phenomena of language in primitive kinds of application in which one can command a clear view of the aim and functioning of the words.

A child uses such primitive forms of language when it learns to talk. Here the teaching of language is not explanation, but training.

6. We could imagine that the language of §2 was the *whole* language of A and B; even the whole language of a tribe. The children are brought up to perform *these* actions, to use *these* words as they do so, and to react in *this* way to the words of others.

An important part of the training will consist in the teacher's pointing to the objects, directing the child's attention to them, and at the same time uttering a word; for instance, the word "slab" as he points to that shape. (I do not want to call this "ostensive definition", because the child cannot as yet *ask* what the name is. I will call it "ostensive teaching of words".—I say that it will form an important part of the training, because it is so with human beings; not because it could not be imagined otherwise.) This ostensive teaching of words can be said to establish an association between the word and the thing. But what does this mean? Well, it can mean various things; but one very likely thinks first of all that a picture of the object comes before the child's mind when it hears the word. But now, if this does happen—is it the purpose of the word?—Yes, it *can* be the purpose.—I can imagine such a use of words (of series of sounds). (Uttering a word is like striking a note on the keyboard of the imagination.) But in the language of §2 it is *not* the purpose of the words to evoke images. (It may, of course, be discovered that that helps to attain the actual purpose.)

But if the ostensive teaching has this effect,—am I to say that it effects an understanding of the word? Don't you understand the call "Slab!" if you act upon it in such-and-such a way?—Doubtless the ostensive teaching helped to bring this about; but only together with a particular training. With different training the same ostensive teaching of these words would have effected a quite different understanding.

"I set the brake up by connecting up rod and lever."—Yes, given the whole of the rest of the mechanism. Only in conjunction with that is it a brake-lever, and separated from its support it is not even a lever; it may be anything, or nothing.

7. In the practice of the use of language (2) one party calls out the words, the other acts on them. In instruction in the language the following process will occur: the learner *names* the objects; that is, he utters the word when the teacher points to the stone.—And there will be this still simpler exercise: the pupil repeats the words after the teacher—both of these being processes resembling language.

We can also think of the whole process of using words in (2) as one of those games by means of which children learn their native language. I will call these games "language-games" and will sometimes speak of a primitive language as a language-game.

And the processes of naming the stones and of repeating words after someone might also be called language-games. Think of much of the use of words in games like ring-a-ring-a-roses.

I shall also call the whole, consisting of language and the actions into which it is woven, the "language-game".

8. Let us now look at an expansion of language (2). Besides the four words "block", "pillar", etc., let it contain a series of words used as the shopkeeper in (1) used the numerals (it can be the series of letters of the alphabet); further, let there be two words, which may as well be "there" and "this" (because this roughly indicates their purpose), that are used in connection with a pointing gesture; and finally a number of color samples. A gives an order like: "d—slab—there". At the same time he shows the assistant a color sample, and when he says "there" he points to a place on the building site. From the stock of slabs B takes one for each letter of the alphabet up to "d", of the same color as the sample, and brings them to the place indicated by A.—On other occasions A gives the order "this—there". At "this" he points to a building stone. And so on.

9. When a child learns this language, it has to learn the series of 'numerals' a, b, c, . . . by heart. And it has to learn their use.—Will this training include ostensive teaching of the words?—Well, people will, for example, point to slabs and count: "a, b, c slabs".—Something more like the ostensive teaching of the words "block", "pillar", etc. would be the ostensive teaching of numerals that serve not to count but to refer to groups of objects that can be taken in at a glance. Children do learn the use of the first five or six cardinal numerals in this way.

Are "there" and "this" also taught ostensively?—Imagine how one might perhaps teach their use. One will point to places and things—but in this case the pointing occurs in the *use* of the words too and not merely in learning the use.—

10. Now what do the words of this language *signify*?—What is supposed to show what they signify, if not the kind of use they have? And we have already described that. So we are asking for the expression "This word signifies *this*" to be made a part of the description. In other words the description ought to take the form: "The word . . . signifies. . . ."

Of course, one can reduce the description of the use of the word "slab" to the statement that this word signifies this object. This will be done when, for example, it is merely a matter of removing the mistaken idea that the word "slab" refers to the shape of building-stone that we in fact call a "block"—but the kind of *'referring'* this is, that is to say the use of these words for the rest, is already known.

Equally one can say that the signs "a", "b", etc. signify numbers; when for example this removes the mistaken idea that "a", "b", "c", play the part actually played in language by "block", "slab", "pillar". And one can also say that "c" means this number and not that one; when for example this serves to explain that the letters are to be used in the order a, b, c, d, etc. and not in the order a, b, d, c.

But assimilating the descriptions of the uses of words in this way cannot make the uses themselves any more like one another. For, as we see, they are absolutely unlike.

11. Think of the tools in a toolbox: there is a hammer, pliers, a saw, a screwdriver, a rule, a glue pot, glue, nails and screws.—The functions of words are as diverse as the functions of these objects. (And in both cases there are similarities.)

Of course, what confuses us is the uniform appearance of words when we hear them spoken or meet them in script and print. For their *application* is not presented to us so clearly. Especially when we are doing philosophy!

12. It is like looking into the cabin of a locomotive. We see handles all looking more or less alike. (Naturally, since they are all supposed to be handled.) But one is the handle of a crank which can be moved continuously (it regulates the opening of a valve); another is the handle of a switch, which has only two effective

positions, it is either off or on; a third is the handle of a brake-lever, the harder one pulls on it, the harder it brakes; a fourth, the handle of a pump: it has an effect only so long as it is moved to and fro.

13. When we say: "Every word in language signifies something" we have so far said *nothing whatever;* unless we have explained exactly *what* distinction we wish to make. (It might be, of course, that we wanted to distinguish the words of language (8) from words 'without meaning' such as occur in Lewis Carroll's poems, or words like "Lilliburlero" in songs.)

14. Imagine someone's saying: "*All* tools serve to modify something. Thus the hammer modifies the position of the nail, the saw the shape of the board, and so on."—And what is modified by the rule, the glue pot, the nails?—"Our knowledge of a thing's length, the temperature of the glue, and the solidity of the box."—Would anything be gained by this assimilation of expressions?—

15. The word "to signify" is perhaps used in the most straight-forward way when the object signified is marked with the sign. Suppose that the tools A uses in building bear certain marks. When A shows his assistant such a mark, he brings the tool that has that mark on it.

It is in this and more or less similar ways that a name means and is given to a thing.—It will often prove useful in philosophy to say to ourselves: naming something is like attaching a label to a thing.

16. What about the color samples that A shows to B: are they part of the *language?* Well, it is as you please. They do not belong among the words; yet when I say to someone: "Pronounce the word 'the'", you will count the second "the" as part of the sentence. Yet it has a role just like that of a color sample in language-game (8); that is, it is a sample of what the other is meant to say.

It is most natural, and causes least confusion, to reckon the samples among the instruments of the language.

((Remark on the reflexive pronoun "*this* sentence".))

17. It will be possible to say: In language (8) we have different *kinds of word*. For the functions of the word "slab" and the word "block" are more alike than those of "slab" and "d". But how we group words into kinds will depend on the aim of the classification,—and on our own inclination.

Think of the different points of view from which one can classify tools or chessmen.

18. Do not be troubled by the fact that languages (2) and (8) consist only of orders. If you want to say that this shows them to be incomplete, ask yourself whether our language is complete;—whether it was so before the symbolism of chemistry and the notation of the infinitesimal calculus were incorporated in it; for these are, so to speak, suburbs of our language. (And how many houses or streets does it take before a town begins to be a town?) Our language can be seen as an ancient city: a maze of little streets and squares, of old and new houses, and of houses with additions from various periods; and this surrounded by a multitude of new boroughs with straight regular streets and uniform houses.

19. It is easy to imagine a language consisting only of orders and reports in battle.—Or a language consisting only of questions and expressions for answering yes and no. And innumerable others.—And to imagine a language means to imagine a form of life.

But what about this: is the call "Slab!" in example (2) a sentence or a word?—If a word, surely it has not the same meaning as the like-sounding word of our ordinary language, for in §2 it is a call. But if a sentence, it is surely not the elliptical sentence: "Slab!" of our language.—As far as the first question goes you can call "Slab!" a word and also a sentence; perhaps it could be appropriately called a 'degenerate sentence' (as one speaks of a degenerate hyperbola); in fact it *is* our 'elliptical' sentence.—But that is surely only a shortened form of the sentence "Bring me a slab", and there is no such sentence in example (2).—But why should I not on the contrary have called the sentence "Bring me a slab" a *lengthening* of the sentence "Slab!"?—Because if you shout "Slab!" you really mean: "Bring me a slab".—But how do you do this: how do you *mean that* while you *say* "Slab!"? Do you say the unshortened sentence to yourself? And why should I translate the call "Slab!" into a different expression in order to say what someone means by it? And if they mean the same thing—why should I not say: "When he says 'Slab!' he means 'Slab!'"? Again, if you can mean "Bring me the slab", why should you not be able to mean "Slab!"?—But when I call "Slab!", then what I want is, *that he should bring me a slab!*—Certainly, but does 'wanting this' consist in thinking in some form or other a different sentence from the one you utter?—

20. But now it looks as if when someone says "Bring me a slab" he could mean this expression as *one* long word corresponding to the single word "Slab!"—Then can one mean it sometimes as one word and sometimes as four? And how does one usually mean it?—I think we shall be inclined to say: we mean the sentence as *four* words when we use it in contrast with other sentences such as "*Hand* me a slab", "Bring *him* a slab", "Bring *two* slabs", etc.; that is, in contrast with sentences containing the separate words of our command in other combinations.—But what does using one sentence in contrast with others consist in? Do the others, perhaps, hover before one's mind? *All* of them? And *while* one is saying the one sentence, or before, or afterwards?—No. Even if such an explanation rather tempts us, we need only think for a moment of what actually happens in order to see that we are going astray here. We say that we use the command in contrast with other sentences because *our language* contains the possibility of those other sentences. Someone who did not understand our language, a foreigner, who had fairly often heard someone giving the order: "Bring me a slab!", might believe that this whole series of sounds was one word corresponding perhaps to the word for "building stone" in his language. If he himself had then given this order perhaps he would have pronounced it differently, and we should say: he pronounces it so oddly because he takes it for a *single* word.—But then, is there not also something different going on in him when he pronounces it,—something corresponding to the fact that he conceives the sentence as a *single* word?—Either the same thing may go on in him, or something different. For what goes on in you when you give such an order? Are you conscious of its consisting of four words *while* you are uttering it? Of course you have a *mastery* of this language—which contains those other sentences as well—but is this having a mastery something that *happens* while you are uttering the sentence?—And I have admitted that the foreigner will probably pronounce a sentence differently if he conceives it differently; but what we call his wrong conception *need* not lie in anything that accompanies the utterance of the command.

The sentence is 'elliptical', not because it leaves out something that we think when we utter it, but because it is shortened—in comparison with a particular paradigm of our grammar.—Of course one might object here: "You grant that the shortened and the unshortened sentence have the same sense.—What is this sense, then? Isn't there a verbal expression for this sense?"—But doesn't the fact that sentences have the same sense consist in their having the same *use*?—(In Russian one says "stone red" instead of "the stone is red"; do they feel the copula to be missing in the sense, or attach it in *thought*?)

21. Imagine a language-game in which A asks and B reports the number of slabs or blocks in a pile, or the colors and shapes of the building stones that are stacked in such-and-such a place.—Such a report might run: "Five slabs". Now what is the difference between the report or statement "Five slabs" and the order "Five slabs!"?—Well, it is the part which uttering these words plays in the language-game. No doubt the tone of voice and the look with which they are uttered, and much else besides, will also be different. But we could also imagine the tone's being the same—for an order and a report can be spoken in a *variety* of tones of voice and with various expressions of face—the difference being only in the application. (Of course, we might use the words "statement" and "command" to stand for grammatical forms of sentence and intonations; we do in fact call "Isn't the weather glorious today?" a question, although it is used as a statement.) We could imagine a language in which *all* statements had the form and tone of rhetorical questions; or every command the form of the question "Would you like to . . . ?" Perhaps it will then be said: "What he says has the form of a question but is really a command"—that is, has the function of a command in the technique of using the language. (Similarly one says "You will do this" not as a prophecy but as a command. What makes it the one or the other?)

22. Frege's idea that every assertion contains an assumption, which is the thing that is asserted, really rests on the possibility found in our language of writing every statement in the form: "It is asserted that such-and-such is the case."—But "that such-and-such is the case" is *not* a sentence in our language—so far it is not a *move* in the language-game. And if I write, not "It is asserted that . . .", but "It is asserted: such-and-such is the case", the words "It is asserted" simply become superfluous.

We might very well also write every statement in the form of a question followed by a "Yes"; for instance: "Is it raining? Yes!" Would this show that every statement contained a question?

Of course we have the right to use an assertion sign in contrast with a question mark, for example, or if we want to distinguish an assertion from a fiction or a supposition. It is only a mistake if one thinks that the assertion consists of two actions, entertaining and asserting (assigning the truth-value, or something of the kind), and that in performing these actions we follow the propositional sign roughly as we sing from the musical score. Reading the written sentence loud or soft is indeed comparable with singing from a musical score, but '*meaning*' (thinking) the sentence that is read is not.

Frege's assertion sign marks the *beginning of the sentence*. Thus its function is like that of the full-stop. It distinguishes the whole period from a clause *within* the period. If I hear someone say "it's raining" but do not know whether I have heard the beginning and end of the period, so far this sentence does not serve to tell me anything.

23. But how many kinds of sentence are there? Say assertion, question, and command?—There are *countless* kinds: countless different kinds of use of what we call "symbols", "words", "sentences". And this multiplicity is not something fixed, given once for all; but new types of language, new language-games, as we may say, come into existence, and others become obsolete and get forgotten. (We can get a *rough picture* of this from the changes in mathematics.)

Here the term "language-*game*" is meant to bring into prominence the fact that the *speaking* of language is part of an activity, or of a form of life.

Review the multiplicity of language-games in the following examples, and in others:

Giving orders, and obeying them—

Describing the appearance of an object, or giving its measurements—

Constructing an object from a description (a drawing)—

Reporting an event—

Speculating about an event—

Forming and testing a hypothesis—

Presenting the results of an experiment in tables and diagrams—

Making up a story; and reading it—

Playacting—

Singing catches—

Guessing riddles—

Making a joke; telling it—

Solving a problem in practical arithmetic—

Translating from one language into another—

Asking, thanking, cursing, greeting, praying.

—It is interesting to compare the multiplicity of the tools in language and of the ways they are used, the multiplicity of kinds of word and sentence, with what logicians have said about the structure of language. (Including the author of the *Tractatus Logico-Philosophicus.*)

• • •

65. Here we come up against the great question that lies behind all these considerations.—For someone might object against me: "You take the easy way out! You talk about all sorts of language-games, but have nowhere said what the essence of a language-game, and hence of language, is: what is common to all these activities, and what makes them into language or parts of language. So you let yourself off the very part of the investigation that once gave you yourself most headache, the part about the *general form of propositions* and of language."

And this is true.—Instead of producing something common to all that we call language, I am saying that these phenomena have no one thing in common which makes us use the same word for all,—but that they are *related* to one another in many different ways. And it is because of this relationship, or these relationships, that we call them all "language". I will try to explain this.

66. Consider for example the proceedings that we call "games". I mean board games, card games, ball games, Olympic games, and so on. What is common to them all?—Don't say: "There *must* be something common, or they would not be called 'games'"—but *look and see* whether there is anything common to all.—For if you look at them you will not see something that is

common to *all,* but similarities, relationships, and a whole series of them at that. To repeat: don't think, but look!—Look for example at board games, with their multifarious relationships. Now pass to card games; here you find many correspondences with the first group, but many common features drop out, and others appear. When we pass next to ball games, much that is common is retained, but much is lost.—Are they all 'amusing'? Compare chess with noughts and crosses. Or is there always winning and losing, or competition between players? Think of patience. In ball games there is winning and losing; but when a child throws his ball at the wall and catches it again, this feature has disappeared. Look at the parts played by skill and luck; and at the difference between skill in chess and skill in tennis. Think now of games like ring-a-ring-a-roses; here is the element of amusement, but how many other characteristic features have disappeared! And we can go through the many, many other groups of games in the same way; can see how similarities crop up and disappear.

And the result of this examination is: we see a complicated network of similarities overlapping and crisscrossing: sometimes overall similarities, sometimes similarities of detail.

67. I can think of no better expression to characterize these similarities than "family resemblances"; for the various resemblances between members of a family: build, features, color of eyes, gait, temperament, etc. etc. overlap and criss-cross in the same way.—And I shall say: 'games' form a family.

And for instance the kinds of number form a family in the same way. Why do we call something a "number"? Well, perhaps because it has a—direct—relationship with several things that have hitherto been called number; and this can be said to give it an indirect relationship to other things we call the same name. And we extend our concept of number as in spinning a thread we twist fiber on fiber. And the strength of the thread does not reside in the fact that some one fiber runs through its whole length, but in the overlapping of many fibers.

But if someone wished to say: "There is something common to all these constructions—namely the disjunction of all their common properties"—I should reply: Now you are only playing with words. One might as well say: "Something runs through the whole thread—namely the continuous overlapping of those fibers".

• • •

71. One might say that the concept 'game' is a concept with blurred edges.—"But is a blurred concept a concept at all?"—Is an indistinct photograph a picture of a person at all? Is it even always an advantage to replace an indistinct picture by a sharp one? Isn't the indistinct one often exactly what we need?

Frege compares a concept to an area and says that an area with vague boundaries cannot be called an area at all. This presumably means that we cannot do anything with it.—But is it senseless to say: "Stand roughly there"? Suppose that I were standing with someone in a city square and said that. As I say it I do not draw any kind of boundary, but perhaps point with my hand—as if I were indicating a particular *spot*. And this is just how one might explain to someone what a game is. One gives examples and intends them to be taken in a particular way.—I do not, however, mean by this that he is supposed to see in those examples that common thing which I—for some reason—was unable to express; but that he is now to *employ* those examples in a particular way. Here giving examples is not an *indirect* means of explaining—in default of a better. For any general definition can be misunderstood too. The point is that *this* is how we play the game. (I mean the language-game with the word "game".)

• • •

116. When philosophers use a word—"knowledge", "being", "object", "I", "proposition", "name"—and try to grasp the *essence* of the thing, one must always ask oneself: is the word ever actually used in this way in the language-game which is its original home?—

What *we* do is to bring words back from their metaphysical to their everyday use.

• • •

118. Where does our investigation get its importance from, since it seems only to destroy everything interesting, that is, all that is great and important? (As it were all the buildings, leaving behind only bits of stone and rubble.) What we are destroying is nothing but houses of cards and we are clearing up the ground of language on which they stand.

119. The results of philosophy are the uncovering of one or another piece of plain nonsense and of bumps that the understanding has got by running its head up against the limits of language. These bumps make us see the value of the discovery.

• • •

122. A main source of our failure to understand is that we do not *command a clear view* of the use of our words.—Our grammar is lacking in this sort of perspicuity. A perspicuous representation produces just that understanding which consists in 'seeing connections'. Hence the importance of finding and inventing *intermediate cases.*

The concept of a perspicuous representation is of fundamental significance for us. It earmarks the form of account we give, the way we look at things. (Is this a 'Weltanschauung'?)

123. A philosophical problem has the form: "I don't know my way about".

124. Philosophy may in no way interfere with the actual use of language; it can in the end only describe it.

For it cannot give it any foundation either.

It leaves everything as it is.

It also leaves mathematics as it is, and no mathematical discovery can advance it. A "leading problem of mathematical logic" is for us a problem of mathematics like any other.

125. It is the business of philosophy, not to resolve a contradiction by means of a mathematical or logico-mathematical discovery, but to make it possible for us to get a clear view of the state of mathematics that troubles us: the state of affairs *before* the contradiction is resolved. (And this does not mean that one is sidestepping a difficulty.)

The fundamental fact here is that we lay down rules, a technique, for a game, and that then when we follow the rules, things do not turn out as we had assumed. That we are therefore as it were entangled in our own rules.

This entanglement in our rules is what we want to understand (i.e., get a clear view of).

It throws light on our concept of *meaning* something. For in those cases things turn out otherwise than we had meant, foreseen. That is just what we say when, for example, a contradiction appears: "I didn't mean it like that."

The civil status of a contradiction, or its status in civil life: there is the philosophical problem.

126. Philosophy simply puts everything before us, and neither explains nor deduces anything.—Since everything lies open to view there is nothing to explain. For what is hidden, for example, is of no interest to us.

One might also give the name "philosophy" to what is possible *before* all new discoveries and inventions.

127. The work of the philosopher consists in assembling reminders for a particular purpose.

128. If one tried to advance *theses* in philosophy, it would never be possible to debate them, because everyone would agree to them.

129. The aspects of things that are most important for us are hidden because of their simplicity and familiarity. (One is unable to notice something—because it is always before one's eyes.) The real foundations of his enquiry do not strike a man at all. Unless *that* fact has at some time struck him.—And this means: we fail to be struck by what, once seen, is most striking and most powerful.

130. Our clear and simple language-games are not preparatory studies for a future regularization of language—as it were first approximations, ignoring friction and air-resistance. The language-games are rather set up as *objects of comparison* which are meant to throw light on the facts of our language by way not only of similarities, but also of dissimilarities.

131. For we can avoid ineptness or emptiness in our assertions only by presenting the model as what it is, as an object of comparison—as, so to speak, a measuring rod; not as a preconceived idea to which reality *must* correspond. (The dogmatism into which we fall so easily in doing philosophy.)

132. We want to establish an order in our knowledge of the use of language: an order with a particular end in view; one out of many possible orders; not *the* order. To this end we shall constantly be giving prominence to distinctions which our ordinary forms of language easily make us overlook. This may make it look as if we saw it as our task to reform language.

Such a reform for particular practical purposes, an improvement in our terminology designed to prevent misunderstandings in practice, is perfectly possible. But these are not the cases we have to do with. The confusions which occupy us arise when language is like an engine idling, not when it is doing work.

133. It is not our aim to refine or complete the system of rules for the use of our words in unheard-of ways.

For the clarity that we are aiming at is indeed *complete* clarity. But this simply means that the philosophical problems should *completely* disappear.

The real discovery is the one that makes me capable of stopping doing philosophy when I want to.—The one that gives philosophy peace, so that it is no longer tormented by questions which bring *itself* in question.—Instead, we now demonstrate a method, by examples; and the series of examples can be broken off.—Problems are solved (difficulties eliminated), not a *single* problem.

There is not *a* philosophical method, though there are indeed methods, like different therapies.

• • •

143. Let us now examine the following kind of language-game: when A gives an order B has to write down series of signs according to a certain formation rule.

The first of these series is meant to be that of the natural numbers in decimal notation.—How does he get to understand this notation?—First of all series of numbers will be written down for him and he will be required to copy them. (Do not balk at the expression "series of numbers"; it is not being used wrongly here.) And here already there is a normal and an abnormal learner's reaction.—At first perhaps we guide his hand in writing out the series 0 to 9; but then the *possibility of getting him to understand* will depend on his going on to write it down independently.—And here we can imagine, e.g., that he does copy the figures independently, but not in the right order: he writes sometimes one sometimes another at random. And then communication stops at *that* point.—Or again, he makes 'mistakes' in the order.—The difference between this and the first case will of course be one of frequency.—Or he makes a *systematic* mistake; for example, he copies every other number, or he copies the series 0, 1, 2, 3, 4, 5, . . . like this: 1, 0, 3, 2, 5, 4,. . . . Here we shall almost be tempted to say that he has understood *wrong*.

Notice, however, that there is no sharp distinction between a random mistake and a systematic one. That is, between what you are inclined to call "random" and what "systematic".

Perhaps it is possible to wean him from the systematic mistake (as from a bad habit). Or perhaps one accepts his way of copying and tries to teach him ours as an offshoot, a variant of his.—And here too our pupil's capacity to learn may come to an end.

144. What do I mean when I say "the pupil's capacity to learn *may* come to an end here"? Do I say this from my own experience? Of course not. (Even if I have had such experience.) Then what am I doing with that proposition? Well, I should like you to say: "Yes, it's true, you can imagine that too, that might happen too!"—But was I trying to draw someone's attention to the fact that he is capable of imagining that?—I wanted to put that picture before him, and his *acceptance* of the picture consists in his now being inclined to regard a given case differently: that is, to compare it with *this* rather than *that* set of pictures. I have changed his *way of looking at things*. (Indian mathematicians: "Look at this.")

145. Suppose the pupil now writes the series 0 to 9 to our satisfaction.—And this will only be the case when he is often successful, not if he does it right once in a hundred attempts. Now I continue the series and draw his attention to the recurrence of the first series in the units; and then to its recurrence in the tens. (Which only means that I use particular emphases, underline figures, write them one under another in such-and-such ways, and similar things.)—And now at some point he continues the series independently—or he does not.—But why do you say that? *so* much is obvious!—Of course; I only wished to say: the effect of any further *explanation* depends on his *reaction*.

Now, however, let us suppose that after some efforts on the teacher's part he continues the series correctly, that is, as we do it. So now we can say he has mastered the system.—But how far need he continue the series for us to have the right to say that? Clearly you cannot state a limit here.

146. Suppose I now ask: "Has he understood the system when he continues the series to the hundredth place?" Or—if I should not speak of 'understanding' in connection with our primitive language-game: Has he got the system, if he continues the series correctly so far?—Perhaps you will say here: to have got the system (or, again, to understand it) can't consist in continuing the series up to *this* or *that* number: *that* is only applying one's understanding. The understanding itself is a state which is the *source* of the correct use.

What is one really thinking of here? Isn't one thinking of the derivation of a series from its algebraic formula?

Or at least of something analogous?—But this is where we were before. The point is, we can think of more than *one* application of an algebraic formula; and every type of application can in turn be formulated algebraically; but naturally this does not get us any further.—The application is still a criterion of understanding.

147. "But how can it be? When *I* say I understand the rule of a series, I am surely not saying so because I have *found out* that up to now I have applied the algebraic formula in such-and-such a way! In my own case at all events I surely know that I mean such-and-such a series; it doesn't matter how far I have actually developed it."—

Your idea, then, is that you know the application of the rule of the series quite apart from remembering actual applications to particular numbers. And you will perhaps say: "Of course! For the series is infinite and the bit of it that I can have developed finite."

148. But what does this knowledge consist in? Let me ask: *When* do you know that application? Always? day and night? or only when you are actually thinking of the rule? do you know it, that is, in the same way as you know the alphabet and the multiplication table? Or is what you call "knowledge" a state of consciousness or a process—say a thought of something, or the like?

149. If one says that knowing the ABC is a state of the mind, one is thinking of a state of a mental apparatus (perhaps of the brain) by means of which we explain the *manifestations* of that knowledge. Such a state is called a disposition. But there are objections to speaking of a state of the mind here, inasmuch as there ought to be two different criteria for such a state: a knowledge of the construction of the apparatus, quite apart from what it does. (Nothing would be more confusing here than to use the words "conscious" and "unconscious" for the contrast between states of consciousness and dispositions. For this pair of terms covers up a grammatical difference.)

150. The grammar of the word "knows" is evidently closely related to that of "can", "is able to". But also closely related to that of "understands". ('Mastery' of a technique.)

151. But there is also *this* use of the word "to know": we say "Now I know!"—and similarly "Now I can do it!" and "Now I understand!"

Let us imagine the following example: A writes series of numbers down; B watches him and tries to find a law for the sequence of numbers. If he succeeds he exclaims: "Now I can go on!"—So this capacity, this understanding, is something that makes its appearance in a moment. So let us try and see what it is that makes its appearance here.—A has written down the numbers 1, 5, 11, 19, 29; at this point B says he knows how to go on. What happened here? Various things may have happened; for example, while A was slowly putting one number after another, B was occupied with trying various algebraic formulas on the numbers which had been written down. After A had written the number 19 B tried the formula $a_n = n^2 + n - 1$; and the next number confirmed his hypothesis.

Or again, B does not think of formulas. He watches A writing his numbers down with a certain feeling of tension, and all sorts of vague thoughts go through his head. Finally he asks himself: "What is the series of differences?" He finds the series 4, 6, 8, 10 and says: Now I can go on.

Or he watches and says "Yes, I know *that* series"—and continues it, just as he would have done if A had written down the series I, 3, 5, 7, 9.—Or he says nothing at all and simply continues the series. Perhaps he had what may be called the sensation "that's easy!". (Such a sensation is, for example, that of a light quick intake of breath, as when one is slightly startled.)

152. But are the processes which I have described here *understanding*?

"B understands the principle of the series" surely doesn't mean simply: the formula "$a_n = \ldots$" occurs to B. For it is perfectly imaginable that the formula should occur to him and that he should nevertheless not understand. "He understands" must have more in it than: the formula occurs to him. And equally, more than any of those more or less characteristic *accompaniments* or manifestations of understanding.

153. We are trying to get hold of the mental process of understanding which seems to be hidden behind those coarser and therefore more readily visible accompaniments. But we do not succeed; or, rather, it does not get as far as a real attempt. For even supposing I had found something that happened in all those cases of understanding,—why should *it* be the understanding? And how can the process of understanding have been hidden, when I said "Now I understand" *because* I understood?! And if I say it is hidden—then how do I know what I have to look for? I am in a muddle.

154. But wait—if "Now I understand the principle" does not mean the same as "The formula . . . occurs to

me" (or "I say the formula", "I write it down", etc.)—does it follow from this that I employ the sentence "Now I understand . . ." or "Now I can go on" as a description of a process occurring behind or side by side with that of saying the formula?

If there has to be anything 'behind the utterance of the formula' it is *particular circumstances,* which justify me in saying I can go on—when the formula occurs to me.

Try not to think of understanding as a 'mental process' at all.—For *that* is the expression which confuses you. But ask yourself: in what sort of case, in what kind of circumstances, do we say, "Now I know how to go on," when, that is, the formula *has* occurred to me?—

In the sense in which there are processes (including mental processes) which are characteristic of understanding, understanding is not a mental process.

(A pain's growing more and less; the hearing of a tune or a sentence: these are mental processes.)

• • •

199. Is what we call "obeying a rule" something that it would be possible for only *one* man to do, and to do only *once* in his life?—This is of course a note on the grammar of the expression "to obey a rule".

It is not possible that there should have been only one occasion on which someone obeyed a rule. It is not possible that there should have been only one occasion on which a report was made, an order given or understood; and so on.—To obey a rule, to make a report, to give an order, to play a game of chess, are *customs* (uses, institutions).

To understand a sentence means to understand a language. To understand a language means to be master of a technique.

200. It is, of course, imaginable that two people belonging to a tribe unacquainted with games should sit at a chess-board and go through the moves of a game of chess; and even with all the appropriate mental accompaniments. And if *we* were to see it we should say they were playing chess. But now imagine a game of chess translated according to certain rules into a series of actions which we do not ordinarily associate with a *game*—say into yells and stamping of feet. And now suppose those two people to yell and stamp instead of playing the form of chess that we are used to; and this in such a way that their procedure is translatable by

suitable rules into a game of chess. Should we still be inclined to say they were playing a game? What right would one have to say so?

201. This was our paradox: no course of action could be determined by a rule, because every course of action can be made out to accord with the rule. The answer was: if everything can be made out to accord with the rule, then it can also be made out to conflict with it. And so there would be neither accord nor conflict here.

It can be seen that there is a misunderstanding here from the mere fact-that in the course of our argument we give one interpretation after another; as if each one contented us at least for a moment, until we thought of yet another standing behind it. What this shows is that there is a way of grasping a rule which is *not an interpretation,* but which is exhibited in what we call "obeying the rule" and "going against it" in actual cases.

Hence there is an inclination to say: every action according to the rule is an interpretation. But we ought to restrict the term "interpretation" to the substitution of one expression of the rule for another.

202. And hence also 'obeying a rule' is a practice. And to *think* one is obeying a rule is not to obey a rule. Hence it is not possible to obey a rule 'privately': otherwise thinking one was obeying a rule would be the same thing as obeying it.

• • •

217. "How am I able to obey a rule?"—if this is not a question about causes, then it is about the justification for my following the rule in the way I do.

If I have exhausted the justifications I have reached bedrock, and my spade is turned. Then I am inclined to say: "This is simply what I do."

(Remember that we sometimes demand definitions for the sake not of their content, but of their form. Our requirement is an architectural one; the definition a kind of ornamental coping that supports nothing.)

218. Whence comes the idea that the beginning of a series is a visible section of rails invisibly laid to infinity? Well, we might imagine rails instead of a rule. And infinitely long rails correspond to the unlimited application of a rule.

219. "All the steps are really already taken" means: I no longer have any choice. The rule, once stamped with a particular meaning, traces the lines along which

it is to be followed through the whole of space.—But if something of this sort really were the case, how would it help?

No; my description only made sense if it was to be understood symbolically.—I should have said: *This is how it strikes me.*

When I obey a rule, I do not choose.

I obey the rule *blindly.*

• • •

243. A human being can encourage himself, give himself orders, obey, blame and punish himself; he can ask himself a question and answer it. We could even imagine human beings who spoke only in monologue; who accompanied their activities by talking to themselves.—An explorer who watched them and listened to their talk might succeed in translating their language into ours. (This would enable him to predict these people's actions correctly, for he also hears them making resolutions and decisions.)

But could we also imagine a language in which a person could write down or give vocal expression to his inner experiences—his feelings, moods, and the rest—for his private use?—Well, can't we do so in our ordinary language?—But that is not what I mean. The individual words of this language are to refer to what can only be known to the person speaking; to his immediate private sensations. So another person cannot understand the language.

244. How do words *refer* to sensations?—There doesn't seem to be any problem here; don't we talk about sensations every day, and give them names? But how is the connection between the name and the thing named set up? This question is the same as: how does a human being learn the meaning of the names of sensations?—of the word "pain" for example. Here is one possibility: words are connected with the primitive, the natural, expressions of the sensation and used in their place. A child has hurt himself and he cries; and then adults talk to him and teach him exclamations and, later, sentences. They teach the child new pain-behavior.

"So you are saying that the word 'pain' really means crying?"—On the contrary: the verbal expression of pain replaces crying and does not describe it.

245. For how can I go so far as to try to use language to get between pain and its expression?

246. In what sense are my sensations *private*?—Well, only I can know whether I am really in pain; another person can only surmise it.—In one way this is wrong, and in another nonsense. If we are using the word "to know" as it is normally used (and how else are we to use it?), then other people very often know when I am in pain.—Yes, but all the same not with the certainty with which I know it myself!—It can't be said of me at all (except perhaps as a joke) that I *know* I am in pain. What is it supposed to mean—except perhaps that I *am* in pain?

Other people cannot be said to learn of my sensations *only* from my behavior,—for *I* cannot be said to learn of them. I *have* them.

The truth is: it makes sense to say about other people that they doubt whether I am in pain; but not to say it about myself.

• • •

258. Let us imagine the following case. I want to keep a diary about the recurrence of a certain sensation. To this end I associate it with the sign "S" and write this sign in a calendar for every day on which I have the sensation.—I will remark first of all that a definition of the sign cannot be formulated.—But still I can give myself a kind of ostensive definition.—How? Can I point to the sensation? Not in the ordinary sense. But I speak, or write the sign down, and at the same time I concentrate my attention on the sensation—and so, as it were, point to it inwardly.—But what is this ceremony for? for that is all it seems to be! A definition surely serves to establish the meaning of a sign.—Well, that is done precisely by the concentrating of my attention; for in this way I impress on myself the connection between the sign and the sensation.—But "I impress it on myself" can only mean: this process brings it about that I remember the connection *right* in the future. But in the present case I have no criterion of correctness. One would like to say: whatever is going to seem right to me is right. And that only means that here we can't talk about 'right'.

• • •

293. If I say of myself that it is only from my own case that I know what the word "pain" means—must I not say the same of other people too? And how can I generalize the *one* case so irresponsibly?

Now someone tells me that *he* knows what pain is only from his own case!—Suppose everyone had a box with something in it: we call it a "beetle". No one can look into anyone else's box, and everyone says he knows what a beetle is only by looking at *his* beetle.—Here it would be quite possible for everyone to have something different in his box. One might even imagine such a thing constantly changing.—But suppose the word "beetle" had a use in these people's language?—If so it would not be used as the name of a thing. The thing in the box has no place in the language-game at all; not even as a *something*: for the box might even be empty.—No, one can 'divide through' by the thing in the box; it cancels out, whatever it is.

That is to say: if we construe the grammar of the expression of sensation on the model of 'object and designation' the object drops out of consideration as irrelevant.

• • •

304. "But you will surely admit that there is a difference between pain-behavior accompanied by pain and pain-behavior without any pain?"—Admit it? What greater difference could there be?—"And yet you again and again reach the conclusion that the sensation itself is a *nothing*."—Not at all. It is not a *something*, but not a *nothing* either! The conclusion was only that a nothing would serve just as well as a something about which nothing could be said. We have only rejected the grammar which tries to force itself on us here.

The paradox disappears only if we make a radical break with the idea that language always functions in one way, always serves the same purpose: to convey thoughts—which may be about houses, pains, good and evil, or anything else you please.

• • •

307. "Are you not really a behaviorist in disguise? Aren't you at bottom really saying that everything except human behavior is a fiction?"—If I do speak of a fiction, then it is of a *grammatical* fiction.

308. How does the philosophical problem about mental processes and states and about behaviorism arise?—The first step is the one that altogether escapes notice. We talk of processes and states and leave their nature undecided. Sometime perhaps we shall know

more about them—we think. But that is just what commits us to a particular way of looking at the matter. For we have a definite concept of what it means to learn to know a process better. (The decisive movement in the conjuring trick has been made, and it was the very one that we thought quite innocent.)—And now the analogy which was to make us understand our thoughts falls to pieces. So we have to deny the yet uncomprehended process in the yet unexplored medium. And now it looks as if we had denied mental processes. And naturally we don't want to deny them.

309. What is your aim in philosophy?—To show the fly the way out of the fly bottle.

READING QUESTIONS

§1–§23: *The Augustinian Theory of Language*

1. Commenting on Augustine's remarks about language learning, Wittgenstein writes in §3 that he "does describe a system of communication, only not everything that we call language is this system." What are some aspects of language which are not captured by Augustine's picture of the essence of human language?

2. What does Wittgenstein mean by the term "language-game" (see §7 and §23 in particular)? What sort of understanding of language is Wittgenstein out to reject?

3. Carefully examine the simple language in §8. In commenting on the workings of this language, Wittgenstein suggests that we "think of the tools in a toolbox: there is a hammer, pliers, a saw, a screwdriver, a rule, a glue pot, glue, nails, and screws.—The functions of words are as diverse as the functions of these objects" (§11). What is the significance of this remark? What larger point is he making about language?

§65–§67 and §71: *Essence and Resemblance*

4. When Wittgenstein remarks that the similarities between various games are like "family resemblances," what does he mean? What view of the nature of games (and of language) is he rejecting?

5. Wittgenstein remarks that "one might say that the concept 'game' is a concept with blurred edges." And he then considers the objection, "but is a blurred concept a concept at all?" What is his reply to this objection?

§116, §118–§119, and §122–§133: *Wittgenstein's Conception of Philosophy*

6. When Wittgenstein states that "what *we* do is to bring words back from their metaphysical to their everyday use" (§116), what does he mean? How is this related to his remark that "if one tried to advance *theses* in philosophy, it would never be possible to question them, because everyone would agree to them" (§128)?

7. Wittgenstein claims in §125 that the "entanglement in our rules is what we want to understand (i.e., get a clear view of)." In what way is this conception of philosophy different from others that you are familiar with?

8. After reviewing his various remarks in these sections, compose a short essay outlining Wittgenstein's conception of philosophy. Specifically address his remark that "philosophy may in no way interfere with the actual use of language; it can in the end only describe it" (§124) and with his remark that "philosophy simply puts everything before us, and neither explains nor deduces anything.—Since everything lies open to view there is nothing to explain" (§126).

§143–§154: *What Is Understanding?*

9. Wittgenstein imagines a situation in which we are trying to teach a pupil the system of natural numbers. The question is, when does the student *understand*? Furthermore, in what does that understanding *consist*? What answers to these questions does Wittgenstein reject? Why?

10. Wittgenstein says that "the grammar of the word 'knows' is closely related to that of 'can', 'is able to' [but] also closely related to that of 'understands'." What does he mean? In what ways are the 'grammar' of these expressions related?

11. "We are trying to get hold of the mental process of understanding which seems to be hidden behind those coarser and therefore more readily available ac-

companiments" (§153). What are these accompaniments that Wittgenstein is talking about? Why does he continue by saying "even supposing I had found something that happened in all those cases of understanding,—why should *it* be the understanding?"

12. In §154 Wittgenstein advances a suggestion as to how to think about what 'understanding' consists in. What is his suggestion? What is your reaction to this suggestion?

§199–§202 and §217–§219: *Understanding and Rule Following*

13. At §199, Wittgenstein asks "is what we call 'obeying a rule' something that it would be possible for only *one* man to do, and to do only *once* in his life?" He answers by saying "it is not possible that there should have been only one occasion on which someone obeyed a rule . . . To obey a rule, to make a report, to give an order, to play a game of chess, are *customs* (uses, institutions)." Why, specifically, would the fact that obeying a rule is a custom lead one to say that this phenomenon is not possible? (*Hint:* See §201 and §202.)

14. In §219, Wittgenstein concludes that "when I obey a rule, I do not choose. I obey the rule *blindly.*" What does he mean by this? How is this remark related to those that he makes at §202?

§243–§246, §258, §293, §304, and §307–§309: *Pain and the Private Language Argument*

15. "In what sense are my sensations *private?*—Well, only I can know whether I am really in pain; another person can only surmise it.—In one way this is false, and in another nonsense" (§246). In what way does Wittgenstein think that this is false and in what way does he think that it is nonsense?

16. In §258, Wittgenstein writes that in the case where I attempt to keep a diary of my sensations, "I have no criterion of correctness. One would like to say: whatever is going to seem right to me is right. And that only means that here we can't talk about 'right'." Why not?

17. Review §293. What impact does this fact have on what we call *meaning* and *understanding*, according to Wittgenstein?

18. Consider Wittgenstein's remarks at §293 regarding the beetle boxes. In reflecting on this case, he remarks that "if we construe the grammar of the expression of sensation on the model of 'object and name' the object drops out of consideration as irrelevant." What point is he making about sensation? Do you agree? What, then, do we mean by 'pain'?

19. Wittgenstein considers an objection to his view when he writes, "'but you will surely admit that there is a difference between pain-behavior accompanied by pain and pain-behavior without any pain?'—Admit it?" He replies, "What greater difference could there be?—'And yet you again and again reach the conclusion that the sensation itself is a *nothing.*'—Not at all," he continues. "It is not a *something,* but not a *nothing* either! The conclusion was only that a nothing would serve just as well as a something about which nothing could be said." Is this correct? Why or why not?

SUGGESTIONS FOR FURTHER READING (THE LATER WITTGENSTEIN)

Primary Sources

(1912–1951) *Philosophical Occasions,* edited by J. C. Klagge and A. Nordmann. Indianapolis, IN: Hackett, 1993.

(1914–1951) *Culture and Value,* edited by P. Winch. Oxford: Basil Blackwell, 1980.

(1929–1948) *Zettel,* edited by G. E. M. Anscombe and G. H. von Wright, translated by G. E. M. Anscombe. Oxford: Basil Blackwell, 1967.

(1930) *Philosophical Remarks,* edited by R. Rhees, translated by R. Hargreaves and R. White. Oxford: Basil Blackwell, 1975.

(1930–1946) *Philosophical Investigations,* edited by G. E. M. Anscombe and R. Rhees, translated by G. E. M. Anscombe. Oxford: Basil Blackwell, 1953.

(1932–1934) *Philosophical Grammar,* edited by R. Rhees, translated by A. Kenny. Oxford: Basil Blackwell, 1974.

(1933–1935) *The Blue and Brown Books,* edited by R. Rhees. Oxford: Basil Blackwell, 1958.

(1937–1944) *Remarks on the Foundations of Mathematics,* edited by G. H. von Wright, R. Rhees, and G. E. M. Anscombe, translated by G. E. M. Anscombe. Oxford: Basil Blackwell, 1956.

(1938, 1942–1946) *Lectures and Conversations on Aesthetics, Psychology, and Religious Belief,* edited by C. Barrett. Oxford: Basil Blackwell, 1966.

(1948–1951) *On Certainty,* edited by G. E. M. Anscombe and G. H. von Wright, translated by D. Paul and G. E. M. Anscombe. Oxford: Basil Blackwell, 1969.

(1977) *Remarks on Colour,* edited by G. E. M Anscombe, translated by L. L. McAlister and M. Schattle. Oxford: Basil Blackwell.

(1980) *Remarks on the Philosophy of Psychology,* edited by G. H. von Wright and H. Nyman, translated by G. E. M. Anscombe. Oxford: Basil Blackwell.

(1982, 1992) *Last Writings on the Philosophy of Psychology,* edited by G. E. M. Anscombe, G. H. von Wright, and H. Nyman, translated by C. G. Luckhardt and M. A. E. Aue. Oxford: Basil Blackwell.

Secondary Sources

Arrington, R., and H. Glock, eds. (1996) *Wittgenstein and Quine.* New York: Routledge.

Ayer, A. J. (1986) *Wittgenstein.* Chicago, IL: University of Chicago Press.

Baker, G. P., and Hacker, P. M. S. (1980, 1988, 1990, and 1996) *An Analytical Commentary on the Philosophical Investigations,* 4 vols. Oxford: Basil Blackwell.

Block, I., ed. (1981) *Perspectives on the Philosophy of Wittgenstein.* Oxford: Basil Blackwell.

Fogelin, R. (1987) *Wittgenstein,* 2nd ed. London: Routledge.

Glock, H. (1996) *A Wittgenstein Dictionary.* Oxford: Blackwell.

Greyling, A. C. (1988) *Wittgenstein.* Oxford: Oxford University Press.

Hacker, P. M. S. (1996) *Wittgenstein's Place in Twentieth-Century Analytic Philosophy.* Oxford: Blackwell.

———. (1997) *Insight and Illusion,* rev. ed. Bristol: Thoemmes Press.

Hanfling, O. (1989) *Wittgenstein's Later Philosophy.* New York: Macmillan.

Heal, J. (1989) *Fact and Meaning.* Oxford: Basil Blackwell.

Johnston, P. (1993) *Wittgenstein: Rethinking the Inner.* London: Routledge.

Kenny, A. (1973) *Wittgenstein.* Cambridge, MA: Harvard University Press.

Kripke, S. (1982) *Wittgenstein on Rules and Private Language.* Oxford: Basil Blackwell.

Malcolm, N. (1958) *Ludwig Wittgenstein: A Memoir.* Oxford: Oxford University Press.

———. (1986) *Nothing Is Hidden.* Oxford: Blackwell.

———. (1995) *Wittgenstein Themes: Essays, 1978–1989,* edited by G. H. von Wright. Ithaca, NY: Cornell University Press.

McGinn, C. (1984) *Wittgenstein on Meaning.* New York: Basil Blackwell.

Monk, R. (1990) *Wittgenstein: The Duty of Genius.* New York: The Free Press.

Pears, D. (1988) *The False Prison.* Oxford: Oxford University Press.

Pitcher, G., ed. (1966) *Wittgenstein: The Philosophical Investigations.* Garden City, NY: Anchor Books.

Rundle, B. (1990) *Wittgenstein on Language: Meaning, Use, and Truth.* Oxford: Blackwell.

Schulte, J. (1989) *Wittgenstein: An Introduction.* New York: State University of New York Press.

Sluga, H., and D. G. Stern, eds. (1996) *The Cambridge Companion to Wittgenstein.* Cambridge: Cambridge University Press.

Stern, D. (1994) *Wittgenstein on Mind and Language.* Oxford: Oxford University Press.

Thorton, T. (1998) *Wittgenstein on Language and Thought: The Philosophy of Content.* Edinburgh: Edinburgh University Press.

GILBERT RYLE

Descartes' Myth

Gilbert Ryle (1900–1976) was born in Brighton, England, and was educated at Queen's College, Oxford. He began his academic pursuits as a classics scholar, but then settled on pursuing a degree in Oxford's newly established program in philosophy, politics, and economics.

Some of Ryle's earliest and most influential research was related to problems of philosophical methodology. His interest in philosophical analysis prompted him to investigate the works of various contemporary European philosophers in both the phenomenological and analytical traditions, including Meinong, Brentano, Frege, Husserl, and Heidegger, as well as the Cambridge analytic philosophers Bertrand Russell, G. E. Moore, and Ludwig Wittgenstein. One of Ryle's earliest papers, "Systematically Misleading Expressions" (1932), deals exclusively with issues relating to philosophical analysis and to the nature of philosophy. The paper is considered by many to be an early manifesto of the ordinary language movement in philosophy.

His teaching career began at Christ Church, where he taught from 1924 until his involvement began in World War II. Ryle served as an officer in the war, and upon his return to Oxford in 1945, was appointed the Waynflete Professor of Metaphysical Philosophy. Shortly after assuming this position, Ryle and his colleague John Mabbott began organizing a graduate program in philosophy at Oxford. The school became, and for nearly 25 years remained, the major instructional program in Great Britain for professors of philosophy.

In 1949, Ryle published his most influential work, *The Concept of Mind*. In this work he severely criticizes Cartesian-style dualism, referring to its theory of the mind as "the dogma of the Ghost in the Machine." In contrast, Ryle himself advances a behavioristic account of the meaning of 'mental' terms. Ryle's 'logical behaviorism', though extreme from a modern perspective, has been enormously influential on contemporary philosophy of mind, especially on the development of modern functionalist accounts.

Ryle took over as editor of the journal *Mind* in 1947, following the retirement of G. E. Moore. He held the position for many years and had a lasting and positive impact on the success of the journal. Remembered today along with Austin and Wittgenstein as one of the great practitioners of ordinary language philosophy,

Ryle died at the age of 77 while vacationing in Yorkshire, England.

1. The Official Doctrine

There is a doctrine about the nature and place of minds which is so prevalent among theorists and even among laymen that it deserves to be described as the official theory. Most philosophers, psychologists and religious teachers subscribe, with minor reservations, to its main articles and, although they admit certain theoretical difficulties in it, they tend to assume that these can be overcome without serious modifications being made to the architecture of the theory. It will be argued here that the central principles of the doctrine are unsound and conflict with the whole body of what we know about minds when we are not speculating about them.

The official doctrine, which hails chiefly from Descartes, is something like this. With the doubtful exceptions of idiots and infants in arms every human being has both a body and a mind. Some would prefer to say that every human being is both a body and a mind. His body and his mind are ordinarily harnessed together, but after the death of the body his mind may continue to exist and function.

Human bodies are in space and are subject to the mechanical laws which govern all other bodies in space. Bodily processes and states can be inspected by external observers. So a man's bodily life is as much a public affair as are the lives of animals and reptiles and even as the careers of trees, crystals and planets.

But minds are not in space, nor are their operations subject to mechanical laws. The workings of one mind are not witnessable by other observers; its career is private. Only I can take direct cognizance of the states and processes of my own mind. A person therefore lives

Gilbert Ryle, "Descartes' Myth" from his *The Concept of Mind*, London, Hutchinson, 1949, pp. 11–24. Reprinted by permission of Taylor and Francis Books, Ltd.

through two collateral histories, one consisting of what happens in and to his body, the other consisting of what happens in and to his mind. The first is public, the second private. The events in the first history are events in the physical world, those in the second are events in the mental world.

It has been disputed whether a person does or can directly monitor all or only some of the episodes of his own private history; but, according to the official doctrine, of at least some of these episodes he has direct and unchallengeable cognizance. In consciousness, self-consciousness and introspection he is directly and authentically apprised of the present states and operations of his mind. He may have great or small uncertainties about concurrent and adjacent episodes in the physical world, but he can have none about at least part of what is momentarily occupying his mind.

It is customary to express this bifurcation of his two lives and of his two worlds by saying that the things and events which belong to the physical world, including his own body, are external, while the workings of his own mind are internal. This antithesis of outer and inner is of course meant to be construed as a metaphor, since minds, not being in space, could not be described as being spatially inside anything else, or as having things going on spatially inside themselves. But relapses from this good intention are common and theorists are found speculating how stimuli, the physical sources of which are yards or miles outside a person's skin, can generate mental responses inside his skull, or how decisions framed inside his cranium can set going movements of his extremities.

Even when 'inner' and 'outer' are construed as metaphors, the problem of how a person's mind and body influence one another is notoriously charged with theoretical difficulties. What the mind wills, the legs, arms and the tongue execute; what affects the ear and the eye has something to do with what the mind perceives; grimaces and smiles betray the mind's moods and bodily castigations lead, it is hoped, to moral improvement. But the actual transactions between the episodes of the private history and those of the public history remain mysterious, since by definition they can belong to neither series. They could not be reported among the happenings described in a person's autobiography of his inner life, but nor could they be re-

ported among those described in some one else's biography of that person's overt career. They can be inspected neither by introspection nor by laboratory experiment. They are theoretical shuttlecocks which are forever being bandied from the physiologist back to the psychologist and from the psychologist back to the physiologist.

Underlying this partly metaphorical representation of the bifurcation of a person's two lives there is a seemingly more profound and philosophical assumption. It is assumed that there are two different kinds of existence or status. What exists or happens may have the status of physical existence, or it may have the status of mental existence. Somewhat as the faces of coins are either heads or tails, or somewhat as living creatures are either male or female, so, it is supposed, some existing is physical existing, other existing is mental existing. It is a necessary feature of what has physical existence that it is in space and time; it is a necessary feature of what has physical existence that it is in time but not in space. What has physical existence is composed of matter, or else is a function of matter; what has mental existence consists of consciousness, or else is a function of consciousness.

There is thus a polar opposition between mind and matter, an opposition which is often brought out as follows. Material objects are situated in a common field, known as 'space', and what happens to one body in one part of space is mechanically connected with what happens to other bodies in other parts of space. But mental happenings occur in insulated fields, known as 'minds', and there is, apart maybe from telepathy, no direct causal connection between what happens in one mind and what happens in another. Only through the medium of the public physical world can the mind of one person make a difference to the mind of another. The mind is its own place and in his inner life each of us lives the life of a ghostly Robinson Crusoe. People can see, hear and jolt one another's bodies, but they are irremediably blind and deaf to the workings of one another's minds and inoperative upon them.

What sort of knowledge can be secured of the workings of a mind? On the one side, according to the official theory, a person has direct knowledge of the best imaginable kind of the workings of his own mind.

Mental states and processes are (or are normally) conscious states and processes, and the consciousness which irradiates them can engender no illusions and leaves the door open for no doubts. A person's present thinkings, feelings and willings, his perceivings, re-memberings and imaginings are intrinsically 'phospho-rescent'; their existence and their nature are inevitably betrayed to their owner. The inner life is a stream of consciousness of such a sort that it would be absurd to suggest that the mind whose life is that stream might be unaware of what is passing down it.

True, the evidence adduced recently by Freud seems to show that there exist channels tributary to this stream, which run hidden from their owner. People are actuated by impulses the existence of which they vigorously disavow; some of their thoughts differ from the thoughts which they acknowledge; and some of the actions which they think they will to perform they do not really will. They are thoroughly gulled by some of their own hypocrisies and they successfully ignore facts about their mental lives which on the official theory ought to be patent to them. Holders of the official theory tend, however, to maintain that anyhow in normal circumstances a person must be directly and authentically seized of the present state and workings of his own mind.

Besides being currently supplied with these alleged immediate data of consciousness, a person is also generally supposed to be able to exercise from time to time a special kind of perception, namely inner perception, or introspection. He can take a (non-optical) 'look' at what is passing in his mind. Not only can he view and scrutinize a flower through his sense of sight and listen to and discriminate the notes of a bell through his sense of hearing; he can also reflectively or introspectively watch, without any bodily organ of sense, the current episodes of his inner life. This self-observation is also commonly supposed to be immune from illusion, confusion or doubt. A mind's reports of its own affairs have a certainty superior to the best that is possessed by its reports of matters in the physical world. Sense-perceptions can, but consciousness and introspection cannot, be mistaken or confused.

On the other side, one person has no direct access of any sort to the events of the inner life of another. He cannot do better than make problematic inferences from the observed behavior of the other person's body to the states of mind which, by analogy from his own conduct, he supposes to be signalized by that behavior. Direct access to the workings of a mind is the privilege of that mind itself; in default of such privileged access, the workings of one mind are inevitably occult to everyone else. For the supposed arguments from bodily movements similar to their own to mental workings similar to their own would lack any possibility of observational corroboration. Not unnaturally, therefore, an adherent of the official theory finds it difficult to resist this consequence of his premises, that he has no good reason to believe that there do exist minds other than his own. Even if he prefers to believe that to other human bodies there are harnessed minds not unlike his own, he cannot claim to be able to discover their individual characteristics, or the particular things that they undergo and do. Absolute solitude is on this showing the ineluctable destiny of the soul. Only our bodies can meet.

As a necessary corollary of this general scheme there is implicitly prescribed a special way of construing our ordinary concepts of mental powers and operations. The verbs, nouns and adjectives, with which in ordinary life we describe the wits, characters and higher-grade performances of the people with whom we have do, are required to be construed as signifying special episodes in their secret histories, or else as signifying tendencies for such episodes to occur. When someone is described as knowing, believing or guessing something, as hoping, dreading, intending or shirking something, as designing this or being amused at that, these verbs are supposed to denote the occurrence of specific modifications in his (to us) occult stream of consciousness. Only his own privileged access to this stream in direct awareness and introspection could provide authentic testimony that these mental-conduct verbs were correctly or incorrectly applied. The onlooker, be he teacher, critic, biographer or friend, can never assure himself that his comments have any vestige of truth. Yet it was just because we do in fact all know how to make such comments, make them with general correctness and correct them when they turn out to be confused or mistaken, that philosophers found it necessary to construct their theories of the nature and place of minds. Finding mental-conduct concepts being regularly and effectively used, they properly sought to fix their logical geography. But the logical geography officially recommended would entail that there could be no regular or effective use of these mental-conduct concepts in our descriptions of, and prescriptions for, other people's minds.

2. The Absurdity of the Official Doctrine

Such in outline is the official theory. I shall often speak of it, with deliberate abusiveness, as 'the dogma of the ghost in the machine'. I hope to prove that it is entirely false, and false not in detail but in principle. It is not merely an assemblage of particular mistakes. It is one big mistake and a mistake of a special kind. It is, namely, a category-mistake. It represents the facts of mental life as if they belonged to one logical type or category (or range of types of categories), when they actually belong to another. The dogma is therefore a philosopher's myth. In attempting to explode the myth I shall probably be taken to be denying well-known facts about the mental life of human beings, and my plea that I aim at doing nothing more than rectify the logic of mental-conduct concepts will probably be disallowed as mere subterfuge.

I must first indicate what is meant by the phrase 'category-mistake'. This I do in a series of illustrations.

A foreigner visiting Oxford or Cambridge for the first time is shown a number of colleges, libraries, playing fields, museums, scientific departments and administrative offices. He then asks, "But where is the university? I have seen where the members of the colleges live, where the registrar works, where the scientists experiment and the rest. But I have not yet seen the university in which reside and work the members of your university." It has then to be explained to him that the university is not another collateral institution, some ulterior counterpart to the colleges, laboratories and offices which he has seen. The university is just the way in which all that he has already seen is organized. When they are seen and when their coordination is understood, the university has been seen. His mistake lay in his innocent assumption that it was correct to speak of Christ Church, the Bodleian Library, the Ashmolean Museum *and* the university, to speak, that is, as if 'the university' stood for an extra member of the class of

which these other units are members. He was mistakenly allocating the university to the same category as that to which the other institutions belong.

The same mistake would be made by a child witnessing the march-past of a division, who, having had pointed out to him such and such battalions, batteries, squadrons, etc., asked when the division was going to appear. He would be supposing that a division was a counterpart to the units already seen, partly similar to them and partly unlike them. He would be shown his mistake by being told that in watching the battalions, batteries and squadrons marching past he had been watching the division marching past. The march-past was not a parade of battalions, batteries, squadrons *and* a division; it was a parade of the battalions, batteries and squadrons *of* a division.

One more illustration. A foreigner watching his first game of cricket learns what are the functions of the bowlers, the batsmen, the fielders, the umpires and the scorers. He then says, "But there is no one left on the field to contribute the famous element of team spirit. I see who does the bowling, the batting and the wicket-keeping; but I do not see whose role it is to exercise *esprit de corps.*" Once more, it would have to be explained that he was looking for the wrong type of thing. Team spirit is not another cricketing operation supplementary to all of the other special tasks. It is, roughly, the keenness with which each of the special tasks is performed, and performing a task keenly is not performing two tasks. Certainly exhibiting team spirit is not the same thing as bowling or catching, but nor is it a third thing such that we can say that the bowler first bowls *and* then exhibits team spirit or that a fielder is at a given moment *either* catching *or* displaying *esprit de corps.*

These illustrations of category-mistakes have a common feature which must be noticed. The mistakes were made by people who did not know how to wield the concepts *university, division* and *team spirit.* Their puzzles arose from inability to use certain items in the English vocabulary.

The theoretically interesting category-mistakes are those made by people who are perfectly competent to apply concepts, at least in the situations with which they are familiar, but are still liable in their abstract thinking to allocate those concepts to logical types to which they do not belong. An instance of a mistake of this sort would be the following story. A student of politics has learned the main differences between the British, the French and the American constitutions, and has learned also the differences and connections between the cabinet, Parliament, the various ministries, the judicature and the Church of England. But he still becomes embarrassed when asked questions about the connections between the Church of England, the Home Office and the British Constitution. For while the Church and the Home Office are institutions, the British Constitution is not another institution in the same sense of that noun. So inter-institutional relations which can be asserted or denied to hold between the Church and the Home Office cannot be asserted or denied to hold between either of them and the British Constitution. 'The British Constitution' is not a term of the same logical type as 'the Home Office' and 'the Church of England'. In a partially similar way, John Doe may be a relative, a friend, an enemy or a stranger to Richard Roe; but he cannot be any of these things to the Average Taxpayer. He knows how to talk sense in certain sorts of discussions about the Average Taxpayer, but he is baffled to say why he could not come across him in the street as he can come across Richard Roe.

It is pertinent to our main subject to notice that, so long as the student of politics continues to think of the British Constitution as a counterpart to the other institutions, he will tend to describe it as a mysteriously occult institution; and so long as John Doe continues to think of the Average Taxpayer as a fellow citizen, he will tend to think of him as an elusive insubstantial man, a ghost who is everywhere yet nowhere.

My destructive purpose is to show that a family of radical category-mistakes is the source of the double-life theory. The representation of a person as a ghost mysteriously ensconced in a machine derives from this argument. Because, as is true, a person's thinking, feeling and purposive doing cannot be described solely in the idioms of physics, chemistry and physiology, therefore they must be described in counterpart idioms. As the human body is a complex organized unit, so the human mind must be another complex organized unit, though one made of a different sort of stuff and with a different sort of structure. Or, again, as the human body, like any other parcel of matter, is a field of causes and effects, so the mind must be another field of causes

and effects, though not (Heaven be praised) mechanical causes and effects.

3. The Origin of the Category-Mistake

One of the chief intellectual origins of what I have yet to prove to be the Cartesian category-mistake seems to be this. When Galileo showed that his methods of scientific discovery were competent to provide a mechanical theory which should cover every occupant of space, Descartes found in himself two conflicting motives. As a man of scientific genius he could not but endorse the claims of mechanics, yet as a religious and moral man he could not accept, as Hobbes accepted, the discouraging rider to those claims, namely that human nature differs only in degree of complexity from clockwork. The mental could not be just a variety of the mechanical.

He and subsequent philosophers naturally but erroneously availed themselves of the following escape route. Since mental-conduct words are not to be construed as signifying the occurrence of mechanical processes, they must be construed as signifying the occurrence of non-mechanical processes; since mechanical laws explain movements in space as the effects of other movements in space, other laws must explain some of the non-spatial workings of minds as the effects of other-non-spatial workings of minds. The difference between the human behaviors which we describe as intelligent and those which we describe as unintelligent must be a difference in their causation; so, while some movements of human tongues and limbs are the effects of mechanical causes, others must be the effects of non-mechanical causes, i.e., some issue from movements of particles of matter, others from workings of the mind.

The differences between the physical and the mental were thus represented as differences inside the common framework of the categories of 'thing', 'stuff', 'attribute', 'state', 'process', 'change', 'cause' and 'effect'. Minds are things, but different sorts of things from bodies; mental processes are causes and effects, but different sorts of causes and effects from bodily movements. And so on. Somewhat as the foreigner expected the university to be an extra edifice, rather like a college but also considerably different, so the repudiators of mechanism represented minds as extra centers of causal processes, rather like machines but also considerably different from them. Their theory was a para-mechanical hypothesis.

That this assumption was at the heart of the doctrine is shown by the fact that there was from the beginning felt to be a major theoretical difficulty in explaining how minds can influence and be influenced by bodies. How can a mental process, such as willing, cause spatial movements like the movements of the tongue? How can a physical change in the optic nerve have among its effects a mind's perception of a flash of light? This notorious crux by itself shows the logical mold into which Descartes pressed his theory of the mind. It was the self-same mold into which he and Galileo set their mechanics. Still unwittingly adhering to the grammar of mechanics, he tried to avert disaster by describing minds in what was merely an obverse vocabulary. The workings of minds had to be described by the mere negatives of the specific descriptions given to bodies; they are not in space, they are not motions, they are not modifications of matter, they are not accessible to public observation. Minds are not bits of clockwork, they are just bits of not-clockwork.

As thus represented, minds are not merely ghosts harnessed to machines, they are themselves just spectral machines. Though the human body is an engine, it it not quite an ordinary engine, since some of its workings are governed by another engine inside it—this interior governor-engine being one of a very special sort. It is invisible, inaudible and it has no size or weight. It cannot be taken to bits and the laws it obeys are not those known to ordinary engineers. Nothing is known of how it governs the bodily engine.

A second major crux points the same moral. Since, according to the doctrine, minds belong to the same category as bodies and since bodies are rigidly governed by mechanical laws, it seemed to many theorists to follow that minds must be similarly governed by rigid non-mechanical laws. The physical world is a deterministic system, so the mental world must be a deterministic system. Bodies cannot help the modifications that they undergo, so minds cannot help pursuing the careers fixed for them. *Responsibility, choice, merit* and *demerit* are therefore inapplicable concepts—unless the compromise solution is adopted of saying that the laws governing mental processes, unlike those governing physical processes, have the congenial attribute of being

only rather rigid. The problem of the freedom of the will was the problem how to reconcile the hypothesis that minds are to be described in terms drawn from the categories of mechanics with the knowledge that higher-grade human conduct is not of a piece with the behavior of machines.

It is a historical curiosity that it was not noticed that the entire argument was broken-backed. Theorists correctly assumed that any sane man could already recognize the differences between, say, rational and non-rational utterances or between purposive and automatic behavior. Else there would have been nothing requiring to be salved from mechanism. Yet the explanation given presupposed that one person could in principle never recognize the difference between the rational and the irrational utterances issuing from other human bodies, since he could never get access to the postulated immaterial causes of some of their utterances. Save for the doubtful exception of himself, he could never tell the difference between a man and a robot. It would have to be conceded, for example, that, for all that we can tell, the inner lives of persons who are classed as idiots or lunatics are as rational as those of anyone else. Perhaps only their overt behavior is disappointing; that is to say, perhaps 'idiots' are not really idiotic, or 'lunatics' lunatic. Perhaps, too, some of those who are classed as sane are really idiots. According to the theory, external observers could never know how the overt behavior of others is correlated with their mental powers and processes and so they could never know or even plausibly conjecture whether their applications of mental-conduct concepts to these other people were correct or incorrect. It would then be hazardous or impossible for a man to claim sanity or logical consistency even for himself, since he would be debarred from comparing his own performances with those of others. In short, our characterizations of persons and their performances as intelligent, prudent and virtuous or as stupid, hypocritical and cowardly could never have been made, so the problem of providing a special causal hypothesis to serve as the basis of such diagnoses would never have arisen. The question, "How do persons differ from machines?" arose just because everyone already knew how to apply mental-conduct concepts before the new causal hypothesis was introduced. This causal hypothesis could not therefore be the source of the criteria used in those applications. Nor, of course, has the casual hypothesis in any degree improved our handling of those criteria. We still distinguish good from bad arithmetic, politic from impolitic conduct and fertile from infertile imaginations in the ways in which Descartes himself distinguished them before and after he speculated how the applicability of these criteria was compatible with the principle of mechanical causation.

He had mistaken the logic of his problem. Instead of asking by what criteria intelligent behavior is actually distinguished from non-intelligent behavior, he asked, "Given that the principle of mechanical causation does not tell us the difference, what other causal principle will tell it us?" He realized that the problem was not one of mechanics and assumed that it must therefore be one of some counterpart to mechanics. Not unnaturally psychology is often cast for just this role.

When two terms belong to the same category, it is proper to construct conjunctive propositions embodying them. Thus a purchaser may say that he bought a left-hand glove and a right-hand glove, but not that he bought a left-hand glove, a right-hand glove and a pair of gloves. 'She came home in a flood of tears and a sedan-chair' is a well-known joke based on the absurdity of conjoining terms of different types. It would have been equally ridiculous to construct the disjunction 'She came home either in a flood of tears or else in a sedan-chair'. Now the dogma of the ghost in the machine does just this. It maintains that there exist both bodies and minds; that there occur physical processes and mental processes; that there are mechanical causes of corporeal movements and mental causes of corporeal movements. I shall argue that these and other analogous conjunctions are absurd; but, it must be noticed, the argument will not show that either of the illegitimately conjoined propositions is absurd in itself. I am not, for example, denying that there occur mental processes. Doing long division is a mental process and so is making a joke. But I am saying that the phrase 'there occur mental processes' does not mean the same sort of thing as 'there occur physical processes', and, therefore, that it makes no sense to conjoin or disjoin the two.

If my argument is successful, there will follow some interesting consequences. First, the hallowed contrast between mind and matter will be dissipated, but dissipated not by either of the equally hallowed adsorptions of mind by matter or of matter by mind, but in quite a different way. For the seeming contrast of the two will

be shown to be as illegitimate as would be the contrast of 'she came home in a flood of tears' and 'she came home in a sedan-chair'. The belief that there is a polar opposition between mind and matter is the belief that they are terms of the same logical type.

It will also follow that both idealism and materialism are answers to an improper question. The 'reduction' of the material world to mental states and processes, as well as the 'reduction' of mental states and processes to physical states and processes, presuppose the legitimacy of the disjunction 'Either there exist minds or there exist bodies (but not both)'. It would be like saying, "Either she bought a left-hand and a right-hand glove or she bought a pair of gloves (but not both)."

It is perfectly proper to say, in one logical tone of voice, that there exist minds and to say, in another logical tone of voice, that there exist bodies. But these expressions do not indicate two different species of existence, for 'existence' is not a generic word like 'colored' or 'sexed'. They indicate two different senses of 'exist', somewhat as 'rising' has different senses in 'the tide is rising', 'hopes are rising', and 'the average age of death is rising'. A man would be thought to be making a poor joke who said that three things are now rising, namely the tide, hopes and the average age of death. It would be just as good or bad a joke to say that there exist prime numbers and Wednesdays and public opinions and navies; or that there exist both minds and bodies. In the succeeding chapters I try to prove that the official theory does rest on a batch of category-mistakes by showing that logically absurd corollaries follow from it. The exhibition of these absurdities will have the constructive effect of bringing out part of the correct logic of mental-conduct concepts.

4. Historical Note

It would not be true to say that the official theory derives solely from Descartes' theories, or even from a more widespread anxiety about the implications of seventeenth-century mechanism. Scholastic and Reformation theology had schooled the intellects of the scientists as well as of the laymen, philosophers and clerics of that age. Stoic-Augustinian theories of the will were embedded in the Calvinist doctrines of sin and grace; Platonic and Aristotelian theories of the intellect shaped the orthodox doctrines of the immortality of the soul. Descartes was reformulating already prevalent theological doctrines of the soul in the new syntax of Galileo. The theologian's privacy of conscience became the philosophers privacy of consciousness, and what had been the bogy of predestination reappeared as the bogy of determinism.

It would also not be true to say that the two-worlds myth did no theoretical good. Myths often do a lot of theoretical good, while they are still new. One benefit bestowed by the para-mechanical myth was that it partly superannuated the then prevalent para-political myth. Minds and their faculties had previously been described by analogies with political superiors and political subordinates. The idioms used were those of ruling, obeying, collaborating and rebelling. They survived and still survive in many ethical and some epistemological discussions. As, in physics, the new myth of occult forces was a scientific improvement on the old myth of final causes, so, in anthropological and psychological theory, the new myth of hidden operations, impulses and agencies was an improvement on the old myth of dictations, deferences and disobediences.

READING QUESTIONS

1. According to the "official theory," what sorts of properties do bodies exhibit, and what sorts of properties do minds exhibit? Ryle remarks that "even when 'inner' and 'outer' are construed as metaphors, the problem of how a person's mind and body influence one another is notoriously charged with theoretical difficulties." What are these difficulties?

2. What is a 'category-mistake'? When he goes on to say that "my destructive purpose is to show that a family of radical category-mistakes is the source of the double-life theory," what does he mean?

3. Briefly encapsulate Ryle's account of the origin of Descartes' dualistic theory. In what way does Descartes make a category-mistake, as Ryle understands that term? Do you agree?

4. Ryle writes that "'existence' is not a generic word like 'colored' or 'sexed'." What does he mean by this? Do you agree? Why or why not?

SUGGESTIONS FOR FURTHER READING (GILBERT RYLE)

Primary Sources and Collected Writings

(1945) *Philosophical Arguments.* Oxford: Clarendon Press.

(1949) *The Concepts of the Mind.* London: Hutchinson.

(1954) *Dilemmas.* Cambridge: Cambridge University Press.

(1966) *Plato's Progress.* Cambridge: Cambridge University Press.

(1971) *Collected Papers.* New York: Barnes and Noble.

(1979) *On Thinking,* edited by K. Kolenda, introduction by G. J. Warnock. Totowa, NJ: Rowman and Littlefield.

(1993) *Aspects of Mind—Gilbert Ryle,* edited by R. Meyer. Oxford: Basil Blackwell.

Secondary Sources

Addis, L., and D. Lewis (1968) *Moore and Ryle: Two Ontologists.* Iowa City, IA: University of Iowa Press.

Kolenda, K., ed. (1972) *Studies in Philosophy: A Symposium on Gilbert Ryle.* Houston, TX: Rice University Press.

Lyons, W. (1980) *Gilbert Ryle: An Introduction to His Philosophy.* Brighton: Harvester Press.

Passmore, J. (1957) *A Hundred Years of Philosophy.* London: Duckworth.

Wood, O., and G. Pitcher, eds. (1970) *Ryle: A Collection of Critical Essays.* Garden City, NY: Anchor Books.

JOHN LANGSHAW (J. L.) AUSTIN

From *Sense and Sensibilia*

John L. Austin (1911–1960) read for a classics degree as an undergraduate at Shrewsbury and Balliol College, Oxford. After graduation, he turned to the study of philosophy. He was a Fellow at All Souls College, Oxford, from 1933 to 1935; a Fellow at Magdalen College,

Oxford, from 1935 to 1952; and White's Professor of Moral Philosophy and a Fellow of Corpus Christi College, Oxford, from 1952 to 1960. In fact, his Oxford career was broken for only three significant periods of time: From 1939 to 1945 he served in World War II in military intelligence (earning the O.B.E., Croix de Guerre, and being admitted to the Legion of Merit for his distinguished service to his country); from 1956 to 1957 he was a visiting professor at Harvard; and from 1958 to 1959 he was appointed a visiting professor at the University of California at Berkeley.

Austin was instrumental in introducing English-speaking readers of philosophy to the work of Gottlob Frege, translating his monumental *Grundlagen der Arithmetik* into English in 1950. But Austin is best remembered for his own original work as a defender and practitioner of ordinary language or "Oxford" philosophy. Developing a philosophical methodology that owed as much to Aristotle as to Wittgenstein, Austin set about to demonstrate that many of the problems of contemporary philosophy (along with their purported "solutions") arise from an unwillingness to closely and carefully examine our considered judgments regarding what would count as an appropriate or inappropriate use of language in various relevant contexts.

Austin did not reject the usefulness or appropriateness of employing a technical vocabulary in philosophy *per se*. Rather, he demanded that any philosophical distinction or term which is put to work should have reasonably clear and precise conditions of correct application. His concern was that most of the technical language of philosophy fails in this regard.

In his essay, "A Plea for Excuses," he remarks that "our common stock of words embodies all the distinctions men have found worth drawing, and the connections they have found worth making, in the lifetimes of many generations: these surely are likely to be more numerous, more sound, since they have stood up to the long test of the survival of the fittest, and more subtle, at least in all ordinary and reasonably practical matters, than any that you or I are likely to think up in our armchairs of an afternoon—the most favored alternative method." Austin concludes that "ordinary language is *not* the last word: in principle it can everywhere be supplemented and improved upon and superseded. Only remember, it *is* the *first* word."

Austin's reputation as a philosopher has diminished somewhat over the last thirty years, but his work remains a mainstay of philosophy, a source of dazzling insight and cogent argument, and—because Austin was such an excellent writer of prose—entertaining reading.

In the following two chapters from *Sense and Sensibilia,* Austin sets himself the task of evaluating the adequacy of the "sense-datum theory" advanced by Ayer in *Foundations of Empirical Knowledge* (1940), by H. H. Price in *Perception* (1932), and by many other philosophers. In the first section reprinted below, Austin considers what we are to make of the distinction between what the so-called "plain man" and the "philosopher" believe when it comes to our "belief in the existence of material things." In the second section, Austin reviews and comments on the famous "argument from illusion," advanced by supporters of the sense-datum theory in order to support their contention that we never "directly perceive" material things. Austin does not so much try to refute the argument as to argue that it never gets off the ground in the first place.

II

Let us have a look, then, at the very beginning of Ayer's *Foundations*—the bottom, one might perhaps call it, of the garden path. In these paragraphs[1] we already seem to see the plain man, here under the implausible aspect of Ayer himself, dribbling briskly into position in front of his own goal, and squaring up to encompass his own destruction.

> It does not normally occur to us that there is any need for us to justify our belief in the existence of material things. At the present moment, for example, I have no doubt whatsoever that I really am per-

Reprinted from *Sense and Sensibilia* by J. L. Austin, edited by G. J. Warnock (1962) by permission of Oxford University Press. Copyright © 1962 Oxford University Press.

ceiving the familiar objects, the chairs and table, the pictures and books and flowers with which my room is furnished; and I am therefore satisfied that they exist. I recognize indeed that people are sometimes deceived by their senses, but this does not lead me to suspect that my own sense-perceptions cannot in general be trusted, or even that they may be deceiving me now. And this is not, I believe, an exceptional attitude. I believe that, in practice, most people agree with John Locke that 'the certainty of things existing *in rerum natura,* when we have the testimony of our senses for it, is not only as great as our frame can attain to, but as our condition needs'.

When, however, one turns to the writings of those philosophers who have recently concerned themselves with the subject of perception, one may begin to wonder whether this matter is quite so simple. It is true that they do, in general, allow that our belief in the existence of material things is well founded; some of them, indeed, would say that there were occasions on which we knew for certain the truth of such propositions as 'this is a cigarette' or 'this is a pen'. But even so they are not, for the most part, prepared to admit that such objects as pens or cigarettes are ever directly perceived. What, in their opinion, we directly perceive is always an object of a different kind from these; one to which it is now customary to give the name of 'sense-datum'.

Now in this passage some sort of contrast is drawn between what we (or the ordinary man) believe (or believes), and what philosophers, at least 'for the most part', believe or are 'prepared to admit'. We must look at both sides of this contrast, and with particular care at what is assumed in, and implied by, what is actually said. The ordinary man's side, then, first.

1. It is clearly implied, first of all, that the ordinary man believes that he perceives material things. Now this, at least if it is taken to mean that he would *say that* he perceives material things, is surely wrong straight off; for 'material thing' is not an expression which the ordinary man would use—nor, probably, is 'perceive'. Presumably, though, the expression 'material thing' is here put forward, not as what the ordinary man would *say,* but as designating in a general way the *class* of things of which the ordinary man both believes and from time to time says that he perceives particular instances. But then we have to ask, of course, what this class comprises. We are given, as examples, 'familiar objects'—chairs, tables, pictures, books, flowers, pens, cigarettes; the expression 'material thing' is not here (or anywhere else in Ayer's text) further defined.[2] But *does* the ordinary man believe that what he perceives is (always) something like furniture, or like these other 'familiar objects'—moderate-sized specimens of dry goods? We may think, for instance, of people, people's voices, rivers, mountains, flames, rainbows, shadows, pictures on the screen at the cinema, pictures in books or hung on walls, vapors, gases—all of which people say that they see or (in some cases) hear or smell, i.e., 'perceive'. Are these all 'material things'? If not, exactly which are not, and exactly why? No answer is vouchsafed. The trouble is that the expression 'material thing' is functioning *already,* from the very beginning, simply as a foil for 'sense-datum'; it is not here given, and is never given, any other role to play, and apart from this consideration it would surely never have occurred to anybody to try to represent as some single *kind of things* the things which the ordinary man says that he 'perceives'.

2. Further, it seems to be also implied (*a*) that when the ordinary man believes that he is not perceiving material things, he believes he is being deceived by his senses; and (*b*) that when he believes that he is not perceiving material things. But both of these are wrong. An ordinary man who saw, for example, a rainbow would not, if persuaded that a rainbow is not a material thing, at once conclude that his senses were deceiving him; nor, when for instance he knows that the ship at sea on a clear day is much farther away than it looks, does he conclude that he is not seeing a material thing (still less that he *is* seeing an immaterial ship). That is to say, there is no more a simple contrast between what the ordinary man believes when all is well (that he is 'perceiving material things') and when something is amiss (that his 'senses are deceiving him' and he is *not* 'perceiving material things') than there is between what he believes that he perceives ('material things') and what philosophers for their part are prepared to admit, whatever that may be. The ground is already being prepared for *two* bogus dichotomies.

3. Next, is it not rather delicately hinted in this passage that the plain man is really a bit naive?[3] It 'does not

normally occur' to him that his belief in 'the existence of material things' needs justifying—but perhaps it *ought* to occur to him. He has 'no doubt whatsoever' that he really perceives chairs and tables—but perhaps he ought to have a doubt or two and not be so easily 'satisfied'. That people are sometimes deceived by their senses 'does not lead him to suspect' that all may not be well—but perhaps a more reflective person *would* be led to suspect. Though ostensibly the plain man's position is here just being described, a little quiet undermining is already being effected by these turns of phrase.

4. But, perhaps more importantly, it is also implied, even taken for granted, that there is *room* for doubt and suspicion, whether or not the plain man feels any. The quotation from Locke, with which most people are said to agree, in fact contains a strong *suggestio falsi.* It suggests that when, for instance, I look at a chair a few yards in front of me in broad daylight, my view is that I have (*only*) as much certainty as I need and can get that there is a chair and that I see it. But in fact the plain man would regard doubt in such a case, not as far-fetched or over-refined or somehow unpractical, but as plain *nonsense;* he would say, quite correctly, "Well, if that's not seeing a real chair then *I don't know what is.*" Moreover, though the plain man's alleged belief that his 'sense-perceptions' can 'in general' or 'now' be trusted is implicitly contrasted with the philosophers' view, it turns out that the philosophers' view is not just that his sense-perceptions *can't* be trusted 'now', or 'in general', or as often as he thinks; for apparently philosophers 'for the most part' really maintain that what the plain man believes to be the case is really *never* the case—'what, in their opinion, we directly perceive is *always* an object of a different kind'. The philosopher is not really going to argue that things go wrong more often than the unwary plain man supposes, but that in some sense or some way he is wrong all the time. So it is misleading to hint, not only that there is always room for doubt, but that the philosophers' dissent from the plain man is just a matter of degree; it is really not *that* kind of disagreement at all.

5. Consider next what is said here about deception. We recognize, it is said, that 'people are sometimes deceived by their senses', though we think that, in general, our 'sense-perceptions' can 'be trusted'.

Now first, though the phrase 'deceived by our senses' is a common metaphor, it *is* a metaphor; and this is worth noting, for in what follows the same metaphor is frequently taken up by the expression 'veridical' and taken very seriously. In fact, of course, our senses are dumb—though Descartes and others speak of 'the testimony of the senses', our senses do not *tell* us anything, true or false. The case is made much worse here by the unexplained introduction of a quite new creation, our 'sense-perceptions'. These entities, which of course don't really figure at all in the plain man's language or among his beliefs, are brought in with the implication that whenever we 'perceive' there is an *intermediate* entity *always* present and *informing* us about something *else*—the question is, can we or can't we trust what it says? Is it 'veridical'? But of course to state the case in this way is simply to soften up the plain man's alleged views for the subsequent treatment; it is preparing the way for, by practically attributing to *him,* the so-called philosophers' view.

Next, it is important to remember that talk of deception only *makes sense* against a background of general non-deception. (You can't fool all of the people all of the time.) It must be possible to *recognize* a case of deception by checking the odd case against more normal ones. If I say, "Our petrol gauge sometimes deceives us," I am understood: though usually what it indicates squares with what we have in the tank, sometimes it doesn't—it sometimes points to two gallons when the tank turns out to be nearly empty. But suppose I say, "Our crystal ball sometimes deceives us": this is puzzling, because really we haven't the least idea what the 'normal' case—*not* being deceived by our crystal ball—would actually be.

The cases, again, in which a plain man might say he was 'deceived by his senses' are not at all common. In particular, he would *not* say this when confronted with ordinary cases of perspective, with ordinary mirror-images, or with dreams; in fact, when he dreams, looks down the long straight road, or at his face in the mirror, he is not, or at least is hardly ever, *deceived* at all. This is worth remembering in view of another strong *suggestio falsi*—namely, that when the philosopher cites as cases of 'illusion' all these and many other very common phenomena, he is either simply mentioning cases which the plain man already concedes as cases of 'deception by the senses', or at any rate is only extending a bit what he would readily concede. In fact this is very far indeed from being the case.

And even so—even though the plain man certainly does not accept anything like so *many* cases as cases of being 'deceived by his senses' as philosophers seem to—it would certainly be quite wrong to suggest that he regards all the cases he *does* accept as being of just the same kind. The battle is, in fact, half lost already if this suggestion is tolerated. Sometimes the plain man would prefer to say that his senses were deceived rather than that he was deceived by his senses—the quickness of the hand deceives the eye, etc. But there is actually a great multiplicity of cases here, at least at the edges of which it is no doubt uncertain (and it would be typically scholastic to try to decide) just which are and which are not cases where the metaphor of being 'deceived by the senses' would naturally be employed. But surely even the plainest of men would want to distinguish (*a*) cases where the *sense organ* is deranged or abnormal or in some way or other not functioning properly; (*b*) cases where the *medium*—or more generally, the conditions—of perception are in some way abnormal or off-color; and (*c*) cases where a wrong inference is made or a wrong construction is put on things, e.g., on some sound that he hears. (Of course these cases do not exclude each other.) And then again there are the quite common cases of misreadings, mishearings, Freudian oversights, etc., which don't seem to belong properly under any of these headings. That is to say, once again there is no neat and simple dichotomy between things going right and things going wrong; things may go wrong, as we really all know quite well, in lots of *different* ways—which don't have to be, and must not be assumed to be, classifiable in any general fashion.

Finally, to repeat here a point we've already mentioned, of course the plain man does *not* suppose that all the cases in which he is 'deceived by his senses' are alike in the particular respect that, in those cases, he is not 'perceiving material things', or *is* perceiving something not real or not material. Looking at the Müller-Lyer diagram (in which, of two lines of equal length, one looks longer than the other), or at a distant village on a very clear day across a valley, is a very different kettle of fish from seeing a ghost or from having D.T.s and seeing pink rats. And when the plain man sees on

the stage the headless woman, what he sees (and this *is* what he sees, whether he knows it or not) is not something 'unreal' or 'immaterial', but a woman against a dark background with her head in a black bag. If the trick is well done, he doesn't (because it's deliberately made very difficult for him) properly size up what he sees, or see *what* it is; but to say this is far from concluding that he sees something *else*.

In conclusion, then, there is less than no reason to swallow the suggestions *either* that what the plain man believes that he perceives most of the time constitutes a *kind* of things (sc. 'material objects'), *or* that he can be said to recognize any other single *kind* of cases in which he is 'deceived'.[4] Now let us consider what it is that is said about philosophers.

Philosophers, it is said, 'are not, for the most part, prepared to admit that such objects as pens or cigarettes are ever directly perceived'. Now of course what brings us up short here is the word 'directly'—a great favorite among philosophers, but actually one of the less conspicuous snakes in the linguistic grass. We have here, in fact, a typical case of a word, which already has a very special use, being gradually stretched, without caution or definition or any limit, until it becomes, first perhaps obscurely metaphorical, but ultimately meaningless. One can't abuse ordinary language without paying for it.[5]

1. First of all, it is essential to realize that here the notion of perceiving *in*directly wears the trousers—'directly' takes whatever sense it has from the contrast with its opposite:[6] while 'indirectly' itself (*a*) has a use only in special cases, and also (b) has *different* uses in different cases—though that doesn't mean, of course, that there is not a good reason why we should use the same word. We might, for example, contrast the man who saw the procession directly with the man who saw it *through a periscope;* or we might contrast the place from which you can watch the door directly with the place from which you can see it only *in the mirror.* Perhaps we might contrast seeing you directly with seeing, say, your shadow on the blind; and *perhaps* we might contrast hearing the music directly with hearing it relayed outside the concert hall. However, these last two cases suggest two further points.

2. The first of these points is that the notion of not perceiving 'directly' seems most at home where, as with the periscope and the mirror, it retains its link with the notion of a kink in *direction*. It seems that we must not be looking *straight at* the object in question. For this reason seeing your shadow on the blind is a doubtful case; and seeing you, for instance, through binoculars or spectacles is certainly not a case of seeing you *indirectly* at all. For such cases as these last we have quite distinct contrasts and different expressions—'with the naked eye' as opposed to 'with a telescope', 'with un-aided vision' as opposed to 'with glasses on'. (These expressions, in fact, are much more firmly established in ordinary use than 'directly' is.)

3. And the other point is that, partly no doubt for the above reason, the notion of indirect perception is not naturally at home with senses other than sight. With the other senses there is nothing quite analogous with the 'line of vision'. The most natural sense of 'hearing indirectly', of course, is that of being *told* something by an intermediary—a quite different matter. But do I hear a shout indirectly, when I hear the echo? If I touch you with a barge pole, do I touch you indirectly? Or if you offer me a pig in a poke, might I feel the pig indirectly—*through* the poke? And what smelling indirectly might be I have simply no idea. For this reason alone there seems to be something badly wrong with the question, "Do we perceive things directly or not?", where perceiving is evidently intended to cover the employment of *any* of the senses.

4. But it is, of course, for other reasons too extremely doubtful how far the notion of perceiving indirectly could or should be extended. Does it, or should it, cover the telephone, for instance? Or television? Or radar? Have we moved too far in these cases from the original metaphor? They at any rate satisfy what seems to be a necessary condition—namely, concurrent existence and concomitant variation as between what is perceived in the straightforward way (the sounds in the receiver, the picture and the blips on the screen) and the candidate for what we might be prepared to describe as being perceived indirectly. And this condition fairly clearly rules out as cases of indirect perception seeing photographs (which statically record scenes from the past) and seeing films (which, though not sta-

tic, are not seen contemporaneously with the events thus recorded). Certainly, there *is* a line to be drawn somewhere. It is certain, for instance, that we should not be prepared to speak of indirect perception in *every* case in which we see something from which the existence (or occurrence) of something else can be inferred; we should *not* say we see the guns indirectly, if we see in the distance only the flashes of guns.

5. Rather differently, if we are to be seriously inclined to speak of something as being perceived indirectly, it seems that it has to be the kind of thing which we (sometimes at least) just perceive, or could perceive, or which—like the backs of our own heads—others could perceive. For otherwise we don't want to say that we perceive the thing *at all,* even indirectly. No doubt there are complications here (raised, perhaps, by the electron microscope, for example, about which I know little or nothing). But it seems clear that, in general, we should want to distinguish between seeing indirectly, e.g., in a mirror, what we might have just *seen,* and seeing signs (or effects), e.g., in a Wilson cloud-chamber, of something not itself perceptible at all. It would at least not come naturally to speak of the latter as a case of perceiving something indirectly.

6. And one final point. For reasons not very obscure, we always prefer in practice what might be called the *cash value* expression to the 'indirect' metaphor. If I were to report that I see enemy ships indirectly, I should merely provoke the question what exactly I mean. "I mean that I can see these blips on the radar screen" "Well, why didn't you say so then?" (Compare "I can see an unreal duck." "What on earth do you mean?" "It's a decoy duck" "Ah, I see. Why didn't you say so at once?") That is, there is seldom if ever any particular point in actually saying 'indirectly' (or 'unreal'); the expression can cover too many rather different cases to be *just* what is wanted in any particular case.

Thus, it is quite plain that the philosophers' use of 'directly perceive', whatever it may be, is not the ordinary, or any familiar, use; for in *that* use it is not only false but simply absurd to say that such objects as pens or cigarettes are never perceived directly. But we are given no explanation or definition of this new use[7]—on the contrary, it is glibly trotted out as if we were all quite familiar with it already. It is clear, too, that the philosophers' use, whatever it may be, offends against several of the canons just mentioned above—no restrictions whatever seem to be envisaged to any special circumstances or to any of the senses in particular, and moreover it seems that what we are to be said to perceive indirectly is *never*—is not the kind of thing which ever *could* be perceived directly.

All this lends poignancy to the question Ayer himself asks, a few lines below the passage we have been considering: 'Why may we not say that we are directly aware of material things?' The answer, he says, is provided 'by what is known as the argument from illusion'; and this is what we must next consider. Just possibly the answer may help us to understand the question.

III

The primary purpose of the argument from illusion is to induce people to accept 'sense-data' as the proper and correct answer to the question what they perceive on certain *abnormal, exceptional* occasions; but in fact it is usually followed up with another bit of argument intended to establish that they *always* perceive sense-data. Well, what is the argument?

In Ayer's statement[8] it runs as follows. It is 'based on the fact that material things may present different appearances to different observers, or to the same observer in different conditions, and that the character of these appearances is to some extent causally determined by the state of the conditions and the observer'. As illustrations of this alleged fact Ayer proceeds to cite perspective ('a coin which looks circular from one point of view may look elliptical from another'); refraction ('a stick which normally appears straight looks bent when it is seen in water'); changes in color-vision produced by drugs ('such as mescal'); mirror-images; double vision; hallucination; apparent variations in tastes; variations in felt warmth ('according as the hand

that is feeling it is itself hot or cold'); variations in felt bulk ('a coin seems larger when it is placed on the tongue than when it is held in the palm of the hand'); and the oft-cited fact that 'people who have had limbs amputated may still continue to feel pain in them'.

He then selects three of these instances for detailed treatment. First, refraction—the stick which normally 'appears straight' but 'looks bent' when seen in water. He makes the 'assumptions' (*a*) that the stick does not *really change its shape* when it is placed in water, and (*b*) that it *cannot be* both crooked and straight.[9] He then concludes ('it follows') that 'at least one of the *visual appearances* of the stick is *delusive*'. Nevertheless, even when 'what we see is not the *real quality* of a *material thing,* it is supposed that we are still seeing something'—and this something is to be called a 'sense-datum'. A sense-datum is to be 'the object of which we are *directly* aware, in perception, if it is not *part* of any *material thing*'. (The italics are mine throughout this and the next two paragraphs.)

Next, mirages. A man who sees a mirage, he says, is 'not perceiving any material thing; for the oasis which he thinks he is perceiving *does not exist*'. But 'his *experience* is not an experience of nothing'; thus 'it is said that he is experiencing sense-data, which are similar in character to what he would be experiencing if he were seeing a real oasis, but are delusive in the sense that *the material thing which they appear to present* is not *really there*'.

Lastly, reflections. When I look at myself in a mirror 'my body *appears to be* some distance behind the glass'; but it cannot actually be in two places at once; thus, my perceptions in this case 'cannot all be *veridical*'. But I do see *something;* and if 'there really is no such material thing as my body in the place where it appears to be, what is it that I am seeing?' Answer—a sense-datum. Ayer adds that 'the same conclusion may be reached by taking any other of any examples'.

Now I want to call attention, first of all, to the name of this argument—the 'argument from *illusion*', and to the fact that it is produced as establishing the conclusion that some at least of our 'perceptions' are *delusive*. For in this there are two clear implications—(*a*) that all the cases cited in the argument are cases of *illusions;* and (*b*) that *illusion* and *delusion* are the same thing. But both of these implications, of course, are quite wrong; and it is by no means unimportant to point this out, for, as we shall see, the argument trades on confusion at just this point.

What, then, would be some genuine examples of illusion? (The fact is that hardly any of the cases cited by Ayer is, at any rate without stretching things, a case of illusion at all.) Well, first, there are some quite clear cases of *optical* illusion—for instance the case we mentioned earlier in which, of two lines of equal length, one is made to look longer than the other. Then again there are illusion produced by professional 'illusionists', conjurors—for instance the headless woman on the stage, who is made to look headless, or the ventriloquist's dummy which is made to appear to be talking. Rather different—not (usually) produced on purpose—is the case where wheels rotating rapidly enough in one direction may look as if they were rotating quite slowly in the opposite direction. Delusions, on the other hand, are something altogether different from this. Typical cases would be delusions of persecution, delusions of grandeur. These are primarily a matter of grossly disordered beliefs (and so, probably, behavior) and may well have nothing in particular to do with perception.[10] But I think we might also say that the patient who sees pink rats has (suffers from) delusions—particularly, no doubt, if, as would probably be the case, he is not clearly aware that his pink rats aren't real rats.[11]

The most important differences here are that the term 'an illusion' (in a perceptual context) does not suggest that something totally unreal is *conjured up*—on the contrary, there just is the arrangement of lines and arrows on the page, the woman on the stage with her head in a black bag, the rotating wheels; whereas the term 'delusion' *does* suggest something totally unreal, not really there at all. (The convictions of the man who has delusions of persecution can be *completely* without foundation.) For this reason delusions are a much more serious matter—something is really wrong, and what's more, wrong *with* the person who has them. But when I see an optical illusion, however well it comes off, there is nothing wrong with me personally, the illusion is not a little (or a large) peculiarity or idiosyncrasy of my own; it is quite public, anyone can see it, and in many cases standard procedures can be laid down for producing it. Furthermore, if we are not actually to be taken in, we need to be *on our guard;* but it is no use to tell the sufferer from delusions to be on his guard. He needs to be cured.

Why is it that we tend—if we do—to confuse illusions with delusions? Well, partly, no doubt the terms are often used loosely. But there is also the point that people may have, without making this explicit, different views or theories about the facts of some cases. Take the case of seeing a ghost, for example. It is not generally known, or agreed, what seeing ghosts *is.* Some people think of seeing ghosts as a case of something being conjured up, perhaps by the disordered nervous system of the victim; so in their view seeing ghosts is a case of delusion. But other people have the idea that what is called seeing ghosts is a case of being taken in by shadows, perhaps, or reflections, or a trick of the light—that is, they assimilate the case in their minds to illusion. In this way, seeing ghosts, for example, may come to be labeled sometimes as 'delusion', sometimes as 'illusion'; and it may not be noticed that it makes a difference which label we use. Rather, similarly, there seem to be different doctrines in the field as to what mirages are. Some seem to take a mirage to be a vision conjured up by the crazed brain of the thirsty and exhausted traveler (delusion), while in other accounts it is a case of atmospheric refraction, whereby something below the horizon is made to appear above it (illusion). (Ayer, you may remember, takes the delusion view, although he cites it along with the rest as a case of illusion. He says not that the oasis appears to be where it is not, but roundly that 'it does not exist'.)

The way in which the 'argument from illusion' positively trades on not distinguishing illusions from delusions is, I think, this. So long as it is being suggested that the cases paraded for our attention are cases of *illusion,* there is the implication (from the ordinary use of the word) that there really is something there that we perceive. But then, when these cases begin to be quietly called delusive, there comes in the very different suggestion of something being conjured up, something unreal or at any rate 'immaterial'. These two implications taken together may then subtly insinuate that in the cases cited there really is something that we are perceiving, but that this is an immaterial something; and this insinuation, even if not conclusive by itself, is certainly well calculated to edge us a little closer towards just the position where the sense-datum theorist wants to have us.

So much, then—though certainly there could be a good deal more—about the differences between illusions and delusions and the reasons for not obscuring them. Now let us look briefly at some of the other cases Ayer lists. Reflections, for instance. No doubt you *can* produce illusions with mirrors, suitably disposed. But is just *any* case of seeing something in a mirror an illusion, as he implies? Quite obviously not. For seeing things in mirrors is a perfectly *normal* occurrence, completely familiar, and there is usually no question of anyone being taken in. No doubt, if you're an infant or an aborigine and have never come across a mirror before, you may be pretty baffled, and even visibly perturbed, when you do. But is that a reason why the rest of us should speak of illusion here? And just the same goes for the phenomena of perspective—again, one *can* play tricks with perspective, but in the ordinary case there is no question of illusion. That a round coin should 'look elliptical' (in one sense) from some points of view is exactly what we expect and what we normally find; indeed, we should be badly put out if we ever found this not to be so. Refraction again—the stick that looks bent in water—is far too familiar a case to be properly called a case of illusion. We may perhaps be prepared to agree that the stick looks bent; but then we can see that it's partly submerged in water, so that is exactly how we should expect it to look.

It is important to realize here how familiarity, so to speak, takes the edge off illusion. Is the cinema a case of illusion? Well, just possibly the first man who ever saw moving pictures may have felt inclined to say that here was a case of illusion. But in fact it's pretty unlikely that even he, even momentarily, was actually taken in; and by now the whole thing is so ordinary a part of our lives that it never occurs to us even to raise the question. One might as well ask whether producing a photograph is producing an illusion—which would plainly be just silly.

Then we must not overlook, in all this talk about illusions and delusions, that there are plenty of more or less unusual cases, not yet mentioned, which certainly aren't either. Suppose that a proofreader makes a mistake—he fails to notice that what ought to be 'causal' is printed as 'casual'; does he have a delusion? Or is there

an illusion before him? Neither, of course; he simply *misreads*. Seeing after-images, too, though not a particularly frequent occurrence and not just an ordinary case of seeing, is neither seeing illusions nor having delusions. And what about dreams? Does the dreamer see illusions? Does he have delusions? Neither; dreams are *dreams*.

Let us turn for a moment to what Price has to say about illusions. He produces,[12] by way of saying 'what the term "illusion" means', the following 'provisional definition': 'An illusory sense-datum of sight or touch is a sense-datum which is such that we tend to take it to be part of the surface of a material object, but if we take it so we are wrong.' It is by no means clear, of course, what this dictum itself means; but still, it seems fairly clear that the definition doesn't actually fit all the cases of illusion. Consider the two lines again. Is there anything here which we tend to take, wrongly, to be part of the surface of a material object? It doesn't seem so. We just see the two lines, we don't think or even tend to think that we see anything else, we aren't even raising the question whether anything is or isn't 'part of the surface' of—what, anyway? the lines? the page?—the trouble is just that one line looks longer than the other, though it isn't. Nor surely, in the case of the headless woman, is it a question whether anything is or isn't part of her surface; the trouble is just that she looks as if she had no head.

It is noteworthy, of course, that, before he even begins to consider the 'argument from illusion', Price has already incorporated in this 'definition' the idea that in such cases there is something to be seen *in addition to* the ordinary things—which is part of what the argument is commonly used, and not uncommonly taken, to *prove*. But this idea surely has no place in an attempt to say what 'illusion' *means*. It comes in again, improperly I think, in his account of perspective (which incidentally he also cites as a species of illusion)—'a distant hillside which is full of protuberances, and slopes upwards at quite a gentle angle, will appear flat and vertical. . . . This means that the sense-datum, the color-expanse which we sense, actually *is* flat and vertical.' But why should we accept this account of the matter? Why should we say that there is *anything* we see which *is* flat and vertical, though not 'part of the surface' of any material object? To speak thus is to assimilate all such cases to cases of delusion, where there *is* something not 'part of any material thing'. But we have already discussed the undesirability of this assimilation.

Next, let us have a look at the account Ayer himself gives of some at least of the cases he cites. (In fairness we must remember here that Ayer has a number of quite substantial reservations of his own about the merits and efficacy of the argument from illusion, so that it is not easy to tell just how seriously he intends his exposition of it to be taken; but this is a point we shall come back to.)

First, then, the familiar case of the stick in water. Of this case Ayer says *(a)* that since the stick looks bent but is straight, 'at least one of the visual appearances of the stick is *delusive*'; and *(b)* that 'what we see [directly anyway] is not the real quality of [a few lines later, not part of] a material thing'. Well now: does the stick 'look bent' to begin with? I think we can agree that it does, we have no better way of describing it. But of course it does *not* look *exactly* like a bent stick, a bent stick out of water—at most, it may be said to look rather like a bent stick partly immersed *in* water. After all, we can't help seeing the water the stick is partly immersed in. So exactly what in this case is supposed to be *delusive*? What is wrong, what is even faintly surprising, in the idea of a stick's being straight but looking bent sometimes? Does anyone suppose that if something is straight, then it jolly well has to *look* straight at all times and in all circumstances? Obviously no one seriously supposes this. So what mess are we supposed to get into here, what is the difficulty? For of course it has to be suggested that there *is* a difficulty—a difficulty, furthermore, which calls for a pretty radical solution, the introduction of sense-data. But what is the problem we are invited to solve in this way?

Well, we are told, in this case you are seeing *something;* and what is this something 'if it is not part of any material thing'? But this question is, really, completely mad. The straight part of the stick, the bit not under water, is presumably part of a material thing; don't we see that? And what about the bit *under* water?—we can see that too. We can see, come to that, the water itself. In fact what we see is *a stick partly immersed in water;* and it is particularly extraordinary that this should appear to be called in question—that a question should be raised about *what* we are seeing—since this, after all,

is simply the description of the situation with which we started. It was, that is to say, agreed at the start that we were looking at a stick, a 'material thing', part of which was under water. If, to take a rather different case, a church were cunningly camouflaged so that it looked like a barn, how could any serious question be raised about what we see when we look at it? We see, of course, *a church* that now *looks like a barn*. We do *not* see an immaterial barn, an immaterial church, or an immaterial anything else. And what in this case could seriously tempt us to say that we do?

Notice, incidentally, that in Ayer's description of the stick-in-water case, which is supposed to be prior to the drawing of any philosophical conclusions, there has already crept in the unheralded but important expression 'visual appearances'—it is, of course, ultimately to be suggested that all we *ever* get when we see is a visual appearance (whatever that may be).

Consider next the case of my reflection in a mirror. My body, Ayer says, 'appears to be some distance behind the glass'; but as it's in front, it can't really be behind the glass. So what am I seeing? A sense-datum. What about this? Well, once again, although there is no objection to saying that my body 'appears to be' some distance behind the glass', in saying this we must remember what sort of situation we are dealing with. It does not 'appear to be' there in a way which might tempt me (though it might tempt a baby or a savage) to go round the back and look for it, and be astonished when this enterprise proved a failure. (To say that A is *in* B doesn't always mean that if you open B you will find A, just as to say that A is *on* B doesn't always mean that you, could pick it off—consider "I saw my face in the mirror," "There's a pain in my toe," "I heard him on the radio," "I saw the image on the screen," etc. Seeing something in a mirror is not like seeing a bun in a shop window.) But does it follow that, since my body is not actually located behind the mirror, I am not seeing a material thing? Plainly not. For one thing, I can see the mirror (nearly always anyway). I can see my own body 'indirectly,' *sc.* in the mirror. I can also see the reflection of my own body or, as some would say, a mirror image. And a mirror image (if we choose this answer) is not a 'sense-datum'; it can be photographed, seen by any number of people, and so on. (Of course there is no question here of either illusion or delusion.)

And if the question is pressed, what actually *is* some distance, five feet say, behind the mirror, the answer is, not a sense-datum, but some region of the adjoining room.

The mirage case—at least if we take the view, as Ayer does, that the oasis the traveler thinks he can see 'does not exist'—is significantly more amenable to the treatment it is given. For here we are supposing the man to be genuinely deluded, he is *not* 'seeing a material thing'.[13] We don't actually have to say, however, even here that he is 'experiencing sense-data'; for though, as Ayer says above, 'it is convenient to give a name' to what he is experiencing, the fact is that it already has a name—a *mirage*. Again, we should be wise not to accept too readily the statement that what he is experiencing is '*similar in character* to what he would be experiencing if he were seeing a real oasis'. For is it at all likely, really, to be very similar? And, looking ahead, if we were to concede this point we should find the concession being used against us at a later stage—namely, at the stage where we shall be invited to agree that we see sense-data always, in normal cases too.

Notes

1. Ayer, A. J. *Foundations of Empirical Knowledge* (London: Macmillan, 1940), pp. 1–2.
2. Compare H. H. Price's list on p. 1 of *Perception* (London: Methuen, 1932)—'chairs and tables, cats and rocks'—though he complicates matters by adding 'water' and 'the earth'. See also p. 280, on 'physical objects', 'visuo-tactual solids'.
3. Price, op. cit., p. 26, says that he *is* naive, though it is not, it seems, certain that he is actually a naive realist.
4. I am not denying that cases in which things go wrong *could* be lumped together under some single name. A single name might in itself be innocent enough, provided its use was not taken to imply either (*a*) that the cases were all alike, or (*b*) that they were all in certain ways alike. What matters is that the facts should not be pre-judged and (therefore) neglected.
5. Especially if one abuses it without realizing what one is doing. Consider the trouble caused by unwitting stretching of the word 'sign', so as to yield—apparently—the conclusion that, when the cheese is in front of our noses, we see *signs* of cheese.
6. Compare, in this respect, 'real', 'proper', 'free', and plenty of others. "It's real"—what exactly are you

saying it isn't? "I wish we had a proper stair-carpet"—what are you complaining of in the one you've got? (That it's *im*proper?) "Is he free?"—well, what have you in mind that he might be instead? In prison? Tied up in prison? Committed to a prior engagement?

7. Ayer takes note of this, rather belatedly, on pp. 60–61.
8. Ayer, op. cit., pp. 3–5.
9. It is not only strange, but also important, that Ayer calls these 'assumptions'. Later on he is going to take seriously the notion of denying at least one of them, which he could hardly do if he had recognized them here as the plain and incontestable facts that they are.
10. The latter point holds, of course, for *some* uses of 'illusion' too; there are the illusions which some people (are said to) lose as they grow older and wiser.
11. Cp. the white rabbit in the play called *Harvey*.
12. *Perception*, p. 27.
13. Not even 'indirectly', no such thing is 'presented'. Doesn't this seem to make the case, though more amenable, a good deal less useful to the philosopher? It's hard to see how normal cases could be said to be *very like* this.

READING QUESTIONS

1. In the passage that Austin quotes verbatim, Ayer is said to draw a distinction between what "the ordinary man" believes and what "philosophers" believe when it comes to "our belief in the existence of material things." According to the view under discussion, as Austin sees it, what are the differences between these two standpoints?
2. In considering what is said about deception, Austin remarks that "it is important to remember that talk of deception only *makes sense* against a background of general non-deception. (You can't fool all of the people all of the time.)" What is Austin's reason for believing this? Do you agree? Why or why not?
3. Austin remarks that "one can't abuse ordinary language without paying for it." What does he mean by this? In what ways does he think that the philosopher is "abusing ordinary language"?

4. In commenting on the idea of "directly" perceiving a thing, Austin remarks that "we have here, in fact, a typical case of a word, which already has a very special use, being gradually stretched, without caution or definition or any limit, until it becomes, first perhaps obscurely metaphorical, but ultimately meaningless." Can you think of other examples of this phenomenon in philosophy, outside of theories of perception?

5. Formalize the argument from illusion.

6. What are Austin's main reservations concerning the manner in which Ayer uses the term 'illusion'? What relevance does the distinction between 'illusion' and 'delusion' have in fortifying Austin's position on the argument from illusion?

7. Austin says that "it is important to realize here how familiarity, so to speak, takes the edge off illusion." What does he mean? What impact does this have on the argument from illusion?

8. Consider the case of the stick in water and the case of the reflection in a mirror. According to Austin, what does Ayer think we should conclude from these cases? What is Austin's reply? Whose position do you find to be more convincing? Why?

SUGGESTIONS FOR FURTHER READING (JOHN L. AUSTIN)

Primary Sources and Collected Writings

(1961) *Philosophical Papers,* 3rd ed., edited by J. O. Urmson and G. J. Warnock. Oxford: Oxford University Press, 1979.

(1962) *Sense and Sensibilia* reconstructed from the manuscript notes by G. J. Warnock. Oxford: Oxford University Press.

(1962) *How to Do Things with Words,* rev. ed. Cambridge, MA: Harvard University Press, 1975.

Secondary Sources

Berlin, I., et al. (1973) *Essays on J. L. Austin.* Oxford: Clarendon Press.

Fann, K. T., ed. (1969) *Symposium on J. L. Austin.* New York: Humanities Press.

Furberg, M. (1971) *Saying and Meaning: A Main Theme in J. L. Austin's Philosophy.* Totowa, NJ: Rowman and Littlefield.

Graham, K. (1977) *J. L. Austin: A Critique of Ordinary Language Philosophy.* Atlantic Highlands, NJ: Humanities Press.

Searle, J. (1969) *Speech Acts.* Cambridge: Cambridge University Press.

Warnock, G. J. (1991). *J. L. Austin.* New York: Routledge.

GERTRUDE ELIZABETH MARGARET (G. E. M.) ANSCOMBE

Modern Moral Philosophy

A distinguished English philosopher and historian of philosophy, G. E. M. Anscombe (1919–) renewed interest in virtue ethics and in the theory of natural law with her monumental 1958 article "Modern Moral Philosophy"; brought Wittgenstein's later work to the attention of English-speaking philosophers throughout the world with her brilliant translation of his *Philosophical Investigations*; and laid the groundwork for much of the work done in the late twentieth century in philosophical psychology and action theory.

Anscombe was educated at St. Hugh's College, Oxford, where she studied both classical literature and philosophy, graduating in 1941. She then held research fellowships at Somerville College, Oxford, and at Newnham College, Cambridge, from 1941 to 1964. In 1964, she became a Fellow of Somerville College, a position that she held until 1970. That same year she became professor of philosophy and a Fellow of New Hall, Cambridge, remaining at Cambridge until her retirement in 1986. In addition to her university appointments, her many honors include being elected a Fellow of the British Academy in 1979, being made a Foreign Honorary Member of the American Academy of Arts and Sciences, and being awarded a J.D. from Notre Dame University in 1986.

Anscombe's work shows strong influences of Wittgenstein, Aristotle, and Aquinas, but remains, nonetheless, highly original and inventive. Her work combines an interest in the traditional areas of epistemology and metaphysics with a desire to better understand the nature of action, intention, deliberation, and the relation between moral philosophy and philosophical psychology. Rejecting many of the traditional late twentieth-century approaches to these topics, Anscombe's work forged a renewed interest in ancient and medieval approaches to the problems of philosophy and worked to combine the care and sophistication of the ordinary language approach with the philosophical temperament and outlook characteristic of the natural law tradition. The outcome has been a reevaluation of many of the fundamental metaethical and metaphysical assumptions made by philosophers pursuing these issues from the modern perspective.

In the following essay, written in 1958, Anscombe argues for three theses. First, she argues that "it is not profitable for us at present to do moral philosophy," because we lack adequate philosophical accounts of psychology, human nature, human action and intention, and "above all of human 'flourishing'." Second, she argues that the "concepts of obligation, and duty—*moral* obligation and *moral* duty . . . and of the *moral* sense of 'ought', ought to be jettisoned if this is psychologically possible" on the grounds that they derive from a divine law conception of ethics, "which no longer generally survives." And, third, she argues (on the basis of the previous two conclusions) that the writings of the major modern moral philosophers from "Sidgwick to the present day are of little importance."

I will begin by stating three theses which I present in this paper. The first is that it is not profitable for us at present to do moral philosophy; that should be laid aside at any rate until we have an adequate philosophy of psychology, in which we are conspicuously lacking. The second is that the concepts of obligation, and

G. E. M. Anscombe, "Modern Moral Philosophy" from *Philosophy* 33 (January 1958), pp. 1–19. Reprinted with the permission of Cambridge University Press.

duty—*moral* obligation and *moral* duty, that is to say—and of what is *morally* right and wrong, and of the *moral* sense of 'ought', ought to be jettisoned if this is psychologically possible; because they are survivals, or derivatives from survivals, from an earlier conception of ethics which no longer generally survives, and are only harmful without it. My third thesis is that the differences between the well-known English writers on moral philosophy from Sidgwick to the present day are of little importance.

Anyone who has read Aristotle's *Ethics* and has also read modern moral philosophy must have been struck by the great contrasts between them. The concepts which are prominent among the moderns seem to be lacking, or at any rate buried or far in the background, in Aristotle. Most noticeably, the term 'moral' itself, which we have by direct inheritance from Aristotle, just doesn't seem to fit, in its modern sense, into an account of Aristotelian ethics. Aristotle distinguishes virtues as moral and intellectual. Have some of what he calls 'intellectual' virtues what *we* should call a 'moral' aspect? It would seem so; the criterion is presumably that a failure in an 'intellectual' virtue—like that of having good judgment in calculating how to bring about something useful, say in municipal government—may be *blameworthy*. But—it may reasonably be asked—cannot *any* failure be made a matter of blame or reproach? Any derogatory criticism, say of the workmanship of a product or the design of a machine, can be called blame or reproach. So we want to put in the word 'morally' again: sometimes such a failure may be *morally* blameworthy, sometimes not. Now has Aristotle got this idea of *moral* blame, as opposed to any other? If he has, why isn't it more central? There are some mistakes, he says, which are causes, not of involuntariness in actions, but of scoundrelism, and for which a man is blamed. Does this mean that there is a *moral* obligation not to make certain intellectual mistakes? Why doesn't he discuss obligation in general, and this obligation in particular? If someone professes to be expounding Aristotle and talks in a modern fashion about 'moral' such-and-such, he must be very imperceptive if he does not constantly feel like someone whose jaws have somehow got out of alignment: the teeth don't come together in a proper bite.

We cannot, then, look to Aristotle for any elucidation of the modern way of talking about 'moral' goodness, obligation, etc. And all the best-known writers on ethics in modern times, from Butler to Mill, appear to me to have faults as thinkers on the subject which make it impossible to hope for any direct light on it from them. I will state these objections with the brevity which their character makes possible.

Butler exalts conscience, but appears ignorant that a man's conscience may tell him to do the vilest things.

Hume defines 'truth' in such a way as to exclude ethical judgements from it, and professes that he has proved that they are so excluded. He also implicitly defines 'passion' in such a way that aiming at anything is having a passion. His objection to passing from 'is' to 'ought' would apply equally to passing from 'is' to 'owes' or from 'is' to 'needs'. (However, because of the historical situation, he has a point here, which I shall return to.)

Kant introduces the idea of 'legislating for oneself,' which is as absurd as if in these days, when majority votes command great respect, one were to call each reflective decision a man made a *vote* resulting in a majority, which as a matter of proportion is overwhelming, for it is always 1–0. The concept of legislation requires superior power in the legislator. His own rigoristic convictions on the subject of lying were so intense that it never occurred to him that a lie could be relevantly described as anything but just a lie (e.g., as 'a lie in such-and-such circumstances'). His rule about universalizable maxims is useless without stipulations as to what shall count as a relevant description of an action with a view to constructing a maxim about it.

Bentham and Mill do not notice the difficulty of the concept 'pleasure'. They are often said to have gone wrong through committing the naturalistic fallacy; but this charge does not impress me, because I do not find accounts of it coherent. But the other point—about pleasure—seems to me a fatal objection from the very outset. The ancients found this concept pretty baffling. It reduced Aristotle to sheer babble about 'the bloom on the cheek of youth' because, for good reasons, he wanted to make it out both identical with and different from the pleasurable activity. Generations of modern philosophers found this concept quite unperplexing, and it reappeared in the literature as a problematic one only a year or two ago when Ryle wrote about it. The reason is simple: since Locke, pleasure was taken to be

some sort of internal impression. But it was superficial, if that was the right account of it, to make it the point of actions. One might adapt something Wittgenstein said about 'meaning' and say "Pleasure cannot be an internal impression, for no internal impression could have the consequences of pleasure."

Mill also, like Kant, fails to realize the necessity for stipulation as to relevant descriptions, if his theory is to have content. It did not occur to him that acts of murder and theft could be otherwise described. He holds that where a proposed action is of such a kind as to fall under some one principle established on grounds of utility, one must go by that; where it falls under none or several, the several suggesting contrary views of the action, the thing to do is to calculate particular consequences. But pretty well any action can be so described as to make it fall under a variety of principles of utility (as I shall say for short) if it falls under any.

I will now return to Hume. The features of Hume's philosophy which I have mentioned, like many other features of it, would incline me to think that Hume was a mere—brilliant—sophist; and his procedures are certainly sophistical. But I am forced, not to reverse, but to add to, this judgment by a peculiarity of Hume's philosophizing: namely that, although he reaches his conclusions—with which he is in love—by sophistical methods, his considerations constantly open up very deep and important problems. It is often the case that in the act of exhibiting the sophistry one finds oneself noticing matters which deserve a lot of exploring: the obvious stands in need of investigation as a result of the points that Hume pretends to have made. In this, he is unlike, say, Butler. It was already well known that conscience could dictate vile actions; for Butler to have written disregarding this does not open up any new topics for us. But with Hume it is otherwise: hence he is a very profound and great philosopher, in spite of his sophistry. For example:

Suppose that I say to my grocer "Truth consists in *either* relations of ideas, as that 20s. = £1, *or* matters of fact, as that I ordered potatoes, you supplied them, and you sent me a bill. So it doesn't apply to such a proposition as that I *owe* you such-and-such a sum."

Now if one makes this comparison, it comes to light that the relation of the facts mentioned to the description 'X owes Y so much money' is an interesting one, which I will call that of being 'brute relative to' that description. Further, the 'brute' facts mentioned here themselves have descriptions relatively to which *other* facts are 'brute'—as, e.g., *he had potatoes carted to my house* and *they were left there* are brute facts relative to 'he supplied me with potatoes'. And the fact *X owes Y money* is in turn 'brute' relative to other descriptions— e.g., '*X is solvent.*' Now the relation of 'relative bruteness' is a complicated one. To mention a few points: if *xyz* is a set of facts brute relative to a description *A*, then *xyz* is a set out of a range some set among which holds if *A* holds; but the holding of some set among these does not necessarily entail *A*, because exceptional circumstances can always make a difference; and what are exceptional circumstances relatively to *A* can generally only be explained by giving a few diverse examples, and *no* theoretically adequate provision can be made for exceptional circumstances, since a further special context can theoretically always be imagined that would reinterpret any special context. Further, though, in normal circumstances, *xyz* would be a justification for *A*, that is not to say that *A* just comes to the same as '*xyz*'; and also there is apt to be an institutional context which gives its point to the description *A*, of which institution *A* is of course not itself a description. (For example, the statement that I give someone a shilling is not a description of the institution of money or of the currency of this country.) Thus, though it would be ludicrous to pretend that there can be no such thing as a transition from, e.g., 'is' to 'owes', the character of the transition is in fact rather interesting and comes to light as a result of reflecting on Hume's arguments.

That I owe the grocer such-and-such a sum would be one of a set of facts which would be 'brute' in relation to the description 'I am a bilker.' 'Bilking' is, of course, a species of 'dishonesty' or 'injustice'. (Naturally the consideration will not have any effect on my actions unless I want to commit or avoid acts of injustice.)

So far, in spite of their strong associations, I conceive 'bilking', 'injustice', and 'dishonesty' in a merely 'factual' way. That I can do this for 'bilking' is obvious enough; 'justice' I have no idea how to define, except that its sphere is that of actions which relate to someone else, but 'injustice', for its defect, can provisionally be offered as a generic name covering various species, e.g., bilking, theft (which is relative to whatever prop-

erty institutions exist), slander, adultery, punishment of the innocent.

In present-day philosophy an explanation is required how an unjust man is a bad man, or an unjust action a bad one; to give such an explanation belongs to ethics; but it cannot even be begun until we are equipped with a sound philosophy of psychology. For the proof that an unjust man is a bad man would require a positive account of justice as a 'virtue'. This part of the subject matter of ethics is, however, completely closed to us until we have an account of what *type of characteristic* a virtue is—a problem, not of ethics, but of conceptual analysis—and how it relates to the actions in which it is instanced: a matter which I think Aristotle did not succeed in really making clear. For this we certainly need an account at least of what a human action is at all, and how its description as 'doing such-and-such' is affected by its motive and by the intention or intentions in it; and for this an account of such concepts is required.

The terms 'should' or 'ought' or 'needs' relate to good and bad: e.g., machinery needs oil, or should or ought to be oiled, in that running without oil is bad for it, or it runs badly without oil. According to this conception, of course, 'should' and 'ought' are not used in a special 'moral' sense when one says that a man should not bilk. (In Aristotle's sense of the term 'moral' (ἠθικός), they are being used in connection with a *moral* subject matter: namely that of human passions and (non-technical) actions.) But they have now acquired a special so-called 'moral' sense—i.e., a sense in which they imply some absolute verdict (like one of guilty/not guilty on a man) on what is described in the 'ought' sentences used in certain types of context: not merely the contexts that *Aristotle* would call 'moral'— passions and actions—but also some of the contexts that he would call 'intellectual'.

The ordinary (and quite indispensable) terms 'should', 'needs', 'ought', 'must'—acquired this special sense by being equated in the relevant contexts with 'is obliged', or 'is bound', or 'is required to', in the sense in which one can be obliged or bound by law, or something can be required by law.

How did this come about? The answer is in history: between Aristotle and us came Christianity, with its *law* conception of ethics. For Christianity derived its ethical notions from the Torah. (One might be inclined to think that a law conception of ethics could arise only among people who accepted an allegedly divine positive law; that this is not so is shown by the example of the Stoics, who also thought that whatever was involved in conformity to human virtues was required by divine law.)

In consequence of the dominance of Christianity for many centuries, the concepts of being bound, permitted, or excused became deeply embedded in our language and thought. The Greek word ἁμαρτάνειν, the aptest to be turned to that use, acquired the sense 'sin', from having meant 'mistake', 'missing the mark', 'going wrong'. The Latin *peccatum* which roughly corresponded to ἁμάρτημα was even apter for the sense 'sin', because it was already associated with *culpa*—'guilt'—a juridical term. The blanket term 'illicit', 'unlawful', meaning much the same as our blanket term 'wrong', explains itself. It is interesting that Aristotle did not have such a blanket term. He has blanket terms for wickedness—'villain', 'scoundrel'; but of course a man is not a villain or a scoundrel by the performance of one bad action, or a few bad actions. And he has terms like 'disgraceful', 'impious'; and specific terms signifying defect of the relevant virtue, like 'unjust'; but no term corresponding to 'illicit'. The extension of this term (i.e., the range of its application) could be indicated in his terminology only by a quite lengthy sentence: that is 'illicit', which, whether it is a thought or a consented-to passion or an action or an omission in thought or action, is something contrary to one of the virtues the lack of which shows a man to be bad *qua* man. That formulation would yield a concept coextensive with the concept 'illicit'.

To have a *law* conception of ethics is to hold that what is needed for conformity with the virtues failure in which is the mark of being bad *qua* man (and not merely, say, *qua* craftsman or logician)—that what is needed for *this,* is required by divine law. Naturally it is not possible to have such a conception unless you believe in God as a lawgiver; like Jews, Stoics, and Christians. But if such a conception is dominant for many centuries, and then is given up, it is a natural result that the concepts of 'obligation', of being bound or required as by a law, should remain though they had lost their root; and if the word 'ought' has become invested in

certain contexts with the sense of 'obligation', it too will remain to be spoken with a special emphasis and a special feeling in these contexts.

It is as if the notion 'criminal' were to remain when criminal law and criminal courts had been abolished and forgotten. A Hume discovering this situation might conclude that there was a special sentiment, expressed by 'criminal', which alone gave the word its sense. So Hume discovered the situation in which the notion 'obligation' survived, and the word 'ought' was invested with that peculiar force having which it is said to be used in a 'moral' sense, but in which the belief in divine law had long since been abandoned: for it was substantially given up among Protestants at the time of the Reformation.[1] The situation, if I am right, was the interesting one of the survival of a concept outside the framework of thought that made it a really intelligible one.

When Hume produced his famous remarks about the transition from 'is' to 'ought', he was, then, bringing together several quite different points. One I have tried to bring out by my remarks on the transition from 'is' to 'owes' and on the relative 'bruteness' of facts. It would be possible to bring out a different point by enquiring about the transition from 'is' to 'needs'; from the characteristics of an organism to the environment that it needs, for example. To say that it needs that environment is not to say, e.g., that you want it to have that environment, but that it won't flourish unless it has it. Certainly, it all depends whether you *want* it to flourish! as Hume would say. But what 'all depends' on whether you want it to flourish is whether the fact that it needs that environment, or won't flourish without it, has the slightest influence on your actions. Now *that* such-and-such 'ought' to be or 'is needed' is supposed to have an influence on your actions: from which it seemed natural to infer that to judge that it 'ought to be' was in fact to grant what you judged 'ought to be' influence on your actions. And no amount of truth as to what *is* the case could possibly have a logical claim to have influence on your actions. (It is not judgment as such that sets us in motion; but our judgment on how to get or do something we *want*.) Hence it *must* be impossible to infer 'needs' or 'ought to be' from 'is'. But in the case of a plant, let us say, the inference from 'is' to 'needs' is certainly not in the least dubious. It is interesting and worth examining; but not at all fishy. Its interest is similar to the interest of the relation between brute and less brute facts: these relations have been very little considered. And while you can contrast 'what it needs' with 'what it's got'—like contrasting *de facto* and *de jure*—that does not make its needing this environment less of a 'truth'.

Certainly in the case of what the plant needs, the thought of a need will only affect action if you want the plant to flourish. Here, then, there is no necessary connection between what you can judge the plant 'needs' and what you want. But there is some sort of necessary connection between what you think *you* need, and what you want. The connection is a complicated one; it is possible *not* to want something that you judge you need. But, e.g., it is not possible never to want *anything* that you judge you need. This, however, is a fact not about the meaning of the word 'to need', but about the phenomenon of *wanting*. Hume's reasoning, we might say, in effect, leads one to think it must be about the word 'to need', or 'to be good for'.

Thus we find two problems already wrapped up in the remark about a transition from 'is' to 'ought'; now supposing that we had clarified the 'relative bruteness' of facts, on the one hand, and the notions involved in 'needing', and 'flourishing', on the other—there would *still* remain a third point. For, following Hume, someone might say: Perhaps you have made out your point about a transition from 'is' to 'owes' and from 'is' to 'needs': but only at the cost of showing 'owes' and 'needs' sentences to express a *kind* of truths, a *kind* of facts. And it remains impossible to infer '*morally ought*' from 'is'.

This comment, it seems to me, would be correct. This word 'ought', having become a word of mere mesmeric force, could not, in the character of having that force, be inferred from anything whatever. It may be objected that it could be inferred from other 'morally ought' sentences: but that cannot be true. The appearance that this is so is produced by the fact that we say 'All men are φ' and 'Socrates is a man' implies 'Socrates is φ'. But here 'φ' is a dummy predicate. We mean that if you substitute a real predicate for 'φ' the implication is valid. A real predicate is required; not just a word containing no intelligible thought: a word retaining the suggestion of force, and apt to have a strong psycholog-

ical effect, but which no longer signifies a real concept at all.

For its suggestion is one of a *verdict* on my action, according as it agrees or disagrees with the description in the 'ought' sentence. And where one does not think there is a judge or a law, the notion of a verdict may retain its psychological effect, but not its meaning. Now imagine that just this word 'verdict' *were* so used—with a characteristically solemn emphasis—as to retain its atmosphere but not its meaning, and someone were to say: "For a *verdict*, after all, you need a law and a judge." The reply might be made: "Not at all, for if there were a law and a judge who gave a verdict, the question for us would be whether accepting that verdict is something that there is a *Verdict* on." This is an analogue of an argument which is so frequently referred to as decisive: if someone does have a divine law conception of ethics, all the same, he has to agree that he has to have a judgment that he *ought* (morally ought) to obey the divine law; so his ethic is in exactly the same position as any other: he merely has a 'practical major premise':[2] 'Divine law ought to be obeyed' where someone else has, e.g., "The greatest happiness principle ought to be employed in all decisions."

I should judge that Hume and our present-day ethicists had done a considerable service by showing that no content could be found in the notion 'morally ought', if it were not that the latter philosophers try to find an alternative (very fishy) content and to retain the psychological force of the term. It would be most reasonable to drop it. It has no reasonable sense outside a law conception of ethics; they are not going to maintain such a conception; and you can do ethics without it, as is shown by the example of Aristotle. It would be a great improvement if, instead of 'morally wrong', one always named a genus such as 'untruthful', 'unchaste', 'unjust'. We should no longer ask whether doing something was 'wrong', passing directly from some description of an action to this notion; we should ask whether, e.g., it was unjust; and the answer would sometimes be clear at once.

I now come to the epoch in modern English moral philosophy marked by Sidgwick. There is a startling change that seems to have taken place between Mill and Moore. Mill assumes, as we saw, that there is no question of calculating particular consequences of an action such as murder or theft; and we saw too that his position was stupid, because it is not at all clear how an action *can* fall under just one principle of utility. In Moore and in subsequent academic moralists of England we find it taken to be pretty obvious that 'the right action' means the one which produces the best possible consequences (reckoning among consequences the intrinsic values ascribed to certain kinds of act by some 'Objectivists'[3]). Now it follows from this that a man does well, subjectively speaking, if he acts for the best in the particular circumstances according to his judgment of the total consequences of this particular action. I say that this follows, not that any philosopher has said precisely that. For discussion of these questions can of course get extremely complicated: e.g., it can be doubted whether 'such-and-such is the right action' is a satisfactory formulation, on the grounds that things have to exist to have predicates—so perhaps the best formulation is 'I am obliged'; or again, a philosopher may deny that 'right' is a 'descriptive' term, and then take a roundabout route through linguistic analysis to reach a view which comes to the same thing as 'the right action is the one productive of the best consequences' (e.g., the view that you frame your 'principles' to effect the end you choose to pursue, the connection between 'choice' and 'best' being supposedly such that choosing reflectively means that you choose how to act so as to produce the best consequences); further, the roles of what are called 'moral principles' and of the 'motive of duty' have to be described; the differences between 'good' and 'morally good' and 'right' need to be explored, the special characteristics of 'ought' sentences investigated. Such discussions generate an appearance of significant diversity of views where what is really significant is an overall similarity. The overall similarity is made clear if you consider that every one of the best known English academic moral philosophers has put out a philosophy according to which, e.g., it is not possible to hold that it cannot be right to kill the innocent as a means to any end whatsoever and that someone who thinks otherwise is in error. (I have to mention both points; because Mr. Hare, for example, while teaching a philosophy which would encourage a person to judge that killing the innocent would be what he ought to choose for overriding purposes, would also teach, I

think, that, if a man chooses to make avoiding killing the innocent for any purpose his 'supreme practical principle', he cannot be impugned for error: that just is his 'principle'. But with that qualification, I think it can be seen that the point I have mentioned holds good of every single English academic moral philosopher since Sidgwick.) Now this is a significant thing: for it means that all these philosophies are quite incompatible with the Hebrew–Christian ethic. For it has been characteristic of that ethic to teach that there are certain things forbidden whatever *consequences* threaten, such as: choosing to kill the innocent for any purpose, however good; vicarious punishment; treachery (by which I mean obtaining a man's confidence in a grave matter by promises of trustworthy friendship and then betraying him to his enemies); idolatry; sodomy; adultery; making a false profession of faith. The prohibition of certain things simply in virtue of their description as such-and-such identifiable kinds of action, regardless of any further consequences, is certainly not the whole of the Hebrew–Christian ethic; but it is a noteworthy feature of it; and, if every academic philosopher since Sidgwick has written in such a way as to exclude this ethic, it would argue a certain provinciality of mind not to see this incompatibility as the most important fact about these philosophers, and the differences between them as somewhat trifling by comparison.

It is noticeable that none of these philosophers displays any consciousness that there is such an ethic, which he is contradicting: it is pretty well taken for obvious among them all that a prohibition such as that on murder does not operate in face of some consequences. But of course the strictness of the prohibition has as its point *that you are not to be tempted by fear or hope of consequences.*

If you notice the transition from Mill to Moore, you will suspect that it was made somewhere by someone; Sidgwick will come to mind as a likely name; and you will in fact find it going on, almost casually, in him. He is rather a dull author; and the important things in him occur in asides and footnotes and small bits of argument which are not concerned with his grand classification of the 'methods of ethics'. A divine-law theory of ethics is reduced to an insignificant variety by a footnote telling us that 'the best theologians' (God knows whom he meant) tell us that God is to be obeyed in his capacity of a *moral* being. ἢ φορτικός ὁ ἔπαινος; one seems to hear Aristotle saying: 'Isn't the praise vulgar?'—but Sidgwick *is* vulgar in that kind of way: he thinks, for example, that humility consists in underestimating your own merits—i.e., in a species of untruthfulness; and that the ground for having laws against blasphemy was that it was offensive to believers; and that to go accurately into the virtue of purity is to offend against its canons, a thing he reproves 'medieval theologians' for not realizing.

From the point of view of the present enquiry, the most important thing about Sidgwick was his definition of intention. He defines intention in such a way that one must be said to intend any foreseen consequences of one's voluntary action. This definition is obviously incorrect, and I dare say that no one would be found to defend it now. He uses it to put forward an ethical thesis which would now be accepted by many people: the thesis that it does not make any difference to a man's responsibility for something that he foresaw, that he felt no desire for it, either as an end or as a means to an end. Using the language of intention more correctly, and avoiding Sidgwick's faulty conception, we may state the thesis thus: it does not make any difference to a man's responsibility for an effect of his action which he can foresee, that he does not intend it. Now this sounds rather edifying; it is I think quite characteristic of very bad degenerations of thought on such questions that they sound edifying. We can see what it amounts to by considering an example. Let us suppose that a man has a responsibility for the maintenance of some child. Therefore deliberately to withdraw support from it is a bad sort of thing for him to do. It would be bad for him to withdraw its maintenance because he didn't want to maintain it any longer; *and* also bad for him to withdraw it because by doing so he would, let us say, compel someone else to do something. (We may suppose for the sake of argument that compelling that person to do that thing is in itself quite admirable.) But now he has to choose between doing something disgraceful and going to prison; if he goes to prison, it will follow that he withdraws support from the child. By Sidgwick's doctrine, there is no difference in his responsibility for ceasing to maintain the child, between the case where he does it for its own sake or as a means to some other purpose, and when it happens as a foreseen and unavoidable consequence of his going to prison rather than do something disgraceful. It follows that he must weigh up the relative badness of withdrawing support from the child and of doing the disgraceful thing; and it may easily be that the disgraceful thing is in fact a less vicious action than intentionally withdrawing support from the child would be; if then the fact that withdrawing support from the child is a side effect of his going to prison does not make any difference to his responsibility, this consideration will incline him to do the disgraceful thing; which can still be pretty bad. And of course, once he has started to look at the matter in this light, the only reasonable thing for him to consider will be the consequences and not the intrinsic badness of this or that action. So that, given that he judges reasonably that no *great* harm will come of it, he can do a much more disgraceful thing than deliberately withdrawing support from the child. And if his calculations turn out in fact wrong, it will appear that he was not responsible for the consequences, because he did not foresee them. For in fact Sidgwick's thesis leads to its being quite impossible to estimate the badness of an action except in the light of *expected* consequences. But if so, then *you* must estimate the badness in the light of the consequences *you* expect; and so it will follow that you can exculpate yourself from the *actual* consequences of the most discraceful actions, so long as you can make out a case for not having foreseen them. Whereas I should contend that a man is responsible for the bad consequences of his bad actions, but gets no credit for the good ones; and contrariwise is not responsible for the bad consequences of good actions.

The denial of *any* distinction between foreseen and intended consequences, as far as responsibility is concerned, was not made by Sidgwick in developing any one 'method of ethics'; he made this important move on behalf of everybody and just on its own account; and I think it plausible to suggest that *this* move on the part of Sidgwick explains the difference between old-fashioned Utilitarianism and that *consequentialism*, as I name it, which marks him and every English academic moral philosopher since him. By it, the kind of consideration which would formerly have been regarded as a temptation, the kind of consideration urged upon men by wives and flattering friends, was given a status by moral philosophers in their theories.

It is a necessary feature of consequentialism that it is a shallow philosophy. For there are always borderline cases in ethics. Now if you are either an Aristotelian, or a believer in divine law, you will deal with a borderline case by considering whether doing such-and-such in such-and-such circumstances is, say, murder, or is an act of injustice; and according as you decide it is or it isn't, you judge it to be a thing to do or not. This would be the method of casuistry; and while it may lead you to stretch a point on the circumference, it will not permit you to destroy the center. But if you are a consequentialist, the question "What is it right to do in such-and-such circumstances?" is a stupid one to raise. The casuist raises such a question only to ask "Would it be *permissible* to do so-and-so?" or "Would it be permissible *not* to do so-and-so?" Only if it would *not* be permissible *not* to do so-and-so could he say "*This* would be *the* thing to do."[4] Otherwise, though he may speak *against* some action, he cannot prescribe any—for in an *actual* case, the circumstances (beyond the ones imagined) might suggest all sorts of possibilities, and you can't know in advance what the possibilities are going to be. Now the consequentialist has no footing on which to say "This would be permissible, this not"; because by his own hypothesis, it is the consequences that are to decide, and he has no business to pretend that he can lay it down what possible twists a man could give doing this or that; the most he can say is: a man must not *bring about* this or that; he has no right to say he will, in an actual case, bring about such-and-such unless he does so-and-so. Further, the consequentialist, in order to be imagining borderline cases at all, has of course to assume some sort of law or standard according to which this is a borderline case. Where then does he get the standard from? In practice the answer invariably is: from the standards current in his society or his circle. And it has in fact been the mark of all these philosophers that they have been extremely conventional; they have nothing in them by which to revolt against the conventional standards of their sort of people; it is impossible that they should be profound. But the chance that a whole range of conventional standards will be decent is small. Finally, the point of considering hypothetical situations, perhaps very improbable ones, *seems* to be to elicit from yourself or someone else a hypothetical decision to do something of a bad kind. I don't doubt this has the effect of predisposing people—who will never get into the situations for which they have made hypothetical choices—to consent to similar bad actions, or to praise and flatter those imagined as doing them, so long as their crowd does so too, when the desperate circumstances imagined don't hold at all.

Those who recognize the origins of the notions of 'obligation' and of the emphatic, 'moral', *ought*, in the divine-law conception of ethics, but who reject the notion of a divine legislator, sometimes look about for the possibility of retaining a law conception without a divine legislator. This search, I think, has some interest in it. Perhaps the first thing that suggests itself is the 'norms' of a society. But just as one cannot be impressed by Butler when one reflects what conscience can tell people to do, so, I think, one cannot be impressed by this idea if one reflects what the 'norms' of a society can be like. That legislation can be 'for oneself' I reject as absurd; whatever you do 'for yourself' may be admirable; but is not legislating. Once one sees this, one may say: I have to frame my own rules, and these are the best I can frame, and I shall go by them until I know something better: as a man might say, "I shall go by the customs of my ancestors." Whether this leads to good or evil will depend on the *content* of the rules or of the customs of one's ancestors. If one is lucky it will lead to good. Such an attitude would be hopeful in this at any rate: it seems to have in it some Socratic doubt where, from having to fall back on such expedients, it should be clear that Socratic doubt is good; in fact rather generally it must be good for anyone to think "Perhaps in some way I can't see, I may be on a bad path, perhaps I am hopelessly wrong in some essential way." The search for 'norms' might lead someone to look for laws of nature, as if the universe were a legislator; but in the present day this is not likely to lead to good results: it might lead one to eat the weaker according to the laws of nature, but would hardly lead anyone nowadays to notions of justice; the pre-Socratic feeling about justice as comparable to the balance or harmony which kept things going is very remote to us.

There is another possibility here: 'obligation' may be contractual. Just as we look at the law to find out what a man subject to it is required by it to do, so we look at a contract to find out what the man who has made it is required by it to do. Thinkers, admittedly remote from us, might have the idea of a *foedus rerum,* of the universe not as a legislator but as the embodiment of a contract. Then if you could find out what the contract was, you would learn your obligations under it. Now, you cannot be under a law unless it has been promulgated to you; and the thinkers who believed in 'natural divine law' held that it was promulgated to every grown man in his knowledge of good and evil. Similarly you cannot be in a contract without having contracted, i.e., given signs of entering upon the contract. Just possibly, it might be argued that the use of language which one makes in the ordinary conduct of life amounts in some sense to giving the signs of entering into various contracts. If anyone had this theory, we should want to see it worked out. I suspect that it would be largely formal; it might be possible to construct a system embodying the law (whose status might be compared to that of 'laws' of logic): 'what's sauce for the goose is sauce for the gander,' but hardly one descending to such particularities as the prohibition on murder or sodomy. Also, while it is clear that you can be subject to a law that you do not acknowledge and have not thought of as law, it does not seem reasonable to say that you can enter upon a contract without knowing that you are doing so; such ignorance is usually held to be destructive of the nature of a contract.

It might remain to look for 'norms' in human virtues: just as *man* has so many teeth, which is certainly not the average number of teeth men have, but is the number of teeth for the species, so perhaps the species *man,* regarded not just biologically, but from the point of view of the activity of thought and choice in regard to the various departments of life—powers and faculties and use of things needed—'has' such-and-such virtues: and this 'man' with the complete set of virtues is the 'norm', as 'man' with, e.g., a complete set of teeth is a norm. But in *this* sense 'norm' has ceased to be roughly equivalent to 'law'. In *this* sense the notion of a 'norm' brings us nearer to an Aristotelian than a law conception of ethics. There is, I think, no harm in that; but if someone looked in this direction to give 'norm' a sense, then he ought to recognize what has happened to the term 'norm', which he wanted to mean 'law—without bringing God in': it has ceased to mean 'law' at all; and *so* the expressions 'moral obligation', 'the moral ought', and 'duty' are best put on the Index, if he can manage it.

But meanwhile—is it not clear that there are several concepts that need investigating simply as part of the philosophy of psychology and—as I should recommend—*banishing ethics totally* from our minds? Namely—to begin with: 'action', 'intention', 'pleasure', 'wanting'. More will probably turn up if we start with these. Eventually it might be possible to advance to considering the concept of a virtue; with which, I suppose, we should be beginning some sort of a study of ethics.

I will end by describing the advantages of using the word 'ought' in a non-emphatic fashion, and not in a special 'moral' sense; of discarding the term 'wrong' in a 'moral sense, and using such notions as 'unjust'.

It is possible, if one is allowed to proceed just by giving examples, to distinguish between the intrinsically unjust, and what is unjust given the circumstances. Seriously to get a man judicially punished for something which it can be clearly seen he has not done is intrinsically unjust. This might be done, of course, and often has been done, in all sorts of ways; by suborning false witnesses, by a rule of law by which something is 'deemed' to be the case which is admittedly not the case as a matter of fact, and by open insolence on the part of the judges and powerful people when they more or less openly say: "A fig for the fact that you did not do it; we mean to sentence you for it all the same." What is unjust given, e.g., normal circumstances is to deprive people of their ostensible property without legal procedure, not to pay debts, not to keep contracts, and a host of other things of the kind. Now, the circumstances can clearly make a great deal of difference in estimating the justice or injustice of such procedures as these; and these circumstances may *sometimes* include expected consequences; for example, a man's claim to a bit of property can become a nullity when its seizure and use can avert some obvious disaster: as, e.g., if you could use a machine of his to produce an explosion in which it would be destroyed, but by means of which you could divert a flood or make a gap which a fire could not jump. Now this certainly does not mean that what would ordinarily be an act of injustice, but is not intrinsically unjust, can always be rendered just by a reasonable calculation of better consequences; far from it; but the problems that would be raised in an attempt to draw a boundary line (or boundary area) here are obviously complicated. And while there are certainly some general remarks which ought to be made here, and some boundaries that can be drawn, the decision on particular cases would for the most part be determined κατὰ τὸν ὀρθὸν λόγον—'according to what's reasonable'—e.g., that *such-and-such* a delay of payment of a *such-and-such* debt to a person *so* circumstanced, on the part of a person *so* circumstanced, would or would not be unjust, is really only to be decided 'according to what's reasonable'; and for this there can *in principle* be no canon other than giving a few examples. That is to say, while it is because of a big gap in philosophy that we can give no general account of the concept of virtue and of the concept of justice, but have to proceed, using the concepts, only by giving examples; still there is an area where it is not because of any gap, but is in principle the case, that there is no account except by way of examples: and that is where the canon is 'what's reason able' reasonable': which of course is *not* a canon.

That is all I wish to say about what is just in some circumstances, unjust in others; and about the way in which expected consequences can play a part in determining what is just. Returning to my example of the intrinsically unjust: if a procedure *is* one of judicially punishing a man for what he is clearly understood not to have done, there can be absolutely no argument about the description of this as unjust. No circumstances, and no expected consequences, which do *not* modify the description of the procedure as one of judicially punishing a man for what he is known not to have done can modify the description of it as unjust. Someone who attempted to dispute this would only be pretending not to know what 'unjust' means: for this is a paradigm case of injustice.

And here we see the superiority of the term 'unjust' over the terms 'morally right' and 'morally wrong'. For in the context of English moral philosophy since Sidgwick it appears legitimate to discuss whether it *might* be 'morally right' in some circumstances to adopt that procedure; but it cannot be argued that the procedure would in any circumstances be just.

Now I am not able to do the philosophy involved—and I think that no one in the present situation of English philosophy *can* do the philosophy involved—but it is clear that a good man is a just man; and a just man is a man who habitually refuses to commit or participate in any unjust actions for fear of any consequences, or to obtain any advantage, for himself or anyone else. Perhaps no one will disagree. But, it will be said, what *is* unjust is sometimes determined by expected consequences; and certainly that is true. But there are cases where it is not: now if someone says, "I agree, but all this wants a lot of explaining," then he is right, and, what is more, the situation at present is that we can't do the explaining; we lack the philosophic equipment. But if someone really thinks, *in advance,*[5] that it is open to question whether such an action as procuring the judicial execution of the innocent should be quite excluded from consideration—I do not want to argue with him; he shows a corrupt mind.

In such cases our moral philosophers seek to impose a dilemma upon us. 'If we have a case where the term "unjust" applies purely in virtue of a factual description, can't one raise the question whether one sometimes conceivably ought to do injustice? If "what is unjust" is determined by consideration of whether it is *right* to do so-and-so in such-and-such circumstances, then the question whether it is "right" to commit injustice can't arise, just because "wrong" has been built into the definition of injustice. But if we have a case where the description "unjust" applies purely in virtue of the facts, without bringing "wrong" in, then the question can arise whether one "ought" perhaps to commit an injustice, whether it might not be "right" to. And of course "ought" and "right" are being used in their *moral* senses here. Now either you must decide what is "morally right" in the light of certain *other* "principles", or you make a "principle" about *this* and decide that an injustice is never "right"; but even if you do the latter you are going beyond the facts; you are making a decision that you will not, or that it is wrong to, commit injustice. But in either case, *if* the term "unjust" is determined simply by the facts, it is not the term "unjust" that determines that the term "wrong" applies, but a decision that injustice is *wrong,* together with the diagnosis of the "factual" description as entailing injustice. But the man who makes an absolute decision that injustice is "wrong" has no footing on which to criticize someone who does *not* make that decision as judging falsely.'

In this argument 'wrong' of course is explained as meaning 'morally wrong', and all the atmosphere of the term is retained while its substance is guaranteed quite null. Now let us remember that 'morally wrong' is the term which is the heir of the notion 'illicit', or 'what there is an obligation *not* to do'; which belongs in a divine-law theory of ethics. Here it really does add something to the description 'unjust' to say there is an obligation not to do it; for what obliges is the divine law—as rules oblige in a game. So if the divine law obliges not to commit injustice by forbidding injustice, it really does add something to the description 'unjust' to say there is an obligation not to do it. And it is because 'morally wrong' is the heir of this concept, but an heir that is cut off from the family of concepts from which it sprang, that 'morally wrong' *both* goes beyond the mere factual description 'unjust' *and* seems to have no discernible content except a certain compelling force, which I should call purely psychological. And such is the force of the term that philosophers actually suppose that the divine law notion can be dismissed as making no essential difference even if it is held—*because* they think that a 'practical principle' running 'I *ought* (i.e., am morally obliged) to obey divine laws' is required for the man who believes in divine laws. But actually *this* notion of obligation is a notion which only operates in the context of law. And I should be inclined to congratulate the present-day moral philosophers on depriving 'morally ought' of its now delusive appearance of content, if only they did not manifest a detestable desire to retain the atmosphere of the term.

It may be possible, if we are resolute, to discard the term 'morally ought', and simply return to the ordinary 'ought', which, we ought to notice, is such an extremely frequent term of human language that it is difficult to imagine getting on without it. Now if we do return to it, can't it reasonably be asked whether one might ever need to commit injustice, or whether it won't be the best thing to do? Of course it can. And the answers will be various. One man—a philosopher—may say that since justice is a virtue, and injustice a vice, and virtues and vices are built up by the performance of the actions in which they are instanced, an act of injustice will tend to make a man bad; and essentially the flourishing of a man *qua* man consists in his being good (e.g., in virtues); but for any *X* to which such terms apply, *X* needs what makes it flourish, so a man needs, or ought to perform, only virtuous actions; and even if, as it must be admitted may happen, he flourishes less, or not at all, in inessentials, by avoiding injustice, his life is spoiled in essentials by not avoiding injustice—so he still needs to perform only just actions. That is roughly how Plato and Aristotle talk; but it can be seen that philosophically there is a huge gap, at present unfillable as far as we are concerned, which needs to be filled by an account of human nature, human action, the type of characteristic a virtue is, and above all of human 'flourishing'. And it is the last concept that appears the most doubtful. For it is a bit much to swallow that a man in pain and hunger and poor and friendless is flourishing, as Aristotle himself admitted. Further, someone might say that one at least needed to stay alive to flourish. Another man unimpressed by all that will say in a hard case "What we need is such-and-such, which we won't get without doing this (which is unjust)—so this is what we ought to do." Another man, who does not follow the rather elaborate reasoning of the philosophers, simply says "I know it is in any case a disgraceful thing to say that one had better commit this unjust action." The man who believes in divine laws will say perhaps "It is forbidden, and however it looks, it cannot be to anyone's profit to commit injustice"; he like the Greek philosophers can think in terms of flourishing. If he is a Stoic, he is apt to have a decidedly strained notion of what flourishing consists in; if he is a Jew or Christian, he need not have any very distinct notion: the way it will profit him to abstain from injustice is something that he leaves it to God to determine, himself only saying "It can't do me any good to go against his law." (He also hopes for a great reward in a new life later on, e.g., at the coming of Messiah; but in this he is relying on special promises.)

It is left to modern moral philosophy—the moral philosophy of all the well-known English ethicists since Sidgwick—to construct systems according to which the man who says "We need such-and-such, and will only get it this way" *may* be a virtuous character: that is to say, it is left open to debate whether such a procedure as the judicial punishment of the innocent may not in some circumstances be the 'right' one to adopt; and though the present Oxford moral philosophers would accord a man *permission* to 'make it his principle' not to do such a thing, they teach a philosophy according to which the particular consequences of such an action *could* 'morally' be taken into account by a man who was debating what to do; and if they were such as to accord with his ends, it might be a step in his moral education to frame a moral principle under which he 'managed' (to use Mr Nowell-Smith's phrase) to bring the action; or it might be a new 'decision of principle', making which was an advance in the formation of his moral thinking (to adopt Mr Hare's conception), to decide: in such-and-such circumstances one ought to procure the judicial condemnation of the innocent. And that is my complaint.

Notes

1. They did not deny the existence of divine law; but their most characteristic doctrine was that it was given, not to be obeyed, but to show man's incapacity to obey it, even by grace; and this applied not merely to the ramified prescriptions of the Torah, but to the requirements of 'natural divine law'. Cf. in this connection the decree of Trent against the teaching that Christ was only to be trusted in as mediator, not obeyed as legislator.

2. As it is absurdly called. Since major premise = premise containing the term which is predicate in the conclusion, it is a solecism to speak of it in the connection with practical reasoning.

3. Oxford Objectivists, of course, distinguish between 'consequences' and 'intrinsic values' and so produce a misleading appearance of not being consequentialists. But they do not hold—and Ross explicitly denies—that the gravity of, e.g., procuring the condemnation of the innocent is such that it cannot be outweighed by, e.g., national interest. Hence their distinction is of no importance.

4. Necessarily a rare case: for the positive precepts, e.g., 'Honor your parents', hardly ever prescribe, and seldom even necessitate any particular action.

5. If he thinks it in the concrete situation, he is of course merely a normally tempted human being. In discussion when this paper was read, as was perhaps to be expected, this case was produced: a government is required to have an innocent man tried, sentenced and executed under threat of a 'hydrogen bomb war'. It would seem strange to me to have much hope of so averting a war threatened by such men as made this demand. But the most important thing about the way in which cases like this are invented in discussions, is the assumption that only two courses are open; here, compliance and open defiance. No one can say in advance of such a situation what the possibilities are going to be—e.g., that there is none of stalling by a feigned willingness to comply, accompanied by a skillfully arranged 'escape' of the victim.

READING QUESTIONS

1. Anscombe says that "we cannot . . . look to Aristotle for any elucidation of the modern way of talking about 'moral' goodness, obligation, etc." Briefly explain why. She continues, saying that "and all the best-known writers on ethics in modern times, from Butler to Mill, appear to me to have faults as thinkers on the subject which make it impossible to hope for any direct light on it from them." She goes on to catalogue the faults that she finds. Briefly list these faults.

2. Why does Anscombe believe that we will be unable to give an explanation of how an unjust man is a bad man until we have "a sound philosophy of psychology"?

3. What is the significance, for Anscombe, of the fact that "between Aristotle and us came Christianity"?

4. Anscombe claims that if a law conception of ethics is "dominant for many centuries, and then is given up, it is a natural result that the concepts of 'obligation', of being bound or required as by a law, should remain though they had lost their root." According to her, what impact does this have on Hume's remarks about 'is' and 'ought'?

5. Why does Anscombe say that the notion of 'morally wrong' has "no reasonable sense outside a law conception of ethcs"? What impact does this have on the status of modern moral philosophy?

6. Anscombe states that "it is a necessary feature of consequentialism that it is a shallow philosophy." What does she mean by 'shallow'? In what ways does she think that consequentialism is shallow?

7. Anscombe remarks that "those who recognize the origins of the notion of 'obligation' and of the emphatic, '*moral*', *ought*, in the divine-law conception of ethics, but who reject the notion of a divine legislator, sometimes look about for the possibility of retaining a law conception without a divine legislator." What strategies might such a person pursue? How does Anscombe respond to these various attempts to ground a law conception outside of a divine legislator?

8. Why does Anscombe believe that terms such as 'unjust' are superior to terms such as 'morally right' and 'morally wrong'? Do you agree? Why or why not?

9. Anscombe considers the following objection to her view: "If we have a case where the term 'unjust' applies purely in virtue of a factual description, can't one raise the question whether one sometimes conceivably ought to do injustice?" What is her reply to this question?

SUGGESTIONS FOR FURTHER READING (G. E. M. ANSCOMBE)

Primary Sources and Collected Writings

(1939) (and N. Daniel) *The Justice of the Present War Examined*. Oxford: published by the authors.

(1957) *Mr. Truman's Degree*. Oxford: published by the author.

(1957) *Intention*, 2nd ed. Oxford: Basil Blackwell, 1963.

(1959) *An Introduction to Wittgenstein's 'Tractatus'*, 2nd ed. Philadelphia, PA: University of Pennsylvania Press, 1971.

(1961) (and P. Geach) *Three Philosophers*. Ithaca, NY: Cornell University Press.

(1981) *The Collected Philosophical Papers of G. E. M. Anscombe*, 3 vols. Minneapolis, MN: University of Minnesota Press.

Secondary Sources

Davidson, D. (1980) *Essays on Actions and Events*. Oxford: Oxford University Press.

Diamond, C., and J. Teichmann (1979) *Intentions and Intentionality*. Ithaca, NY: Cornell University Press.

Foot, P. (1978) *Virtues and Vices*, Berkeley, CA: University of California Press.

Richter, D. (1999) *Ethics After Anscombe*. Dordrecht: Kluwer Academic Publishers.

Teichmann, R., ed. (2000) *Logic, Cause and Action: Essays in Honour of Elizabeth Anscombe*. Cambridge: Cambridge University Press.

PART V / Contemporary Philosophy

WILLARD VAN ORMAN (W. V. O.) QUINE

Two Dogmas of Empiricism

Willard Van Orman Quine (1908–) was born and raised in Akron, Ohio. He studied mathematics and philosophy at Oberlin College before going on to Harvard University. At Harvard he wrote his dissertation on a topic in logic and the philosophy of mathematics under the direction of Alfred North Whitehead (co-author with Bertrand Russell of *Principia Mathematica*), graduating in just two years with his Ph.D. in 1932. His studies in logic at Harvard brought him into closer acquaintance both with the work of the leading logicists in Europe and also with a key figure in American pragmatism—his teacher, Clarence Irving Lewis.

Quine's work earned him a fellowship. After graduation he traveled to Europe to become more acquainted with the leading figures in mathematical philosophy working on the Continent. His explorations took him to Vienna, where he discussed philosophy with Moritz Schlick, Friedrich Waismann, and Kurt Gödel; to Prague, where he spent much time in close contact with Rudolf Carnap; and to Warsaw, where he talked about the logical foundations of mathematics with Alfred Tarski, the brilliant Polish mathematician, logician, and philosopher of language. The direct and indirect influence of positivism on Quine was enormous and, although he would come to reject much of the positivist's credo in later years, it would play a major role in shaping both his philosophical temperament and his appreci-

ation and understanding of the methods of the natural sciences.

Shortly after returning to the United States, Quine took a teaching position at Harvard, where he remained until his retirement in 1978. In 1955 he was appointed Edgar Pierce Professor of Philosophy. His only extended absence from Harvard came during the Second World War, when he volunteered for military service, held the rank of lieutenant commander, and worked briefly in naval intelligence. A great lover of travel, maps, and languages, Quine has visited more than a hundred countries and has had his work translated and published throughout the world. He remains one of the great figures of contemporary philosophy.

In the following essay, written in 1951, Quine advances a series of arguments designed to undermine our confidence in what he calls the "two dogmas of empiricism." The first dogma is a belief "in some fundamental cleavage between truths which are *analytic*, or grounded in meanings independent of fact, and truths which are *synthetic*, or grounded in fact." The second dogma is "*reductionism*: the belief that each meaningful statement is equivalent to some logical construct upon terms which refer to immediate experience." The impact of abandoning these commitments, if Quine is correct, should be felt in two ways. On one hand we should see "a blurring of the supposed boundary between speculative metaphysics and natural science." That is, we should expect that philosophy should move in a more naturalistic direction. And on the other hand, our overall philosophical outlook should undergo "a shift towards pragmatism." Quine's goal is not to persuade us to reject empiricism, but rather to become more thoroughgoing or enlightened empiricists.

Modern empiricism has been conditioned in large part by two dogmas. One is a belief in some fundamental cleavage between truths which are *analytic,* or grounded in meanings independently of matters of fact, and truths which are *synthetic,* or grounded in fact. The other dogma is *reductionism*: the belief that each meaningful statement is equivalent to some logical construct upon terms which refer to immediate experience. Both dogmas, I shall argue, are ill-founded. One effect of abandoning them is, as we shall see, a blurring of the supposed boundary between speculative metaphysics and natural science. Another effect is a shift toward pragmatism.

1. Background for Analyticity

Kant's cleavage between analytic and synthetic truths was foreshadowed in Hume's distinction between relations of ideas and matters of fact, and in Leibniz's distinction between truths of reason and truths of fact. Leibniz spoke of the truths of reason as true in all possible worlds. Picturesqueness aside, this is to say that the truths of reason are those which could not possibly be false. In the same vein we hear analytic statements defined as statements whose denials are self-contradictory. But this definition has small explanatory value; for the notion of self-contradictoriness, in the quite broad sense needed for this definition of analyticity, stands in exactly the same need of clarification as does the notion of analyticity itself. The two notions are the two sides of a single dubious coin.

Kant conceived of an analytic statement as one that attributes to its subject no more than is already concep-

tually contained in the subject. This formulation has two shortcomings: it limits itself to statements of subject-predicate form, and it appeals to a notion of containment which is left at a metaphorical level. But Kant's intent, evident more from the use he makes of the notion of analyticity than from his definition of it, can be restated thus: a statement is analytic when it is true by virtue of meanings and independently of fact. Pursuing this line, let us examine the concept of *meaning* which is presupposed.

Meaning, let us remember, is not to be identified with naming. Frege's example of "Evening Star" and "Morning Star," and Russell's of "Scott" and "the author of *Waverley*," illustrate that terms can name the same thing but differ in meaning. The distinction between meaning and naming is no less important at the level of abstract terms. The terms "9" and "the number of the planets" name one and the same abstract entity but presumably must be regarded as unlike in meaning; for astronomical observation was needed, and not mere reflection on meanings, to determine the sameness of the entity in question.

The above examples consist of singular terms, concrete and abstract. With general terms, or predicates, the situation is somewhat different but parallel. Whereas a singular term purports to name an entity, abstract or concrete, a general term does not; but a general term is *true of* an entity, or of each of many, or of none. The class of all entities of which a general term is true is called the *extension* of the term. Now paralleling the contrast between the meaning of a singular term and the entity named, we must distinguish equally between the meaning of a general term and its extension. The general terms "creature with a heart" and "creature with kidneys," for example, are perhaps alike in extension but unlike in meaning.

Confusion of meaning with extension, in the case of general terms, is less common than confusion of meaning with naming in the case of singular terms. It is indeed commonplace in philosophy to oppose intension (or meaning) to extension, or, in a variant vocabulary, connotation to denotation.

The Aristotelian notion of essence was the forerunner, no doubt, of the modern notion of intension or meaning. For Aristotle it was essential in men to be rational, accidental to be two-legged. But there is an important difference between this attitude and the doctrine of meaning. From the latter point of view it may indeed be conceded (if only for the sake of argument) that rationality is involved in the meaning of the word "man" while two-leggedness is not; but two-leggedness may at the same time be viewed as involved in the meaning of "biped" while rationality is not. Thus from the point of view of the doctrine of meaning it makes no sense to say of the actual individual, who is at once a man and a biped, that his rationality is essential and his two-leggedness accidental or vice versa. Things had essences, for Aristotle, but only linguistic forms have meanings. Meaning is what essence becomes when it is divorced from the object of reference and wedded to the word.

For the theory of meaning a conspicuous question is the nature of its objects: what sort of things are meanings? A felt need for meant entities may derive from an earlier failure to appreciate that meaning and reference are distinct. Once the theory of meaning is sharply separated from the theory of reference, it is a short step to recognizing as the primary business of the theory of meaning simply the synonymy of linguistic forms and the analyticity of statements; meanings themselves, as obscure intermediary entities, may well be abandoned.

The problem of analyticity then confronts us anew. Statements which are analytic by general philosophical acclaim are not, indeed, far to seek. They fall into two classes. Those of the first class, which may be called *logically true*, are typified by:

1. No unmarried man is married.

The relevant feature of this example is that it not merely is true as it stands, but remains true under any and all reinterpretations of "man" and "married." If we suppose a prior inventory of *logical* particles, comprising "no," "un-," "not," "if," "then," "and," etc., then in general a logical truth is a statement which is true and remains true under all reinterpretations of its components other than the logical particles.

But there is also a second class of analytic statements, typified by:

2. No bachelor is married.

The characteristic of such a statement is that it can be turned into a logical truth by putting synonyms for synonyms; thus (2) can be turned into (1) by putting "unmarried man" for its synonym "bachelor." We still lack a proper characterization of this second class of analytic statements, and therewith of analyticity generally, inasmuch as we have had in the above description to lean on a notion of 'synonymy' which is no less in need of clarification than analyticity itself.

In recent years Carnap has tended to explain analyticity by appeal to what he calls state-descriptions.[1] A state-description is any exhaustive assignment of truth values to the atomic, or noncompound, statements of the language. All other statements of the language are, Carnap assumes, built up of their component clauses by means of the familiar logical devices, in such a way that the truth value of any complex statement is fixed for each state-description by specifiable logical laws. A statement is then explained as analytic when it comes out true under every state description. This account is an adaptation of Leibniz's "true in all possible worlds." But note that this version of analyticity serves its purpose only if the atomic statements of the language are, unlike "John is a bachelor" and "John is married," mutually independent. Otherwise there would be a state-description which assigned truth to "John is a bachelor" and "John is married," and consequently "No bachelors are married" would turn out synthetic rather than analytic under the proposed criterion. Thus the criterion of analyticity in terms of state-descriptions serves only for languages devoid of extralogical synonym-pairs, such as "bachelor" and "unmarried man"—synonym-pairs of the type which give rise to the 'second class' of analytic statements. The criterion in terms of state-descriptions is a reconstruction at best of logical truth, not of analyticity.

I do not mean to suggest that Carnap is under any illusions on this point. His simplified model language with its state-descriptions is aimed primarily not at the general problem of analyticity but at another purpose, the clarification of probability and induction. Our problem, however, is analyticity; and here the major difficulty lies not in the first class of analytic statements, the logical truths, but rather in the second class, which depends on the notion of synonymy.

2. Definition

There are those who find it soothing to say that the analytic statements of the second class reduce to those of the first class, the logical truths, by *definition*; "bachelor," for example, is *defined* as "unmarried man." But how do we find that "bachelor" is defined as "unmarried man"? Who defined it thus, and when? Are we to appeal to the nearest dictionary, and accept the lexicographer's formulation as law? Clearly this would be to put the cart before the horse. The lexicographer is an empirical scientist, whose business is the recording of antecedent facts; and if he glosses "bachelor" as "unmarried man" it is because of his belief that there is a relation of synonymy between those forms, implicit in general or preferred usage prior to his own work. The notion of synonymy presupposed here has still to be clarified, presumably in terms relating to linguistic behavior. Certainly the 'definition' which is the lexicographer's report of an observed synonymy cannot be taken as the ground of the synonymy.

Definition is not, indeed, an activity exclusively of philologists. Philosophers and scientists frequently have occasion to 'define' a recondite term by paraphrasing it into terms of a more familiar vocabulary. But ordinarily such a definition, like the philologist's, is pure lexicography, affirming a relation of synonymy antecedent to the exposition in hand.

Just what it means to affirm synonymy, just what the interconnections may be which are necessary and sufficient in order that two linguistic forms be properly describable as synonymous, is far from clear; but, whatever these interconnections may be, ordinarily they are grounded in usage. Definitions reporting selected instances of synonymy come then as reports upon usage.

There is also, however, a variant type of definitional activity which does not limit itself to the reporting of pre-existing synonymies. I have in mind what Carnap calls *explication*—an activity to which philosophers are given, and scientists also in their more philosophical moments. In explication the purpose is not merely to paraphrase the definiendum into an outright synonym, but actually to improve upon the definiendum by refining or supplementing its meaning. But even explication, though not merely reporting a pre-existing synonymy between definiendum and definiens, does rest nevertheless on *other* pre-existing synonymies. The matter may be viewed as follows. Any word worth explicating has some contexts which, as wholes, are clear and precise enough to be useful; and the purpose of explication is to preserve the usage of these favored contexts while sharpening the usage of other contexts. In

order that a given definition be suitable for purposes of explication, therefore, what is required is not that the definiendum in its antecedent usage be synonymous with the definiens, but just that each of these favored contexts of the definiendum, taken as a whole in its antecedent usage, be synonymous with the corresponding context of the definiens.

Two alternative definientia may be equally appropriate for the purposes of a given task of explication and yet not be synonymous with each other; for they may serve interchangeably within the favored contexts but diverge elsewhere. By cleaving to one of these definientia rather than the other, a definition of explicative kind generates, by fiat, a relation of synonymy between definiendum and definiens which did not hold before. But such a definition still owes its explicative function, as seen, to pre-existing synonymies.

There does, however, remain still an extreme sort of definition which does not hark back to prior synonymies at all: namely, the explicitly conventional introduction of novel notations for purposes of sheer abbreviation. Here the definiendum becomes synonymous with the definiens simply because it has been created expressly for the purpose of being synonymous with the definiens. Here we have a really transparent case of synonymy created by definition; would that all species of synonymy were as intelligible. For the rest, definition rests on synonymy rather than explaining it.

The word "definition" has come to have a dangerously reassuring sound, owing no doubt to its frequent occurrence in logical and mathematical writings. We shall do well to digress now into a brief appraisal of the role of definition in formal work.

In logical and mathematical systems either of two mutually antagonistic types of economy may be striven for, and each has its peculiar practical utility. On the one hand we may seek economy of practical expression—ease and brevity in the statement of multifarious relations. This sort of economy calls usually for distinctive concise notations for a wealth of concepts. Second, however, and oppositely, we may seek economy in grammar and vocabulary; we may try to find a minimum of basic concepts such that, once a distinctive notation has been appropriated to each of them, it becomes possible to express any desired further concept by mere combination and iteration of our basic notations. This second sort of economy is impractical in one way, since a poverty in basic idioms tends to a necessary lengthening of discourse. But it is practical in another way: it greatly simplifies theoretical discourse *about* the language, through minimizing the terms and the forms of construction wherein the language consists.

Both sorts of economy, though prima facie incompatible, are valuable in their separate ways. The custom has consequently arisen of combining both sorts of economy by forging in effect two languages, the one a part of the other. The inclusive language, though redundant in grammar and vocabulary, is economical in message lengths, while the part, called primitive notation, is economical in grammar and vocabulary. Whole and part are correlated by rules of translation whereby each idiom not in primitive notation is equated to some complex built up of primitive notation. These rules of translation are the so-called *definitions* which appear in formalized systems. They are best viewed not as adjuncts to one language but as correlations between two languages, the one a part of the other.

But these correlations are not arbitrary. They are supposed to show how the primitive notations can accomplish all purposes, save brevity and convenience, of the redundant language. Hence the definiendum and its definiens may be expected, in each case, to be related in one or another of the three ways lately noted. The definiens may be a faithful paraphrase of the definiendum into the narrower notation, preserving a direct synonymy[2] as of antecedent usage; or the definiens may, in the spirit of explication, improve upon the antecedent usage of the definiendum; or finally, the definiendum may be a newly created notation, newly endowed with meaning here and now.

In formal and informal work alike, thus, we find that definition—except in the extreme case of the explicitly conventional introduction of new notations—hinges on prior relations of synonymy. Recognizing then that the notion of definition does not hold the key to synonymy and analyticity, let us look further into synonymy and say no more of definition.

3. Interchangeability

A natural suggestion, deserving close examination, is that the synonymy of two linguistic forms consists simply in their interchangeability in all contexts without change of truth value—interchangeability, in Leibniz's phrase, *salva veritate*.[3] Note that synonyms so conceived need not even be free from vagueness, as long as the vaguenesses match.

But it is not quite true that the synonyms "bachelor" and "unmarried man" are everywhere interchangeable *salva veritate*. Truths which become false under substitution of "unmarried man" for "bachelor" are easily constructed with the help of "bachelor of arts" or "bachelor's buttons"; also with the help of quotation, thus:

"Bachelor" has less than ten letters.

Such counterinstances can, however, perhaps be set aside by treating the phrases "bachelor of arts" and "bachelor's buttons" and the quotation "bachelor" each as a single indivisible word, and then stipulating that the interchangeability *salva veritate,* which is to be the touchstone of synonymy, is not supposed to apply to fragmentary occurrences inside of a word. This account of synonymy, supposing it acceptable on other counts, has indeed the drawback of appealing to a prior conception of 'word' which can be counted on to present difficulties of formulation in its turn. Nevertheless, some progress might be claimed in having reduced the problem of synonymy to a problem of wordhood. Let us pursue this line a bit, taking 'word' for granted.

The question remains whether interchangeability *salva veritate* (apart from occurrences within words) is a strong enough condition for synonymy, or whether, on the contrary, some heteronymous expressions might be thus interchangeable. Now let us be clear that we are not concerned here with synonymy in the sense of complete identity in psychological associations or poetic quality; indeed no two expressions are synonymous in such a sense. We are concerned only with what may be called *cognitive* synonymy. Just what this is cannot be said without successfully finishing the present study, but we know something about it from the need which arose for it in connection with analyticity in §1. The sort of synonymy needed there was merely such that any analytic statement could be turned into a logical truth by putting synonyms for synonyms. Turning the tables and assuming analyticity, indeed, we could explain cognitive synonymy of terms as follows (keeping to the familiar example): To say that "bachelor" and "unmarried man" are cognitively synonymous is to say no more nor less than that the statement:

3. All and only bachelors are unmarried men

is analytic.[4]

What we need is an account of cognitive synonymy not presupposing analyticity—if we are to explain analyticity conversely with help of cognitive synonymy as undertaken in §1. And indeed such an independent account of cognitive synonymy is at present up for consideration, namely, interchangeability *salva veritate* everywhere except within words. The question before us, to resume the thread at last, is whether such interchangeability is a sufficient condition for cognitive synonymy. We can quickly assure ourselves that it is, by examples of the following sort. The statement:

4. Necessarily all and only bachelors are bachelors

is evidently true, even supposing "necessarily" so narrowly construed as to be truly applicable only to analytic statements. Then, if "bachelor" and "unmarried man" are interchangeable *salva veritate*, the result:

5. Necessarily all and only bachelors are unmarried men

of putting "unmarried man" for an occurrence of "bachelor" in (4) must, like (4), be true. But to say that (5) is true is to say that (3) is analytic, and hence that "bachelor" and "unmarried man" are cognitively synonymous.

Let us see what there is about the above argument that gives it its air of hocus-pocus. The condition of interchangeability *salva veritate* varies in its force with variations in the richness of the language at hand. The above argument supposes we are working with a language rich enough to contain the adverb "necessarily," this adverb being so construed as to yield truth when and only when applied to an analytic statement. But can we condone a language which contains such an adverb? Does the adverb really make sense? To suppose that it does is to suppose that we have already made satisfactory sense of "analytic." Then what are we so hard at work on right now?

Our argument is not flatly circular, but something like it. It has the form, figuratively speaking, of a closed curve in space.

Interchangeability *salva veritate* is meaningless until relativized to a language whose extent is specified in relevant respects. Suppose now we consider a language containing just the following materials. There is an indefinitely large stock of one-place predicates (for example, "F" where "Fx" means that x is a man) and many-place predicates (for example, "G" where "Gxy" means that x loves y), mostly having to do with extralogical subject matter. The rest of the language is logical. The atomic sentences consist each of a predicate followed by one or more variables "x," "y," etc.; and the complex sentences are built up of the atomic ones by truth functions ("not," "and," "or," etc.) and quantification. In effect such a language enjoys the benefits also of descriptions and indeed singular terms generally, these being contextually definable in known ways. Even abstract singular terms naming classes, classes of classes, etc., are contextually definable in case the assumed stock of predicates includes the two-place predicate of class membership. Such a language can be adequate to classical mathematics and indeed to scientific discourse generally, except in so far as the latter involves debatable devices such as contrary-to-fact conditionals or modal adverbs like "necessarily."[5] Now a language of this type is extensional, in this sense: Any two predicates which agree extensionally (that is, are true of the same objects) are interchangeable *salva veritate*.[6]

In an extensional language, therefore, interchangeability *salva veritate* is no assurance of cognitive synonymy of the desired type. That "bachelor" and "unmarried man" are interchangeability *salva veritate* in an extensional language assures us of no more than that (3) is true. There is no assurance here that the extensional agreement of "bachelor" and "unmarried man" rests on meaning rather than merely on accidental matters of fact, as does the extensional agreement of "creature with a heart" and "creature with kidneys."

For most purposes extensional agreement is the nearest approximation to synonymy we need care about. But the fact remains that extensional agreement falls far short of cognitive synonymy of the type required for explaining analyticity in the manner of §1. The type of cognitive synonymy required there is such as to equate the synonymy of "bachelor" and "unmarried man" with the analyticity of (3), not merely with the truth of (3).

So we must recognize that interchangeability *salva veritate,* if construed in relation to an extensional language, is not a sufficient condition of cognitive synonymy in the sense needed for deriving analyticity in the manner of §1. If a language contains an intensional adverb "necessarily" in the sense lately noted, or other particles to the same effect, then interchangeability *salva veritate* in such a language does afford a sufficient condition of cognitive synonymy; but such a language is intelligible only in so far as the notion of analyticity is already understood in advance.

The effort to explain cognitive synonymy first, for the sake of deriving analyticity from it afterward as in §1, is perhaps the wrong approach. Instead we might try explaining analyticity somehow without appeal to cognitive synonymy. Afterward we could doubtless derive cognitive synonymy from analyticity satisfactorily enough if desired. We have seen that cognitive synonymy of "bachelor" and "unmarried man" can be explained as analyticity of (3). The same explanation works for any pair of one-place predicates, of course, and it can be extended in obvious fashion to many-place predicates. Other syntactical categories can also be accommodated in fairly parallel fashion. Singular terms may be said to be cognitively synonymous when the statement of identity formed by putting "=" between them is analytic. Statements may be said simply to be cognitively synonymous when their biconditional (the result of joining them by "if and only if") is analytic.[7] If we care to lump all categories into a single formulation, at the expense of assuming again the notion of 'word' which was appealed to early in this section, we can describe any two linguistic forms as cognitively synonymous when the two forms are interchangeable (apart from occurrences within 'words') *salva* (no longer *veritate* but) *analyticitate.* Certain technical questions arise, indeed, over cases of ambiguity or homonymy; let us not pause for them, however, for we are already digressing. Let us rather turn our backs on the problem of synonymy and address ourselves anew to that of analyticity.

4. Semantical Rules

Analyticity at first seemed most naturally definable by appeal to a realm of meanings. On refinement, the appeal to meanings gave way to an appeal to synonymy or definition. But definition turned out to be a will-o'-the-wisp, and synonymy turned out to be best understood only by dint of a prior appeal to analyticity itself. So we are back at the problem of analyticity.

I do not know whether the statement "Everything green is extended" is analytic. Now does my indecision over this example really betray an incomplete understanding, an incomplete grasp of the 'meanings', of "green" and "extended?" I think not. The trouble is not with "green" or "extended," but with "analytic."

It is often hinted that the difficulty in separating analytic statements from synthetic ones in ordinary language is due to the vagueness of ordinary language and that the distinction is clear when we have a precise artificial language with explicit 'semantical rules'. This, however, as I shall now attempt to show, is a confusion.

The notion of analyticity about which we are worrying is a purported relation between statements and languages: A statement S is said to be *analytic for* a language L, and the problem is to make sense of this relation generally, that is, for variable "S" and "L". The gravity of the problem is not perceptibly less for artificial languages than for natural ones. The problem of making sense of the idiom "S is analytic for L," with variable "S" and "L," retains its stubbornness even if we limit the range of the variable "L" to artificial languages. Let me now try to make this point evident.

For artificial languages and semantical rules we look naturally to the writings of Carnap. His semantical rules take various forms, and to make my point I shall have to distinguish certain of the forms. Let us suppose, to begin with, an artificial language L_0 whose semantical rules have the form explicitly of a specification, by recursion or otherwise, of all the analytic statements of L_0. The rules tell us that such and such statements, and only those, are the analytic statements of L_0. Now here the difficulty is simply that the rules contain the word "analytic," which we do not understand! We understand what expressions the rules attribute analyticity to, but we do not understand what the rules attribute to those expressions. In short, before we can understand a rule which begins "A statement S is analytic for language L_0 if and only if . . . ," we must understand the general relative term "analytic for"; we must understand "S" is analytic for "L" where "S" and "L" are variables.

Alternatively we may, indeed, view the so-called rule as a conventional definition of a new simple symbol "analytic-for-L_0" which might better be written untendentiously as "K" so as not to seem to throw light on the interesting word "analytic." Obviously any number of classes K, M, N, etc. of statements of L_0 can be specified for various purposes or for no purpose; what does it mean to say that K, as against M, N, etc., is the class of the 'analytic' statement of L_0?

By saying what statements are analytic for L_0 we explain "analytic-for-L_0" but not "analytic," not "analytic for." We do not begin to explain the idiom "S is analytic for L" with variable "S" and "L," even if we are content to limit the range of "L" to the realm of artificial languages.

Actually we do know enough about the intended significance of "analytic" to know that analytic statements are supposed to be true. Let us then turn to a second form of semantical rule, which says not that such and such statements are analytic but simply that such and such statements are included among the truths. Such a rule is not subject to the criticism of containing the un-understood word "analytic"; and we may grant for the sake of argument that there is no difficulty over the broader term "true." A semantical rule of this second type, a rule of truth, is not supposed to specify all the truths of the language; it merely stipulates, recursively or otherwise, a certain multitude of statements which, along with others unspecified, are to count as true. Such a rule may be conceded to be quite clear. Derivatively, afterward, analyticity can be demarcated thus: a statement is analytic if it is (not merely true but) true according to the semantical rule.

Still there is really no progress. Instead of appealing to an unexplained word "analytic," we are now appealing to an unexplained phrase "semantical rule." Not every true statement which says that the statements of some class are true can count as a semantical rule—otherwise all truths would be 'analytic' in the sense of being true according to semantical rules. Semantical rules are distinguishable, apparently, only by the fact of appearing on a page under the heading "Semantical Rules"; and this heading is itself then meaningless.

We can say indeed that a statement is *analytic-for-L_0* if and only if it is true according to such and such specifically appended 'semantical rules,' but then we find ourselves back at essentially the same case which was originally discussed: "S is analytic-for-L_0 if and only if. . . ." Once we seek to explain "S is analytic for L" generally for variable "L" (even allowing limitation of "L" to artificial languages), the explanation "true according to the semantical rules of L" is unavailing; for the relative term "semantical rule of" is as much in need of clarification, at least, as "analytic for."

It may be instructive to compare the notion of semantical rule with that of postulate. Relative to a given set of postulates, it is easy to say what a postulate is: it is a member of the set. Relative to a given set of semantical rules, it is equally easy to say what a semantical rule is. But given simply a notation, mathematical or otherwise, and indeed as thoroughly understood a notation as you please in point of the translations or truth conditions of its statements, who can say which of its true statements rank as postulates? Obviously the question is meaningless—as meaningless as asking which points in Ohio are starting points. Any finite (or effectively specifiable infinite) selection of statements (preferably true ones, perhaps) is as much *a* set of postulates as any other. The word "postulate" is significant only relative to an act of inquiry; we apply the word to a set of statements just in so far as we happen, for the year or the moment, to be thinking of those statements in relation to the statements which can be reached from them by some set of transformations to which we have seen fit to direct our attention. Now the notion of semantical rule is as sensible and meaningful as that of postulate, if conceived in a similarly relative spirit—relative, this time, to one or another particular enterprise of schooling unconversant persons in sufficient conditions for truth of statements of some natural or artificial language L. But from this point of view no one signalization of a subclass of the truths of L is intrinsically more a semantical rule than another; and, if "analytic" means "true by semantical rules," no one truth of L is analytic to the exclusion of another.[8]

It might conceivably be protested that an artificial language L (unlike a natural one) is a language in the ordinary sense *plus* a set of explicit semantical rules—the whole constituting, let us say, an ordered pair; and that the semantical rules of L then are specifiable simply as the second component of the pair L. But, by the same token and more simply, we might construe an artificial language *L* outright as an ordered pair whose second component is the class of its analytic statements; and then the analytic statements of *L* become specifiable simply as the statements in the second component of *L*. Or better still, we might just stop tugging at our bootstraps altogether.

Not all the explanations of analyticity known to Carnap and his readers have been covered explicitly in the above considerations, but the extension to other forms is not hard to see. Just one additional factor should be mentioned which sometimes enters: sometimes the semantical rules are in effect rules of translation into ordinary language, in which case the analytic statements of the artificial language are in effect recognized as such from the analyticity of their specified translations in ordinary language. Here certainly there can be no thought of an illumination of the problem of analyticity from the side of the artificial language.

From the point of view of the problem of analyticity the notion of an artificial language with semantical rules is a *feu follet par excellence*. Semantical rules determining the analytic statements of an artificial language are of interest only in so far as we already understand the notion of analyticity; they are of no help in gaining this understanding.

Appeal to hypothetical languages of an artificially simple kind could conceivably be useful in clarifying analyticity, if the mental or behavioral or cultural factors relevant to analyticity—whatever they may be— were somehow sketched into the simplified model. But a model which takes analyticity merely as an irreducible character is unlikely to throw light on the problem of explicating analyticity.

It is obvious that truth in general depends on both language and extralinguistic fact. The statement "Brutus killed Caesar" would be false if the world had been different in certain ways, but it would also be false if the word "killed" happened rather to have the sense of "begat." Thus one is tempted to suppose in general that the truth of a statement is somehow analyzable into a linguistic component and a factual component. Given this supposition, it next seems reasonable that in some statements the factual component should be null; and these are the analytic statements. But, for all its a priori reasonableness, a boundary between analytic and synthetic statements simply has not been drawn. That

there is such a distinction to be drawn at all is an unempirical dogma of empiricists, a metaphysical article of faith.

5. The Verification Theory and Reductionism

In the course of these somber reflections we have taken a dim view first of the notion of meaning, then of the notion of cognitive synonymy, and finally of the notion of analyticity. But what, it may be asked, of the verification theory of meaning? This phrase has established itself so firmly as a catchword of empiricism that we should be very unscientific indeed not to look beneath it for a possible key to the problem of meaning and the associated problems.

The verification theory of meaning, which has been conspicuous in the literature from Pierce onward, is that the meaning of a statement is the method of empirically confirming or infirming it. An analytic statement is that limiting case which is confirmed no matter what.

As urged in §1, we can as well pass over the question of meanings as entities and move straight to sameness of meaning, or synonymy. Then what the verification theory says is that statements are synonymous if and only if they are alike in point of method of empirical confirmation or infirmation.

This is an account of cognitive synonymy not of linguistic forms generally, but of statements.[9] However, from the concept of synonymy of statements we could derive the concept of synonymy for other linguistic forms, by considerations somewhat similar to those at the end of §3. Assuming the notion of 'word' indeed, we could explain any two forms as synonymous when the putting of the one form for an occurrence of the other in any statement (apart from occurrences within 'words') yields a synonymous statement. Finally, given the concept of synonymy thus for linguistic forms generally, we could define analyticity in terms of synonymy and logical truth as in §1. For that matter, we could define analyticity more simply in terms of just synonymy of statements together with logical truth; it is not necessary to appeal to synonymy of linguistic forms other than statements. For a statement may be described as analytic simply when it is synonymous with a logically true statement.

So, if the verification theory can be accepted as an adequate account of statement synonymy, the notion of analyticity is saved after all. However, let us reflect. Statement synonymy is said to be likeness of method of empirical confirmation or infirmation. Just what are these methods which are to be compared for likeness? What, in other words, is the nature of the relation between a statement and the experiences which contribute to or detract from its confirmation?

The most naive view of the relation is that it is one of direct report. This is *radical reductionism.* Every meaningful statement is held to be translatable into a statement (true or false) about immediate experience. Radical reductionism, in one form or another, well antedates the verification theory of meaning explicitly so called. Thus Locke and Hume held that every idea must either originate directly in sense experience or else be compounded of ideas thus originating; and taking a hint from Tooke we might rephrase this doctrine in semantical jargon by saying that a term, to be significant at all, must be either a name of a sense datum or a compound of such names or an abbreviation of such a compound. So stated, the doctrine remains ambiguous as between sense data as sensory events and sense data as sensory qualities, and it remains vague as to the admissible ways of compounding. Moreover, the doctrine is unnecessarily and intolerably restrictive in the term-by-term critique which it imposes. More reasonably, and without yet exceeding the limits of what I have called radical reductionism, we may take full statements as our significant units—thus demanding that our statements as wholes be translatable into sense-datum language, but not that they be translatable term by term.

This emendation would unquestionably have been welcome to Locke and Hume and Tooke, but historically it had to await an important reorientation in semantics—the reorientation whereby the primary vehicle of meaning came to be seen no longer in the term but in the statement. This reorientation, explicit in Frege ([1], §60), underlies Russell's concept of incomplete symbols defined in use; also it is implicit in the verification theory of meaning, since the objects of verification are statements.

Radical reductionism, conceived now with statements as units, set itself the task of specifying a sense-datum language and showing how to translate the rest of significant discourse, statement by statement, into it. Carnap embarked on this project in the *Aufbau.*

The language which Carnap adopted as his starting point was not a sense-datum language in the narrowest conceivable sense, for it included also the notations of logic, up through higher set theory. In effect it included the whole language of pure mathematics. The ontology implicit in it (that is, the range of values of its variables) embraced not only sensory events but classes, classes of classes, and so on. Empiricists there are who would boggle at such prodigality. Carnap's starting point is very parsimonious, however, in its extralogical or sensory part. In a series of constructions in which he exploits the resources of modern logic with much ingenuity, Carnap succeeds in defining a wide array of important additional sensory concepts which, but for his constructions, one would not have dreamed were definable on so slender a basis. He was the first empiricist who, not content with asserting the reducibility of science to terms of immediate experience, took serious steps toward carrying out the reduction.

If Carnap's starting point is satisfactory, still his constructions were, as he himself stressed, only a fragment of the full program. The construction of even the simplest statements about the physical world was left in a sketchy state. Carnap's suggestions on this subject were, despite their sketchiness, very suggestive. He explained spatio-temporal point-instants as quadruples of real numbers and envisaged assignment of sense qualities to point-instants according to certain canons. Roughly summarized, the plan was that qualities should be assigned to point-instants in such a way as to achieve the laziest world compatible with our experience. The principle of least action was to be our guide in constructing a world from experience.

Carnap did not seem to recognize, however, that his treatment of physical objects fell short of reduction not merely through sketchiness, but in principle. Statements of the form "Quality q is at point-instant x; y; z; t" were, according to his canons, to be apportioned truth values in such a way as to maximize and minimize certain overall features, and with growth of experience the truth values were to be progressively revised in the same spirit. I think this is a good schematization (deliberately oversimplified, to be sure) of what science really does; but it provides no indication, not even the sketchiest, of how a statement of the form "Quality *q* is at *x; y; z; t*" could ever be translated into Carnap's initial language of sense data and logic. The connective "is at" remains an added undefined connective; the canons counsel us in its use but not in its elimination.

Carnap seems to have appreciated this point afterward; for in his later writings he abandoned all notion of the translatability of statements about immediate experience. Reductionism in its radical form has long since ceased to figure in Carnap's philosophy.

But the dogma of reductionism has, in a subtler and more tenuous form, continued to influence the thought of empiricists. The notion lingers that to each statement, or each synthetic statement, there is associated a unique range of possible sensory events such that the occurrence of any of them would add to the likelihood of truth of the statement, and that there is associated also another unique range of possible sensory events whose occurrence would detract from that likelihood. This notion is of course implicit in the verification theory of meaning.

The dogma of reductionism survives in the supposition that each statement, taken in isolation from its fellows, can admit of confirmation or infirmation at all. My countersuggestion, issuing essentially from Carnap's doctrine of the physical world in the *Aufbau*, is that our statements about the external world face the tribunal of sense experience not individually but only as a corporate body.[10]

The dogma of reductionism, even in its attenuated form, is intimately connected with the other dogma—that there is a cleavage between the analytic and the synthetic. We have found ourselves led, indeed, from the latter problem to the former through the verification theory of meaning. More directly, the one dogma clearly supports the other in this way: as long as it is taken to be significant in general to speak of the confirmation and infirmation of a statement, it seems significant to speak also of a limiting kind of statement which is vacuously confirmed, *ipso facto*, come what may; and such a statement is analytic.

The two dogmas are, indeed, at root identical. We lately reflected that in general the truth of statements

does obviously depend both upon language and upon extralinguistic fact; and we noted that this obvious circumstance carries in its train, not logically but all too naturally, a feeling that the truth of a statement is somehow analyzable into a linguistic component and a factual component. The factual component must, if we are empiricists, boil down to a range of confirmatory experiences. In the extreme case where the linguistic component is all that matters, a true statement is analytic. But I hope we are now impressed with how stubbornly the distinction between analytic and synthetic has resisted any straightforward drawing. I am impressed also, apart from prefabricated examples of black and white balls in an urn, with how baffling the problem has always been of arriving at any explicit theory of the empirical confirmation of a synthetic statement. My present suggestion is that it is nonsense, and the root of much nonsense, to speak of a linguistic component and a factual component in the truth of any individual statement. Taken collectively, science has its double dependence upon language and experience; but this duality is not significantly traceable into the statements of science taken one by one.

The idea of defining a symbol in use was, as remarked, an advance over the impossible term-by-term empiricism of Locke and Hume. The statement, rather than the term, came with Frege to be recognized as the unit accountable to an empiricist critique. But what I am now urging is that even in taking the statement as unit we have drawn our grid too finely. The unit of empirical significance is the whole of science.

6. Empiricism Without the Dogmas

The totality of our so-called knowledge or beliefs, from the most casual matters of geography and history to the profoundest laws of atomic physics or even of pure mathematics and logic, is a man-made fabric which impinges on experience only along the edges. Or, to change the figure, total science is like a field of force whose boundary conditions are experience. A conflict with experience at the periphery occasions readjustments in the interior for the field. Truth values have to be redistributed over some of our statements. Reevaluation of some statements entails reevaluation of others, because of their logical interconnections—the logical laws being in turn simply certain further statements of the system, certain further elements of the field. Having reevaluated one statement we must reevaluate some others, which may be statements logically connected with the first or may be the statements of logical connections themselves. But the total field is so underdetermined by its boundary conditions, experience, that there is much latitude of choice as to what statements to reevaluate in the light of any single contrary experience. No particular experiences are linked with any particular statements in the interior of the field, except indirectly through considerations of equilibrium affecting the field as a whole.

If this view is right, it is misleading to speak of the empirical content of an individual statement—especially if it is a statement at all remote from the experiential periphery of the field. Furthermore it becomes folly to seek a boundary between synthetic statements, which hold contingently on experience, and analytic statements, which hold come what may. Any statement can be held true come what may, if we make drastic enough adjustments elsewhere in the system. Even a statement very close to the periphery can be held true in the face of recalcitrant experience by pleading hallucination or by amending certain statements of the kind called logical laws. Conversely, by the same token, no statement is immune to revision. Revision even of the logical law of the excluded middle has been proposed as a means of simplifying quantum mechanics; and what difference is there in principle between such a shift and the shift whereby Kepler superseded Ptolemy, or Einstein Newton, or Darwin Aristotle?

For vividness I have been speaking in terms of varying distances from a sensory periphery. Let me try now to clarify this notion without metaphor. Certain statements, though *about* physical objects and not sense experience, seem peculiarly germane to sense experience—and in a selective way: some statements to some experiences, others to others. Such statements, especially germane to particular experiences, I picture as near the periphery. But in this relation of 'germaneness' I envisage nothing more than a loose association reflecting the relative likelihood, in practice, of our choosing one statement rather than another for revision in the event of recalcitrant experi-

ence. For example, we can imagine recalcitrant experiences to which we would surely be inclined to accommodate our system by reevaluating just the statement that there are brick houses on Elm Street, together with related statements on the same topic. We can imagine other recalcitrant experiences to which we would be inclined to accommodate our system by reevaluating just the statement that there are no centaurs, along with kindred statements. A recalcitrant experience can, I have urged, be accommodated by any of various alternative reevaluations in various alternative quarters of the total system; but, in the cases which we are now imagining, our natural tendency to disturb the total system as little as possible would lead us to focus our revisions upon these specific statements concerning brick houses or centaurs. These statements are felt, therefore, to have a sharper empirical reference than highly theoretical statements of physics or logic or ontology. The latter statements may be thought of as relatively centrally located within the total network, meaning merely that little preferential connection with any particular sense data obtrudes itself.

As an empiricist I continue to think of the conceptual scheme of science as a tool, ultimately, for predicting future experience in the light of past experience. Physical objects are conceptually imported into the situation as convenient intermediaries—not by definition in terms of experience, but simply as irreducible posits comparable, epistemologically, to the gods of Homer. For my part I do, qua lay physicist, believe in physical objects and not in Homer's gods; and I consider it a scientific error to believe otherwise. But in point of epistemological footing the physical objects and the gods differ only in degree and not in kind. Both sorts of entities enter our conception only as cultural posits. The myth of physical objects is epistemologically superior to most in that is has proved more efficacious than other myths as a device for working a manageable structure into the flux of experience.

Positing does not stop with macroscopic physical objects. Objects at the atomic level are posited to make the laws of macroscopic objects, and ultimately the laws of experience, simpler and more manageable; and we need not expect or demand full definition of atomic and subatomic entities in terms of macroscopic ones, any more than definition of macroscopic things in terms of sense data. Science is a continuation of common sense, and it continues the common-sense expedient of swelling ontology to simplify theory.

Physical objects, small and large, are not the only posits. Forces are another example; and indeed we are told nowadays that the boundary between energy and matter is obsolete. Moreover, the abstract entities which are the substance of mathematics—ultimately classes and classes of classes and so on up—are another posit in the same spirit. Epistemologically these are myths on the same footing with physical objects and gods, neither better nor worse except for differences in the degree to which they expedite our dealings with sense experiences.

The overall algebra of rational and irrational numbers is underdetermined by the algebra of rational numbers, but is smoother and more convenient; and it includes the algebra of rational numbers as a jagged or gerrymandered part. Total science, mathematical and natural and human, is similarly but more extremely underdetermined by experience. The edge of the system must be kept squared with experience; the rest, with all its elaborate rate myths or fictions, has as its objective the simplicity of laws.

Ontological questions, under this view, are on a par with questions of natural science.[11] Consider the question whether to countenance classes as entities. This, as I have argued elsewhere, is the question whether to quantify with respect to variables which take classes as values. Now Carnap [3] has maintained that this is a question not of matters of fact but of choosing a convenient language form, a convenient conceptual scheme or framework for science. With this I agree, but only on the proviso that the same be conceded regarding scientific hypotheses generally. Carnap ([3], p. 32n) has recognized that he is able to preserve a double standard for ontological questions and scientific hypotheses only by assuming an absolute distinction between the analytic and the synthetic; and I need not say again that this is a distinction which I reject.[12]

The issue over there being classes seems more a question of convenient conceptual scheme; the issue over there being centaurs, or brick houses on Elm Street, seems more a question of fact. But I have been urging that this difference is only one of degree, and

that it turns upon our vaguely pragmatic inclination to adjust one strand of the fabric of science rather than another in accommodating some particular recalcitrant experience. Conservatism figures in such choices, and so does the quest for simplicity.

Carnap, Lewis, and others take a pragmatic stand on the question of choosing between language forms, scientific frameworks; but their pragmatism leaves off at the imagined boundary between the analytic and the synthetic. In repudiating such a boundary I espouse a more thorough pragmatism. Each man is given a scientific heritage plus a continuing barrage of sensory stimulation; and the considerations which guide him in warping his scientific heritage to fit his continuing sensory promptings are, where rational, pragmatic.

Notes

1. Carnap [1], pp. 9ff; [2], pp. 70ff.
2. According to an important variant sense of "definition," the relation preserved may be the weaker relation of mere agreement in reference. But definition in this sense is better ignored in the present connection, being irrelevant to the question of synonymy.
3. Cf. Lewis [1], p. 373.
4. This is cognitive synonymy in a primary, broad sense. Carnap ([1], pp. 56ff) and Lewis ([2], pp. 83ff) have suggested how, once this notion is at hand, a narrower sense of cognitive synonymy which is preferable for some purposes can in turn be derived. But this special ramification of concept-building lies aside from the present purposes and must not be confused with the broad sort of cognitive synonymy here concerned.
5. On such devices see also Quine [1].
6. This is the substance of Quine [2], *121.
7. The 'if and only if' itself is intended in the truth functional sense. See Carnap [1], p. 14.
8. The foregoing paragraph was not part of the present essay as originally published. It was prompted by Martin.
9. The doctrine can indeed be formulated with terms rather than statements as the units. Thus Lewis describes the meaning of a term as "a *criterion in*

mind, by reference to which one is able to apply or refuse to apply the expression in question in the case of presented, or imagined, things or situations" ([2], p. 133).—for an instructive account of the vicissitudes of the verification theory of meaning, centered however on the question of meaning *fulness* rather than synonymy and analyticity, see Hempel.

10. This doctrine was well argued by Duhem, pp. 303–328. Or see Lowinger, pp. 132–140.
11. "L'ontologie fait corps avec la science elle-même et ne peut en être separée." Meyerson, p. 439.
12. For an effective expression of further misgivings over this distinction, see White.

References

Carnap, R. [1]. *Meaning and Necessity.* (Chicago: University of Chicago Press, 1947.)
————[2]. *Logical   Foundations   of   Probability.* (Chicago: University of Chicago Press, 1950.)
————[3]. "Empiricism, semantics, and ontology," *Revue Internationale de Philosophie,* vol. IV (1950), pp. 20–40.
Duhem, P. *La Théorie physique: son objet et sa structure.* (Paris: 1906.)
Frege, Gottlob. *Foundations of Arithmetic.* (New York: Philosophical Library, 1950.)
Hempel, C. G. "Problems and Changes in the Empiricist Criterion of Meaning." *Revue International de Philosophie,* vol. IV (1950), pp. 41–63.
Lewis, C. I. [1]. *A Survey of Symbolic Logic.* (Berkeley: 1918.)
————[2]. *An Analysis of Knowledge and Valuation.* (LaSalle, Ill.: Open Court Publishing Co., 1946).
Lowinger, A. *The Methodology of Pierre Duhem.* (New York: Columbia University Press, 1941.)
Martin, R. M., "On 'Analytic'." *Philosophical Studies,* vol. III (1952), pp. 42–47.
Meyerson, Émile. *Identité et realité.* (Paris: 1908; 4th ed., 1932.)
Quine, W. V. [1]. *From a Logical Point of View.* (New York: Harper & Row, 1961.)
————[2]. *Mathematical Logic.* (New York: W. W. Norton & Company, Inc., 1940; Cambridge: Harvard University Press, 1947; rev. ed., 1951.)
White, Morton. "The Analytic and the Synthetic: An Untenable Dualism." In Sidney Hook, ed., *John Dewey: Philosopher of Science and   Freedom.* (New York: The Dial Press, Inc., 1950), pp. 316–330.

READING QUESTIONS

1. Why, according to Quine, should meaning not be identified with naming? Why does Quine say that "meaning is what essence becomes when it is divorced from the object of reference and wedded to the word"? What is the impact of separating the "theory of meaning" from the "theory of reference," according to Quine?
2. Quine writes that "there are those who find it soothing to say that the analytic statements of the second class reduce to those of the first class, the logical truths, by *definition,* 'bachelor', for example, is *defined* as 'unmarried man'." Why does he go on to say that "definitions reporting selected instances of synonymy come then as reports upon usage"? What is the significance of this?
3. What is the activity Carnap calls 'explication'? How does it differ from 'definition'? Why does Quine say that "even explication, though not merely reporting a preexisting synonymy between definiendum and definiens, does rest nevertheless on *other* preexisting synonymies"? What is the significance of this?
4. Is interchangeability *salva veritate* a strong enough condition for (cognitive) synonymy? Quine says that "the condition of interchangeability *salva veritate* varies in its force with variations in the richness of the language at hand." What does he mean by this? In what way does this fact provide a reason to be suspicious of the interchangeability requirement when it comes to the goal of explicating the notion of analyticity?
5. Why does Quine think that attempts to adequately mark the distinction between analytic and synthetic statements in the context of "a precise artificial language with explicit 'semantic rules'" will fail?
6. What is radical reductionism? According to radical reductionism, what gets reduced to what? Briefly

describe Carnap's radical reductionism as expressed in his *Aufbau,* as Quine understands it.

7. In what way is Quine's claim "that our statements about the external world face the tribunal of sense experience not individually but only as a corporate body" a rejection of radical reductionism?

8. "The unit of empirical significance is the whole of science." What does this mean? Is Quine correct? Why or why not?

9. How does Quine conceive of "our so-called knowledge of beliefs"? How, if at all, does this conception support his contention that "any statement can be held true come what may, if we make drastic enough adjustments elsewhere in the system"?

10. Quine writes that "for my part I do, qua lay physicist, believe in physical objects and not in Homer's gods; and I consider it a scientific error to believe otherwise. But in point of epistemological footing the physical objects and the gods differ only in degree and not in kind." Why does Quine believe this? Do you agree? Why or why not?

11. In what ways does Quine's repudiation of a boundary between the analytic and the synthetic and his rejection of radical reductionism as a related dogma of empiricism lead him to "espouse a more thorough pragmatism"? In what ways is Quine a pragmatist?

W. V. O. QUINE

Ontological Relativity

Originally presented as two lectures given at Columbia University in 1968, "Ontological Relativity" is a refined exposition of Quine's philosophical views on language and reality as expressed in his detailed and highly influential monograph on the subject, *Word and Object* (1960).

As a behaviorist when it comes to understanding issues of meaning, Quine begins his essay by rejecting the view that words are merely markers for associated ideas (or for the things that we associate with ideas) as the "myth of a museum in which the exhibits are meanings and the words are labels." And so, he continues, the process of translation from one language to another is *not* merely a matter of changing between sets of labels, each of which in turn simply functions as a set of tags for a fixed set of meanings.

Instead, Quine argues that there are no facts of the matter whatsoever about what a given speaker's words mean (i.e., that translation is indeterminate) or about what it is to which they are referring (i.e., that reference is behaviorally inscrutable). In fact, there are "no meanings, nor likenesses nor distinctions of meaning, beyond what are implicit in people's dispositions to overt behavior." This thesis about reference has ontological implications. Quine concludes that it does not make any sense to say "what the objects of a theory are, absolutely speaking." Rather, all that it makes sense to say is "how one theory of objects is interpretable or reinterpretable in another." This is the thesis of ontological relativity. To the question "what exists?" therefore, there is no "museum of meanings" that we can consult and so there is no absolute answer.

I

I listened to Dewey on Art as Experience when I was a graduate student in the spring of 1931. Dewey was then at Harvard as the first William James Lecturer. I am proud now to be at Columbia as the first John Dewey Lecturer.

Philosophically I am bound to Dewey by the naturalism that dominated his last three decades. With Dewey I hold that knowledge, mind, and meaning are part of the same world that they have to do with, and that they are to be studied in the same empirical spirit that animates natural science. There is no place for a prior philosophy.

When a naturalistic philosopher addresses himself to the philosophy of mind, he is apt to talk of language. Meanings are, first and foremost, meanings of language. Language is a social art which we all acquire on the evidence solely of other people's overt behavior under publicly recognizable circumstances. Meanings, therefore, those very models of mental entities, end up as grist for the behaviorist's mill. Dewey was explicit on the point: "Meaning . . . is not a psychic existence; it is primarily a property of behavior."[1]

Once we appreciate the institution of language in these terms, we see that there cannot be, in any useful sense, a private language. This point was stressed by Dewey in the twenties. "Soliloquy," he wrote, "is the product and reflex of converse with others" (170). Further along he expanded the point thus: "Language is specifically a mode of interaction of at least two beings, a speaker and a hearer; it presupposes an organized group to which these creatures belong, and from whom they have acquired their habits of speech. It is therefore a relationship" (185). Years later, Wittgenstein likewise rejected private language. When Dewey was writing in this naturalistic vein, Wittgenstein still held his copy theory of language.

The copy theory in its various forms stands closer to the main philosophical tradition, and to the attitude of common sense today. Uncritical semantics is the myth of a museum in which the exhibits are meanings and the words are labels. To switch languages is to change the labels. Now the naturalist's primary objection to this view is not an objection to meanings on account of their being mental entities, though that could be objection enough. The primary objection persists even if we take the labeled exhibits not as mental ideas but as Platonic ideas or even as the denoted concrete objects. Semantics is vitiated by a pernicious mentalism as long as we regard a man's semantics as somehow determinate in his mind beyond what might be implicit in his dispositions to overt behavior. It is the very facts about meaning, not the entities meant, that must be construed in terms of behavior.

There are two parts to knowing a word. One part is being familiar with the sound of it and being able to reproduce it. This part, the phonetic part, is achieved by observing and imitating other people's behavior, and there are no important illusions about the process. The other part, the semantic part, is knowing how to use the word. This part, even in the paradigm case, is more complex than the phonetic part. The word refers, in the paradigm case, to some visible object. The learner has now not only to learn the word phonetically, by hearing it from another speaker; he also has to see the object; and in addition to this, in order to capture the relevance of the object to the word, he has to see that the speaker also sees the object. Dewey summed up the point thus: "The characteristic theory about B's understanding of A's sounds is that he responds to the thing from the standpoint of A" (178). Each of us, as he learns his language, is a student of his neighbor's behavior; and conversely, insofar as his tries are approved or corrected, he is a subject of his neighbor's behavioral study.

The semantic part of learning a word is more complex than the phonetic part, therefore, even in simple cases: we have to see what is stimulating the other speaker. In the case of words not directly ascribing observable traits to things, the learning process is increasingly complex and obscure; and obscurity is the breeding place of mentalistic semantics. What the naturalist insists on is that, even in the complex and obscure parts of language learning, the learner has no data to work with but the overt behavior of other speakers.

When with Dewey we turn thus toward a naturalistic view of language and a behavioral view of meaning, what we give up is not just the museum figure of speech. We give up an assurance of determinacy. Seen according to the museum myth, the words and sentences of a language have their determinate meanings. To discover the meanings of the native's words we may have to observe his behavior, but still the meanings of the words are supposed to be determinate in the native's *mind,* his mental museum, even in cases where behavioral criteria are powerless to discover them for us. When on the other hand we recognize with Dewey that "meaning . . . is primarily a property of behavior," we recognize that there are no meanings, nor likenesses nor distinctions of meaning, beyond what are implicit in people's dispositions to overt behavior. For naturalism the question whether two expressions are alike or unlike in meaning has no determinate answer, known or unknown, except insofar as the answer is settled in principle by people's speech dispositions, known or unknown. If by these standards there are indeterminate cases, so much the worse for the terminology of meaning and likeness of meaning.

To see what such indeterminacy would be like, suppose there were an expression in a remote language that could be translated into English equally defensibly in either of two ways, unlike in meaning in English. I am not speaking of ambiguity within the native language. I am supposing that one and the same native use of the expression can be given either of the English translations, each being accommodated by compensating adjustments in the translation of other words. Suppose both translations, along with these accommodations in each case, accord equally well with all observable behavior on the part of speakers of the remote language and speakers of English. Suppose they accord perfectly not only with behavior actually observed, but with all dispositions to behavior on the part of all the speakers concerned. On these assumptions it would be forever impossible to know of one of these translations that it was the right one, and the other wrong. Still, if the museum myth were true, there would be a right and wrong of the matter; it is just that we would never know, not having access to the museum. See language naturalistically, on the other hand, and you have to see the notion of likeness of meaning in such a case simply as nonsense.

I have been keeping to the hypothetical. Turning now to examples, let me begin with a disappointing one and work up. In the French construction "ne . . . rien" you can translate "rien" into English as "anything" or as "nothing" at will, and then accommodate your choice by translating "ne" as "not" or by construing it as pleonastic. This example is disappointing because you can object that I have merely cut the French units too small. You can believe the mentalistic myth of the meaning museum and still grant that "rien" of itself has no meaning, being no whole label; it is part of "ne . . . rien," which has its meaning as a whole.

I began with this disappointing example because I think its conspicuous trait—its dependence on cutting language into segments too short to carry meanings—is the secret of the more serious cases as well. What makes other cases more serious is that the segments they involve are seriously long: long enough to be predicates and to be true of things and hence, you would think, to carry meanings.

An artificial example which I have used elsewhere[2] depends on the fact that a whole rabbit is present when and only when an undetached part of a rabbit is present; also when and only when a temporal stage of a rabbit is present. If we are wondering whether to translate a native expression "gavagai" as "rabbit" or as "undetached rabbit part" or as "rabbit stage," we can never settle the matter simply by ostension—that is, simply by repeatedly querying the expression "gavagai" for the native's assent or dissent in the presence of assorted stimulations.

Before going on to urge that we cannot settle the matter by non-ostensive means either, let me belabor this ostensive predicament a bit. I am not worrying, as Wittgenstein did, about simple cases of ostension. The color word "sepia," to take one of his examples,[3] can certainly be learned by an ordinary process of conditioning, or induction. One need not even be told that sepia is a color and not a shape or a material or an article. True, barring such hints, many lessons may be needed, so as to eliminate wrong generalizations based on shape, material, etc., rather than color, and so as to eliminate wrong notions as to the intended boundary of an indicated example, and so as to delimit the admissible variations of color itself. Like all conditioning, or induction, the process will depend ultimately also on one's own inborn propensity to find one stimulation qualitatively more akin to a second stimulation than to a third; otherwise there can never be any selective reinforcement and extinction of responses.[4] Still, in principle nothing more is needed in learning "sepia" than in any conditioning or induction.

But the big difference between "rabbit" and "sepia" is that whereas "sepia" is a mass term like "water," "rabbit" is a term of divided reference. As such it cannot be mastered without mastering its principle of individuation: where one rabbit leaves off and another begins. And this cannot be mastered by pure ostension, however persistent.

Such is the quandary over "gavagai": where one gavagai leaves off and another begins. The only difference between rabbits, undetached rabbit parts, and rabbit stages is in their individuation. If you take the total scattered portion of the spatiotemporal world that is made up of rabbits, and that which is made up of un-detached rabbit parts, and that which is made up of rabbit stages, you come out with the same scattered portion of the world each of the three times. The only difference is in how you slice it. And how to slice it is what ostension or simple conditioning, however persistently repeated, cannot teach.

Thus consider specifically the problem of deciding between "rabbit" and "undetached rabbit part" as translation of "gavagai." No word of the native language is known, except that we have settled on some working hypothesis as to what native words or gestures to construe as assent and dissent in response to our pointings and queryings. Now the trouble is that whenever we point to different parts of the rabbit, even sometimes screening the rest of the rabbit, we are pointing also each time to the rabbit. When, conversely, we indicate the whole rabbit with a sweeping gesture, we are still pointing to a multitude of rabbit parts. And note that we do not have even a native analogue of our plural ending to exploit, in asking "gavagai?" It seems clear that no even tentative decision between "rabbit" and "undetached rabbit part" is to be sought at this level.

How would we finally decide? My passing mention of plural endings is part of the answer. Our individuating of terms of divided reference, in English, is bound up with a cluster of interrelated grammatical particles and constructions: plural endings, pronouns, numerals, the "is" of identity, and its adaptations "same" and "other." It is the cluster of interrelated devices in which quantification becomes central when the regimentation of symbolic logic is imposed. If in his language we could ask the native "Is this *gavagai* the same as that one?" while making appropriate multiple ostensions, then indeed we would be well on our way to deciding between "rabbit," "undetached rabbit part," and "rabbit stage." And of course the linguist does at length reach the point where he can ask what purports to be that question. He develops a system for translating our pluralizations, pronouns, numerals, identity, and related devices contextually into the native idiom. He develops such a system by abstraction and hypothesis. He abstracts native particles and constructions from observed native sentences and tries associating these variously with English particles and constructions. Insofar as the native sentences and the thus associated English

ones seem to match up in respect of appropriate occasions of use, the linguist feels confirmed in these hypotheses of translation—what I call *analytical hypotheses.*[5]

But it seems that this method, though laudable in practice and the best we can hope for, does not in principle settle the indeterminacy between "rabbit," "undetached rabbit part," and "rabbit stage." For if one workable overall system of analytical hypotheses provides for translating a given native expression into "is the same as," perhaps another equally workable but systematically different system would translate that native expression rather into something like "belongs with." Then when in the native language we try to ask "Is this *gavagai* the same as that?" we could as well be asking "Does this *gavagai* belong with that?" Insofar, the native's assent is no objective evidence for translating "gavagai" as "rabbit" rather than "undetached rabbit part" or "rabbit stage."

This artificial example shares the structure of the trivial earlier example "ne . . . rien." We were able to translate "rien" as "anything" or as "nothing," thanks to a compensatory adjustment in the handling of "ne." And I suggest that we can translate "gavagai" as "rabbit" or "undetached rabbit part" or "rabbit stage," thanks to compensatory adjustments in the translation of accompanying native locutions. Other adjustments still might accommodate translation of "gavagai" as "rabbithood," or in further ways. I find this plausible because of the broadly structural and contextual character of any considerations that could guide us to native translations of the English cluster of interrelated devices of individuation. There seem bound to be systematically very different choices, all of which do justice to all dispositions to verbal behavior on the part of all concerned.

An actual field linguist would of course be sensible enough to equate "gavagai" with "rabbit," dismissing such perverse alternatives as "undetached rabbit part" and "rabbit stage" out of hand. This sensible choice and others like it would help in turn to determine his subsequent hypotheses as to what native locutions should answer to the English apparatus of individuation, and thus everything would come out all right. The implicit maxim guiding his choice of "rabbit," and similar choices for other native words, is that an enduring and relatively homogeneous object, moving as a whole against a contrasting background, is a likely reference for a short expression. If he were to become conscious of this maxim, he might celebrate it as one of the linguistic universals, or traits of all languages, and he would have no trouble pointing out its psychological plausibility. But he would be wrong; the maxim is his own imposition, toward settling what is objectively indeterminate. It is a very sensible imposition, and I would recommend no other. But I am making a philosophical point.

It is philosophically interesting, moreover, that what is indeterminate in this artificial example is not just meaning, but extension; reference. My remarks on indeterminacy began as a challenge to likeness of meaning. I had us imagining "an expression that could be translated into English equally defensibly in either of two ways, unlike in meaning in English." Certainly likeness of meaning is a dim notion, repeatedly challenged. Of two predicates which are alike in extension, it has never been clear when to say that they are alike in meaning and when not; it is the old matter of featherless bipeds and rational animals, or of equiangular and equilateral triangles. Reference, extension, has been the firm thing; meaning, intension, the infirm. The indeterminacy of translation now confronting us, however, cuts across extension and intension alike. The terms "rabbit," "undetached rabbit part," and "rabbit stage" differ not only in meaning; they are true of different things. Reference itself proves behaviorally inscrutable.

Within the parochial limits of our own language, we can continue as always to find extensional talk clearer than intensional. For the indeterminacy between "rabbit," "rabbit stage," and the rest depended only on a correlative indeterminacy of translation of the English apparatus of individuation—the apparatus of pronouns, pluralization, identity, numerals, and so on. No such indeterminacy obtrudes so long as we think of this apparatus as given and fixed. Given this apparatus, there is no mystery about extension; terms have the same extension when true of the same things. At the level of radical translation, on the other hand, extension itself goes inscrutable.

My example of rabbits and their parts and stages is a contrived example and a perverse one, with which, as I said, the practicing linguist would have no patience. But there are also cases, less bizarre ones, that obtrude

in practice. In Japanese there are certain particles, called "classifiers," which may be explained in either of two ways. Commonly they are explained as attaching to numerals, to form compound numerals of distinctive styles. Thus take the numeral for 5. If you attach one classifier to it you get a style of "5" suitable for counting animals; if you attach a different classifier, you get a style of "5" suitable for counting slim things like pencils and chopsticks; and so on. But another way of viewing classifiers is to view them not as constituting part of the numeral, but as constituting part of the term—the term for "chopsticks" or "oxen" or whatever. On this view the classifier does the individuative job that is done in English by "sticks of" as applied to the mass term "wood," or "head of" as applied to the mass term "cattle."

What we have on either view is a Japanese phrase tantamount say to "five oxen," but consisting of three words;[6] the first is in effect the neutral numeral "5," the second is a classifier of the animal kind, and the last corresponds in some fashion to "ox." On one view the neutral numeral and the classifier go together to constitute a declined numeral in the "animal gender," which then modifies "ox" to give, in effect, "five oxen." On the other view the third Japanese word answers not to the individuative term "ox" but to the mass term "cattle"; the classifier applies to this mass term to produce a composite individuative term, in effect "head of cattle"; and the neutral numeral applies directly to all this without benefit of gender, giving "five head of cattle," hence again in effect "five oxen."

If so simple an example is to serve its expository purpose, it needs your connivance. You have to understand "cattle" as a mass term covering only bovines, and "ox" as applying to all bovines. That these usages are not the invariable usages is beside the point. The point is that the Japanese phrase comes out as "five bovines," as desired, when parsed in either of two ways. The one way treats the third Japanese word as an individuative term true of each bovine, and the other way treats that word rather as a mass term covering the unindividuated totality of beef on the hoof. These are two very different ways of treating the third Japanese word; and the three-word phrase as a whole turns out all right in both cases only because of compensatory differences in our account of the second word, the classifier.

This example is reminiscent in a way of our trivial initial example, "ne . . . rien." We were able to represent "rien" as "anything" or as "nothing," by compensatorily taking "ne" as negative or as vacuous. We are able now to represent a Japanese word either as an individuative term for bovines or as a mass term for live beef, by compensatorily taking the classifier as declining the numeral or as individuating the mass term. However, the triviality of the one example does not quite carry over to the other. The early example was dismissed on the ground that we had cut too small; "rien" was too short for significant translation on its own, and "ne . . . rien" was the significant unit. But you cannot dismiss the Japanese example by saying that the third word was too short for significant translation on its own and that only the whole three-word phrase, tantamount to "five oxen," was the significant unit. You cannot take this line unless you are prepared to call a word too short for significant translation even when it is long enough to be a term and carry denotation. For the third Japanese word is, on either approach, a term: on one approach a term of divided reference, and on the other a mass term. If you are indeed prepared thus to call a word too short for significant translation even when it is a denoting term, then in a back-handed way you are granting what I wanted to prove: the inscrutability of reference.

Between the two accounts of Japanese classifiers there is no question of right and wrong. The one account makes for more efficient translation into idiomatic English; the other makes for more of a feeling for the Japanese idiom. Both fit all verbal behavior equally well. All whole sentences, and even component phrases like "five oxen," admit of the same net overall English translations on either account. This much is invariant. But what is philosophically interesting is that the reference or extension of shorter terms can fail to be invariant. Whether that third Japanese word is itself true of each ox, or whether on the other hand it is a mass term which needs to be adjoined to the classifier to make a term which is true of each ox—here is a question that remains undecided by the totality of human dispositions to verbal behavior. It is indeterminate in principle; there is no fact of the matter. Either answer can be accommodated by an account of the classifier. Here again, then, is the inscrutability of refer-

ence—illustrated this time by a humdrum point of practical translation.

The inscrutability of reference can be brought closer to home by considering the word "alpha," or again the word "green." In our use of these words and others like them there is a systematic ambiguity. Sometimes we use such words as concrete general terms, as when we say the grass is green, or that some inscription begins with an alpha. Sometimes on the other hand we use them as abstract singular terms, as when we say that green is a color and alpha is a letter. Such ambiguity is encouraged by the fact that there is nothing in ostension to distinguish the two uses. The pointing that would be done in teaching the concrete general term "green," or "alpha," differs none from the pointing that would be done in teaching the abstract singular term "green" or "alpha." Yet the objects referred to by the word are very different under the two uses; under the one use the word is true of many concrete objects, and under the other use it names a single abstract object.

We can of course tell the two uses apart by seeing how the word turns up in sentences: whether it takes an indefinite article, whether it takes a plural ending, whether it stands as singular subject, whether it stands as modifier, as predicate complement, and so on. But these criteria appeal to our special English grammatical constructions and particles, our special English apparatus of individuation, which, I already urged, is itself subject to indeterminacy of translation. So, from the point of view of translation into a remote language, the distinction between a concrete general and an abstract singular term is in the same predicament as the distinction between "rabbit," "rabbit part," and "rabbit stage." Here then is another example of the inscrutability of reference, since the difference between the concrete general and the abstract singular is a difference in the objects referred to.

Incidentally we can concede this much indeterminacy also to the "sepia" example, after all. But this move is not evidently what was worrying Wittgenstein.

The ostensive indistinguishability of the abstract singular from the concrete general turns upon what may be called "deferred ostension," as opposed to direct ostension. First let me define direct ostension. The *ostended point,* as I shall call it, is the point where the line of the pointing finger first meets an opaque surface. What characterizes *direct ostension*, then, is that the term which is being ostensively explained is true of something that contains the ostended point. Even such direct ostension has its uncertainties, of course, and these are familiar. There is the question how wide an environment of the ostended point is meant to be covered by the term that is being ostensively explained. There is the question how considerably an absent thing or substance might be allowed to differ from what is now ostended, and still be covered by the term that is now being ostensively explained. Both of these questions can in principle be settled as well as need be by induction from multiple ostensions. Also, if the term is a term of divided reference like "apple," there is the question of individuation: the question where one of its objects leaves off and another begins. This can be settled by induction from multiple ostensions of a more elaborate kind, accompanied by expressions like "same apple" and "another," if an equivalent of this English apparatus of individuation has been settled on; otherwise the indeterminacy persists that was illustrated by "rabbit," "undetached rabbit part," and "rabbit stage."

Such, then, is the way of direct ostension. Other ostension I call *deferred*. It occurs when we point at the gauge, and not the gasoline, to show that there is gasoline. Also it occurs when we explain the abstract singular term "green" or "alpha" by pointing at grass or a Greek inscription. Such pointing is direct ostension when used to explain the concrete general term "green" or "alpha," but it is deferred ostension when used to explain the abstract singular terms; for the abstract object which is the color green or the letter alpha does not contain the ostended point, nor any point.

Deferred ostension occurs very naturally when, as in the case of the gasoline gauge, we have a correspondence in mind. Another such example is afforded by the Gödel numbering of expressions. Thus if 7 has been assigned as the Gödel number of the letter alpha, a man conscious of the Gödel numbering would not hesitate to say "Seven" on pointing to an inscription of the Greek letter in question. This is, on the face of it, a doubly deferred ostension: one step of deferment carries us from the inscription to the letter as abstract object, and a second step carries us thence to the number.

By appeal to our apparatus of individuation, if it is available, we can distinguish between the concrete general and the abstract singular use of the word "alpha"; this we saw. By appeal again to that apparatus, and in particular to identity, we can evidently settle also whether the word "alpha" in its abstract singular use is being used really to name the letter or whether, perversely, it is being used to name the Gödel number of the letter. At any rate we can distinguish these alternatives if also we have located the speaker's equivalent of the numeral "7" to our satisfaction; for we can ask him whether alpha *is* 7.

These considerations suggest that deferred ostension adds no essential problem to those presented by direct ostension. Once we have settled upon analytical hypotheses of translation covering identity and the other English particles relating to individuation, we can resolve not only the indecision between "rabbit" and "rabbit stage" and the rest, which came of direct ostension, but also any indecision between concrete general and abstract singular, and any indecision between expression and Gödel number, which come of deferred ostension. However, this conclusion is too sanguine. The inscrutability of reference runs deep, and it persists in a subtle form even if we accept identity and the rest of the apparatus of individuation as fixed and settled; even, indeed, if we forsake radical translation and think only of English.

Consider the case of a thoughtful protosyntactician. He has a formalized system of first-order proof theory, or protosyntax, whose universe comprises just expressions, that is, strings of signs of a specified alphabet. Now just what sorts of things, more specifically, are these expressions? They are types, not tokens. So, one might suppose, each of them is the set of all its tokens. That is, each expression is a set of inscriptions which are variously situated in space-time but are classed together by virtue of a certain similarity in shape. The concatenate $x \frown y$ of two expressions x and y, in a given order, will be the set of all inscriptions each of which has two parts which are tokens respectively of x and y and follow one upon the other in that order. But $x \frown y$ may then be the null set, though x and y are not null; for it may be that inscriptions belonging to x and y happen to turn up head to tail nowhere, in the past, present, or future. This danger increases with the lengths of x and y. But it is easily seen to violate a law of protosyntax which says that $x = z$ whenever $x \frown y = z \frown y$.

Thus it is that our thoughtful protosyntactician will not construe the things in his universe as sets of inscriptions. He can still take his atoms, the single signs, as sets of inscriptions, for there is no risk of nullity in these cases. And then, instead of taking his strings of signs as sets of inscriptions, he can invoke the mathematical notion of sequence and take them as sequences of signs. A familiar way of taking sequences, in turn, is as a mapping of things on numbers. On this approach an expression or string of signs becomes a finite set of pairs each of which is the pair of a sign and a number.

This account of expressions is more artificial and more complex than one is apt to expect who simply says he is letting his variables range over the strings of such and such signs. Moreover, it is not the inevitable choice; the considerations that motivated it can be met also by alternative constructions. One of these constructions is Gödel numbering itself, and it is temptingly simple. It uses just natural numbers, whereas the foregoing construction used sets of one-letter inscriptions and also natural numbers and sets of pairs of these. How clear is it that at just *this* point we have dropped expressions in favor of numbers? What is clearer is merely that in both constructions we were artificially devising models to satisfy laws that expressions in an unexplicated sense had been meant to satisfy.

So much for expressions. Consider now the arithmetician himself, with his elementary number theory. His universe comprises the natural numbers outright. Is it clearer than the protosyntactician's? What, after all, is a natural number? There are Frege's version, Zermelo's, and von Neumann's, and countless further alternatives, all mutually incompatible and equally correct. What we are doing in any one of these explications of natural number is to devise set-theoretic models to satisfy laws which the natural numbers in an unexplicated sense had been meant to satisfy. The case is quite like that of protosyntax.

It will perhaps be felt that any set-theoretic explication of natural number is at best a case of *obscurum per obscurius*; that all explications must assume something, and the natural numbers themselves are an admirable assumption to start with. I must agree that a construction of sets and set theory from natural numbers and arithmetic would be far more desirable than the famil-

iar opposite. On the other hand our impression of the clarity even of the notion of natural number itself has suffered somewhat from Gödel's proof of the impossibility of a complete proof procedure for elementary number theory, or, for that matter, from Skolem's and Henkin's observations that all laws of natural numbers admit nonstandard models.[7]

We are finding no clear difference between *specifying* a universe of discourse—the range of the variables of qualification—and *reducing* that universe to some other. We saw no significant difference between clarifying the notion of expression and supplanting it by that of number. And now to say more particularly what numbers themselves are is in no evident way different from just dropping numbers and assigning to arithmetic one or another new model, say in set theory.

Expressions are known only by their laws, the laws of concatenation theory, so that any constructs obeying those laws—Gödel numbers, for instance—are *ipso facto* eligible as explications of expression. Numbers in turn are known only by their laws, the laws of arithmetic, so that any constructs obeying those laws—certain sets, for instance—are eligible in turn as explications of number. Sets in turn are known only by their laws, the laws of set theory.

Russell pressed a contrary thesis, long ago. Writing of numbers, he argued that for an understanding of number the laws of arithmetic are not enough; we must know the applications, we must understand numerical discourse embedded in discourse of other matters. In applying number, the key notion, he urged, is *Anzahl*: there are *n* so-and-sos. However, Russell can be answered. First take, specifically, *Anzahl*. We can define "there are *n* so-and-sos" without ever deciding what numbers are, apart from their fulfillment of arithmetic. That there are *n* so-and-sos can be explained simply as meaning that the so-and-sos are in one-to-one correspondence with the numbers up to *n*.[8]

Russell's more general point about application can be answered too. Always, if the structure is there, the applications will fall into place. As paradigm it is perhaps sufficient to recall again this reflection on expressions and Gödel numbers: that even the pointing out of an inscription is no final evidence that our talk is of expressions and not of Gödel numbers. We can always plead deferred ostension.

It is in this sense true to say, as mathematicians often do, that arithmetic is all there is to number. But it would be a confusion to express this point by saying, as is sometimes said, that numbers are any things fulfilling arithmetic. This formulation is wrong because distinct domains of objects yield distinct models of arithmetic. Any progression can be made to serve; and to identify all progressions with one another, e.g., to identify the progression of odd numbers with the progression of evens, would contradict arithmetic after all.

So, though Russell was wrong in suggesting that numbers need more than their arithmetical properties, he was right in objecting to the definition of numbers as any things fulfilling arithmetic. The subtle point is that any progression will serve as a version of number so long and only so long as we stick to one and the same progression. Arithmetic is, in this sense, all there is to number: there is no saying absolutely what the numbers are; there is only arithmetic.[9]

II

I first urged the inscrutability of reference with the help of examples like the one about rabbits and rabbit parts. These used direct ostension, and the inscrutability of reference hinged on the indeterminacy of translation of identity and other individuative apparatus. The setting of these examples, accordingly, was radical translation: translation from a remote language on behavioral evidence, unaided by prior dictionaries. Moving then to deferred ostension and abstract objects, we found a certain dimness of reference pervading the home language itself.

Now it should be noted that even for the earlier examples the resort to a remote language was not really essential. On deeper reflection, radical translation begins at home. Must we equate our neighbor's English words with the same strings of phonemes in our own mouths? Certainly not; for sometimes we do not thus equate them. Sometimes we find it to be in the interests of communication to recognize that our neighbor's use of some word, such as "cool" or "square" or "hopefully," differs from ours, and so we translate that word of his into a different string of phonemes in our idiolect. Our usual domestic rule of translation is indeed

the homophonic one, which simply carries each string of phonemes into itself; but still we are always prepared to temper homophony with what Neil Wilson has called the "principle of charity."[10] We will construe a neighbor's word heterophonically now and again if thereby we see our way to making his message less absurd.

The homophonic rule is a handy one on the whole. That it works so well is no accident, since imitation and feedback are what propagate a language. We acquired a great fund of basic words and phrases in this way, imitating our elders and encouraged by our elders amid external circumstances to which the phrases suitably apply. Homophonic translation is implicit in this social method of learning. Departure from homophonic translation in this quarter would only hinder communication. Then there are the relatively rare instances of opposite kind, due to divergence in dialect or confusion in an individual, where homophonic translation incurs negative feedback. But what tends to escape notice is that there is also a vast mid-region where the homophonic method is indifferent. Here, gratuitously, we can systematically reconstrue our neighbor's apparent references to rabbits as really references to rabbit stages, and his apparent references to formulas as really references to Gödel numbers and vice versa. We can reconcile all this with our neighbor's verbal behavior, by cunningly readjusting our translations of his various connecting predicates so as to compensate for the switch of ontology. In short, we can reproduce the inscrutability of reference at home. It is of no avail to check on this fanciful version of our neighbor's meanings by asking him, say, whether he really means at a certain point to refer to formulas or to their Gödel numbers; for our question and his answer—"By all means, the numbers"—have lost their title to homophonic translation. The problem at home differs none from radical translation ordinarily so called except in the willfulness of this suspension of homophonic translation.

I have urged in defense of the behavioral philosophy of language, Dewey's, that the inscrutability of reference is not the inscrutability of a fact; there is no fact of the matter. But if there is really no fact of the matter, then the inscrutability of reference can be brought even closer to home than the neighbor's case; we can apply it to ourselves. If it is to make sense to say even of oneself that one is referring to rabbits and formulas and not to rabbit stages and Gödel numbers, then it should make sense equally to say it of someone else. After all, as Dewey stressed, there is no private language.

We seem to be maneuvering ourselves into the absurd position that there is no difference on any terms, interlinguistic or intralinguistic, objective or subjective, between referring to rabbits and referring to rabbit parts or stages; or between referring to formulas and referring to their Gödel numbers. Surely this is absurd, for it would imply that there is no difference between the rabbit and each of its parts or stages, and no difference between a formula and its Gödel number. Reference would seem now to become nonsense not just in radical translation but at home.

Toward resolving this quandary, begin by picturing us at home in our language, with all its predicates and auxiliary devices. This vocabulary includes "rabbit," "rabbit part," "rabbit stage," "formula," "number," "ox," "cattle"; also the two-place predicates of identity and difference, and other logical particles. In these terms we can say in so many words that this is a formula and that a number, this a rabbit and that a rabbit part, this and that the same rabbit, and this and that different parts. *In just those words.* This network of terms and predicates and auxiliary devices is, in relativity jargon, our frame of reference, or coordinate system. Relative to *it* we can and do talk meaningfully and distinctively of rabbits and parts, numbers and formulas. Next, as in recent paragraphs, we contemplate alternative denotations for our familiar terms. We begin to appreciate that a grand and ingenious permutation of these denotations, along with compensatory adjustments in the interpretations of the auxiliary particles, might still accommodate all existing speech dispositions. This was the inscrutability of reference, applied to ourselves; and it made nonsense of reference. Fair enough; reference *is* nonsense except relative to a coordinate system. In this principle of relativity lies the resolution of our quandary.

It is meaningless to ask whether, in general, our terms "rabbit," "rabbit part," "number," etc., really refer respectively to rabbits, rabbit parts, numbers, etc., rather than to some ingeniously permuted denotations. It is meaningless to ask this absolutely; we can meaningfully ask it only relative to some background language. When we ask, "Does 'rabbit' really refer to rabbits?" someone can counter with the question: "Refer to rab-

bits in what sense of 'rabbits'?" thus launching a regress; and we need the background language to regress into. The background language gives the query sense, if only relative sense; sense relative in turn to it, this background language. Querying reference in any more absolute way would be like asking absolute position, or absolute velocity, rather than position or velocity relative to a given frame of reference. Also it is very much like asking whether our neighbor may not systematically see everything upside down, or in complementary color, forever undetectably.

We need a background language, I said, to regress into. Are we involved now in an infinite regress? If questions of reference of the sort we are considering make sense only relative to a background language, then evidently questions of reference for the background language make sense in turn only relative to a further background language. In these terms the situation sounds desperate, but in fact it is little different from questions of position and velocity. When we are given position and velocity relative to a given coordinate system, we can always ask in turn about the placing of origin and orientation of axes of that system of coordinates; and there is no end to the succession of further coordinate systems that could be adduced in answering the successive questions thus generated.

In practice of course we end the regress of coordinate systems by something like pointing. And in practice we end the regress of background languages, in discussions of reference, by acquiescing in our mother tongue and taking its words at face value.

Very well; in the case of position and velocity, in practice, pointing breaks the regress. But what of position and velocity apart from practice? what of the regress then? The answer, of course, is the relational doctrine of space; there is no absolute position or velocity; there are just the relations of coordinate systems to one another, and ultimately of things to one another. And I think that the parallel question regarding denotation calls for a parallel answer, a relational theory of what the objects of theories are. What makes sense is to say not what the objects of a theory are, absolutely speaking, but how one theory of objects is interpretable or reinterpretable in another.

The point is not that bare matter is inscrutable: that things are indistinguishable except by their properties.

That point does not need making. The present point is reflected better in the riddle about seeing things upside down, or in complementary colors; for it is that things can be inscrutably switched even while carrying their properties with them. Rabbits differ from rabbit parts and rabbit stages not just as bare matter, after all, but in respect of properties; and formulas differ from numbers in respect of properties. What our present reflections are leading us to appreciate is that the riddle about seeing things upside down, or in complementary colors, should be taken seriously and its moral applied widely. The relativistic thesis to which we have come is this, to repeat: it makes no sense to say what the objects of a theory are, beyond saying how to interpret or reinterpret that theory in another. Suppose we are working within a theory and thus treating of its objects. We do so by using the variables of the theory, whose values those objects are, though there be no ultimate sense in which that universe can have been specified. In the language of the theory there are predicates by which to distinguish portions of this universe from other portions, and these predicates differ from one another purely in the roles they play in the laws of the theory. Within this background theory we can show how some subordinate theory, whose universe is some portion of the background universe, can be a reinterpretation be reduced to another subordinate theory whose universe is some lesser portion. Such talk of subordinate theories and their ontologies *is* meaningful, but only relative to the background theory with its own primitively adopted and ultimately inscrutable ontology.

To talk thus of theories raises a problem of formulation. A theory, it will be said, is a set of fully interpreted sentences. (More particularly, it is a deductively closed set: it includes all its own logical consequences, insofar as they are couched in the same notation.) But if the sentences of a theory are fully interpreted, then in particular the range of values of their variables is settled. How then can there be no sense in saying what the objects of a theory are?

My answer is simply that we cannot require theories to be fully interpreted, except in a relative sense, if anything is to count as a theory. In specifying a theory we must indeed fully specify, in our own words, what sentences are to comprise the theory, in our own words,

what sentences are to comprise the theory, and what things are to be taken as values of the variables, and what things are to be taken as values of the variables, and what things are to be taken as satisfying the predicate letters; insofar we do fully interpret the theory, *relative* to our own words and relative to our overall home theory which lies behind them. But this fixes the objects of the described theory only relative to those of the home theory; and these can, at will, be questioned in turn.

One is tempted to conclude simply that meaninglessness sets in when we try to pronounce on everything in our universe; that universal predication takes on sense only when furnished with the background of a wider universe, where the predication is no longer universal. And this is even a familiar doctrine, the doctrine that no proper predicate is true of everything. We have all heard it claimed that a predicate is meaningful only by contrast with what it excludes, and hence that being true of everything would make a predicate meaningless. But surely this doctrine is wrong. Surely self-identity, for instance, is not to be rejected as meaningless. For that matter, any statement of fact at all, however brutally meaningful, can be put artificially into a form in which it pronounces on everything. To say merely of Jones that he sings, for instance, is to say of everything that it is other than Jones or sings. We had better beware of repudiating universal predication, lest we be tricked into repudiating everything there is to say.

Carnap took an intermediate line in his doctrine of universal words, or *Allwörter,* in *The Logical Syntax of Language.* He did treat the predicating of universal words as "quasi-syntactical"—as a predication only by courtesy, and without empirical content. But universal words were for him not just any universally true predicates, like "is other than Jones or sings." They were a special breed of universally true predicates, ones that are universally true by the sheer meanings of their words and no thanks to nature. In his later writing this doctrine of universal words takes the form of a distinction between "internal" questions, in which a theory comes to grips with facts about the world, and "external" questions, in which people come to grips with the relative merits of theories.

Should we look to these distinctions of Carnap's for light on ontological relativity? When we found there was no absolute sense in saying what a theory is about, were we sensing the infactuality of what Carnap calls "external questions"? When we found that saying what a theory is about did make sense against a background theory, were we sensing the factuality of internal questions of the background theory? I see no hope of illumination in this quarter. Carnap's universal words were not just any universally true predicates, but, as I said, a special breed; and what distinguishes this breed is not clear. What I said distinguished them was that they were universally true by sheer meanings and not by nature; but this is a very questionable distinction. Talking of "internal" and "external" is no better.

Ontological relativity is not to be clarified by any distinction between kinds of universal predication—unfactual and factual, external and internal. It is not a question of universal predication. When questions regarding the ontology of a theory are meaningless absolutely, and become meaningful relative to a background theory, this is not in general because the background theory has a wider universe. One is tempted, as I said a little while back, to suppose that it is; but one is then wrong.

What makes ontological questions meaningless when taken absolutely is not universality but circularity. A question of the form "What is an *F*?" can be answered only by recourse to a further term: "An *F* is a *G*." The answer makes only relative sense: sense relative to the uncritical acceptance of "*G*."

We may picture the vocabulary of a theory as comprising logical signs such as quantifiers and the signs for the truth functions and identity, and in addition descriptive or nonlogical signs, which, typically, are singular terms, or names, and general terms, or predicates. Suppose next that in the statements which comprise the theory, that is, are true according to the theory, we abstract from the meanings of the nonlogical vocabulary and from the range of the variables. We are left with the logical form of the theory, or, as I shall say, the *theory form*. Now we may interpret this theory form anew by picking a new universe for its variables of quantification to range over, and assigning objects from this universe to the names, and choosing subsets of this universe as extensions of the one-place predicates, and so on. Each such interpretation of the theory form is called a model of it, if it makes it come out true.

Which of these models is meant in a given actual theory cannot, of course, be guessed from the theory form. The intended references of the names and predicates have to be learned rather by ostension, or else by paraphrase in some antecedently familiar vocabulary. But the first of these two ways has proved inconclusive, since, even apart from indeterminacies of translation affecting identity and other logical vocabulary, there is the problem of deferred ostension. Paraphrase in some antecedently familiar vocabulary, then, is our only recourse; and such is ontological relativity. To question the reference of all the terms of our all-inclusive theory becomes meaningless, simply for want of further terms relative to which to ask or answer the question.

It is thus meaningless within the theory to say which of the various possible models of our theory form is our real or intended model. Yet even here we can make sense still of there being many models. For we might be able to show that for each of the models, however unspecifiable, there is bound to be another which is a permutation or perhaps a diminution of the first.

Suppose for example that our theory is purely numerical. Its objects are just the natural numbers. There is no sense in saying, from within that theory, just which of the various models of number theory is in force. But we can observe even from within the theory that, whatever 0, 1, 2, 3, etc. may be, the theory would still hold true if the 17 of this series were moved into the role of 0, and the 18 moved into the role of 1, and so on.

Ontology is indeed doubly relative. Specifying the universe of a theory makes sense only relative to some background theory, and only relative to some choice of a manual of translation of the one theory into the other. Commonly of course the background theory will simply be a containing theory, and in this case no question of a manual of translation arises. But this is after all just a degenerate case of translation still—the case where the rule of translation is the homophonic one.

We cannot know what something is without knowing how it is marked off from other things. Identity is thus of a piece with ontology. Accordingly it is involved in the same relativity, as may be readily illustrated. Imagine a fragment of economic theory. Suppose its universe comprises persons, but its predicates are incapable of distinguishing between persons whose incomes are equal. The interpersonal relation of equality of income enjoys, within the theory, the substitutivity property of the identity relation itself; the two relations are indistinguishable. It is only relative to a background theory, in which more can be said of personal identity than equality of income, that we are able even to appreciate the above account of the fragment of economic theory, hinging as the account does on a contrast between persons and incomes.

A usual occasion for ontological talk is reduction, where it is shown how the universe of some theory can by a reinterpretation be dispensed with in favor of some other universe, perhaps a proper part of the first. I have treated elsewhere[11] of the reduction of one ontology to another with help of a *proxy function:* a function mapping the one universe into part or all of the other. For instance, the function "Gödel number of" is a proxy function. The universe of elementary proof theory or protosyntax, which consists of expressions or strings of signs, is mapped by this function into the universe of elementary number theory, which consists of numbers.

The proxy function used in reducing one ontology to another need not, like Gödel numbering, be one-to-one. We might, for instance, be confronted with a theory treating of both expressions and ratios. We would cheerfully reduce all this to the universe of natural numbers, by invoking a proxy function which enumerates the expressions in the Gödel way, and enumerates the ratios by the classical method of short diagonals. This proxy function is not one-to-one, since it assigns the same natural number both to an expression and to a ratio. We would tolerate the resulting artificial convergence between expressions and ratios, simply because the original theory made no capital of the distinction between them; they were so invariably and extravagantly unlike that the identity question did not arise. Formally speaking, the original theory used a two-sorted logic.

For another kind of case where we would not require the proxy function to be one-to-one, consider again the fragment of economic theory lately noted. We would happily reduce its ontology of persons to a less numerous one of incomes. The proxy function would assign to each person his income. It is not one-to-one; distinct persons give way to identical incomes.

The reason such a reduction is acceptable is that it merges the images of only such individuals as never had been distinguishable by the predicates of the original theory. Nothing in the old theory is contravened by the new identities.

If on the other hand the theory that we are concerned to reduce or reinterpret is straight protosyntax, or a straight arithmetic of ratios or of real numbers, then a one-to-one proxy function is mandatory. This is because any two elements of such a theory are distinguishable in terms of the theory. This is true even for the real numbers, even though not every real number is uniquely specifiable; any two real numbers x and y are still distinguishable, in that $x < y$ or $y < x$ and never $x < x$. A proxy function that did not preserve the distinctness of the elements of such a theory would fail of its purpose of reinterpretation.

One ontology is *always* reducible to another when we are given a proxy function f that is one-to-one. The essential reasoning is as follows. Where P is any predicate of the old system, its work can be done in the new system by a new predicate which we interpret as true of just the correlates fx of the old objects x that P was true of. Thus suppose we take fx as the Gödel number of x, and as our old system we take a syntactical system in which one of the predicates is "is a segment of." The corresponding predicate of the new or numerical system, then, would be one which amounts, so far as its extension is concerned, to the words "is the Gödel number of a segment of that whose Gödel number is." The numerical predicate would not be given this devious form, of course, but would be rendered as an appropriate purely arithmetical condition.

Our dependence upon a background theory becomes especially evident when we reduce our universe U to another V by appeal to a proxy function. For it is only in a theory with an inclusive universe, embracing U and V, that we can make sense of the proxy function. The function maps U into V and hence needs all the old objects of U as well as their new proxies in V.

The proxy function need not exist as an object in the universe even of the background theory. It may do its work merely as what I have called a "virtual class,"[12] and Gödel has called a "notion."[13] That is to say, all that is required toward a function is an open sentence with two free variables, provided that it is fulfilled by exactly one value of the first variable for each object of the old universe as value of the second variable. But the point is that it is only in the background theory, with its inclusive universe, that we can hope to write such a sentence and have the right values at our disposal for its variables.

If the new objects happen to be among the old, so that V is a subclass of U, then the old theory with universe U can itself sometimes qualify as the background theory in which to describe its own ontological reduction. But we cannot do better than that; we cannot declare our new ontological economies without having recourse to the uneconomical old ontology.

This sounds, perhaps, like a predicament: as if no ontological economy is justifiable unless it is a false economy and the repudiated objects really exist after all. But actually this is wrong; there is no more cause for worry here than there is in *reductio ad absurdum,* where we assume a falsehood that we are out to disprove. If what we want to show is that the universe U is excessive and that only a part exists, or need exist, then we are quite within our rights to assume all of U for the space of the argument. We show thereby that if all of U were needed then not all of U would be needed; and so our ontological reduction is sealed by *reductio ad absurdum.*

Toward further appreciating the bearing of ontological relativity on programs of ontological reduction, it is worth while to reexamine the philosophical bearing of the Löwenheim-Skolem theorem. I shall use the strong early form of the theorem,[14] which depends on the axiom of choice. It says that if a theory is true and has an indenumerable universe, then all but a denumerable part of that universe is dead wood, in the sense that it can be dropped from the range of the variables without falsifying any sentences.

On the face of it, this theorem declares a reduction of all acceptable theories to denumerable ontologies. Moreover, a denumerable ontology is reducible in turn to an ontology specifically of natural numbers, simply by taking the enumeration as the proxy function, if the enumeration is explicitly at hand. And even if it is not at hand, it exists; thus we can still think of all our objects as natural numbers, and merely reconcile ourselves to not always knowing, numerically, which number an otherwise given object is. May we not thus settle for an all-purpose Pythagorean ontology outright?

Suppose, afterward, someone were to offer us what would formerly have qualified as an ontological reduction—a way of dispensing in future theory with all things of a certain sort S, but still leaving an infinite universe. Now in the new Pythagorean setting his discovery would still retain its essential content, though relinquishing the form of an ontological reduction; it would take the form merely of a move whereby some numerically unspecified numbers were divested of some property of numbers that corresponded to S.

Blanket Pythagoreanism on these terms is unattractive, for it merely offers new and obscurer accounts of old moves and old problems. On this score again, then, the relativistic proposition seems reasonable: that there is no absolute sense in speaking of the ontology of a theory. It very creditably brands this Pythagoreanism itself as meaningless. For there is no absolute sense in saying that all the objects of a theory are numbers, or that they are sets, or bodies, or something else; this makes no sense unless relative to some background theory. The relevant predicates—"number," "set," "body," or whatever—would be distinguished from *one another* in the background theory by the roles they play in the laws of that theory.

Elsewhere[11] I urged in answer to such Pythagoreanism that we have no ontological reduction in an interesting sense unless we can specify a proxy function. Now where does the strong Löwenheim-Skolem theorem leave us in this regard? If the background theory assumes the axiom of choice and even provides a notation for a general selector operator, can we in these terms perhaps specify an actual proxy function embodying the Löwenheim-Skolem argument?

The theorem is that all but a denumerable part of an ontology can be dropped and not be missed. One could imagine that the proof proceeds by partitioning the universe into denumerably many equivalence classes of indiscriminable objects, such that all but one member of each equivalence class can be dropped as superfluous; and one would then guess that where the axiom of choice enters the proof is in picking a survivor from each equivalence class. If this were so, then with help of Hilbert's selector notation we could indeed express a proxy function. But in fact the Löwenheim-Skolem proof has another structure. I see in the proof even of the strong Löwenheim-Skolem theorem no reason to suppose that a proxy function can be formulated anywhere that will map an indenumerable ontology, say the real numbers, into a denumerable one.

On the face of it, of course, such a proxy function is out of the question. It would have to be one-to-one, as we saw, to provide distinct images of distinct real numbers; and a one-to-one mapping of an indenumerable domain into a denumerable one is a contradiction. In particular it is easy to show in the Zermelo-Fraenkel system of set theory that such a function would neither exist nor admit even of formulation as a virtual class in the notation of the system.

The discussion of the ontology of a theory can make variously stringent demands upon the background theory in which the discussion is couched. The stringency of these demands varies with what is being said about the ontology of the object theory. We are now in a position to distinguish three such grades of stringency.

The least stringent demand is made when, with no view to reduction, we merely explain what things a theory is about, or what things its terms denote. This amounts to showing how to translate part or all of the object theory into the background theory. It is a matter really of showing how we *propose*, with some arbitrariness, to relate terms of the object theory to terms of the background theory; for we have the inscrutability of reference to allow for. But there is here no requirement that the background theory have a wider universe or a stronger vocabulary than the object theory. The theories could even be identical; this is the case when some terms are clarified by definition on the basis of other terms of the same language.

A more stringent demand was observed in the case where a proxy function is used to reduce an ontology. In this case the background theory needed the unreduced universe. But we saw, by considerations akin to *reductio ad absurdum*, that there was little here to regret.

The third grade of stringency has emerged now in the kind of ontological reduction hinted at by the Löwenheim-Skolem theorem. If a theory has by its own account an indenumerable universe, then even by taking that whole unreduced theory as background theory we cannot hope to produce a proxy function that would be adequate to reducing the ontology to a denumerable one. To find such a proxy function, even just a virtual one, we would need a background theory essentially stronger than the theory we were trying to reduce. This demand cannot, like the second grade of stringency above, be accepted in the spirit of *reductio ad absurdum*. It is a demand that simply discourages any general argument for Pythagoreanism from the Löwenheim-Skolem theorem.

A place where we see a more trivial side of ontological relativity is in the case of a finite universe of named objects. Here there is no occasion for quantification, except as an inessential abbreviation; for we can expand quantifications into finite conjunctions and alternations. Variables thus disappear, and with them the question of a universe of values of variables. And the very distinction between names and other signs lapses in turn, since the mark of a name is its admissibility in positions of variables. Ontology thus is emphatically meaningless for a finite theory of named objects, considered in and of itself. Yet we are now talking meaningfully of such finite ontologies. We are able to do so precisely because we are talking, however vaguely and implicitly, within a broader containing theory. What the objects of the finite theory are makes sense only as a statement of the background theory in its own referential idiom. The answer to the question depends on the background theory, the finite foreground theory, and, of course, the particular manner in which we choose to translate or embed the one in the other.

Ontology is internally indifferent also, I think, to any theory that is complete and decidable. Where we can always settle truth values mechanically, there is no evident internal reason for interest in the theory of quantifiers nor, therefore, in values of variables. These matters take on significance only as we think of the decidable theory as embedded in a richer background theory in which the variables and their values are serious business.

Ontology may also be said to be internally indifferent even to a theory that is not decidable and does not have a finite universe, if it happens still that each of the infinitely numerous objects of the theory has a name. We can no longer expand quantifications into conjunctions and alternations, barring infinitely long expressions. We can, however, revise our semantical account of the truth conditions of quantification, in such a way as to turn our backs on questions of reference. We can explain universal quantifications as true when true under all substitutions; and correspondingly for existential. Such is the course that has been favored by Leśniewski and by Ruth Marcus.[15] Its nonreferential orientation is seen in the fact that it makes no essential use of namehood. That is, additional quantifications could be explained whose variables are place-holders for words of any syntactical category. *Substitutional* quantification, as I call it, thus brings no way of distinguishing names from other vocabulary, nor any way of distinguishing between genuinely referential or value-taking variables and other place-holders. Ontology is thus meaningless for a theory whose only quantification is substitutionally construed; meaningless, that is, insofar as the theory is considered in and of itself. The question of its ontology makes sense only relative to some translation of the theory into a background theory in which we use referential quantification. The answer depends on both theories and, again, on the chosen way of translating the one into the other.

A final touch of relativity can in some cases cap this, when we try to distinguish between substitutional and referential quantification. Suppose again a theory with an infinite lot of names, and suppose that, by Gödel numbering or otherwise, we are treating of the theory's notations and proofs within the terms of the theory. If we succeed in showing that every result of substituting a name for the variable in a certain open sentence is true in the theory, but at the same time we disprove the universal quantification of the sentence,[16] then certainly we have shown that the universe of the theory contained some nameless objects. This is a case where an absolute decision can be reached in favor of referential quantification and against substitutional quantification, without ever retreating to a background theory.

But consider now the opposite situation, where there is no such open sentence. Imagine on the contrary that, whenever an open sentence is such that each result of substituting a name in it can be proved, its universal quantification can be proved in the theory too. Under these circumstances we can construe the universe as devoid of nameless objects and hence reconstrue the quantifications as substitutional, but we need not. We could still construe the universe as containing nameless objects. It could just happen that the nameless ones are *inseparable* from the named ones, in this sense: it could happen that all properties of nameless objects that we can express in the notation of the theory are shared by named objects.

We could construe the universe of the theory as containing, e.g., all real numbers. Some of them are nameless, since the real numbers are indenumerable while the names are denumerable. But it could still happen that the nameless reals are inseparable from the named reals. This would leave us unable within the theory to prove a distinction between referential and substitutional quantification.[17] Every expressible quantification that is true when referentially construed remains true when substitutionally construed, and vice versa.

We might still make the distinction from the vantage point of a background theory. In it we might specify some real number that was nameless in the object theory; for there are always ways of strengthening a theory so as to name more real numbers, though never all. Further, in the background theory, we might construe the universe of the object theory as exhausting the real numbers. In the background theory we could, in this way, clinch the quantifications in the object theory as referential. But this clinching is doubly relative: it is relative to the background theory and to the interpretation or translation imposed on the object theory from within the background theory.

One might hope that this recourse to a background theory could often be avoided, even when the nameless reals are inseparable from the named reals in the object theory. One might hope by indirect means to show within the object theory that there are nameless reals. For we might prove within the object theory that the reals are indenumerable and that the names are denumerable and hence that there is no function whose arguments are names and whose values exhaust the real numbers. Since the relation of real numbers to their names would be such a function if each real number had a name, we would seem to have proved within the object theory itself that there are nameless reals and hence that quantification must be taken referentially.

However, this is wrong; there is a loophole. This reasoning would prove only that a relation of all real numbers to their names cannot exist as an entity in the universe of the theory. This reasoning denies no number a name in the notation of the theory, as long as the name relation does not belong to the universe of the theory. And anyway we should know better than to expect such a relation, for it is what causes Berry's and Richard's and related paradoxes.

Some theories can attest to their own nameless objects and so claim referential quantification on their own; other theories have to look to background theories for this service. We saw how a theory might attest to its own nameless objects, namely, by showing that some open sentence became true under all constant substitutions but false under universal quantification. Perhaps this is the only way a theory can claim referential import for its own quantifications. Perhaps, when the nameless objects happen to be inseparable from the named, the quantification used in a theory cannot meaningfully be declared referential except through the medium of a background theory. Yet referential quantification is the key idiom of ontology. Thus ontology can be multiply relative, multiply meaningless apart from a background theory. Besides being unable to say in absolute terms just what the objects are, we are sometimes unable even to distinguish objectively between referential quantification and a substitutional counterfeit. When we do relativize these matters to a background theory, moreover, the relativization itself has two components: relativity to the choice of background theory and relativity to the choice of how to translate the object theory into the background theory. As for the ontology in turn of the background theory, and even the referentiality of its quantification—these matters can call for a background theory in turn.

There is not always a genuine regress. We saw that, if we are merely clarifying the range of the variables of a theory or the denotations of its terms, and are taking the referentiality of quantification itself for granted, we can commonly use the object theory itself as background theory. We found that when we undertake an ontological reduction, we must accept at least the unreduced theory in order to cite the proxy function; but this we were able cheerfully to accept in the spirit of *reductio ad absurdum* arguments. And now in the end we have found further that if we care to question quantification itself, and settle whether it imports a universe of discourse or turns merely on substitution at the linguistic level, we in some cases have genuinely to regress

to a background language endowed with additional resources. We seem to have to do this unless the nameless objects are separable from the named in the object theory.

Regress in ontology is reminiscent of the now familiar regress in the semantics of truth and kindred notions—satisfaction, naming. We know from Tarski's work how the semantics, in this sense, of a theory regularly demands an in some way more inclusive theory. This similarity should perhaps not surprise us, since both ontology and satisfaction are matters of reference. In their elusiveness, at any rate—in their emptiness now and again except relative to a broader background—both truth and ontology may in a suddenly rather clear and even tolerant sense be said to belong to transcendental metaphysics.[18]

Note added in proof. Besides such ontological reduction as is provided by proxy functions . . . there is that which consists simply in dropping objects whose absence will not falsify any truths expressible in the notation. Commonly this sort of deflation can be managed by proxy functions, but R. E. Grandy has shown me that sometimes it cannot. Let us by all means recognize it then as a further kind of reduction. In the background language we must, of course, be able to say what class of objects is dropped, just as in other cases we had to be able to specify the proxy function. This requirement seems sufficient still to stem any resurgence of Pythagoreanism on the strength of the Löwenheim-Skolem theorem.

Notes

1. J. Dewey, *Experience and Nature* (La Salle, Ill.: Open Court, 1925, 1958), p. 179.

2. Quine, *Word and Object* (Cambridge, Mass.: MIT Press, 1960), §12.

3. L. Wittgenstein, *Philosophical Investigations* (New York: Macmillan, 1953), p. 14.

4. Cf. *Word and Object,* §17.

5. *Word and Object,* §15. For a summary of the general point of view see also §I of "Speaking of Objects," Chapter 1 in [Quine, *Ontological Relativity and Other Essays* (New York: Columbia University Press, 1969)].

6. To keep my account graphic I am counting a certain postpositive particle as a suffix rather than a word.

7. See Leon Henkin, "Completeness in the theory of types," *Journal of Symbolic Logic* 15 (1950), 81–91, and references therein.

8. For more on this theme see my *Set Theory and Its Logic* (Cambridge, Mass.: Harvard, 1963, 1969), §11.

9. Paul Benacerraf, "What numbers cannot be," *Philosophical Review* 74 (1965), 47–73, develops this point. His conclusions differ in some ways from those I shall come to.

10. N. L. Wilson, "Substances without substrata," *Review of Metaphysics* 12 (1959), 521–539, p. 532.

11. Quine, *The Ways of Paradox* (New York: Random House, 1966), p. 204 ff.; or see *Journal of Philosophy*, 1964, pp. 214 ff.

12. Quine, *Set Theory and Its Logic,* §§2 f.

13. Kurt Gödel, *The Consistency of the Continuum Hypothesis* (Princeton, N.J.: The University Press, 1940), p. 11.

14. Thoralf Skolem, "Logisch-kombinatorische Untersuchungen über die Erfüllbarkeit oder Beweisbarkeit mathematischer Sätze nebst einem Theorem über dichte Mengen," *Skrifter utgit av Videnskapsselskapet i Kristiania*, 1919. 37 pp. Translation in Jean van Heijenoort, ed., *From Frege to Gödel: Source Book in the History of Mathematical Logic* (Cambridge, Mass.: Harvard, 1967), pp. 252–263.

15. Ruth B. Marcus, "Modalities and intensional languages," *Synthese* 13 (1961), 303–322. I cannot locate an adequate statement of Stanislaw Leśniewski's philosophy of quantification in his writings; I have it from his conversations. E. C. Luschei, in *The Logical Systems of Leśniewski* (Amsterdam: North-Holland, 1962), pp. 108 f, confirms my attribution but still cites no passage. On this version of quantification see further "Existence and Quantification," in [Quine, *Ontological Relativity and other Essays*].

16. Such is the typical way of a numerically insegregative system, misleadingly called "ω-inconsistent." See my *Selected Logic Papers* (New York: Random House, 1996), pp. 118f, or *Journal of Symbolic Logic*, 1953, pp. 122 f.

17. This possibility was suggested by Saul Kripke.

18. In developing these thoughts I have been helped by discussions with Saul Kripke, Thomas Nagel, and especially Burton Dreben.

READING QUESTIONS

1. Quine writes that "semantics is vitiated by a pernicious mentalism as long as we regard a man's semantics as somehow determinate in his mind beyond what might be implicit in his dispositions to overt behavior. It is the very facts about meaning, not the entities meant, that must be construed in terms of behavior." What does Quine mean by "a pernicious mentalism" in this context?

2. In considering the case of an expression in "a remote language" which can be translated into English in either of two ways (which are unlike in meaning), Quine writes that "if the museum myth were true, there would be a right and wrong of the matter . . . see language naturalistically, on the other hand, and you have to see the notion of likeness of meaning in such a case as simply nonsense." Why?

3. What is it that Quine calls 'analytical hypotheses'? What does he mean when he says that "if one workable over-all system of analytical hypotheses provides for translating a given native expression into 'is the same as', perhaps another equally workable but systematically different system would translate that native expression rather into something like 'belongs with'"? How might this work?

4. What does it mean to say that "translation is indeterminate"?

5. What does it mean to say that "reference is inscrutable"? In what ways does Quine connect the idea that translation is indeterminate with the idea that reference is inscrutable? In what ways do these commitments follow from his refusal to accept the myth of the museum?

6. Quine writes that "on deeper reflection, radical translation begins at home." What does this mean? Why does Quine think that this is true? How, according to Quine, does this lead to the conclusion that "we can reproduce the inscrutability of reference at home" as well?

7. Characterize in a general way how Quine thinks that one's first language is learned.

8. Quine writes that "the inscrutability of reference is not the inscrutability of a fact; there is no fact of the matter. But if there really is no fact of the matter, then the inscrutability of reference can be brought even closer to home than the neighbor's case; we can apply it to ourselves." What sorts of things does this thesis entail? Why does Quine think that it is true?

9. Quine says that "it is meaningless to ask whether, in general, our terms 'rabbit', 'rabbit part', 'number', etc., really refer respectively to rabbits, rabbit parts, numbers, etc., rather than to some ingeniously permuted denotations. It is meaningless to ask this absolutely; we can meaningfully ask it only relative to some background language." What is Quine talking about when he talks about a 'background language'? In what way does regressing into a background language make the question meaningful?

10. Quine finally urges *ontological relativity*. He states that "the relativistic thesis to which we have come is this, to repeat: it makes no sense to say what the objects of a theory are, beyond saying how to interpret or reinterpret that theory in another." How does this thesis connect with his thesis that translation is indeterminate and his thesis that reference is inscrutable?

11. "What makes ontological questions meaningless when taken absolutely is not universality, but circularity. A question of the form 'What is an *F*?' can only be answered by recourse to a further term: 'An *F* is a *G*.' The answer makes only relative sense: sense relative to an uncritical acceptance of '*G*'." Explain this carefully. Do you agree? Why or why not?

12. Quine claims that ontology is "doubly relative." According to him, in what way is this so? Is Quine correct about this?

SUGGESTIONS FOR FURTHER READING (W. V. O. QUINE)

Primary Sources and Collected Writings

(1934) *A System of Logistic.* Cambridge, MA: Harvard University Press.

(1940) *Mathematical Logic.* New York: W. W. Norton.

(1941) *Elementary Logic,* rev. ed. New York: Harper & Row, 1965.

(1950) *Methods of Logic,* 4th ed. Cambridge, MA: Harvard University Press, 1982.

(1953) *From a Logical Point of View,* rev. ed. Cambridge, MA: Harvard University Press, 1961.

(1960) *Word and Object.* Cambridge, MA:MIT Press.

(1963) *Set Theory and Its Logic,* rev. ed. Cambridge, MA: Harvard University Press, 1969.

(1966) *Selected Logic Papers,* enlarged ed. Cambridge, MA: Harvard University Press, 1995.

(1966) *The Ways of Paradox and Other Essays,* rev. and enlarged ed. Cambridge, MA: Harvard University Press, 1976.

(1969) *Ontological Relativity and Other Essays.* New York: Columbia University Press.

(1970) *Philosophy of Logic,* 2nd ed. Cambridge, MA: Harvard University Press, 1986.

(1970) (and J. S. Ullian) *The Web of Belief,* 2nd ed. New York: Random House, 1978.

(1974) *The Roots of Reference.* La Salle, IL: Open Court.

(1981) *Theories and Things.* Cambridge, MA: Harvard University Press.

(1985) *The Time of My Life: An Autobiography.* Cambridge, MA: MIT Press.

(1986) *Philosophy of Logic.* Cambridge, MA: Harvard University Press.

(1987) *Quiddities: An Intermittently Philosophical Dictionary.* Cambridge, MA: Harvard University Press.

(1990) *Pursuit of Truth,* 2nd ed. Cambridge, MA: Harvard University Press, 1992.

(1990) *Dear Carnap, Dear Van: The Quine-Carnap Correspondence and Related Work,* edited by R. Creath. Berkeley, CA: University of California Press.

(1995) *From Stimulus to Science.* Cambridge, MA: Harvard University Press.

Secondary Sources

Arrington, R. L., and H.-J. Glock, eds. (1996). *Wittgenstein and Quine.* New York: Routledge.

Barret, R. B., and R. Gibson, eds. (1990) *Perspectives on Quine.* Oxford: Blackwell.

Davidson, D., and J. Hintikka, eds. (1975) *Words and Objections.* Dordrecht: D. Reidel.

Dilham, I. (1984) *Quine on Ontology, Necessity and Experience: A Philosophical Critique.* New York: Macmillan.

Field, H. (1980) *Science Without Numbers.* Princeton, NJ: Princeton University Press.

Gibson, R. (1982) *The Philosophy of W. V. Quine.* Gainsville, FL: University Presses of Florida.

———. (1988) *Enlightened Empiricism: An Examination of W. V. Quine's Theory of Knowledge.* Tampa, FL: University of South Florida Press.

Gochet, P. (1986) *Ascent to Truth: A Critical Examination of Quine's Philosophy.* Munich: Munich Verlag.

Hahn, L. E., and P. A. Schilpp, eds. (1986) *The Philosophy of W. V. Quine.* La Salle, IL: Open Court.

Hookway, C. (1988) *Quine: Language, Experience, and Reality.* Stanford, CA: Stanford University Press.

Kirk, R. (1986) *Translation Determined.* Oxford: Oxford University Press.

Leonardi, P., and M. Santambroggia, eds. (1995) *On Quine.* Cambridge: Cambridge University Press.

Orenstein, A., and P. Kotatko, eds. (1998) *Knowledge, Language and Logic: Questions for Quine.* Dordrecht: Kluwer Academic Publishers.

Shahan, R. W., and C. Swoyer, eds. (1979) *Essays on the Philosophy of W. V. Quine.* Norman, OK: University of Oklahoma Press.

DONALD DAVIDSON

On the Very Idea of a Conceptual Scheme

Donald Davidson (1917–) was born in Springfield, Massachusetts. He attended Harvard University, where he pursued studies in English, comparative literature, and the classics. He also studied philosophy, attending classes taught by Alfred North Whitehead and others. He completed his undergraduate studies in 1939 and decided to go on to advanced study in philosophy. As a graduate student at Harvard, Davidson became a pupil of W. V. O. Quine. He received his M.A. in 1941 and, in 1942, enlisted in the U.S. Navy for a three-year term in order to serve in the Second World War. After the war Davidson returned to his philosophical studies at Harvard. He graduated with the Ph.D. in 1949 with a dissertation on Plato's *Philebus.*

Davidson took his first teaching position at Queen's College in New York and from there traveled to to

Stanford University, becoming a member of the faculty and teaching there from 1951 to 1967. After leaving Stanford, Davidson took various positions at Princeton (1967–1970), at Rockefeller (1970–1976), and at the University of Chicago (1976–1981). At one point, Davidson had the honor of being named to the distinguished position of John Locke Lecturer at the University of Oxford. In 1981 Davidson took a position in the philosophy department at the University of California at Berkeley, where he currently serves as professor of philosophy.

In the following essay, Davidson addresses the so-called "third dogma of empiricism"—the idea that one can draw a distinction between a conceptual scheme for organizing experience, on one hand, and the empirical content of that scheme, on the other. In the course of his argument, Davidson explores the idea that a conceptual scheme is best thought of as a language, or family of translatable languages, and so the existence of different conceptual schemes can in turn be characterized in terms of the complete or partial failure of translatability between languages or sets of languages. The question, then, is whether we can really make sense of the idea of a complete or partial failure of translatability between languages in this way.

Davidson believes that the implications of this question are far-reaching. "I want to urge," he writes, "that [the] dualism of scheme and content, of organizing system and something wanting to be organized, cannot be made intelligible and defensible. It is itself a dogma of empiricism, the third dogma. The third, and perhaps the last, for if we give it up it is not clear that there is anything distinctively left to call empiricism."

Philosophers of many persuasions are prone to talk of conceptual schemes. Conceptual schemes, we are told, are ways of organizing experience; they are systems of

Donald Davidson, "On the Very Idea of a Conceptual Scheme" from *Proceedings and Addresses of the American Philosophical Association* 47, no. 2 (1974), pp. 5–20. Reprinted with the kind permission of Donald Davidson and the American Philosophical Association.

categories that give form to the data of sensation; they are points of view from which individuals, cultures, or periods survey the passing scene. There may be no translating from one scheme to another, in which case the beliefs, desires, hopes, and bits of knowledge that characterize one person have no true counterparts for the subscriber to another scheme. Reality itself is relative to a scheme: what counts as real in one system may not in another.

Even those thinkers who are certain there is only one conceptual scheme are in the sway of the scheme concept; even monotheists have religion. And when someone sets out to describe "our conceptual scheme," his homey task assumes, if we take him literally, that there might be rival systems.

Conceptual relativism is a heady and exotic doctrine, or would be if we could make good sense of it. The trouble is, as so often in philosophy, it is hard to improve intelligibility while retaining the excitement. At any rate that is what I shall argue.

We are encouraged to imagine we understand massive conceptual change or profound contrasts by legitimate examples of a familiar sort. Sometimes an idea, like that of simultaneity as defined in relativity theory, is so important that with its addition a whole department of science takes on a new look. Sometimes revisions in the list of sentences held true in a discipline are so central that we may feel that the terms involved have changed their meanings. Languages that have evolved in distant times or places may differ extensively in their resources for dealing with one or another range of phenomena. What comes easily in one language may come hard in another, and this difference may echo significant dissimilarities in style and value.

But examples like these, impressive as they occasionally are, are not so extreme but that the changes and the contrasts can be explained and described using the equipment of a single language. Whorf, wanting to demonstrate that Hopi incorporates a metaphysics so alien to ours that Hopi and English cannot, as he puts it, "be calibrated," uses English to convey the contents of sample Hopi sentences. Kuhn is brilliant at saying what things were like before the revolution using what else? our postrevolutionary idiom. Quine gives us a feel for the "pre-individuative phase in the evolution of our conceptual scheme," while Bergson tells us where we can go to get a view of a mountain undistorted by one or another provincial perspective.

The dominant metaphor of conceptual relativism, that of differing points of view, seems to betray an underlying paradox. Different points of view make sense, but only if there is a common coordinate system on which to plot them; yet the existence of a common system belies the claim of dramatic incomparability. What we need, it seems to me, is some idea of the considerations that set the limits to conceptual contrast. There are extreme suppositions that founder on paradox or contradiction; there are modest examples we have no trouble understanding. What determines where we cross from the merely strange or novel to the absurd?

We may accept the doctrine that associates having a language with having a conceptual scheme. The relation may be supposed to be this: if conceptual schemes differ, so do languages. But speakers of different languages may share a conceptual scheme provided there is a way of translating one language into the other. Studying the criteria of translation is therefore a way of focusing on criteria of identity for conceptual schemes. If conceptual schemes aren't associated with languages in this way, the original problem is needlessly doubled, for then we would have to imagine the mind, with its ordinary categories, operating with a language with *its* organizing structure. Under the circumstances we would certainly want to ask who is to be master.

Alternatively, there is the idea that *any* language distorts reality, which implies that it is only wordlessly, if at all, that the mind comes to grips with things as they really are. This is to conceive language as an inert (though necessarily distorting) medium independent of the human agencies that employ this view of language that surely cannot be maintained. Yet if the mind can grapple without distortion with the real, the mind itself must be without categories and concepts. This featureless self is familiar from theories in quite different parts of the philosophical landscape. There are, for example, theories that make freedom consist in decisions taken apart from all desires, habits, and dispositions of the agent; and theories of knowledge that suggest that the mind can observe the totality of its own perceptions and ideas. In each case, the mind is divorced from the traits that constitute it; a familiar enough conclusion to certain lines of reasoning, as I said, but one that should always persuade us to reject the premises.

We may identify conceptual schemes with languages, then, or better, allowing for the possibility that more than one language may express the same scheme, sets of intertranslatable languages. Languages we will think of as separate from souls; speaking a language is not a trait a man can lose while retaining the power of thought. So there is no chance that someone can take up a vantage point for comparing conceptual schemes by temporarily shedding his own. Can we say that two people have different conceptual schemes if they speak languages that fail of intertranslatability?

In what follows I consider two kinds of case that might be expected to arise: complete, and partial, failures of translatability. There would be complete failure if no significant range of sentence in one language could be translated into the other; there would be partial failure if some range could be translated and some range could not (I shall neglect possible asymmetrics). My strategy will be to argue that we cannot make sense of total failure, and then to examine more briefly cases of partial failure.

First, then, the purported cases of complete failure. It is tempting to take a very short line indeed: nothing, it may be said, could count as evidence that some form of activity could not be interpreted in our language that was not at the same time evidence that that form of activity was not speech behavior. If this were right, we probably ought to hold that a form of activity that cannot be interpreted as language in our language is not speech behavior. Putting matters this way is unsatisfactory, however, for it comes to little more than making translatability into a familiar tongue a criterion of languagehood. As fiat, the thesis lacks the appeal of self-evidence; if it is a truth, as I think it is, it should emerge as the conclusion of an argument.

The credibility of the position is improved by reflection on the close relations between language and the attribution of attitudes such as belief, desire, and intention. On the one hand, it is clear that speech requires a multitude of finely discriminated intentions and beliefs. A person who asserts that perseverance keeps honor bright must, for example, represent himself as believing that perseverance keeps honor bright, and he must intend to represent himself as believing it. On the other hand, it seems unlikely that we can intelligibly attribute attitudes as complex as these to a speaker unless we can translate his words into ours. There can be no doubt that the relation between being able to translate someone's language

and being able to describe his attitudes is very close. Still, until we can say more about *what* this relation is, the case against untranslatable languages remains obscure.

It is sometimes thought that translatability into a familiar language, say English, cannot be a criterion of languagehood on the grounds that the relation of translatability is not transitive. The idea is that some language, say Saturnian, may be translatable into English, and some further language, like Plutonian, may be translatable into Saturnian, while Plutonian is not translatable into English. Enough translatable differences may add up to an untranslatable one. By imagining a sequence of languages, each close enough to the one before to be acceptably translated into it, we can imagine a language so different from English as to resist totally translation into it. Corresponding to this distant language would be a system of concepts altogether alien to us.

This exercise does not, I think, introduce any new element into the discussion. For we should have to ask how we recognized that what the Saturnian was doing was *translating* Plutonian (or anything else). The Saturnian speaker might tell us that that was what he was doing or rather, we might for a moment assume that that was what he was telling us. But then it would occur to us to wonder whether our translations of Saturnian were correct.

According to Kuhn, scientists operating in different scientific traditions (within different "paradigms") "live in different worlds." Strawson's *The Bounds of Sense* begins with the remark that "It is possible to imagine kinds of worlds very different from the world as we know it."[1] Since there is at most one world, these pluralities are metaphorical or merely imagined. The metaphors are, however, not at all the same. Strawson invites us to imagine possible nonactual worlds, worlds that might be described, using our present language, by redistributing truth values over sentences in various systematic ways. The clarity of the contrasts between worlds in this case depends on supposing our scheme of concepts, our descriptive resources, to remain fixed. Kuhn, on the other hand, wants us to think of different observers of the same world who come to it with incommensurable systems of concepts. Strawson's many imagined worlds are seen (or heard)—anyway described—from the same points of view; Kuhn's one world is seen from different points of view. It is the second metaphor we want to work on.

The first metaphor requires a distinction within language of concept and content: using a fixed system of concepts (words with fixed meanings) we describe alternative universes. Some sentences will be true simply because of the concepts or meanings involved, others because of the way of the world. In describing possible worlds, we play with sentences of the second kind only.

The second metaphor suggests instead a dualism of quite a different sort, a dualism of total scheme (or language) and uninterpreted content. Adherence to the second dualism, while not inconsistent with adherence to the first, may be encouraged by attacks on the first. Here is how it may work.

To give up the analytic-synthetic distinction as basic to the understanding of language is to give up the idea that we can clearly distinguish between theory and language. Meaning, as we might loosely use the world, is contaminated by theory, by what is held to be true. Feyerabend puts it this way:

> Our argument against meaning invariance is simple and clear. It proceeds from the fact that usually some of the principles involved in the determinations of the meanings of older theories or points of view are inconsistent with the new . . . theories. It points out that it is natural to resolve this contradiction by eliminating the troublesome . . . older principles, and to replace them by principles, or theorems, of a new . . . theory. And it concludes by showing that such a procedure will also lead to the elimination of the old meanings.[2]

We may now seem to have a formula for generating distinct conceptual schemes. We get a new out of an old scheme when the speakers of a language come to accept as true an important range of sentences they previously took to be false (and, of course, vice versa). We must not describe this change simply as a matter of their coming to view old falsehoods as truths, for a truth is a proposition, and what they come to accept, in accepting a sentence as true, is not the same thing that they rejected when formerly they held the sentence to be false. A change has come over the meaning of the sentence because it now belongs to a new language.

This picture of how new (perhaps better) schemes result from new and better science is very much the picture philosophers of science, like Putnam and Feyerabend, and historians of science, like Kuhn, have painted for us. A related idea emerges in the suggestion of some other philosophers, that we could improve our conceptual lot if we were to tune our language to an improved science. Thus both Quine and Smart, in somewhat different ways, regretfully admit that our present ways of talking make a serious science of behavior impossible. (Wittgenstein and Ryle have said similar things without regret.) The cure, Quine and Smart think, is to change how we talk. Smart advocates (and predicts) the change in order to put us on the scientifically straight path of materialism. Quine is more concerned to clear the way for a purely extensional language. (Perhaps I should add that I think our *present* scheme and language are best understood as extensional and materialist.)

If we were to follow this advice, I do not myself think science or understanding would be advanced, though possibly morals would. But the present question is only whether, if such changes were to take place, we should be justified in calling them alterations in the basic conceptual apparatus. The difficulty in so calling them is easy to appreciate. Suppose that in my office of Minister of Scientific Language I want the new man to stop using words that refer, say, to emotions, feelings, thoughts, and intentions, and to talk instead of the physiological states and happenings that are assumed to be more or less identical with the mental riff and raff. How do I tell whether my advice has been heeded if the new person speaks a new language? For all I know, the shiny new phrases, though stolen from the old language in which they refer to physiological stirrings may in his mouth play the role of the messy old mental concepts.

The key phrase is: "for all I know." What is clear is that retention of some or all of the old vocabulary in itself provides no basis for judging the new scheme to be the same as, or different from, the old. So what sounded at first like a thrilling discovery—that truth is relative to a conceptual scheme—has not so far been shown to be anything more than the pedestrian and familiar face that the truth of a sentence is relative to (among other things) the language to which it belongs. Instead of living in different worlds, Kuhn's scientists may, like those who need Webster's dictionary, be only words apart.

Giving up the analytic-synthetic distinction has not proven a help in making sense of conceptual relativism. The analytic-synthetic distinction is, however, explained in terms of something that may serve to buttress conceptual relativism, namely the idea of empirical content. The dualism of the synthetic and the analytic is a dualism of sentences some of which are true (or false) both because of what they mean and because of their empirical content, while others are true (or false) by virtue of meaning alone, having no empirical content. If we give up the dualism, we abandon the conception of meaning that goes with it, but we do not have to abandon the idea of empirical content: we can hold, if we want, that *all* sentences have empirical content. Empirical content is in turn explained by reference to the facts, the world, experience, sensation, the totality of sensory stimuli, or something similar. Meanings gave us a way to talk about categories, the organizing structure of language, and so on, but it is possible, as we have seen, to give up meanings and analyticity while retaining the idea of language as embodying a conceptual scheme. Thus in place of the dualism of the analytic-synthetic we get the dualism of conceptual scheme and empirical content. The new dualism is the foundation of an empiricism shorn of the untenable dogmas of the analytic-synthetic distinction and reductionism—shorn, that is, of the unworkable idea that we can uniquely allocate empirical content sentence by sentence.

I want to urge that this second dualism of scheme and content, of organizing system and something waiting to be organized, cannot to be made intelligible and defensible. It is itself a dogma of empiricism, the third dogma. The third, and perhaps the last, for if we give it up it is not clear that there is anything distinctive left to call empiricism.

The scheme-content dualism has been formulated in many ways. Here are some examples. The first comes from Whorf, elaborating on a theme of Sapir's. Whorf says that:

language produces an organization of experience. We are inclined to think of language simply as a technique of expression, and not to realize that language first of all is a classification and arrangement

of the stream of sensory experience which results in a certain world-order. . . . In other words, language does in a cruder but also in a broader and more versatile way the same thing that science does. . . . We are thus introduced to a new principle of relativity, which holds that all observers are not led by the same physical evidence to the same picture of the universe, unless their linguistic backgrounds are similar, or can in some way be calibrated.[3]

Here we have all the required elements: language as the organizing force, not to be distinguished clearly from science: what is organized, referred to variously as "experience," "the stream of sensory experience," and "physical evidence"; and finally, the failure of intertranslatability is a necessary condition for difference of conceptual schemes; the common relation to experience or the evidence is what is supposed to help us make sense of the claim that it is languages or schemes that are under consideration when translation fails. It is essential to this idea that there be something neutral and common that lies outside all schemes. This common something cannot, of course, be the *subject matter* of contrasting languages, or translation would be possible. Thus Kuhn has recently written:

Philosophers have now abandoned hope of finding a pure sense-datum language . . . but many of them continue to assume that theories can be compared by recourse to a basic vocabulary consisting entirely of words which are attached to nature in ways that are unproblematic and, to the extent necessary, independent of theory. . . . Feyerabend and I have argued at length that no such vocabulary is available. In the transition from one theory to the next words change their meanings or conditions of applicability in subtle ways. Though most of the same signs are used before and after a revolution . . . e.g., force, mass, element, compound, cell . . . the ways in which some of them attach to nature has somehow changed. Successive theories are thus, we say, incommensurable.[4]

"Incommensurable" is, of course, Kuhn and Feyerabend's word for "not intertranslatable." The neutral content waiting to be organized is supplied by nature.

Feyerabend himself suggests that we may compare contrasting schemes by "choosing a point of view outside the system or the language." He hopes we can do this because "there is still human experience as an actually existing process"[5] independent of all schemes.

The same, or similar, thoughts are expressed by Quine in many passages: "The totality of our so-called knowledge or beliefs . . . is a manmade fabric which impinges on experience only along the edges";[6] "total science is like a field of force whose boundary conditions are experience";[7] "as an empiricist I . . . think of the conceptual scheme of science as a tool . . . for predicting future experience in the light of past experience."[8] And again:

> We persist in breaking reality down somehow into a multiplicity of identifiable and discriminable objects. . . . We talk so inveterately of objects that to say we so seems almost to say nothing at all; for how else is there to talk? It is hard to say how else there is to talk, not because our objectifying pattern is an invariable trait of human nature, but because we are bound to adapt any alien pattern to our own in the very process of understanding or translating the alien sentences.[9]

The test of difference remains failure or difficulty of translation: "to speak of that remote medium as radically different from ours is to say no more than that the translations do not come smoothly."[10] Yet the roughness may be so great that the alien has an "as yet unimagined pattern beyond individuation."[11]

The idea is then that something is a language, and associated with a conceptual scheme, whether we can translate it or not, if it stands in a certain relation (predicting, organizing, facing, or fitting) to experience (nature, reality, sensory promptings). The problem is to say what the relation is, and to be clearer about the entities related.

The images and metaphors fall into two main groups: conceptual schemes (languages) either *organize* something, or they *fit* it (as in "he warps his scientific heritage to fit his . . . sensory promptings"[12]). The first group contains also *systematize, divide up* (the stream of experience); further examples of the second group are *predict, account for, face* (the tribunal of experience). As for the entities that get organized, or which the scheme must fit, I think again we may detect two main ideas; either it is reality (the universe, the world, nature), or it is experience (the passing show, surface irritations, sensory promptings, sense data, the given).

We cannot attach a clear meaning to the notion of organizing a single object (the world, nature, etc.) unless that object is understood to contain or consist in other objects. Someone who sets out to organize a closet arranges the things in it. If you are told not to organize the shoes and shirts, but the closet itself, you would be bewildered. How would you organize the Pacific Ocean? Straighten out its shores, perhaps, or relocate its islands, or destroy the fish.

A language may contain simple predicates whose extensions are matched by no simple predicates, or even by any predicates at all, in some other language. What enables us to make this point in particular cases is an ontology common to the two languages, with concepts that individuate the same objects. We can be clear about breakdowns in translation when they are local enough, for a background of generally successful translation provides what is needed to make the failures intelligible. But we were after larger game: we wanted to make sense of there being a language we could not translate at all. Or, to put the point differently, we were looking for a criterion of languagehood that did not depend on, or entail, translatability into a familiar idiom. I suggest that the image of organizing the closet of nature will not apply such a criterion.

How about the other kind of object, experience? Can we think of a language organizing it? Much the same difficulties recur. The notion of organization applies only to pluralities. But whatever plurality we take experience to consist in—events like losing a button or stubbing a toe, having a sensation of warmth or hearing an oboe—we will have to individuate according to familiar principles. A language that organizes *such* entities must be a language very like our own.

Experience (and its classmates like surface irritations, sensations, and sense data) also makes another and more obvious trouble for the organizing idea. For how could something count as a language that organized *only* experiences, sensations, surface irritations, or sense data? Surely knives and forks, railroads and mountains, cabbages and kingdoms also need organizing.

This last remark will no doubt sound inappropriate as a reason to the claim that a conceptual scheme is a way of coping with sensory experience; and I agree that it is. But what was under consideration was the idea of *organizing* experience, not the idea of *coping with* (or fitting or facing) experience. The reply was apropos of the former, not the latter, concept. So now let's see whether we can do better with the second idea.

When we turn from talk of organization to talk of fitting we turn our attention from the referential apparatus of language—predicates, quantifiers, variables, and singular terms—to whole sentences. It is sentences that predict (or are used to predict), sentences that cope or deal with things, that fit our sensory promptings, that can be compared or confronted with the evidence. It is sentences also that face the tribunal of experience, though of course they must face it together.

The proposal is not that experiences, sense data, surface irritations, or sensory promptings are the sole subject matter of language. There is, it is true, the theory that talk about brick houses on Elm Street is ultimately to be construed as being about sense data or perceptions, but such reductionistic views are only extreme, and implausible, versions of the general position we are considering. The general position is that sensory experience provides all the *evidence* for the acceptance of sentences (where sentences may include whole theories). A sentence or theory fits our sensory promptings, successfully faces the tribunal of experience, predicts future experience, or copes with the pattern of our surface irritations, provided it is borne out by the evidence.

In the common course of affairs, a theory may be borne out by the available evidence and yet be false. But what is in view here is not just actually available evidence; it is the totality of possible sensory evidence past, present, and future. We do not need to pause to contemplate what this might mean. The point is that for a theory to fit or face up to the totality of possible sensory evidence is for that theory to be true. If a theory quantifies over physical objects, numbers or sets, what it says about these entities is true provided the theory as a whole fits the sensory evidence. One can see how, from this point of view, such entities might be called posits. It is reasonable to call something a posit if it can be contrasted with something that is not. Here the something that is not is sensory experience, at least that is the idea.

The trouble is that the notion of fitting the totality of experience, like the notions of fitting the facts, or being true to the facts, adds nothing intelligible to the simple concept of being true. To speak of sensory experience rather than the evidence, or just the facts, ex-

presses a view about the source or nature of evidence, but it does not add a new entity to the universe against which to test conceptual schemes. The totality of sensory evidence is what we want provided it is all the evidence there is; and all the evidence there is is just what it takes to make our sentences or theories true. Nothing, however, no *thing*, makes sentences and theories true; not experience, not surface irritations, not the world, can make a sentence true. That experience takes a certain course, that our skin is warmed or punctured, that the universe is finite, these facts, if we like to talk that way, make sentences and theories true. But this point is put better without mention of facts. The sentence "My skin is warm" is true if and only if my skin is warm. Here there is no reference to a fact, a world, an experience, or a piece of evidence.[13]

Our attempt to characterize languages or conceptual schemes in terms of the notion of fitting some entity has come down, then, to the simple thought that something is an acceptable conceptual scheme or theory if it is true. Perhaps we better say *largely* true in order to allow sharers of a scheme to differ on details. And the criterion of a conceptual scheme different from our own now becomes largely true but not translatable. The question whether this is a useful criterion is just the question how well we understand the notion of truth, as applied to language, independent of the notion of translation. The answer is, I think, that we do not understand it independently at all.

We recognize sentences like " 'Snow is white' is true if and only if snow is white" to be trivially true. Yet the totality of such English sentences uniquely determines the extension of the concept of truth for English. Tarski generalized this observation and made it a test of theories of truth: according to Tarski's Convention T, a satisfactory theory of truth for a language L must entail, for every sentence s of L, a theorem of the form "s is true if and only if p" where "s" is replaced by a description of s and "p" by s itself if L is English, and by a translation of s into English if L is not English.[14] This isn't, of course, a definition of truth, and it doesn't hint that there is a single definition or theory that applies to languages generally. Nevertheless, Convention T suggests, though it cannot state, an important feature common to all the specialized concepts of truth. It succeeds in doing this by making essential use of the notion of translation into a language we know. Since Convention

T embodies our best intuition as to how the concept of truth is used, there does not seem to be much hope for a test that a conceptual scheme is radically different from ours if that test depends on the assumption that we can divorce the notion of truth from that of translation.

Neither a fixed stock of meanings, nor a theory-neutral reality, can provide, then, a ground for comparison of conceptual schemes. It would be a mistake to look further for such a ground if by that we mean something conceived as common to incommensurable schemes. In abandoning this search, we abandon the attempt to make sense of the metaphor of a single space within which each scheme has a position and provides a point of view.

I turn now to the more modest approach: the idea of partial rather than total failure of translation. This introduces the possibility of making changes and contrasts in conceptual schemes intelligible by reference to the common part. What we need is a theory of translation or interpretation that makes no assumptions about shared meanings, concepts, or beliefs.

The interdependence of belief and meaning springs from the interdependence of two aspects of the interpretation of speech behavior; the attribution of beliefs and the interpretation of sentences. I remarked before that we can afford to associate conceptual schemes with languages because of these dependencies. Now we can put the point in a somewhat sharper way. Allow that a man's speech cannot be interpreted without knowing a good deal about what he believes (and intends and wants), and that fine distinctions between beliefs are impossible without understood speech; how then are we to interpret speech or intelligibly to attribute beliefs and other attitudes? Clearly we must have a theory that simultaneously accounts for attitudes and interprets speech, a theory that rests on evidence which assumes neither.

I suggest, following Quine, that we may without circularity or unwarranted assumptions accept certain very general attitudes towards sentences as the basic evidence for a theory of radical interpretation. For the sake of the present discussion at least we may depend on the attitude of accepting as true, directed at sentences, as the crucial notion. (A more full-blooded theory would look to other attitudes toward sentences as well, such as wishing true, wondering whether true, intending to make true, and so on.) Attitudes are indeed involved here, but the fact that the main issue is not

begged can be seen from this: if we merely know that someone holds a certain sentence to be true, we know neither what he means by the sentence nor what belief his holding it true represents. His holding the sentence true is thus the vector of two forces; the problem of interpretation is to abstract from the evidence a workable theory of meaning and an acceptable theory of belief.

The way this problem is solved is best appreciated from undramatic examples. If you see a ketch sailing by and your companion says, "Look at that handsome yawl," you may be faced with a problem of interpretation. One natural possibility is that your friend has mistaken a ketch for a yawl, and has formed a false belief. But if his vision is good and his line of sight favorable it is even more plausible that he does not use the word "yawl" quite as you do, and has made no mistake at all about the position of the jigger on the passing yacht. We do this sort of off-the-cuff interpretation all the time, deciding in favor of reinterpretation of words in order to preserve a reasonable theory of belief. As philosophers we are peculiarly tolerant of systematic malapropism, and practiced at interpreting the result. The process is that of constructing a viable theory of belief and meaning from sentences held true.

Such examples emphasize the interpretation of anomalous details against a background of common beliefs and a going method of translation. But the principles involved must be the same in less trivial cases. What matters is this: if all we know is what sentences a speaker holds true, and we cannot assume that his language is our own, then we cannot take even a first step toward interpretation without knowing or assuming a great deal about the speaker's beliefs. Since knowledge of beliefs comes only with the ability to interpret words, the only possibility at the start is to assume general agreement on beliefs. We get a first approximation to a finished theory by assigning to sentences of a speaker conditions of truth that actually obtain (in our own opinion) just when the speaker holds those sentences true. The guiding policy is to do this as far as possible—subject to considerations of simplicity, hunches about the effects of social conditioning, and of course our common sense, or scientific knowlege of explicable error.

The method is not designed to eliminate disagreement, nor can it; its purpose is to make meaningful disagreement possible, and this depends entirely on a foundation—*some* foundation—in agreement. The agreement may take the form of widespread sharing of sentences held true by speakers of "the same language," or agreement in the large mediated by a theory of truth contrived by an interpreter for speakers of another language.

Since charity is not an option, but a condition of having a workable theory, it is meaningless to suggest that we might fall into massive error by endorsing it. Until we have successfully established a systematic correlation of sentences held true with sentences held true, there are no mistakes to make. Charity is forced on us, whether we like it or not, if we want to understand others, we must count them right in most matters. If we can produce a theory that reconciles charity and the formal conditions for a theory, we have done all that could be done to ensure communication. Nothing more is possible, and nothing more is needed.

We make maximum sense of the words and thoughts of others when we interpret in a way that optimizes agreement (this includes room, as we said, for explicable error, i.e., differences of opinion). Where does this leave the case for conceptual relativism? The answer is, I think, that we must say much the same thing about differences in conceptual scheme as we say about differences in belief: we improve the clarity and bite of declarations of difference, whether of scheme or opinion, by enlarging the basis of shared (translatable) language or of shared opinion. Indeed, no clear line between the cases can be made out. If we choose to translate some alien sentence rejected by its speakers by a sentence to which we are strongly attached on a community basis, we may be tempted to call this a difference in schemes; if we decide to accommodate the evidence in other ways, it may be more natural to speak of a difference of opinion. But when others think differently from us, no general principle, or appeal to evidence, can force us to decide that the difference lies in our beliefs rather than in our concepts.

We must conclude, I think, that the attempt to give a solid meaning to the idea of conceptual relativism, and hence to the idea of a conceptual scheme, fares no better when based on partial failure of translation than when based on total failure. Given the underlying methodology of interpretation, we could not be in a position to judge that others had concepts or beliefs radically different from our own.

It would be wrong to summarize by saying I have shown how communication is possible between people who have different schemes, a way that works without need of what there cannot be, namely a neutral ground, or a common coordinate system. For we have found no intelligible basis on which it can be said that schemes are different. It would be equally wrong to announce the glorious news that all mankind, all speakers of language, at least, share a common scheme and ontology. For if we cannot intelligibly say that schemes are different, neither can we intelligibly say that they are one.

In giving up dependence on the concepts of an uninterpreted reality, something outside all schemes and science, we do not relinquish the notion of objective truth—quite the contrary. Given the dogma of a dualism of scheme and reality, we get conceptual relativity, and truth relative to a scheme. Without the dogma, this kind of relativity goes by the board. Of course truth of sentences remains relative to language, but that is as objective as can be. In giving up the dualism of scheme and world, we do not give up the world, but reestablish unmediated touch with the familiar objects whose antics make our sentences and opinions true or false.

Notes

1. Peter Strawson, *The Bounds of Sense* (London, 1966), p. 15.
2. Paul Feyerabend, "Explanation, Reduction, and Empiricism," in H. Feigl and Grover Maxwell, eds., *Scientific Explanation, Space, and Time.* Minnesota Studies in the Philosophy of Science, vol. 3 (Minneapolis, University of Minnesota Press, 1962), p. 82.
3. Benjamin Lee Whorf, *Language, Thought, and Reality: Selected Writings of Benjamin Lee Whorf,* J. B. Carroll, ed. (Cambridge, Mass.: MIT Press, 1956), p. 55.
4. Thomas Kuhn, "Reflection on my Critics," in I. Lakatos and A. Musgrave, eds., *Criticism and the Growth of Knowledge* (Cambridge: Cambridge University Press, 1970), pp. 266, 267.
5. Paul Feyerabend, "Problems of Empiricism," in R. G. Colodny, ed., *Beyond the Edge of Certainty,* Englewood Cliffs, N.J.: Prentice-Hall, 1965), p. 214.
6. W. V. O. Quine, "Two Dogmas of Empiricism," reprinted in *From a Logical Point of View,* 2d ed. (Cambridge: Harvard University Press, 1961), p. 42.
7. *Ibid.*

8. *Ibid.,* p. 44.
9. W. V. O. Quine, "Speaking of Objects," reprinted in *Ontological Relativity and Other Essays* (New York: Columbia University Press, 1969), p. 1.
10. *Ibid.,* p. 25.
11. *Ibid.,* p. 24.
12. Quine, "Two Dogmas of Empiricism," p. 46.
13. These remarks are defended in my "True to the Facts," *The Journal of Philosophy* (1969) 66:748–764.
14. Alfred Tarski, "The Concept of Truth in Formalized Languages," in *Logics, Semantics, Metamathematics* (Oxford: Oxford University Press, 1956).

READING QUESTIONS

1. According to Davidson, what are 'conceptual schemes'? What does he mean when he says "we may accept the doctrine that associates having a language with having a conceptual scheme"? What view is Davidson talking about, in turn, when he discusses 'conceptual relativism'?
2. Davidson writes that "the dominant metaphor of conceptual relativism, that of differing points of view, seems to betray an underlying paradox. Different points of view make sense, but only if there is a common coordinate system on which to plot them; yet the existence of a common system belies the claim of dramatic incomparability." In what way is this a paradox, if Davidson is correct? Do you agree with him that conceptual relativism betrays an underlying paradox?
3. Davidson asks, "Can we say that two people have different conceptual schemes if they speak languages that fail of intertranslatability?" What is his answer to this question? Why?
4. What is the difference between complete and partial failures of translatability?
5. Davidson claims that many philosophers embrace the rejection of the analytic-synthetic distinction without embracing the rejection of the scheme-content distinction. In what ways are these distinctions thought to be independent?
6. What are the two metaphors used to characterize conceptual schemes or languages? How do they differ? In what ways does Davidson think that these metaphors fail to make sense of the idea of a language?

7. What is the 'problem of interpretation' that Davidson discusses? In what ways does Davidson think that belief and meaning are interdependent? Why does Davidson say that "charity is forced on us, whether we like it or not, if we want to understand others, we must count them right in most matters"? What does he mean by 'charity' here?
8. How do Davison's views on the interdependence of belief and meaning lead to his conclusions regarding the incoherence of conceptual relativism? In thinking about this, consider his remark that "we improve the clarity and bite of declarations of difference, whether of scheme or opinion, by enlarging the basis of shared (translatable) language or shared opinion."

SUGGESTIONS FOR FURTHER READING (DONALD DAVIDSON)

Primary Sources and Collected Writings

(1972) (and G. Harman) *Semantics of Natural Language.* Dordrecht: D. Reidel.
(1980) *Essays on Actions and Events.* Oxford: Oxford University Press.
(1982) "Two Paradoxes of Irrationality." In *Philosophical Essays on Freud,* edited by R Wollheim and J. Hopkins. Cambridge: Cambridge University Press.
(1984) *Inquiries into Truth and Interpretation.* Oxford: Oxford University Press.
(1985) "Rational Animals." In *Actions and Events: Perspectives on the Philosophy of Donald Davidson,* edited by E. Lepore and B. McLaughlin. Oxford: Basil Blackwell.
(1986) "A Coherence Theory of Truth and Knowledge." In *Truth and Interpretation: Perspectives on the Philosophy of Donald Davidson,* edited by E. Lepore. Oxford: Basil Blackwell.
(1990) "The Structure and Content of Truth." In *Journal of Philosophy,* 87: 279–328.
(1991) "Epistemology Externalized." In *Dialectica,* 45: 191–202.
(1993) "Thinking Causes." In *Mental Causation,* edited by J. Heil and A. Mele. Oxford: Oxford University Press.
(1995) "Laws and Causes." In *Dialectica,* 49: 263–278.

Secondary Sources

Evnine, S. (1991) *Donald Davidson.* Stanford, CA: Stanford University Press.

Fodor, J., and E. Lepore (1992) *Holism: A Shopper's Guide.* Oxford: Blackwell.

Hahn, L. E. (1999) *The Philosophy of Donald Davidson.* La Salle, IL: Open Court.

Lepore, E., ed. (1986) *Truth and Interpretation: Perspectives on the Philosophy of Donald Davidson.* Oxford: Basil Blackwell.

Lepore, E., and B. McLaughlin, eds. (1985) *Actions and Events: Perspectives on the Philosophy of Donald Davidson.* Oxford: Basil Blackwell.

Malpas, J. (1992) *Donald Davidson and the Mirror of Meaning: Holism, Truth, Interpretation.* Cambridge: Cambridge University Press.

Ramberg, B. (1989) *Donald Davidson's Philosophy of Language: An Introduction.* Oxford: Basil Blackwell.

Stoecker, R. ed. (1993) *Reflecting Davidson.* Berlin: W. de Gruyter.

Zeglen, U. (1999) *Donald Davidson: Truth, Meaning, and Knowledge.* New York: Routledge.

SAUL AARON KRIPKE

From *Naming and Necessity*

Saul Kripke (1940–) was born in Bay Shore, New York, but his family moved to Omaha, Nebraska, a short time later. The Bobby Fisher of philosophy, Kripke demonstrated at an early age an incredible ability for mathematics and logic. His first published paper (entitled "A Completeness Theorem in Modal Logic") appeared in *The Journal of Symbolic Logic* in 1959 when Kripke was just nineteen years old.

Kripke was educated at Harvard, where he received his bachelor's degree in mathematics in 1962. He then pursued his education in philosophy at Oxford. He began his teaching and research career by taking positions as a lecturer at Princeton and at Harvard. After leaving Harvard, Kripke accepted a position as an assistant professor at Rockefeller University. He was pro-

moted to the rank of professor there in 1972. In 1973, Kripke was selected to give the John Locke Lectures at Oxford, the youngest person ever to receive this honor. Since 1977 he has been the McCosh Professor of Philosophy at Princeton.

Kripke's work has made a lasting impact in a number of areas of philosophy, including philosophical logic, the philosophy of language, metaphysics, and the philosophy of mind. His two most famous works concern themselves respectively with the issue of the semantics of proper names (in *Naming and Necessity*) and with the correct interpretation of the sections of Wittgenstein's *Philosophical Investigations* that concern themselves with rules and rule-following (in his *Wittgenstein on Rules and Private Language*).

In the following selections from *Naming and Necessity*, Kripke argues that proper names are what he calls "rigid designators," i.e., labels that denote the same objects in all possible worlds in which they exist. In the process, he rejects the theories of proper names proposed by Russell, Frege, and Searle (among others). His own account takes the form of a causal theory of the meaning of proper names. Kripke holds that the meaning of a proper name is fixed through an initial act of "baptism" and preserved through a series of causal linkages or "reference borrowings," which connect our significant use of the name back to the initial act of reference fixing itself.

Lecture I

. . . The first topic in the pair of topics is naming. By a name here I will mean a proper name, i.e., the name of a person, a city, a country, etc. It is well known that modern logicians also are very interested in definite descriptions: phrases of the form "the *x* such that ϕx,"

Selections reprinted by permission of the publisher from *Naming and Necessity* by Saul Kripke, Cambridge, Mass.: Harvard University Press, Copyright © 1972, 1980 by Saul A. Kripke.

such as "the man who corrupted Hadleyburg." Now, if one and only one man ever corrupted Hadleyburg, then that man is the referent, in the logician's sense, of that description. We will use the term 'name' so that it does *not* include definite descriptions of that sort, but only those things which in ordinary language would be called 'proper names'. If we want a common term to cover names and descriptions, we may use the term 'designator'.

It is a point, made by Donnellan,[1] that under certain circumstances a particular speaker may use a definite description to refer, not to the proper referent, in the sense that I've just defined it, of that description, but to something else which he wants to single out and which he thinks is the proper referent of the description, but which in fact isn't. So you may say, "The man over there with the champagne in his glass is happy," though he actually only has water in his glass. Now, even though there is no champagne in his glass, and there may be another man in the room who does have champagne in his glass, the speaker *intended* to refer, or maybe, in some sense of 'refer', *did* refer, to the man he thought had the champagne in his glass. Nevertheless, I'm just going to use the term 'referent of the description' to mean the object uniquely satisfying the conditions in the definite description. This is the sense in which it's been used in the logical tradition. So, if you have a description of the for in "the *x* such that ϕ*x*," and there is exactly one *x* such that ϕ*x*, that is the referent of the description. . . .

Many people have said that the theory of Frege and Russell is false, but, in my opinion, they have abandoned its letter while retaining its spirit, namely, they have used the notion of a cluster concept. Well, what is this? The obvious problem for Frege and Russell, the one which comes immediately to mind, is already mentioned by Frege himself. He said,

In the case of genuinely proper names like "Aristotle" opinions as regards their sense may diverge. As such may, e.g., be suggested: Plato's disciple and the teacher of Alexander the Great. Whoever accepts this sense will interpret the meaning of the statement "Aristotle was born in Stagira," differently from one who interpreted the sense of "Aristotle" as the Stagirite teacher of Alexander the Great. As long as the nominatum remains the same, these fluctua-

tions in sense are tolerable. But they should be avoided in the system of a demonstrative science and should not appear in a perfect language.[2]

So, according to Frege, there is some sort of looseness or weakness in our language. Some people may give one sense to the name "Aristotle," others may give another. But of course it is not only that; even a single speaker when asked "What description are you willing to substitute for the name?" may be quite at a loss. In fact, he may know many things about him; but any particular thing that he knows he may feel clearly expresses a contingent property of the object. If "Aristotle" meant *the man who taught Alexander the Great,* then saying "Aristotle was a teacher of Alexander the Great" would be a mere tautology. But surely it isn't; it expresses the fact that Aristotle taught Alexander the Great, something we could discover to be false. So, *being the teacher of Alexander the Great* cannot be part of [the sense of] the name.

The most common way out of this difficulty is to say "really it is not a weakness in ordinary language that we can't substitute a *particular* description for the name; that's all right. What we really associate with the name is a *family* of descriptions." A good example of this is in *Philosophical Investigations,* where the idea of family resemblances is introduced and with great power.

> Consider this example. If one says "Moses did not exist," this may mean various things. It may mean: the Israelites did not have a *single* leader when they withdrew from Egypt—or: their leader was not called Moses—or: there cannot have been anyone who accomplished all that the Bible relates of Moses— . . . But when I make a statement about Moses, am I always ready to substitute some *one* of those descriptions for "Moses"? I shall perhaps say: by "Moses" I understand the man who did what the Bible relates of Moses, or at any rate, a good deal of it. But how much? Have I decided how much must be proved false for me to give up my proposition as false? Has the name "Moses" got a fixed and unequivocal use for me in all possible cases?[3]

According to this view, and a *locus classicus* of it is Searle's article on proper names,[4] the referent of a name is determined not by a single description but by some cluster or family. Whatever in some sense satisfies enough or most of the family is the referent of the name. I shall return to this view later. It may seem, as an analysis of ordinary language, quite a bit more plausible than that of Frege and Russell. It may seem to keep all the virtues and remove the defects of this theory.

Let me say (and this will introduce us to another new topic before I really consider this theory of naming) that there are two ways in which the cluster concept theory, or even the theory which requires a single description, can be viewed. One way of regarding it says that the cluster or the single description actually gives the meaning of the name; and when someone says "Walter Scott," he means *the man such that such and such and such and such.*

Now another view might be that even though the description in some sense doesn't give the *meaning* of the name, it is what *determines its reference* and although the phrase "Walter Scott" isn't *synonymous* with "the man such that such and such and such and such," or even maybe with the family (if something can be synonymous with a family), the family or the single description is what is used to determine to whom someone is referring when he says "Walter Scott." Of course, if when we hear his beliefs about Walter Scott we find that they are actually much more nearly true of Salvador Dali, then according to this theory the reference of this name is going to be Mr. Dali, not Scott. There are writers, I think, who explicitly deny that names have meaning at all even more strongly than I would but still use this picture of how the referent of the name gets determined. A good case in point is Paul Ziff, who says, very emphatically, that names don't have meaning at all, [that] they are not a part of language in some sense. But still, when he talks about how we determine what the reference of the name was, then he gives this picture. Unfortunately I don't have the passage in question with me, but this is what he says.[5]

The difference between using this theory as a theory of meaning and using it as a theory of reference will come out a little more clearly later on. But some of the attractiveness of the theory is lost if it isn't supposed to give the meaning of the name; for some of the solutions of problems that I've just mentioned will not be right, or at least won't clearly be right, if the description doesn't give the meaning of the name. For example, if someone

said "Aristotle does not exist" *means* "there is no man doing such and such," or in the example from Wittgenstein, "Moses does not exist," *means* "no man did such and such," that might depend (and in fact, I think, does depend) on taking the theory in question as a theory of the meaning of the name "Moses," not just as a theory of its reference. Well, I don't know. Perhaps all that is immediate now is the other way around: if "Moses" means the same as "the man who did such and such" then to say that Moses did not exist is to say that the man who did such and such did not exist, that is, that no one person did such and such. If, on the other hand, "Moses" is not synonymous with any description, then even if its reference is in some sense determined by a description, statements containing the name cannot in general be *analyzed* by replacing the name by a description, though they may be materially equivalent to statements containing a description. So the analysis of singular existence statements mentioned above will have to be given up, unless it is established by some special argument, independent of a general theory of the meaning of names; and the same applies to identity statements. In any case, I think it's false that "Moses exists" means that at all. So we won't have to see if such a special argument can be drawn up.[6]

Before I go any further into this problem, I want to talk about another distinction which will be important in the methodology of these talks. Philosophers have talked (and, of course, there has been considerable controversy in recent years over the meaningfulness of these notions) [about] various categories of truth, which are called 'a priori', 'analytic', 'necessary'—and sometimes even 'certain' is thrown into this batch. The terms are often used as if *whether* there are things answering to these concepts is an interesting question, but we might as well regard them all as meaning the same thing. Now, everyone remembers Kant (a bit) as making a distinction between 'a priori' and 'analytic'. So maybe this distinction is still made. In contemporary discussion very few people, if any, distinguish between the concepts of statements being a priori and their being necessary. At any rate I shall *not* use the terms 'a priori' and 'necessary' interchangeably here.

Consider what the traditional characterizations of such terms as 'a priori' and 'necessary' are. First the notion of a prioricity is a concept of epistemology. I guess the traditional characterization from Kant goes something like: a priori truths are those which can be known independently of any experience. This introduces another problem before we get off the ground, because there's another modality in the characterization of 'a priori', namely, it is supposed to be something which *can* be known independently of any experience. That means that in some sense it's *possible* (whether we do or do not in fact know it independently of any experience) to know this independently of any experience. And possible for whom? For God? For the Martians? Or just for people with minds like ours? To make this all clear might [involve] a host of problems all of its own about what sort of possibility is in question here. It might be best therefore, instead of using the phrase 'a priori truth', to the extent that one uses it at all, to stick to the question of whether a particular person or knower knows something a priori or believes it true on the basis of a priori evidence.

I won't go further too much into the problems that might arise with the notion of a prioricity here. I will say that some philosophers somehow change the modality in this characterization from *can* to *must*. They think that if something belongs to the realm of *a priori* knowledge, it couldn't possibly be known empirically. This is just a mistake. Something may belong in the realm of such statements that *can* be known *a priori* but still may be known by particular people on the basis of experience. To give a really common sense example: anyone who has worked with a computing machine knows that the computing machine may give an answer to whether such and such a number is prime. No one has calculated or proved that the number is prime; but the machine has given the answer: this number is prime. We, then, if we believe that the number is prime, believe it on the basis of our knowledge of the laws of physics, the construction of the machine, and so on. We therefore do not believe this on the basis of purely a priori evidence. We believe it (if anything is a posteriori at all) on the basis of a posteriori evidence. Nevertheless, maybe this could be known a priori by someone who made the requisite calculations. So 'can be known a priori' doesn't mean '*must* be known a priori'.

The second concept which is in question is that of necessity. Sometimes this is used in an epistemological way and might then just mean a priori. And of course,

sometimes it is used in a physical way when people distinguish between physical and logical necessity. But what I am concerned with here is a notion which is not a notion of epistemology but of metaphysics, in some (I hope) nonpejorative sense. We ask whether something might have been true, or might have been false. Well, if something is false, it's obviously not necessarily true. If it is true, might it have been otherwise? Is it possible that, in this respect, the world should have been different from the way it is? If the answer is "no," then this fact about the world is a necessary one. If the answer is "yes," then this fact about the world is a contingent one. This in and of itself has nothing to do with anyone's knowledge of anything. It's certainly a philosophical thesis, and not a matter of obvious definitional equivalence, either that everything a priori is necessary or that everything necessary is a priori. Both concepts may be vague. That may be another problem. But at any rate they are dealing with two different domains, two different areas, the epistemological and the metaphysical. Consider, say, Fermat's last theorem—or the Goldbach conjecture. The Goldbach conjecture says that an even number greater than 2 must be the sum of two prime numbers. If this is true, it is presumably necessary, and, if it is false, presumably necessarily false. We are taking the classical view of mathematics here and assume that in mathematical reality it is either true or false.

If the Goldbach conjecture is false, then there is an even number, n, greater than 2, such that for no primes p_1 and p_2, both $< n$, does $n = p_1 + p_2$. This fact about n, if true, is verifiable by direct computation, and thus is necessary if the results of arithmetical computations are necessary. On the other hand, if the conjecture is true, then every even number exceeding 2 is the sum of two primes. Could it then be the case that, although in fact every such even number is the sum of two primes, there might have been such an even number which was not the sum of two primes? What would that mean? Such a number would have to be one of 4, 6, 8, 10, . . . ; and, by hypothesis, since we are assuming Goldbach's conjecture to be true, each of these can be shown, again by direct computation, to be the sum of two primes. Goldbach's conjecture, then, cannot be contingently true or false; whatever truth-value it has belongs to it by necessity.

But what we can say, of course, is that right now, as far as we know, the question can come out either way. So, in the absence of a mathematical proof deciding this question, none of us has any a priori knowledge about this question in either direction. We don't know whether Goldbach's conjecture is true or false. So right now we certainly don't know anything a priori about it. . . .

Let's use some terms quasi-technically. Let's call something a 'rigid designator' if in every possible world it designates the same object, a 'nonrigid' or 'accidental designator' if that is not the case. Of course we don't require that the objects exist in all possible worlds. Certainly Nixon might not have existed if his parents had not gotten married, in the normal course of things. When we think of a property as essential to an object we usually mean that it is true of that object in any case where it would have existed. A rigid designator of a necessary existent can be called 'strongly rigid.'

One of the intuitive theses I will maintain in these talks is that *names* are rigid designators. Certainly they seem to satisfy the intuitive test mentioned above: although someone other than the U.S. president in 1970 might have been the U.S. president in 1970 (e.g., Humphrey might have), no one other than Nixon might have been Nixon. In the same way, a designator rigidly designates a certain object if it designates that object wherever the object exists; if, in addition, the object is a necessary existent, the designator can be called 'strongly rigid.' For example, "the president of the U.S. in 1970" designates a certain man, Nixon; but someone else (e.g., Humphrey) might have been the president in 1970, and Nixon might not have; so this designator is not rigid.

In these lectures, I will argue, intuitively, that proper names are rigid designators, for although the man (Nixon) might not have been the president, it is not the case that he might not have been Nixon (though he might not have been *called* "Nixon"). Those who have argued that to make sense of the notion of rigid designator, we must antecedently make sense of "criteria of transworld identity" have precisely reversed the cart and the horse; it is *because* we can refer (rigidly) to Nixon, and stipulate that we are speaking of what might have happened to *him* (under

certain circumstances), that "transworld identifications" are unproblematic in such cases.[7]

The tendency to demand purely qualitative descriptions of counterfactual situations has many sources. One, perhaps, is the confusion of the epistemological and the metaphysical, between a prioricity and necessity. If someone identifies necessity with a prioricity, and thinks that objects are named by means of uniquely identifying properties, he may think that it is the properties used to identify the object which, being known about it a priori, must be used to identify it in all possible worlds, to find out which object is Nixon. As against this, I repeat: (1) Generally, things aren't 'found out' about a counterfactual situation, they are stipulated; (2) possible worlds need not be given purely qualitatively, as if we were looking at them through a telescope. And we will see shortly that the properties an object has in every counterfactual world have nothing to do with properties used to identify it in the actual world. . . .

Lecture II

Last time we ended up talking about a theory of naming which is given by a number of theses:

1. To every name or designating expression "X," there corresponds a cluster of properties, namely the family of those properties φ such that A believes "φX."

2. One of the properties, or some conjointly, are believed by A to pick out some individual uniquely.

3. If most, or a weighted most, of the φ's are satisfied by one unique object y, then y is the referent of "X."

4. If the vote yields no unique object, "X" does not refer.

5. The statement, "If X exists, then X has most of the φ's" is known a priori by the speaker.

6. The statement, "If X exists, then X has most of the φ's" expresses a necessary truth (in the idiolect of the speaker).

C. For any successful theory, the account must not be circular. The properties which are used in the vote must not themselves involve the notion of reference in such a way that it is ultimately impossible to eliminate.

(C) is not a thesis but a condition on the satisfaction of the other theses. In other words, theses (1)–(6) cannot be satisfied in a way which leads to a circle, in a way which does not lead to any independent determination of reference. The example I gave last time of a blatantly circular attempt to satisfy these conditions was a theory of names mentioned by William Kneale. I was a little surprised at the statement of the theory when I was reading what I had copied down, so I looked it up again. I looked it up in the book to see if I'd copied it down accurately. Kneale *did* use the past tense. He said that though it is not trifling to be told that Socrates was the greatest philosopher of ancient Greece, it is trifling to be told that Socrates was called "Socrates." Therefore, he concludes, the name "Socrates" must simply mean "the individual called 'Socrates'." Russell, as I've said, in some places gives a similar analysis. Anyway, as stated using the past tense, the condition wouldn't be circular, because one certainly could decide to use the term "Socrates" to refer to whoever was called "Socrates" by the Greeks. But, of course, in that sense it's not at all trifling to be told that Socrates was called "Socrates." If this is any kind of fact, it might be false. Perhaps we know that *we* call him "Socrates"; that hardly shows that the Greeks did so. In fact, of course, they may have pronounced the name differently. It may be, in the case of this particular name, that transliteration from the Greek is so good that the English version is not pronounced *very* differently from the Greek. But that won't be so in the general case. Certainly it is not trifling to be told that Isaiah was called "Isaiah." In fact, it is false to be told that Isaiah was called "Isaiah"; the prophet wouldn't have recognized this name at all. And of course the Greeks didn't call their country anything like "Greece." Suppose we amend the thesis so that it reads: it's trifling to be told that Socrates is called "Socrates" by us, or at least, by me, the speaker. Then in some sense this is fairly trifling. I don't think it is necessary or analytic. In the same way, it is trifling to be told that horses are called "horses," without this leading to the conclusion that the word "horse" simply *means* "the animal called a 'horse'." As a theory of the reference of the name "Socrates" it will lead immediately to a vicious circle. If one was determining the referent of a name like 'Glunk' to himself and made the following decision, "I shall use the term 'Glunk' to refer to the man that I call 'Glunk'," this would get one nowhere. One had better have some independent determination of the referent of "Glunk." This is a good example of a blatantly circular determination. Actually sentences like "Socrates is called 'Socrates'" are very interesting and one can spend, strange as it may seem, hours talking about their analysis. I actually did, once, do that. I won't do that, however, on this occasion. (See how high the seas of language can rise. And at the lowest points too.) Anyway this is a useful example of a violation of the noncircularity condition. The theory will satisfy all of these statements, perhaps, but it satisfies them only because there is some independent way of determining the reference independently of the particular condition: being the man called "Socrates."

I have already talked about, in the last lecture, thesis (6). Theses (5) and (6), by the way, have converses. What I said for thesis (5) is that the statement that if X exists, X has most of the φ's, is a priori true for the speaker. It will also be true under the given theory that certain converses of this statement hold true also a priori for the speaker, namely: if any unique thing has most of the properties φ in the properly weighted sense, it is X. Similarly a certain converse to this will be *necessarily* true, namely: if anything has most of the properties φ in the properly weighted sense, it is X. So really one can say that it is both a priori and necessary that something is X if and only if it uniquely has most of the properties φ. This really comes from the previous theses (1)–(4), I suppose. And (5) and (6) really just say that a sufficiently reflective speaker grasps this theory of proper names. Knowing this, he therefore sees that (5) and (6) are true. The objections to theses (5) and (6) will *not* be that some speakers are unaware of this theory and therefore don't know these things.

What I talked about in the last lecture is thesis (6). It's been observed by many philosophers that, if the cluster of properties associated with a proper name is taken in a very narrow sense, so that only one property is given any weight at all, let's say one definite description to pick out the referent—for example, Aristotle was the philosopher who taught Alexander the Great—then certain things will seem to turn out to be necessary truths which are not necessary truths—in this case, for example, that Aristotle taught Alexander the Great. But as Searle said, it is not a necessary truth but a contingent one that Aristotle ever went into pedagogy. Therefore, he concludes that one must drop the original paradigm of a single description and turn to that of a cluster of descriptions.

To summarize some things that I argued last time, this is not the correct answer (whatever it may be) to this problem about necessity. For Searle goes on to say,

> Suppose we agree to drop "Aristotle" and use, say, "the teacher of Alexander," then it is a necessary truth that the man referred to is Alexander's teacher—but it is a contingent fact that Aristotle ever went into pedagogy, though I am suggesting that it is a necessary fact that Aristotle has the logical sum, inclusive disjunction, of properties commonly attributed to him. . . . [8]

This is what is not so. It just is not, in any intuitive sense of necessity, a necessary truth that Aristotle had the properties commonly attributed to him. There is a certain theory, perhaps popular in some views of the philosophy of history, which might both be deterministic and yet at the same time assign a great role to the individual in history. Perhaps Carlyle would associate with the meaning of the name of a great man his achievements. According to such a view it will be necessary, once a certain individual is born, that he is destined to perform various great tasks and so it will be part of the very nature of Aristotle that he should have produced ideas which had a great influence on the Western world. Whatever the merits of such a view may be as a view of history or the nature of great men, it does not seem that it should be trivially true on the basis of a theory of proper names. It would seem that it's a contingent fact that Aristotle ever did *any* of the things commonly attributed to him today, *any* of these great achievements that we so much admire. . . .

To clear up one thing which some people have asked me: When I say that a designator is rigid, and designates the same thing in all possible worlds, I mean that, as used in *our* language, it stands for that thing, when *we* talk about counterfactual situations. I don't mean, of course, that there mightn't be counterfactual situations in which in the other possible worlds people actually spoke a different language. One doesn't say that "two plus two equals four" is contingent because people might have spoken a language in which "two plus two equals four" meant that seven is even. Similarly, when we speak of a counter-factual situation, we speak of it in English, even if it is part of the description of that counterfactual situation that we were all speaking German in that counterfactual situation. We say, "suppose we had all been speaking German" or "suppose we had been using English in a nonstandard way." Then we are describing a possible world or counterfactual situation in which people, including ourselves, did speak in a certain way different from the way we speak. But still, in describing that world, we use *English* with *our* meanings and *our* references. It is in this sense that I speak of a rigid designator as having the same reference in all possible worlds, I also don't mean to imply that the thing designated exists in all possible worlds, just that the name refers rigidly to that thing. If you say "suppose Hitler had never been born" then "Hitler" refers here, still rigidly, to something that would not exist in the counterfactual situation described.

Given these remarks, this means we must cross off thesis (6) as incorrect. The other theses have nothing to do with necessity and can survive. In particular thesis (5) has nothing to do with necessity and it can survive. If I use the name "Hesperus" to refer to a certain planetary body when seen in a certain celestial position in the evening, it will not therefore be a necessary truth that Hesperus is ever seen in the evening. That depends on various contingent facts about people being there to see and things like that. So even if I should say to myself that I will use "Hesperus" to name the heavenly body I see in the evening in yonder position of the sky, it will not be necessary that Hesperus was ever seen in the evening. But it may be a priori in that this is how I have determined the referent. If I have determined that Hesperus is the thing that I saw in the evening over there, then I will know, just from making that determination of the referent, that if there is any Hesperus at all it's the thing I saw in the evening. This at least survives as far as the arguments we have given up to now go.

How about a theory where thesis (6) is eliminated? Theses (2), (3), and (4) turn out to have a large class of counterinstances. Even when theses (2)–(4) are true, thesis (5) is usually false; the truth of theses (3) and (4) is an empirical 'accident', which the speaker hardly knows a priori. That is to say, other principles really determine the speaker's reference, and the fact that the referent coincides with that determined by (2)–(4) is an 'accident', which we were in no position to know a priori. Only in a rare class of cases, usually initial baptisms, are all of (2)–(5) true.

What picture of naming do these theses [(1)–(5)] give you? The picture is this. I want to name an object. I think of some way of describing it uniquely and then I go through, so to speak, a sort of mental ceremony: By "Cicero" I shall mean the man who denounced Catiline; and that's what the reference of "Cicero" will be. I will use "Cicero" to designate rigidly the man who (in fact) denounced Catiline, so I can speak of possible worlds in which he did not. But still my intentions are given by first, giving some condition which uniquely determines an object, then using a certain word as a name for the object determined by this condition. Now there may be some cases in which we actually do this. Maybe, if you want to stretch and call it description, when you say: I shall call that heavenly body over there "Hesperus."[9] That is really a case where the theses not only are true but really even give a correct picture of how the reference is determined. Another case, if you want to call this a name, might be when the police in London use the name "Jack" or "Jack the Ripper" to refer to the man, whoever he is, who committed all these murders, or most of them. Then they are giving the reference of the name by a description.[10] But in many or most cases, I think the theses are false. So let's look at them.[11]

Thesis (1), as I say, is a definition. Thesis (2) says that one of the properties believed by *A* of the object, or some conjointly, are believed to pick out some individual uniquely. A sort of example people have in mind is just what I said: I shall use the term "Cicero" to denote the man who denounced Catiline (or first denounced him in public, to make it unique). This picks out an object uniquely in this particular reference. Even some writers such as Ziff in *Semantic Analysis,* who don't believe that names have meaning in any sense, think that this is a good picture of the way reference can be determined.

Let's see if thesis (2) is true. It seems, in some a priori way, that it's got to be true, because if you don't think that the properties you have in mind pick out anyone uniquely—let's say they're all satisfied by two people—then how can you say which one of them you're talking about? There seem to be no grounds for saying you're talking about the one rather than about the other. Usually the properties in question are supposed to be some famous deeds of the person in question. For example, Cicero was the man who denounced Catiline. The average person, according to this, when he refers to Cicero, is saying something like "the man who denounced Catiline" and thus has picked out a certain man uniquely. It is a tribute to the education of philosophers that they have held this thesis for such a long time. In fact, most people, when they think of Cicero, just think of a *famous Roman orator,* without any pretension to think either that there was only one famous Roman orator or that one must know something else about Cicero to have a referent for the name. Consider Richard Feynman, to whom many of us are able to refer. He is a leading contemporary theoretical physicist. Everyone *here* (I'm sure!) can state the contents of one of Feynman's theories so as to differentiate him from Gell-Mann. However, the man in the street, not possessing these abilities, may still use the name "Feynman." When asked he will say: well he's a physicist or something. He may not think that this picks out anyone uniquely. I still think he uses the name "Feynman" as a name for Feynman.

But let's look at some of the cases where we do have a description to pick out someone uniquely. Let's say, for example, that we know that Cicero was the man who first denounced Catiline. Well, that's good. That really picks someone out uniquely. However, there is a problem, because this description contains another name, namely "Catiline." We must be sure that we satisfy the conditions in such a way as to avoid violating the noncircularity condition here. In particular, we must not say that Catiline was the man denounced by Cicero. If we do this, we will really not be picking out anything uniquely, we will simply be picking out a pair of objects *A* and *B*, such that *A* denounced *B*. We do not think that this was the only pair where such denunciations ever occurred; so we had better add some other conditions in order to satisfy the uniqueness condition.

If we say Einstein was the man who discovered the theory of relativity, that certainly picks out someone uniquely. One can be sure, as I said, that everyone *here* can make a compact and independent statement of this theory and so pick out Einstein uniquely; but many people actually don't know enough about this stuff, so when asked what the theory of relativity is, they will say: "Einstein's theory," and thus be led into the most straightforward sort of vicious circle.

So thesis (2), in a straightforward way, fails to be satisfied when we say Feynman is a famous physicist without attributing anything else to Feynman. In another way it may not be satisfied in the proper way even when it is satisfied: If we say Einstein was "the man who discovered relativity theory," that does pick someone out uniquely; but it may not pick him out in such a way as to satisfy the noncircularity condition, because the theory of relativity may in turn be picked out as "Einstein's theory." So thesis (2) seems to be false. . . .

Let's go on to thesis (3): If most of the φ's, suitably weighted, are satisfied by a unique object γ, then γ is the referent of the name for the speaker. Now since we have already established that thesis (2) is wrong, why should any of the rest work? . . . Suppose most of the φ's are in fact satisfied by a unique object. Is that object necessarily the referent of "*X*" for *A*? Let's suppose someone says that Gödel is the man who proved the incompleteness of arithmetic, and this man is suitably well educated and is even able to give an independent account of the incompleteness theorem. He doesn't just say, "Well, that's Gödel's theorem," or whatever. He actually states a certain theorem, which he attributes to Gödel as the discoverer. Is it the case, then, that if most of the φ's are satisfied by a unique object, γ, then γ is the referent of the name "*X*" for *A?* Let's take a simple case. In the case of Gödel that's practically the only thing many people have heard about him—that he discovered the incompleteness of arithmetic. Does it follow that whoever discovered the incompleteness of arithmetic is the referent of "Gödel"?

Imagine the following blatantly fictional situation. (I hope Professor Gödel is not present.) Suppose that Gödel was not in fact the author of this theorem. A man named "Schmidt," whose body was found in Vienna under mysterious circumstances many years ago,

actually did the work in question. His friend Gödel somehow got hold of the manuscript and it was thereafter attributed to Gödel. On the view in question, then, when our ordinary man uses the name "Gödel," he really means to refer to Schmidt, because Schmidt is the unique person satisfying the description, "the man who discovered the incompleteness of arithmetic." Of course you might try changing it to "the man who *published* the discovery of the incompleteness of arithmetic." By changing the story a little further one can make even this formulation false. Anyway, most people might not even know whether the thing was published or got around by word of mouth. Let's stick to "the man who discovered the incompleteness of arithmetic." So, since the man who discovered the incompleteness of arithmetic is in fact Schmidt, we, when we talk about "Gödel," are in fact always referring to Schmidt. But it seems to me that we are not. We simply are not. One reply, which I will discuss later, might be: You should say instead, "the man to whom the incompleteness of arithmetic is commonly attributed," or something like that. Let's see what we can do with that later.

But it may seem to many of you that this is a very odd example, or that such a situation occurs rarely. This also is a tribute to the education of philosophers. Very often we use a name on the basis of considerable misinformation. The case of mathematics used in the fictive example is a good case in point. What do we know about Peano? What many people in this room may 'know' about Peano is that he was the discoverer of certain axioms which characterize the sequence of natural numbers, the so-called "Peano axioms." Probably some people can even state them. I have been told that these axioms were not first discovered by Peano but by Dedekind. Peano was of course not a dishonest man. I am told that his footnotes include a credit to Dedekind. Somehow the footnote has been ignored. So on the theory in question the term "Peano," as we use it, really refers to—now that you've heard it you see that you were really all the time talking about—Dedekind. But you were not. Such illustrations could be multiplied indefinitely.

Even worse misconceptions, of course, occur to the layman. In a previous example I supposed people to identify Einstein by reference to his work on relativity.

Actually, I often used to hear that Einstein's most famous achievement was the invention of the atomic bomb. So when we refer to Einstein, we refer to the inventor of the atomic bomb. But this is not so. Columbus was the first man to realize that the earth was round. He was also the first European to land in the western hemisphere. Probably none of these things are true, and therefore, when people use the term "Columbus" they really refer to some Greek if they use the roundness of the earth, or to some Norseman, perhaps, if they use the "discovery of America." But they don't. So it does not seem that if most of the φ's are satisfied by a unique object γ, then γ is the referent of the name. This seems simply to be false.[12]

Thesis (4): If the vote yields no unique object the name does not refer. Really this case has been covered before—has been covered in my previous examples. First, the vote may not yield a *unique* object, as in the case of Cicero or Feynman. Secondly, suppose it yields *no* object, that nothing satisfies most, or even any, substantial number, of the φ's. Does that mean the name doesn't refer? No: in the same way that you may have false beliefs about a person which may actually be true of someone else, so you may have false beliefs which are true of absolutely no one. And these may constitute the totality of your beliefs. Suppose, to vary the example about Gödel, no one had discovered the incompleteness of arithmetic—perhaps the proof simply materialized by a random scattering of atoms on a piece of paper—the man Gödel being lucky enough to have been present when this improbable event occurred. Further, suppose arithmetic is in fact complete. One wouldn't really expect a random scattering of atoms to produce a correct proof. A subtle error, unknown through the decades, has still been unnoticed—or perhaps not actually unnoticed, but the friends of Gödel. . . . So even if the conditions are not satisfied by a unique object the name may still refer. I gave you the case of Jonah last week. Biblical scholars, as I said, think that Jonah really existed. It isn't because they think that someone ever was swallowed by a big fish or even went to Nineveh to preach. These conditions may be true of no one whatsoever and yet the name "Jonah" really has a referent. In the case above of Einstein's invention of the bomb, possibly no one really deserves to be called the "inventor" of the device.

Thesis 5 says that the statement "If *X* exists, then *X* has most of the φ's," is a priori true for *A*. Notice that even in a case where (3) and (4) *happen* to be true, a typical speaker hardly knows a priori that they are, as required by the theory. I *think* that my belief about Gödel *is* in fact correct and that the "Schmidt" story is just a fantasy. But the belief hardly constitutes a priori knowledge. . . .

Someone, let's say, a baby, is born; his parents call him by a certain name. They talk about him to their friends. Other people meet him. Through various sorts of talk the name is spread from link to link as if by a chain. A speaker who is on the far end of this chain, who has heard about, say Richard Feynman, in the marketplace or elsewhere, may be referring to Richard Feynman even though he can't remember from whom he first heard of Feynman or from whom he ever heard of Feynman. He knows that Feynman is a famous physicist. A certain passage of communication reaching ultimately to the man himself does reach the speaker. He then is referring to Feynman even though he can't identify him uniquely. He doesn't know what a Feynman diagram is, he doesn't know what the Feynman theory of pair production and annihilation is. Not only that: he'd have trouble distinguishing between Gell-Mann and Feynman. So he doesn't have to know these things, but, instead, a chain of communication going back to Feynman himself has been established, by virtue of his membership in a community which passed the name on from link to link, not by a ceremony that he makes in private in his study: "By 'Feynman' I shall mean the man who did such and such and such and such." . . . On our view, it is not how the speaker thinks he got the reference, but the actual chain of communication, which is relevant.

I think I said the other time that philosophical theories are in danger of being false, and so I wasn't going to present an alternative theory. Have I just done so? Well, in a way; but my characterization has been far less specific than a real set of necessary and sufficient conditions for reference would be. Obviously the name is passed on from link to link. But of course not every sort of causal chain reaching from me to a certain man will do for me to make a reference. There may be a causal chain from our use of the term "Santa Claus" to a certain historical saint, but still the children, when they use this, by this time probably do not refer to that saint. So other conditions must be satisfied in order to make this into a really rigorous theory of reference. I don't know that I'm going to do this because, first, I'm sort of too lazy at the moment; secondly, rather than giving a set of necessary and sufficient conditions which will work for a term like reference, I want to present just a *better picture* than the picture presented by the received views.

Haven't I been very unfair to the description theory? Here I have stated it very precisely—more precisely, perhaps, than it has been stated by any of its advocates. So then it's easy to refute. Maybe if I tried to state mine with sufficient precision in the form of six or seven or eight theses, it would also turn out that when you examine the theses one by one, they will all be false. That might even be so, but the difference is this. What I think the examples I've given show is not simply that there's some technical error here or some mistake there, but that the whole picture given by this theory of how reference is determined seems to be wrong from the fundamentals. It seems to be wrong to think that we give ourselves some properties which somehow qualitatively uniquely pick out an object and determine our reference in that manner. What I am trying to present is a better picture—a picture which, if more details were to be filled in, might be refined so as to give more exact conditions for reference to take place.

One might never reach a set of necessary and sufficient conditions. I don't know, I'm always sympathetic to Bishop Butler's "Everything is what it is and not another thing"—in the nontrivial sense that philosophical analyses of some concept like reference, in completely different terms which make no mention of reference, are very apt to fail. Of course in any particular case when one is given an analysis one has to look at it and see whether it is true or false. One can't just cite this maxim to oneself and then turn the page. But more cautiously, I want to present a better picture without giving a set of necessary and sufficient conditions for reference. Such conditions would be very complicated, but what is true is that it's in virtue of our connection with other speakers in the community, going back to the referent himself, that we refer to a certain man.

There may be some cases where the description picture is true, where some man really gives a name by going into the privacy of his room and saying that the referent is to be the unique thing with certain identifying properties. "Jack the Ripper" was a possible example which I gave. Another was "Hesperus." Yet another case which can be forced into this description is that of meeting someone and being told his name. Except for a belief in the description theory, in its importance in other cases, one probably wouldn't think that that was a case of giving oneself a description, i.e., "the guy I'm just meeting now." But one can put it in these terms if one wishes, and if one has never heard the name in any other way. Of course, if you're introduced to a man and told, "That's Einstein," you've heard of him before, it may be wrong, and so on. But maybe in some cases such a paradigm works—especially for the man who first gives someone or something a name. Or he points to a star and says, "That is to be Alpha Centauri." So he can really make himself this ceremony: "By 'Alpha Centauri' I shall mean the star right over there with such and such coordinates." But in general this picture fails. In general our reference depends not just on what we think ourselves, but on other people in the community, the history of how the name reached one, and things like that. It is by following such a history that one gets to the reference. . . .

A rough statement of a theory might be the following: An initial "baptism" takes place. Here the object may be named by ostension, or the reference of the name may be fixed by a description.[13] When the name is "passed from link to link," the receiver of the name must, I think, intend when he learns it to use it with the same reference as the man from whom he heard it. If I hear the name "Napoleon" and decide it would be a nice name for my pet aardvark, I do not satisfy this condition.[14] (Perhaps it is some such failure to keep the reference fixed which accounts for the divergence of present uses of "Santa Claus" from the alleged original use.)

Notice that the preceding outline hardly *eliminates* the notion of reference; on the contrary, it takes the notion of intending to use the same reference as a given. There is also an appeal to an initial baptism which is explained in terms either of fixing a reference by a description, or ostension (if ostension is not to be subsumed under the other category).[15] (Perhaps there are other possibilities for initial baptisms.) Further, the George Smith case casts some doubt as to the sufficiency of the conditions. Even if the teacher does refer to his neighbor, is it clear that he has passed on his reference to the pupils? Why shouldn't their belief be about any other man named "George Smith"? If he says that Newton was hit by an apple, somehow his task of transmitting a reference is easier, since he has communicated a common misconception about Newton.

To repeat. I may not have presented a theory, but I do think that I have presented a better picture than that given by description theorists.

I think the next topic I shall want to talk about is that of statements of identity. Are these necessary or contingent? The matter has been in some dispute in recent philosophy. First, everyone agrees that descriptions can be used to make contingent identity statements. If it is true that the man who invented bifocals was the first postmaster general of the United States—that these were one and the same—it's contingently true. That is, it might have been the case that one man invented bifocals and another was the first postmaster general of the United States. So certainly when you make identity statements using descriptions—when you say "the *x* such that φ*x* and the *x* such that ψ*x* are one and the same"—that can be a contingent fact. But philosophers have been interested also in the question of identity statements between names. When we say "Hesperus is Phosphorus" or "Cicero is Tully," is what we are saying necessary or contingent? Further, they've been interested in another type of identity statement, which comes from scientific theory. We identify, for example, light with electromagnetic radiation between certain limits of wavelengths, or with a stream of photons. We identify heat with the motion of molecules; sound with a certain sort of wave disturbance in the air; and so on. Concerning such statements the following thesis is commonly held. First, that these are obviously contingent identities: we've found out that light is a stream of photons, but of course it might not have been a stream of photons. Heat is in fact the motion of molecules; we found that out, but heat might not have been the mo-

tion of molecules. Secondly, many philosophers feel damned lucky that these examples are around. Now, why? These philosophers, whose views are expounded in a vast literature, hold to a thesis called "the identity thesis" with respect to some psychological concepts. They think, say, that pain is just a certain material state of the brain or of the body, or what have you—say the stimulation of C-fibers. (It doesn't matter what.) Some people have then objected, "Well, look, there's perhaps a *correlation* between pain and these states of the body; but this must just be a contingent correlation between two different things, because it was an empirical discovery that this correlation ever held. Therefore, by 'pain' we must mean something different from this state of the body or brain; and, therefore, they must be two different things."

Then it's said, "Ah, but you see, this is wrong! Everyone knows that there can be contingent identities." First, as in the bifocals and postmaster general case, which I have mentioned before. Second, in the case, believed closer to the present paradigm, of theoretical identifications, such as light and a stream of photons, or water and a certain compound of hydrogen and oxygen. These are all contingent identities. They might have been false. It's no surprise, therefore, that it can be true as a matter of contingent fact and not of any necessity that feeling pain, or seeing red, is just a certain state of the human body. Such psychophysical identifications can be contingent facts just as the other identities are contingent facts. And of course there are widespread motivations—ideological, or just not wanting to have the 'nomological dangler' of mysterious connections not accounted for by the laws of physics, one to one correlations between two different kinds of thing, material states, and things of an entirely different kind, which lead people to want to believe this thesis.

I guess the main thing I'll talk about first is identity statements between names. . . .

Let's suppose we refer to the same heavenly body twice, as "Hesperus" and "Phosphorus." We say: Hesperus is that star over there in the evening; Phosphorus is that star over there in the morning. Actually, Hesperus is Phosphorus. Are there really circumstances under which Hesperus wouldn't have been Phosphorus? Supposing that Hesperus is Phosphorus, let's try to describe a possible situation in which it would not have been. Well, it's easy. Someone goes by and he calls two *different* stars "Hesperus" and "Phosphorus." It may even be under the same conditions as prevailed when we introduced the names "Hesperus" and "Phosphorus." But are those circumstances in which Hesperus is not Phosphorus or would not have been Phosphorus? It seems to me that they are not.

Now, of course I'm committed to saying that they're not, by saying that such terms as "Hesperus" and "Phosphorus," when used as names, are rigid designators. They refer in every possible world to the planet Venus. Therefore, in that possible world too, the planet Venus is the planet Venus and it doesn't matter what any other person has said in this other possible world. How should *we* describe this situation? He can't have pointed to Venus twice, and in the one case called it "Hesperus," and in the other "Phosphorus," as we did. If he did so, then "Hesperus is Phosphorus" would have been true in that situation too. He pointed maybe neither time to the planet Venus—at least one time he didn't point to the planet Venus, let's say when he pointed to the body he called "Phosphorus." Then in that case we can certainly say that the name "Phosphorus" might not have referred to Phosphorus. We can even say that in the very position when viewed in the morning that we found Phosphorus, it might have been the case that Phosphorus was not there—that something else was there, and that even, under certain circumstances it would have been *called* "Phosphorus." But that still is not a case in which Phosphorus was not Hesperus. There might be a possible world in which, a possible counterfactual situation in which, "Hesperus" and "Phosphorus" weren't names of the things they in fact are names of. Someone, if he did determine their reference by identifying descriptions, might even have used the very identifying descriptions we used. But still that's not a case in which Hesperus wasn't Phosphorus. For there couldn't have been such a case, given that Hesperus is Phosphorus.

Now this seems very strange because in advance, we are inclined to say, the answer to the question whether Hesperus is Phosphorus might have turned either way. So aren't there really two possible worlds—one in which Hesperus was Phosphorus, the other in which

Hesperus wasn't Phosphorus—in advance of our discovering that these were the same? First, there's one sense in which things might turn out either way, in which it's clear that that doesn't imply that the way it finally turns out isn't necessary. For example, the four color theorem might turn out to be true and might turn out to be false. It might turn out either way. It still doesn't mean that the way it turns out is not necessary. Obviously, the 'might' here is purely 'epistemic'—it merely expresses our present state of ignorance, or uncertainty.

But it seems that in the Hesperus-Phosphorus case, something even stronger is true. The evidence I have before I know that Hesperus is Phosphorus is that I see a certain star or a certain heavenly body in the evening and call it "Hesperus," and in the morning and call it "Phosphorus." I know these things. There certainly is a possible world in which a man should have seen a certain star at a certain position in the evening and called it "Hesperus" and a certain star in the morning and called it "Phosphorus"; and should have concluded—should have found out by empirical investigation—that he names two different stars, or two different heavenly bodies. At least one of these stars or heavenly bodies was not Phosphorus, otherwise it couldn't have come out that way. But that's true. And so it's true that given the evidence that someone has antecedent to his empirical investigation, he can be placed in a sense in exactly the same situation, that is a qualitatively identical epistemic situation, and call two heavenly bodies "Hesperus" and "Phosphorus," without their being identical. So in that sense we can say that it might have turned out either way. Not that it might have turned out either way as to Hesperus's being Phosphorus. Though for all we knew in advance, Hesperus wasn't Phosphorus, that couldn't have turned out any other way, in a sense. But being put in a situation where we have exactly the same evidence, qualitatively speaking, it could have turned out that Hesperus was not Phosphorus; that is, in a counterfactual world in which "Hesperus" and "Phosphorus" were not used in the way that we use them, as names of this planet, but as names of some other objects, one could have had qualitatively identical evidence and concluded that "Hesperus" and "Phosphorus" named two different objects.[16] But we, using the names as we do right now, can say in advance, that if Hesperus and Phosphorus are one and the same, then in no other possible world can they be different. We use "Hesperus" as the name of a certain body and "Phosphorus" as the name of a certain body. We use them as names of those bodies in all possible worlds. If, in fact, they are the *same* body, then in any other possible world we have to use them as a name of that object. And so in any other possible world it will be true that Hesperus is Phosphorus. So two things are true: first, that we do not know a priori that Hesperus is Phosphorus, and are in no position to find out the answer except empirically. Second, this is so because we could have evidence qualitatively indistinguishable from the evidence we have and determine the reference of the two names by the positions of two planets in the sky, without the planets being the same.

Of course, it is only a contingent truth (not true in every other possible world) that the star seen over there in the evening is the star seen over there in the morning, because there are possible worlds in which Phosphorus was not visible in the morning. But that contingent truth shouldn't be identified with the statement that Hesperus is Phosphorus. It could only be so identified if you thought that it was a necessary truth that Hesperus is visible over there in the evening or that Phosphorus is visible over there in the morning. But neither of those are necessary truths even if that's the way we pick out the planet. These are the contingent marks by which we identify a certain planet and give it a name.

Notes

1. Keith Donnellan, "Reference and Definite Descriptions," *Philosophical Review* 75 (1966), pp. 281–304. See also Leonard Linsky, "Reference and Referents," in *Philosophy and Ordinary Language,* ed. Caton (University of Illinois Press, Urbana: 1963.) Donnellan's distinction seems applicable to names as well as to descriptions. Two men glimpse someone at a distance and think they recognize him as Jones. "What is Jones doing? Raking the leaves." If the distant leaf-raker is actually Smith, then in some sense they are *referring* to Smith, even though they both use "Jones" *as a name of* Jones. In the text, I speak of the 'referent' of a name to mean the thing named by the name—e.g., Jones, not Smith—even though a speaker may sometimes properly be said to use the name to refer to someone else. Perhaps it would have been less misleading to use a technical term, such as 'denote' rather than 'refer'. My use of 'refer'. is such as to satisfy the schema, "The referent of 'X' is X," where "X" is replaceable by any name or description. I am tentatively inclined to believe, in opposition to Donnellan, that his remarks about reference have little to do with semantics or truth-conditions, though they may be relevant to a theory of speech acts. Space limitations do not permit me to explain what I mean by this, much less defend the view, except for a brief remark: Call the referent of a name or description in my sense the 'semantic referent'; for a name, this is the thing named, for a description, the thing uniquely satisfying the description.

   Then the speaker may *refer* to something other than the semantic referent if he has appropriate false beliefs. I think this is what happens in the naming (Smith-Jones) cases and also in the Donnellan 'champagne' case; the one requires no theory that names are ambiguous, and the other requires no modification of Russell's theory of descriptions.

2. Gottlob Frege, "On Sense and Nominatum," translated by Herbert Feigl in *Readings in Philosophical Analysis,* ed. Herbert Feigl and Wilfrid Sellars (Appleton Century Crofts: 1949), p. 86.

3. Ludwig Wittgenstein, *Philosophical Investigations,* trans. G. E. M. Anscombe (Macmillan: 1953), §79.

4. John R. Searle, "Proper Names," *Mind* 67 (1958), 166–73.

5. Ziff's most detailed statement of his version of the cluster-of-descriptions theory of the reference of names is in "About God," reprinted in *Philosophical Turnings* (Cornell University Press, Ithaca, and Oxford University Press, London: 1966) pp. 94–96. A briefer statement is in his *Semantic Analysis* (Cornell University Press, Ithaca: 1960) pp. 102–05 (esp. pp. 103–04). The latter passage suggests that names of things with which we are acquainted should be treated somewhat differently (using ostension and baptism) from names of historical figures, where the reference is determined by (a cluster of) associated descriptions. On p. 93 of *Se-*

mantic Analysis Ziff states that "simple strong generalization(s) about proper names" are impossible; "one can only say what is so for the most part . . .". Nevertheless Ziff clearly states that a cluster-of-descriptions theory is a reasonable such rough statement, at least for historical figures. For Ziff's view that proper names ordinarily are not words of the language and ordinarily do not have meaning, see pp. 85–89 and 93–94 of *Semantic Analysis*.

6. Those determinists who deny the importance of the individual in history may well argue that had Moses never existed, someone else would have arisen to achieve all that he did. Their claim cannot be refuted by appealing to a correct philosophical theory of the meaning of 'Moses exists'.

7. Of course I don't imply that language contains a name for every object. Demonstratives can be used as rigid designators, and free variables can be used as rigid designators of unspecified objects. Of course when we specify a counterfactual situation, we do not describe the whole possible world, but only the portion which interests us.

8. Searle, "Proper Names," in Caton, op. cit., p. 160.

9. An even better case of determining the reference of a name by description, as opposed to ostension, is the discovery of the planet Neptune. Neptune was hypothesized as the planet which caused such and such discrepancies in the orbits of certain other planets. If Leverrier indeed gave the name "Neptune" to the planet before it was ever seen, then he fixed the reference of "Neptune" by means of the description just mentioned. At that time he was unable to see the planet even through a telescope. At this stage, an a priori material equivalence held between the statements "Neptune exists" and "some one planet perturbing the orbit of such and such other planets exists in such and such a position," and also such statements as "if such and such perturbations are caused by a planet, they are caused by Neptune" had the status of a priori truths. Nevertheless, they were not *necessary* truths, since "Neptune" was introduced as a name rigidly designating a certain planet. Leverrier could well have believed that if Neptune had been knocked off its course one million years earlier, it would have caused no such perturbations and even that some

other object might have caused the perturbations in its place.

10. Following Donnellan's remarks on definite descriptions, we should add that in some cases, an object may be identified, and the reference of a name fixed, using a description which may turn out to be false of its object. The case where the reference of "Phosphorus" is determined as the "morning star," which later turns out not to be a star, is an obvious example. In such cases, the description which fixes the reference clearly is in no sense known a priori to hold of the object, though a more cautious substitute may be. If such a more cautious substitute is available, it is really the substitute which fixes the reference in the sense intended in the text.

11. Some of the theses are sloppily stated in respect of fussy matters like use of quotation marks and related details. (For example, theses (5) and (6), as stated, presuppose that the speaker's language is English.) Since the purport of the theses is clear, and they are false anyway. I have not bothered to set these things straight.

12. The cluster-of-descriptions theory of naming would make "Peano discovered the axioms for number theory" express a trivial truth, not a misconception, and similarly for other misconceptions about the history of science. Some who have conceded such cases to me have argued that there are *other* uses of the same proper names satisfying the cluster theory. For example, it is argued, if we say, "Gödel proved the incompleteness of arithmetic," we are, of course, referring to Gödel, not to Schmidt. But, if we say, "Gödel relied on a diagonal argument in this step of the proof," don't we here, perhaps, refer to *whoever proved the theorem*? Similarly, if someone asks, "What did Aristotle (or Shakespeare) have in mind here?", isn't he talking about the author of the passage in question, whoever he is? By analogy to Donnellan's usage for descriptions, this might be called an "attributive" use of proper names. If this is so, then assuming the Gödel-Schmidt story, the sentence "Gödel proved the incompleteness theorem" is false, but "Gödel used a diagonal argument in the proof" is (at least in some contexts) true, and the reference of the

name 'Gödel' is ambiguous. Since some counter-examples remain, the cluster-of-descriptions theory would still, in general, be false, which was my main point in the text; but it would be applicable in a wider class of cases than I thought. I think, however, that no such ambiguity need be postulated. It is, perhaps, true that sometimes when someone uses the name "Gödel," his main interest is in whoever proved the theorem, and *perhaps,* in some sense, he 'refers' to him. I do not think that this case is different from the case of Smith and Jones. If I mistake Jones for Smith, I may *refer* (in an appropriate sense) to Jones when I say that Smith is raking the leaves; nevertheless I do not use "Smith" ambiguously, as a name sometimes of Smith and sometimes of Jones, but univocally as a name of Smith. Similarly, if I erroneously think that Aristotle wrote such-and-such passage, I may perhaps sometimes use "Aristotle" to *refer* to the actual author of the passage, even though there is no ambiguity in my use of the name. In both cases, I will withdraw my original statement, and my original use of the name, if apprised of the facts. Recall that, in these lectures, 'referent' is used in the technical sense of the thing named by a name (or uniquely satisfying a description), and there should be no confusion.

13. A good example of a baptism whose reference was fixed by means of a description was that of naming Neptune in n. 9. The case of a baptism by ostension can perhaps be subsumed under the description concept also. Thus the primary applicability of the description theory is to cases of initial baptism. Descriptions are also used to fix a reference in cases of designation which are similar to naming except that the terms introduced are not usually called 'names'. The terms "one meter," "100 degrees Centigrade," have already been given as examples, and other examples will be given later in these lectures. Two things should be emphasized concerning the case of introducing a name via a description in an initial baptism. First, the description used is not synonymous with the name it introduces but rather fixes its reference. Here we differ from the usual description theorists. Second, most cases of initial baptism are far from those which originally

inspired the description theory. Usually a baptizer is acquainted in some sense with the object he names and is able to name it ostensively. Now the inspiration of the description theory lay in the fact that we can often use names of famous figures of the past who are long dead and with whom no living person is acquainted; and it is precisely these cases which, on our view, cannot be correctly explained by a description theory.

14. I can transmit the name of the aardvark to other people. For each of these people, as for me, there will be a certain sort of causal or historical connection between my use of the name and the emperor of the French, but not one of the required type.

15. Once we realize that the description used to fix the reference of a name is not synonymous with it, then the description theory can be regarded as presupposing the notion of naming or reference. The requirement I made that the description used not itself involve the notion of reference in a circular way is something else and is crucial if the description theory is to have any value at all. The reason is that the description theorist supposes that each speaker essentially uses the description he gives in an initial act of naming to determine his reference. Clearly, if he introduces the name "Cicero" by the determination, "By 'Cicero' I shall refer to the man I call 'Cicero'," he has by this ceremony determined no reference at all.

   Not all description theorists thought that they were eliminating the notion of reference altogether. Perhaps some realized that some notion of ostension, or primitive reference, is required to back it up. Certainly Russell did.

16. There is a more elaborate discussion of this point in the third lecture, where its relation to a certain sort of counterpart theory is also mentioned.

READING QUESTIONS

1. According to Kripke, what exactly is the problem with Frege's and Russell's treatment of proper names? According to Kripke, what is the problem with Searle's "cluster" theory of names?

2. What are some of the problems Kripke identifies with the concepts of being *a priori* and being *necessary?* Do you believe that his remarks are correct? Why?

3. What does Kripke mean when he speaks of a "possible world"? How is the concept of a "possible world" related to the concept of a "counterfactual situation"? How should we understand talk of "possible worlds"?

4. At the beginning of Lecture II, Kripke outlines a theory of naming that involves a commitment to the truth of various theses. He then examines whether or not the theses can be adequately defended. Briefly outline his criticisms, where appropriate. Do you agree with his criticisms? Why or why not?

5. What is Kripke's own account of naming? How does he explain the significance or reference of names in terms of reference fixing through description or ostension? Why does Kripke believe that his own theory is superior to the theories of Russell, Frege, and Searle?

6. How does Kripke handle what he calls "statements of identity"? What is the significance of his analysis, if he is correct?

SUGGESTIONS FOR FURTHER READING (SAUL KRIPKE)

Primary Sources and Collected Writings

(1959) "A Completeness Theorem in Modal Logic." In *Journal of Symbolic Logic*, 24.1: 1–14.

(1963) "Semantical Analysis of Modal Logic 1." In *Zeitschrift für Mathematische Logik und Grundlagen der Mathematik*, 9: 67–96.

(1965) "Semantical Considerations on Modal Logic." In *Acta Philosophica Fennica*, 16: 83–94.

(1965) "Semantical Analysis of Modal Logic 2." In *The Theory of Models*, edited by J. Addison, L. Henkin, and A. Tarski. Amsterdam: North Holland, pp. 206–20.

(1971) "Identity and Necessity." In *Identity and Individuation*, edited by M. Munitz. New York: New York University Press.

(1972) "Naming and Necessity." In *Semantics of Natural Language*, 2nd ed., edited by D. Davidson. Dordrecht: D. Reidel, pp. 253–355.

(1975) "Outline of a Theory of Truth." In *Journal of Philosophy*, 72: 690–716.

(1976) "Is There a Problem about Substitutional Quantification?" In *Truth and Meaning: Essays in Semantics*, edited by G. Evans and J. McDowell. London: Oxford University Press, pp. 325–419.

(1977) "Speaker's Reference and Semantic Reference." In *Contemporary Perspectives in the Philosophy of Language*, edited by P. French, T. Uehling, and H. Wettstein. Minneapolis, MN: University of Minnesota Press, pp. 255–76.

(1979) "A Puzzle about Belief." In *Meaning and Use*, edited by A. Margalit. Dordrecht: D. Reidel, pp. 239–83.

(1980) *Naming and Necessity*. Cambridge, MA: Harvard University Press.

(1982) *Wittgenstein on Rules and Private Language*. Cambridge, MA: Harvard University Press.

Secondary Sources

Branch, T. (1977) "New Frontiers in American Philosophy." In *The New York Times Magazine*, August 14.

Devitt, M., and K. Sterelny. (1987) *Language and Reality: An Introduction to the Philosophy of Language*. Oxford: Basil Blackwell.

Forbes, G. (1985) *The Metaphysics of Modality*. Oxford: Clarendon Press.

Humpreys, P., and J. Fertzer, eds. (1988) *The New Theory of Reference: Kripke, Marcus, and Its Origins*. Dordrecht: Kluwer Academic Publishing.

Jubien, M. (1993) *Ontology, Modality, and the Fallacy of Reference*. Cambridge: Cambridge University Press.

Katz, J. (1990) *The Metaphysics of Meaning*. Cambridge, MA: MIT Press.

Lewis, D. (1968) "Counterpart Theory and Quantified Modal Logic." In *Journal of Philosophy*, 65: 113–26.

———. (1986) *On the Plurality of Worlds*. Oxford: Basil Blackwell.

Linksy, L., ed. (1971) *Reference and Modality*. Oxford: Oxford University Press.

Marcus, R. B. (1993) *Modalities*. New York: Oxford University Press.

Martin, R. M., ed. (1984) *Recent Essays on Truth and the Liar Paradox*. Oxford: Clarendon Press.

McGinn, C. (1984) *Wittgenstein on Meaning: An Interpretation and Evaluation.* Oxford: Basil Blackwell.

Plantinga, A. (1974) *The Nature of Necessity.* Oxford: Oxford University Press.

Salmon, N. (1982) *Reference and Essence.* Oxford: Basil Blackwell.

Hilary Putnam

Brains in a Vat

Hilary Putnam (1926–) remains one of the most innovative and interesting philosophers of his generation. Unlike many of his contemporaries whose work is highly specialized and technical, Putnam's writings explore and inform just about every dimension of contemporary philosophy with flair, readability, and intelligence. Furthermore, like another great figure of twentieth-century philosophy, Bertrand Russell, his philosophical standpoint has undergone constant revision and development, demonstrating a high degree of self-awareness and a refreshingly honest willingness to engage in constructive self-criticism.

Putnam was born in Chicago, Illinois, and raised in Europe and the United States. He obtained his B.A. from the University of Pennsylvania in 1948 and his Ph.D. from the University of California at Los Angeles in 1952. His doctoral supervisor was the great philosopher of science, Hans Reichenbach (1891–1953). Putnam himself began his career pursuing topics in the philosophy of science and the philosophy of mathematics, but soon found himself growing interested in a larger spectrum of questions and issues ranging from politics, to ethics, to the arts.

Putnam's first full-time teaching position was at Northwestern University. After leaving Northwestern, he became a professor at Princeton University for a short time, and then professor of the philosophy of science at Massachusetts Institute of Technology from 1961 to 1965. After leaving MIT, he moved to Harvard University where, in 1976, he was appointed the Walter Beverley Pearson Professor of Mathematical Logic.

He is currently the Cogan University Professor of Philosophy at Harvard. His career has been marked by many professional achievements, including his appointment as the president of the American Philosophical Association (1976) and as the president of the Association of Symbolic Logic (1980).

The most significant change in his overall philosophical outlook came with the publication in 1981 of his book *Reason, Truth, and History.* In it, he turns away from a view he terms "metaphysical realism" toward a sophisticated and subtle view closely related to verificationism, which he calls "internal realism" or "pragmatic realism." This view, he claims, stands in the gap between indefensibly traditional realist conceptions of truth and metaphysics, on one hand, and the perceived threat of extreme relativism, on the other. It also provides a basis for the rejection of scientism in philosophy and its associated dismissal of the normative and religious dimension of experience as somehow conceptually ill-formed.

In the following opening essay from *Reason, Truth, and History,* Putnam takes on the challenge of skepticism with respect to the external world. He argues that "the supposition that we are actually brains in a vat, although it violates no physical law, and is perfectly consistent with everything we have experienced, cannot possibly be true. *It cannot possibly be true,* because it is, in a certain way, self-refuting." His argument, in part, hinges on his rejection of "meaning internalism" and in part on his insistence that reference requires a causal connection to be forged between the significant use of any term and that to which the term actually refers.

An ant is crawling on a patch of sand. As it crawls, it traces a line in the sand. By pure chance the line that it traces curves and recrosses itself in such a way that it ends up looking like a recognizable caricature of Win-

Hilary Putnam, "Brains in a Vat" from his *Reason, Truth, and History,* Cambridge, Cambridge University Press, 1981. Reprinted with the permission of Cambridge University Press.

ston Churchill. Has the ant traced a picture of Winston Churchill, a picture that *depicts* Churchill?

Most people would say, on a little reflection, that it has not. The ant, after all, has never seen Churchill, or even a picture of Churchill, and it had no intention of depicting Churchill. It simply traced a line (and even *that* was unintentional), a line that *we* can 'see as' a picture of Churchill.

We can express this by saying that the line is not 'in itself' a representation[1] of anything rather than anything else. Similarity (of a certain very complicated sort) to the features of Winston Churchill is not sufficient to make something represent or refer to Churchill. Nor is it necessary: in our community the printed shape 'Winston Churchill', the spoken words 'Winston Churchill', and many other things are used to represent Churchill (though not pictorially), while not having the sort of similarity to Churchill that a picture—even a line drawing—has. If *similarity* is not necessary or sufficient to make something represent something else, how can *anything* be necessary or sufficient for this purpose? How on earth can one thing represent (or 'stand for', etc.) a different thing?

The answer may seem easy. Suppose the ant had seen Winston Churchill, and suppose that it had the intelligence and skill to draw a picture of him. Suppose it produced the caricature *intentionally*. Then the line would have represented Churchill.

On the other hand, suppose the line had the shape WINSTON CHURCHILL. And suppose this was just accident (ignoring the improbability involved). Then the 'printed shape' WINSTON CHURCHILL would *not* have represented Churchill, although that printed shape does represent Churchill when it occurs in almost any book today.

So it may seem that what is necessary for representation, or what is mainly necessary for representation, is *intention*.

But to have the intention that *anything,* even private language (even the words 'Winston Churchill' spoken in my mind and not out loud), should *represent* Churchill, I must have been able to *think about* Churchill in the first place. If lines in the sand, noises, etc., cannot 'in themselves' represent anything, then how is it that thought forms can 'in themselves' represent anything? Or can they? How can thought reach out and 'grasp' what is external?

Some philosophers have, in the past, leaped from this sort of consideration to what they take to be a proof that the mind is *essentially non-physical in nature.* The argument is simple; what we said about the ant's curve applies to any physical object. No physical object can, in itself, refer to one thing rather than to another; nevertheless, *thoughts in the mind* obviously do succeed in referring to one thing rather than another. So thoughts (and hence the mind) are of an essentially different nature than physical objects. Thoughts have the characteristic of *intentionality*—they can refer to something else; nothing physical has 'intentionality', save as that intentionality is derivative from some employment of that physical thing by a mind. Or so it is claimed. This is too quick; just postulating mysterious powers of mind solves nothing. But the problem is very real. How is intentionality, reference, possible?

Magical Theories of Reference

We saw that the ant's 'picture' has no necessary connection with Winston Churchill. The mere fact that the 'picture' bears a 'resemblance' to Churchill does not make it into a real picture, nor does it make it a representation of Churchill. Unless the ant is an intelligent ant (which it isn't) and knows about Churchill (which it doesn't), the curve it traced is not a picture or even a representation of anything. Some primitive people believe that some representations (in particular, *names*) have a necessary connection with their bearers; that to know the 'true name' of someone or something gives one power over it. This power comes from the *magical connection* between the name and the bearer of the name; once one realizes that a name *only* has a contextual, contingent, conventional connection with its bearer, it is hard to see why knowledge of the name should have any mystical significance.

What is important to realize is that what goes for physical pictures also goes for mental images, and for mental representations in general; mental representations no more have a necessary connection with what they represent than physical representations do. The contrary supposition is a survival of magical thinking.

Perhaps the point is easiest to grasp in the case of mental *images*. (Perhaps the first philosopher to grasp the enormous significance of this point, even if he was not the first to actually make it, was Wittgenstein.) Suppose there is a planet somewhere on which human beings have evolved (or been deposited by alien spacemen, or what have you). Suppose these humans, although otherwise like us, have never seen *trees*. Suppose they have never imagined trees (perhaps vegetable life exists on their planet only in the form of molds). Suppose one day a picture of a tree is accidentally dropped on their planet by a spaceship which passes on without having other contact with them. Imagine them puzzling over the picture. What in the world is this? All sorts of speculations occur to them: a building, a canopy, even an animal of some kind. But suppose they never come close to the truth.

For *us* the picture is a representation of a tree. For these humans the picture only represents a strange object, nature and function unknown. Suppose one of them has a mental image which is exactly like one of my mental images of a tree as a result of having seen the picture. His mental image is not a *representation of a tree.* It is only a representation of the strange object (whatever it is) that the mysterious picture represents.

Still, someone might argue that the mental image is *in fact* a representation of a tree, if only because the picture which caused this mental image was itself a representation of a tree to begin with. There is a causal chain from actual trees to the mental image even if it is a very strange one.

But even this causal chain can be imagined absent. Suppose the 'picture of the tree' that the spaceship dropped was not really a picture of a tree, but the accidental result of some spilled paints. Even if it looked exactly like a picture of a tree, it was, in truth, no more a picture of a tree than the ant's 'caricature' of Churchill was a picture of Churchill. We can even imagine that the spaceship which dropped the 'picture' came from a planet which knew nothing of trees. Then the humans would still have mental images qualitatively identical with my image of a tree, but they would not be images which represented a tree any more than anything else.

The same thing is true of *words.* A discourse on paper might seem to be a perfect description of trees, but if it was produced by monkeys randomly hitting keys on a typewriter for millions of years, then the words do not refer to anything. If there were a person who memorized those words and said them in his

mind without understanding them, then they would not refer to anything when thought in the mind, either.

Imagine the person who is saying those words in his mind has been hypnotized. Suppose the words are in Japanese, and the person has been told that he understands Japanese. Suppose that as he thinks those words he has a 'feeling of understanding'. (Although if someone broke into his train of thought and asked him what the words he was thinking *meant,* he would discover he couldn't say.) Perhaps the illusion would be so perfect that the person could even fool a Japanese telepath! But if he couldn't use the words in the right contexts, answer questions about what he 'thought', etc., then he didn't understand them.

By combining these science fiction stories I have been telling, we can contrive a case in which someone thinks words which are in fact a description of trees in some language *and* simultaneously has appropriate mental images, but *neither* understands the words *nor* knows what a tree is. We can even imagine that the mental images were caused by paint-spills (although the person has been hypnotized to think that they are images of something appropriate to his thought—only, if he were asked, he wouldn't be able to say of what). And we can imagine that the language the person is thinking in is one neither the hypnotist nor the person hypnotized has ever heard of—perhaps it is just coincidence that these 'nonsense sentences', as the hypnotist supposes them to be, are a description of trees in Japanese. In short, everything passing before the person's mind might be qualitatively identical with what was passing through the mind of a Japanese speaker who was *really* thinking about trees—but none of it would refer to trees.

All of this is really impossible, of course, in the way that it is really impossible that monkeys should by chance type out a copy of *Hamlet.* That is to say that the probabilities against it are so high as to mean it will never really happen (we think). But is is not logically impossible, or even physically impossible. It *could* happen (compatibly with physical law and, perhaps, compatibly with actual conditions in the universe, if there are lots of intelligent beings on other planets). And if it did happen, it would be a striking demonstration of an important conceptual truth; that even a large and complex system of representations, both verbal and visual, still does not have an *intrinsic,* built-in, magical connection with what it represents—a connection independent of how it was caused and what the dispositions of the speaker or thinker are. And this is true whether the system of representations (words and images, in the case of the example) is physically realized—the words are written or spoken, and the pictures are physical pictures—or only realized in the mind. Thought words and mental pictures do not *intrinsically* represent what they are about.

The Case of the Brains in a Vat

Here is a science fiction possibility discussed by philosophers: imagine that a human being (you can imagine this to be yourself) has been subjected to an operation by an evil scientist. The person's brain (your brain) has been removed from the body and placed in a vat of nutrients which keeps the brain alive. The nerve endings have been connected to a super-scientific computer which causes the person whose brain it is to have the illusion that everything is perfectly normal. There seem to be people, objects, the sky, etc; but really all the person (you) is experiencing is the result of electronic impulses traveling from the computer to the nerve endings. The computer is so clever that if the person tries to raise his hand, the feedback from the computer will cause him to 'see' and 'feel' the hand being raised. Moreover, by varying the program, the evil scientist can cause the victim to 'experience' (or hallucinate) any situation or environment the evil scientist wishes. He can also obliterate the memory of the brain operation, so that the victim will seem to himself to have always been in this environment. It can even seem to the victim that he is sitting and reading these very words about the amusing but quite absurd supposition that there is an evil scientist who removes people's brains from their bodies and places them in a vat of nutrients which keep the brains alive. The nerve endings are supposed to be connected to a super-scientific computer which causes the person whose brain it is to have the illusion that . . .

When this sort of possibility is mentioned in a lecture on the theory of knowledge, the purpose, of course, is to raise the classical problem of skepticism with respect to the external world in a modern way.

(*How do you know you aren't in this predicament?*) But this predicament is also a useful device for raising issues about the mind/world relationship.

Instead of having just one brain in a vat, we could imagine that all human beings (perhaps all sentient beings) are brains in a vat (or nervous systems in a vat in case some beings with just a minimal nervous system already count as 'sentient'). Of course, the evil scientist would have to be outside—or would he? Perhaps there is no evil scientist, perhaps (though this is absurd) the universe just happens to consist of automatic machinery tending a vat full of brains and nervous systems.

This time let us suppose that the automatic machinery is programmed to give us all a *collective* hallucination, rather than a number of separate unrelated hallucinations. Thus, when I seem to myself to be talking to you, you seem to yourself to be hearing my words. Of course, it is not the case that my words actually reach your ears—for you don't have (real) ears, nor do I have a real mouth and tongue. Rather, when I produce my words, what happens is that the efferent impulses travel from my brain to the computer, which both causes me to 'hear' my own voice uttering those words and 'feel' my tongue moving, etc., and causes you to 'hear' my words, 'see' me speaking, etc. In this case, we are, in a sense, actually in communication. I am not mistaken about your real existence (only about the existence of your body and the 'external world', apart from brains). From a certain point of view, it doesn't even matter that 'the whole world' is a collective hallucination; for you do, after all, really hear my words when I speak to you, even if the mechanism isn't what we suppose it to be. (Of course, if we were two lovers making love, rather than just two people carrying on a conversation, then the suggestion that it was just two brains in a vat might be disturbing.)

I want now to ask a question which will seem very silly and obvious (at least to some people, including some very sophisticated philosophers), but which will take us to real philosophical depths rather quickly. Suppose this whole story were actually true. Could we, if we were brains in a vat in this way, *say* or *think* that we were?

I am going to argue that the answer is "No, we couldn't." In fact, I am going to argue that the supposition that we are actually brains in a vat, although it violates no physical law, and is perfectly consistent with everything we have experienced, cannot possibly be true. *It cannot possibly be true, because it is, in a certain way, self-refuting*.

The argument I am going to present is an unusual one, and it took me several years to convince myself that it is really right. But it is a correct argument. What makes it seem so strange is that it is connected with some of the very deepest issues in philosophy. (It first occurred to me when I was thinking about a theorem in modern logic, the 'Skolem—Löwenheim Theorem', and I suddenly saw a connection between this theorem and some arguments in Wittgenstein's *Philosophical Investigations*.)

A 'self-refuting supposition' is one whose truth implies its own falsity. For example, consider the thesis that *all general statements are false*. This is a general statement. So if it is true, then it must be false. Hence, it is false. Sometimes a thesis is called 'self-refuting' if it is *the supposition that the thesis is entertained or enunciated* that implies its falsity. For example, 'I do not exist' is self-refuting if thought by *me* (for any '*me*'). So one can be certain that one oneself exists, if one thinks about it (as Descartes argued).

What I shall show is that the supposition that we are brains in a vat has just this property. If we can consider whether it is true or false, then it is not true (I shall show). Hence it is not true.

Before I give the argument, let us consider why it seems so strange that such an argument can be given (at least to philosophers who subscribe to a 'copy' conception of truth). We conceded that it is compatible with physical law that there should be a world in which all sentient beings are brains in a vat. As philosophers say, there is a 'possible world' in which all sentient beings are brains in a vat. (This 'possible world' talk makes it sound as if there is a *place* where any absurd supposition is true, which is why it can be very misleading in philosophy.) The humans in that possible world have exactly the same experiences that *we* do. They think the same thoughts we do (at least, the same words, images, thought-forms, etc., go through their minds). Yet, I am claiming that there is an argument we can give that shows we are not brains in a vat. How can there be? And why couldn't the people in the possible world who really *are* brains in a vat give it too?

The answer is going to be (basically) this: although the people in that possible world can think and 'say' any words we can think and say, they cannot (I claim) *refer* to what we can refer to. In particular, they cannot think or say that they are brains in a vat (*even by thinking "we are brains in a vat"*).

Turing's Test

Suppose someone succeeds in inventing a computer which can actually carry on an intelligent conversation with one (on as many subjects as an intelligent person might). How can one decide if the computer is 'conscious'?

The British logician Alan Turing proposed the following test:[2] let someone carry on a conversation with the computer and a conversation with a person whom he does not know. If he cannot tell which is the computer and which is the human being, then (assume the test to be repeated a sufficient number of times with different interlocutors) the computer is conscious. In short, a computing machine is conscious if it can pass the 'Turing Test'. (The conversations are not to be carried on face to face, of course, since the interlocutor is not to know the visual appearance of either of his two conversational partners. Nor is voice to be used, since the mechanical voice might simply sound different from a human voice. Imagine, rather, that the conversations are all carried on via electric typewriter. The interlocutor types in his statements, questions, etc., and the two partners—the machine and the person—respond via the electric keyboard. Also, the machine may *lie*—asked 'Are you a machine', it might reply, "No, I'm an assistant in the lab here.")

The idea that this test is really a definitive test of consciousness has been criticized by a number of authors (who are by no means hostile in principle to the idea that a machine might be conscious). But this is not our topic at this time. I wish to use the general idea of the Turing test, the general idea of a *dialogic test of competence*, for a different purpose, the purpose of exploring the notion of *reference*.

Imagine a situation in which the problem is not to determine if the partner is really a person or a machine, but is rather to determine if the partner uses the words to refer as we do. The obvious test is, again, to carry on a conversation, and, if no problems arise, if the partner 'passes' in the sense of being indistinguishable from someone who is certified in advance to be speaking the same language, referring to the usual sorts of objects, etc., to conclude that the partner does refer to objects as we do. When the purpose of the Turing test is as just described, that is, to determine the existence of (shared) reference, I shall refer to the test as the *Turing Test for Reference*. And, just as philosophers have discussed the question whether the original Turing test is a *definitive* test for consciousness, i.e., the question of whether a machine which 'passes' the test not just once but regularly is *necessarily* conscious, so, in the same way, I wish to discuss the question of whether the Turing Test for Reference just suggested is a definitive test for shared reference.

The answer will turn out to be 'No'. The Turing Test for Reference is not definitive. It is certainly an excellent test in practice; but it is not logically impossible (though it is certainly highly improbable) that someone could pass the Turing Test for Reference and not be referring to anything. It follows from this, as we shall see, that we can extend our observation that words (and whole texts and discourses) do not have a necessary connection to their referents. Even if we consider not words by themselves but rules deciding what words may appropriately be produced in certain contexts—even if we consider, in computer jargon, *programs for using words*—unless those programs themselves *refer to something extra-linguistic* there is still no determinate reference that those words possess. This will be a crucial step in the process of reaching the conclusion that the Brain-in-a-Vat Worlders cannot refer to anything external at all (and hence cannot say *that* they are Brain-in-a-Vat Worlders).

Suppose, for example, that I am in the Turing situation (playing the 'Imitation Game', in Turing's terminology) and my partner is actually a machine. Suppose this machine is able to win the game ('passes' the test). Imagine the machine to be programmed to produce beautiful responses in English to statements, questions, remarks, etc. in English, but that it has no sense organs (other than the hookup to my electric typewriter), and no motor organs (other than the electric typewriter). (As far as I can make out, Turing does not assume that

the possession of either sense organs or motor organs is necessary for consciousness or intelligence.) Assume that not only does the machine lack electronic eyes and ears, etc., but that there are no provisions in the machine's program, the program for playing the Imitation Game, for incorporating inputs from such sense organs, or for controlling a body. What should we say about such a machine?

To me, it seems evident that we cannot and should not attribute reference to such a device. It is true that the machine can discourse beautifully about, say, the scenery in New England. But it could not recognize an apple tree or an apple, a mountain or a cow, a field or a steeple, if it were in front of one.

What we have is a device for producing sentences in response to sentences. But none of these sentences is at all connected to the real world. *If one coupled two of these machines and let them play the Imitation Game with each other, then they would go on 'fooling' each other forever, even if the rest of the world disappeared!* There is no more reason to regard the machine's talk of apples as referring to real world apples than there is to regard the ant's 'drawing' as referring to Winston Churchill.

What produces the illusion of reference, meaning, intelligence, etc., here is the fact that there is a convention of representation which *we* have under which the machine's discourse refers to apples, steeples, New England, etc. Similarly, there is the *illusion* that the ant has caricatured Churchill, for the same reason. But we are able to perceive, handle, deal with apples and fields. Our talk of apples and fields is intimately connected with our *non-verbal* transactions with apples and fields. There are 'language entry rules' which take us from experiences of apples to such utterances as 'I see an apple', and 'language exit rules' which take us from decisions expressed in linguistic form ('I am going to buy some apples') to actions other than speaking. Lacking either language entry rules or language exit rules, there is no reason to regard the conversation of the machine (or of the two machines, in the case we envisaged of two machines playing the Imitation Game with each other) as more than syntactic play. Syntactic play that *resembles* intelligent discourse, to be sure; but only as (and no more than) the ant's curve resembles a biting caricature.

In the case of the ant, we could have argued that the ant would have drawn the same curve even if Winston Churchill had never existed. In the case of the machine, we cannot quite make the parallel argument; if apples, trees, steeples and fields had not existed, then, presumably, the programmers would not have produced that same program. Although the machine does not *perceive* apples, fields, or steeples, its creator-designers did. There is *some* causal connection between the machine and the real world apples, etc., via the perceptual experience and knowledge of the creator-designers. But such a weak connection can hardly suffice for reference. Not only is it logically possible, though fantastically improbable, that the same machine *could* have existed even if apples, fields, and steeples had not existed; more important, the machine is utterly insensitive to the *continued* existence of apples, fields, steeples, etc. Even if all these things *ceased* to exist, the machine would still discourse just as happily in the same way. That is why the machine cannot be regarded as referring at all.

The point that is relevant for our discussion is that there is nothing in Turing's Test to rule out a machine which is programmed to do nothing *but* play the Imitation Game, and that a machine which can do nothing *but* play the Imitation Game is *clearly* not referring any more than a record player is.

Brains in a Vat (Again)

Let us compare the hypothetical 'brains in a vat' with the machines just described. There are obviously important differences. The brains in a vat do not have sense organs, but they do have *provision* for sense organs; that is, there are afferent nerve endings, there are inputs from these afferent nerve endings, and these inputs figure in the 'program' of the brains in the vat just as they do in the program of our brains. The brains in a vat are *brains*; moreover, they are *functioning* brains, and they function by the same rules as brains do in the actual world. For these reasons, it would seem absurd to deny consciousness or intelligence to them. But the fact that they are conscious and intelligent does not mean that their words refer to what our words refer. The question we are interested in is this: do their ver-

balizations containing, say, the word 'tree' actually refer to *trees*? More generally: can they refer to *external objects at all*? (As opposed to, for example, objects in the image produced by the automatic machinery.)

To fix our ideas, let us specify that the automatic machinery is supposed to have come into existence by some kind of cosmic chance or coincidence (or, perhaps, to have always existed). In this hypothetical world, the automatic machinery itself is supposed to have no intelligent creator-designers. In fact, as we said at the beginning of this chapter, we may imagine that all sentient beings (however minimal their sentience) are inside the vat.

This assumption does not help. For there is no connection between the *word* 'tree' as used by these brains and actual trees. They would still use the word 'tree' just as they do, think just the thoughts they do, have just the images they have, even if there were no actual trees. Their images, words, etc., are qualitatively identical with images, words, etc., which do represent trees in *our* world; but we have already seen (the ant again!) that qualitative similarity to something which represents an object (Winston Churchill or a tree) does not make a thing a representation all by itself. In short, the brains in a vat are not thinking about real trees when they think 'there is a tree in front of me' because there is nothing by virtue of which their thought 'tree' represents actual trees.

If this seems hasty, reflect on the following: we have seen that the words do not necessarily refer to trees even if they are arranged in a sequence which is identical with a discourse which (were it to occur in one of our minds) would unquestionably *be about trees* in the actual world. Nor does the 'program', in the sense of the rules, practices, dispositions of the brains to verbal behavior, necessarily refer to trees or bring about reference to trees through the connections it establishes between words and words, or *linguistic* cues and *linguistic* responses. If these brains think about, refer to, represent trees (real trees, outside the vat), then it must be because of the way the 'program' connects the system of language to *non-verbal* input and outputs. There are indeed such non-verbal inputs and outputs in the Brain-in-a-Vat world (those efferent and afferent nerve endings again!), but we also saw that the 'sense-data' produced by the automatic machinery do not represent trees (or anything external) even when they resemble our tree-images exactly. Just as a splash of paint might resemble a tree picture without *being* a tree picture, so, we saw, a 'sense-datum' might be qualitatively identical with an 'image of a tree' without being an image of a tree. How can the fact that, in the case of the brains in a vat, the language is connected by the program with sensory inputs which do not intrinsically or extrinsically represent trees (or anything external) possibly bring it about that the whole system of representations, the language-in-use, *does* refer to or represent trees or anything external?

The answer is that it cannot. The whole system of sense-data, motor signals to the efferent endings, and verbally or conceptually mediated thought connected by 'language entry rules' to the sense-data (or whatever) as inputs and by 'language exit rules' to the motor signals as outputs, has no more connection to *trees* than the ant's curve has to Winston Churchill. Once we see that the *qualitative similarity* (amounting, if you like, to qualitative identity) between the thoughts of the brains in a vat and the thoughts of someone in the actual world by no means implies sameness of reference, it is not hard to see that there is no basis at all for regarding the brain in a vat as referring to external things.

The Premises of the Argument

I have now given the argument promised to show that the brains in a vat cannot think or say that they are brains in a vat. It remains only to make it explicit and to examine its structure.

By what was just said, when the brain in a vat (in the world where every sentient being is and always was a brain in a vat) thinks 'There is a tree in front of me', his thought does not refer to actual trees. On some theories that we shall discuss it might refer to trees in the image, or to the electronic impulses that cause tree experiences, or to the features of the program that are responsible for those electronic impulses. These theories are not ruled out by what was just said, for there is a close causal connection between the use of the word 'tree' in vat-English and the presence of trees in the image, the presence of electronic impulses of a certain kind, and the presence of certain features in the ma-

chine's program. On these theories the brain is *right*, not *wrong* in thinking "There is a tree in front of me." Given what 'tree' refers to in vat-English and what 'in front of' refers to, assuming one of these theories is correct, then the truth-conditions for 'There is a tree in front of me' when it occurs in vat-English are simply that a tree in the image be 'in front of' the 'me' in question—in the image—or, perhaps, that the kind of electronic impulse that normally produces this experience be coming from the automatic machinery, or, perhaps, that the feature of the machinery that is supposed to produce the 'tree in front of one' experience be operating. And these truth-conditions are certainly fulfilled.

By the same argument, 'vat' refers to vats in the image in vat-English, or something related (electronic impulses or program features), but certainly not to real vats, since the use of 'vat' in vat-English has no causal connection to real vats (apart from the connection that the brains in a vat wouldn't be able to use the word 'vat', if it were not for the presence of one particular vat—the vat they are in; but this connection obtains between the use of *every* word in vat-English and that one particular vat; it is not a special connection between the use of the *particular* word 'vat' and vats). Similarly, 'nutrient fluid' refers to a liquid in the image in vat-English, or something related (electronic impulses or program features). It follows that if their 'possible world' is really the actual one, and we are really the brains in a vat, then what we now mean by 'we are brains in a vat' is that *we are brains in a vat in the image* or something of that kind (if we mean anything at all). But part of the hypothesis that we are brains in a vat is that we aren't brains in a vat in the image (i.e., what we are 'hallucinating' isn't that we are brains in a vat). So, if we are brains in a vat, then the sentence 'We are brains in a vat' says something false (if it says anything). In short, if we are brains in a vat, then 'We are brains in a vat' is false. So it is (necessarily) false.

The supposition that such a possibility makes sense arises from a combination of two errors: (1) taking *physical possibility* too seriously; and (2) unconsciously operating with a magical theory of reference, a theory on which certain mental representations necessarily refer to certain external things and kinds of things. There is a 'physically possible world' in which we are brains in a vat—what does this mean except that there is a *description* of such a state of affairs which is compatible with the laws of physics? Just as there is a tendency in our culture (and has been since the seventeenth century) to take *physics* as our metaphysics, that is, to view the exact sciences as the long-sought description of the 'true and ultimate furniture of the universe', so there is, as an immediate consequence, a tendency to take 'physical possibility' as the very touchstone of what might really actually be the case. Truth is physical truth; possibility physical possibility; and necessity physical necessity, on such a view. But we have just seen, if only in the case of a very contrived example so far, that this view is wrong. The existence of a 'physically possible world' in which we are brains in a vat (and always were and will be) does not mean that we might really, actually, possibly *be* brains in a vat. What rules out this possibility is not physics but *philosophy*.

Some philosophers, eager both to assert and minimize the claims of their profession at the same time (the typical state of mind of Anglo-American philosophy in the twentieth century), would say: "Sure. You have shown that some things that seem to be physical possibilities are really *conceptual* impossibilities. What's so surprising about that?"

Well, to be sure, my argument can be described as a 'conceptual' one. But to describe philosophical activity as the search for 'conceptual' truths makes it all sound like *inquiry about the meaning of words*. And that is not at all what we have been engaging in.

What we have been doing is considering the *preconditions* for *thinking about, representing, referring to*, etc. We have investigated these preconditions *not* by investigating the meaning of these words and phrases (as a linguist might, for example) but by *reasoning a priori*. Not in the old 'absolute' sense (since we don't claim that magical theories of reference are *a priori* wrong), but in the sense of inquiring into what is *reasonably* possible *assuming* certain general premises, or making certain very broad theoretical assumptions. Such a procedure is neither 'empirical' nor quite 'a priori', but has elements of both ways of investigating. In spite of the fallibility of my procedure, and its dependence upon assumptions which might be described as 'empirical' (e.g., the assumption that the mind has no access to external things or properties apart from that provided by the senses), my procedure has a close relation to what

Kant called a 'transcendental' investigation; for it is an investigation, I repeat, of the *preconditions* of reference and hence of thought—preconditions built in to the nature of our minds themselves, though not (as Kant hoped) wholly independent of empirical assumptions.

One of the premises of the argument is obvious: that magical theories of reference are wrong, wrong for mental representations and not only for physical ones. The other premise is that one cannot refer to certain kinds of things, e.g., *trees*, if one has no causal interaction at all with them,[3] or with things in terms of which they can be described. But why should we accept these premises? Since these constitute the broad framework within which I am arguing, it is time to examine them more closely.

The Reasons for Denying Necessary Connections Between Representations and Their Referents

I mentioned earlier that some philosophers (most famously, Brentano) have ascribed to the mind a power, 'intentionality', which precisely enables it to *refer*. Evidently, I have rejected this as no solution. But what gives me this right? Have I, perhaps, been too hasty?

These philosophers did not claim that we can think about external things or properties without using representations at all. And the argument I gave above comparing visual sense data to the ant's 'picture' (the argument via the science fiction story about the 'picture' of a tree that came from a paint-splash and that gave rise to sense-data qualitatively similar to our 'visual images of trees', but unaccompanied by any *concept* of a tree) would be accepted as showing that *images* do not necessarily refer. If there are mental representations that necessarily refer (to external things) they must be of the nature of *concepts* and not of the nature of images. But what are *concepts*?

When we introspect we do not perceive 'concepts' flowing through our minds as such. Stop the stream of thought when or where we will, what we catch are words, images, sensations, feelings. When I speak my thoughts out loud I do not think them twice. I hear my words as you do. To be sure it feels different to me when I utter words that I believe and when I utter words I do not believe (but sometimes, when I am nervous, or in front of a hostile audience, it feels as if I am lying when I know I am telling the truth); and it feels different when I utter words I understand and when I utter words I do not understand. But I can imagine without difficulty someone thinking just these words (in the sense of saying them in his mind) and having just the feeling of understanding, asserting, etc., that I do, and realizing a minute later (or on being awakened by a hypnotist) that he did not understand what had just passed through his mind at all, that he did not even understand the language these words are in. I don't claim that this is very likely; I simply mean that there is nothing at all unimaginable about this. And what this shows is not that concepts *are* words (or images, sensations, etc.), but that to attribute a 'concept' or a 'thought' to someone is quite different from attributing any mental 'presentation', any introspectible entity or event, to him. Concepts are not mental presentations that intrinsically refer to external objects for the very decisive reason that they are not mental presentations at all. Concepts are signs used in a certain way; the signs may be public or private, mental entities or physical entities, but even when the signs are 'mental' and 'private', the sign itself apart from its use is not the concept. And signs do not themselves intrinsically refer.

We can see this by performing a very simple thought experiment. Suppose you are like me and cannot tell an elm tree from a beech tree. We still say that the reference of 'elm' in my speech is the same as the reference of 'elm' in anyone else's, viz., elm trees, and that the set of all beech trees is the extension of 'beech' (i.e., the set of things the word 'beech' is truly predicated of) both in your speech and my speech. Is it really credible that the difference between what 'elm' refers to and what 'beech' refers to is brought about by a difference in our *concepts*? My concept of an elm tree is exactly the same as my concept of a beech tree (I blush to confess). (This shows that the determination of reference is social and not individual, by the way; you and I both defer to experts who *can* tell elms from beeches.) If someone heroically attempts to maintain that the difference between the reference of 'elm' and the reference of 'beech' in *my* speech is explained by a differ-

ence in my psychological state, then let him imagine a Twin Earth where the words are switched. Twin Earth is very much like Earth; in fact, apart from the fact that 'elm' and 'beech' are interchanged, the reader can suppose Twin Earth is exactly like Earth. Suppose I have a *Doppelganger* on Twin Earth who is molecule for molecule identical with me (in the sense in which two neckties can be 'identical'). If you are a dualist, then suppose my *Doppelganger* thinks the same verbalized thoughts I do, has the same sense data, the same dispositions, etc. It is absurd to think his psychological state is one bit different from mine: yet his word 'elm' represents *beeches*, and my word 'elm' represents elms. (Similarly, if the 'water' on Twin Earth is a different liquid—say, XYZ and not H_2O—then 'water' represents a different liquid when used on Twin Earth and when used on Earth, etc.) Contrary to a doctrine that has been with us since the seventeenth century, *meanings just aren't in the head.*

We have seen that possessing a concept is not a matter of possessing images (say, of trees—or even images, 'visual' or 'acoustic', of sentences, or whole discourses, for that matter) since one could possess any system of images you please and not possess the *ability* to use the sentences in situationally appropriate ways (considering both linguistic factors—what has been said before—and non-linguistic factors as determining 'situational appropriateness'). A man may have all the images you please, and still be completely at a loss when one says to him 'point to a tree', even if a lot of trees are present. He may even have the image of what he is supposed to do, and still not know what he is supposed to do. For the image, if not accompanied by the ability to act in a certain way, is just a *picture*, and acting in accordance with a picture is itself an ability that one may or may not have. (The man might picture himself pointing to a tree, but just for the sake of contemplating something logically possible; himself pointing to a tree after someone has produced the—to him meaningless—sequence of sounds 'please point to a tree'.) He would still not know that he was supposed to point to a tree, and he would still not *understand* 'point to a tree'.

I have considered the ability to use certain sentences to be the criterion for possessing a full-blown concept, but this could easily be liberalized. We could allow symbolism consisting of elements which are not words in a natural language, for example, and we could allow such mental phenomena as images and other types of internal events. What is essential is that these should have the same complexity, ability to be combined with each other, etc., as sentences in a natural language. For, although a particular presentation—say, a blue flash—might serve a particular mathematician as the inner expression of the whole proof of the prime number theorem, still there would be no temptation to say this (and it would be false to say this) if that mathematician could not unpack his 'blue flash' into separate steps and logical connections. But, no matter what sort of inner phenomena we allow as possible *expressions* of thought, arguments exactly similar to the foregoing will show that it is not the phenomena themselves that constitute understanding, but rather the ability of the thinker to *employ* these phenomena, to produce the right phenomena in the right circumstances.

The foregoing is a very abbreviated version of Wittgenstein's argument in *Philosophical Investigations*. If it is correct, then the attempt to understand thought by what is called 'phenomenological' investigation is fundamentally misguided; for what the phenomenologists fail to see is that what they are describing is the inner *expression* of thought, but that the *understanding* of that expression—one's understanding of one's own thoughts—is not an *occurrence* but an *ability*. Our example of a man pretending to think in Japanese (and deceiving a Japanese telepath) already shows the futility of a phenomenological approach to the problem of *understanding*. For even if there is some introspectible quality which is present when and only when one *really* understands (this seems false on introspection, in fact), still that quality is only *correlated* with understanding, and it is still possible that the man fooling the Japanese telepath have that quality too and *still* not understand a word of Japanese.

On the other hand, consider the perfectly possible man who does not have any 'interior monologue' at all. He speaks perfectly good English, and if asked what his opinions are on a given subject, he will give them at length. But he never thinks (in words, images, etc.) when he is not speaking out loud; nor does anything 'go through his head', except that (of course) he hears his own voice speaking, and has the usual sense impressions from his surroundings, plus a general 'feeling

of understanding'. (Perhaps he is in the habit of talking to himself.) When he types a letter or goes to the store, etc., he is not having an internal 'stream of thought'; but his actions are intelligent and purposeful, and if anyone walks up and asks him 'What are you doing?' he will give perfectly coherent replies.

This man seems perfectly imaginable. No one would hesitate to say that he was conscious, disliked rock and roll (if he frequently expressed a strong aversion to rock and roll), etc., just because he did not think conscious thoughts except when speaking out loud.

What follows from all this is that (a) no set of mental events—images or more 'abstract' mental happenings and qualities—*constitutes* understanding; and (b) no set of mental events is *necessary* for understanding. In particular, *concepts cannot be identical with mental objects of any kind*. For, assuming that by a mental object we mean something introspectible, we have just seen that whatever it is, it may be absent in a man who does understand the appropriate word (and hence has the full-blown concept), and present in a man who does not have the concept at all.

Coming back now to our criticism of magical theories of reference (a topic which also concerned Wittgenstein), we see that, on the one hand, those 'mental objects' we *can* introspectively detect—words, images, feelings, etc.—do not intrinsically refer any more than the ant's picture does (and for the same reasons), while the attempts to postulate special mental objects, 'concepts', which *do* have a necessary connection with their referents, and which only trained phenomenologists can detect, commit a *logical* blunder; for concepts are (at least in part) *abilities* and not occurrences. The doctrine that there are mental presentations which necessarily refer to external things is not only bad natural science; it is also bad phenomenology and conceptual confusion.

Notes

1. In this [essay] the terms 'representation' and 'reference' always refer to a relation between a word (or other sort of sign, symbol, or representation) and something that actually exists (i.e., not just an 'object of thought'). There is a sense of 'refer' in which I can 'refer' to what does not exist; this is not the sense

in which 'refer' is used here. An older word for what I call 'representation' or 'reference' is *denotation*.

Secondly, I follow the custom of modern logicians and use 'exist' to mean 'exist in the past, present, or future'. Thus Winston Churchill 'exists', and we can 'refer to' or 'represent' Winston Churchill, even though he is no longer alive.

2. A. M. Turing, "Computing Machinery and Intelligence," *Mind* (1950), reprinted in A. R. Anderson (ed.), *Minds and Machines.*

3. If the Brains in a Vat will have causal connection with, say, trees *in the future*, then perhaps they can *now* refer to trees by the description 'the things I will refer to as "trees" at such-and-such a future time'. But we are to imagine a case in which the Brains in a Vat *never* get out of the vat, and hence *never* get into causal connection with trees, etc.

READING QUESTIONS

1. What are "magical theories of reference"? Why does Putnam believe that "thought words and mental pictures do not *intrinsically* represent what they are about"? What does the word 'intrinsically' mean in this context?

2. What exactly is the problem of skepticism with respect to the external world?

3. What is the Turing Test for Reference? What is the Imitation Game? Why does Putnam believe that "a machine which can do nothing *but* play the Imitation Game is *clearly* not referring any more than a record player is." What more is needed, then, to be able to refer?

4. Why does Putnam deny that the brains in the vat could "refer to or represent trees or anything external"? Why does Putnam believe that the brains in a vat could not "think or say that they are brains in a vat"?

5. Putnam writes, " 'We are brains in a vat' says something false (if it says anything). In short, if we are brains in a vat, then 'We are brains in a vat' is false. So it is (necessarily) false." Add the missing premises and formalize this argument. Do you believe that this argument is sound? Why or why not?

6. "The existence of a 'physically possible world' in which we are brains in a vat (and always were and will be) does not mean that we might really, actually, possibly be brains in a vat. What rules out this possibility is not physics but *philosophy*." Do you agree? Why or why not? How could philosophy rule such a thing out?

7. Putnam argues that "concepts are not mental presentations that intrinsically refer to external objects for the very decisive reason that they are not mental presentations at all." What is his argument for this conclusion?

SUGGESTIONS FOR FURTHER READING (HILARY PUTNAM)

Primary Sources and Collected Writings

(1971) *Philosophy of Logic.* New York: Harper & Row.

(1975) "The Meaning of Meaning." In *Language, Mind and Knowledge*, edited by K. Gunderson. Minneapolis, MN: University of Minnesota Press.

(1975) *Mathematics, Matter, and Method: Philosophical Papers*, Vol. 1. Cambridge: Cambridge University Press.

(1975) *Mind, Language, and Reality: Philosophical Papers*, Vol. 2. Cambridge: Cambridge University Press.

(1978) *Meaning and the Moral Sciences.* London: Routledge.

(1981) *Reason, Truth and History.* Cambridge: Cambridge University Press.

(1982) *Renewing Philosophy.* Cambridge, MA: Harvard University Press.

(1983) *Realism and Reason, Philosophical Papers*, Vol. 3. Cambridge: Cambridge University Press.

(1983) (and P. Benacerraf, eds.) *Philosophy of Mathematics: Selected Readings.* Cambridge: Cambridge University Press.

(1987) *The Many Faces of Realism.* La Salle, IL: Open Court.

(1988) *Representation and Reality.* Cambridge, MA: MIT Press.

(1990) *Realism with a Human Face*, edited by J. Conant. Cambridge, MA: Harvard University Press.

(1992) *Renewing Philosophy.* Cambridge, MA: Harvard University Press.

(1994) *Words and Life,* edited by J. Conant. Cambridge, MA: Harvard University Press.

(1995) *Pragmatism: An Open Question.* Oxford: Basil Blackwell.

Secondary Sources

Boolos, G., ed. (1990) *Meaning and Method: Essays in Honor of Hilary Putnam.* Cambridge: Cambridge University Press.

Clark, P., and B. Hale, eds. (1994) *Reading Putnam.* Oxford: Basil Blackwell.

Hill, C. S., ed. (1992) "The Philosophy of Hilary Putnam." *Philosophical Topics,* 20 (1).

McCormick, P. J., ed. (1996) *Starmaking: Realism, Anti-Realism and Irrealism.* Cambridge, MA: MIT Press.

McGinn, C. (1989) *Mental Content.* Oxford: Basil Blackwell.

Pessin, A., and S. Goldberg, eds. (1996) *The Twin Earth Chronicles: Twenty Years of Reflection on Hilary Putnam's "The Meaning of 'Meaning.'"* New York: Paragon House.

Salmon, N. U. (1981) *Reference and Essence.* Princeton, NJ: Princeton University Press.

Thomas Nagel (1937–) was born in Belgrade, Yugoslavia, but became a naturalized United States citizen in 1944. He earned his B.A. degree in 1958 from Cornell University, his B.Phil. from Corpus Christi College, Oxford, in 1960, and his Ph.D. from Harvard University in 1963. Some of the material in his first book, *The Possibility of Altruism* (1970), originated as parts of his B.Phil and Ph.D. theses.

Nagel's career in professional philosophy began at the University of California, Berkeley, in 1963. Nagel remained at Berkeley until 1966, at which time he moved on to a teaching position at Princeton University. In addition to *The Possibility of Altruism*, Nagel completed his second book, *Mortal Questions*, an influential and important collection of his essays, while on the faculty at Princeton. In 1980, he left Princeton for New York University, where he currently holds the rank of professor of philosophy and law and teaches in both the philosophy program at NYU and in the law school. He is a Fellow of the American Academy of Arts and Sciences and the British Academy, and was the John Locke Lecturer at Oxford University in 1990. He has also held brief visiting appointments throughout the world.

In the following essay drawn from his 1979 book, *Mortal Questions,* Nagel addresses "a problem that emerges in several areas of philosophy whose connection with one another is not obvious." The problem is that of the "opposition between subjective and objective points of view." He claims that the most difficult and irresolvable problems of ethics and metaphysics arise out of our capacity to simultaneously maintain both our own subjective point of view alongside a more objective or "scientific" conception of ourselves and of our place in the world as a whole. Rejecting reductionistic attempts at understanding the place of recalcitrant subjective facts and values, in the end he argues that we should "resist the voracity of the objective appetite, and stop assuming that understanding the world and our position in it can always be advanced by detaching from that position and subsuming whatever appears from there under a single more comprehensive conception."

Thomas Nagel

Subjective and Objective

There is a problem that emerges in several areas of philosophy whose connection with one another is not obvious. I believe that it can be given a general form, and

Thomas Nagel, "Subjective and Objective" from his *Mortal Questions,* Cambridge, Cambridge University Press, 1979. Reprinted with the permission of Cambridge University Press.

that some treatment of it is possible in abstraction from its particular instances—with results that can be applied to the instances eventually. This discussion is a preliminary sketch for what I intend to treat more thoroughly in the future.

The problem is one of opposition between subjective and objective points of view. There is a tendency to seek an objective account of everything before admitting its reality. But often what appears to be a more subjective point of view cannot be accounted for in this way. So either the objective conception of the world is incomplete, or the subjective involves illusions that should be rejected.

Instead of trying to define these terms at the outset, I shall begin with some examples, drawn from ethics and metaphysics. The parallels between them should emerge as I proceed.

Consider first a problem about the meaning of life. There is a way of considering human pursuits from within life, which allows justification of some activities in terms of others, but does not permit us to question the significance of the whole thing, unless we are asking, from within life, whether the allocation of energy or attention to different segments of it makes sense in virtue of their relative importance. This view comes under challenge from a position that regards life in detachment from specific or general human purposes. People, and oneself in particular, are perceived as having no significance, and absurd because they seem to accord their lives great importance in action, even though they can also appreciate a broader point of view from which they have no importance.

Each of the two points of view claims priority. The internal view asks, what is the importance for individual life of insignificance from an external point of view? Life is lived from inside, and issues of significance are significant only if they can be raised from inside. It therefore does not matter that from a point of view outside my life, my life does not matter.

The external view, on the other hand, comprehends within its scope of observation all the aims and commitments by reference to which internal significance is measured. It presents itself as the *right* way for the individual to look at the world and his place in it: the big picture. He develops this kind of detachment naturally, to counter the egocentric distortion of a purely internal

view, and to correct the parochialism engendered by the contingencies of his overspecific nature and circumstances. But it is not merely corrective. It claims a position of dominance, as the only complete conception of how things really are. This dominance is not imposed from outside, but derives from the intrinsic appeal of impersonality to individual reflection. Life seems absurd because it seems absurd to *oneself*, taking up a point of view that is both natural and appealing.

The second example to consider is the problem of free will. This problem arises initially in the form of a threat to free agency from the hypothesis that actions are determined by antecedent circumstances. There have been many attempts to analyze agency in terms compatible with determinism—by reference to intentions, motives, second-order volitions, capacities, absence of obstacles, or coercion. Real advances have been made in specifying necessary conditions of agency, but the possibility that these conditions are themselves determined seems still to present a threat to some element of the ordinary concept of action.[1] They may be necessary, but they do not seem sufficient.

The next step, however, is the discovery that free agency is not implied by the *absence* of determinism, even though it appears to be threatened by the presence of determinism. Uncaused acts are no more attributable to the agent than those caused by antecedent circumstances. One is therefore led to wonder what further factor, in addition to the absence of determinism, is required for free agency, and whether this further factor might not be sufficient for freedom by itself. The most difficult problem of free will is saying what the problem is, which seems to survive every attempt to specify sufficient conditions for free action.

The recent attempt to analyze action in terms of *agent* causation rather than event causation is instructive because it reveals the true source of discomfort with determinism.[2] The problem is that when one views an action as an event causally connected with other events, there is no room in the picture for someone's *doing* it. But it turns out that there is no room for someone's *doing* it if it is an event causally *un*connected with other events, either. Hence some philosophers have tried to capture this aspect by making an agent, rather than an event, the cause. I do not find the concept of agent causation intelligible, but I think I understand its motivation. While its positive content is obscure, its negative implications are clear. It removes action from the causal sequence of events by denying that it is caused by antecedent circumstances; and by substituting an agent as the cause, it avoids the alternative that action is something that just *happens.* It is a doomed attempt to capture the *doing* of the action in a new kind of causation.

But the problem is not that the idea of agency clashes with this or that particular conception of what happens in action, viewed externally as a type of event. It is not predictability that creates the problem, for I make many choices and do many things that are completely predictable. It is just that when I pick the shiny apple instead of the rotten one, it is *my doing*—and there is no room for this in an external account of the event, deterministic or not. The real problem stems from a clash between the view of action from inside and *any* view of it from outside. Any external view of an act as something that happens, with or without causal antecedents, seems to omit the doing of it.

Even if an action is described in terms of motives, reasons, abilities, absence of impediments, or coercion, this does not capture the agent's own idea of himself as its source. His actions appear to him different from other things that happen in the world, but not merely a different kind of happening, with different causes or none at all. They seem in some indescribable way not to *happen* at all (unless they are quite out of his control), though things happen when he does them. And if he sees others as agents too, their actions will seem to have the same quality. The tendency to express this conception of agency in terms of freedom from antecedent causes is a mistake, but an understandable one. When the act is viewed under the aspect of determination by antecedents, its status as an event becomes prominent. But as appears upon further investigation, no account of it as an event is satisfactory from the internal viewpoint of the agent doing it.

The connection of this problem with moral responsibility is that when we view actions, our own or others, merely as part of the general course of events, it seems impossible to attribute them to individuals in a way that makes sense of the attitudes we take toward someone we regard as the source of an action. Certain attitudes toward the agent, rather than just about him, lose

their footing. If an individual is destructive enough we may think it would be better if he did not exist; but if he is just a disastrous part of the world, blame directed at him or guilt he directs at himself make no sense, however causally or indeterministically complex his behavior and motives are.

The true nature of the third problem I want to mention—that of personal identity—is also hidden in many discussions. The problem is usually presented as a search for the conditions that must obtain if two experiential episodes separated in time are to belong to a single person. Various types of continuity and similarity—physical, mental, causal, emotional—have been considered and they all seem to leave an aspect of personal identity unaccounted for. Given that any proposed set of conditions is met, there still seems to be a further question as to whether the same *subject* or *self* is preserved under these conditions. This further question can be raised by imagining that you have the first of two experiences and asking about the other (which bears the candidate relation to it), "Yes, but will it be *mine?*" As with free will, the real problem seems to be to identify the problem that always remains no matter how ingenious a solution has been proposed.

It may seem that this further question involves the assumption of a metaphysical ego which preserves personal identity. But this would be a mistake, for the ego, if it is a continuing individual with its own identity over time, would be just one more thing about which the same problem could be raised (will *that* ego still be me?). If on the other hand its *only* identity over time is that of still being me, then it cannot be the individual whose persistence *preserves* personal identity. For its identity would then simply consist in the fact that experiences had by it were all mine; and that cannot explain what makes them all mine.

The problem seems unreal when persons are viewed as beings in the world, whether physical or mental. They persist and change through time, and those are the terms in which they must be described. But as with the problem of free will, the persistent dissatisfaction with candidate analyses of this form derives from a submerged internal aspect of the problem which is left untouched by all external treatments. From the point of view of the person himself, the question of his identity or nonidentity with someone undergoing some experience in the future appears to have a content that cannot be exhausted by any account in terms of memory, similarity of character, or physical continuity. Such analyses are never sufficient, and from this point of view they may appear not even to supply necessary conditions for identity.

When someone poses inwardly the question whether a past or future experience was or will be *his,* he has the sensation of picking out something whose identity over time is well defined, just by concentrating on his present experience and specifying the temporal extension of *its subject.* The concept of the self is a psychological one, and it is characteristic of such concepts to give rise to the philosophical idea that their subjective essence, expressed most clearly in first-person applications, is detachable from objective accompaniments and even to a considerable extent from necessary connection with other psychological phenomena. (Another example: the conviction that it is a perfectly well-defined but in principle unanswerable question whether sugar tastes like *this* to other people.) This may be an illusion. It may have no sense to speak of "the same self as this one" in complete detachment from all external conditions. But it is still the internal idea of the self that gives rise to the problem of personal identity. Any attempt to conceive persons completely as a kind of thing in the world persisting through time will come up against this obstacle. The self that appears to the subjects seems to disappear under external analysis.

My fourth example is the mind-body problem. A particularly difficult aspect of that problem comes from the subjective character of experience. So long as mental states are looked at objectively, in their causal relations to stimuli and behavior, no special issues arise which do not arise about the physical analysis of other natural phenomena. Even problems of intentionality may seem to be soluble if one puts aside their subjective aspect, for then one may be able to describe certain kinds of computers as intentional systems. What seems impossible is to include in a physical conception of the world the facts about what mental states are like for the creature having them. The creature and his states seem to belong to a world that can be viewed impersonally and externally. Yet subjective aspects of the mental can be apprehended only from the point of view of the creature itself (perhaps taken up by someone else),

whereas what is physical is simply there, and can be externally apprehended from more than one point of view. Is there any way of including mental phenomena in the world as well, as part of what is simply *there?*

Here too the idea of impersonally comprehensible reality asserts its claim to dominance. We are not faced only with the problem of the relation between mind and body, or the inclusion of the mental in the physical world. The broader issues between personal and impersonal, or subjective and objective, arise also for a dualist theory of mind. The question of how one can include in the objective world a mental substance having subjective properties is as acute as the question how a physical substance can have subjective properties.

The physical is an ideal representative for the objective in general; therefore much obscurity has been shed on the problem by faulty analogies between the mental-physical relation and relations between the physical and other objective aspects of reality. As determinism is a substitute for externality or objectivity in posing the problem of free will, so the physical is a substitute for objectivity in posing the mind-body problem. All the disputes over causal role, theoretical identification, and functional realization, while of interest in themselves, fail to give expression to the central issue that makes the mind-body problem so hard. And as with free will and personal identity, the internal element remains, even if ignored, as the true source of persistent dissatisfaction with all physical or other external theories of the mind. At the same time, the idea that persons (along with everything about them) must be parts of objective reality continues to exert its powerful appeal. Objectivity is naturally linked with reality; it is easy to feel that anything has to be located in the objective world in order to qualify as real, and that it must have as its real nature some character which, whether physical or not, can be regarded impersonally and externally.

The final example I want to discuss comes from ethics, and concerns the difference between consequentialist and more agent-centered views of right and wrong. A familiar type of objection to utilitarianism and other consequentialist views charges them with unjustifiably making questions about what to do subordinate to questions about what would be best overall. Such criticisms assert that an ethical theory should leave some room for each individual to pursue his own life without having to consider at every point how he is serving more comprehensive goals; or else they urge the need for certain restrictions or requirements on action that are not justified by their contribution to the general good. In other words, both what is permitted and what is required of a person can sometimes deviate from what would be best. I group these two rather different exceptions to consequentialism together because, while they can also be opposed to each other, they deviate from the consequentialist viewpoint in the same direction. This is clear in the case of permission to pursue one's own life, less clear in the case of general requirements or restrictions on action, whatever the goal.

Utilitarianism, or any purely consequentialist view, is very demanding. It requires you to justify the pursuit of your own personal life and interests only as components of the general good, and does not permit reasons for action to *end* with a reference to what you want or are devoted to. Those considerations are completely encompassed by an impersonal point of view which accords you no special position, unless it can be impersonally justified. Resistance comes, naturally enough, from the point of view of the individual, who may be willing to accord impersonal considerations some weight, but who is also powerfully motivated by the independent claims of his own life—of the view from where he is in the world. But this does not remain a conflict between impersonal values and mere individual interest, because the resistance can be generalized. Someone who regards consequentialist requirements as unacceptable because of their claim to dominance over his own point of view will naturally extend this objection to others. He will gravitate toward a *general* exception to consequentialism in favor of the personal viewpoint, and this will constitute an alternative ethic, rather than merely a resistance to ethics. Such an ethic need be no less universal than utilitarianism, but it will be subjective in a way that consequentialist positions are not. Each person will be permitted, within limits, to concentrate on the pursuit of *his* life, and there will not be a single, objectively describable end by reference to which everyone's actions must be justified.

In this sense the deontological requirements that resist a consequentialist account are also subjective. Constraints against murder, lying, betrayal, assault, or coercion, though intended to apply universally, oppose the agent's specific relations to other people to the conception of a single end that everyone should exclusively promote. They are agent-centered, but in a different way. The real source of these restrictions, unlike that of the agent-centered permissions, is not the agent but the potential victim whose rights are protected. But the wrongness of violating those rights implies a constraint on each person against violating them, rather than a requirement that he try to minimize their overall violation (even if this means committing a few himself). Deontological requirements are agent-centered because they instruct each person to determine the rightness or wrongness of his acts solely from the point of view of his position in the world and his direct relation to others. The very idea that the basic moral concepts are right and wrong rather than good and bad entails that the character of one's actions rather than the world as a whole must be one's primary concern.[3]

If there is a difference in point of view between the two types of exception to consequentialism, it is that the first derives simply from the standpoint of the individual agent, whereas the second emerges when he considers in a certain way his own point of view together with those of the persons to whom he is directly related in action. Deontological constraints are intermediate between purely individual motives and completely impersonal values.

There are familiar disputes about whether utilitarianism really does have the consequences attributed to it by anti-consequentialist critics—aspects of the wider dispute between radical and moderate interpretations of utilitarianism. Likewise there are disputes about the formulation of alternative views: how absolutist they are, whether they should be stated in terms of individual rights, or liberty, or self-realization, or interpersonal commitment. But the essence of the conflict is clearer than the exact nature of the alternatives. The issue is how the individual position of the agent should enter into a decision about what he should or may do.

Obviously it cannot fail to enter in certain ways. Even on a consequentialist view, what one should do will depend on what one is in a position to do, and on the relative desirability of the possible outcomes. Nevertheless, the consequentialist judgment that one should do something is essentially the judgment that it would be best if one did it—that it ought to *happen*. The right thing to do is to turn oneself as far as possible into an instrument for the realization of what is best *sub specie aeternitatis*.

Agent-centered views, on the other hand, determine what is right, wrong, and permissible partly at least on the basis of the individual's life, his role in the world, and his relation with others. Agent-centered morality gives primacy to the question of what to do, a question asked by the individual agent, and does not assume that the only way to answer it is to say what it would be best if he did *sub specie aeternitatis*. It may also hold that the place for considerations of what would be best, in a decision about what to do, is not obvious and must be established by analysis of agent-centered choice and its grounds.

The real issue, therefore, is the relative priority, in regard to action, of two ways of looking at the world. On the one hand there is the position that one's decisions should be tested ultimately from an external point of view, to which one appears as just one person among others. The question then becomes, "What would be best? Which of the acts within my power would do the most good, considering matters from out here, impersonally?" This point of view claims priority by virtue of greater comprehensiveness. The agent's situation is supposedly given its due in a larger perspective.[4]

On the other hand there is the position that since an agent lives his life from where he is, even if he manages to achieve an impersonal view of his situation, whatever insights result from this detachment need to be made part of a personal view before they can influence decision and action. The pursuit of what seems impersonally best may be an important aspect of individual life, but its place in that life must be determined from a personal standpoint, because life is always the life of a particular person, and cannot be lived *sub specie aeternitatis*.[5]

The opposition looks like a stalemate because each of the points of view claims dominance over the other, by virtue of inclusion. The impersonal standpoint takes in a world that includes the individual and his personal views. The personal standpoint, on the other hand, regards the deliverances of impersonal reflection as only a part of any individual's total view of the world.

This list of problems could be extended. Obviously the difficulty of reconciling subjective and objective

points of view arises with regard to space and time, death, and throughout the theory of knowledge. Perhaps the problem takes its purest form in a sense of incredulity that one should be anyone in particular, a specific individual of a particular species existing at a particular time and place in the universe. There is a pattern in these questions which justifies us in locating a common philosophical difficulty behind all of them, concealed by their diversity, and sometimes ignored in their treatment with unfortunate results. In what follows I shall discuss some strategies for dealing with the problem. But first I shall discuss the parallels among its different forms.

Although I shall speak of the subjective viewpoint and the objective viewpoint, this is just shorthand, for there are not two such viewpoints, nor even two such categories into which more particular viewpoints can be placed. Instead, there is a polarity. At one end is the point of view of a particular individual, having a specific constitution, situation, and relation to the rest of the world. From here the direction of movement toward greater objectivity involves, first, abstraction from the individual's specific spatial, temporal, and personal position in the world, then from the features that distinguish him from other humans, then gradually from the forms of perception and action characteristic of humans, and away from the narrow range of a human scale in space, time, and quantity, toward a conception of the world which as far as possible is not the view from anywhere within it. There is probably no endpoint to this process, but its aim is to regard the world as centerless, with the viewer as just one of its contents.

The distinction between subjective and objective is relative. A general human point of view is more objective than the view from where you happen to be, but less objective than the viewpoint of physical science. The opposition between subjective and objective can arise at any place on the spectrum where one point of view claims dominance over another, more subjective one, and that claim is resisted. In the dispute over consequentialism in ethics, it appears in the clash between internal and external views of human life, both fully admitting the importance of human concerns and ends. In the mind-body problem, it appears in the clash between an internal human view of human beings and the external view of physical theory. In the problem of personal identity, it appears in the clash between the point of view of a particular individual toward his own past and future and the view that others may take of him as a continuing conscious being, characterized by bodily and psychological continuities.

Another point I wish to emphasize is this. What is more subjective is not necessarily more private. In general it is intersubjectively available. I assume that the subjective ideas of experience of action, and of the self are in some sense public or common property. That is why the problems of mind and body, free will, and personal identity are not just problems about one's own case.

I cannot here take up Wittgenstein's arguments about the publicity of rules and therefore of concepts.[6] I believe he is right, and that even our most subjective phenomenological concepts are public in a sense. But they are public in a very different way from that in which concepts used to describe the physical world are public. The coordination of the points of view of different individuals toward their own experiences is totally different from the coordination of their points of view toward the external world. Nothing in the former case corresponds to different individuals sharing a point of view toward the same object. Wittgenstein's position on sensations is that they just *are* appearances, so their properties are not the properties of objects which appear to whoever has them, and similarity in their properties is not similarity in the properties of such objects. Rather it is similarity in appearances. That is a similarity between irreducibly subjective phenomena. Only if we acknowledge their subjectivity—the fact that each is essentially an appearance *to* someone—can we understand the special way in which sensations are publicly comparable and not private. The private object or sense datum view is an instance of the false objectification of what is essentially subjective.

Since a kind of intersubjective agreement characterizes even what is most subjective, the transition to a more objective viewpoint is not accomplished merely through intersubjective agreement. Nor does it proceed by an increase of imaginative scope that provides access to many subjective points of view other than one's own. Its essential character, in all the examples cited, is externality of detachment. The attempt is made to view the world not from a place within it, or from the vantage point of a special type of life and awareness, but from nowhere in particular and no form of life in par-

ticular at all. The object is to discount for the features of our prereflective outlook that make things appear to us as they do, and thereby to reach an understanding of things as they really are. We flee the subjective under the pressure of an assumption that everything must be something not to any point of view, but in itself. To grasp this by detaching more and more from our own point of view is the unreachable ideal at which the pursuit of objectivity aims.

Some version of this polarity can be found in relation to most subject matter—ethical, epistemological, metaphysical. The relative subjectivity or objectivity of different appearances is a matter of degree, but the same pressures toward a more external viewpoint are to be found everywhere. It is recognized that one's own point of view can be distorted as a result of contingencies of one's makeup or situation. To compensate for these distortions it is necessary either to reduce dependence on those forms of perception or judgment in which they are most marked, or to analyze the mechanisms of distortion and discount for them explicitly. The subjective comes to be defined by contrast with this development of objectivity.

Problems arise because the same individual is the occupant of both viewpoints. In trying to understand and discount for the distorting influences of his specific nature he must rely on certain influence. He examines himself and his interactions with the world, using a specially selected part of himself for the purpose. That part may subsequently be scrutinized in turn, and there may be no end to the process. But obviously the selection of trustworthy subparts presents a problem.

The selection of what to rely on is based partly on the idea that the less an appearance depends on contingencies of this particular self, the more it is capable of being arrived at from a variety of points of view. If there is a way things really are, which explains their diverse appearances to differently constituted and situated observers, then it is most accurately apprehended by methods not specific to particular types of observers. That is why scientific measurement interposes between us and the world instruments whose interactions with the world are of a kind that could be detected by a creature not sharing the human senses. Objectivity requires not only a departure from one's individual viewpoint, but also, so far as possible, departure from a specifically human or even mammalian viewpoint. The idea is that if one can still maintain some view when one relies less and less on what is specific to one's position or form, it will be truer to reality. The respects in which the results of various viewpoints are incompatible with each other represent distortions of the way matters really are. And if there is such a thing as the correct view, it is certainly not going to be the unedited view from wherever one happens to be in the world. It must be a view that includes oneself, with all one's contingencies of constitution and circumstance, among the things viewed, without according it any special centrality. And it must accord the same detached treatment to the type of which one is an instance. The true view of things can no more be the way they naturally appear to human beings than the way they look from here.

The pursuit of objectivity therefore involves a transcendence of the self, in two ways: a transcendence of particularity and a transcendence of one's type. It must be distinguished from a different kind of transcendence by which one enters imaginatively into other subjective points of view, and tries to see how things appear from other specific standpoints. Objective transcendence aims at a representation of what is external to each specific point of view: what is there or what is of value in itself, rather than *for* anyone. Though it employs whatever point of view is available as the representational vehicle—humans typically use visual diagrams and notation in thinking about physics—the aim is to represent how things are, not *for* anyone or any type of being. And the enterprise assumes that what is represented is detachable from the mode of representation, so that the same laws of physics could be represented by creatures sharing none of our sensory modalities.

While there are problems about how to achieve this kind of transcendence, it is certainly one of the important ways of advancing our understanding. We cannot help wanting to extend it farther and farther, and to bring more and more of life and the world within its range. But the consistent pursuit of greater objectivity runs into trouble, and gives rise to the philosophical problems I have described, when it is turned back on the self, as it must be to pursue its comprehensive ambitions.

The trouble occurs when the objective view encounters something, revealed subjectively, that it cannot accommodate. Its claims to comprehensiveness will then be threatened. The indigestible lump may be either a fact or a value. The problems of personal identity and mind-body arise because certain subjectively apparent facts about the self seem to vanish as one ascends to a more objective standpoint. The problems about consequentialism and the meaning of life arise from a corresponding disappearance of certain personal values with the ascent to a more and more detached and impersonal point of view. The problem of free will combines both effects.

In either case it appears that something must give way, for two natural and necessary ways of thinking lead to a collision and cannot without adjustment be accommodated in a single view of how things are. But even allowing for adjustments, the options seem to be limited and unpalatable. If one wishes to insist that everything real must be brought under an objective description there seem to be three courses available with respect to any recalcitrant subjective aspect: reduction, elimination, and annexation.

First, reduction: one may try to save the appearances as much as possible, by accommodating them under an objective interpretation. Thus one might offer a consequentialist account of rights or special obligations or the allowable forms of self-interest. Or one might analyze experience in terms of behavioral criteria, or agency in terms of certain kinds of causes, or personal identity in terms of physical or mental continuity.

Secondly, elimination: if no reduction seems plausible one may dismiss the deliverance of a subjective viewpoint as an illusion, perhaps offering an explanation of how it arises. For example, one might say there is no such thing as pure personal identity, or free agency. One might even say that there is no such thing as the subjective character of experience, that experiences can be adequately characterized by their causal roles and do not possess phenomenological properties in addition. And one might dismiss deontological requirements and other nonconsequentialist ethical intuitions as superstitious, selfish, or rule-bound.

Thirdly, annexation: if one fails to reduce the subjective to familiar objective terms, and is unwilling to deny its reality outright, one may invent a new element of objective reality especially for the purpose of including this recalcitrant element: the will, the ego, the soul, or perhaps the command of God. Such metaphysical inventions, however, can seem to serve the purpose for which they were designed only because their obscurity prevents it from being obvious that the same problems of subjectivity will arise with regard to them, if they really belong to objective reality. It is no good trying to amplify our conception of the objective world to include whatever is revealed subjectively, for the problem is not that something has been left out. An objective conception of space and time cannot be faulted for *leaving out* the identification of the here and now. Any conception that included it would not be objective, and any objective realization would fail to capture it. This applies also to the prediction that mental phenomena will eventually come to be counted as physical, once we understand them systematically—even if they are not reduced to terms already admitted as physical.[7] We cannot solve these problems by simply annexing to the objective (or even physical) world everything that is not already in it.

The only alternative to these unsatisfactory moves is to resist the voracity of the objective appetite, and stop assuming that understanding of the world and our position in it can always be advanced by detaching from that position and subsuming whatever appears from there under a single more comprehensive conception. Perhaps the best or truest view is not obtained by transcending oneself as far as possible. Perhaps reality should not be identified with objective reality. The problem is to explain why objectivity is inadequate as a comprehensive ideal of understanding, without faulting it for not including subjective elements it could not possibly include. There is always room for improvement in our objective understanding of things, naturally, but the proposal I am considering is not that the objective picture is incomplete, but rather that it is, in essence, only partial.

This proposal is harder to accept than it may seem, for it implies that there is no single way things are in themselves. Even if one admits to the world facts or values involving a particular point of view, it is tempting to assume that something's being so from a particular point of view must consist in something else's being the case from no point of view. (The something else may of course involve some objective relations.) Those who believe there are no objective values may try to analyze the existence of subjective values in terms of objective facts about the individuals for whom they are values. Others have analyzed apparently subjective val-

ues in terms of objective ones.[8] And the philosophy of mind is full of refusals to admit that there may be no objective fact that is what *really* obtains when something looks red to someone.

The idealist tradition, including contemporary phenomenology, has of course admitted subjective points of view as basic, and has gone to the opposite length of denying an irreducible objective reality. I have concentrated on the tendency to resolve the conflict by objectifying everything because it has dominated recent analytic philosophy in spite of Wittgenstein. But I find the idealist solution unacceptable for the same reason: objective reality cannot be analyzed or shut out of existence any more than subjective reality can. Even if not everything is something from no point of view, some things are.

The deep source of both idealism and its objectifying opposite is the same: a conviction that a single world cannot contain both irreducible points of view and irreducible objective reality—that one of them must be what there *really* is and the other somehow reducible to or dependent on it. This is a very powerful idea. To deny it is in a sense to deny that there is a single world.

We must admit that the move toward objectivity reveals what things are like in themselves as opposed to how they appear; not just how they appear to one, relatively austere point of view as opposed to others. Therefore when the objective gaze is turned on human beings and other experiencing creatures, who are undeniably parts of the world, it can reveal only what they are like in themselves. And if the way things are for these subjects is not part of the way things are in themselves, an objective account, whatever it shows, will omit something. So reality is not just objective reality, and the pursuit of objectivity is not an equally effective method of reaching the truth about everything.

It is conceivable that everything has *some* objective properties. I do not know whether it makes sense to attribute physical and phenomenological properties to the same thing, but perhaps even experiences are events that can be in part described objectively, perhaps physically. But the properties that make them experiences exist only from the point of view of the types of beings who have them.

Since we are not the only creatures in the universe, a general conception of reality would require a general conception of experience which admitted our own subjective viewpoint as a special case. This is completely beyond us and will probably remain so for as long as human beings continue to exist.

It makes objectivity attractive by comparison. We can pursue a unified if very etiolated conception of reality by detaching progressively from our own point of view. We just have to keep in mind what we are leaving behind, and not be fooled into thinking we have made it disappear. This is particularly important in connection with philosophical problems about free will, personal identity, agent-centered morality, or mind and body, which cannot be dealt with in detachment from the subjective point of view on which they depend for their existence.

The power of the impulse to transcend oneself and one's species is so great, and its rewards so substantial, that it is not likely to be seriously baffled by the admission that objectivity has its limits. While I am arguing for a form of romanticism, I am not an extremist. The task of accepting the polarity without allowing either of its terms to swallow the other should be a creative one. It is the aim of eventual unification that I think is misplaced, both in our thoughts about how to live and in our conception of what there is. The coexistence of conflicting points of view, varying in detachment from the contingent self, is not just a practically necessary illusion but an irreducible fact of life.

Notes

1. The literature on this subject is enormous. Three of the best recent articles are P. F. Strawson, "Freedom and Resentment," *Proceedings of the British Academy (1962)*; Harry G. Frankfurt, "Freedom of the Will and the Concept of a Person," *Journal of Philosophy* (January 14, 1971), 63:5–20; Gary Watson, "Free Agency," *Journal of Philosophy* (April 24, 1975), 62:209–220.

2. Roderick M. Chisholm, "Freedom and Action," in Keith Lehrer, ed., *Freedom and Determinism* (New York: Random House, 1966).

3. A moral theory of this type is developed by Charles Fried in *Right and Wrong* (Cambridge: Harvard University Press, 1978). An intermediate view has been put forward by Samuel Scheffler, in "Agents and Outcomes," Ph.D. dissertation, Princeton University, 1977: he defends agent-centered permissions but rejects agent-centered requirements as having no intelligible basis.

4. In Thomas Nagel, *The Possibility of Altruism* (Oxford: Oxford University Press, 1970), I defended a version of this position.

5. This position is persuasively presented by Bernard Williams in "A Critique of Utilitarianism," in J. J. C. Smart and Bernard Williams, *Utilitarianism: For and Against* (Cambridge: Cambridge University Press, 1973). See also Bernard Williams, "Persons, Character, and Morality," in Amelia Rorty, ed., *The Identities of Persons* (Berkeley: University of California Press, 1976), where he presses the claims not only of the view from within one's own life but of the view from the present time. This tendency of a subjective viewpoint to shrink into the present moment has been noted by Derek Parfit in his skeptical work on prudence (not yet published).

6. Ludwig Wittgenstein, *Philosophical Investigations* (Oxford: Blackwell, 1953).

7. See Noam Chomsky, *Language and Mind* (New York: Harcourt, Brace & World, 1968), pp. 83–84.

8. For example, G. E. More in *Principia Ethica* (Cambridge: Cambridge University Press, 1903), p. 99.

READING QUESTIONS

1. Nagel writes that "there is a tendency to seek an objective account of everything before admitting its reality." Do you agree that this so? Why or why not?

2. According to Nagel, the problem of the meaning of life, the problem of the freedom of the will, the problem of personal identity, the mind-body problem, and the problem of reconciling the demands of consequentialist and nonconsequentialist conceptions of right and wrong, are all characteristically ones that develop because we can find ourselves caught in the clash between the demands of our subjective and objective points of view. Catalog the ways in which Nagel believes the demands of the subjective and the objective conflict in each of these cases. Do you agree with his diagnoses?

3. In general, what are some of the characteristic differences to be found in the "polarity" of the subjective and the objective points of view, as Nagel

describes them? In answering this question, consider specifically Nagel's remark that "the pursuit of objectivity therefore involves a transcendence of the self, in two ways: a transcendence of particularity and a transcendence of one's type." What does he mean by this?

4. Nagel writes, "if one wishes to insist that everything real must be brought under an objective description there seem to be three courses available with respect to any recalcitrant subjective aspect: reduction, elimination, and annexation." Briefly characterize these three strategies. In what ways are they effective or ineffective in bringing subjective aspects of the world under objective description?

5. Nagel suggests that "perhaps the best or truest view is not obtained by transcending oneself as far as possible. Perhaps reality should not be identified with objective reality." On the contrary, he proposes that "the coexistence of conflicting points of view, varying in detachment from the contingent self, is not just a practically necessary illusion but an irreducible fact of life." Do you agree with this? Why or why not? How should we characterize reality if we are prepared to not identify it outright with "objective reality"?

SUGGESTIONS FOR FURTHER READING (THOMAS NAGEL)

Primary Sources and Collected Writings

(1970) *The Possibility of Altruism.* Princeton, NJ: Princeton University Press, 1978.

(1979) *Moral Questions.* Cambridge: Cambridge University Press.

(1980) "The Limits of Objectivity." In *The Tanner Lectures on Human Values,* Vol. 1, edited by S. McMurrin. Salt Lake City, UT: Utah University Press.

(1986) *The View from Nowhere.* Oxford: Oxford University Press.

(1987) *What Does It All Mean? A Very Short Introduction to Philosophy.* Oxford: Oxford University Press.

(1991) *Equality and Partiality.* Princeton University Press.

(1995) *Other Minds: Critical Essays, 1969–1994.* Oxford: Oxford University Press.

(1997) *The Last Word.* Oxford: Oxford University Press.

Secondary Sources

Darwall, S. (1987) "The View from Nowhere." *Ethics* 98: 137–57.

Lycan, W. (1987) *Consciousness.* Cambridge, MA: MIT Press.

McGinn, C. (1987) "The View from Nowhere." *Mind* 96: 263–72.

Peacocke, C. (1989) "No Resting Place: A Critical Notice of *The View from Nowhere* by Thomas Nagel." *Philosophical Review* 98: 65–82.

Robins, M. H. (1988) "The Objectivity of Agent-Relative Values." In *Inquiries into Values,* edited by S. H. Lee. Lewiston, NY: Edwin Mullen Press.

RICHARD M. (R. M.) HARE

A Moral Argument

R. M. Hare (1919–) was born in Backwell, England, and was educated at Balliol College, University of Oxford. During the Second World War, Hare served as a lieutenant in the Royal Artillery and in the Indian Mountain Artillery. After the war, he returned to education and accepted a position as a Fellow of Balliol College and as a tutor of philosophy. He held this position until 1966, when he became White's Professor of Moral Philosophy and a Fellow of Corpus Christi College at Oxford. Hare left Oxford in 1983 to accept a position as graduate research professor at the University of Florida in Gainesville, Florida. In addition to his academic appointments, Hare is an honorary foreign member of the American Academy of Arts and Sciences and a Fellow of the British Academy.

During his tenure at Balliol, Hare published his first book, *The Language of Morals* (1952), which has become one of the most important and influential works in moral philosophy in the twentieth century. In this work, Hare attempts to combine what he believes is correct in emotivistic metaethics, namely, the sense that moral propositions are not descriptions, but rather serve some other function in language, with a rejection of the doctrine (found in, for example, Stevenson) that moral propositions serve simply to influence the attitudes and behavior of others. Hare's position, on the contrary, is that the propositions of ethics are attempts to tell people what to do or to command them. Furthermore, Hare believes that his theory is superior to traditional emotivistic accounts of ethics in that it provides a basis for thinking that judgments of ethics, though not descriptive, are nevertheless capable of being more or less rational.

In his subsequent writings, Hare has developed and refined his general moral theory, working to show that moral judgments are both universal in form (i.e., have the form of a universal principle applying to all persons similarly situated) and prescriptive or imperative (i.e., that the sincere acceptance of a moral judgment commits the believer to act on the basis of it whenever it applies to his or her actions). His view, therefore, has come to be called *universal prescriptivism.* Hare's position in metaethics has, he believes, implications in first-order moral theory as well, and in subsequent work he has also worked to articulate a defensible form of utilitarianism, which is consistent with this second-order conception of morality.

In the following chapter from his 1963 book, *Freedom and Reason,* Hare briefly discusses his conception of moral judgments as universal prescriptions and outlines a corresponding theory of moral reasoning. He considers a number of possible replies that an opponent to his view might make in an effort to see how his theory of moral reasoning holds up under various attacks.

1. Historically, one of the chief incentives to the study of ethics has been the hope that its findings might be of help to those faced with difficult moral problems. That this is still a principal incentive for many people is shown by the fact that modern philosophers are often reproached for failing to make ethics relevant to morals.[1] This is because one of the main tenets of many

recent moral philosophers has been that the most popular method by which it was sought to bring ethics to bear on moral problems was not feasible—namely the method followed by the group of theories loosely known as 'naturalist'.

The method of naturalism is so to characterize the *meanings* of the key moral terms that, given certain factual premises, not themselves moral judgments, moral conclusions can be deduced from them. If this could be done, it was thought that it would be of great assistance to us in making moral decisions; we should only have to find out the non-moral facts, and the moral conclusion as to what we ought to do would follow. Those who say that it cannot be done leave themselves the task of giving an alternative account of moral reasoning.

Naturalism seeks to make the findings of ethics *relevant* to moral decisions by making the former not morally *neutral.* It is a very natural assumption that if a statement of ethics is relevant to morals, then it cannot be neutral as between different moral judgments; and naturalism is a tempting view for those who make this assumption. Naturalistic definitions are not morally neutral, because with their aid we could show that statements of non-moral facts *entailed* moral conclusions. And some have thought that unless such an entailment can be shown to hold, the moral philosopher has not made moral reasoning possible.

One way of escaping this conclusion is to say that the relation between the non-moral premises and the non-moral conclusion is not one of entailment, but that some other logical relation, peculiar to morals, justifies the inference. . . . Since I have argued elsewhere against this approach, I shall not discuss it here. Its advocates have, however, hit upon an important insight: that moral reasoning does not necessarily proceed by way of *deduction* of moral conclusions from non-moral premises. Their further suggestion, that therefore it makes this transition by means of some other, peculiar, non-deductive kind of inference, is not the only possibility. It may be that moral reasoning is not, typically, any kind of 'straight-line' or 'linear' reasoning from premises to conclusion.

2. A parallel from the philosophy of science will perhaps make this point clear. It is natural to suppose that what the scientist does is to reason from premises, which are the data of observation, to conclusions, which are his 'scientific laws', by means of a special sort of inference called 'inductive'. Against this view, Professor Popper has forcibly argued that in science there are no inferences other than deductive; the typical procedure of scientists is to propound hypotheses, and then look for ways of testing them—i.e., experiments which, if they are false, will show them to be so. A hypothesis which, try as we may, we fail to falsify, we accept provisionally, though ready to abandon it if, after all, further experiment refutes it; and of those that are so accepted we rate highest the ones which say most, and which would, therefore, be most likely to have been falsified if they were false. The only inferences which occur in this process are deductive ones, from the *truth* of certain observations to the falsity of a hypothesis. There is no reasoning which proceeds from the data of observation to the *truth* of a hypothesis. Scientific inquiry is rather a kind of *exploration*, or looking for hypotheses which will stand up to the test of experiment.[2]

We must ask whether moral reasoning exhibits any similar features. I want to suggest that it too is a kind of exploration, and not a kind of linear inference, and that the only inferences which take place in it are deductive. What we are doing in moral reasoning is to look for moral judgments and moral principles which, when we have considered their logical consequences and the facts of the case, we can still accept. As we shall see, this approach to the problem enables us to reject the assumption, which seemed so natural, that ethics cannot be relevant to moral decisions without ceasing to be neutral. This is because we are not going to demand any inferences in our reasoning other than deductive ones, and because none of these deductive inferences rely for their validity upon naturalistic definitions of moral terms.

Two further parallels may help to make clear the sense in which ethics is morally neutral. In the kind of scientific reasoning just described, mathematics plays a major part, for many of the deductive inferences that occur are mathematical in character. So we are bound to admit that mathematics is relevant to scientific inquiry. Nevertheless, it is also neutral, in the sense that no discoveries about matters of physical fact can be made with the aid of mathematics alone, and that no mathematical inference can have a conclusion which says more, in the way of prediction of observations, than its premises implicitly do.

An even simpler parallel is provided by the rules of games. The rules of a game are neutral as between the players, in the sense that they do not, by themselves, determine which player is going to win. In order to decide who wins, the players have to play the game in accordance with the rules, which involves their making, themselves, a great many individual decisions. On the other hand, the 'neutrality' of the rules of a game does not turn it into a game of chance, in which the bad player is as likely to win as the good.

Ethical theory, which determines the meanings and functions of the moral words, and thus the 'rules' of the moral 'game', provides only a clarification of the conceptual framework within which moral reasoning takes place; it is therefore, in the required sense, neutral as between different moral opinions. But it is highly relevant to moral reasoning because, as with the rules of a game, there could be no such thing as moral reasoning without this framework, and the framework dictates the form of the reasoning. It follows that naturalism is not the only way of providing for the possibility of moral reasoning; and this may, perhaps, induce those who have espoused naturalism as a way of making moral thought a rational activity to consider other possibilities.

The rules of moral reasoning are, basically, two, corresponding to the two features of moral judgments which I argued for in the first half of this book, prescriptivity and universalizability.[3] When we are trying, in a concrete case, to decide what we ought to do, what we are looking for (as I have already said) is an action to which we can commit ourselves (prescriptivity) but which we are at the same time prepared to accept as exemplifying a principle of action to be prescribed for others in like circumstances (universalizability). If, when we consider some proposed action, we find that, when universalized, it yields prescriptions which we cannot accept, we reject this action as a solution to our moral problem—if we cannot universalize the prescription, it cannot become an 'ought'.

It is to be noticed that, troublesome as was the problem of moral weakness when we were dealing theoretically with the logical character of the moral concepts, it cannot trouble us here.[4] For if a person is going to reason seriously at all about a moral question, he has to presuppose that the moral concepts are going, in his reasoning, to be used prescriptively. One cannot start a moral argument about a certain proposal on the basis that, whatever the conclusion of it, it makes no difference to what anybody is to do. When one has arrived at a conclusion, one may then be too weak to put it into practice. But *in arguing* one has to discount this possibility; for, as we shall see, to abandon the prescriptivity of one's moral judgments is to unscrew an essential part of the logical mechanism on which such arguments rely. This is why, if a person were to say 'Let's have an argument about this grave moral question which faces us, but let's not think of any conclusion we may come to as requiring anybody to *do* one thing rather than another', we should be likely to accuse him of flippancy, or worse.

3. I will now try to exhibit the bare bones of the theory of moral reasoning that I wish to advocate by considering a very simple (indeed over-simplified) example. As we shall see, even this very simple case generates the most baffling complexities; and so we may be pardoned for not attempting anything more difficult to start with.

The example is adapted from a well-known parable.[5] *A* owes money to *B*, and *B* owes money to *C,* and it is the law that creditors may exact their debts by putting their debtors into prison. *B* asks himself, 'Can I say that I ought to take this measure against *A* in order to make him pay?' He is no doubt *inclined* to do this, or *wants* to do it. Therefore, if there were no question of universalizing his prescriptions, he would assent readily to the *singular* prescription 'Let me put *A* into prison'. But when he seeks to turn this prescription into a moral judgment, and say, 'I *ought* to put *A* into prison because he will not pay me what he owes', he reflects that this would involve accepting the principle 'Anyone who is in my position ought to put his debtor into prison if he does not pay'. But then he reflects that *C* is in the same position of unpaid creditor with regard to himself (*B*), and that the cases are otherwise identical; and that if anyone in this position ought to put his debtors into prison, then so ought *C* to put him (*B*) into prison. And to accept the moral prescription '*C* ought to put me into prison' would commit him (since, as we have seen, he must be using the word 'ought' prescriptively) to accepting the singular prescription 'Let *C* put me into prison'; and this he is not

ready to accept. But if he is not, then neither can he accept the original judgment that he (*B*) ought to put *A* into prison for debt. Notice that the whole of this argument would break down if 'ought' were not being used both universalizably *and prescriptively*; for if it were not being used prescriptively, the step from '*C* ought to put me into prison' to 'Let *C* put me into prison' would not be valid.

The structure and ingredients of this argument must now be examined. We must first notice an analogy between it and the Popperian theory of scientific method. What has happened is that a provisional or suggested moral principle has been rejected because one of its particular consequences proved unacceptable. But an important difference between the two kinds of reasoning must also be noted; it is what we should expect, given that the data of scientific observation are recorded in descriptive statements, whereas we are here dealing with prescriptions. What knocks out a suggested hypothesis, on Popper's theory, is a singular statement of fact: the hypothesis has the consequence that *p;* but not-*p*. Here the logic is just the same, except that in place of the observation-statements '*p*' and 'not-*p*' we have the singular *prescriptions* 'Let *C* put *B* into prison for debt' and its contradictory. Nevertheless, given that *B* is disposed to reject the first of these prescriptions, the argument against him is just as cogent as in the scientific case.

We may carry the parallel further. Just as science, seriously pursued, is the search for hypotheses and the testing of them by the attempt to falsify their particular consequences, so morals, as a serious endeavor, consists in the search for principles and the testing of them against particular cases. Any rational activity has its discipline, and this is the discipline of moral thought: to test the moral principles that suggest themselves to us by following out their consequences and seeing whether we can accept *them.*

No argument, however, starts from nothing. We must therefore ask what we have to have before moral arguments of the sort of which I have given a simple example can proceed. The first requisite is that the facts of the case should be given; for all moral discussion is about some particular set of facts, whether actual or supposed. Secondly we have the logical framework provided by the meaning of the word 'ought' (i.e., prescriptivity and universalizability, both of which we saw to be necessary). Because moral judgments have to be universalizable, *B* cannot say that he ought to put *A* into prison for debt without committing himself to the view that *C*, who is *ex hypothesi* in the same position vis-à-vis himself, ought to put *him* into prison; and because moral judgments are prescriptive, this would be, in effect, prescribing to *C* to put him into prison; and this he is unwilling to do, since he has a strong inclination not to go to prison. This inclination gives us the third necessary ingredient in the argument: if *B* were a completely apathetic person, who literally did not mind what happened to himself or to anybody else, the argument would not touch him. The three necessary ingredients which we have noticed, then, are (1) facts; (2) logic; (3) inclinations. These ingredients enable us, not indeed to arrive at an evaluative conclusion, but to *reject* an evaluative proposition. We shall see later that these are not, in all cases, the only necessary ingredients.

4. In the example which we have been using, the position was deliberately made simpler by supposing that *B* actually stood to some other person in exactly the same relation as *A* does to him. Such cases are unlikely to arise in practice. But it is not necessary for the force of the argument that *B* should *in fact* stand in this relation to anyone; it is sufficient that he should consider hypothetically such a case, and see what would be the consequences in it of those moral principles between whose acceptance and rejection he has to decide. Here we have an important point of difference from the parallel scientific argument, in that the crucial case which leads to rejection of the principle can itself be a supposed, not an observed, one. That hypothetical cases will do as well as actual ones is important, since it enables us to guard against a possible misinterpretation of the argument which I have outlined. It might be thought that what moves *B* is the *fear* that *C* will actually do to him as he does to *A*—as happens in the gospel parable. But this fear is not only irrelevant to the moral argument; it does not even provide a particularly strong non-moral motive unless the circumstances are somewhat exceptional. *C* may, after all, not find out what *B* has done to *A*; or *C*'s moral principles may be different from *B*'s, and independent of them, so that

what moral principle *B* accepts makes no difference to the moral principles on which *C* acts.

Even, therefore, if *C* did not exist, it would be no answer to the argument for *B* to say 'But in my case there is no fear that anybody will ever be in a position to do to me what I am proposing to do to *A*'. For the argument does not rest on any such fear. All that is essential to it is that *B* should disregard the fact that he plays the particular role in the situation which he does, without disregarding the inclinations which people have in situations of this sort. In other words, he must be prepared to give weight to *A*'s inclinations and interests as if they were his own. This is what turns selfish prudential reasoning into moral reasoning. It is much easier, psychologically, for *B* to do this if he is actually placed in a situation like *A*'s vis-à-vis somebody else; but this is not necessary, provided that he has sufficient imagination to envisage what it is like to be *A*. For our first example, a case was deliberately chosen in which little imagination was necessary; but in most normal cases a certain power of imagination and readiness to use it is a fourth necessary ingredient in moral arguments, alongside those already mentioned, viz., logic (in the shape of universalizability and prescriptivity), the facts, and the inclinations or interests of the people concerned.

It must be pointed out that the absence of even one of these ingredients may render the rest ineffective. For example, impartiality by itself is not enough. If, in becoming impartial, *B* became also completely dispassionate and apathetic, and moved as little by other people's interests as by his own, then, as we have seen, there would be nothing to make him accept or reject one moral principle rather than another. That is why those who, like Adam Smith and Professor Kneale, advocate what have been called 'Ideal Observer Theories' of ethics, sometimes postulate as their imaginary ideal observer not merely an impartial spectator, but an impartially *sympathetic* spectator.[6] To take another example, if the person who faces the moral decision has no imagination, then even the fact that someone can do the very same thing to him may pass him by. If, again, he lacks the readiness to universalize, then the vivid imagination of the sufferings which he is inflicting on others may only spur him on to intensify them, to increase his own vindictive enjoyment. And if he is ignorant of the material facts (for example about what is likely to happen to a person if one takes out a writ against him), then there is nothing to tie the moral argument to particular choices.

5. The best way of testing the argument which we have outlined will be to consider various ways in which somebody in *B*'s position might seek to escape from it. There are indeed a number of such ways; and all of them may be successful, at a price. It is important to understand what the price is in each case. We may classify these maneuvers which are open to *B* into two kinds. There are first of all the moves which depend on his using the moral words in a different way from that on which the argument relied. We saw that for the success of the argument it was necessary that 'ought' should be used universalizably and prescriptively. If *B* uses it in a way that is either not prescriptive or not universalizable, then he can escape the force of the argument, at the cost of resigning from the kind of discussion that we thought we were having with him. We shall discuss these two possibilities separately. Secondly, there are moves which can still be made by *B*, even though he is using the moral words in the same way as we are. We shall examine three different subclasses of these.

Before dealing with what I shall call the *verbal* maneuvers in detail, it may be helpful to make a general remark. Suppose that we are having a simple mathematical argument with somebody, and he admits, for example, that there are five eggs in this basket, and six in the other, but maintains that there are a dozen eggs in the two baskets taken together; and suppose that this is because he is using the expression 'a dozen' to mean 'eleven'. It is obvious that we cannot compel him logically to admit that there are not a dozen eggs, in *his* sense of 'dozen'. But it is equally obvious that this should not disturb us. For such a man only appears to be dissenting from us. His dissent is only apparent, because the proposition which his words express is actually consistent with the conclusion which we wish to draw; he *says* "There are a dozen eggs"; but he *means* what we should express by saying "There are eleven eggs"; and this we are not disputing. It is important to remember that in the moral case also the dissent may be only apparent, if the words are being used in differ-

ent ways, and that it is no defect in a method of argument if it does not make it possible to prove a conclusion to a person when he is using words in such a way that the conclusion does not follow.

It must be pointed out, further (since this is a common source of confusion), that in this argument nothing whatever hangs upon our *actual* use of words in common speech, any more than it does in the arithmetical case. That we use the sound 'dozen' to express the meaning that we customarily do use it to express is of no consequence for the argument about the eggs; and the same may be said of the sound 'ought'. There is, however, something which I, at any rate, customarily express by the sound 'ought', whose character is correctly described by saying that it is a universal or universalizable prescription. I hope that what I customarily express by the sound 'ought' is the same as what most people customarily express by it; but if I am mistaken in this assumption, I shall still have given a correct account, so far as I am able, of that which I express by this sound.[7] Nevertheless, this account will interest other people mainly in so far as my hope that they understand the same thing as I do by 'ought' is fulfilled; and since I am moderately sure that this is indeed the case with many people, I hope that I may be of use to them in elucidating the logical properties of the concept which they thus express.

At this point, however, it is of the utmost importance to stress that the fact that two people express the same thing by 'ought' does not entail that they share the same moral opinions. For the formal, logical properties of the word 'ought' (those which are determined by its *meaning*) are only one of the four factors (listed earlier) whose combination governs a man's moral opinion on a given matter. Thus ethics, the study of the logical properties of the moral words, remains morally neutral (its conclusions neither are substantial moral judgments, nor entail them, even in conjunction with factual premises); its bearing upon moral questions lies in this, that it makes logically impossible certain combinations of moral and other prescriptions. Two people who are using the word 'ought' in the same way may yet disagree about what ought to be done in a certain situation, either because they differ about the facts, or because one or other of them lacks imagination, or because their different inclinations make one reject some singular prescription which the other can accept. For all that, ethics (i.e., the logic of moral language) is an immensely powerful engine for producing moral agreement; for if two people are willing to use the moral word 'ought', and to use it in the same way (viz., the way that I have been describing), the other possible sources of moral disagreement are all eliminable. People's inclinations about most of the important matters in life tend to be the same (very few people, for example, like being starved or run over by motor cars); and, even when they are not, there is a way of generalizing the argument, . . . which enables us to make allowance for differences in inclinations. The facts are often, given sufficient patience, ascertainable. Imagination can be cultivated. If these three factors are looked after, as they can be, agreement on the use of 'ought' is the only other necessary condition for producing moral agreement, at any rate in typical cases. And, if I am not mistaken, this agreement in use is already there in the discourse of anybody with whom we are at all likely to find ourselves arguing; all that is needed is to think clearly, and so make it evident.

After this methodological digression, let us consider what is to be done with the man who professes to be using 'ought' in some different way from that which I have described—because he is not using it prescriptively, or not universalizably. For the reasons that I have given, if he takes either of these courses, he is no longer in substantial moral disagreement with us. Our apparent moral disagreement is really only verbal; for although, as we shall see shortly, there may be a residuum of substantial disagreement, this cannot be moral. It cannot even be an evaluative disagreement, in the sense of 'evaluative' above defined.

Let us take first the man who is using the word 'ought' prescriptively, but not universalizably. He can say that he ought to put his debtor into prison, although he is not prepared to agree that his creditor ought to put *him* into prison. We, on the other hand, since we are not prepared to admit that our creditors in these circumstances ought to put us into prison, cannot say that we ought to put our debtors into prison. So there is an appearance of substantial moral disagreement, which is intensified by the fact that, since we are both using the word 'ought' prescriptively, our respective views will lead to different particular actions. Dif-

ferent *singular* prescriptions about what to do are (since both our judgments are prescriptive) derivable from what we are respectively saying. But this is not enough to constitute a moral disagreement. For there to be a moral disagreement, or even an evaluative one of any kind, we must differ, not only about what *is* to be done in some particular case, but about some universal principle concerning what *ought* to be done in cases of a certain sort; and since B is (on the hypothesis considered) advocating no such universal principle, he is saying nothing with which we can be in moral or evaluative disagreement. Considered purely as prescriptions, indeed, our two views are in substantial disagreement; but the moral, evaluative (i.e., the *universal* prescriptive) disagreement is only verbal, because, when the expression of B's view is understood as he means it, the view turns out not to be a view about the morality of the action at all. So B, by this maneuver, can go on prescribing to himself to put A into prison, but has to abandon the claim that he is justifying the action morally, as we understand the word 'morally'. One may, of course, use any word as one pleases, at a price. But he can no longer claim to be giving that sort of justification of his action for which, as I think, the common expression is 'moral justification'.

I need not deal at length with the second way in which B might be differing from us in his use of 'ought', viz., by not using it prescriptively. If he were not using it prescriptively, it will be remembered, he could assent to the singular prescription 'Let not C put me into prison for debt', and yet assent also to the nonprescriptive moral judgment 'C ought to put me into prison for debt'. And so his disinclination to be put into prison for debt by C would furnish no obstacle to his saying that he (B) ought to put A into prison for debt. And thus he could carry out his own inclination to put A into prison with apparent moral justification. The justification would be, however, only apparent. For if B is using the word 'ought' non-prescriptively, then 'I ought to put A into prison for debt' does not entail the singular prescription 'Let me put A into prison for debt'; the 'moral' judgment becomes quite irrelevant to the choice of what to do. There would also be the same lack of substantial moral disagreement as we noticed in the preceding case. B would not be disagreeing with us other than verbally, so far as the moral question is concerned (though there might be points of *factual* disagreement between us, arising from the *descriptive* meaning of our judgments). The 'moral' disagreement could be only verbal, because whereas we should be dissenting from the universalizable prescription '*B* ought to put *A* into prison for debt', *this* would not be what *B* was expressing, though the words he would be using would be the same. For *B* would not, by these words, be expressing a prescription at all.

6. So much for the ways (of which my list may well be incomplete) in which *B* can escape from our argument by using the word 'ought' in a different way from us. The remaining ways of escape are open to him even if he is using 'ought' in the same way as we are, viz., to express a universalizable prescription.

We must first consider that class of escape routes whose distinguishing feature is that *B*, while using the moral words in the same way as we are, refuses to make positive moral judgments at all in certain cases. There are two main variations of this maneuver. *B* may either say that it is indifferent, morally, whether he imprisons *A* or not; or he may refuse to make any moral judgment at all, even one of indifference, about the case. It will be obvious that if he adopts either of these moves, he can evade the argument as so far set out. For that argument only forced him to *reject* the moral judgment 'I ought to imprison *A* for debt'. It did not force him to assent to any moral judgment; in particular, he remained free to assent, either to the judgment that he ought not to imprison *A* for debt (which is the one that we want him to accept) or to the judgment that it is neither the case that he ought, nor the case that he ought not (that it is, in short, indifferent); and he remained free, also, to say 'I am just not making any moral judgments at all about this case'.

We have not yet, however, exhausted the arguments generated by the demand for universalizability, provided that the moral words are being used in a way which allows this demand. For it is evident that these maneuvers could, in principle, be practiced in any case whatever in which the morality of an act is in question. And this enables us to place *B* in a dilemma. Either he practices this maneuver in *every* situation in which he is faced with a moral decision; or else he practices it only *sometimes*. The first alternative, however, has to be sub-divided; for 'every situation' might mean 'every situation in which he himself has to face a moral decision regarding one of his own actions', or it might mean 'every situation in which a moral question arises for him, whether about his own actions or about somebody else's'. So there are three courses that he can adopt: (1) He either refrains altogether from making moral judgments, or makes none except judgments of indifference (that is to say, he either observes a complete moral silence, or says 'Nothing matters morally'; either of these two positions might be called a sort of amoralism); (2) he makes moral judgments in the normal way about other people's actions, but adopts one or other of the kinds of amoralism, just mentioned, with regard to his own; (3) he expresses moral indifference, or will make no moral judgment at all, with regard to *some* of his own actions and those of other people, but makes moral judgments in the normal way about others.

Now it will be obvious that in the first case there is nothing that we can do, and that this should not disturb us. Just as one cannot win a game of chess against an opponent who will not make any moves—and just as one cannot argue mathematically with a person who will not commit himself to any mathematical statements—so moral argument is impossible with a man who will make no moral judgments at all, or—which for practical purposes comes to the same thing—makes only judgments of indifference. Such a person is not entering the arena of moral dispute, and therefore it is impossible to contest with him. He is compelled also—and this is important—to abjure the protection of morality for his own interests.

In the other two cases, however, we have an argument left. If a man is prepared to make positive moral judgments about other people's actions, but not about his own, or if he is prepared to make them about some of his own decisions, but not about others, then we can ask him on what principle he makes the distinction between these various cases. This is a particular application of the demand for universalizability. He will still have left to him the ways of escape from this demand which are available in all its applications, and which we shall consider later. But there is no way of escape which is available in this application, but not in others. He must either produce (or at least admit the existence of) some principle which makes him hold different moral opinions about apparently similar cases, or else admit that the judgments he is making are not moral ones. But in the latter case, he is in the same position, in the present dispute, as the man who will not make any moral judgments at all; he has resigned from the contest.

In the particular example which we have been considering, we supposed that the cases of *B* and of *C*, his own creditor, were identical. The demand for universalization therefore compels *B* to make the same moral judgment, whatever it is, about both cases. He has therefore, unless he is going to give up the claim to be arguing morally, either to say that neither he nor *C* ought to exercise their legal rights to imprison their debtors; or that both ought (a possibility to which we shall recur in the next section); or that it is indifferent whether they do. But the last alternative leaves it open to *B* and *C* to do what they like in the matter; and we may suppose that, though *B* himself would like to have this freedom, he will be unwilling to allow it to *C*. It is as unlikely that he will *permit C* to put him (*B*) into prison as that he will *prescribe* it. We may say, therefore, that while move (1), described above, constitutes an abandonment of the dispute, moves (2) and (3) really add nothing new to it.

7. We must next consider a way of escape which may seem much more respectable than those which I have so far mentioned. Let us suppose that *B* is a firm believer in the rights of property and the sanctity of contracts. In this case he may say roundly that debtors ought to be imprisoned by their creditors whoever they are, and that, specifically, *C* ought to imprison him (*B*), and he (*B*) ought to imprison *A*. And he may, unlike the superficially similar person described earlier, be meaning by 'ought' just what we usually mean by it— i.e., he may be using the word prescriptively, realizing that in saying that *C* ought to put him into prison, he is prescribing that *C* put him in prison. *B*, in this case, is perfectly ready to go to prison for his principles, in order that the sanctity of contracts may be enforced. In real life, *B* would be much more likely to take this line if the situation in which he himself played the role of debtor were not actual but only hypothetical; but this, as we saw earlier, ought not to make any difference to the argument.

We are not yet, however, in a position to deal with this escape route. All we can do is to say why we cannot now deal with it, and leave this loose end to be picked up later. *B*, if he is sincere in holding the principle about the sanctity of contracts (or any other universal moral principle which has the same effect in this particular case), may have two sorts of grounds for it. He may hold it on utilitarian grounds, thinking that, unless contracts are rigorously enforced, the results will be so disastrous as to outweigh any benefits that *A*, or *B* himself, may get from being let off. This could, in certain circumstances, be a good argument. But we cannot tell whether it is, until we have generalized the type of moral argument which has been set out in this chapter, to cover cases in which the interests of more than two parties are involved. As we saw, it is only the interests of *A* and *B* that come into the argument as so far considered (the interests of the third party, *C*, do not need separate consideration, since *C* was introduced only in order to show *B*, if necessary fictionally, a situation in which the roles were reversed; therefore *C*'s interests, being a mere replica of *B*'s, will vanish, as a separate factor, once the *A/B* situation, and the moral judgments made on it, are universalized). But if utilitarian grounds of the sort suggested are to be adduced, they will bring with them a reference to all the other people whose interests would be harmed by laxity in the enforcement of contracts. This escape route, therefore, if this is its basis, introduces considerations which cannot be assessed until we have generalized our form of argument to cover 'multilateral' moral situations. At present, it can only be said that if *B* can show that leniency in the enforcement of contracts would really have the results he claims for the community at large, he might be justified in taking the severer course. . . .

On the other hand, *B* might have a quite different, nonutilitarian kind of reason for adhering to his principle. He might be moved, not by any weight which he might attach to the interests of other people, but by the thought that to enforce contracts of this sort is necessary in order to conform to some moral or other *ideal* that he has espoused. Such ideals might be of various sorts. He might be moved, for example, by an ideal of abstract justice, of the *fiat justitia, ruat caelum* variety. We have to distinguish such an ideal of justice, which pays no regard to people's interests, from that which is concerned merely to do justice *between* people's interests. It is very important, if considerations of justice are introduced into a moral argument, to know of which sort they are. Justice of the second kind can perhaps be accommodated within a moral view which it is not misleading to call utilitarian. But this is not true of an ideal of the first kind. It is characteristic of this sort of non-utilitarian ideals that, when they are introduced into moral arguments, they render ineffective the appeal to universalized self-interest which is the foundation of the argument that we have been considering. This is because the person who has wholeheartedly espoused such an ideal (we shall call him the 'fanatic') does not mind if people's interests—even his own—are harmed in the pursuit of it.

It need not be justice which provides the basis of such an escape route as we are considering. Any moral ideal would do, provided that it were pursued regardless of other people's interests. For example, *B* might be a believer in the survival of the fittest, and think that, in order to promote this, he (and everyone else) ought to pursue their own interests by all means in their power and regardless of everyone else's interests. This ideal might lead him, in this particular case, to put *A* in prison, and he might agree that *C* ought to do the same to him, if he were not clever enough to avoid this fate. He might think that universal obedience to such a principle would maximize the production of supermen and so make the world a better place. If these were his grounds, it is possible that we might argue with him factually, showing that the universal observance of the principle would not have the results he claimed. But we might be defeated in this factual argument if he had an ideal which made him call the world 'a better place' when the jungle law prevailed; he could then agree to our factual statements, but still maintain that the condition of the world described by us as resulting from the observance of his principle would be better than its present condition. In this case, the argument might take two courses. If we could get him to imagine himself in the position of the weak, who went to the wall in such a state of the world, we might bring him to realize that to hold his principle involved prescribing that things should be done to him, in hypothetical situations, which he could not sincerely prescribe. If so, then the argument would be on the rails again, and could proceed on lines which we have already sketched. But he might stick to his principle and say 'If I were weak, then I ought to go to the wall'. If he did this, he

would be putting himself beyond the reach of what we shall call 'golden rule' or 'utilitarian' arguments by becoming what we shall call a 'fanatic'. Since a great part of the rest of this book will be concerned with people who take this sort of line, it is unnecessary to pursue their case further at this point.

8. The remaining maneuver that *B* might seek to practice is probably the commonest. It is certainly the one which is most frequently brought up in philosophical controversies on this topic. This consists in a fresh appeal to the facts—i.e., in asserting that there are in fact morally relevant differences between his case and that of others. In the example which we have been considering, we have artificially ruled out this way of escape by assuming that the case of *B* and *C* is exactly similar to that of *A* and *B*; from this it follows *a fortiori* that there are no morally relevant differences. Since the *B/C* case may be a hypothetical one, this condition of exact similarity can always be fulfilled, and therefore this maneuver is based on a misconception of the type of argument against which it is directed. Nevertheless it may be useful, since this objection is so commonly raised, to deal with it at this point, although nothing further will be added thereby to what has been said already.

It may be claimed that no two actual cases would ever be exactly similar; there would always be some differences, and *B* might allege that some of these were morally relevant. He might allege, for example, that, whereas his family would starve if *C* put him into prison, this would not be the case if he put *A* into prison, because *A*'s family would be looked after by *A*'s relatives. If such a difference existed, there might be nothing logically disreputable in calling it morally relevant, and such arguments are in fact often put forward and accepted.

The difficulty, however, lies in drawing the line between those arguments of this sort which are legitimate, and those which are not. Suppose that *B* alleges that the fact that *A* has a hooked nose or a black skin entitles him, *B*, to put him in prison, but that *C* ought not to do the same thing to him, *B*, because his nose is straight and his skin white. Is this an argument of equal logical respectability? Can I say that the fact that I have a mole in a particular place on my chin entitles me to further my own interests at others' expense, but that they are forbidden to do this by the fact that they lack this mark of natural preeminence?

The answer to this maneuver is implicit in what has been said already about the relevance, in moral arguments, of hypothetical as well as of actual cases. The fact that no two actual cases are ever identical has no bearing on the problem. For all we have to do is to imagine an identical case in which the roles are reversed. Suppose that my mole disappears, and that my neighbor grows one in the very same spot on his chin. Or, to use our other example, what does *B* say about a hypothetical case in which he has a black skin or a hooked nose, and *A* and *C* are both straight-nosed and white-skinned? Since this is the same argument, in essentials, as we used at the very beginning, it need not be repeated here. *B* is in fact faced with a dilemma. Either the property of his own case, which he claims to be morally relevant, is a properly universal property (i.e., one describable without reference to individuals), or it is not. If it is a universal property, then, because of the meaning of the word 'universal', it is a property which might be possessed by another case in which he played a different role (though in fact it may not be); and we can therefore ask him to ignore the fact that it is he himself who plays the role which he does in this case. This will force him to count as morally relevant only those properties which he is prepared to allow to be relevant even when other people have them. And this rules out all the attractive kinds of special pleading. On the other hand, if the property in question is not a properly universal one, then he has not met the demand for universalizability, and cannot claim to be putting forward a moral argument at all.

9. It is necessary, in order to avoid misunderstanding, to add two notes to the foregoing discussion. The misunderstanding arises through a too literal interpretation of the common forms of expression—which constantly recur in arguments of this type—'How would you like it if . . . ?' and 'Do as you would be done by'. Though I shall later, for convenience, refer to the type of arguments here discussed as 'golden rule' arguments, we must not be misled by these forms of expression.

First of all, we shall make the nature of the argument clearer if, when we are asking *B* to imagine himself in the position of his victim, we phrase our question, never in the form 'What *would* you say, or feel, or think, or how *would* you like it, if you were he?', but always in the form 'What *do* you say (*in propria persona*) about a hypothetical case in which you are in your vic-

tim's position?' The importance of this way of phrasing the question is that, if the question were put in the first way, *B* might reply 'Well, of course, if anybody did this to me I should resent it very much and make all sorts of adverse moral judgments about the act; but this has absolutely no bearing on the validity of the moral opinion which I am *now* expressing'. To involve him in contradiction, we have to show that he *now* holds an opinion about the hypothetical case which is inconsistent with his opinion about the actual case.

The second thing which has to be noticed is that the argument, as set out, does not involve any sort of deduction of a moral judgment, or even of the negation of a moral judgment, from a factual statement about people's inclinations, interests, etc. We are not saying to *B* 'You are as a matter of fact averse to this being done to you in a hypothetical case; and from this it follows logically that you ought not to do it to another'. Such a deduction would be a breach of Hume's Law ('No "ought" from an "is" '), to which I have repeatedly declared my adherence. The point is, rather, that because of his aversion to its being done to him in the hypothetical case, he cannot accept the singular *prescription* that in the hypothetical case it should be done to him; and this, because of the logic of 'ought', precludes him from accepting the moral judgment that he ought to do likewise to another in the actual case. It is not a question of a factual statement about a person's inclinations being inconsistent with a moral judgment; rather, his inclinations being what they are, he cannot assent sincerely to a certain singular prescription, and if he cannot do this, he cannot assent to a certain universal prescription which entails it, when conjoined with factual statements about the circumstances whose truth he admits. Because of this entailment, if he assented to the factual statements and to the universal prescription, but refused (as he must, his inclinations being what they are) to assent to the singular prescription, he would be guilty of a logical inconsistency.

If it be asked what the relation is between his aversion to being put in prison in the hypothetical case, and his inability to accept the hypothetical singular prescription that if he were in such a situation he should be put into prison, it would seem that the relation is not unlike that between a belief that the cat is on the mat, and an inability to accept the proposition that the cat is not on the mat. Further attention to this parallel will perhaps make the position clearer. Suppose that somebody advances the hypothesis that cats never sit on mats, and that we refute him by pointing to a cat on a mat. The logic of our refutation proceeds in two stages. Of these, the second is: 'Here is a cat sitting on a mat, so it is not the case that cats never sit on mats'. This is a piece of logical deduction; and to it, in the moral case, corresponds the step from 'Let this not be done to me' to 'It is not the case that I ought to do it to another in similar circumstances'. But in both cases there is a first stage whose nature is more obscure, and different in the two cases, though there is an analogy between them.

In the 'cat' case, it is logically possible for a man to look straight at the cat on the mat, and yet believe that there is no cat on the mat. But if a person with normal eyesight and no psychological aberrations does this, we say that he does not understand the meaning of the words, 'The cat is on the mat'. And even if he does not have normal eyesight, or suffers from some psychological aberration (such a phobia of cats, say, that he just *cannot* admit to himself that he is face to face with one), yet, if we can convince him that everyone else can see a cat there, he will have to admit that there *is* a cat there, or be accused of misusing the language.

If, on the other hand, a man says 'But I *want* to be put in prison, if ever I am in that situation', we can, indeed, get as far as accusing him of having eccentric desires; but we cannot, when we have proved to him that nobody else has such a desire, face him with the choice of either saying, with the rest, 'Let this not be done to me', or else being open to the accusation of not understanding what he is saying. For it is not an incorrect use of words to want eccentric things. Logic does not prevent me wanting to be put in a gas chamber if a Jew. It is perhaps true that I logically cannot want for its own sake an experience which I think of as *unpleasant;* for to say that I think of it as unpleasant may be logically inconsistent with saying that I want it for its own sake. If this is so, it is because 'unpleasant' is a prescriptive expression. But 'to be put in prison' and 'to be put in a gas chamber if a Jew', are not prescriptive expressions; and therefore these things can be wanted without offense to logic. It is, indeed, in the logical possibility of wanting *anything* (neutrally described) that the 'freedom' which is alluded to in my title essentially consists. And it is this, as we shall see, that lets by the person whom I shall call the 'fanatic'.

There is not, then, a complete analogy between the man who says 'There is no cat on the mat' when there is, and the man who wants things which others do not. But there is a partial analogy, which, having noticed this difference, we may be able to isolate. The analogy is between two relations: the relations between, in both cases, the 'mental state' of these men and what they say. If I believe that there is a cat on the mat I cannot sincerely say that there is not; and, if I want not to be put into prison more than I want anything else, I cannot sincerely say 'Let me be put into prison'. When, therefore, I said above 'His inclinations being what they are, he cannot assent sincerely to a certain singular prescription', I was making an analytic statement (although the 'cannot' is not a logical 'cannot'); for if he were to assent sincerely to the prescription, that would entail *exviterminorum* that his inclinations had changed—in the very same way that it is analytically true that, if the other man were to say sincerely that there was a cat on the mat, when before he had sincerely denied this, he must have changed his belief.

If, however, instead of writing 'His inclinations being what they are, he cannot . . .', we leave out the first clause and write simply 'He cannot . . .', the statement is no longer analytic; we are making a statement about his psychology which might be false. For it is logically possible for inclinations to change; hence it is possible for a man to come sincerely to hold an ideal which requires that he himself should be sent to a gas chamber if a Jew. That is the price we have to pay for our freedom. But, as we shall see, in order for reason to have a place in morals it is not necessary for us to close this way of escape by means of a logical barrier; it is sufficient that, men and the world being what they are, we can be very sure that hardly anybody is going to take it with his eyes open. And when we are arguing with one of the vast majority who are not going to take it, the reply that somebody else *might* take it does not help his case against us. In this respect, all moral arguments are *ad hominem.*

Notes

1. I have tried to fill in some of the historical background of these reproaches, and to assess the justification for them, in my article in *The Philosophy of C. D. Broad,* ed. P. Schilpp.

2. K. R. Popper, *The Logic of Scientific Discovery* (esp. pp. 32 f.). See also his article in C. A. Mace (ed.), *British Philosophy in the Mid-Century*, p. 155.

3. [See his *Freedom and Reason* (Oxford: Clarendon Press, 1963), Part I.]

4. [*Ibid.,* Chapter 5.]

5. Matthew xviii. 23.

6. It will be plain that there are affinities, though there are also differences, between this type of theory and my own. For such theories see W. C. Kneale, *Philosophy*, xxv (1950), 162; R. Firth and R. B. Brandt, *Philosophy and Phenomenological Research*, xii (1951/2), 317, and xv (1954/5), 407, 414, 422; and J. Harrison, *Aristotelian Society*, supp. vol. xxviii (1954), 132. Firth, unlike Kneale, says that the observer must be 'dispassionate', but see Brandt, op. cit., p. 411 n. For a shorter discussion see Brandt, *Ethical Theory*, p. 173. Since for many Christians God occupies the role of 'ideal observer', the moral judgments which they make may be expected to coincide with those arrived at by the method of reasoning which I am advocating.

7. Cf. Moore, *Principia Ethica*, p. 6.

READING QUESTIONS

1. What is the view in metaethics known as naturalism? What is the difference between thinking of moral reasoning as a kind of linear process of deductive or inductive reasoning and thinking of moral reasoning as a kind of exploration?

2. What are Hare's two proposed rules of moral reasoning?

3. Carefully review Hare's thought experiment in §3 involving the debtors. Why does Hare think that it is irrational for B to accept the proposition "let me (B) put A into prison"? How is this irrationality related to universalizability and prescriptivity?

4. Because Hare believes that moral judgments are essentially commands rather than descriptions, it follows that they lack truth values (in anything like the traditional sense). Still, he writes that "in place of the observation-statements '*p*' and '*not-p*' we have the singular *prescriptions* 'Let C put B into prison for debt' and its contradictory. . . . Given that B is disposed to reject the first of these prescriptions, the

argument against him is just as cogent as in the scientific case." Is this really true? Why or why not?

5. In the case of "the man who is using the word 'ought' prescriptively, but not universalizably," Hare remarks that such a person "can no longer claim to be giving that sort of justification of his action for which . . . the common expression is 'moral justification'." What is his argument for this conclusion? Do you agree?

6. In the case where B is not using the word 'ought' prescriptively, Hare argues that 'I ought to put A into prison for debt' does not entail 'Let me put A into prison for debt.'" Why?

7. What are some of the other routes of escape from Hare's argument that B might attempt? How does Hare reply in each of the cases that you consider? Do you find his replies to be adequate?

8. Why does Hare conclude his essay by writing that "all moral arguments are *ad hominem.*" What is it about a moral argument, as Hare sees it, that makes all such things essentially *ad hominem*? Do you agree?

SUGGESTIONS FOR FURTHER READING (R. M. HARE)

Primary Sources and Collected Writings

(1952) *The Language of Morals.* Oxford: Clarendon Press.

(1963) *Freedom and Reason.* Oxford: Clarendon Press.

(1971) *Essays on Philosophical Method.* Berkeley, CA: University of California Press.

(1971) *Practical Inferences.* Berkeley, CA: University of California Press.

(1972) *Applications of Moral Philosophy.* Berkeley, CA: University of California Press.

(1972) *Essays on the Moral Concepts.* Berkeley, CA: University of California Press.

(1981) *Moral Thinking: Its Levels, Methods and Point.* Oxford: Clarendon Press.

(1982) *Plato.* Oxford: Oxford University Press, 1999.

(1989) *Essays in Ethical Theory.* Oxford: Clarendon Press.

(1989) *Essays on Political Morality.* Oxford: Clarendon Press.

(1992) *Essays on Religion and Education.* Oxford: Clarendon Press.

(1993) *Essays on Bioethics.* Oxford: Clarendon Press.

(1997) *Sorting Out Ethics.* Oxford: Clarendon Press.

(1999) *Objective Prescriptions and Other Essays.* Oxford: Clarendon Press.

Secondary Sources

Adu-Amankwah, P. (1997) *The Moral Philosophy of R. M. Hare: A Vindication of Utilitarianism?* New York: P. Lang.

Fehige, C., and G. Meggle, eds. (1995) *Towards Moral Thinking.* Frankfurt: Suhrkamp.

Hudson, W. (1983) *Modern Moral Philosophy.* New York: Macmillan.

Seanor, D., and N. Fotion, eds. (1988) *Hare and Critics: Essays on Moral Thinking.* Oxford: Oxford University Press.

Urmson, J. O. (1968) *The Emotive Theory of Ethics.* London: Hutchinson.

CATHERINE Z. ELGIN

The Relativity of Fact and the Objectivity of Value

Catherine Z. Elgin (1948–) has been investigating the ways in which what appear to be unbridgeable philosophical dichotomies are in actuality intertwined and mutually dependent categories of the understanding. She has also been uncovering the various ways in which our conception of knowledge and our picture of the world undergo substantial modification when we reject these distinctions as absolute or categorical. In many respects, her work is aimed at continuing the process of breaking through (or breaking down) the traditional categories of analytic philosophy. In that way, her efforts can be viewed as a continuation of the kind of project Quine is pursuing in his "Two Dogmas of Empiricism."

Born in Yonkers, New York, Elgin attended Vassar College and Harvard University, where she earned her

Ph.D. in 1975 with a dissertation on Wittgenstein's *Tractatus.* Elgin began her professional career in 1974 as an assistant professor at Vassar College. She has held teaching positions at a number of American colleges and universities, including Michigan State University, the University of North Carolina at Chapel Hill, Wellesley College, Princeton, Dartmouth, and Massachusetts Institute of Technology. She currently holds an appointment as Professor of the Philosophy of Education in the Graduate School of Education at Harvard University. Her publications include a number of books and dozens of articles on a wide variety of topics in philosophy, including the philosophy of art, metaphysics, the philosophy of language, the philosophy of science, epistemology, and the history of philosophy. Her philosophical work often takes inspiration from that of her mentor and friend, the late Nelson Goodman (1906–1999).

In the following essay, Elgin investigates the traditional philosophical dichotomy of a realm of facts, on one hand, and a realm of values, on the other. She argues that "far from being poles apart, the two are inextricably intertwined: the demarcation of facts rests squarely on considerations of value, and evaluations are infused with considerations of fact. She goes on to argue that "tenable judgments of both kinds are at once relative and objective." Her essay, therefore, breaks ground in two directions simultaneously, taking on the distinction between facts and values at the same time that she takes on the supposedly "categorical" distinction between that which is relative and that which is objective.

Fact and value purport to be polar opposites: facts being absolute, material, objective, and impersonal; values relative, spiritual, subjective, and personal; facts

being verifiable by the rigorous, austere methods of science; values being subject to no such assessment. The facts, they say, don't lie. So every factual disagreement has a determinate resolution. Whether barium is heavier than plutonium is a question of fact, and whatever the answer, there are no two ways about it. Values, if they don't precisely lie, are thought perhaps to distort. So evaluative disputes may be genuinely irresolvable. Whether, for example, a Van Gogh is better than a Vermeer might just be a matter of opinion. And on matters like these everyone is entitled to his own opinion. Such is the prevailing stereotype.

I believe that stereotype ought to be rejected, for it stifles our understanding of both fact and value. Far from being poles apart, the two are inextricably intertwined: the demarcation of facts rests squarely on considerations of value, and evaluations are infused with considerations of fact. So factual judgments are not objective unless value judgments are, and value judgments are not relative unless factual judgments are. I want to suggest that tenable judgments of both kinds are at once relative and objective.[1]

First, let's look at the facts. When we proclaim their independence from and indifference to human concerns, we forget that we are the ones who set and enforce the standards for what counts as a fact. We stipulate: "a thing cannot both be and not be"; or "no entity is without identity"; or "whatever is is physical." In effect we decree that whatever fails to satisfy our standards hasn't got what it takes to be a fact.

At the same time we arrange for our standards to be met. We construct systems of categories that settle the conditions on the individuation of entities and their classification into kinds. Thus, for example, we devise a biological taxonomy according to which a dachshund is the same kind of thing as a Doberman, but a horse is a different kind of thing from a zebra.

For all their clarity scientific examples may mislead. We are apt to think that constructing a biological taxonomy is simply a matter of introducing terminology for what is already the case. Then prior to our categorization dachshunds and Dobermans were already alike; horses and zebras, already different. The problem is that any two things are alike in some respects and different in others. So likeness alone is powerless to settle matters of categorization. In classing dachshunds

and Dobermans together, horses and zebras apart, we distinguish important from unimportant similarities. That is, we make a value judgment.

The selection of significant likenesses and differences is not, in general, whimsical. It is grounded in an appreciation of why a particular classificatory scheme is wanted, and this, in turn, depends on what we already believe about the subject at hand. If our goal is to understand heredity, for example, it is reasonable to group together animals that interbreed. Then despite their obvious differences dachshunds and Dobermans belong together, and despite their blatant similarities horses and zebras belong apart.

More general considerations come into play as well. If our system is to serve the interests of science, the cognitive values and priorities of science must be upheld. Membership in its kinds should be determinate and epistemically accessible. There should be no ambiguity and no (irresolvable) uncertainty about an individual's membership in a kind. The classification should be conducive to the formulation and testing or elegant, simple, fruitful generalizations and should perhaps mesh with other scientific classifications of the same and adjacent domains. In constructing a system of categories suitable for science, then, we make factual judgments about what the values of science are and how they can be realized.

Science streamlines its categories in hopes of achieving exceptionless, predictive, quantitative laws. Narrative has quite different ends in view, being concerned with the particular, the exceptional, the unique. So schemes suited to narrative enterprises exhibit different features from those suited to science. Scientific vices—ambiguity, imprecision, immeasurability, and indeterminacy—are often narrative virtues.[2] The complex characterization of the emotional life that we find, for example, in the novels of Henry James requires a baroque conceptual scheme whose involuted categories intersect in intricate and subtle ways. And equally complex categories may be required to achieve the sort of understanding that biographers, historians, psychoanalysts, and serious gossips strive to achieve.

A category scheme provides the resources for stating various truths and falsehoods, for exhibiting particular patterns and discrepancies, for drawing specific distinctions, for demarcating conceptual boundaries. Purposes, values, and priorities are integral to the design. They constitute the basis for organizing the domain in one way rather than another. And the acceptability of any particular scheme depends on the truths it enables us to state, the methods it permits [us] to employ, the projects it furthers, and the values it promotes. Together these constitute a system of thought. A failure of the components to mesh undermines the system, preventing it from doing what it ought to do.

We design category schemes with more or less specific purposes in mind and integrate into the scheme such values and priorities as we think will serve those purposes. But the values that our schemes realize are not always or only the ones we intend to produce. Some are simply mistakes; others, inadvertent holdovers from prior systems; yet others, unintended by-products of features we intentionally include. When pregnancy and aging are classified as medical conditions, they come to be considered and treated as diseases or disabilities—as deviations from a state of health. If Marx is right, the values of the ruling class are invisibly embedded in the social and economic categories of a society. And my students are convinced that a fundamental truth is revealed by the fact that witchcraft comes just after philosophy in the Library of Congress classification system.

As a first approximation, facts are what answer to true sentences. And different systems produce different truths. It is a truth of physics, not of botany, that copper is lighter than zinc. This alone does not lead to relativity, for such systems may complement one another or be indifferent to one another. Relativity emerges when systems clash—when what is true according to one system is false according to another. Evolutionary taxonomy so groups animals that crocodiles and lizards are close relatives; crocodiles and birds, distant ones. Cladistic classification shows crocodiles and birds to be close; crocodiles and lizards distant. Each system divulges some affinities among animals and obscures others. Neither invalidates the other. So whether it is a fact that crocodiles and lizards are closely related depends on a choice of system. According to one system any violation of the law is a crime; according to another only serious violations—felonies—are crimes. So whether spitting on the sidewalk is a crime depends on which system is in use. According to one medical classification, health is the absence of disease; according to another, health is the absence of disease or disability. So whether a congenital defect renders a person unhealthy depends on which system is in effect. A single domain can be organized in a multitude of ways, while different schematizations may employ a single vocabulary. So under one schematization a given sentence—say, "Spitting on the sidewalk is a crime"—comes out true; under another it comes out false. Truth then is relative to the system in effect.

Still, facts are objective. For once the system is in place, there is no room for negotiation. Events that are simultaneous relative to one frame of reference are successive relative to another. But it is determinate for each frame of reference whether given events are successive or simultaneous. Similarly, although some psychologistic systems consider neuroses to be mental illnesses and others do not, once a system is chosen there is a fact of the matter as to whether a compulsive hand-washer is mentally ill.

Such objectivity might seem spurious if we can switch frameworks at will. What is true according to one framework is false according to another. So can't we simply choose our facts to fit our fantasy? There are at least two reasons why we can't. The first is that rightness requires more than truth.[3] We need to employ an appropriate framework—one that yields the right facts. For example, the fact that someone went to Choate neither qualifies nor disqualifies him for a federal judgeship. So a classification of candidates according to their secondary schools is inappropriate, even if it would enable us to choose the candidate we want. Correctness requires that the facts we appeal to be relevant. Psychoanalytic categories are powerless to settle the issue of criminal insanity because they mark the wrong distinctions. People who cannot be held criminally liable for their actions are supposed to be, in some important respect, different from the rest of us. And the categories in question reveal no difference. For they characterize everyone's behavior in terms of motives and desires the agent can neither acknowledge nor control. So the facts that psychoanalytic theory reveals do not suit the purposes of the criminal court: they do not discriminate the class of criminally insane. Rightness of categorization thus depends on suitability to a purpose. And an aspiring lepidopterist whose collection consists of larvae seems to have missed the point. Lepidopterists concentrate on mature forms—they collect butterflies, not caterpillars. Although biologists class butterflies and caterpillars together, butterfly collectors do not. Rightness here requires fit with past practice. The fellow fails as a lepidopterist because he employs radically nontraditional categories in selecting specimens for his collection.

Moreover, even though we construct the categories that fix the facts, we cannot construct whatever we want. If we take the notion of construction seriously, this will come as no surprise. Although we make all manner of inventions, we can't make a nonfattening Sacher torte, a solar-powered subway, or a perpetual-motion machine. And although we design programs that endow computers with amazing abilities, we can't get a computer to translate a natural language or beat a grand master at chess.

Some of these incapacities are irremediable; others will eventually be overcome. My point in mentioning them is to emphasize that construction is something we do, and we can't do everything we want. Our capacities are limited, and our aspirations often interfere with one another. So there is no reason to think that we can convert any fantasy into fact by designing a suitable system. Plainly we cannot.

In constructing a political system, for example, we'd like to maximize both personal liberty and public safety. We'd like, that is, to arrange for as many actions as possible to fall under the predicate 'free to . . .' and as many harms as possible to fall under the predicate 'safe from. . . .' But we can't maximize both at once. The cost of security is a loss of liberty, and the cost of liberty, a risk of harm. With the freedom to carry a gun comes the danger of getting shot. So we have to trade the values of liberty and safety off against each other to arrive at a system that achieves an acceptable level of both.

In constructing a physicalistic system we'd like all the magnitudes of elementary particles to be at once determinate and epistemically accessible. But this is out of the question. For although we can measure either the position or the momentum of an electron, we can't measure both at once.

In building a system of thought we begin with a provisional scaffolding made of the (relevant) beliefs we already hold, the aims of the project we are embarked on, the liberties and constraints we consider the system subject to, and the values and priorities we seek

to uphold. We suspend judgment on matters in dispute. The scaffolding is not expected to stand by itself. We anticipate having to augment and revise it significantly before we have an acceptable system. Our initial judgments are not comprehensive; they are apt to be jointly untenable; they may fail to serve the purposes to which they are being put or to realize the values we want to respect. So our scaffolding has to be supplemented and (in part) reconstructed before it will serve.

The considered judgments that tether today's theory are the fruits of yesterday's theorizing. They are not held true come what may but are accorded a degree of initial credibility because previous inquiry sanctioned them. They are not irrevisable, but they are our current best guesses about the matter at hand. So they possess a certain inertia. We need a good reason to give them up.[4]

System-building is dialectical. We mold specific judgments to accepted generalizations, and generalizations to specific judgments. We weigh considerations of value against antecedent judgments of fact. Having a (partial) biological taxonomy that enables us to form the generalization "like comes from like"—that is, progeny belong to the same biological kind as their parents—we have reason to extend the system so as to classify butterflies and caterpillars as the same kind of thing. Rather than invoke a more superficial similarity and violate an elegant generalization, we plump for the generalization and overlook obvious differences.

Justification is holistic. Support for a conclusion comes, not from a single line of argument, but from a host of considerations of varying degrees of strength and relevance. What justifies the categories we construct is the cognitive and practical utility of the truths they enable us to formulate, the elegance and informativeness of the accounts they engender, the value of the ends they promote. We engage in system-building when we find the resources at hand inadequate.[5] We have projects they do not serve, questions they do not answer, values they do not realize. Something new is required. But a measure of the adequacy of a novelty is its fit with what we think we already know. If the finding is at all surprising, the background of accepted beliefs is apt to require modification to make room for it, and the finding may require revision to be fitted into place. A process of delicate adjustments occurs, its goal being a system in wide reflective equilibrium.[6]

Considerations of cognitive value come into play in deciding what modifications to attempt. Since science places a premium on repeatable results, an observation that cannot be reproduced is given short shrift, while one that is readily repeated may be weighted so heavily that it can undermine a substantial body of theory. And a legal system that relies on juries consisting of ordinary citizens is unlikely to favor the introduction of distinctions so recondite as to be incomprehensible to the general public.

To go from a motley collection of convictions to a system of considered judgments in reflective equilibrium requires balancing competing claims against one another. And there are likely to be several ways to achieve an acceptable balance. One system might, for example, sacrifice scope to achieve precision; another trade precision for scope. Neither invalidates the other. Nor is there any reason to believe that a uniquely best system will emerge in the long run. To accommodate the impossibility of ascertaining both the position and the momentum of an electron, drastic revisions are required in our views about physics. But which ones? A number of alternatives have been suggested. We might maintain that each electron has a determinate position and a determinate momentum at every instant, but admit that only one of these magnitudes can be known. In that case science is committed to the existence of things that it cannot in principle discover. Or we might contend that the magnitudes are created in the process of measurement. Then an unmeasured particle has neither a position nor a momentum, and one that has a position lacks momentum (for the one measurement precludes the other). Physical magnitudes are then knowable because they are artifacts of our knowledge-gathering techniques. But from the behavior of particles in experimental situations nothing follows about their behavior elsewhere. Yet a third option is to affirm that a particle has a position and affirm that it has a momentum, but deny that it has both a position and a momentum. In that case, however, we must alter our logic in such a way that the conjunction of individually true sentences is not always true. That science countenances nothing unverifiable, that experiments yield information about what occurs in nature, that logic is independent of matters of fact—such antecedently reasonable theses are shown by the findings of quantum

mechanics to be at odds with one another. Substantial alterations are thus required to accommodate our theory of scientific knowledge to the data it seeks to explain. Although there are several ways of describing and explaining quantum phenomena, none does everything we want. Different accommodations retain different scientific desiderata. And deciding which one to accept involves deciding which features of science we value most and which ones we are prepared, if reluctantly, to forego. "Unexamined electrons have no position" derives its status as fact from a judgment of value—the judgment that it is better to construe magnitudes as artifacts of measurement than to modify classical logic, or commit science to the truth of claims it is powerless to confirm, or to make any of the other available revisions needed to resolve the paradox.

Pluralism results. The same constellation of cognitive and practical objectives can sometimes be realized in different ways, and different constellations of cognitive and practical objectives are sometimes equally worthy of realization. A sentence that is right according to one acceptable system may be wrong according to another.

But it does not follow that every statement, method, or value is right according to some acceptable system. Among the considered judgments that guide our theorizing are convictions that certain things—for example, affirming a contradiction, ignoring the preponderance of legal or experimental evidence, or exterminating a race—are just wrong. Such convictions must be respected unless we find powerful reasons to revise them. And there is no ground for thinking that such reasons are in the offing. So it is not the case that anything goes.

Nor does it follow that systems can be evaluated only by standards that they acknowledge. An account that satisfies the standards it sets for itself might rightly be faulted for being blind to problems it ought to solve, for staking out a domain in which there are only trivial problems, for setting too low standards for itself. An inquiry that succeeds by its own lights may yet be in the dark.

So far I have argued for the value ladenness of facts. I developed a scientific example in some detail, because science is considered a bastion of objectivity. If scientific facts can be shown to be relative and value laden, there is a strong *prima facie* case for saying that relativity and value ladenness do not undermine objectivity. Then, if the objectivity of normative claims is to be impugned, it must be on other grounds.

I want to turn to questions of value. Not surprisingly, I contend that value judgments are vindicated in the same way as factual judgments. Indeed, normative and descriptive claims belong to the same systems of thought and so stand or fall together. Still, some systems seem more heavily factual; others, more heavily evaluative. For now I will concentrate on the latter.

In constructing a normative category scheme, as in constructing any other scheme, we are guided by our interests, purposes, and the problem at hand. Together these factors organize the domain, so that certain considerations are brought to the fore. In restructuring zoning laws, for example, it is advisable to employ consequentialist categories. For we need the capacity to tell whether things would in fact improve if the building code were altered in one way or another. We need, then, the capacity to classify and to evaluate in terms of outcomes. If we are concerned with developing moral character, it may be advisable to use predicates that can be applied with reasonable accuracy in self-ascription. For the capacity for self-scrutiny is likely to be valuable in moral development.

For like cases to be treated alike the evaluations yielded by a moral or legal system must be coherent, consistent with one another, and grounded in the relevant facts. Fairness and equity are demanded of such a system; arbitrariness and caprice are anathemas to it. So logical and evidential constraints are binding on evaluation as well as on description.

The problems we face and the constraints on their solution often have their basis in the facts. Whether, for example, we ought to perform surgery to prolong the life of a severely defective newborn becomes a problem only when we acquire the medical resources to perform such surgery. Prior to the development of the medical techniques the question was moot. There was no reason to require a moral code to provide an answer. So a moral problem arises in response to changes in the facts.

Our previously acceptable moral code may never have needed, and so never have developed, the refinements required to handle the new case. Unanticipated facts can thus put pressure on a system by generating problems it cannot (but should) solve, thus yielding inconsistent evaluations or producing counterintuitive verdicts. Values that do not ordinarily clash may do so in special circumstances. Typically the physician can both prolong the lives of her patients and alleviate their pain. But not always. So a moral system that simply says she ought to do both is inadequate. It does not tell her how to proceed when the realization of one value interferes with the realization of the other. Our values then need to be reconsidered. In the reconception previously accepted conclusions are called into question, competing claims adjudicated, a new balance struck. Our goal again is a system of considered judgments in reflective equilibrium. Achieving that goal may involve drawing new evaluative and descriptive distinctions or erasing distinctions already drawn, reordering priorities or imposing new ones, reconceiving the relevant facts and values or recognizing new ones as relevant. We test the construction for accuracy by seeing whether it reflects (closely enough) the initially credible judgments we began with. And we test it for adequacy by seeing whether it realizes our objectives in theorizing. An exact fit is neither needed nor wanted. We realize that the views we began with are incomplete, and we suspect that they are flawed, while we recognize that our initial conception of our objectives is inchoate and perhaps inconsistent. So we treat our starting points as touchstones which guide but do not determine the shape of our construction.

Here, too, pluralism results, for the constraints on construction do not guarantee a unique result. Where competing considerations are about equal in weight, different trade-offs might reasonably be made, different balances struck. If any system satisfies our standards, several are apt to do so.

In child rearing, for example, we regularly have to balance a concern for a child's welfare against the value of granting him autonomy. And responsible parents settle the matter differently, some allowing their children greater freedom, some less. A variety of combinations of permissions and prohibitions seem satisfactory, none being plainly preferable to the rest. It follows then that a single decision—say, to permit a child to play football— might be right or wrong depending on which acceptable system is in effect. Rightness is then relative to system.

But it does not follow that every act is right according to some acceptable system or other. It is irresponsible to permit a toddler to play with matches and overprotective to forbid a teenager to cross the street. From the fact that several solutions are right, it does not follow that none is wrong. Some proposed resolutions to the conflict between welfare and autonomy are plainly out of bounds.

Nor does it follow that to be right according to some acceptable system is to be right *simpliciter*. Rightness further requires that the system invoked be appropriate in the circumstances. Although my freshmen's papers would rightly be judged abysmal failures if evaluated according to the editorial standards of *The Journal of Philosophy,* those are clearly the wrong standards to use. To grade my students fairly, I must employ standards appropriate to undergraduate work. (Then only some of their papers are abysmal failures.)

Can we rest satisfied with the prospect of multiple correct evaluations? Disconcertingly, the answer varies. If the systems that produce the several evaluations do not clash, there is no difficulty. We easily recognize that an accurate shot by an opposing player is good from one point of view (excellence in playing the game) and bad from another (our partisan interest that the opposition collapse into incompetence). And there is no need to decide whether it is a good or bad shot all things considered.

In other cases multiplicity of correct evaluations may be rendered harmless by a principle of tolerance. We can then say that what is right according to any acceptable system is right. Thus one parent's decision on how best to balance paternalist and libertarian considerations in child rearing does not carry with it the commitment that all parents who decide otherwise are wrong. And one physician's decision on how to balance the value of alleviating pain against the value of prolonging life does not carry with it the commitment that all physicians who strike a different balance are wrong.

Tolerance is an option because the prescriptions for action apply to numerically distinct cases. So long as parents decide only for their own children, they can recognize that other parents might reasonably decide the same matters somewhat differently. Pluralism does not lead to paralysis here because the assignment of responsibility is such that conflicting right answers are not brought to bear on a single case.

Tolerance seems not to be an option, however, when systems dictate antithetical responses to a single case. For we must inevitably do one thing or another. The problem becomes acute in socially coordinated activity. If the several parties in a joint venture employ clashing systems, their contributions are likely to cancel each other out, diminishing the prospect of success. Although nothing favors the convention of driving on the right side of the road over that of driving on the left, leaving the choice to the individual driver would be an invitation to mayhem. We need then to employ a single system, even if the selection among acceptable alternatives is ultimately arbitrary.

In such cases, then, we invoke a metasystematic principle of intolerance. Even if there are several ways of equilibrating our other concerns, we mandate that an acceptable equilibrium has not been reached until a single system is selected. The justification for this mandate is the recognition that unanimity or widespread agreement is itself a desideratum that is sometimes worth considerable sacrifice to achieve.

To be sure, an intolerant system remains vulnerable to criticism, revision, and replacement by a better system. The argument for intolerance is simply that where divided allegiance leads to ineffectiveness, a single system must reign. Successors there can be, but no contemporaries.

In the cases I've spoken of so far, both tolerance and intolerance look like fairly easy options. We readily agree to be intolerant about rules of the road, not only because we appreciate the value of conformity in such matters but also because we recognize that nothing important has to be given up. It simply doesn't matter whether we drive on the left or on the right, so long as we all drive on the same side. And we readily tolerate a range of child-rearing practices, because so long as certain broad constraints are somehow satisfied, small differences don't much matter. The difference between a 10 P.M. curfew and a 10:30 one is unlikely to significantly affect a child's well-being. In such cases we can agree, or respectfully agree to disagree, precisely because no deeply held convictions are violated in the process.

Sometimes, however, conflicts run deep. Thus, the abortion problem arises because in an unwanted pregnancy, the value of personal autonomy clashes with the value of fetal life. Neither is trivial. So to achieve any resolution, a substantial good must be sacrificed. Each party to the dispute achieves equilibrium at a price the other is unwilling to pay: the one maintaining that even fetal life cannot compensate for the loss of liberty, the other maintaining that even liberty cannot compensate for the loss of fetal life. Nor can the parties civilly agree to disagree. For each is convinced that the position of the other is fundamentally immoral.

Both parties to the dispute can adduce powerful reasons to support their position. But neither has the resources to convince its opponents. Nor has anyone come up with a compromise that both sides can in good conscience accept.

The existence of such seemingly intractable problems might seem to support a subjective ethical relativism. Having found no objective way to resolve such dilemmas, we might conclude that all morality is relative to system, and the choice of a system is, in the end, subjective.

Without denying the difficulty that such problems pose I want to resist the slide into subjectivism. Our practice bears me out. Even in the face of widespread disagreement we don't treat such issues as subjective. If we did, we would probably be more charitable to those holding opposing views. How do we proceed?

Sometimes we deny that the problem remains unsolved. We contend that one of the positions, although still sincerely held, has actually been discredited. The holdouts, we maintain, overlook some morally relevant features of the situation or improperly weigh the relevant ones. This response may well be correct. Advocates of apartheid, however adamant, are simply wrong. And they remain wrong even if they are too ignorant, biased, or closed-minded to recognize it.

So the failure of an argument to convince its opponents may be due to defects in their understanding, not to weaknesses in the argument. This has its parallel in science. The inability of any argument to convince my accountant of the truth of the Heisenberg Uncertainty Principle does not discredit the objectivity of the principle; it discredits her claim to have mastered quantum mechanics.

Alternatively, we might concede that a question is unanswered without concluding that it is unanswerable. We then take it to be an outstanding problem for the relevant field of inquiry. All fields have such problems. And if our current inability to solve the problem

of the origin of life does not impugn the objectivity of biology, our current inability to solve the problem of abortion should not impugn the objectivity of ethics. What such problems show is that more work remains to be done. This is no surprise.

The objectivity of ethics does not ensure that we can answer every question. Neither does the objectivity of science. If a question is ill-conceived or just too difficult, or if our attempts are wrongheaded or unlucky, the answer may forever elude us. But that success is not guaranteed is just an epistemological fact of life.

Nor does objectivity insure that every properly conceived question has a determinate answer. So perhaps nothing determines whether the young man whom Sartre describes ought to join the Resistance or stay home and care for his aged mother.[7] If the relevant considerations are in fact equally balanced, either alternative is as good (or as bad) as the other. The choice he faces then is subjective. But this does not make ethics subjective. For to say that personal predilections are involved in deciding among equally worthy alternatives is quite different from saying that personal predilections are what make the alternatives worthy. Subjective considerations function as tiebreakers after the merit of the contenders has been certified by other means.

I have suggested that factual and evaluative sentences are justified in the same way. In both cases acceptability of an individual sentence derives from its place in a system of considered judgments in reflective equilibrium. Since equilibrium is achieved by adjudication, several systems are apt to be adequate. But since they are the products of different trade-offs, they are apt to disagree about the acceptability of individual sentences. So relativism follows from pluralism. Something that is right relative to one acceptable system may be wrong relative to another.

Still, the verdicts are objective. For the systems that validate them are themselves justified. The accuracy of such a system is attested by its ability to accommodate antecedent convictions and practices; its adequacy, by its ability to realize our objectives. Several applicable systems may possess these abilities, so several answers to a given question or several courses of action may be right. But not every system possesses them, so not every answer or action is right. The pluralism and relativism I favor thus do not lead to the conclusion that anything goes. If many things are right, many more remain wrong.[8]

Notes

1. Ruth Anna Putnam argues for a similar thesis in "Creating Facts and Values," *Philosophy* 60 (1985): 187–204.
2. Israel Scheffler, *Beyond the Letter* (London: Routledge and Kegan Paul, 1979), pp. 6–7.
3. Nelson Goodman, *Ways of Worldmaking* (Indianapolis: Hackett, 1978), pp. 109–140.
4. Nelson Goodman, "Sense and Certainty," in *Problems and Projects* (Indianapolis: Hackett, 1972), pp. 60–68.
5. But not only then. We may attempt to modify a working system out of curiosity—to see how it works and whether it can be made to work better.
6. Cf. Nelson Goodman, *Fact, Fiction, and Forecast* (Cambridge: Harvard University Press, 1984), pp. 65–68; John Rawls, *A Theory of Justice* (Cambridge: Harvard University Press, 1971); Catherine Z. Elgin, *With Reference to Reference* (Indianapolis: Hackett, 1983), pp. 183–193.
7. Jean Paul Sartre, *Existentialism and Humanism* (London: Methuen, 1968), pp. 35–37.
8. I am grateful to Israel Scheffler, Jonathan Adler, and William Lycan for comments on an earlier draft of this paper.

4. She writes that "to go from a motley collection of convictions to a system of considered judgments in reflective equilibrium requires balancing competing claims against one another." What are some examples of the kinds of competing claims that she has in mind?
5. What does Elgin mean by "pluralism" and "subjectivism"? In general, why does Elgin reject the view that pluralism necessarily leads to subjectivism? Do you agree with this?

SUGGESTIONS FOR FURTHER READING (CATHERINE Z. ELGIN)

Primary Sources

(1983) *With Reference to Reference.* Indianapolis: Hackett.

(1988) (with Nelson Goodman), *Reconceptions.* Indianapolis: Hackett.

(1990) (with Nelson Goodman) *Esthétique et Connaissance: Pour changer de Sujet.* Combas: Editions de l'Eclat.

(1996) *Between the Absolute and the Arbitrary.* Ithaca: Cornell University Press.

(1997) *Considered Judgment.* Princeton: Princeton University Press.

(1997) (ed.) *The Philosophy of Nelson Goodman.* New York: Garland.

READING QUESTIONS

1. In her essay Elgin often talks about "category schemes" and "frameworks." What does she mean? She also writes that "we need to employ an appropriate framework." What sorts of features, according to Elgin, makes a framework appropriate?
2. What are some of the ways in which Elgin characterizes "facts" and "values"? How are these ways related to our "standards"? Briefly outline her overall argument that facts depend on values and values depend on facts.
3. Elgin uses the terms "considered judgment" and "reflective equilibrium" repeatedly. What do these terms mean, exactly?

DAVID LEWIS (WITH STEPHANIE LEWIS)

Holes

David Lewis (1941–) was born in Oberlin, Ohio. His father was a professor of government at Oberlin College and his mother was a historian who also taught at the college. Lewis earned his bachelor's degree in philosophy at Swarthmore in 1962. He then enrolled at Harvard University, taking his master's degree in 1964 and his doctorate in philosophy in 1967.

His teaching career began at UCLA, where he was appointed assistant professor in 1966. In 1970 he left California for Princeton University, where he has remained ever since. In 1973 he was promoted to the rank of full professor at Princeton. Many of his other professional achievements in philosophy are equally noteworthy. In 1983 he was elected to the American Academy of Arts and Sciences, and in 1992 he was elected a Corresponding Fellow of the British Academy. In addition to his teaching and research at Princeton, he has held various short visiting appointments at many universities outside the United States, especially in Australia and England.

Since the mid-1960s, Lewis has been writing on various central topics in metaphysics, the philosophy of logic and mathematics, and the philosophy of mind. His books include a philosophical study of convention as the basis for solutions to coordination problems, an essay on the analysis and metaphysics of counterfactuals, and a short treatise on the intricacies of set theory. He has also written highly influential articles on the mind-body identity thesis, modality, the problem of personal identity, propositional attitudes, and the nature of time. On the whole, Lewis is one of the most important and influential philosophers working in contemporary metaphysics.

In the following short dialogue, written with Stephanie Lewis, David Lewis illustrates a particular conception of the methodology and outcomes of philosophy. In the process, he works to demonstrates in this little vignette how theories that depart from "common opinions" could nevertheless "earn credence by their clarity and economy"—a mark of his philosophical work as a whole.

ARGLE: I believe in nothing but concrete material objects.

BARGLE: There are many of your opinions I applaud; but one of your less pleasing characteristics is your fondness for the doctrines of nominalism and mate-

David and Stephanie Lewis, "Holes" from *Australasian Journal of Philosophy* 48 (1970), pp. 206–12. Reprinted with the kind permission of David and Stephanie Lewis and the Australasian Association of Philosophy.

rialism. Every time you get started on any such topic, I know we are in for a long argument. Where shall we start this time: numbers, colors, lengths, sets, force-fields, sensations, or what?

ARGLE: Fictions all! I've thought hard about every one of them.

BARGLE: A long evening's work. Before we start, let me find you a snack. Will you have some crackers and cheese?

ARGLE: Thank you. What splendid Gruyère!

BARGLE: You know, there are remarkably many holes in this piece.

ARGLE: There are.

BARGLE: Got you!

BARGLE: You admit there are many holes in that piece of cheese. Therefore, there are some holes in it. Therefore, there are some holes. In other words, holes exist. But holes are not made of matter; to the contrary, they result from the absence of matter.

ARGLE: I did say that there are holes in the cheese; but that is not to imply that there are holes.

BARGLE: However not? If you say that there are A's that are B's, you are committed logically to the conclusion that there are A's.

ARGLE: When *I* say that there are holes in something, I mean nothing more nor less than that it is perforated. The synonymous shape-predicates ' . . . is perforated' and 'there are holes in . . . '—just like any other shape-predicate, say ' . . . is a dodecahedron'—may truly be predicated of pieces of cheese, without any implication that perforation is due to the presence of occult, immaterial entities. I am sorry my innocent predicate confuses you by sounding like an idiom of existential quantification, so that you think that inferences involving it are valid when they are not. But I have my reasons. You, given a perforated piece of cheese and believing as you do that it is perforated because it contains immaterial entities called holes, employ an idiom of existential quantification to say falsely 'There are holes in it.' Agreeable fellow that I am, I wish to have a sentence that sounds like yours and that is true exactly when you falsely suppose your existential quantification over immaterial things to be true. That way we could talk about the cheese without philosophizing, if only you'd let me. You and I would understand our sentences differently, but the difference wouldn't interfere with our conversation until you start drawing conclusions which follow from your false sentence but not from my homonymous true sentence.[1]

BARGLE: Oh, very well. But behold: there are as many holes in my piece of cheese as in yours. Do you agree?

ARGLE: I'll take your word for it without even counting: there are as many holes in mine as in yours. But what I mean by that is that either both pieces are singly-perforated, or both are doubly-perforated, or both are triply-perforated, and so on.

BARGLE: What a lot of different shape-predicates you know! How ever did you find time to learn them all? And what does 'and so on' mean?[2]

ARGLE: Let me just say that the two pieces are equally-perforated. Now I have used only one two-place predicate.

BARGLE: Unless I singly-perforate each of these crackers, how will you say that there are as many holes in my cheese as crackers on my plate? Be so kind as not to invent another predicate on the spot. I am quite prepared to go on until you have told me about all the predicates you have up your sleeve. I have a good imagination, and plenty of time.

ARGLE: Oh, dear . . . (ponders)

ARGLE: I was wrong. There *are* holes.

BARGLE: You recant?

ARGLE: No. Holes are material objects.

BARGLE: I expected that sooner. You are thinking, doubtless, that every hole is filled with matter: silver amalgam, air, interstellar gas, luminiferous ether or whatever it may be.

ARGLE: No. Perhaps there are no truly empty holes; but I cannot deny that there might be.

BARGLE: How can something utterly devoid of matter be made of matter?

ARGLE: You're looking for the matter in the wrong place. (I mean to say, that's what you would be doing if there were any such things as places, which there aren't.) The matter isn't inside the hole. It would be absurd to say it was: nobody wants to say that holes are inside themselves. The matter surrounds the hole.

The lining of a hole, you agree, is a material object. For every hole there is a hole-lining; for every hole-lining there is a hole. I say the hole-lining *is* the hole.

BARGLE: Didn't you say that the hole-lining surrounds the hole? Things don't surround themselves.

ARGLE: Holes do. In my language, 'surrounds' said of a hole (described as such) means 'is identical with.' 'Surrounds' said of other things means just what you think it means.

BARGLE: Doesn't it bother you that your dictionary must have two entries under 'surrounds' where mine has only one?

ARGLE: A little, but not much. I'm used to putting up with such things.

BARGLE: Such *whats*?

ARGLE: Such dictionary entries. They're made of dried ink, you recall.

BARGLE: Oh. I suppose you'll also say that ' . . . is in . . .' or ' . . . is through . . . ' said of a hole means ' . . . is part of . . .'.

ARGLE: Exactly so, Bargle.

BARGLE: Then do you still say that 'There are holes in the cheese' contains an unanalyzed shape-predicate synonymous with ' . . . is perforated'?

ARGLE: No; it is an existential quantification, as you think it is. It means that there exist material objects such that they are holes and they are parts of the piece of cheese.

BARGLE: But we wouldn't say, would we, that a hole is made out of cheese?

ARGLE: No; but the fact that we wouldn't say it doesn't mean it isn't true. We wouldn't have occasion to say, unless philosophizing, that these walls are perpendicular to the floor; but they are. Anyhow we *do* say that caves are holes in the ground and that some of them are made out of limestone.

BARGLE: Take this paper-towel roller. Spin it on a lathe. The hole-lining spins. Surely you'd never say the hole spins?

ARGLE: Why not?

BARGLE: Even though the hole might continue to be entirely filled with a dowel that didn't spin or move at all?

ARGLE: What difference does that make?

BARGLE: None, really. But now I have you: take a toilet-paper roller, put it inside the paper-towel roller, and spin it the other way. The big hole spins clockwise. The little hole spins counter-clockwise. But the little hole is part of the big hole, so it spins clockwise along with the rest of the big hole. So if holes can spin, as you think, the little hole turns out to be spinning in both directions at once, which is absurd.

ARGLE: I see why you might think that the little hole is part of the big hole, but you can't expect me to agree. The little hole is inside the big hole, but that's all. Hence I have no reason to say that the little hole is spinning clockwise.

BARGLE: Consider a thin-walled hole with a gallon of water inside. The volume of the hole is at least a gallon, whereas the volume of the hole-lining is much less. If the hole is the hole-lining, then whatever was true of one would have to be true of the other. They could not differ in volume.

ARGLE: For 'hole' read 'bottle;' for 'hole-lining' also read 'bottle.' You have the same paradox. Holes, like bottles, have volume—or, as I'd rather say, are voluminous or equi-voluminous with other things—in two different senses. There's the volume of the hole or bottle itself, and there's the volume of the largest chunk of fluid which could be put inside the hole or bottle without compression. For holes, as for bottles, contextual clues permit us to keep track of which we mean.

BARGLE: What is the volume of the hole itself? How much of the cheese do you include as part of one of these holes? And how do you decide? Arbitrarily, that's how. Don't try saying you include as little of the cheese as possible, for however much you include, you could have included less.

ARGLE: What we call a single hole is really many hole-linings. Some include more of the cheese, some include less. Therefore I need not decide, arbitrarily or otherwise, how much cheese is part of the hole. Many different decisions are equally correct.

BARGLE: How can a single hole be identical with many hole-linings that are not identical with one another?

ARGLE: Really there are many different holes, and each is identical with a different hole-lining. But all these different holes are the same hole.

BARGLE: You contradict yourself. Don't you mean to say that they all *surround* the same hole—where by 'surround' I mean 'surround,' not 'be identical with'?

ARGLE: Not at all. I would contradict myself if I said that two different holes were identical. But I didn't; what I said was that they were the same hole. Two holes are the same hole when they have a common part that is itself a hole.

BARGLE: You agreed before that there were as many holes in my cheese as crackers on my plate. Are there still?

ARGLE: Yes; there are two of each left.

BARGLE: Two crackers, to be sure, but how can you say there are two holes?

ARGLE: Thus: there is a hole, and there is another hole that is not the same hole, and every hole in the cheese is the same hole as one or the other.

BARGLE: Be so kind as to say 'co-perforated,' not 'same,' and stop pretending to talk about identity when you are not. I understand you now: co-perforation is supposed to be an equivalence relation among hole-linings, and when you say there are two holes you are trying to say that there are two non-identical co-perforation-classes of hole-linings. Really you identify holes not with hole-linings but with *classes* of hole-linings.

ARGLE: I would if I could, but I can't. No; holes are hole-linings; but when I speak of them as holes, I find it convenient to use 'same' meaning 'co-perforated' wherever a man of your persuasion would use 'same' meaning 'identical.' You know my reason for this trickery: my sentences about sameness of holes will be true just when you wrongly suppose your like-sounding sentences to be. The same goes for sentences about number of holes, since we both analyze these in terms of sameness.[3]

BARGLE: You still haven't told me how you say there are as many holes in my cheese as crackers on my plate, without also saying how many there are.

ARGLE: Here goes. There exist three things X, Y, and Z. X is part of the sum of the crackers, Y is part of the cheese, and Z is part of Y. Every maximal connected part of Y is a hole, and every hole in the cheese is the same hole as some maximal connected part of Y. X overlaps each of the crackers and Z overlaps each maximal connected part of Y. Everything which is either the intersection of X and a cracker or the intersection of Z and some maximal connected part of Y is the same size as any other such thing. X is the same size as Z.[4]

BARGLE: Your devices won't work because co-perforation is not an equivalence relation. *Any* two overlapping parts of my cheese have a common part that is a hole-lining, though in most cases the hole-lining is entirely filled with cheese. To be co-perforated is therefore nothing more than to overlap, and overlapping is no equivalence relation. The result is that although, as you say, you can find two hole-linings in this cheese that are not co-perforated, you can find another one that is co-perforated with both of them.

ARGLE: If you were right that a hole made of cheese sould be entirely filled with the same kind of cheese, you could find far more than two non-co-perforated hole-linings; and there would be no such thing as cheese without holes in it. But you are wrong. A hole is a hole not just by virtue of its own shape but also by virtue of the way it contrasts with the matter inside it and around it. The same is true of other shape-predicates; I wouldn't say that any part of the cheese is a dodecahedron, though I admit that there are parts—parts that do not contrast with their surroundings—that are *shaped like* dodecahedra.

BARGLE: Consider the paper-towel roller. How many holes?

ARGLE: One. You know what I mean: many, but they're all the same.

BARGLE: I think you must say there are at least two. The left half and the right half are not the same hole. They have no common part, so no common part that is a hole.

ARGLE: They're not holes, they're two parts of a hole.

BARGLE: Why aren't they holes themselves? They are singly-perforated and they are made of matter unlike the matter inside them. If I cut them apart you'd have to say they were holes?

ARGLE: Yes.

BARGLE: You admit that a hole can be a proper part of a bigger—say, thicker-skinned—hole?

ARGLE: Yes.

BARGLE: You admit that they are shaped like holes?

ARGLE: Yes, but they aren't holes. I can't say why they aren't. I know which things are holes, but I can't give you a definition. But why should I? You already know what hole-linings are. I say the two halves of the roller are only parts of a hole because I—like you—would say they are only parts of a hole-lining. What isn't a hole-lining isn't a hole.

BARGLE: In that case, I admit that co-perforation may be an equivalence relation at least among singly-perforated hole-linings.

ARGLE: All holes are singly-perforated. A doubly-perforated thing has two holes in it that are not the same hole.

BARGLE: Are you sure? Take the paper-towel roller and punch a little hole in its side. Now you have a hole in a hole-lining. You'd have to say you have a hole in a hole. You have a little hole which is part of a big hole; the big hole is not singly-perforated; and the little hole and the big hole are the same hole, since the little hole is a common part of each.

ARGLE: I think not. You speak of *the* big hole; but what we have are two big holes, not the same, laid end to end. There is also the little hole, not the same as either big hole, which overlaps them both. Of course we sometimes call something a hole, in a derivative sense, if it is a connected sum of holes. Any decent cave consists of many holes that are not the same hole, so I must have been speaking in this derivative sense when I said that caves are holes.

BARGLE: What peculiar things you are driven to say when philosophy corrupts your mind! Tell me the truth: would you have dreamed for a moment of saying there were two big holes rather than one if you were not suffering under the influence of a philosophical theory?

ARGLE: No; I fear I would have remained ignorant.

BARGLE: I see that I can never hope to refute you, since I no sooner reduce your position to absurdity than you embrace the absurdity.

ARGLE: Not absurdity; disagreement with common opinion.

BARGLE: Very well. But I, for one, have more trust in common opinions than I do in any philosophical reasoning whatever. In so far as you disagree with them, you must pay a great price in the plausibility of your theories.

ARGLE: Agreed. We have been measuring that price. I have shown that it is not so great as you thought; I am prepared to pay it. My theories can earn credence by their clarity and economy; and if they disagree a little with common opinion, then common opinion may be corrected even by a philosopher.

BARGLE: The price is still too high.

ARGLE: We agree in principle; we're only haggling.

BARGLE: We do. And the same is true of our other debates over ontic parsimony. Indeed, this argument has served us as an illustration—novel, simple, and self-contained—of the nature of our customary disputes.

ARGLE: And yet the illustration has interest in its own right. Your holes, had I been less successful, would have punctured my nominalistic materialism with the greatest of ease.

BARGLE: Rehearsed and refreshed, let us return to—say—the question of classes.[5]

Notes

1. *Cf.* W. V. Quine, "On What There Is," *From a Logical Point of View,* 2nd ed. (Cambridge, Mass: Harvard University Press, 1961), p. 13.

2. *Cf.* Donald Davidson, "Theories of Meaning and Learnable Languages," in Y. Bar-Hillel, *Logic, Methodology and Philosophy of Science, Proceedings of the 1964 International Congress* (Amsterdam, 1965), pp. 383–94.

3. *Cf.* Quine's maxim of identification of indiscernibles in "Identity, Ostension, and Hypostasis," *From a Logical Point of View,* p. 71; P. T. Geach, "Identity," *Review of Metaphysics* 21 (1967): 3–12.

4. This translation adapts a device from Nelson Goodman and W. V. Quine, "Steps Toward a Constructive Nominalism," *Journal of Symbolic Logic* 12 (1947): 109–10.

5. There would be little truth to the guess that Argle is one of the authors and Bargle is the other. We thank Charles Chastain, who also is neither Argle nor Bargle, for many helpful comments.

READING QUESTIONS

1. What are Argle and Bargle arguing about? What is Argle's position and what is Bargle's? Initially, do you sympathize more with Argle's view or with Bargle's?

2. In reply to an attack by Bargle, Argle proposes that "holes are material objects," specifically, that "the hole-lining is the hole." What is his positive argument for this conclusion? Why does Bargle, in turn, think that his case of the spinning paper-towel roller is problematic for Argle's analysis? How about the case of the thin-walled hole with a gallon of water inside?

3. Argle agrees with Bargle that "there are as many holes in my cheese as crackers on my plate." Bargle objects that Argle's analysis of 'hole' is incompatible with this claim. What is Bargle's argument for this conclusion and what is Argle's reply?

4. When Bargle objects that Argle's "devices won't work because co-perforation is not an equivalence relation," to what specific aspect of Argle's theory is his objection?

5. Exasperated, Bargle remarks, "I see that I can never hope to refute you, since I no sooner reduce your position to absurdity than you embrace the absurdity." Argle replies, "Not absurdity; disagreement with common opinion." What general lessons about the *reductio ad absurdum* form of argument and, perhaps especially, its use in metaphysics, are illustrated in this short dialogue?

6. Are philosophical debates (or at least debates about "ontic parsimony") really cases of "haggling," as Argle proposes? Why or why not?

SUGGESTIONS FOR FURTHER READING (DAVID LEWIS)

Primary Sources and Collected Writings

(1966) "An Argument for the Identity Theory." In *Journal of Philosophy* 63: 17–25.

(1968) "Counterpart Theory and Quantified Modal Logic." In *Journal of Philosophy* 65: 113–26.

(1969) *Convention: A Philosophical Study.* Cambridge, MA: Harvard University Press.

(1973) *Counterfactuals.* Cambridge, MA: Harvard University Press.

(1976) "Survival and Identity." In *The Identities of Persons,* edited by A. O. Rorty. Berkeley, CA: University of California Press.

(1983) *Philosophical Papers,* Vol. 1. Oxford: Oxford University Press.

(1986) *Philosophical Papers,* Vol. 2. Oxford: Oxford University Press.

(1986) *On the Plurality of Worlds.* Oxford: Basil Blackwell.

(1991) *Parts of Classes.* Oxford: Basil Blackwell.

(1994) "Reduction of Mind." In *A Companion to Philosophy of Mind,* edited by S. Guttenplan. Oxford: Basil Blackwell.

(1998) *Papers in Philosophical Logic.* Cambridge: Cambridge University Press.

(1999) *Papers in Metaphysics and Epistemology.* Cambridge: Cambridge University Press.

Secondary Sources

Chihara, C. (1998) *The Worlds of Possibility: Modal Realism and the Semantics of Modal Logic.* Oxford: Clarendon Press.

Elgin, C. (1992) "Critical Notice of *Parts of Classes.*" In *Philosophical Books* 33: 193–198.

Hughes, G., and M. Cresswell (1996) *A New Introduction to Modal Logic.* London: Routledge.

Loux, M., ed. (1979) *The Possible and the Actual: Readings in the Metaphysics of Modality.* Ithaca, NY: Cornell University Press.

Plantinga, A. (1989) *The Nature of Necessity.* Oxford: Clarendon Press.

Stalnaker, R. (1968) "A Theory of Conditionals." In *Studies in Logical Theory,* edited by N. Rescher. Oxford: Basil Blackwell.

———. (1988) "A Critical Notice of *On the Plurality of Worlds.*" In *Mind* 97: 117–128.

van Inwagen, P. (1986) "Critical Notice of *Philosophical Papers I.*" In *Mind,* 95: 246–257.